21st-CENTURY OXFORD AUTHORS

GENERAL EDITOR

SEAMUS PERRY

21st-CENTURY OXFORD AUTHORS

William Morris

EDITED BY

INGRID HANSON

OXFORD

UNIVERSITY PRESS

OXFORD
UNIVERSITY PRESS

Great Clarendon Street, Oxford, OX2 6DP,
United Kingdom

Oxford University Press is a department of the University of Oxford.
It furthers the University's objective of excellence in research, scholarship,
and education by publishing worldwide. Oxford is a registered trade mark of
Oxford University Press in the UK and in certain other countries

© Ingrid Hanson 2024

The moral rights of the author have been asserted

Published in the United States of America by Oxford University Press
198 Madison Avenue, New York, NY 10016, United States of America

British Library Cataloguing in Publication Data
Data available

Library of Congress Control Number: 2023934167

ISBN 978-0-19-289481-6

Printed and bound in the UK by
Clays Ltd, Elcograf S.p.A.

ACKNOWLEDGEMENTS

I'm grateful for the insights of those who have edited Morris's works, letters, and lectures so finely before me, including Clive Wilmer, David Leopold, Krishan Kumar, and Florence Boos. I have benefitted most especially from the magisterial work of Eugene Lemire's wonderfully precise and detailed bibliography of Morris's work and Norman Kelvin's four-volume *Collected Letters*. I'm grateful to Princeton University Press for allowing me to include two letters from that collection here. My thanks, too, to all the institutions and organizations who have given permission for the use of Morris's images: Cleveland Museum of Art, the Tate Gallery, the Victoria and Albert Museum, the William Morris Gallery, the William Morris Society, the Working Class Movement Library, the National Trust, and the University of Manchester Special Collections, to whose staff I owe particular thanks.

My heartfelt thanks are due, too, to the many friends and colleagues whose advice, expertise, intellectual companionship, and kind help has contributed to the making of this book, most particularly Anke Bernau, David Matthews, Marcus Waithe, Cathy Shrank, Noelle Gallagher, Hal Gladfelder, Nawal El-Amrani, Kevin Cawley, and Mike Sanders. I'm grateful to the many students who have enthusiastically and critically thought through Morris with me over the last fifteen years; to Chris Mees at Art History Research; to Neil Reed for insights on rivers, fish, and fishing; to Seamus Perry for his insight and guidance; and to Eleanor Collins, Karen Raith, Susan Frampton, and Matthew Humphrys at OUP for their patience, expertise, and generosity. As always I remain deeply grateful to Jess Hanson and Isaac Hanson, whose lively and provocative interest in my work is unselfish, unstinting, and unfailing. I dedicate my part in the making of this book to the beloved memory of Richard Hanson.

CONTENTS

ILLUSTRATIONS

ABBREVIATIONS

AWS	May Morris, ed. *William Morris: Artist, Writer, Socialist*, 2 vols (Oxford: Basil Blackwell, 1936).
BL	British Library.
Capital	Karl Marx, *Capital*, Vol. 35 of Karl Marx and Friedrich Engels, *Collected Works*, 50 vols (London: Lawrence and Wishart, 1996).
Carlyle	*The Works of Thomas Carlyle*, Centenary edition, ed. H. D. Traill, 30 vols (London: Chapman and Hall, 1896–1901).
CL	Norman Kelvin, ed. *Collected Letters of William Morris*, 4 vols (Princeton: Princeton University Press, 1984–1996).
CW	May Morris, ed. *Collected Works of William Morris* (London: Longmans Green and Co, 1910–1915).
The Defence	William Morris, *The Defence of Guenevere, and Other Poems* (London: Bell and Daldy, 1858).
Egerton	William Morris, Egerton MS 2866 (*Sigurd the Volsung*), British Library.
Farther Adventures	Daniel Defoe, *The Farther Adventures of Robinson Crusoe* (London: W. Taylor, 1719).
Ferdowsī	*Le Livre des Rois par Abou'lKasim Firdousi*, trans. Julius Mohl, 7 vols (Paris: Imprimerie Royale, 1837–1878).
Fourier	Charles Fourier, *Selections from the Works of Fourier*, trans. Julia Franklin (London: Swan Sonnenschein, 1901).
Froissart	Jean Froissart, *Chronicles of England, France and Spain: And the adjoining countries, from the latter part of the reign of Edward II, to the coronation of Henry IV*, trans. Thomas Johnes, 2 vols (London: William Smith, 1844).
Green	John R. Green, *A Short History of the English People*, 2 vols (New York: Harper and Brothers, 1883).
Henderson	Philip Henderson, *William Morris, His Life, Work and Friends* (London: Thames and Hudson, 1967).
Hopes	William Morris, *Hopes and Fears for Art* (London: Ellis and White, 1882).
Hubbard	Elbert Hubbard, *This Then is a William Morris Book* (New York: The Roycrofters, 1907).
KP	Kelmscott Press.
Labour and Pleasure	William Morris, *Labour and Pleasure versus Labour and Sorrow* (Birmingham: Cund Brothers, 1880).
Lemire	Eugene D. Lemire, ed. *The Unpublished Lectures of William Morris* (Detroit, 1969).

Leopold	William Morris, *News from Nowhere*, ed. David Leopold (Oxford: Oxford University Press, 2008).
Letters	Philip Henderson, ed. *The Letters of William Morris to his Family and Friends* (London: Longmans Green and Co, 1950).
Mackail	J. W. Mackail, *The Life of William Morris*, 2 vols (London: Longmans, Green and Co, 1899).
MA	Thomas Malory, *The Byrth, Lyf, and Actes of Kyng Arthur; of His Noble Knyghtes of the Rounde Table, Theyr Mervellous Enquests and Adventures, Thachyeuyng of the Sanc Greal; and in the End le Morte Darthur, with the Dolorous Deth and Departyng out of Thys Worlde of Them Al*, With an Introduction and Notes by Robert Southey, 2 vols (London: Longman, Hurst, Rees, Orme, and Brown, 1817).
Meier	Paul Meier, *William Morris: The Marxist Dreamer*, 2 vols, trans. Frank Gubb (Sussex: Harvester Press, 1978).
Memorials	Georgiana Burne-Jones, *Memorials of Edward Burne-Jones*, 2 vols (London: Macmillan, 1906).
O and C	*The Oxford and Cambridge Magazine*, 1856.
Paul Thompson	Paul Thompson, *The Work of William Morris* (London: Heinemann, 1967).
Rural Rides	William Cobbett, *Rural Rides* (London: Reeves and Turner, 1893).
Ruskin, *Works*	*The Works of John Ruskin*, ed. E. T. Cook and Alexander Wedderburn, 39 vols (London: George Allen, 1903–1912).
Signs	William Morris, *Signs of Change* (London: Reeves and Turner, 1888).
Sturluson	Snorri Sturluson, *The Prose Edda: Norse Mythology*, trans. Jesse Byock (London: Penguin, 2005).
Tennyson, *Poems*	*The Poems of Tennyson in Three Volumes* ed. Christopher Ricks, 2nd edn (London: Longman, 1987).
Thompson	E. P. Thompson, *William Morris: Romantic to Revolutionary*, rev. edn (London: Merlin, 1976).
Waithe	Marcus Waithe, *William Morris's Utopia of Strangers: Victorian Medievalism and the Ideal of Hospitality* (Cambridge: Boydell and Brewer, 2006).
Wilmer	William Morris, *News from Nowhere and Other Writings*, ed. Clive Wilmer (London: Penguin, 2004).

CHRONOLOGY

1834 24 March, William Morris is born at Elm House, Walthamstow, then part of Essex, to William Morris (1797–1847) and Emma Morris, née Shelton (1805–1894). He is the third of nine surviving children.

1839 19 October, Jane Burden is born in a cottage in St Helen's Passage, Holywell, Oxford, to stableman Robert Burden and his wife Ann Burden (née Maizey).

1840 Morris's family move a few miles to Woodford Hall, in Woodford, Essex, a large house with 50 acres of land giving onto Epping Forest.

1843 Morris begins attending a boys' preparatory school run by the Misses Arundale in Walthamstow. The school moves to Woodford shortly afterwards, and Morris remains there until 1847.

1847 8 September, death of William Morris, Snr.

1848 Morris begins schooling at Marlborough College (founded in 1843) in February.

1848 The Morris family moves to Water House, Walthamstow (now the William Morris Gallery).

1851 Morris leaves Marlborough and begins studying privately with the Rev F. B. Guy.

1852 Morris refuses to join the family in attending the public events of the Duke of Wellington's funeral on 18 November.

1853 Morris goes up to Exeter College, Oxford, in January, an entry deferred from the previous autumn as the college was too full. Meets Edward Burne-Jones. Reads Ruskin's *The Stones of Venice*, just completed in 1853.

1854 In the summer Long Vacation, Morris visits Belgium and France, taking in the cathedrals in Amiens, Beauvais, and Chartres. He brings back engravings by Albert Dürer.

1855 Morris, Burne-Jones, and William Fulford go on a summer walking tour of northern France, taking in churches and museums. Morris meets Dante Gabriel Rossetti in Oxford.

1856 Morris, Burne-Jones, and other friends at Oxford and Cambridge write and edit the twelve monthly issues of *The Oxford and Cambridge Magazine*. Morris contributes: 'The Story of the Unknown Church' and the poem 'Winter Weather' (January); an essay on 'The Churches of North France, No. 1: The Shadow of Amiens' (February; no further numbers follow); 'A Dream' and the review essay 'Men and Women. By Robert Browning'

(March); 'Frank's Sealed Letter' (April); 'Riding Together' (May); 'Gertha's Lovers' (July and August) and the poem 'Hands' (July); 'Svend and his Brethren' (August); 'Lindenborg Pool', the poem 'The Chapel in Lyonesse' and the untitled poem 'Pray but one Prayer for me' [later, 'Summer Dawn'] (September); 'The Hollow Land' (September–October); and 'Golden Wings' (December). Morris graduates from Oxford, begins working for the architect George Street, moves to Red Lion Square, Holborn, in London with Burne-Jones. At the end of the year, he leaves Street's.

1857 Morris moves back to Oxford to live with Burne-Jones and Rossetti at 87 High Street, opposite Queen's College. They begin painting medievalist murals on the walls of the Oxford Union.

1858 February, *The Defence of Guenevere, and Other Poems* published by Bell and Daldy.

1858 Morris completes his Arthurian painting, *La Belle Iseult*, modelled by Jane Burden.

1859 26 April, Morris and Jane Burden marry at St Michael's Church, Ship Street, Oxford. November, Morris joins the Artists Rifles volunteer army corps. Begins work, with his friend Philip Speakman Webb, on designs for a new home, Red House.

1860 Morris and Jane move to the Red House, Bexleyheath, Kent.

1861 17 January, Jane Alice (Jenny) Morris born.

1861 Morris, Marshall, Faulkner & Co ('the Firm') opens for business in April, designing wallpapers, carpets, furnishings, and stained-glass windows.

1862 25 March, Mary (May) Morris born.

1864 February, Morris registers his first wallpaper designs, *Trellis* and *Daisy*.

1865 Morris and family move out of Red House to 26 Queen Square, Bloomsbury.

1867 May, *The Life and Death of Jason* published by Bell and Daldy, well received by critics, including Algernon Swinburne.

1868 Parts I and II of *The Earthly Paradise* published by F. S. Ellis, to laudatory reviews. Browning and Tennyson both admire it.

1869 Morris and Eiríkr Magnússon bring out the first of their Icelandic translations, 'The Saga of Gunnlaug the Wormtongue and Rafn the Skald' in the January edition of *Fortnightly Review*, 27–56. May, *Grettis Saga* published by F. S. Ellis.

1870 Parts III and IV of *The Earthly Paradise* published by F. S. Ellis. Morris and Magnússon's translation of *Völsunga Saga: The Story of the Volsungs and Niblungs* published by F. S. Ellis.

1871 Morris takes Kelmscott Manor near Lechlade in Oxfordshire in a joint tenancy with Rossetti. Morris makes his first trip to Iceland, accompanied by Charley Faulkner. Rossetti stays at Kelmscott Manor with Jane Morris.

1872 October, Morris completes his illuminated manuscript of *The Rubáiyát of Omar Khayyám* and presents it to Georgiana Burne-Jones. November, *Love is Enough* published by Ellis and White. December, the Morris family move from Queen Square to Kelmscott House, Hammersmith.

1873 Morris's second trip to Iceland with Charley Faulkner.

1875 Plans for the dissolution of the Firm are set in motion.

1875 Morris goes to stay with Thomas Wardle, the master-dyer, to learn his art. The Firm is dissolved and becomes Morris's company. November, *The Aeneids of Virgil: Done into English Verse* published by Ellis and White (dated 1876).

1876 Late November, *Sigurd the Volsung* published (dated 1877). Morris becomes Treasurer of the Eastern Question Association and begins to agitate and speak publicly on the side of Gladstone and Liberals. Jenny Morris has her first epileptic fit.

1877 4 December, Morris gives his first public lecture on art, 'The Decorative Arts' (later 'The Lesser Arts'). Establishes the Society for the Protection of Ancient Buildings (SPAB).

1878 7 January, 'Address to English Liberals' delivered to the Chichester Liberal Association.

1880 Morris, Jane, and friends take a trip down the Thames from London to Kelmscott Manor. 19 February, Morris delivers 'Labour and Pleasure *versus* Labour and Sorrow'.

1881 10 December, 'Some Hints on Pattern Designing' delivered.

1882 *Brer Rabbit* fabric design registered. February, *Hopes and Fears for Art* published by Ellis and White. 9 April, Rossetti dies.

1883 January, Morris joins the Social Democratic Federation. *Kennet* and *Strawberry Thief* fabric designs registered. August, Jane meets Wilfred Scawen Blunt.

1884 December, Morris, Eleanor Marx, Edward Aveling, and others leave the SDF to set up the Socialist League. 16 January, 'Useful Work versus Useless Toil' delivered.

1885 February, the first edition of *Commonweal* comes out. *Chants for Socialists* published by Socialist League. 21 September, Morris arrested at Thames Court for his defence of Socialist League members arrested at a free speech demonstration.

1887 *Willow Bough* wallpaper registered. 13 November, Bloody Sunday demonstrations in Trafalgar Square, in which Morris takes an active part.

1888 December, *The House of the Wolfings* published by Reeves and Turner (dated 1889). *A Dream of John Ball*, first serialized in *Commonweal* October 1886–January 1887, published by Reeves and Turner. *Signs of Change* published by Reeves and Turner.

1889 *The Roots of the Mountains* published by Reeves and Turner.

1890 *News from Nowhere* serialized in *Commonweal*, 11 January–4 October. In May, Morris gives up the editorship of *Commonweal* and in November leaves the Socialist League to set up the Hammersmith Socialist Society.

INTRODUCTION

In his 1880 lecture, 'The Beauty of Life', William Morris urged his listeners at the Birmingham Society of Arts and School of Design: 'pray do not forget, that any one who cuts down a tree wantonly or carelessly, especially in a great town or its suburbs, need make no pretence of caring about art'.[1] He establishes this vital connection between art and what he later called 'the beauty of the earth' again and again across his work, developing a concept of beauty and its correlative, pleasure, as a basic requirement for decent life on the earth.[2] Such a life must be shaped by interrelationships, he argues, and it is one that comes with a cost to be borne by all; no aspect of this life can be purchased on the cheap, or indeed purchased in the conventional, financial sense, at all:

for you must dismiss at once as a delusion the hope that has been sometimes cherished, that you can have a building which is a work of art, and is therefore above all things properly built, at the same price as a building which only pretends to be this: never forget when people talk about cheap art in general, by the way, that all art costs time, trouble, and thought, and that money is only a counter to represent these things.[3]

There is no possibility of art or of justice without due attention to the earth, Morris argues in this lecture, turning from material structures and possessions to 'possessions which should be common to all of us, [...] the green grass, and the leaves, and the waters, [...] the very light and air of heaven, which the Century of Commerce has been too busy to pay any heed to'.[4] The idea of earth and its plants, water, and air as 'common to all of us' gestures towards the rich linguistic and political history of the *common*, both adjective and noun, evoking not only what is shared but also, more specifically, the medieval space of unenclosed 'common grazing ground', as Morris uses it in *A Dream of John Ball*; it suggests, too, this shared possession as common wealth or commonweal, a term Morris uses in both these forms at various points in his writings, and redeploys in his later life as the title of his socialist newspaper.[5] The earth is always interactive with humanity in Morris's work, from the earliest mysteriously shifting landscapes of his short romances through the drama of his Icelandic epics and into the politically inflected or politically directed writings of his later years and the magical landscapes of his last romances. Landscape, indeed, becomes a further signifier of the moral

---

[1] William Morris, 'The Beauty of Life', 267.
[2] William Morris, 'Art and the Beauty of the Earth', in *CW*, XXII, 155–74.
[3] 'The Beauty', 269.   [4] 'The Beauty', 266.
[5] Morris, *A Dream of John Ball*, 368; 'Prologue: The Wanderers' in *The Earthly Paradise*, 103, l. 74; *News from Nowhere*, 448 and 'How I Became a Socialist', 563. Morris's uses More's term in his Foreword to Thomas More, *Utopia*, Kelmscott Press (1893), iii.

imperatives of art in the 1880 lecture: 'how can you care about the image of a landscape when you show by your deeds that you don't care for the landscape itself?' he asks his listeners, 'or what right have you to shut yourself up with beautiful form and colour when you make it impossible for other people to have any share in these things?'[6]

At the same time, his work both expresses and demands what may seem to some, he argues, 'an absurd superfluity of life', which he increasingly depicts as something that should be available to all.[7] This is represented by the desire to live among 'the best art', he claims in an 1881 lecture, by which he means art that tells stories: 'stories that tell of men's aspirations for more than material life can give them, their struggles for the future welfare of their race, their unselfish love, their unrequited service'. While 'in such subjects there is hope', Morris suggests, 'the aspect of them is likely to be sorrowful enough: defeat the seed of victory, and death the seed of life, will be shown on the face of most of them'.[8] This movement between victory and defeat, death and life, in the pursuit of beauty, pleasure and wholeness in work, relationships, and living conditions, finds expression in the form, style, and content of Morris's work. The interrelationships are significant here in that Morris's engagement with the beauty of life and art is never expressed in unchanging contentment with the status quo—even in the imagined utopia of *News from Nowhere*—but always in a commitment to the possibility of disruption and change and an acceptance of imperfection. Indeed, active, energizing, hope, variously construed in his writings as a contrasting experience to fear, despair, resignation, and inaction, runs through Morris's own life in a constant dialectical relationship with productive, disruptive imperfection, 'the sign of life in a mortal body, that is to say, of a state of progress and change', as John Ruskin puts it.[9]

LIFE AND INFLUENCES

William Morris was born on 24 March 1834 in Walthamstow, Essex, to William Morris and Emma Morris, née Shelton. He grew up in a comfortable home with eight siblings. His father, who worked for a city firm, Sanderson and Co, in London, also had shares in copper mines, the Devon Consoles: it is from these that the family's wealth arose, and left them 'very well off, rich in fact' after his death in 1847.[10] While the family practised evangelical

---

[6] 'The Beauty', 266.   [7] 'Some Hints on Pattern Designing', 275.

[8] 'Some Hints', 276.

[9] John Ruskin, 'The Nature of Gothic' in *Works*, X: *The Stones of Venice*, ii, 203. On imperfection in Morris's work, see also Waithe, 147.

[10] Letter to Andreas Scheu, in *CL*, II, 228. Morris sold his shares in the copper mines in 1875: see *CL*, II, 255–6.

Christianity Morris's own early investment in religion was always weighted towards the experience of beauty: in song, in church buildings, in the ritual and language and fellowship of the church. As he wrote to Austrian exile and socialist Andreas Scheu in a letter of 1883, 'I was brought up in what I should call rich establishmentarian puritanism; a religion which even as a boy I never took to'.[11] Instead he was attracted to the aesthetic side of religion, while his interest in it lasted; his deep familiarity with the cadences and tales of the Bible, evident in his writings, can be traced to those early evangelical roots as well as to the regular chapel-going required by public schools.

Morris was sent in 1848 to the minor public school Marlborough—'then a new and very rough school'[12]—and his letters home to his oldest sister Emma give evidence of the dislike he later made explicit in his critique of public schools as 'boy farms'. A letter of 1 November 1848 notes that there are 'now only 7 weeks to the Holidays', and concludes: 'there I go again! just like me! always harping on the Holidays. I am sure you must think me a great fool to be always thinking about home always, but I really can't help it.'[13] There is a touching sense of the alienation from his environment in that incongruous 'only', and the repetition of 'always' here. Later, in April 1849, he writes to Emma that 'it is no good either to you or to me to say any *horrid stale arguments* about being obliged to go to school for of course we know all about that.'[14] He escaped the confines of school to do two things: to explore the countryside, where he revelled in the landscape and natural beauty around Marlborough, in prehistoric monuments and remains in the area 'and everything else that had any history in it';[15] and to visit churches, admiring the architecture and taking rubbings of church brasses. Alongside this physical interaction with landscape and architecture Morris read voraciously. As he later wrote to Scheu, 'ever since I could remember I was a great devourer of books'.[16] The wide frames of reference and richness of easy allusion in his works make evident the enormous breadth of his reading, deliberately casual and frequently loose though such allusions are.

In his school and then his undergraduate years, his thinking about hand and eye, about the connections between conditions of labour, the work produced and the environment in which people work was greatly influenced by reading Ruskin, whose first two volumes of *Modern Painters* he discovered before going up to university and whose 1853 work, *The Stones of Venice*, came out in his first year as a student at Exeter College, Oxford, where he

[11] *CL*, II, 227.   [12] *CL*, II, 227.
[13] See 'The Boy Farms at Fault', *Commonweal*, 30 July 1887, 241; letter to Emma Morris, 1 November 1848, in *CL*, I, 3.
[14] Letter to Emma Morris, 13 April 1849, in *CL*, I, 8.   [15] *CL*, II, 228.
[16] *CL*, II, 228.

began reading Greats.[17] Morris's earliest biographer J. W. Mackail notes that 'Ruskin's famous chapter "Of the Nature of Gothic" [...] was a new gospel and a fixed creed', from which he read aloud again and again to his new friends at Oxford, much as he would later read aloud folk tales, poems, stories, and his own work to fellow-socialists and sympathizers.[18] That the language, rhythm, sound, and voice—the texture of texts—was as important to him as their content is evident in the many accounts of his unfailing joy in reading and dramatizing texts; his friend Edward Burne-Jones remembered 'the curious half-chanting voice, with immense stress laid on the rhymes, which always remained his method of reading poetry, whether his own or that of others'.[19] As to Oxford in general, 'I took very ill to the studies of the place,' Morris wrote to Scheu, 'but fell to very vigorously on history and specially mediaeval history'.[20] His fellow-readers of history, myth, and art criticism included Burne-Jones, who was to be his lifelong artistic collaborator, William Fulford, another lifelong friend, Charley Faulkner, who later accompanied him to Iceland and followed him into socialism, and Cormell Price, later head of the United Services College attended by Rudyard Kipling. It is to Price that some of Morris's most revealing letters from Oxford days are written.

On a trip to France with Burne-Jones and Fulford in the summer of 1855 he writes to Price of the architecture and landscape of northern France, beginning with a declaration of delight—'O! the glories of the Churches we have seen!'—and going on, before giving a detailed account of the architecture of the churches, to describe 'the lovely country' and its trees: 'so gloriously the trees are grouped, all manner of trees, but more especially the graceful poplars and aspens'.[21] The grouping here, suggesting arrangement, interaction, belonging, and variety, is essential to the pleasures of the landscape as well as its internal coherence and beauty: these are preoccupations that would run through Morris's ecological, political, and imaginative engagements with the world right up to the end of his life. In 1895, the year before he died, he made explicit what is implicit here: writing to the *Daily Chronicle* to protest against plans for thinning out the hornbeam trees in Epping Forest, his childhood playground, he argued, among other points, that no tree should be felled 'unless it were necessary for the growth of its fellows'.[22] The exigencies and responsibilities of community exist, Morris suggests, beyond the human.

The idea of another such glorious interactive grouping, or fellowship, this time of people living out their beliefs, began to take shape at Oxford. Morris and his undergraduate friends were avid readers of Malory's *Morte Darthur*

---

[17] Morris and Ruskin became close acquaintances and corresponded over shared interests, including stained glass, the SPAB, and support for younger artists. See *CL*, I, 252; 254; 569; II, 184–8.
[18] Mackail, I, 40.   [19] Mackail, I, 40.   [20] *CL*, II, 228.
[21] Letter to Cormell Price, 10 August 1855, 5–6 in this volume.
[22] Morris, 'Letter to the *Daily Chronicle*', 568 in this volume.

in Robert Southey's 1817 edition, and some of them, at least, were at first intent on forming 'a Brotherhood' modelled on the Arthurian knights, with Sir Galahad, Burne-Jones suggested, as their patron;[23] they soon decided instead to pour their energies into a communally authored magazine, *The Oxford and Cambridge Magazine*, which ran monthly throughout 1856. Much earnest discussion among the 'Brotherhood' preceded the magazine's beginnings, and Price recorded in his diary that 'there is to be no shewing off, no quips, no sneers, no lampooning in our Magazine'. It was funded largely by Morris, edited by Morris at first and then handed over to Fulford, whom Morris paid £100 to be editor.[24] *The Oxford and Cambridge Magazine* included one Arthurian poem of Morris's—'The Chapel in Lyoness'—and an Arthurian-influenced story, 'Golden Wings'.[25] However, though his other poems and short stories published in it bore, in all cases but one, the distinctly medievalist tint that would continue to characterize his work throughout his life, it was not until the publication of his first full collection, *The Defence of Guenevere, and Other Poems*, in 1858, that this early Arthurian preoccupation found full expression in his work.[26]

It was in the *Oxford and Cambridge*, in one of his first published pieces, that the harmonies of landscape and architecture he had noticed in France first found their way into his published work, in the setting for 'The Story of the Unknown Church':

Through the boughs and trunks of the poplars, we caught glimpses of the great golden corn sea, waving, waving, waving for leagues and leagues; and among the corn grew burning scarlet poppies, and blue corn-flowers; and the corn-flowers were so blue, that they gleamed, and seemed to burn with a steady light, as they grew beside the poppies among the gold of the wheat. Through the corn sea ran a blue river.[27]

This close observation of nature would remain a feature of Morris's writing throughout his life. Alongside the painterly intensity of colour in this description, there is an appreciation of the real conditions of plant growth; as contemporary ecologist Robin Wall Kimmerer has argued, the division between an understanding of plant science and an appreciation of plant beauty, which she similarly observes in the growing together of goldenrod and asters, is an artificial one.[28] Although Morris evinces no particular interest in large-scale scientific developments of his day, his apparently casual botanical

---

[23] *Memorials*, I, 77.   [24] Mackail, I, 83; 91.

[25] *O and C*, May 1856, 577–9; December 1856, 733–42.

[26] 'Frank's Sealed Letter', in the *O and C*, April 1856, 225–34, like his unfinished novel of 1872, unpublished in his lifetime, is a rare foray for Morris into fiction in a contemporary setting. Morris, *Novel on Blue Paper*, ed. by Penelope Fitzgerald (London, 1982).

[27] 'The Story of the Unknown Church', 39.

[28] Robin Wall Kimmerer, *Braiding Sweetgrass: Indigenous Wisdom, Scientific Knowledge, and the Teachings of Plants* (Minneapolis, MN, 2013), 39–47.

and biological knowledge shows an intimate familiarity with the necessary relationships between plants, animals, and humans, with growth patterns in plants and feeding habits of animals. The dramas of these interactions become part of the tales of human life in his work.

At Oxford Morris's last gasp of religious passion took the form of a brief fascination with the High Church Oxford Movement, with its emphasis on sacramental religion, though, as he wrote to Scheu, 'this latter phase [...] did not last me long'.[29] In 1855, after his trip across France, Morris decided not to go into the church. Instead, on graduating, he went to work as an apprentice architect to George Street in his offices in Beaumont Street, Oxford. By the end of 1856, he had left Street's. He continued to write and, on the encouragement of Dante Gabriel Rossetti, whom he had long admired and recently met, to paint. In 1858 Bell and Daldy brought out the vivid, jagged poems of *The Defence of Guenevere*, to mixed reviews. They are angular, bodily, contrary poems, locating meaning in the physical and hope in disruption. The title poem in the voice of Arthur's queen offers vivid evocations of her 'eager body', her 'long hand', her breast rising 'like waves of purple sea', and her 'long throat' through which 'the words go up | in ripples to my mouth'; natural rhythms are set alongside unnatural movements, wandering mouths, and straining hands. In 'Sir Peter Harpdon's End', a poetic drama of the Hundred Years War, Sir Peter notes, 'I like the straining game | Of striving well to hold up things that fall'.[30]

The combination of eagerness and languor, of flat planes and sharp angles that is present in his poems is evident too in his major Arthurian painting, 'La Belle Iseult', modelled by Jane Burden and completed in 1858.[31] It was while working for Street and living at Red Lion Square in London with Burne-Jones that Morris had first met Jane Burden, an ostler's daughter from Oxford; he soon afterwards asked her to marry him. She worked, before and after their marriage, as an artist's model for him and Rossetti, who, in 1860, married another of his models, the working-class artist and poet, Elizabeth Siddal. Morris, at the very end of his 1883 account of his life and work to Scheu, adds: 'I should have written above that I married in 1859 and have two daughters by that marriage very sympathetic with me as to my aims in life.'[32] The discontents of his marriage to Jane, her long-standing relationship with Rossetti after Siddal's suicide in 1862, and then, after Rossetti's death, with the poet Wilfred Scawen Blunt, begun the year Morris wrote this letter, are present by omission in this passing closing mention of his wife. Nonetheless his letters—some of which, especially during the early 1870s, give evidence of

---

[29] *CL*, II, 228.

[30] 'The Defence of Guenevere', l. 77; l. 121; ll. 226–7; ll. 230–1; 'Sir Peter Harpdon's End', ll. 218–19.

[31] See figure 1.   [32] *CL*, II, 229.

his emotional turmoil over the relationship—demonstrate a continuing companionship with Jane and the shared concerns of family life after the birth of their daughters Jenny and May. Jenny, the older, was of particular concern after she developed epilepsy in 1867, and was often thereafter away from home, on the basis that her health was better elsewhere. Morris's letters about her as well as to her are full of tender sympathy and love.[33]

In 1859–60 the newly married Morris oversaw the building of his own family home, Red House, at Bexhill in Kent, to his design ideas, worked up professionally by his friend, the architect Philip Speakman Webb.[34] The walls of the Red House were decorated, in a fashion Morris so often stipulated as ideal in later lectures, with stories from the past, painted by Morris, Jane, and their friends.[35] In 1861, building on his artistic friendships and his experience at Street's, Morris founded Morris, Marshall, Faulkner and Co, known colloquially as 'the Firm', with his friends Edward Burne-Jones, Peter Paul Marshall, Charles Faulkner, Dante Gabriel Rossetti, Ford Madox Brown, and Philip Webb. They produced stained glass windows, fabrics, and furniture, and it was as part of his work for the Firm that Morris began investigating dyeing in 1875. He lodged at first with the family of master-dyer Thomas Wardle in Leek, Staffordshire, and his letters of this period are full of descriptions of plunging his hands into vats of colour, of sourcing the right kinds of natural dyes, including what would become his signature madder for reds and indigo for blues. As well as learning from Wardle, he consulted old manuals of all kinds to learn this art: in August 1875 he writes to Wardle that 'I have been looking about for a Gerard for you', referring to the sixteenth-century botanist John Gerard's encyclopaedic *Herball*, which May Morris recalls her father reading aloud frequently to the family, and which offered information about vegetable dyes no longer in common use.[36]

That same year, in negotiations fraught with acrimony, the Firm was reconstituted under Morris alone, and renamed Morris and Co. Morris, meanwhile, was 'up to the neck in turning out designs for papers chintzes & carpets', busy completing a translation of *The Aeneid*, and deep in a new poetic work of his own, following the publication of his well-received long poems, the classical *Life and Death of Jason* (1867), 'a work of consummate art and of genuine beauty', as Henry James wrote, and *The Earthly Paradise*

---

[33] On Jane Morris, see Wendy Parkin, *Jane Morris: The Burden of History* (Edinburgh, 2013), and Jan Marsh and Frank C. Sharp, eds. *The Collected Letters of Jane Morris* (Martlesham, Suffolk, 2024); see *CL*, II, 160; 437.

[34] See figure 2.

[35] See, for instance, 'Some Hints', 276, and *News from Nowhere*, 427. See figure 3. In 2013 new murals were uncovered on the walls of Morris's Red House, now in the possession of the National Trust.

[36] John Gerard, *The Herball or General Historie of Plants, Gathered by John Gerarde, Master in Chirurgerie* (London, 1597); *CL*, I, 265.

(1868–70), with its Chaucerian structure of travellers' tales.[37] These two works made his name as a poet in his own day.[38] His new work was something rather different: an epic Icelandic poem, drawing together his own experience of landscape, story, history, and fellowship, which had found a particular focus in the language and literature of Iceland. In 1868 he had met Icelander and Icelandic scholar Eiríkr Magnússon, and soon began studying with him. They embarked on what would be a long-running collaboration in translating Icelandic literature, the 'delightful freshness and independence of thought' of which, alongside its 'air of freedom', 'worship of courage' and 'utter unconventionality', Morris noted later in characteristically visceral language, 'took my heart by storm'.[39] January 1869 saw the publication of their first collaboration, the short prose story 'The Saga of Gunnlaug the Wormtongue and Rafn the Skald' in *Fortnightly Review*, and in spring that year *The Grettis Saga* was published by F. S. Ellis. In 1870 they brought out the Icelandic epic, *The Völsunga Saga: The Story of the Volsungs and Niblungs*, 'the Great Story of the North, which should be to all our race what the tale of Troy was to the Greeks', and went on to publish further saga prose tales.[40] In 1871 and 1873 Morris visited Iceland, escaping his marital woes, leaving Jane Morris and Rossetti at the house he had taken in 1871 in a joint tenancy with Rossetti, Kelmscott Manor near Lechlade, Oxfordshire.

He immersed himself in both landscape and lifestyle in Iceland, glorying in the drama of its scenery. As he noted on his return in 1873: 'the glorious simplicity of the terrible & tragic, but beautiful land with its well-remembered stories of brave men, killed all querulous feeling in me'.[41] In 1876 he published his own Icelandic poem, *Sigurd the Volsung and the Fall of the Niblungs*, written in rhyming hexameter couplets, shot through with kennings in the Old Norse or Icelandic style, in language hailed by contemporaries as particularly Northern and imbued, as the *International Review* put it, with 'a Saxon muscularity and strength'.[42] Yet its muscularity, masculinity, and, by extension, tracing of a particular Northern national identity, much praised in contemporary reviews, are complicated by blendings of language, form, landscape, and content, as well as by its emphasis on Ragnarök, the inevitable destruction of the world it so beautifully portrays, as Heather O'Donoghue has suggested.[43]

---

[37] *CL*, I, 255; Henry James [unsigned review] *North American Review*, 105.2 (1867), 691–2.

[38] For reviews, see Peter Faulkner, *William Morris: The Critical Heritage* (London, 1973), 50–202.

[39] *CL*, II, 23.

[40] William Morris and Eiríkr Magnússon, Introduction to *The Völsungasaga*, in *CW*, VII, 286.

[41] Letter to Aglaia Coronio, in *CL*, II, 198.

[42] 'Recent American Books', *International Review*, 4 (1877), 697.

[43] Heather O'Donoghue, 'The Great Story of the North: William Morris's Sigurd the Volsung as National Epic', in Stahl and Bønding, *Mythology and 'Nation Building': N. F. S. Grundtvig and his Contemporaries* (Aarhus, 2019), 410–29.

While he was at work on *Sigurd*, experimenting with dyes and continuing to produce stained glass windows and furnishings for the Firm, Morris turned his attention to wider public matters, writing in a letter to the *Athenaeum* in March 1877 that he would like to see the establishment of an association:

to keep a watch on old monuments to protest against all 'restoration' that means more than keeping out wind and weather, and by all means, literary and other, to awaken a feeling that our ancient buildings are not mere ecclesiastical toys, but sacred monuments of the nation's growth and hope.[44]

Shortly afterwards he did indeed set up the Society for the Protection of Ancient Buildings; its manifesto urged 'all those who have to deal' with historical buildings 'to put Protection in the place of Restoration, to stave off decay by daily care, to prop a perilous wall or mend a leaky roof by such means as are obviously meant for support or covering' and to 'resist all tampering with either the fabric or ornament of the building'.[45] The work of the SPAB, or Anti-Scrape, was to occupy Morris intermittently for the rest of his life.

He was, by now, becoming established not only as a poet but as an expert in and on the decorative arts, and at the end of 1877 he gave the first of what would become many public lectures on art. At the same time, he became increasingly outraged by the injustices evident in international relations and in 1876 he was particularly galvanized by the Eastern Question—debates over how to respond to the status and power of Turkey and the Ottoman Empire in Europe—following the 'Bulgarian Atrocities', the brutal suppression of an uprising of Bulgarians in the Ottoman Empire. Benjamin Disraeli and the Tory government took the side of Turkey against Russia in this question, and Morris, with William Gladstone, the Liberals, and the Eastern Question Association, formed in 1876, took the opposite position. Morris took on the role of treasurer of the Eastern Question Association, and argued passionately over the succeeding two years against Britain's bellicose support of Turkey against Russia. 'I joined heartily in that question on the Liberal side', he later wrote to Scheu, and indeed his earliest political song, 'Wake, London Lads!', with its call to 'arise and fall to work' in the cause of freedom, was published and used at a protest meeting in Exeter Hall, London, in January 1878.[46]

That same year, entering a hot contemporary debate, Morris makes a distinction, central in many of his works, between a battle of equals and a war of possession and domination. In his 'Address to English Liberals' he identifies subjects of the Ottoman empire as slaves—'either actually slaves [...] or newly made freedman [...] or people who would be slaves if they

---

[44] Morris, 'Society for the Protection of Ancient Monuments', *Athenaeum*, 10 March 1877, 326.
[45] 'Manifesto of the SPAB' in *AWS*, I, 111.
[46] *CL*, II, 230; 'Wake, London Lads!', in *AWS*, II, 572–3.

were not heroes'. He notes that those among the British who had supported the South in the recent American Civil War saw the white Confederate army as the underdog against the richer North but failed to identify the cause of the slaves; the same dynamic, he suggests, is in play in the current war. 'This it is', he says, 'that makes me sad and not exultant when I hear of the stout fighting, the heroism if you will, of the Turkish soldiers; I cannot look upon them as men fighting for their hearths and homes, but rather as land-lords fighting for their unjust rents.'[47] Questions of class injustice that were soon to preoccupy Morris are foreshadowed in this speech of 1878; indeed as E. P. Thompson notes, he had already framed his opposition to British warmongering on the side of Turkey in explicitly class terms in his 1877 manifesto 'To the Working Men of England', in which he noted that a certain portion of the 'richer classes' would, if they could, 'thwart your just aspirations, [. . .] silence you, [. . .] deliver you bound hand and foot for ever to irresponsible capital'.[48]

The combination of single-minded passion, opposition to wars of domination, and a willingness to support uprisings against oppression that characterized Morris's response to the Eastern Question was soon to find a different focus.[49] On 1 January 1881 he wrote to Georgiana Burne-Jones his 'word of hope for the new year':

that it may do a good turn of work toward the abasement of the rich and the raising up of the poor, [. . .] till people can at last rub out from their dictionaries altogether these dreadful words rich and poor.[50]

By the turn of the following year, Morris had become disillusioned with Gladstone and Liberalism, not least because of the Liberal government's pursuit of a 'Stockjobbers' war in Egypt in 1882, evidence, for Morris, that it was not a party of the people against oppression.[51] His hope soon found a new political expression: in January 1883 he joined the Democratic Federation, soon to become the Social Democratic Federation, established by Henry Myers Hyndman. In May he joined its executive committee, and in August that year he wrote to Sarah Anne Unwin Byles that 'I am in short "one of the people called" Socialists, and am bound as by religious conviction to preach that doctrine whenever I open my mouth in public'.[52]

---

[47] 'Address to English Liberals', *AWS*, II, 373.   [48] Thompson, 193.

[49] While my own work has critiqued Morris's long-running investment in an idea of transformative battle violence it is worth noting that he remained resolutely opposed to wars of empire and violent domination while continuing to see occasional spontaneous violence or violent resistance to oppression as a sign of hope. At the same time, he designates economic competition Commercial War. See 'How We Live and How We Might Live', 313–15, 317, 322.

[50] *CL*, II, 3.   [51] *CL*, II, 230. A stockjobber is a stockbroker intent on personal gain.

[52] *CL*, II, 194; 214.

Where previously Morris had lectured primarily about art, everyday life, and the beauty of the earth, he now began to turn his energies to preaching socialism, beginning immediately in 1883 what would become by late 1886 and 1887 a busy programme of lecturing, identifying in socialism's revolutionary message of justice and equality a new cause that intertwined with the cause of art.[53] In his first year as a declared socialist, he began reading Marx in French; he delivered his controversial new lectures, 'Art, Wealth and Riches' and 'Art under Plutocracy', garnering a chorus of media consternation and disapproval; he gave a speech promoting the Democratic Federation's aims; he wrote to various newspapers about his socialism and responded to articles commenting on it; and he urged friends and associates, including Ruskin and Algernon Swinburne, to join the Democratic Federation, for whom he also designed a membership card and contributed to a manifesto entitled *Socialism Made Plain*.[54]

By August 1883 Morris was noting discontent among SDF members.[55] In December 1884 he and a group of comrades broke away and launched a rival organization, the Socialist League, followed swiftly in February 1885 by the establishment of its own newspaper, *Commonweal*. Like the early *Oxford and Cambridge Magazine*, this paper was underwritten from its inception by Morris, despite its cost of one penny to buy. It was distributed on the streets and sent out to subscribers nationally and internationally, reaching a regular circulation of around 2,000–3,000 per issue.[56] Morris's contributions to *Commonweal* were many and various: as well as editorials, plays, poems, news roundups, reports on socialist meetings, and comments on historical movements and current affairs, he included in its early months the supplements 'Unattractive Labour' (May 1885) and 'Attractive Labour' (June 1885), titles drawing on French utopian thinker Charles Fourier's argument for 'attractive labour', characterized by variety.[57] These articles synthesized briefly some of the ideas of the interconnection of art, pleasure, labour, and the urgent need for social change which he explored at greater length in lectures such as 'Useful Work *versus* Useless Toil' (1884) and 'How We Live and How We Might Live' (1885), this latter also published in *Commonweal*.

It was in *Commonweal*, too, that *A Dream of John Ball* (1886–7) and *News from Nowhere* (1890) were first serialized, among stories of the suffering and

---

[53] On Morris's schedule for 1887, see Florence Boos, ed., *William Morris's Socialist Diary* (London, 1982).

[54] See Lemire, 239–40; Morris and H. M. Hyndman, *Socialism Made Plain: Being the Social and Political Manifesto of the Democratic Federation* (London, 1883).

[55] *CL*, II, 219.

[56] For circulation figures, see Deborah Mutch and Norman Kelvin, '*Commonweal*', in Laurel Brake and Marysa Demoor (eds), *Dictionary of Nineteenth-Century Journalism in Great Britain and Ireland* (Ghent, 2009), 136.

[57] Charles Fourier, *Selections from the Works of Fourier*, trans. Julia Franklin (London, 1901), 166.

struggling of socialists of the day. These tales—one a fictionalized dream-vision of the 1381 Peasants' Revolt, and the other a playful medievalist utopia set in the twenty-second century—thus take their place in the propaganda (a term claimed and used positively by the Socialist League and others in Victorian Britain) of the *Commonweal*. Both serialized tales appeared alongside reviews of and advertisements for other socialist books, talks, and utopian tales; both form part of a utopian conversation about change in the context of *Commonweal*'s stated aims: 'to awaken the sluggish, to strengthen the waverers, to instruct the seekers after truth'.[58] Morris's tales reached far beyond their immediate socialist readership, however, and were quickly brought out in book form by Reeves and Turner, *John Ball* in 1888 and *News from Nowhere* in 1891. They are texts that insist on the possibility of future change inherent in history and on the necessity of communal battles against domination to bring about that change.

At the end of 1890, after much public debate in *Commonweal* about the differences between Communism and anarchism, Morris left the increasingly anarchist-oriented Socialist League to set up the Hammersmith Socialist Society, his last political fellowship. As well as the book publication of *News from Nowhere*, the following year saw Morris bring to fruition a growing interest in typography and book design in the founding of the Kelmscott Press, 'with the hope of producing some [books] which would have a definite claim to beauty'.[59] The first book hand-printed on the press was *The Glittering Plain*, one of five complete romances that Morris wrote in the last five years of his life, all named for environmental features and shaped by interactions between active, magical or semi-magical environments, migrants, questors, and travellers, and the imperatives of desire, openly and sometimes troublesomely expressed by women and men alike.[60]

POSTHUMOUS REPUTATION

Morris's last romance, *The Sundering Flood*, was finished on his deathbed and published posthumously by the Kelmscott Press, which had absorbed and delighted him, though not to the exclusion of political engagement, in his final years. When he died on 3 October 1896, his obituaries reflected what one newspaper cartoon had portrayed in 1886 as 'the Earthly Paradox': his polarized and polarizing standing as beloved establishment poet and

---

[58] *Commonweal*, February 1885, 1.

[59] 'Note by William Morris on his Aims in Founding the Kelmscott Press', 585.

[60] *The Story of the Glittering Plain* (1891), *The Wood beyond the World* (1894), *The Well at the World's End* (1896), *The Water of the Wondrous Isles* (1897), and *The Sundering Flood* (1898).

anti-establishment revolutionary radical.[61] Indeed, fellow-artist and socialist Walter Crane defended Morris in his 1896 obituary against those who experienced an 'insuperable difficulty' in imagining that 'the man who wrote *The Earthly Paradise* should have lent a hand to try and bring it about'.[62] That perceived incongruity, and the range of responses to it, continued to shape his reputation in the years that followed. In 1899, Morris's first biographer, J. W. Mackail, noted the consternation of some of Morris's oldest friends at his turn to socialism, but nonetheless offered a well-documented, if occasionally disparaging, account of Morris's practical politics, highlighting his commitment to the cause and his comrades, and his constant emphasis on the need to 'make Socialists'.[63] After the painstaking and wide-ranging editing work of Morris's daughter May Morris in publishing his *Collected Works* in 1910–15, Morris's reputation as poet and writer continued strong into the 1920s and 1930s but his radical revolutionary politics and innovative style began to be eclipsed by his role as an artist, designer, and 'idle singer', to use his own phrase from the *Earthly Paradise*.[64]

An attempt to reclaim Morris's serious radical credentials was made in the 1930s by Robin Page Arnot, writer, campaigner, conscientious objector to the First World War, and founder member of the Communist Party of Great Britain. Arnot wrote a pamphlet in 1934, the centenary of Morris's birth, entitled *William Morris: A Vindication*, in an avowed effort to rescue Morris's political reputation and demonstrate that he was specifically Marxist and revolutionary rather than 'a sort of sickly dilettante Socialist'.[65] He was responding in part to the Victoria and Albert Museum's first exhibition of Morris's art and craft work, opened by Conservative minister and nephew of Burne-Jones, Stanley Baldwin, with affectionate and rather anodyne anecdotes about Morris and his work that served to dispel any sense of his revolutionary and anti-establishment thought and actions.[66] In 1936, Blackwell's brought out *William Morris: Artist, Writer, Socialist*, May Morris's two-volume collection of unpublished extracts from her father's work, drawing attention to his socialist thinking in particular and to the links between his aesthetics and his politics. The same year saw the influential publication of Nikolaus Pevsner's *Pioneers of Modern Design: William Morris to Walter Gropius* (Faber and Faber) further establishing Morris's artistic reputation.

---

[61] See Fiona MacCarthy, *William Morris: A Life for our Time* (London, 1994), 529.
[62] *CL*, II, 455; Walter Crane, 'William Morris: Poet, Artist and Craftsman, and Social Reconstructor', *Progressive Review*, (November 1896), 149.
[63] Mackail, II, 251.   [64] *EP*, 98 in this edition.
[65] Robin Page Arnot, *William Morris: A Vindication* (London, 1934), 6; Arnot later developed this into a book, *William Morris: The Man and the Myth* (London, 1964).
[66] 'Mr Baldwin's Memories of William Morris', *Manchester Guardian*, 10 February 1934, 10; on Baldwin and Arnot, see Michelle Weinroth, *Englishness, Sublimity, and the Rhetoric of Dissent* (Montreal, 1996), 50–118.

The 1950s brought the beginnings of new wave of interest in Morris's work and new evaluations of its political and aesthetic imbrications. The quiet but significant publication in 1955 of E. P. Thompson's trenchant, deeply researched, and politically astute biography, *William Morris: Romantic to Revolutionary*, followed by a well-received revised edition of 1976, set in motion a wider reclamation of Morris's reputation as a serious, deeply committed, and practical political activist and thinker as well as writer and artist. Thompson drew widely and deeply on original records to demonstrate in particular the range of Morris's activities as a socialist, making the argument that Morris's revolutionary politics followed from his early commitment to Romantic ideals and the developing moral sense that drove that commitment. Scholarly books on Morris's poetry and prose, his politics and the intersections of his life and work, as well as new editions of individual works, followed thick and fast over the next two decades.[67]

Norman Kelvin published the first volume of his illuminating and painstakingly researched *Collected Letters of William Morris* in 1984, and the last in 1996, demonstrating the range and interconnectedness of Morris's personal, artistic, and political concerns. Fiona MacCarthy's prize-winning, comprehensive literary biography of 1994 knitted together the strands of Morris's life in a lively, compelling narrative, establishing him firmly as a central figure in British literary and artistic history and a major influence on twenty-first-century culture.[68] In the years since that biography Morris's work has been discussed in relation to its medieval sources and texts, its manuscript histories and its historical, political, cultural, press, literary, and environmental contexts.[69] Scholars have begun to pay fresh attention to Morris's Icelandic epic, *Sigurd the Volsung*, still perhaps the most neglected of his works but newly relevant to our own day in its representations of violence, contested masculinities, fluid identities, and interspecies connections.[70] Indeed *Sigurd*, I suggest, might rightly be seen as a fulcrum of Morris's work rather than an idiosyncratic sidenote. New popular fantasy press editions of Morris's late romances are now routinely advertised as works that influenced J. R. R. Tolkien, and his commitment to ecology is garnering wide critical

---

[67] See, for instance the competing 1967 accounts in Henderson, *William Morris*, and Paul Thompson. On Morris as Marxist, see Meier.

[68] MacCarthy, *William Morris*.

[69] See Alice Chandler, *A Dream of Order: The Medieval Ideal in the Nineteenth Century* (Lincoln, NE, 1970); Waithe; Anna Vaninskaya, *William Morris and the Idea of Community: Romance, History and Propaganda, 1880–1914* (Edinburgh, 2010); Elizabeth Carolyn Miller, *Slow Print: Literary Radicalism and Late Victorian Print Culture* (Princeton, 2013); Owen Holland, *William Morris's Utopianism: Propaganda, Politics and Prefiguration* (Basingstoke, 2017). See also the William Morris Archive, ed. by Florence Boos, at https://morrisarchive.lib.uiowa.edu/.

[70] See particularly Ian Felce, *William Morris and the Icelandic Sagas* (2018) and O'Donoghue.

recognition.[71] In the range of his concerns, the range of his modes of expressing them, and the range of readers he attracts, Morris continues to generate pleasure and disturbance, controversy and delight.

THE LIVING WISDOM OF ALL THINGS

J. W. Mackail notes of Morris's early life in Essex that he and his brothers spent much time out of doors, fishing, shooting rabbits and small birds to eat, and also gardening in their own small plots. He records that 'one who shared this outdoor life at Woodford with Morris told me, in a phrase of accurate simplicity, that as a boy he "knew the names of birds." There was, indeed, little that he ever saw of which he did not know the name.'[72] Certainly his letters, lectures, writings, and pattern designs are full of references to birds, animals, and plants, as well as topographical features, not in general but specifically: named by species or carefully depicted by characteristics of habit, form, or growth. In the works included in this selection, Morris makes mention of at least twenty-nine species of trees, twenty-eight different kinds of bird, twenty other kinds of plants and flowers, and twenty other animals and insects. He pays close attention to natural detail: the way light filters through the leaves of a beech tree, which plants grow in company with each other, what kinds of insects particular fish feed on and at what time of day. Central to his work, in all its different preoccupations with story, myth, disruption, passion, history, equality, justice, rhythm, sound, and a myriad other concerns, is the interconnection of the human and the environmental, articulated by the hedge priest John Ball when he tells the assembled crowd that even if they should die in battle, they will remain 'a part and parcel of the living wisdom of all things, very stones of the pillars that uphold the joyful earth'.[73] These words resonate particularly in this twenty-first-century moment of ecological crisis, ecological guilt, and ecological injustice in global terms, and so it is to this aspect of Morris's work that I turn in what follows.

Just as Morris was interested in migrations, disruptions, and minglings among people, so not infrequently the human and the non-human mingle in his work. This is most fully realized in *News from Nowhere*, where 'I looked up at the overhanging boughs of the great trees, with the sun coming glittering through the leaves, and listened to the song of the summer blackbirds as it mingled with the sound of the backwater near us', or where:

---

[71] On ecology, see Bradley J. Macdonald, 'William Morris and the Vision of Ecosocialism', *Contemporary Justice Review*, 7 (2004), 287–304; Miller, 'William Morris, Extraction Capitalism, and the Aesthetics of Surface', *Victorian Studies*, 57.3 (2015), 395–404; Patrick O'Sullivan, 'Desire and Necessity: William Morris and Nature' in *The Routledge Companion to William Morris*, ed. Florence Boos (London, 2020), 442–64.

[72] Mackail, I, 10.   [73] *A Dream of John Ball*, 359.

the folk on the bank talked indeed, mingling their kind voices with the cuckoo's song, the sweet strong whistle of the blackbirds, and the ceaseless note of the corn-crake as he crept through the long grass of the mowing-field; whence came the waves of fragrance from the flowering clover amidst of the ripe grass.[74]

Elsewhere in the tale pleasurable human work, represented by sounding tools, joins the mingling of species, senses, and movement: the travellers in the tale hear 'the full tune of tinkling trowels mingle with the humming of the bees and the singing of the larks'. In the protosocialist romance of battle between the Germans and Goths, *The House of the Wolfings* (1888), children, whose voices are like those of 'young throstles' (song thrushes), play and mingle with the community's dogs. More metaphorically, wrong is mingled with wrong in *Sigurd the Volsung*, but so too is delight mingled with sorrow in the hand of Regin 'blended' with the harp strings to tell tales.[75] The beginning of a battle in *Sigurd* is the moment when 'at last the edges mingled'.[76]

In 'The Lesser Arts' Morris suggests that in the English countryside, 'all is measured, mingled, varied, gliding easily one thing into another: little rivers, little plains; swelling, speedily-changing uplands, all beset with handsome orderly trees; little hills, little mountains, netted over with the walls of sheep-walks'. The designer's eye on the landscape is evident in that use of 'netted', evoking the background net of many of Morris's designs. The English landscape is not vast or majestic, he argues; rather 'all is little; yet not foolish and blank, but serious rather, and abundant of meaning for such as choose to seek it; it is neither prison nor palace, but a decent home'.[77] Elsewhere in his work, more dramatic landscapes also mingle with the human to suggest meaning and connection: waste spaces, full of drama and stories, abound in *Sigurd*; the river in *The Sundering Flood* cleaves 'a great waste of rocks mingled with sand, where groweth neither tree nor bush nor grass'. Later in the text, Morris has the young lovers Osberne and Elfhild converse across the river that divides them and talks as they do: 'There was but some thirty feet of water between them, but all gurgling and rushing and talking, so the child raised a shrill and clear voice as she clapped her hands together and cried: "O thou beauteous creature, what art thou?"' Osberne laughs, and replies 'in a loud voice'.[78] The openness of their delight in each other is set in the context of the expressive river. The convention of the babbling brook is made rather less poetic than literal in the mingling of human voice with nature here. Romance conventions of the living earth gesture towards a more authentic or natural connection between the human and non-human than the alienated life of the nineteenth century allows.

---

[74] *News*, 554.   [75] *News*, 538; *Wolfings*, 406; *Sigurd*, 176.   [76] *Sigurd*, 135.
[77] 'The Lesser Arts', 246.   [78] *The Sundering Flood*, 571; 582.

Yet Morris's ecological thinking is rooted always in close attention to non-human things in themselves as well as in relation to the human. His own knowledge of and interest in animals, birds, and plants is evident not only in his writings but also in the designs of his carpets, fabrics, and wallpapers, which draw on rivers, including the Kennet (see figure 8), plants, including 'Willow Bough' (see figure 7) and, in 'Strawberry Thief' (see figure 6), the thrushes which Morris sees and hears, along with their close relatives, blackbirds, so often in his Kelmscott garden over the years. Nature, intertwined with history, story, and belonging is there too in private and public letters, not only in the passionate late correspondence about Epping Forest, but across his life.[79] Writing to his epileptic daughter Jenny, away from home in pursuit of better health in the 1880s and 1890s, he frequently comments on the state of the plants in the garden at Kelmscott Manor. In 1883, he sends Jenny a hand-drawn illustration of a plant he doesn't know, commenting that 'Edgar says it is the Dog-wood but I can't find it in Gerard': as with his attentive reading of Izaak Walton on fish, Morris combines close observation with information from expert texts. The much-read and shared Gerard (like Walton) was not only a source of information, however, but of connection with the past; May Morris recalls: 'we learnt to know old Gerard well; it was a link of friendship to meet certain uncommon plants that flourished at Kelmscott in his London garden'.[80] Just as in his art and design work Morris drew on ancient Persian and Byzantine designs incorporating plant, animal, and human life and activity, to 're-knit or re-knot the elements and restore dynamic force or vitality', as Caroline Arscott puts it, drawing on the image of carpet-knotting, so in his life, letters, and writing the idea of friendship knots together plants and people, past and present, the living and the dead.[81]

Friendship or fellowship as an experience, a practice, and a mode of social and artistic organization, occurs so frequently in Morris's work that it can be seen not only as a theme but a form and indeed a hermeneutic. *News from Nowhere*, a tale closely focused on one small part of southern England and on a deep sense of belonging between people and land, nonetheless insists on the international connections of its people: before they can read, the people of Morris's future world 'can talk French'—rather than 'learn French'; this is an organic, not a taught process—'which is the nearest language talked on the other side of the water'; children also learn German and Welsh or Irish 'very quickly, because their elders all know them; and besides our guests from over sea often bring their children with them, and the little ones get together, and rub their speech into one another.'[82] There is a casual assumption of friendship

[79] 'On Epping Forest', 567–8.
[80] *CL*, II, 81; May Morris, Introduction to *CW*, XXII, xviii–xix.
[81] Caroline Arscott, 'Morris Carpets', *RIHA Journal* 89 (March 2014), <https://doi.org/10.11588/riha.2014.1.69970>, para 23 of 29.
[82] *News*, 438.

across countries here, and of easy, corporeal internationalism. Even in the almost complete world of this utopian text, there remains a possibility of new interaction, a further world just out of sight, and an awareness of the international shaping the national, as well as corporeal desire shaping relationships. While in his review of Edward Bellamy's *Looking Backward*, Morris noted that 'modern nationalities are mere artificial devices for the commercial war that we seek to put an end to, and will disappear with it', *News from Nowhere* suggests that a new kind of nationality and indeed a new kind of relational internationalism might remain in a postcapitalist world of equality and cooperation.[83]

Although Morris's life was so deeply rooted in the south of England, his works, his thinking and his relationships drew in and on the international, from his wide reading in the ancient tales of Persia and India as well as Greece and Rome, contemporary African American folk tales and European epics, poems, and novels, to his own circles of friendship among political exiles in London.[84] Wales remained important to him as a place of origin for his family, and he drew on its dominated history to imagine the experiences of the oppressed of his own time; Scotland became an important centre for Socialist League activities and lecture tours.[85] He was interested in work in its various forms, including art, domestic work, and, in a matter of enduring concern, battle as well as struggle, but he was also alive to global interconnections, conditions of work, fellowships, and oppressions well beyond Europe, from ancient Persia and historic Turkey to British involvement in contemporary Egypt, Sudan, and China.

His interest in the effects of the international on the local is borne out too in his lectures on art, architecture, and socialism, which touch on Irish republican politics, Persian design, and the craftsmanship of Indian and Javanese textile workers; his thinking about politics, from his early, instinctive Liberalism to his firmly committed and clear-eyed socialism, is rooted in a critique of Britain's empire, and indeed of other empires, past and present, from the Romans to the Ottomans.[86] While in his imagined past worlds of the 1870s and 1880s, Morris neither glosses over nor underplays the reality of slavery and violent subjugation in the processes of change, in his lectures of

---

[83] 'Looking Backward', 417. On Morris's internationalism, see Tanya Agathocleous, *Urban Realism and the Cosmopolitan Imagination in the Nineteenth Century: Visible City, Invisible World* (Cambridge, 2010), 147–61; Holland, 191–218; and Leela Gandhi, *Affective Communities: Anticolonial Thought, Fin-de-Siècle Radicalism, and the Politics of Friendship* (Durham, NC, 2006), 123.

[84] For a list of his favourite books, see *CL*, II, 514–18.

[85] On Wales, see 'Address', 374–5.

[86] See 281 and 315 in this volume. In his critique of the Ottoman Empire, Morris examines his own ideas of Islam with critical self-awareness in the 'Address', 377–8, although his internationalism does not make him immune to the occasional mobilization of racial or religious stereotypes, as Waithe (166–8) has noted.

this period, he draws on the international oppressions of past and present to critique current conditions of work. In 'How We Live and How We Might Live' he challenges the deliberate unawareness of the middle classes of his own time by contrasting them with recent American slave-owners as well as with ancient Romans in being at a remove from their own oppressive actions: 'many of the oppressors of the poor [...] are not conscious of their being oppressors [...]; they live in an orderly, quiet way themselves, as far as possible removed from the feelings of a Roman slave-owner or a Legree' (this latter a brutal slave-owner in Harriet Beecher Stowe's abolitionist novel of 1852, *Uncle Tom's Cabin*). Morris goes on to suggest that 'they know that the poor exist, but their sufferings do not present themselves to them in a trenchant and dramatic way'.[87] His own work, by contrast, insistently dramatizes. While the societies he depicts in *Sigurd the Volsung* and *The House of the Wolfings*, for instance, are founded on slavery, and he notes elsewhere that 'the civilisation of the ancients was founded on slavery', his tales are of people in the midst of change: the movements of violent upheaval of which they tell are preferable, for Morris, to the oppressive stasis of what he calls 'modern society', and its conditions of work.[88]

The nature and history of these conditions, their interconnections with human and non-human life, and the means of changing them, forms a central strand of Morris's thinking. In his 1881 lecture 'Art and the Beauty of the Earth', he argues that in the early Middle Ages, art was the work of 'the nameless people', not least because 'the tyrants, and pedants, and bullies of the time were too busy over other things to make it'. Namelessness, in this instance, suggests not a loss but a transfer of identity from the people to the work of their hands: 'for no names of its makers are left, not one. Their work only is left, and all that came of it, and all that is to come of it.'[89] The everyday communal work of art, he suggests, was itself a form of freedom, and 'what came of it first was the complete freedom of art in the midst of a society that had at least begun to free itself from religious and political fetters'. In a virtuoso account of the power of art that is neither history nor analysis but a call to action, he argues that 'art was free. Whatever a man thought of, that he might bring to light by the labour of his hands, to be praised and wondered at by his fellows. Whatever man had thought in him of any kind, and skill in him of any kind to express it, he was deemed good enough to be used for his own pleasure and the pleasure of his fellows.' Moreover, art in this account unites people across races and religions, invoking again an idea of intrinsic value rather than disposability of people or things: 'nothing and nobody was wasted;

---

[87] 'How We Live', 311.

[88] 'The Beauty', 262; See 'Useful Work *versus* Useless Toil', 300, and 'How I Became a Socialist', 565.

[89] 'Art and the Beauty', 158.

all people east of the Atlantic felt this art; from Bokhara to Galway, from Iceland to Madras, all the world glittered with its brightness and quivered with its vigour. It cast down the partitions of race and religion also.' Not only were 'Christian and Mussulman [...] made joyful by it' but 'Kelt, Teuton, and Latin raised it up together; Persian, Tartar, and Arab gave and took its gifts from one another.' Art acts here, in Morris's account. It functions not only as the means and result of knotting together cultures and people but also as friend and token of friendship in a gift economy, suggesting its pre- and supra-capitalist status. Finally, Morris asserts that 'whatever slavery still existed in the world (more than enough, as always) art had no share in it'.[90] He does not flinch from the brutality of ancient worlds, but he presents them as worlds in transition. So, he argues, although 'in those days of which I speak life was often rough & evil enough, beset by violence, superstition, ignorance, slavery; yet I cannot help thinking that sorely as poor folk needed a solace, they did not altogether lack one': it was 'pleasure in their work'.[91]

In 'The Lesser Arts', Morris notes that his thoughts on pleasure in labour are an echo of Ruskin's in 'The Nature of Gothic', where Ruskin's key contention is that division of labour, the separation of the person from the meaning of their work, makes the workers merely machines, and therefore 'less than men', people 'divided into mere segments of men'.[92] Morris extends this argument from the diminishment of the individual to the dissolution of community: in 'Unattractive Labour', he argues that workers have no possibility of enjoying their labour or the earth but instead are set in competition by desperate need. In notes for an undelivered lecture in 1891 he recognizes the paucity of life engendered by poverty of living and working conditions, which in turn ensures unequal power and the destruction of relationships, not only between workers and masters but between workers themselves: 'The reason why the workers cannot at once compel better terms from the privileged, is that they are so poor and must at once work if they are not to become mere paupers, and since their number is so great, they *compete* for the labour.[93] Morris lists the common Malthusian solutions to this analysis—fewer children and more self-discipline on the part of the poor— and rejects them, as 'vain dreams!'. They assume a mere modification of the state of relations between 'the useful classes who are oppressed' and 'the useless classes who oppress them' and Morris notes that 'the crimes of civilization cannot be atoned for in such easy terms'.[94] It is the refusal of change on 'easy terms' that makes Morris's myths of battle so compelling,

---

[90] See *John Ball*, 552–7; 'Art and the Beauty', 158–9.
[91] 'Art and the Beauty', 163.
[92] 'The Lesser Arts', 242; Ruskin, 'The Nature of Gothic', 194; 196.
[93] 'Socialism up to date', BL Add Ms 45334, 8.
[94] 'Socialism up to date', quoted in *AWS*, II, 342.

and his imagination of the productive possibilities of personal, physical combat so insistent and so disruptive.

At the same time there is in Morris's thinking a struggle with non-human nature and the nature of work that is different from the uprising of the oppressed and from the 'state of perpetual war' he identifies in his own commercial society. It bears some resemblance to twenty-first-century thinking about the nature of the non-human as active rather than passive, even as it remains distinct in its language of contest and victory.[95] In 'Some Hints on Pattern Designing', he argues about simple materials such as worsted thread in these terms: 'you may, with them, tell a story in a new way, even if it be not a new story; you may conquer the obstinacy of your material and make it obey you as far as the needs of beauty go, and the telling of your tale'; as a result, he argues, 'you will be pleased with the victory of your skill, but you will not have forgotten your subject amidst mere laboriousness, and you will know that your victory has been no barren one, but has produced a beautiful thing, which nothing but your struggle with difficulties could have brought forth'.[96] Work as struggle contributes to the formation of the human person in this account, which at the same time imagines a separate being inherent not only in the living earth but in apparently inanimate things.[97]

In 'The Beauty of Life' Morris further suggests that it is 'that kindly struggle with nature, to which all true craftsmen are born' which is 'both the building-up and the wearing-away of their lives'. Similarly, May Morris notes that Morris liked the Norwegian novelist Bjørnstjerne Martinius Bjørnson's 1857 novel of peasant farming life, *Synnøve Solbakken*, with its portrayal of: 'the taciturn life in constant struggle with Nature, and a sober rejoicing in her not lightly yielded gifts'.[98] In both Morris's and May Morris's words here there is an assumption of equality between people and the earth in this struggle: not a one-way move to domination by the human but a need for exertion in order to win the gifts of the earth. Morris's recurring image of sensual love for the earth in *News from Nowhere*, described by Old Hammond as an 'intense and overweening love of the very skin and surface of the earth on which man dwells, such as a lover has in the fair flesh of the woman he loves' seems borne out here in the sense that working the earth might be seen as akin to winning a beloved's favour—and as so often in Morris's work, there is just behind that image, the possibility of the need to engage in hand-to-hand combat in order to win the prize.[99] Politics and ecology are partners in

---

[95] 'How We Live', 312.   [96] 'Some Hints', 282.
[97] Morris's views might be read as foreshadowing ideas of 'thing power', as outlined in Jane Bennett, *Vibrant Matter: A Political Ecology of Things* (Durham, NC, 2010), 4, while at the same time reaching back to medieval ideas of animate matter.
[98] 'The Beauty', 253; May Morris, Introduction to *CW*, XXII, xxix.
[99] *News*, 508. Morris said of himself: 'I am no patriot as the word is generally used; and yet I am not ashamed to say that as for the face of the land we live in I love it with something of the passion of a lover.' Lemire, 158.

this account, both driven by an acceptance of the primacy of the physical. Unlike people of the nineteenth century, the people of Morris's future delight in 'the changing drama of the year, the life of the earth and its dealings with men'. Multifarious nature has its own life, its own story and its own active power; it is, in Jane Bennett's terms, an 'actant', capable of generating 'that strange combination of delight and disturbance' so evident in Morris's people of the future; in Bennett's account this kind of enchantment is capable of moving people to ethical action, while in Morris's ethically coherent utopia the drama of nature, as well as its sounds and stories, form part of the knotted-together everyday experience of people, nature, and things.[100]

Even flotsam and natural waste carry stories. While Elizabeth Carolyn Miller rightly notes that Morris creates fictional worlds, as well as actual working practices, that minimize or re-use waste, and while in lectures and letters he often associates waste with war, commercial war, and capitalism, he also celebrates natural waste, wastes, and wild land as a refusal of instrumentalization: there is joy and wonder akin to that future Nowherean delight in the drama of the earth in his account to Norton of journeying across 'great wastes' of Iceland or the description of 'the wastes and the woodland beauty' in 'The Day is Coming' (341).[101] In *The House of the Wolfings*, the people of the Mark 'fished the river's eddies also with net and with line; and drew drift from out of it of far-travelled wood and other matters'.[102] The use of 'matters' is particularly evocative here, rather than, as one might expect, matter: 'far-travelled wood', itself active and acted upon, becomes, by association with other matters, not only a material with its own journey and story, but subject for discussion, worthy of the attention of the people and of other non-humans. Attending to the matters of wood, trees, animals, and earth in Morris's work is also a way of attending to the value of human lives and conditions of work. Waste material and wasteland can signify freedom in a wider ecology of use but not over-use. In *John Ball* the dreamer awakes to find himself in a rich and particular rural landscape, on 'a strip of wayside waste by an oak copse'. In *News from Nowhere* wastes are spaces of freedom and exploration. Ellen mistakenly imagines that her nineteenth-century visitor would find it difficult to imagine a time when England was treated 'as if it had been an ugly characterless waste, with no delicate beauty to be guarded, with no heed taken of the ever fresh pleasure of the recurring seasons, and changeful weather, and diverse quality of the soil, and so forth'. How, she muses, 'could people be so cruel to themselves?'[103] Class justice, the destruction of industrial capitalism, the resurgence of individual and

---

[100] Jane Bennett borrows the term actant from Bruno Latour, in Bennett, *Vibrant Matter*, 9; Bennett, Preface, xi.

[101] Elizabeth C. Miller, 'Sustainable Socialism: William Morris on Waste', *The Journal of Modern Craft*, 4.1 (2011), 7–25 (13–18); letter to Charles Eliot Norton, October 1871, 120.

[102] *Wolfings*, 402.   [103] *John Ball*, 350; *News*, 546.

communal arts, and a renewed ecological wholeness go hand in hand in this sense of the world. It is not, however, a vision rooted in unmitigated primitivism: in gesturing towards the possibilities of change, the potential innovations of science and the capacity for disruption or discontent, Morris aligns his vision of the future with a sense of the self-renewing and changing earth.

Guest and Hammond together, as often in *News from Nowhere*, seem to speak for Morris when, having begun to get the measure of the new world in which he finds himself, Guest makes an observation and Hammond replies. Guest records that:

I wondered indeed at the deftness and abundance of beauty of the work of men who had at last learned to accept life itself as a pleasure, and the satisfaction of the common needs of mankind and the preparation for them, as work fit for the best of the race. I mused silently; but at last I said:

'What is to come after this?'

The old man laughed. 'I don't know,' said he; 'we will meet it when it comes.'

It is this, perhaps, that is the most enduring quality of Morris's work: its invitational openness to the possibility of change and the human capacity to meet it and shape it collectively, in which he sees hope. There is always 'we' in Morris's work: the brotherhood, the tribe, the house and line, the travellers, the interconnected human/animal/environmental community, the tellers of a tale, reciters of poems, listeners and readers, the artistic or political movement, the campaigners, and craftspeople. Hope is in the imperfect and changing collective, its rhythms, dramas, and actions. It is surely in this quality of practical and much-practised hope that it resonates with the concerns of the twenty-first century and generates many new kinds of pleasure and desire for change in twenty-first-century readers even as it did for its first readers.

NOTE ON THE TEXT

For the text here I have used, in most cases, the earliest published edition. May Morris gives an account of Sydney Cockerell, manager of the Kelmscott Press, relating Morris's fury at finding 'a late version of "La Belle Dame Sans Merci" in the proofs of the Kelmscott Keats. [...] He had a certain feeling about the first-published form of other men's work, if not about that of his own.' She goes on to note, however, 'if the alteration made by Keats had been in his judgement an improvement to the poem [...] he would have let it stand'.[1] Where the first version of a text is published in more ephemeral form in *Commonweal*, I have usually used the book form edited and authorized by Morris.

Where there are significant variations in the versions I have used from earlier, serialized versions, as in the case of *News from Nowhere* and *A Dream of John Ball*, or from later versions published in Morris's lifetime, or in May Morris's *Collected Works*, I have drawn attention to this in notes on the text. I have silently corrected occasional misspellings or typos. May Morris notes that, in manuscript versions of the *Defence of Guenevere* poems, 'there are scarcely any stops and few capitals. My father was notoriously careless in spelling common words, and he did not trouble himself much about stops.' She adds, however, that 'he had [...] certain peculiarities in punctuation, and when these got entangled with the printers' views, the rather muddled scheme has sometimes a quaint appearance.'[2] Mackail observes about the same collection that, 'Morris was then a bad and an impatient corrector of proofs; the punctuation of the poems is deplorable, and there are a good many serious misprints.'[3] Mackail's implication is that Morris becomes a better corrector of proofs. In another introduction, however, to *The House of the Wolfings*, May Morris notes that she has left in her father's rather erratic capitalization, as giving a 'lively' appearance to the text; she adds that 'I am certain that often there was a more or less unconscious idea of emphasis or of avoiding emphasis in his use now of capitals, now of lower case letters'.[4] I have taken these various comments and steered a path that seems to hew most closely to Morris's concerns, retaining almost entirely his 'lively' punctuation, and recording any minor changes beyond typos in the footnotes.

---

[1] May Morris, Introduction to *CW*, I, xxv.   [2] May Morris Introduction to *CW*, I, xxxi.
[3] Mackail, I, 134.   [4] May Morris, Introduction to *CW*, XIV, xxvii–xxviii.

POEMS, PROSE, LECTURES, LETTERS

Letter to Cormell Price, 3 April 1855

Clay Street
Walthamstow, Essex
Tuesday in Holy Week

My dearest Crom,

Yes, it's quite true, I ought to be ashamed of myself, I am ashamed of myself:
I won't make any excuses: please forgive me. As the train went away from the
station, I saw you standing in your scholar's gown, and looking for me. If
I hadn't been on the other side, I think I should have got out of the window to
say good-bye again…Ted will shew something to criticise, or stop, I may as
well write it for you myself; it is exceedingly seedy. Here it is.

'Twas in Church on Palm Sunday,
Listening what the priest did say
  Of the kiss that did betray,

That the thought did come to me
  How the olives used to be   5
  Growing in Gethsemane.

That the thoughts upon me came
Of the lantern's steady flame,
  Of the softly whispered name.

Of how kiss and words did sound   10
  While the olives stood around
While the robe lay on the ground.

Then the words the Lord did speak
And that kiss in Holy Week
  Dreams of many a kiss did make: 15

Lover's kiss beneath the moon,
  With it sorrow cometh soon:
  Juliet's within the tomb:

Angelico's in quiet light
'Mid the aureoles very bright   20
God is looking from the height.

There the monk his love doth meet:
Once he fell before her feet
Ere within the Abbey sweet

He, while music rose alway   25
From the Church, to God did pray
That his life might pass away.

There between the angel rows
With the light flame on his brows,
With his friend, the deacon goes: 30

Hand in hand they go together,
Loving hearts they go together
Where the Presence shineth ever.

Kiss upon the death-bed given,
Kiss on dying forehead given   35
When the soul goes up to Heaven.

Many thoughts beneath the sun
Thought together; Life is done,
Yet for ever love doth run.

Willow standing 'gainst the blue,   40
Where the light clouds come and go,
Mindeth me of kiss untrue.

Christ, thine awful cross is thrown
Round the whole world, and thy Sun
Woful kisses looks upon.   45

* * * * * * * *

Eastward slope the shadows now,
Very light the wind does blow,
Scarce it lifts the laurels low;

I cannot say the things I would,
I cannot think the things I would,   50
How the Cross at evening stood.

Very blue the sky above,
Very sweet the faint clouds move,
Yet I cannot think of love.

There, dear, perhaps I ought to be ashamed of it, don't spare me. I have begun a good many other things, I don't know if I shall ever finish them, I shall have to show them to Ted and to you first: you know my failing. I have been in a horrible state of mind about my writing; for I seem to get more and more imbecile as I go on. Do you know, I don't know what to write to you about; there are no facts here to write about; I have no one to talk to, except to ask for things to eat and drink and clothe myself withal; I have read no new books since I saw you, in fact no books at all.

The other day I went 'a-brassing' near the Thames on the Essex side; I got two remarkable brasses and three or four others that were not remarkable: one was a Flemish brass of a knight, date 1370, very small; another a brass (very small, with the legend gone) of a priest in his shroud; I think there are only two other shrouded brasses in England. The Church that this last brass came from was I think one of the prettiest Churches (for a small village Church) that I have ever seen; the consecration crosses (some of them) were visible, red in a red circle; and there was some very pretty colouring on a corbel, in very good preservation; the parson of the parish shewed us over this Church; he was very civil and very, very dirty and snuffy, inexpressibly so, I can't give you an idea of his dirt and snuffiness.

Letter to Cormell Price, 10 August 1855

Avranches, Normandy,
August 10, 1855

Dearest Crom

I haven't quite forgotten you yet, though I have been so long writing but the fact is, I am quite uncomfortable even now about writing a letter to you, for I don't know what to say; I suppose you won't be satisfied with the names merely of the places we have been to; and I scarcely think I can give you anything else. Why couldn't you come, Crom? O! the glories of the Churches we have seen! for we have seen the last of them now, we finished up with Mont S. Michel yesterday and are waiting here (which is a very beautiful place however,) till Saturday evening or Sunday morning when we shall go back to Granville and take steamer for Jersey and Southampton. Crom, we have seen nine Cathedrals, and let me see how many non-Cathedral Churches; I must count them on my fingers; there, I think I have missed some but I have made out 24 all splendid Churches; some of them surpassing first-rate English Cathedrals.

I am glad that Fulford has lightened my load a little bit, by telling you what we did as far as Chartres: so I won't begin till after we left that place. Well, Crom, you must know that we had thought that we should be forced to go back to Paris to get to Rouen and that we should be obliged to go by railway all the way, which grew so distasteful to us after a bit, that we made efforts, and found that we could get across the country with very little railway indeed; so we went; I enjoyed the journey very much, and so did the others I think, though Ted's eyes were bad, as they have been all the time whenever the sun has been out: we went the greater part of the way in a queer little contrivance with one horse the greater part of the way. Behold our itinerary. We started from Chartres quite early (six o'clock) with drizzling rain that almost hid the spires of the Cathedral, how splendid they looked in the midst of it! but we were obliged to leave them, and the beautiful statues, and the stained glass, and the great, cliff-like buttresses, for quite a long time, I'm afraid—so we went for about 20 miles by railroad to a place called Maintenon, where we mounted the quaint little conveyance and went off, with the rain still falling a little, through the beautiful country to Dreux, for a distance of about 17 miles; there was plenty to look at by the road, I almost think I like that part of the country better than any other part of the lovely country we have seen in France; so gloriously the trees are grouped, all manner of trees, but more especially the graceful poplars and aspens, of all kinds; and the hedgeless fields of grain, and beautiful herbs that they grow for forage whose names I don't know, the most beautiful fields I ever saw yet, looking as if they belonged to no man, as if they were planted not to be cut down in the end, and to be stored in barns and eaten by the cattle, but that rather they were planted for their beauty only, that they might grow always among the trees, mingled with the flowers, purple thistles, and blue corn-flowers, and red poppies, growing together with the corn round the roots of the fruit trees, in their shadows, and sweeping up to the brows of the long low hills till they reached the sky, changing sometimes into long fields of vines, or delicate, lush green forage; and they all looked as [if] they would grow there for ever, as if they had always grown there, without change of season, knowing no other time than the early August. So we went on through this kind of country till we came to Dreux, and the rain had cleared up long before we reached it, and it was a bright sunny day. Some distance from Dreux the country changed very much into what I will tell you afterwards, but a great part of Picardy and the Isle of France seemed to be a good deal the same kind of country, and the land between Rouen and Caudebec, along the side of the Seine, was much like this, so much so, that I think I had it in my mind a good deal just now; perhaps it is even lovelier than this, the hills are much higher, but I scarcely think the flowers are so rich, or perhaps, when we went through it, the flowers had gone off a good deal. Well, we had to stop at Dreux about an hour and we saw the church there, a very good one, flamboyant mostly, but with an earlier apse very evilly used, and with a transept front very elaborately carved once, now very forlorn and battered, but (Deo gratias) not yet restored: there is a delightful old secular tower at Dreux too, and that is flamboyant also, with a roof like the side of a cliff, it is so steep. So we left Dreux, and set our faces as though we would go to Evreux; we were obliged to undergo about half an hour's ride in the railway before we got there, to my intense indignation. We had only a very short time to stay at Evreux, and even that short time we had to divide (alas! for our Lower Nature) between eating our dinner and gazing on the gorgeous Cathedral: it is an exceedingly lovely one, though not nearly so large as most of the Cathedrals we saw, the aisles are very rich flamboyant, with a great deal of light canopy work about them; the rest of the Church is earlier, the nave being Norman, and the choir fully developed early Gothic; though the transepts and lantern are flamboyant also by the way: there is a great deal of good stained glass about the Church. When we left Evreux we found that the country had changed altogether, getting much more hilly, almost as glorious in its way as the other land perhaps, but very different; for it is a succession of quite flat valleys surrounded on all sides by hills of a very decent height with openings in them to let out the river, the valleys are very well wooded, and the fields a good deal like the other ones I have described, quite without hedges, and with fruit-trees growing all about them; so we kept going on, first winding up a long hill, then on a table land for a greater or less time, then down into the glorious lake-like valley till at last we got to Louviers; there is a splendid church there, though it is not a large one; the outside has a kind of mask of the most gorgeous flamboyant (though late) thrown all over it, with such parapets and windows, it is so gorgeous and light, that I was utterly unprepared for the inside, and almost startled by it; so solemn it looked and calm after the fierce flamboyant of the outside; for all the interior, except the Chapels, is quite early Gothic and very beautiful; I have never, either before or since, been so much struck with the difference between the early and late Gothic, and by the greater nobleness of the former. So after we had looked at the Church for a little time we mounted the omnibus to go to the railway station where we were to take the train to Rouen—it was about 5 miles I should think from Louviers to the station. What a glorious ride that was, with the sun, which was getting low by that time, striking all across the valley that Louviers lies in; I think that valley was the most glorious of all we saw that day, there was not much grain there, it was nearly all grass land and the trees, O! the trees! it was all like the country in a beautiful poem, in a beautiful Romance such as might make a background to Chaucer's Palamon and Arcite; how we could see the valley winding away along the side of the Eure a long way, under the hills: but we had to leave it and go to Rouen by a nasty, brimstone, noisy, shrieking railway train that cares not twopence for hill or valley, poplar tree or lime tree, corn poppy or blue cornflower, or purple thistle and purple vetch, white convolvulus, white clematis, or golden S. John's wort; that cares not twopence either for tower, or spire, or apse, or dome, for it will be as noisy and obtrusive under the spires of Chartres or the towers of Rouen as it is [under] Versailles or the Dome of the Invalides; verily railways are ABOMINATIONS; and I think I have never fairly realised this fact till this our tour: fancy, Crom, all the roads (or nearly all) that come into Rouen dip down into the valley where it lies, from gorgeous hills which command the most splendid views of Rouen, but we, coming into Rouen by railway, crept into it in the most seedy way, seeing actually nothing at all of it till we were driving through the town in an omnibus.

I had some kind of misgivings that I might be disappointed with Rouen, after my remembrances of it from last year; but I wasn't a bit. O! what a place it is. I think Ted liked the Cathedral, on the whole, better than any other church we saw. We were disappointed in one thing, however, we had expected Vespers every afternoon, we found they were only sung in that diocese on Saturday and Sunday. And weren't they sung, just. O! my word! On the Sunday especially, when a great deal of the Psalms were sung to the Peregrine tone, and then, didn't they sing the hymns!

I bought the Newcomes at Rouen, Tauchnitz edition, it is a splendid book. Well Crom, I can't write any more, I am fairly run down; I am tired too, and have got to pack up as well, which is always somewhat of a bore; when I see you (which I hope will be soon) I will tell you about the rest. Ah me! if only you had been here, how I have longed for you! so very, very much. This is a seedy letter to send to such a fellow as you are, Crom, please forgive me, and be jolly when I see you. Shall I see you at Birmingham?

Your most loving,
Topsy.

From *The Oxford and Cambridge Magazine*

THE HOLLOW LAND: A TALE

Chapter I. Struggling in the World

> We find in ancient story wonders many told,
> Of heroes in great glory, with spirit free and bold;
> Of joyances and high-tides, of weeping and of woe,
> Of noble Recken striving, mote ye now wonders know.
> Nibelungen Lied (See *Carlyle's Miscellanies*)

Do you know where it is—the Hollow Land?

I have been looking for it now so long, trying to find it again—the Hollow Land—for there I saw my love first.

I wish to tell you how I found it first of all; but I am old, my memory fails me: you must wait and let me think if I perchance can tell you how it happened.

Yea, in my ears is a confused noise of trumpet-blasts singing over desolate moors, in my ears and eyes a clashing and clanging of horse-hoofs, a ringing and glittering of steel: drawn-back lips, set teeth, shouts, shrieks, and curses.

How was it that no one of us ever found it till that day? for it is near our country: but what time have we to look for it, or any other good thing; with such biting carking cares hemming us in on every side—cares about great things—mighty things: mighty things, O my brothers! or rather little things enough, if we only knew it.

Lives past in turmoil, in making one another unhappy; in bitterest misunderstanding of our brothers' hearts, making those sad whom God has not made sad, – alas! alas! what chance for any of us to find the Hollow Land? what time even to look for it?

Yet who has not dreamed of it? Who, half miserable yet the while, for that he knows it is but a dream, has not felt the cool waves round his feet, the roses crowning him, and through the leaves of beech and lime the many whispering winds of the Hollow Land?

Now, my name was Florian, and my house was the House of the Lilies; and of that house was my father Lord, and after him my eldest brother Arnald: and me they called Florian de Liliis.

Moreover, when my father was dead, there arose a feud between the Lilies' house and Red Harald: and this that follows is the history of it.

Lady Swanhilda, Red Harald's mother, was a widow, with one son, Red Harald; and when she had been in widowhood two years, being of princely blood, and besides comely and fierce, King Urraynes sent to demand her in marriage. And I remember seeing the procession leaving the town, when I was quite a child; and many young knights and squires attended the Lady Swanhilda as pages, and amongst them Arnald, my eldest brother.

And as I gazed out of the window, I saw him walking by the side of her horse, dressed in white and gold very delicately; but as he went it chanced that he stumbled. Now he was one of those that held a golden canopy over the lady's head, so that it now sunk into wrinkles, and the lady had to bow her head full low, and even then the gold brocade caught in one of the long, slim gold flowers that were wrought round about the crown she wore. She flushed up in her rage, and her smooth face went suddenly into the carven wrinkles of a wooden water-spout, and she caught at the brocade with her left hand, and pulled it away furiously, so that the warp and woof were twisted out of their place, and many gold threads were left dangling about the crown; but Swanhilda stared about when she rose, then smote my brother across the mouth with her gilded sceptre, and the red blood flowed all about his garments; yet he only turned exceeding pale, and dared say no word, though he was heir to the House of the Lilies: but my small heart swelled with rage, and I vowed revenge, and, as it seems, he did too.

So when Swanhilda had been queen three years, she suborned many of King Urraynes' knights and lords, and slew her husband as he slept, and reigned in his stead. And her son, Harald, grew up to manhood, and was counted a strong knight, and well spoken of, by then I first put on my armour.

Then, one night, as I lay dreaming, I felt a hand laid on my face, and starting up saw Arnald before me fully armed. He said, 'Florian, rise and arm.' I did so, all but my helm, as he was.

He kissed me on the forehead; his lips felt hot and dry; and when they brought torches, and I could see his face plainly, I saw he was very pale. He said:

'Do you remember, Florian, this day sixteen years ago? It is a long time, but I shall never forget it unless this night blots out its memory.'

I knew what he meant, and because my heart was wicked, I rejoiced exceedingly at the thought of vengeance, so that I could not speak, but only laid my palm across his lips.

'Good; you have a good memory, Florian. See now, I waited long and long: I said at first, I forgive her; but when the news came concerning the death of the King, and how that she was shameless, I said I will take it as a sign, if God does not punish her within certain years, that He means me to do so; and I have been watching and watching now these two years for an opportunity, and behold it has come at last; and I think God has certainly given her into our hands, for she rests this night, this very Christmas Eve, at a small walled town on the frontier, not two hours' gallop from this: they keep little ward there, and the night is wild: moreover, the prior of a certain house of monks, just without the walls, is my fast friend in this matter, for she has done him some great injury. In the courtyard below, a hundred and fifty knights and squires, all faithful and true, are waiting for us: one moment and we shall be gone.'

Then we both knelt down, and prayed God to give her into our hands: we put on our helms, and went down into the courtyard.

It was the first time I expected to use a sharp sword in anger, and I was full of joy as the muffled thunder of our horse-hoofs rolled through the bitter winter night.

In about an hour and a half we had crossed the frontier, and in half an hour more the greater part had halted in a wood near the Abbey, while I and a few others went up to the Abbey-gates and knocked loudly four times with my sword-hilt, stamping on the ground meantime. A long, low whistle answered me from within, which I in my turn answered: then the wicket opened, and a monk came out, holding a lantern. He seemed yet in the prime of life, and was a tall, powerful man. He held the lantern to my face, then smiled, and said, 'The banners hang low.' I gave the countersign, 'The crest is lopped off.' 'Good my son,' said he; 'the ladders are within here. I dare not trust any of the brethren to carry them for you, though they love not the witch either, but are timorsome.'

'No matter,' I said, 'I have men here.' So they entered and began to shoulder the tall ladders: the prior was very busy. 'You will find them just the right length, my son, trust me for that.' He seemed quite a jolly pleasant man, I could not understand him nursing furious revenge; but his face darkened strangely whenever he happened to mention her name.

As we were starting he came and stood outside the gate, and putting his lantern down that the light of it might not confuse his sight, looked earnestly into the night, then said: 'The wind has fallen, the snowflakes get thinner and smaller every moment, in an hour it will be freezing hard, and will be quite clear; everything depends upon the surprise being complete; stop a few minutes yet, my son.' He went away chuckling, and returned presently with two more sturdy monks carrying something: they threw their burdens down before my feet; they consisted of all the white albs in the Abbey:—'There, trust an old man, who has seen more than one stricken fight in his carnal days; let the men who scale the walls put these over their arms, and they will not be seen in the least. God make your sword sharp, my son.'

So we departed, and when I met Arnald again, he said, that what the prior had done was well thought of; so we agreed that I should take thirty men, an old squire of our house, well skilled in war, along with them, scale the walls as quietly as possible, and open the gates to the rest.

I set off accordingly, after that with low laughing we had put the albs all over us, wrapping the ladders also in white. Then we crept very warily and slowly up to the wall; the moat was frozen over, and on the ice the snow lay quite thick; we all thought that the guards must be careless enough, when they did not even take the trouble to break the ice in the moat. So we listened—there was no

sound at all, the Christmas midnight mass had long ago been over, it was nearly
three o'clock, and the moon began to clear, there was scarce any snow falling
now, only a flake or two from some low hurrying cloud or other: the wind
sighed gently about the round towers there, but it was bitter cold, for it had
begun to freeze again: we listened for some minutes, about a quarter of an hour
I think, then at a sign from me, they raised the ladders carefully, muffled as
they were at the top with swathings of wool. I mounted first, old Squire Hugh
followed last; noiselessly we ascended, and soon stood all altogether on the
walls; then we carefully lowered the ladders again with long ropes; we got our
swords and axes from out of the folds of our priests' raiments, and set forward,
till we reached the first tower along the wall; the door was open, in the chamber
at the top there was a fire slowly smouldering, nothing else; we passed through
it, and began to go down the spiral staircase, I first, with my axe shortened in
my hand.—'What if we were surprised there,' I thought, and I longed to be out
in the air again —'what if the door were fast at the bottom'?

As we passed the second chamber, we heard some one within snoring loudly:
I looked in quietly, and saw a big man with long black hair, that fell off his pillow
and swept the ground, lying snoring, with his nose turned up and his mouth
open, but he seemed so sound asleep that we did not stop to slay him.— Praise
be!—the door was open, without even a whispered word, without a pause, we
went on along the streets, on the side that the drift had been on, because our
garments were white, for the wind being very strong all that day, the houses
on that side had caught in their cornices and carvings, and on the rough stone
and wood of them, so much snow, that except here and there where the black
walls grinned out, they were quite white; no man saw us as we stole along,
noiselessly because of the snow, till we stood within 100 yards of the gates and
their house of guard. And we stood because we heard the voice of some one
singing:

> Queen Mary's crown was gold,   5
> King Joseph's crown was red,
> But Jesus' crown was diamond
> That lit up all the bed
> *Mariae Virginis*

So they had some guards after all; this was clearly the sentinel that sang to
keep the ghosts off.—Now for a fight.—We drew nearer, a few yards nearer,
then stopped to free ourselves from our monk's clothes.

> Ships sail through the Heaven   10
> With red banners dress'd,
> Carrying the planets seven
> To see the white breast
> *Mariae Virginis*   15

Thereat he must have seen the waving of some alb or other as it shivered down to the ground, for his spear fell with a thud, and he seemed to be standing open-mouthed, thinking something about ghosts; then, plucking up heart of grace he roared out like ten bull-calves, and dashed into the guard-house.

We followed smartly, but without hurry, and came up to the door of it just as some dozen half-armed men came tumbling out under our axes: thereupon, while our men slew them, I blew a great blast upon my horn, and Hugh with some others drew bolt and bar and swung the gates wide open.

Then the men in the guard-house understood they were taken in a trap, and began to stir with great confusion; so lest they should get quite waked and armed I left Hugh at the gate with ten men, and myself led the rest into that house. There while we slew all those that yielded not, came Arnald with the others, bringing our horses with them: then all the enemy threw their arms down. And we counted our prisoners and found them over fourscore; therefore, not knowing what to do with them (for they were too many to guard, and it seemed unknightly to slay them all), we sent up some bowmen to the walls, and turning our prisoners out of gates bid them run for their lives, which they did fast enough, not knowing our numbers, and our men sent a few flights of arrows among them that they might not be undeceived.

Then the one or two prisoners that we had left, told us, when we had crossed our axes over their heads, that the people of the good town would not willingly fight us, in that they hated the queen; that she was guarded at the palace by some fifty knights, and that beside, there were no others to oppose us in the town: so we set out for the palace, spear in hand.

We had not gone far, before we heard some knights coming, and soon, in a turn of the long street, we saw them riding towards us; when they caught sight of us they seemed astonished, drew rein, and stood in some confusion.

We did not slacken our pace for an instant, but rode right at them with a yell, to which I lent myself with all my heart.

After all they did not run away, but waited for us with their spears held out; I missed the man I had marked, or hit him rather just on the top of the helm; he bent back, and the spear slipped over his head, but my horse still kept on, and I felt presently such a crash that I reeled in my saddle, and felt mad. He had lashed out at me with his sword as I came on, hitting me in the ribs (for my arm was raised), but only flatlings.

I was quite wild with rage, I turned, almost fell upon him, caught him by the neck with both hands, and threw him under the horse-hoofs, sighing with fury. I heard Arnald's voice close to me, 'Well fought, Florian': and I saw his great stern face bare among the iron, for he had made a vow in remembrance of that blow always to fight unhelmed: I saw his great sword swinging, in wide gyves, and hissing as it started up, just as if it were alive and liked it.

So joy filled all my soul, and I fought with my heart, till the big axe I swung felt like nothing but a little hammer in my hand, except for its bitterness: and as for the enemy, they went down like grass, so that we destroyed them utterly, for those knights would neither yield nor fly, but died as they stood, so that some fifteen of our men also died there.

Then at last we came to the palace, where some grooms and such like kept the gates armed, but some ran, and some we took prisoners, one of whom died for sheer terror in our hands, being stricken by no wound: for he thought we would eat him.

These prisoners we questioned concerning the queen, and so entered the great hall.

There Arnald sat down in the throne on the daïs, and laid his naked sword before him on the table: and on each side of him sat such knights as there was room for, and the others stood round about, while I took ten men, and went to look for Swanhilda.

I found her soon, sitting by herself in a gorgeous chamber. I almost pitied her when I saw her looking so utterly desolate and despairing; her beauty too had faded, deep lines cut through her face. But when I entered she knew who I was, and her look of intense hatred was so fiend-like, that it changed my pity into horror of her.

'Knight', she said 'who are you, and what do you want, thus discourteously entering my chamber?'

'I am Florian de Liliis, and I am to conduct you to judgment.'

She sprung up, 'Curse you and your whole house,—you I hate worse than any,—girl's face, —guards, guards!' and she stamped on the ground, her veins on the forehead swelled, her eyes grew round and flamed out, as she kept crying for her guards, stamping the while, for she seemed quite mad.

Then at last she remembered that she was in the power of her enemies, she sat down, and lay with her face between her hands, and wept passionately.

'Witch,'—I said, between my closed teeth, 'will you come, or must we carry you down to the great hall?'

Neither would she come, but sat there, clutching at her dress and tearing her hair.

Then I said, 'Bind her, and carry her down.' And they did so.

I watched Arnald as we came in, there was no triumph in his stern white face, but resolution enough, he had made up his mind.

They placed her on a seat in the midst of the hall over against the daïs. He said, 'Unbind her, Florian.' They did so, she raised her face, and glared defiance at us all, as though she would die queenly after all.

Then rose up Arnald and said, 'Queen Swanhilda, we judge you guilty of death, and because you are a queen and of a noble house you shall be slain by my knightly sword, and I will even take the reproach of slaying a woman, for no other hand than mine shall deal the blow.'

Then she said, 'O false knight, shew your warrant from God, man, or devil.'

'This warrant from God, Swanhilda,' he said, holding up his sword, 'listen!—fifteen years ago, when I was just winning my spurs, you struck me, disgracing me before all the people; you cursed me, and meant that curse well enough. Men of the House of the Lilies, what sentence for that?'

'Death!' they said.

'Listen!—afterwards you slew my cousin, your husband, treacherously, in the most cursed way, stabbing him in the throat, as the stars in the canopy above him looked down on the shut eyes of him. Men of the House of the Lily, what sentence for that?'

'Death!' they said.

'Do you hear them, queen? there is warrant from man; for the devil, I do not reverence him enough to take warrant from him, but, as I look at that face of yours, I think that even he has left you.'

And indeed just then all her pride seemed to leave her, she fell from the chair, and wallowed on the ground moaning, she wept like a child, so that the tears lay on the oak floor; she prayed for another month of life; she came to me and kneeled, and kissed my feet, and prayed piteously, so that water ran out of her mouth.

But I shuddered, and drew away; it was like having an adder about one; I could have pitied her had she died bravely, but for one like her to whine and whine!—pah!—

Then from the daïs rang Arnald's voice terrible, much changed. 'Let there be an end of all this.' And he took his sword and strode through the hall towards her; she rose from the ground and stood up, stooping a little, her head sunk between her shoulders, her black eyes turned up and gleaming, like a tigress about to spring. When he came within some six paces of her something in his eye daunted her, or perhaps the flashing of his terrible sword in the torch-light; she threw her arms up with a great shriek, and dashed screaming about the hall. Arnald's lip never once curled with any scorn, no line in his face changed: he said: 'Bring her here and bind her.'

But when one came up to her to lay hold on her she first of all ran at him, hitting him with her head in the belly. Then while he stood doubled up for want of breath, and staring with his head up, she caught his sword from the girdle, and cut him across the shoulders, and many others she wounded sorely before they took her.

Then Arnald stood by the chair to which she was bound, and poised his sword, and there was a great silence.

Then he said, 'Men of the House of the Lilies, do you justify me in this, shall she die?' Straightway rang a great shout through the hall, but before it died away the sword had swept round, and therewithal was there no such thing as Swanhilda left upon the earth, for in no battle-field had Arnald struck truer blow. Then he turned to the few servants of the palace and said, 'Go now, bury this accursed woman, for she is a king's daughter.' Then to us all, 'Now, knights, to horse and away, that we may reach the good town by about dawn.' So we mounted and rode off.

What a strange Christmas-day that was, for there, about nine o'clock in the morning, rode Red Harald into the good town to demand vengeance; he went at once to the king, and the king promised that before nightfall that very day the matter should be judged; albeit the king feared somewhat, because every third man you met in the streets had a blue cross on his shoulder, and some likeness of a lily, cut out or painted, stuck in his hat; and this blue cross and lily were the bearings of our house, called 'de Liliis'. Now we had seen Red Harald pass through the streets, with a white banner borne before him, to show that he came peaceably as for this time; but I trow he was thinking of other things but peace.

And he was called Red Harald first at this time, because over all his arms he wore a great scarlet cloth, that fell in heavy folds about his horse and all about him. Then, as he passed our house, some one pointed it out to him, rising there with its carving and its barred marble, but stronger than many a castle on the hill-tops, and its great overhanging battlement cast a mighty shadow down the wall and across the street; and above all rose the great tower, our banner floating proudly from the top, whereon was emblazoned on a white ground a blue cross, and on a blue ground four white lilies. And now faces were gazing from all the windows, and all the battlements were thronged; so Harald turned, and rising in his stirrups, shook his clenched fist at our house; natheless, as he did so, the east wind, coming down the street, caught up the corner of that scarlet cloth and drove it over his face, and therewithal disordering his long black hair, well-nigh choked him, so that he bit both his hair and that cloth.

So from base to cope rose a mighty shout of triumph and defiance, and he passed on.

Then Arnald caused it to be cried, that all those who loved the good House of the Lilies should go to mass that morning in St. Mary's church, hard by our house. Now this church belonged to us, and the abbey that served it, and always we appointed the abbot of it on condition that our trumpets should sound altogether when on high masses they sing the 'Gloria in Excelsis'. It was the largest and most beautiful of all the churches in the town, and had two exceeding high towers, which you could see from far off, even when you saw not the town or any of its other towers: and in one of these towers were twelve great bells, named after the twelve Apostles, one name being written on each one of them, as Peter, Matthew, and so on; and in the other tower was one great bell only, much larger than any of the others, and which was called Mary. Now this bell was never rung but when our house was in great danger, and it had this legend on it, 'When Mary rings the earth shakes;' and indeed from this we took our war cry, which was, 'Mary rings;' somewhat justifiably indeed, for the last time that Mary rung, on that day before nightfall there were four thousand bodies to be buried, which bodies wore neither cross nor lily.

So Arnald gave me in charge to tell the abbot to cause Mary to be tolled for an hour before mass that day.

The abbot leaned on my shoulder as I stood within the tower and looked at the twelve monks laying their hands to the ropes. Far up in the dimness I saw the wheel before it began to swing round about; then it moved a little; the twelve men bent down to the earth and a roar rose that shook the tower from base to spire-vane: backwards and forwards swept the wheel, as Mary now looked downwards towards earth, now looked up at the shadowy cone of the spire, shot across by bars of light from the dormers.

And the thunder of Mary was caught up by the wind and carried through all the country; and when the good man heard it, he said goodbye to wife and child, slung his shield behind his back, and set forward with his spear sloped over his shoulder, and many a time, as he walked toward the good town, he tightened the belt that went about his waist, that he might stride the faster, so long and furiously did Mary toll.

And before the great bell, Mary, had ceased ringing all the ways were full of armed men.

But at each door of the church of St. Mary stood a row of men armed with axes, and when any came, meaning to go into the church, the two first of these would hold their axes (whose helves were about four feet long), over his head, and would ask him, 'Who went over the moon last night?' then if he answered nothing or at random they would bid him turn back, which he for the more part would be ready enough to do: but some, striving to get through that row of men, were slain outright; but if he were one of those that were friends to the House of the Lilies he would answer to that question, 'Mary and John.'

By the time the mass began the whole church was full, and in the nave and transept thereof were three thousand men, all of our house and all armed. But Arnald and myself, and Squire Hugh, and some others sat under a gold-fringed canopy near the choir; and the abbot said mass, having his mitre on his head. Yet, as I watched him, it seemed to me that he must have something on beneath his priest's vestments, for he looked much fatter than usual, being really a tall lithe man.

Now, as they sung the 'Kyrie', someone shouted from the other end of the church, 'My lord Arnald, they are slaying our people without;' for, indeed, all the square about the church was full of our people, who for the press had not been able to enter, and were standing there in no small dread of what might come to pass.

Then the abbot turned round from the altar, and began to fidget with the fastenings of his rich robes.

And they made a lane for us up to the west door; then I put on my helm, and we began to go up the nave, then suddenly the singing of the monks and all stopped. I heard a clinking and a buzz of voices in the choir; I turned, and saw that the bright noon sun was shining on the gold of the priests' vestments, as they lay on the floor, and on the mail that the priests carried.

So we stopped, the choir gates swung open, and the abbot marched out at the head of *his* men, all fully armed, and began to strike up the Psalm 'Exsurgat Deus'.

When we got to the west door, there was indeed a tumult, but as yet no slaying. The square was all a-flicker with steel, and we beheld a great body of knights, at the head of them Red Harald and the king, standing over against us: but our people, pressed against the houses, and into the corners of the square, were, some striving to enter the doors, some beside themselves with rage, shouting out to the others to charge; withal, some were pale and some were red with the blood that had gathered to the wrathful faces of them.

Then said Arnald to those about him, 'Lift me up.' So they laid a great shield on two lances, and these four men carried, and thereon stood Arnald, and gazed about him.

Now the king was unhelmed, and his white hair (for he was an old man) flowed down behind him on to his saddle; but Arnald's hair was cut short, and was red.

And all the bells rang.

Then the king said, 'O Arnald of the Lilies, will you settle this quarrel by the judgment of God?' And Arnald thrust up his chin, and said, 'Yea.' 'How then,' said the king, 'and where?' 'Will it please you try now?' said Arnald.

Then the king understood what he meant, and took in his hand from behind tresses of his long white hair, twisting them round his hand in his wrath, but yet said no word, till I suppose his hair put him in mind of something, and he raised it in both his hands above his head, and shouted out aloud, 'O knights, hearken to this traitor!' Whereat, indeed, the lances began to move ominously. But Arnald spoke.

'O you king and lords, what have we to do with you? were we not free in the old time, up among the hills there? Wherefore give way, and we will go to the hills again; and if any man try to stop us, his blood be on his own head; wherefore now,' (and he turned) 'all you House of the Lily, both soldiers and monks, let us go forth together fearing nothing, for I think there is not bone enough or muscle enough in these fellows here that have a king that they should stop us withal, but only skin and fat.'

And truly, no man dared to stop us, and we went.

Chapter II. Failing in the World

Now at that time we drove cattle in Red Harald's land.

And we took no hoof but from the lords and rich men, but of these we had a mighty drove, both oxen and sheep, and horses, and besides, even hawks and hounds, and a huntsman or two to take care of them.

And, about noon, we drew away from the corn-lands that lay beyond the pastures and mingled with them, and reached a wide moor, which was called 'Goliah's Land'; I scarce know why, except that it belonged neither to Red Harald or us, but was debatable.

And the cattle began to go slowly, and our horses were tired, and the sun struck down very hot upon us, for there was no shadow, and the day was cloudless.

All about the edge of the moor, except on the side from which we had come, was a rim of hills, not very high, but very rocky and steep, otherwise the moor itself was flat; and through these hills was one pass, guarded by our men, which pass led to the hill castle of the Lilies.

It was not wonderful, that of this moor many wild stories were told, being such a strange lonely place, some of them one knew, alas! to be over-true. In the old time, before we went to the good town, this moor had been the mustering-place of our people, and our house had done deeds enough of blood and horror to turn our white lilies red, and our blue cross to a fiery one. But some of those wild tales I never believed; they had to do mostly with men losing their way without any apparent cause (for there were plenty of land-marks), finding some well-known spot, and then, just beyond it, a place they had never even dreamed of.

'Florian! Florian!' said Arnald. 'For God's sake stop! as every one else is stopping to look at the hills yonder; I always thought there was a curse upon us. What does God mean by shutting us up here? Look at the cattle; O Christ, they have found it out too! See, some of them are turning to run back again towards Harald's land. Oh! unhappy, unhappy, from that day forward!'

He leaned forward, rested his head on his horse's neck, and wept like a child.

I felt so irritated with him, that I could almost have slain him then and there. Was he mad? Had these wild doings of ours turned his strong wise head?

'Are you my brother Arnald, that I used to think such a grand man when I was a boy?' I said, 'or are you changed too, like everybody, and everything else? What do *you* mean?'

'Look! look!' he said, grinding his teeth in agony.

I raised my eyes: where was the one pass between the rim of stern rocks? Nothing: the enemy behind us—that grim wall in front: what wonder that each man looked in his fellow's face for help, and found it not? Yet I refused to believe that there was any truth either in the wild stories that I had heard when I was a boy, or in this story told me so clearly by my eyes now.

I called out cheerily: 'Hugh, come here!' He came. 'What do you think of this? Some mere dodge on Harald's part? Are we cut off?'

'Think! Sir Florian? God forgive me for ever thinking at all! I have given up that long and long ago, because thirty years ago I thought this, that the House of Lilies would deserve anything in the way of bad fortune that God would send them: so I gave up thinking, and took to fighting. But if you think that Harald had anything to do with this, why—why—in God's name, I wish *I* could think so!' I felt a dull weight on my heart. Had our house been the devil's servants all along? I thought we were God's servants.

The day was very still, but what little wind there was, was at our backs. I watched Hugh's face, not being able to answer him. He was the cleverest man at war that I have known, either before or since that day, sharper than any hound in ear and scent, clearer sighted than any eagle; he was listening now intently. I saw a slight smile cross his face; heard him mutter, 'Yes! I think so: verily that is better, a great deal better.' Then he stood up in his stirrups and shouted, 'Hurrah for the Lilies! Mary rings!' 'Mary rings!' I shouted, though I did not know the reason for his exultation: my brother lifted his head, and smiled too, grimly. Then as I listened I heard clearly the sound of a trumpet, and an enemy's trumpet too.

'After all it was only mist or some such thing,' I said; for the pass between the hills was clear enough now.

'Hurrah! only mist,' said Arnald, quite elated; 'Mary rings!' And we all began to think of fighting: for after all what joy is equal to that?

There were five hundred of us; two hundred spears, the rest archers; and both archers and men-at-arms were picked men. 'How many of them are we to expect?' said I. 'Not under a thousand, certainly, probably more, Sir Florian.' (My brother Arnald, by the way, had knighted me before we left the good town, and Hugh liked to give me the handle to my name. How was it, by the way, that no one had ever made *him* a knight?)

'Let everyone look to his arms and horse, and come away from these silly cows' sons!' shouted Arnald. Hugh said, 'They will be here in an hour, fair Sir.'

So we got clear of the cattle, and dismounted, and both ourselves took food and drink, and our horses; afterwards we tightened our saddle-girths, shook our great pots of helmets on, except Arnald, whose rusty-red hair had been his only head-piece in battle for years and years, and stood with our spears close by our horses, leaving room for the archers to retreat between our ranks; and they got their arrows ready, and planted their stakes before a little peat moss: and there we waited, and saw their pennons at last floating high above the corn of the fertile land, then heard their many horse-hoofs ring upon the hard-parched moor, and the archers began to shoot.

*   *   *   *   *   *

It had been a strange battle; we had never fought better, and yet withal it had ended in a retreat; indeed all along every man but Arnald and myself, even Hugh, had been trying at least to get the enemy between him and the way toward the pass; and now we were all drifting that way, the enemy trying to cut us off, but never able to stop us, because he could only throw small bodies of men in our way, whom we scattered and put to flight in their turn.

I never cared less for my life than then; indeed, in spite of all my boasting and hardness of belief, I should have been happy to have died, such a strange weight of apprehension was on me; and yet I got no scratch even. I had soon put off my great helm, and was fighting in my mail-coif only: and here I swear that three knights together charged me, aiming at my bare face, yet never touched me; for, as for one, I put his lance aside with my sword, and the other two in some most wonderful manner got their spears locked in each other's armour, and so had to submit to be knocked off their horses.

And we still neared the pass, and began to see distinctly the ferns that grew on the rocks, and the fair country between the rift in them, spreading out there blue-shadowed.

Whereupon came a great rush of men of both sides, striking side blows at each other, spitting, cursing, and shrieking, as they tore away like a herd of wild hogs. So, being careless of life, as I said, I drew rein, and turning my horse, waited quietly for them; and I knotted the reins, and laid them on the horse's neck, and stroked him, that he whinnied, then got both my hands to my sword.

Then, as they came on, I noted hurriedly that the first man was one of Harald's men, and one of our men behind him leaned forward to prod him with his spear, but could not reach so far; till he himself was run through the eye with a spear, and throwing his arms up fell dead with a shriek. Also I noted concerning this first man that the laces of his helmet were loose, and when he saw me he lifted his left hand to his head, took off his helm, and cast it at me, and still tore on; the helmet flew over my head, and I sitting still there swung out, hitting him on the neck; his head flew right off, for the mail no more held than a piece of silk.

'Mary rings,' and my horse whinnied again, and we both of us went at it, and fairly stopped that rout, so that there was a knot of quite close and desperate fighting, wherein we had the best of that fight and slew most of them, albeit my horse was slain and my mail-coif cut through. Then I bade a squire fetch me another horse, and began meanwhile to upbraid those knights for running such a strange disorderly race, instead of standing and fighting cleverly.

Moreover we had drifted even in this successful fight still nearer to the pass, so that the conies who dwelt there were beginning to consider whether they should not run into their holes.

But one of those knights said: 'Be not angry with me, Sir Florian, but do you think you will go to Heaven?'

'The saints! I hope so,' I said. But one who stood near him whispered to him to hold his peace, so I cried out:

'O friend! I hold this world and all therein so cheap now, that I see not anything in it but shame which can any longer anger me; wherefore speak out.'

'Then, Sir Florian, men say that at your christening some fiend took on him the likeness of a priest and strove to baptize you in the Devil's name; but God had mercy on you so that the fiend could not choose but baptize you in the name of the most holy Trinity: and yet men say that you hardly believe any doctrine such as other men do, and will at the end only go to Heaven round about as it were, not at all by the intercession of our Lady; they say too that you can see no ghosts or other wonders, whatever happens to other Christian men.'

I smiled— 'Well, friend, I scarcely call this a disadvantage, moreover what has it to do with the matter in hand?'

How was this in Heaven's name? we had been quite still, resting, while this talk was going on, but we could hear the hawks chattering from the rocks, we were so close now.

And my heart sunk within me: there was no reason why this should not be true; there was no reason why anything should not be true.

'This, Sir Florian,' said the knight again, 'how would you feel inclined to fight if you thought that everything about you was mere glamour; this earth here, the rocks, the sun, the sky? I do not know where I am for certain, I do not know that it is not midnight instead of undern; I do not know if I have been fighting men or only *simulacra*—but I think, we all think, that we have been led into some devil's trap or other, and—and—may God forgive me my sins!—I wish I had never been born.'

There now! he was weeping—they all wept—how strange it was to see those rough, bearded men blubbering there, and snivelling till the tears ran over their armour and mingled with the blood, so that it dropped down to the earth in a dim, dull, red rain.

My eyes indeed were dry, but then so was my heart; I felt far worse than weeping came to, but nevertheless I spoke cheerily.

'Dear friends, where are your old men's hearts gone to now? See now! this is a punishment for our sins, is it? well, for our forefathers' sins or our own? if the first, O brothers, be very sure that if we bear it manfully God will have something very good in store for us hereafter; but if for our sins, is it not certain that He cares for us yet, for note that He suffers the wicked to go their own ways pretty much; moreover brave men, brothers, ought to be the masters of *simulacra*—come, is it so hard to die once for all?'

Still no answer came from them, they sighed heavily only. I heard the sound of more than one or two swords as they rattled back to their scabbards: nay, one knight, stripping himself of surcoat and hauberk, and drawing his dagger, looked at me with a grim smile, and said, 'Sir Florian, do so!' then he drew the dagger across his throat and he fell back dead.

They shuddered, those brave men, and crossed themselves. And I had no heart to say a word more, but mounted the horse which had been brought to me, and rode away slowly for a few yards; then I became aware that there was a great silence over the whole field.

So I lifted my eyes and looked; and behold no man struck at another.

Then from out of a band of horsemen came Harald, and he was covered all over with a great scarlet cloth as before, put on over the head, and flowing all about his horse, but rent with the fight. He put off his helm and drew back his mail-coif; then took a trumpet from the hand of a herald and blew strongly.

And in the midst of his blast I heard a voice call out: 'O Florian! come and speak to me for the last time!'

So when I turned I beheld Arnald standing by himself, but near him stood Hugh and ten others with drawn swords.

Then I wept, and so went to him, weeping; and he said, 'Thou seest, brother, that we must die, and I think by some horrible and unheard-of death; the House of the Lilies is just dying too; and now I repent me of Swanhilda's death; now I know that it was a poor cowardly piece of revenge, instead of a brave act of justice; thus has God shown us the right.

'O Florian! curse me! So will it be straighter; truly thy mother when she bore thee did not think of this; rather saw thee in the tourney at this time, in her fond hopes, glittering with gold and doing knightly; or else mingling thy brown locks with the golden hair of some maiden weeping for the love of thee. God forgive me! God forgive me!'

'What harm, brother?' I said, 'this is only failing in the world; what if we had not failed, in a little while it would have made no difference; truly just now I felt very miserable, but now it has passed away, and I am happy.'

'O brave heart!' he said, 'yet we shall part just now, Florian, farewell!'

'The road is long,' I said, 'farewell.' Then we kissed each other, and Hugh and the others wept.

Now all this time the trumpets had been ringing, ringing, great doleful peals, then it ceased, and above all sounded Red Harald's voice.

(So I looked round towards that pass, and when I looked I no longer doubted any of those wild tales of glamour concerning Goliath's Land; for though the rocks were the same, and though the conies still stood gazing at the doors of their dwellings, though the hawks still cried out shrilly, though the fern still shook in the wind, yet, beyond, oh such a land! not to be described by any because of its great beauty, lying, a great *hollow* land, the rocks going down on this side in precipices, then reaches and reaches of loveliest country, trees and flowers, and corn, then the hills, green and blue, and purple, till their ledges reached the white snowy mountains at last. Then, with all manner of strange feelings, 'my heart in the midst of my body was even like melting wax.')

'O you House of the Lily! you are conquered—yet I will take vengeance only on a few, therefore let all those who wish to live come and pile their swords, and shields, and helms behind me in three great heaps, and swear fealty afterwards to me: yes, all but the false Knights Arnald and Florian.'

We were holding each other's hands and gazing; and we saw all our knights, yea, all but Squire Hugh and his ten heroes, pass over the field singly, or in groups of three or four, with their heads hanging down in shame, and they cast down their notched swords and dinted lilied shields, and brave-crested helms into three great heaps, behind Red Harald, then stood behind, no man speaking to his fellow or touching him.

Then dolefully the great trumpets sang over the dying House of the Lily, and Red Harald led his men forward, but slowly: on they came, spear and mail glittering in the sunlight; and I turned and looked at that good land, and a shuddering delight seized my soul.

But I felt my brother's hand leave mine, and saw him turn his horse's head and ride swiftly toward the pass; that was a strange pass now.

And at the edge he stopped, turned round, and called out aloud, 'I pray thee, Harald, forgive me! now farewell all.'

Then the horse gave one bound forward, and we heard the poor creature's scream when he felt that he must die, and we heard afterwards (for we were near enough for that even) a clang and a crash.

So I turned me about to Hugh, and he understood me though I could not speak.

We shouted all together, 'Mary rings,' then laid our bridles on the necks of our horses, spurred forward, and—in five minutes they were all slain, and I was down among the horse-hoofs.

Not slain though, not wounded. Red Harald smiled grimly when he saw me rise and lash out again; he and some ten others dismounted and [came] holding their long spears out, I went back—back, back,—I saw what it meant, and sheathed my sword, and their laughter rolled all about, and I too smiled.

Presently they all stopped, and I felt the last foot of turf giving under my feet; I looked down and saw the crack there widening; then in a moment I fell, and a cloud of dust and earth rolled after me; then again their mirth rose into thunder-peals of laughter. But through it all I heard Red Harald shout, 'Silence! evil dogs!'

For as I fell I stretched out my arms, and caught a tuft of yellow broom some three feet from the brow, and hung there by the hands, my feet being loose in the air.

Then Red Harald came & stood on the precipice above me, his great axe over his shoulder; and he looked down on me not ferociously, almost kindly, while the wind from the Hollow Land blew about his red raiment, tattered and dusty now.

And I felt happy, though it pained me to hold straining by the broom, yet I said: 'I will hold out to the last.'

It was not long; the plant itself gave way, and I fell, and as I fell I fainted.

Chapter III. Leaving the World

Fytte the first

I had thought when I fell that I should never wake again; but I woke at last: for a long time I was quite dizzied and could see nothing at all: horrible doubts came creeping over me; I half expected to see presently great half-formed shapes come rolling up to me to crush me; some thing fiery, not strange, too utterly horrible to be strange, but utterly vile and ugly, the sight of which would have killed me when I was upon the earth, come rolling up to torment me. In fact I doubted if I were in hell.

I knew I deserved to be, but I prayed, and then it came into my mind that I could not pray if I were in hell.

Also there seemed to be a cool green light all about me, which was sweet. Then presently I heard a glorious voice ring out clear, close to me—

> Christ keep the Hollow Land   15
>   Through the sweet spring-tide,
> When the apple-blossoms bless
>   The lowly bent hill side.

Thereat my eyes were slowly unsealed, and I saw the blessedest sight I have ever seen before or since: for I saw my Love.

She sat about five yards from me on a great grey stone that had much moss on it, one of the many scattered along the side of the stream by which I lay; she was clad in loose white raiment close to her hands and throat; her feet were bare, her hair hung loose a long way down, but some of it lay on her knees: I said 'white' raiment, but long spikes of light scarlet went down from the throat, lost here and there in the shadows of the folds, and, growing smaller and smaller, died before they reached her feet.

I was lying with my head resting on soft moss that some one had gathered and placed under me. She, when she saw me moving and awake, came and stood over me with a gracious smile.—She was so lovely and tender to look at, and so kind, yet withal no one, man or woman, had ever frightened me half so much.

She was not fair in white and red, like many beautiful women are, being rather pale, but like ivory for smoothness, and her hair was quite golden, not light yellow, but dusky golden.

I tried to get up on my feet, but was too weak, and sunk back again. She said:

'No, not just yet, do not trouble yourself or try to remember anything just at present.'

There withal she kneeled down and hung over me closer.

'To-morrow you may, perhaps, have something hard to do or bear, I know, but now you must be as happy as you can be, quietly happy. Why did you start and turn pale when I came to you? Do you not know who I am? Nay, but you do, I see; and I have been waiting here so long for you; so you must have expected to see me.— You cannot be frightened of me, are you?'

But I could not answer a word, but all the time strange knowledge, strange feelings, were filling my brain and my heart, she said:

'You are tired; rest, and dream happily.'

So she sat by me, and sung to lull me to sleep, while I turned on my elbow, and watched the waving of her throat: and the singing of all the poets I had ever heard, and of many others too, not born till years after I was dead, floated all about me as she sung, and I did indeed dream happily.

When I awoke it was the time of the cold dawn, and the colours were gathering themselves together, whereat in fatherly approving fashion the sun sent all across the east long bars of scarlet and orange that after faded through yellow to green and blue.

And she sat by me still; I think she had been sitting there and singing all the time; all through hot yesterday, for I had been sleeping day-long and night-long, all through the falling evening under moonlight and starlight the night through.

And now it was dawn, and I think too that neither of us had moved at all; for the last thing I remembered before I went to sleep was the tips of her fingers brushing my cheek, as she knelt over me with down-drooping arm, and still now I felt them there. Moreover she was just finishing some fainting measure that died before it had time to get painful in its passion.

Dear Lord! how I loved her! yet did I not dare to touch her, or even speak to her. She smiled with delight when she saw I was awake again, and slid down her hand on to mine; but some shuddering dread made me draw it away again hurriedly; then I saw the smile leave her face: what would I not have given for courage to hold her body quite tight to mine? but I was so weak. She said:

'Have you been very happy?'

'Yea,' I said.

It was the first word I had spoken there, and my voice sounded strange.

'Ah!' she said, 'you will talk more when you get used to the air of the Hollow Land. Have you been thinking of your past life at all? if not, try to think of it. What thing in Heaven or Earth do you wish for most?'

Still I said no word; but she said in a wearied way:

'Well now, I think you will be strong enough to get to your feet and walk; take my hand and try.'

Therewith she held it out: I strove hard to be brave enough to take it, but could not; I only turned away shuddering, sick, and grieved to the heart's core of me; then struggling hard with hand and knee and elbow, I scarce rose, and stood up totteringly; while she watched me sadly, still holding out her hand.

But as I rose, in my swinging to and fro the steel sheath of my sword struck her on the hand so that the blood flowed from it, which she stood looking at for a while, then dropped it downwards, and turned to look at me, for I was going.

Then as I walked she followed me, so I stopped and turned and said almost fiercely:

'I am going alone to look for my brother.'

The vehemence with which I spoke, or something else, burst some blood-vessel within my throat, and we both stood there with the blood running from us on to the grass and summer flowers.

She said: 'If you find him, wait with him till I come.'

'Yea,' and I turned and left her, following the course of the stream upwards, and as I went I heard her low singing that almost broke my heart for its sadness.

And I went painfully because of my weakness, and because also of the great stones; and sometimes I went along a spot of earth where the river had been used to flow in flood-time, and which was now bare of everything but stones; and the sun, now risen high, poured down on everything a great flood of fierce light and scorching heat, and burnt me sorely, so that I almost fainted.

But about noontide I entered a wood close by the stream, a beech-wood, intending to rest myself. The herbage was thin and scattered there, sprouting up from amid the leaf-sheaths and nuts of the beeches, which had fallen year after year on that same spot; the outside boughs swept low down, the air itself seemed green when you entered within the shadow of the branches, they over-roofed the place so with tender green, only here and there showing spots of blue.

But what lay at the foot of a great beech tree but some dead knight in armour, only the helmet off? A wolf was prowling round about it, who ran away snarling when he saw me coming.

So I went up to that dead knight, and fell on my knees before him, laying my head on his breast, for it was Arnald.

He was quite cold but had not been dead for very long; I would not believe him dead, but went down to the stream and brought him water, tried to make him drink—what would you? he was as dead as Swanhilda: neither came there any answer to my cries that afternoon but the moaning of the wood-doves in the beeches.

So then I sat down and took his head on my knees, and closed his eyes, and wept quietly while the sun sunk lower.

But a little after sunset I heard a rustle through the leaves, that was not the wind, and looking up my eyes met the pitying eyes of that maiden.

Something stirred rebelliously within me; I ceased weeping, and said:

'It is unjust, unfair: What right had Swanhilda to live? Did not God give her up to us? How much better was he than ten Swanhildas? and look you—See!—He is DEAD.'

Now this I shrieked out, being mad; and though I trembled when I saw some stormy wrath that vexed her very heart and loving lips, gathering on her face, I yet sat there looking at her and screaming, screaming, till all the place rung.

But when growing hoarse and breathless I ceased; she said, with straightened brow and scornful mouth:

'So! Bravely done! must I then, though I am a woman, call you a liar, for saying God is unjust? You to punish her, had not God then punished her already? How many times when she woke in the dead night do you suppose she missed seeing King Urrayne's pale face and hacked head lying on the pillow by her side? Whether by night or day, what things but screams did she hear when the wind blew loud round about the Palace corners? and did not that face too, often come before her, pale and bleeding as it was long ago, and gaze at her from unhappy eyes! poor eyes! with changed purpose in them—no more hope of converting the world when that blow was once struck, truly it was very wicked—no more dreams, but only fierce struggles with the Devil for very life, no more dreams but failure at last, and death, happier so in the Hollow Land.'

She grew so pitying as she gazed at his dead face that I began to weep again unreasonably, while she saw not that I was weeping, but looked only on Arnald's face, but after turned on me frowning.

'Unjust! yes truly unjust enough to take away life and all hope from her; you have done a base cowardly act, you and your brother here, disguise it as you may; you deserve all God's judgments—you—'

But I turned my eyes and wet face to her, and said:

'Do not curse me—there—do not look like Swanhilda: for see now, you said at first that you had been waiting long for me, give me your hand now, for I love you so.'

Then she came and knelt by where I sat, and I caught her in my arms, and she prayed to be forgiven.

'O Florian! I have indeed waited long for you, and when I saw you my heart was filled with joy, but you would neither touch me nor speak to me, so that I became almost mad,—forgive me, we will be so happy now. O! do you know, this is what I have been waiting for all these years; it made me glad, I know, when I was a little baby in my mother's arms to think I was born for this; and afterwards, as I grew up, I used to watch every breath of wind through the beech-boughs, every turn of the silver poplar leaves, thinking it might be you or some news of you.'

Then I rose and drew her up with me; but she knelt again by my brother's side, and kissed him, and said:

'O brother! the Hollow Land is only second best of the places God has made; for Heaven also is the work of His hand.'

Afterwards we dug a deep grave among the beech-roots and there we buried Arnald de Liliis.

And I have never seen him since, scarcely even in dreams. Surely God has had mercy on him, for he was very leal and true and brave; he loved many men, and was kind and gentle to his friends, neither did he hate any but Swanhilda.

But as for us two, Margaret and me, I cannot tell you concerning our happiness, such things cannot be told; only this I know, that we abode continually in the Hollow Land until I lost it.

Moreover this I can tell you. Margaret was walking with me, as she often walked near the place where I had first seen her; presently we came upon a woman sitting, dressed in scarlet and gold raiment, with her head laid down on her knees; likewise we heard her sobbing.

'Margaret, who is she?' I said: 'I knew not that any dwelt in the Hollow Land but us two only.'

She said, 'I know not who she is, only sometimes, these many years, I have seen her scarlet robe flaming from far away, amid the quiet green grass: but I was never so near her as this. Florian, I am afraid; let us come away.'

Fytte the second

Such a horrible grey November day it was, the fog-smell all about, the fog creeping into our very bones.

And I sat there, trying to recollect, at any rate something, under those fir-trees that I ought to have known so well.

Just think now; I had lost my best years somewhere; for I was past the prime of life, my hair and beard were scattered with white, my body was growing weaker, my memory of all things was very faint.

My raiment, purple and scarlet and blue once, was so stained that you could scarce call it any colour, was so tattered that it scarce covered my body, though it seemed once to have fallen in heavy folds to my feet, and still, when I rose to walk, though the miserable November mist lay in great drops upon my bare breast, yet was I obliged to wind my raiment over my arm, it draggled so (wretched, slimy, textureless thing!) in the brown mud.

On my head was a light morion, which pressed on my brow and pained me; so I put my hand up to take it off, but when I touched it I stood still in my walk shuddering; I nearly fell to the earth with shame and sick horror; for I laid my hand on a lump of slimy earth with worms coiled up in it. I could scarce forbear from shrieking, but breathing such a prayer as I could think of, I raised my hand again and seized it firmly. Worse horror still! the rust had eaten it into holes, and I gripped my own hair as well as the rotting steel, the sharp edge of which cut into my fingers; but setting my teeth, gave a great wrench, for I knew that if I let go of it then, no power on the earth or under it could make me touch it again. God be praised! I tore it off and cast it far from me; I saw the earth, and the worms and green weeds and sun-begotten slime, whirling out from it radiatingly, as it spun round about.

I was girt with a sword too, the leathern belt of which had shrunk and squeezed my waist: dead leaves had gathered in knots about the buckles of it, the gilded handle was encrusted with clay in many parts, the velvet sheath miserably worn.

But, verily, when I took hold of the hilt, and dreaded lest instead of a sword I should find a serpent in my hand; lo! then I drew out my own true blade and shook it flawless from hilt to point, gleaming white in that mist.

Therefore it sent a thrill of joy to my heart, to know that there was one friend left me yet: I sheathed it again carefully, and undoing it from my waist, hung it about my neck.

Then catching up my rags in my arms, I drew them up till my legs and feet were altogether clear from them, afterwards folded my arms over my breast, gave a long leap and ran, looking downward, but not giving heed to my way.

Once or twice I fell over stumps of trees, and such-like, for it was a cut-down wood that I was in, but I rose always, though bleeding and confused, and went on still; sometimes tearing madly through briars and gorse bushes, so that my blood dropped on the dead leaves as I went.

I ran in this way for about an hour; then I heard a gurgling and splashing of waters; I gave a great shout, and leapt strongly, with shut eyes, and the black water closed over me.

When I rose again, I saw near me a boat with a man in it; but the shore was far off; I struck out toward the boat, but my clothes which I had knotted and folded about me, weighed me down terribly.

The man looked at me, and began to paddle toward me with the oar he held in his left hand, having in his right a long, slender spear, barbed like a fish hook; perhaps, I thought, it is some fishing spear; moreover his raiment was of scarlet, with upright stripes of yellow and black all over it.

When my eye caught his, a smile widened his mouth as if someone had made a joke; but I was beginning to sink, and indeed my head was almost under water just as he came and stood above me, but before it went quite under I saw his spear gleam, then *felt* it in my shoulder, and for the present, felt nothing else.

When I woke I was on the bank of that river; the flooded waters went hurrying past me; no boat on them now; from the river the ground went up in gentle slopes till it grew a great hill, and there, on that hill-top—Yes, I might forget many things, almost everything, but not that, not the old castle of my fathers up among the hills, its towers blackened now and shattered, yet still no enemy's banner waved from it.

So I said I would go and die there; and at this thought I drew my sword, which yet hung about my neck, and shook it in the air till the true steel quivered, then began to pace toward the castle. I was quite naked, no rag about me; I took no heed of that, only thanking God that my sword was left, and so toiled up the hill. I entered the castle soon by the outer court; I knew the way so well, that I did not lift my eyes from the ground, but walked on over the lower drawbridge, through the unguarded gates, and stood in the great hall at last—my father's hall—as bare of everything but my sword as when I came into the world fifty years before: I had as little clothes, as little wealth, less memory and thought, I verily believe, than then.

So I lifted up my eyes and gazed; no glass in the windows, no hangings on the walls; the vaulting yet held good throughout, but seemed to be going; the mortar had fallen out from between the stones, and grass and fern grew in the joints; the marble pavement was in some places gone, and water stood about in puddles, though one scarce knew how it had got there.

No hangings on the walls—no; yet, strange to say, instead of them, the walls blazed from end to end with scarlet paintings, only striped across with green damp-marks in many places, some falling bodily from the wall, the plaster hanging down with the fading colour on it.

In all of them, except for the shadows and the faces of the figures, there was scarce any colour but scarlet and yellow; here and there it seemed the painter, whoever it was, had tried to make his trees or his grass green, but it would not do: some ghastly thoughts must have filled his head, for all the green went presently into yellow, out-sweeping through the picture dismally. But the faces were painted to the very life, or it seemed so;—there were only five of them, however, that were very marked or came much in the foreground; and four of these I knew well, though I did not then remember the names of those that had borne them. They were Red Harald, Swanhilda, Arnald, and myself. The fifth I did not know; it was a woman's, and very beautiful.

Then I saw that in some parts a small penthouse roof had been built over the paintings, to keep them from the weather. Near one of these stood a man painting, clothed in red, with stripes of yellow and black: then I knew that it was the same man who had saved me from drowning by spearing me through the shoulder; so I went up to him, and saw furthermore that he was girt with a heavy sword.

He turned round when he saw me coming, and asked me fiercely what I did there.

I asked why he was painting in my castle.

Thereupon, with that same grim smile widening his mouth as heretofore, he said: 'I paint God's judgments.'

And as he spoke, he rattled the sword in his scabbard; but I said,

'Well, then, you paint them very badly. Listen; I know God's judgments much better than you do. See now; I will teach you God's judgments, and you shall teach me painting.'

While I spoke he still rattled his sword, and when I had done, shut his right eye tight, screwing his nose on one side; then said:

'You have got no clothes on, and may go to the devil! what do *you* know about God's judgments?'

'Well, they are not all yellow and red, at all events; you ought to know better.'

He screamed out, 'O you fool! yellow and red! Gold and blood; what do they make?'

'Well,' I said; 'what?'

'HELL!' And, coming close up to me, he struck me with his open hand in the face, so that the colour with which his hand was smeared was dabbed about my face. The blow almost threw me down; and, while I staggered, he rushed at me furiously with his sword. Perhaps it was good for me that I had got no clothes on; for, being utterly unencumbered, I leapt this way and that, and avoided his fierce eager strokes till I could collect myself somewhat; while he had a heavy scarlet cloak on that trailed on the ground, and which he often trod on so that he stumbled.

He very nearly slew me during the first few minutes, for it was not strange that, together with other matters, I should have forgotten the art of fence: but yet, as I went on, and sometimes bounded about the hall under the whizzing of his sword, as he rested sometimes, leaning on it, as the point sometimes touched my bare flesh, nay, once as the whole sword fell flatlings on my head and made my eyes start out, I remembered the old joy that I used to have, and the *swy*, *swy*, of the sharp edge as one gazed between one's horse's ears; moreover, at last, one fierce swift stroke, just touching me below the throat, tore up the skin all down my body and fell heavy on my thigh, so that I drew my breath in and turned white; then first, as I swung my sword round my head, our blades met, oh! to hear that *tchink* again! and I felt the notch my sword made in his, and swung out at him; but he guarded it and returned on me: I guarded right and left, and grew warm, and opened my mouth to shout, but knew not what to say; and our sword-points fell on the floor together: then, when we had panted awhile, I wiped from my face the blood that had been dashed over it, shook my sword and cut at him, then we spun round and round in a mad waltz to the measured music of our meeting swords, and sometimes either wounded the other somewhat, but not much, till I beat down his sword on to his head that he fell grovelling, but not cut through. Verily, thereupon my lips opened mightily with 'Mary rings!'

Then, when he had gotten to his feet, I went at him again, he staggering back, guarding wildly; I cut at his head; he put his sword up confusedly, so I fitted both hands to my hilt, and smote him mightily under the arm: then his shriek mingled with my shout, made a strange sound together; he rolled over and over, dead, as I thought.

I walked about the hall in great exultation at first, striking my sword point on the floor every now and then, till I grew faint with loss of blood; then I went to my enemy and stripped off some of his clothes to bind up my wounds withal; afterwards I found in a corner bread and wine, and I eat and drank thereof.

Then I went back to him, and looked, and a thought struck me, and I took some of his paints and brushes, and, kneeling down, painted his face thus, with stripes of yellow and red, crossing each other at right angles; and in each of the squares so made I put a spot of black, after the manner of the painted letters in the prayer books and romances, when they are ornamented.

So I stood back as painters use, folded my arms, and admired my own handiwork. Yet there struck me as being something so utterly doleful in the man's white face, and the blood running all about him, and washing off the stains of paint from his face and hands, and splashed clothes, that my heart misgave me, and I hoped that he was not dead; I took some water from a vessel he had been using for his painting, and, kneeling, washed his face.

Was it some resemblance to my father's dead face, which I had seen when I was young, that made me pity him? I laid my hand upon his heart and felt it beating feebly; so I lifted him up gently, and carried him towards a heap of straw that he seemed used to lie upon; there I stripped him and looked to his wounds, and used leech-craft, the memory of which God gave me for this purpose, I suppose, and within seven days I found that he would not die.

Afterwards, as I wandered about the castle, I came to a room in one of the upper storeys, that had still the roof on, and windows in it with painted glass; and there I found green raiment and swords and armour, and I clothed myself.

So when he got well I asked him what his name was, and he me, and we both of us said, 'Truly, I know not.'

Then said I, 'But we must call each other some name, even as men call days.'

'Call me Swerker,' he said, 'some priest I knew once had that name.'

'And me Wulf,' said I, 'though wherefore I know not.'

Then he said: 'Wulf, I will teach you painting now, come and learn.'

Then I tried to learn painting till I thought I should die, but at last learned it through very much pain and grief.

And, as the years went on and we grew old and grey, we painted purple pictures and green ones instead of the scarlet and yellow, so that the walls looked altered, and always we painted God's judgments.

And we would sit in the sunset and watch them with the golden light changing them, as we yet hoped God would change both us and our works.

Often too we would sit outside the walls and look at the trees and sky, and the ways of the few men and women we saw; therefrom sometimes befell adventures.

Once there went past a great funeral of some king going to his own country, not as he had hoped to go, but stiff and colourless, spices filling up the place of his heart.

And first went by very many knights, with long bright hauberks on, that fell down before their knees as they rode, and they all had tilting-helms on with the same crest, so that their faces were quite hidden: and this crest was two hands clasped together tightly as though they were the hands of one praying forgiveness from the one he loves best; and the crest was wrought in gold.

Moreover, they had on over their hauberks surcoats which were half scarlet and half purple, strewn about with golden stars.

Also long lances, that had forked knights'-pennons, half purple and half scarlet, strewn with golden stars.

And these went by with no sound but the fall of their horse-hoofs.

And they went slowly, so slowly that we counted them all, five thousand five hundred and fifty-five.

There went by many fair maidens whose hair was loose and yellow, and who were all clad in green raiment ungirded, and shod with golden shoes. These also we counted, being five hundred; moreover some of the outermost of them, viz. one maiden to every twenty, had long silver trumpets, which they swung out to right and left, blowing them, and their sound was very sad.

Then many priests, and bishops, and abbots, who wore white albs and golden copes over them; and they all sung together mournfully: 'Propter amnen Babylonis;' and these were three hundred. After that came a great knot of the lords, who wore tilting helmets and surcoats emblazoned with each one his own device; only each had in his hand a small staff two feet long, whereon was a pennon of scarlet and purple. These also were three hundred.

And in the midst of these was a great car hung down to the ground with purple, drawn by grey horses whose trappings were half scarlet, half purple.

And on this car lay the King, whose head and hands were bare; and he had on him a surcoat, half purple and half scarlet, strewn with golden stars.

And his head rested on a tilting helmet whose crest was the hands of one praying passionately for forgiveness.

But his own hands lay by his side as if he had just fallen asleep.

And all about the car were little banners, half purple and half scarlet, strewn with golden stars.

Then the King, who counted but as one, went by also.

And after him came again many maidens clad in ungirt white raiment strewn with scarlet flowers, and their hair was loose and yellow and their feet bare: and, except for the falling of their feet and the rustle of the wind through their raiment, they went past quite silently. These also were five hundred.

Then lastly came many young knights with long bright hauberks falling over their knees as they rode, and surcoats, half scarlet and half purple, strewn with golden stars; they bore long lances with forked pennons which were half purple, half scarlet, strewn with golden stars; their heads and their hands were bare, but they bore shields, each one of them, which were of bright steel wrought cunningly in the midst with that bearing of the two hands of one who prays for forgiveness; which was done in gold. These were but five hundred.

Then they all went by winding up and up the hill roads, and, when the last of them had departed out of our sight we put down our heads and wept, and I said, 'Sing us one of the songs of the Hollow Land.'

Then he whom I had called Swerker put his hand into his bosom, and slowly drew out a long, long tress of black hair, and laid it on his knee and smoothed it, weeping on it: so then I left him there and went and armed myself, and brought armour for him.

And then came back to him and threw the armour down so that it clanged, and said: 'O! Harald, let us go!'

He did not seem surprised that I called him by the right name, but rose and armed himself, and then he looked a good knight; so we set forth.

And in a turn of the long road we came suddenly upon a most fair woman, clothed in scarlet, who sat and sobbed, holding her face between her hands, and her hair was very black.

And when Harald saw her, he stood and gazed at her for long through the bars of his helmet, then suddenly turned, and said: 'Florian, I must stop here; do you go on to the Hollow Land. Farewell.'

'Farewell.' And then I went on, never turning back, and him I never saw more. And so I went on, quite lonely, but happy, till I had reached the Hollow Land.

Into which I let myself down most carefully, by the jutting rocks and bushes and strange trailing flowers, and there lay down and fell asleep.

Fytte the third

And I was waked by someone singing: I felt very happy; I felt young again; I had fair delicate raiment on, my sword was gone, and my armour; I tried to think where I was, and could not for my happiness; I tried to listen to the words of the song. Nothing, only an old echo in my ears, only all manner of strange scenes from my wretched past life before my eyes in a dim, far-off manner: then at last, slowly, without effort, I heard what she sang.

Christ keep the Hollow Land
All the summer-tide;   20
Still we cannot understand
Where the waters glide:

Only dimly seeing them
Coldly slipping through
Many green-lipp'd cavern mouths,   25
Where the hills are blue.

'Then,' she said, 'come now and look for it, love, a hollow city in the Hollow Land.'

I kissed Margaret, and we went.

*   *   *   *   *   *   *   *   *   *   *   *   *   *   *   *

Through the golden streets under the purple shadows of the houses we went, and the slow fanning backward and forward of the many-coloured banners cooled us: we two alone; there was no one with us, no soul will ever be able to tell what we said, how we looked.

At last we came to a fair palace, cloistered off in the old time, before the city grew golden from the din and hubbub of traffic; those who dwelt there in the old ungolden times had had their own joys, their own sorrows, apart from the joys and sorrows of the multitude: so, in like manner was it now cloistered off from the eager leaning and brotherhood of the golden dwellings: so now it had its own gaiety, its own solemnity, apart from theirs; unchanged, unchangeable were its marble walls, whatever else changed about it.

We stopped before the gates and trembled, and clasped each other closer; for there among the marble leafage and tendrils that were round and under and over the archway that held the golden valves, were wrought two figures of a man and woman winged and garlanded, whose raiment flashed with stars;

and their faces were like faces we had seen or half seen in some dream long and long and long ago, so that we trembled with awe and delight; and I turned, and seeing Margaret, saw that her face was that face seen or half seen long and long and long ago; and in the shining of her eyes I saw that other face, seen in that way and no other long and long and long ago—my face.

And then we walked together toward the golden gates, and opened them, and no man gainsaid us.

And before us lay a great space of flowers.

THE STORY OF THE UNKNOWN CHURCH

I was the master-mason of a church that was built more than six hundred years ago; it is now two hundred years since that church vanished from the face of the earth; it was destroyed utterly,—no fragment of it was left; not even the great pillars that bore up the tower at the cross, where the choir used to join the nave. No one knows now even where it stood, only in this very autumn-tide, if you knew the place, you would see the heaps made by the earth-covered ruins heaving the yellow corn into glorious waves, so that the place where my church used to be is as beautiful now as when it stood in all its splendour. I do not remember very much about the land where my church was; I have quite forgotten the name of it, but I know it was very beautiful, and even now, while I am thinking of it, comes a flood of old memories, and I almost seem to see it again,—that old beautiful land! Only dimly do I see it in spring and summer and winter, but I see it in autumn-tide clearly now; yes, clearer, clearer, oh! so bright and glorious! yet it was beautiful too in spring, when the brown earth began to grow green: beautiful in summer, when the blue sky looked so much bluer, if you could hem a piece of it in between the new white carving; beautiful in the solemn starry nights, so solemn that it almost reached agony—the awe and joy one had in their great beauty. But of all these beautiful times, I remember the whole only of autumn-tide; the others come in bits to me; I can think only of parts of them but all of autumn; and of all days and nights in autumn, I remember one more particularly. That autumn day the church was nearly finished, and the monks, for whom we were building the church, and the people, who lived in the town hard by, crowded round us oftentimes to watch us carving.

Now the great Church, and the buildings of the Abbey where the monks lived, were about three miles from the town, and the town stood on a hill overlooking the rich autumn country: it was girt about with great walls that had overhanging battlements, and towers at certain places all along the walls, and often we could see from the churchyard or the Abbey garden, the flash of helmets and spears, and the dim shadowy waving of banners, as the knights and lords and men-at-arms passed to and fro along the battlements; and we could see too in the town the three spires of the three churches; and the spire of the Cathedral, which was the tallest of the three, was gilt all over with gold, and always at night-time a great lamp shone from it that hung in the spire midway between the roof of the church and the cross at the top of the spire. The Abbey where we built the Church was not girt by stone walls, but by a circle of poplar trees, and whenever a wind passed over them, were it ever so little a breath, it set them all a-ripple; and when the wind was high, they bowed and swayed very low, and the wind, as it lifted the leaves, and showed their silvery white sides, or as again in the lulls of it, it let them drop, kept on changing the trees from green to white, and white to green; moreover, through the boughs and trunks of the poplars we caught glimpses of the great golden corn sea, waving, waving, waving for leagues and leagues; and among the corn grew burning scarlet poppies, and blue corn-flowers; and the corn-flowers were so blue, that they gleamed, and seemed to burn with a steady light, as they grew beside the poppies among the gold of the wheat. Through the corn sea ran a blue river, and always green meadows and lines of tall poplars followed its windings. The old Church had been burned, and that was the reason why the monks caused me to build the new one; the buildings of the Abbey were built at the same time as the burned-down Church, more than a hundred years before I was born, and they were on the north side of the Church, and joined to it by a cloister of round arches, and in the midst of the cloister was a lawn, and in the midst of that lawn, a fountain of marble, carved round about with flowers and strange beasts; and at the edge of the lawn, near the round arches, were a great many sun-flowers that were all in blossom on that autumn day; and up many of the pillars of the cloister crept passion-flowers and roses. Then farther from the Church, and past the cloister and its buildings, were many detached buildings, and a great garden round them, all within the circle of the poplar trees; in the garden were trellises covered over with roses, and convolvolus, and the great-leaved fiery nasturtium; and specially all along by the poplar trees were there trellises, but on these grew nothing but deep crimson roses; the hollyhocks too were all out in blossom at that time, great spires of pink, and orange, and red, and white, with their soft, downy leaves. I said that nothing grew on the trellises by the poplars but crimson roses, but I was not quite right, for in many places the wild flowers had crept into the garden from without; lush green briony, with green-white blossoms, that grows so fast, one could almost think that we see it grow, and deadly nightshade, La bella donna, O! so beautiful; red berry, and purple, yellow-spiked flower, and deadly, cruel-looking, dark green leaf, all growing together in the glorious days of early autumn. And in the midst of the great garden was a conduit, with its sides carved with histories from the Bible, and there was on it too, as on the fountain in the cloister, much carving of flowers and strange beasts. Now the Church itself was surrounded on every side but the north by the cemetery, and there were many graves there, both of monks and of laymen, and often the friends of those, whose bodies lay there, had planted flowers about the graves of those they loved. I remember one such particularly, for at the head of it was a cross of carved wood, and at the foot of it, facing the cross, three tall sun-flowers; then in the midst of the cemetery was a cross of stone, carved on one side with the Crucifixion of our Lord

Jesus Christ, and on the other with Our Lady holding the Divine Child. So that day, that I specially remember, in autumn-tide, when the church was nearly finished, I was carving in the central porch of the west front; (for I carved all those bas-reliefs in the west front with my own hand;) beneath me my sister Margaret was carving at the flower-work, and the little quatrefoils that carry the signs of the zodiac and emblems of the months: now my sister Margaret was rather more than twenty years old at that time, and she was very beautiful, with dark brown hair and deep calm violet eyes. I had lived with her all my life, lived with her almost alone latterly, for our father and mother died when she was quite young, and I loved her very much, though I was not thinking of her just then, as she stood beneath me carving. Now the central porch was carved with a bas-relief of the Last Judgment, and it was divided into three parts by horizontal bands of deep flower-work. In the lowest division, just over the doors, was carved The Rising of the Dead; above were angels blowing long trumpets, and Michael the Archangel weighing the souls, and the blessed led into heaven by angels, and the lost into hell by the devil; and in the topmost division was the Judge of the world.

All the figures in the porch were finished except one, and I remember when I woke that morning my exultation at the thought of my Church being so nearly finished; I remember, too, how a kind of misgiving mingled with the exultation, which, try all I could, I was unable to shake off; I thought then it was a rebuke for my pride, well, perhaps it was. The figure I had to carve was Abraham, sitting with a blossoming tree on each side of him, holding in his two hands the corners of his great robe, so that it made a mighty fold, wherein, with their hands crossed over their breasts, were the souls of the faithful, of whom he was called Father: I stood on the scaffolding for some time, while Margaret's chisel worked on bravely down below. I took mine in my hand, and stood so, listening to the noise of the masons inside, and two monks of the Abbey came and stood below me, and a knight, holding his little daughter by the hand, who every now and then looked up at him, and asked him strange questions. I did not think of these long, but began to think of Abraham, yet I could not think of him sitting there, quiet and solemn, while the Judgment-Trumpet was being blown; I rather thought of him as he looked when he chased those kings so far; riding far ahead of any of his company, with his mail-hood off his head, and lying in grim folds down his back, with the strong west wind blowing his wild black hair far out behind him, with the wind rippling the long scarlet pennon of his lance; riding there amid the rocks and the sands alone; with the last gleam of the armour of the beaten kings disappearing behind the winding of the pass; with his company a long, long way behind, quite out of sight, though their trumpets sounded faintly among the clefts of the rocks; and so I thought I saw him, till in his fierce chase he leapt, horse and man, into a deep river, quiet, swift, and smooth; and there was something in the moving of the water-lilies as the breast of the horse swept them aside, that suddenly took away the thought of Abraham and brought a strange dream of lands I had never seen; and the first was of a place where I was quite alone, standing by the side of a river, and there was the sound of singing a very long way off, but no living thing of any kind could be seen, and the land was quite flat, quite without hills, and quite without trees too, and the river wound very much, making all kinds of quaint curves, and on the side where I stood there grew nothing but long grass, but on the other side grew, quite on to the horizon, a great sea of red corn-poppies, only paths of white lilies wound all among them, with here and there a great golden sunflower. So I looked down at the river by my feet, and saw how blue it was, and how, as the stream went swiftly by, it swayed to and fro the long green weeds, and I stood and looked at the river for long, till at last I felt some one touch me on the shoulder, and, looking round, I saw standing by me my friend Amyot, whom I love better than anyone else in the world, but I thought in my dream that I was frightened when I saw him, for his face had changed so, it was so bright and almost transparent, and his eyes gleamed and shone as I had never seen them do before. Oh! he was so wondrously beautiful, so fearfully beautiful! and as I looked at him the distant music swelled, and seemed to come close up to me, and then swept by us, and fainted away, at last died off entirely; and then I felt sick at heart, and faint, and parched, and I stooped to drink of the water of the river, and as soon as the water touched my lips, lo! the river vanished, and the flat country with its poppies and lilies, and I dreamed that I was in a boat by myself again, floating in an almost land-locked bay of the northern sea, under a cliff of dark basalt. I was lying on my back in the boat, looking up at the intensely blue sky, and a long low swell from the outer sea lifted the boat up and let it fall again and carried it gradually nearer and nearer towards the dark cliff; and as I moved on, I saw at last, on the top of the cliff, a castle with many towers, and on the highest tower of the castle there was a great white banner floating, with a red chevron on it, and three golden stars on the chevron; presently I saw too on one of the towers, growing in a cranny of the worn stones, a great bunch of golden and blood-red wall-flowers, and I watched the wall-flowers and banner for long; when suddenly I heard a trumpet blow from the castle, and saw a rush of armed men on to the battlements, and there was a fierce fight, till at last it was ended, and one went to the banner and pulled it down, and cast it over the cliff into the sea, and it came down in long sweeps, with the wind making little ripples in it;—slowly, slowly it came, till at last it fell over me and covered me from my feet till over my breast, and I let it stay there and looked again at the castle, and then I saw that there was an amber-coloured banner floating over the castle in place of the red chevron, and it was much larger than the other: also now, a man stood on the battlements, looking towards me; he had a tilting helmet on, with the visor down, and an amber-coloured surcoat over his armour: his right hand was ungauntletted, and he held it high above his head, and in his hand was the bunch of wall-flowers that I had seen growing on the wall; and his hand was white and small, like a woman's, for in my dream I could see even very far off things much clearer than we see real material things on the earth: presently he threw the wall-flowers over the cliff, and they fell in the boat just behind my head, and then I saw, looking down from the battlements of the castle, Amyot. He looked down towards me very sorrowfully, I thought, but, even as in the other dream, said nothing; so I thought in my dream that I wept for very pity, and for love of him, for he looked as a man just risen from a long illness, and who will carry till he dies a dull pain about with him. He was very thin, and his long black hair drooped all about his face, as he leaned over the battlements looking at me: he was quite pale, and his cheeks were hollow, but his eyes large and soft and sad. So I reached out my arms to him, and suddenly I was walking with him in a lovely garden, and we said nothing, for the music which I had heard at first was sounding close to us now, and there were many birds in the boughs of the trees: oh, such birds! gold and ruby, and emerald, but they sung not at all, but were quite silent, as though they too were listening to the music. Now all this time Amyot and I had been looking at each other, but just then I turned my head away from him, and as soon as I did so, the music ended with a long wail, and when I turned again Amyot was gone; then I felt even more sad and sick at heart than I had before when I was by the river, and I leaned against a tree, and put my hands before my eyes. When I looked again the garden was gone, and I knew not where I was, and presently all my dreams were gone. The chips were flying bravely from the stone under my chisel at last, and all my thoughts now were in my carving, when I heard my name, 'Walter,' called, and when I looked down I saw one standing below me, whom I had seen in my dreams just before—Amyot. I had no hopes of seeing him for a long time, perhaps I might never see him again, I thought, for he was away (as I thought) fighting in the holy wars, and it made me almost beside myself to see him standing close by me in the flesh. I got down from my scaffolding as soon as I could, and all thoughts else were soon drowned in the joy of having him by me; Margaret, too, how glad she must have been, for she had been betrothed to him for some time before he went to the wars, and he had been five years away; five years! and how we had thought of him through those many weary days! how often his face had come before me! his brave, honest face, the most beautiful among all the faces of men and women I have ever seen. Yes, I remember how five years ago I held his hand as we came together out of the cathedral of that great, far-off city, whose name I forget now; and then I remember the stamping of the horses' feet; I remember how his hand left mine at last, and then, some one looking back at me earnestly as they all rode on together—looking back, with his hand on the saddle behind him, while the trumpets sang in long solemn peals as they all rode on together, with the glimmer of arms and the fluttering of banners, and the clinking of the rings of the mail, that sounded like the falling of many drops of water into the deep, still waters of some pool that the rocks nearly meet over; and the gleam and flash of the swords, and the glimmer of the lance-heads and the flutter of the rippled banners, that streamed out from them, swept past me, and were gone, and they seemed like a pageant in a dream, whose meaning we know not; and those sounds too, the trumpets, and the clink of the mail, and the thunder of the horse-hoofs, they seemed dream-like too—and it was all like a dream that he should leave me, for we had said that we should always be together; but he went away, and now he is come back again.

We were by his bed-side, Margaret and I; I stood and leaned over him, and my hair fell sideways over my face and touched his face; Margaret kneeled beside me, quivering in every limb, not with pain, I think, but rather shaken by a passion of earnest prayer. After some time (I know not how long), I looked up from his face to the window underneath which he lay; I do not know what time of the day it was, but I know that it was a glorious autumn day, a day soft with melting, golden haze: a vine and a rose grew together, and trailed half across the window, so that I could not see much of the beautiful blue sky, and nothing of town or country beyond; the vine leaves were touched with red here and there, and three over-blown roses, light pink roses, hung amongst them. I remember dwelling on the strange lines the autumn had made in red on one of the gold-green vine leaves, and watching one leaf of one of the over-blown roses, expecting it to fall every minute; but as I gazed, and felt disappointed that the rose leaf had not fallen yet, I felt my pain suddenly shoot through me, and I remembered what I had lost; and then came bitter, bitter dreams—dreams which had once made me happy—dreams of the things I had hoped would be, of the things that would never be now; they came between the fair vine leaves and rose blossoms, and that which lay before the window; they came as before, perfect in colour and form, sweet sounds and shapes. But now in every one was something unutterably miserable; they would not go away, they put out the steady glow of the golden haze, the sweet light of the sun through the vine leaves, the soft leaning of the full blown roses. I wandered in them for a long time; at last I felt a hand put me aside gently, for I was standing at the head of—of the bed; then some one kissed my forehead, and words were spoken—I know not what words. The bitter dreams left me for the bitterer reality at last; for I had found him that morning lying dead, only the morning after I had seen him when he had come back from his long absence—I had found him lying dead, with his hands crossed downwards, with his eyes closed, as though the angels had done that for him; and now when I looked at him he still lay there, and Margaret knelt by him with her face touching his: she was not quivering now, her lips moved not at all as they had done just before; and so, suddenly those words came to my mind which she had spoken when she kissed me, and which at the time I had only heard with my outward hearing, for she had said, 'Walter, farewell, and Christ keep you; but for me, I must be with him, for so I promised him last night that I would never leave him any more, and God will let me go.' And verily Margaret and Amyot did go, and left me very lonely and sad.

It was just beneath the westernmost arch of the nave, there I carved their tomb: I was a long time carving it; I did not think I should be so long at first, and I said, 'I shall die when I have finished carving it,' thinking that would be a very short time. But so it happened after I had carved those two whom I loved, lying with clasped hands like husband and wife above their tomb, that I could not yet leave carving it; and so that I might be near them I became a monk, and used to sit in the choir and sing, thinking of the time when we should all be together again. And as I had time I used to go to the westernmost arch of the nave and work at the tomb that was there under the great, sweeping arch; and in process of time I raised a marble canopy that reached quite up to the top of the arch, and I painted it too as fair as I could, and carved it all about with many flowers and histories, and in them I carved the faces of those I had known on earth (for I was not as one on earth now, but seemed quite away out of the world). And as I carved, sometimes the monks and other people too would come and gaze, and watch how the flowers grew; and sometimes too as they gazed, they would weep for pity, knowing how all had been.

So my life passed, and I lived in that Abbey for twenty years after he died, till one morning, quite early, when they came into the church for matins, they found me lying dead, with my chisel in my hand, underneath the last lily of the tomb.

FIGURE 1. *La Belle Iseult*, 1858. ©Tate Gallery, London. Oil on canvas. Morris's only large easel painting, with Jane Burden as model, in the character of the Arthurian Queen Iseult.

From *The Defence of Guenevere,
and Other Poems*

The Defence of Guenevere

But, knowing now that they would have her speak,
She threw her wet hair backward from her brow,
Her hand close to her mouth touching her cheek,

As though she had had there a shameful blow,
And feeling it shameful to feel ought but shame 5
All through her heart, yet felt her cheek burned so,

She must a little touch it; like one lame
She walked away from Gauwaine, with her head
Still lifted up; and on her cheek of flame

The tears dried quick; she stopped at last and said: 10
'O knights and lords, it seems but little skill
To talk of well-known things past now and dead.

'God wot I ought to say, I have done ill,
And pray you all forgiveness heartily!
Because you must be right, such great lords—still 15

'Listen, suppose your time were come to die,
And you were quite alone and very weak;
Yea, laid a dying while very mightily

'The wind was ruffling up the narrow streak
Of river through your broad lands running well: 20
Suppose a hush should come, then some one speak:

'"One of these cloths is heaven, and one is hell,
Now choose one cloth for ever; which they be,
I will not tell you, you must somehow tell

'"Of your own strength and mightiness; here, see!" 25
Yea, yea, my lord, and you to ope your eyes,
At foot of your familiar bed to see

'A great God's angel standing, with such dyes,
Not known on earth, on his great wings, and hands,
Held out two ways, light from the inner skies 30

'Showing him well, and making his commands
Seem to be God's commands, moreover, too,
Holding within his hands the cloths on wands;

'And one of these strange choosing cloths was blue,
Wavy and long, and one cut short and red;   35
No man could tell the better of the two.

'After a shivering half-hour you said:
"God help! Heaven's colour, the blue;" and he said, "hell."
Perhaps you then would roll upon your bed,

'And cry to all good men that loved you well,   40
"Ah Christ! if only I had known, known, known;"
Launcelot went away, then I could tell,

'Like wisest man how all things would be, moan,
And roll and hurt myself, and long to die,
And yet fear much to die for what was sown.   45

'Nevertheless you, O Sir Gauwaine, lie,
Whatever may have happened through these years,
God knows I speak truth, saying that you lie.'

Her voice was low at first, being full of tears,
But as it cleared, it grew full loud and shrill,   50
Growing a windy shriek in all men's ears,

A ringing in their startled brains, until
She said that Gauwaine lied, then her voice sunk,
And her great eyes began again to fill,

Though still she stood right up, and never shrunk,   55
But spoke on bravely, glorious lady fair!
Whatever tears her full lips may have drunk,

She stood, and seemed to think, and wrung her hair,
Spoke out at last with no more trace of shame,
With passionate twisting of her body there: 60

'It chanced upon a day that Launcelot came
To dwell at Arthur's court: at Christmas-time
This happened; when the heralds sung his name,

'"Son of King Ban of Benwick", seemed to chime
Along with all the bells that rang that day,   65
O'er the white roofs, with little change of rhyme.

'Christmas and whitened winter passed away,
And over me the April sunshine came,
Made very awful with black hail-clouds, yea

'And in the Summer I grew white with flame,   70
And bowed my head down—Autumn, and the sick
Sure knowledge things would never be the same,

'However often Spring might be most thick
Of blossoms and buds, smote on me, and I grew
Careless of most things, let the clock tick, tick,   75

'To my unhappy pulse, that beat right through
My eager body; while I laughed out loud,
And let my lips curl up at false or true,

'Seemed cold and shallow without any cloud.
Behold my judges, then the cloths were brought;   80
While I was dizzied thus, old thoughts would crowd,

'Belonging to the time ere I was bought
By Arthur's great name and his little love,
Must I give up for ever then, I thought,

'That which I deemed would ever round me move   85
Glorifying all things; for a little word,
Scarce ever meant at all, must I now prove

'Stone-cold for ever? Pray you, does the Lord
Will that all folks should be quite happy and good?
I love God now a little, if this cord   90

'Were broken, once for all what striving could
Make me love anything in earth or heaven.
So day by day it grew, as if one should

'Slip slowly down some path worn smooth and even,
Down to a cool sea on a summer day;   95
Yet still in slipping was there some small leaven

'Of stretched hands catching small stones by the way,
Until one surely reached the sea at last,
And felt strange new joy as the worn head lay

'Back, with the hair like sea-weed; yea all past   100
Sweat of the forehead, dryness of the lips,
Washed utterly out by the dear waves o'ercast

'In the lone sea, far off from any ships!
Do I not know now of a day in Spring?
No minute of that wild day ever slips   105

'From out my memory; I hear thrushes sing,
And wheresoever I may be, straightway
Thoughts of it all come up with most fresh sting;

'I was half mad with beauty on that day,
And went without my ladies all alone,   110
In a quiet garden walled round every way;

'I was right joyful of that wall of stone,
That shut the flowers and trees up with the sky,
And trebled all the beauty: to the bone,

'Yea right through to my heart, grown very shy   115
With weary thoughts, it pierced, and made me glad;
Exceedingly glad, and I knew verily,

'A little thing just then had made me mad;
I dared not think, as I was wont to do,
Sometimes, upon my beauty; if I had   120

'Held out my long hand up against the blue,
And, looking on the tenderly darken'd fingers,
Thought that by rights one ought to see quite through,

'There, see you, where the soft still light yet lingers,
Round by the edges; what should I have done,   125
If this had joined with yellow spotted singers,

'And startling green drawn upward by the sun?
But shouting, loosed out, see now! all my hair,
And trancedly stood watching the west wind run

'With faintest half-heard breathing sound—why there   130
I lose my head e'en now in doing this;
But shortly listen—In that garden fair

'Came Launcelot walking; this is true, the kiss
Wherewith we kissed in meeting that spring day,
I scarce dare talk of the remember'd bliss,   135

'When both our mouths went wandering in one way,
And aching sorely, met among the leaves;
Our hands being left behind strained far away.

'Never within a yard of my bright sleeves
Had Launcelot come before—and now, so nigh!   140
After that day why is it Guenevere grieves?

'Nevertheless you, O Sir Gauwaine, lie,
Whatever happened on through all those years,
God knows I speak truth, saying that you lie.

'Being such a lady could I weep these tears   145
If this were true? A great queen such as I
Having sinn'd this way, straight her conscience sears;

'And afterwards she liveth hatefully,
Slaying and poisoning, certes never weeps,—
Gauwaine be friends now, speak me lovingly.   150

'Do I not see how God's dear pity creeps
All through your frame, and trembles in your mouth?
Remember in what grave your mother sleeps,

'Buried in some place far down in the south,
Men are forgetting as I speak to you;   155
By her head sever'd in that awful drouth

'Of pity that drew Agravaine's fell blow,
I pray your pity! let me not scream out
For ever after, when the shrill winds blow

'Through half your castle-locks! let me not shout   160
For ever after in the winter night
When you ride out alone! in battle-rout

'Let not my rusting tears make your sword light!
Ah! God of mercy how he turns away!
So, ever must I dress me to the fight,   165

'So—let God's justice work! Gauwaine, I say,
See me hew down your proofs: yea, all men know
Even as you said how Mellyagraunce one day,

'One bitter day in *la Fausse Garde*, for so
All good knights held it after, saw—   170
Yea, sirs, by cursed unknightly outrage; though

'You, Gauwaine, held his word without a flaw,
This Mellyagraunce saw blood upon my bed—
Whose blood then pray you? is there any law

'To make a queen say why some spots of red   175
Lie on her coverlet? or will you say:
"Your hands are white, lady, as when you wed,

' "Where did you bleed?" and must I stammer out—"Nay,
I blush indeed, fair lord, only to rend
My sleeve up to my shoulder, where there lay   180

' "A knife-point last night": so must I defend
The honour of the lady Guenevere?
Not so, fair lords, even if the world should end

'This very day, and you were judges here
Instead of God. Did you see Mellyagraunce   185
When Launcelot stood by him? what white fear

'Curdled his blood, and how his teeth did dance,
His side sink in? as my knight cried and said,
"Slayer of unarm'd men, here is a chance!

' "Setter of traps, I pray you guard your head,   190
By God I am so glad to fight with you,
Stripper of ladies, that my hand feels lead

' "For driving weight; hurrah now! draw and do,
For all my wounds are moving in my breast,
And I am getting mad with waiting so."   195

'He struck his hands together o'er the beast,
Who fell down flat, and grovell'd at his feet,
And groan'd at being slain so young—"at least,"

'My knight said, "Rise you, sir, who are so fleet
At catching ladies, half-arm'd will I fight,   200
My left side all uncovered!" then I weet,

'Up sprang Sir Mellyagraunce with great delight
Upon his knave's face; not until just then
Did I quite hate him, as I saw my knight

'Along the lists look to my stake and pen   205
With such a joyous smile, it made me sigh
From agony beneath my waist-chain, when

'The fight began, and to me they drew nigh;
Ever Sir Launcelot kept him on the right,
And traversed warily, and ever high   210

'And fast leapt caitiff's sword, until my knight
Sudden threw up his sword to his left hand,
Caught it, and swung it; that was all the fight.

'Except a spout of blood on the hot land;
For it was hottest summer; and I know   215
I wonder'd how the fire, while I should stand,

'And burn, against the heat, would quiver so,
Yards above my head; thus these matters went;
Which things were only warnings of the woe

'That fell on me. Yet Mellyagraunce was shent,   220
For Mellyagraunce had fought against the Lord;
Therefore, my lords, take heed lest you be blent

'With all this wickedness; say no rash word
Against me, being so beautiful; my eyes,
Wept all away to grey, may bring some sword   225

'To drown you in your blood; see my breast rise,
Like waves of purple sea, as here I stand;
And how my arms are moved in wonderful wise,

'Yea also at my full heart's strong command,
See through my long throat how the words go up   230
In ripples to my mouth; how in my hand

'The shadow lies like wine within a cup
Of marvellously colour'd gold; yea now
This little wind is rising, look you up,

'And wonder how the light is falling so   235
Within my moving tresses: will you dare,
When you have looked a little on my brow,

'To say this thing is vile? or will you care
For any plausible lies of cunning woof,
When you can see my face with no lie there   240

'For ever? am I not a gracious proof—
"But in your chamber Launcelot was found"—
Is there a good knight then would stand aloof,

'When a queen says with gentle queenly sound:
"O true as steel come now and talk with me,   245
I love to see your step upon the ground

'"Unwavering, also well I love to see
That gracious smile light up your face, and hear
Your wonderful words, that all mean verily

'"The thing they seem to mean: good friend, so dear   250
To me in everything, come here to-night,
Or else the hours will pass most dull and drear;

'"If you come not, I fear this time I might
Get thinking over much of times gone by,
When I was young, and green hope was in sight;   255

'"For no man cares now to know why I sigh;
And no man comes to sing me pleasant songs,
Nor any brings me the sweet flowers that lie

'"So thick in the gardens; therefore one so longs
To see you, Launcelot; that we may be   260
Like children once again, free from all wrongs

'"Just for one night." Did he not come to me?
What thing could keep true Launcelot away
If I said, "come?" There was one less than three

'In my quiet room that night, and we were gay;   265
Till sudden I rose up, weak, pale, and sick,
Because a bawling broke our dream up, yea

'I looked at Launcelot's face and could not speak,
For he looked helpless too, for a little while;
Then I remember how I tried to shriek,   270

'And could not, but fell down; from tile to tile
The stones they threw up rattled o'er my head,
And made me dizzier; till within a while

'My maids were all about me, and my head
On Launcelot's breast was being soothed away   275
From its white chattering, until Launcelot said—

'By God! I will not tell you more to-day,
Judge any way you will—what matters it?
You know quite well the story of that fray,

'How Launcelot still'd their bawling, the mad fit   280
That caught up Gauwaine—all, all, verily,
But just that which would save me; these things flit.

'Nevertheless you, O Sir Gauwaine, lie,
Whatever may have happen'd these long years,
God knows I speak truth, saying that you lie!   285

'All I have said is truth, by Christ's dear tears.'
She would not speak another word, but stood
Turn'd sideways; listening, like a man who hears

His brother's trumpet sounding through the wood
Of his foes' lances. She lean'd eagerly,   290
And gave a slight spring sometimes, as she could

At last hear something really; joyfully
Her cheek grew crimson, as the headlong speed
Of the roan charger drew all men to see,
The knight who came was Launcelot at good need.   295

Golden Wings

Midways of a walled garden,
  In the happy poplar land,
  Did an ancient castle stand,
With an old knight for a warden.

Many scarlet bricks there were   5
  In its walls, and old grey stone;
  Over which red apples shone
At the right time of the year.

On the bricks the green moss grew,
  Yellow lichen on the stone,   10
  Over which red apples shone;
Little war that castle knew.

Deep green water fill'd the moat,
  Each side had a red-brick lip,
  Green and mossy with the drip   15
Of dew and rain; there was a boat

Of carven wood, with hangings green
  About the stern; it was great bliss
  For lovers to sit there and kiss
In the hot summer noons, not seen.   20

Across the moat the fresh west wind
  In very little ripples went;
  The way the heavy aspens bent
Towards it, was a thing to mind.

The painted drawbridge over it   25
  Went up and down with gilded chains,
  'Twas pleasant in the summer rains
Within the bridge-house there to sit.

There were five swans that ne'er did eat
  The water-weeds, for ladies came   30
  Each day, and young knights did the same,
And gave them cakes and bread for meat.

They had a house of painted wood,
  A red roof gold-spiked over it,
  Wherein upon their eggs to sit   35
Week after week; no drop of blood,

Drawn from men's bodies by sword-blows,
   Came ever there, or any tear;
   Most certainly from year to year
'Twas pleasant as a Provence rose.   40

The banners seem'd quite full of ease,
   That over the turret-roofs hung down;
   The battlements could get no frown
From the flower-moulded cornices.

Who walked in that garden there?   45
   Miles and Giles and Isabeau,
   Tall Jehane du Castel beau,
Alice of the golden hair,

Big Sir Gervaise, the good knight,
   Fair Ellayne le Violet,   50
   Mary, Constance fille de fay,
Many dames with footfall light.

Whosoever wander'd there,
   Whether it be dame or knight,
   Half of scarlet, half of white   55
Their raiment was; of roses fair

Each wore a garland on the head,
   At Ladies' Gard the way was so:
   Fair Jehane du Castel beau
Wore her wreath till it was dead.   60

Little joy she had of it,
   Of the raiment white and red,
   Or the garland on her head,
She had none with whom to sit

In the carven boat at noon;   65
   None the more did Jehane weep,
   She would only stand and keep
Saying, 'He will be here soon.'

Many times in the long day
   Miles and Giles and Gervaise passed,   70
   Holding each some white hand fast,
Every time they heard her say:

'Summer cometh to an end,
   Undern cometh after noon;

Golden wings will be here soon,   75
What if I some token send?'

Wherefore that night within the hall,
    With open mouth and open eyes,
    Like some one listening with surprise,
She sat before the sight of all.   80

Stoop'd down a little she sat there,
    With neck stretch'd out and chin thrown up,
    One hand around a golden cup;
And strangely with her fingers fair

She beat some tune upon the gold;   85
    The minstrels in the gallery
    Sung: 'Arthur, who will never die,
In Avallon he groweth old.'

And when the song was ended, she
    Rose and caught up her gown and ran;   90
    None stopp'd her eager face and wan
Of all that pleasant company.

Right so within her own chamber
    Upon her bed she sat; and drew
    Her breath in quick gasps; till she knew   95
That no man follow'd after her.

She took the garland from her head,
    Loosed all her hair, and let it lie
    Upon the coverlit; thereby
She laid the gown of white and red;   100

And she took off her scarlet shoon,
    And bared her feet; still more and more
    Her sweet face redden'd; evermore
She murmur'd: 'He will be here soon;

'Truly he cannot fail to know   105
    My tender body waits him here;
    And if he knows, I have no fear
For poor Jehane du Castel beau.'

She took a sword within her hand,
    Whose hilts were silver, and she sung   110
    Somehow like this, wild words that rung
A long way over the moonlit land:—

Gold wings across the sea!
Grey light from tree to tree,
Gold hair beside my knee,   115
I pray thee come to me,
Gold wings!

       The water slips,
The red-bill'd moorhen dips.
Sweet kisses on red lips;
Alas! the red rust grips,   120
And the blood-red dagger rips,
Yet, O knight, come to me!

Are not my blue eyes sweet?
The west wind from the wheat
Blows cold across my feet;   125
Is it not time to meet
Gold wings across the sea?

White swans on the green moat,
Small feathers left afloat
By the blue-painted boat;   130
Swift running of the stoat;
Sweet gurgling note by note
Of sweet music.

       O gold wings,
Listen how gold hair sings,
And the Ladies' Castle rings,   135
Gold wings across the sea.

I sit on a purple bed,
Outside, the wall is red,
Thereby the apple hangs,
And the wasp, caught by the fangs,   140

Dies in the autumn night.
And the bat flits till light,
And the love-crazed knight

Kisses the long wet grass:
The weary days pass,—   145
Gold wings across the sea!

Gold wings across the sea!
Moonlight from tree to tree,

Sweet hair laid on my knee,
O, sweet knight, come to me!   150

     Gold wings, the short night slips,
     The white swan's long neck drips,
     I pray thee, kiss my lips,
     Gold wings across the sea.

No answer through the moonlit night;   155
     No answer in the cold grey dawn;
     No answer when the shaven lawn
Grew green, and all the roses bright.

Her tired feet look'd cold and thin,
     Her lips were twitch'd, and wretched tears,   160
     Some, as she lay, roll'd past her ears,
Some fell from off her quivering chin.

Her long throat, stretched to its full length,
     Rose up and fell right brokenly;
     As though the unhappy heart was nigh   165
Striving to break with all its strength.

And when she slipp'd from off the bed,
     Her cramp'd feet would not hold her; she
     Sank down and crept on hand and knee,
On the window-sill she laid her head.   170

There, with crooked arm upon the sill,
     She look'd out, muttering dismally:
     'There is no sail upon the sea,
No pennon on the empty hill.

'I cannot stay here all alone,   175
     Or meet their happy faces here,
     And wretchedly I have no fear;
A little while, and I am gone.'

Therewith she rose upon her feet,
     And totter'd; cold and misery   180
     Still made the deep sobs come, till she
At last stretch'd out her fingers sweet,

And caught the great sword in her hand;
     And, stealing down the silent stair,
     Barefooted in the morning air,   185
And only in her smock, did stand

Upright upon the green lawn grass;
   And hope grew in her as she said:
   'I have thrown off the white and red,
And pray God it may come to pass   190

'I meet him; if ten years go by
   Before I meet him; if, indeed,
   Meanwhile both soul and body bleed,
Yet there is end of misery,

'And I have hope. He could not come,   195
   But I can go to him and show
   These new things I have got to know,
And make him speak, who has been dumb.'

O Jehane! the red morning sun
   Changed her white feet to glowing gold,   200
   Upon her smock, on crease and fold,
Changed that to gold which had been dun.

O Miles, and Giles, and Isabeau,
   Fair Ellayne le Violet,
   Mary, Constance fille de fay!   205
Where is Jehane du Castel beau?

O big Gervaise ride apace!
   Down to the hard yellow sand,
   Where the water meets the land.
This is Jehane by her face;   210

Why has she a broken sword?
   Mary! she is slain outright;
   Verily a piteous sight;
Take her up without a word!

Giles and Miles and Gervaise there,   215
   Ladies' Gard must meet the war;
   Whatsoever knights these are,
Man the walls withouten fear!

Axes to the apple-trees,
   Axes to the aspens tall!   220
   Barriers without the wall
May be lightly made of these.

O poor shivering Isabeau;
   Poor Ellayne le Violet,

Bent with fear! we miss to-day   225
Brave Jehane du Castel beau.

O poor Mary, weeping so!
  Wretched Constance fille de fay!
  Verily we miss today
Fair Jehane du Castel beau.   230

The apples now grow green and sour
  Upon the mouldering castle-wall,
  Before they ripen there they fall:
There are no banners on the tower.

The draggled swans most eagerly eat   235
  The green weeds trailing in the moat;
  Inside the rotting leaky boat
You see a slain man's stiffen'd feet.

The Haystack in the Floods

Had she come all the way for this,
To part at last without a kiss?
Yea, had she borne the dirt and rain
That her own eyes might see him slain
Beside the haystack in the floods?   5

Along the dripping leafless woods,
The stirrup touching either shoe,
She rode astride as troopers do;
With kirtle kilted to her knee,
To which the mud splash'd wretchedly;   10
And the wet dripp'd from every tree
Upon her head and heavy hair,
And on her eyelids broad and fair;
The tears and rain ran down her face.
By fits and starts they rode apace,   15
And very often was his place
Far off from her; he had to ride
Ahead, to see what might betide
When the roads cross'd; and sometimes, when
There rose a murmuring from his men,   20
Had to turn back with promises;
Ah me! She had but little ease;
And often for pure doubt and dread
She sobb'd, made giddy in the head
By the swift riding; while, for cold,   25
Her slender fingers scarce could hold
The wet reins; yea, and scarcely, too,
She felt the foot within her shoe
Against the stirrup: all for this,
To part at last without a kiss   30
Beside the haystack in the floods.

For when they near'd that old soak'd hay,
They saw across the only way
That Judas, Godmar, and the three
Red running lions dismally   35
Grinn'd from his pennon, under which
In one straight line along the ditch,
They counted thirty heads.

        So then,
While Robert turn'd round to his men,

She saw at once the wretched end,   40
And, stooping down, tried hard to rend
Her coif the wrong way from her head,
And hid her eyes; while Robert said:
'Nay, love, 'tis scarcely two to one,
At Poictiers where we made them run   45
So fast—why, sweet my love, good cheer,
The Gascon frontier is so near,
Nought after this.'

                But, 'O,' she said,
'My God! my God! I have to tread
The long way back without you; then   50
The court at Paris; those six men;
The gratings of the Chatelet;
The swift Seine on some rainy day
Like this, and people standing by,
And laughing, while my weak hands try   55
To recollect how strong men swim.
All this, or else a life with him,
For which I should be damned at last,
Would God that this next hour were past!'

He answer'd not, but cried his cry,   60
'St. George for Marny!' cheerily;
And laid his hand upon her rein.
Alas! no man of all his train
Gave back that cheery cry again;
And, while for rage his thumb beat fast   65
Upon his sword-hilts, some one cast
About his neck a kerchief long,
And bound him.

               Then they went along
To Godmar; who said: 'Now, Jehane,
Your lover's life is on the wane   70
So fast, that, if this very hour
You yield not as my paramour,
He will not see the rain leave off—
Nay, keep your tongue from gibe and scoff,
Sir Robert, or I slay you now.'   75

She laid her hand upon her brow,
Then gazed upon the palm, as though
She thought her forehead bled, and—'No!'
She said, and turn'd her head away,

As there were nothing else to say,   80
And everything were settled: red
Grew Godmar's face from chin to head:
'Jehane, on yonder hill there stands
My castle, guarding well my lands;
What hinders me from taking you,   85
And doing that I list to do
To your fair wilful body, while
Your knight lies dead?'

              A wicked smile
Wrinkled her face, her lips grew thin,
A long way out she thrust her chin: 90
'You know that I should strangle you
While you were sleeping; or bite through
Your throat, by God's help—ah!' she said,
'Lord Jesus, pity your poor maid!
For in such wise they hem me in,   95
I cannot choose but sin and sin,
Whatever happens: yet I think
They could not make me eat or drink,
And so should I just reach my rest.'
'Nay, if you do not my behest,   100
O Jehane! though I love you well,'
Said Godmar, 'would I fail to tell
All this that I know?' 'Foul lies,' she said.
'Eh? Lies, my Jehane? by God's head,
At Paris folks would deem them true!   105
Do you know, Jehane, they cry for you:
Jehane the brown! Jehane the brown!
Give us Jehane to burn or drown!'—
Eh—gag me Robert!—sweet my friend,
This were indeed a piteous end   110
For those long fingers, and long feet,
And long neck, and smooth shoulders sweet;
An end that few men would forget
That saw it—So, an hour yet:
Consider, Jehane, which to take   115
Of life or death!'

             So, scarce awake,
Dismounting, did she leave that place,
And totter some yards: with her face
Turn'd upward to the sky she lay,
Her head on a wet heap of hay,   120

And fell asleep: and while she slept,
And did not dream, the minutes crept
Round to the twelve again; but she
Being waked at last, sigh'd quietly,
And strangely childlike came, and said: 125
'I will not.' Straightway Godmar's head,
As though it hung on strong wires, turn'd
Most sharply round, and his face burn'd.

For Robert—both his eyes were dry,
He could not weep, but gloomily   130
He seem'd to watch the rain; yea, too,
His lips were firm; he tried once more
To touch her lips; she reach'd out, sore
And vain desire so tortured them,
The poor grey lips, and now the hem   135
Of his sleeve brush'd them.

                              With a start
Up Godmar rose, thrust them apart;
From Robert's throat he loosed the bands
Of silk and mail; with empty hands
Held out, she stood and gazed, and saw   140
A long bright blade without a flaw
Glide out from Godmar's sheath, his hand
In Robert's hair; she saw him bend
Back Robert's head; she saw him send
The thin steel down; the blow told well,   145
Right backward the knight Robert fell,
And moan'd as dogs do, being half dead,
Unwitting, as I deem: so then
Godmar turned grinning to his men,
Who ran, some five or six, and beat   150
His head to pieces at their feet.

Then Godmar turn'd again and said:
'So, Jehane, the first fitte is read!
Take note, my lady, that your way
Lies backward to the Chatelet!'   155
She shook her head and gazed awhile
At her cold hands with a rueful smile,
As though this thing had made her mad.

This was the parting that they had
Beside the haystack in the floods.   160

Sir Peter Harpdon's End

In an English castle in Poictou.

SIR PETER HARPDON, *a Gascon knight in the English service and*
JOHN CURZON, *his lieutenant.*

JOHN CURZON Of those three prisoners, that before you came
    We took down at St John's hard by the mill,
    Two are good masons; we have tools enough,
    And you have skill to set them working.
SIR PETER   So—
    What are their names?
JOHN CURZON   Why, Jacques Acquadent,   5
    And Peter Plombiere, but—
SIR PETER   What colour'd hair
    Has Peter now? Has Jacques got bow legs?
JOHN CURZON Why sir, you jest—what matters Jacques' hair,
    Or Peter's legs to us?
SIR PETER   O! John, John, John!
    Throw all your mason's tools down the deep well,   10
    Hang Peter up and Jacques; they're no good,
    We shall not build, man.
JOHN CURZON   *Going.*
           Shall I call the guard
    To hang them, sir? and yet, sir, for the tools,
    We'd better keep them still; sir, fare you well.
                    Muttering as he goes.

What have I done that he should jape at me?   15
And why not build? The walls are weak enough,
And we've two masons and a heap of tools.
                    Goes, still muttering.

SIR PETER To think a man should have a lump like that
    For his lieutenant! I must call him back,
    Or else, as surely as St. George is dead,   20
    He'll hang our friends the masons—here, John! John!
JOHN CURZON At your good service, sir.
SIR PETER   Come now, and talk
    This weighty matter out; there we've no stone
    To mend our walls with,—neither brick nor stone.
JOHN CURZON There is a quarry, sir, some ten miles off.   25
SIR PETER We are not strong enough to send ten men
    Ten miles to fetch us stone enough to build,

In three hours' time they would be taken or slain,
The cursed Frenchmen ride abroad so thick.
JOHN CURZON But we can send some villaynes to get stone.   30
SIR PETER Alas! John, that we cannot bring them back,
    They would go off to Clisson or Sanxere,
    And tell them we were weak in walls and men,
    Then down go we; for, look you, times are changed,
    And now no longer does the country shake   35
    At sound of English names; our captains fade
    From off our muster-rolls. At Lusac Bridge
    I daresay you may even yet see the hole
    That Chandos beat in dying; far in Spain
    Pembroke is prisoner; Phelton prisoner here;   40
    Manny lies buried in the Charterhouse;
    Oliver Clisson turn'd these years agone;
    The Captal died in prison; and, over all,
    Edward the prince lies underneath the ground;
    Edward the king is dead, at Westminster   45
    The carvers smooth the curls of his long beard.
    Everything goes to rack—eh! And we too.
    Now, Curzon, listen; if they come, these French,
    Whom have I got to lean on here, but you?
    A man can die but once; will you die then,   50
    Your brave sword in your hand, thoughts in your heart
    Of all the deeds we have done here in France—
    And yet may do? So God will have your soul,
    Whoever has your body.
JOHN CURZON   Why, sir, I
    Will fight to the last moment, until then   55
    Will do whate'er you tell me. Now I see
    We must e'en leave the walls; well, well, perhaps
    They're stronger than I think for; pity though!
    For some few tons of stone, if Guesclin comes.
SIR PETER Farewell, John, pray you watch the Gascons well,   60
    I doubt them.
JOHN CURZON Truly, sir, I will watch well.   *Goes.*
SIR PETER Farewell, good lump! and yet, when all is said,
    'Tis a good lump. Why then, if Guesclin comes;
    Some dozen stones from his petrariae,
    And, under shelter of his crossbows, just   65
    An hour's steady work with pickaxes,
    Then a great noise—some dozen swords and glaives
    A-playing on my basnet all at once,

And little more cross-purposes on earth
For me.
       Now this is hard: a month ago,   70
And a few minutes' talk had set things right
'Twixt me and Alice;—if she had a doubt,
As (may Heaven bless her!) I scarce think she had,
'Twas but their hammer, hammer in her ears,
Of 'how Sir Peter failed at Lusac Bridge:'   75
And 'how he was grown moody of late days;'
And 'how Sir Lambert' (think now!) 'his dear friend,
His sweet dear cousin, could not but confess
That Peter's talk tended towards the French,
Which he' (for instance Lambert) 'was glad of,   80
Being' (Lambert, you see) 'on the French side.'
                      Well,
If I could but have seen her on that day,
Then, when they sent me off!
                I like to think,
Although it hurts me, makes my head twist, what,
If I had seen her, what I should have said,   85
What she, my darling, would have said and done.
As thus perchance—
          To find her sitting there,
In the window-seat, not looking well at all,
Crying perhaps, and I say quietly;
'Alice!' She looks up, chokes a sob, looks grave,   90
Changes from pale to red; but, ere she speaks,
Straightway I kneel down there on both my knees,
And say: 'O lady, have I sinn'd, your knight?
That still you ever let me walk alone
In the rose garden, that you sing no songs   95
When I am by, that ever in the dance
You quietly walk away when I come near?
Now that I have you, will you go, think you?'

  Ere she could answer I would speak again,
Still kneeling there.
             'What! they have frighted you,   100
By hanging burs, and clumsily carven puppets,
Round my good name; but afterwards, my love,
I will say what this means; this moment, see!
Do I kneel here, and can you doubt me? Yea'
(For she would put her hands upon my face),   105

'Yea, that is best, yea feel, love, am I changed?'
And she would say: 'Good knight, come, kiss my lips!'
And afterwards as I sat there would say:
'Please a poor silly girl by telling me
What all those things they talk of really were,   110
For it is true you did not help Chandos,
And true, poor love! you could not come to me
When I was in such peril.'
                            I should say:
'I am like Balen, all things turn to blame—
I did not come to you? At Bergerath   115
The constable had held us close shut up,
If from the barriers I made three steps,
I should have been but slain; at Lusac, too,
We struggled in a marish half the day,
And came too late at last: you know, my love,   120
How heavy men and horses are all arm'd.
All that Sir Lambert said was pure, unmix'd,
Quite groundless lies; as you can think, sweet love.'

   She, holding tight my hand as we sat there,
Started a little at Sir Lambert's name,   125
But otherwise she listen'd scarce at all
To what I said. Then with moist, weeping eyes,
And quivering lips, that scarcely let her speak,
She said: 'I love you.'
                            Other words were few,
The remnant of that hour; her hand smooth'd down   130
My foolish head; she kiss'd me all about
My face, and through the tangles of my beard
Her little fingers crept
                            O! God, my Alice,
Not this good way: my lord but sent and said
That Lambert's sayings were taken at their worth,   135
Therefore that day I was to start, and keep
This hold against the French; and I am here,—

                                    Looks out of the window.

A sprawling lonely gard with rotten walls,
And no one to bring aid if Guesclin comes,
Or any other.
                            There's a pennon now!   140
At last.

But not the constable's, whose arms,
I wonder, does it bear? Three golden rings
On a red ground; my cousin's by the rood!
Well, I should like to kill him, certainly,
But to be killed by him—

A trumpet sounds.

                    That's for a herald;   145
I doubt this does not mean assaulting yet.

Enter JOHN CURZON.

What says the herald of our cousin, sir?
JOHN CURZON So please you, sir, concerning your estate,
  He has good will to talk with you.
SIR PETER   Outside,
  I'll talk with him, close by the gate St. Ives.   150
  Is he unarm'd?
JOHN CURZON   Yea, sir, in a long gown.
SIR PETER Then bid them bring me hither my furr'd gown
  With the long sleeves, and under it I'll wear,
  By Lambert's leave, a secret coat of mail;
  And will you lend me, John, your little axe?   155
  I mean the one with Paul wrought on the blade?
  And I will carry it inside my sleeve,
  Good to be ready always—you, John, go
  And bid them set up many suits of arms,
  Bows, archgays, lances, in the base-court, and   160
  Yourself, from the south postern setting out,
  With twenty men, be ready to break through
  Their unguarded rear when I cry out 'St. George!'
JOHN CURZON How, sir! Will you attack him unawares,
  And slay him unarm'd?
SIR PETER   Trust me, John, I know   165
  The reason why he comes here with sleeved gown,
  Fit to hide axes up. So, let us go.   *They go.*

    Outside the castle by the great gate; SIR LAMBERT *and* SIR PETER
      seated; guards attending each, the rest of SIR LAMBERT'S
         men drawn up about a furlong off.

SIR PETER And if I choose to take the losing side
  Still, does it hurt you?
SIR LAMBERT   O! no hurt to me;
  I see you sneering, 'Why take trouble then,   170
  Seeing you love me not?' Look you, our house
  (Which, taken altogether, I love much)

Had better be on the right side now,
If, once for all, it wishes to bear rule
As such a house should; cousin, you're too wise   175
To feed your hope up fat, that this fair France
Will ever draw two ways again; this side
The French, wrong headed, all a-jar
With envious longings; and the other side
The order'd English, orderly led on   180
By those two Edwards through all wrong and right,
And muddling right and wrong to a thick broth
With that long stick, their strength. This is all changed,
The true French win, on either side you have
Cool-headed men, good at a tilting-match,   185
And good at setting battles in array,
And good at squeezing taxes at due time;
Therefore by nature we French being here
Upon our own big land—

                                        Sir Peter laughs aloud.
                    Well Peter! well!
What makes you laugh?
SIR PETER   Hearing you sweat to prove   190
    All this I know so well; but you have read
    The siege of Troy?
SIR LAMBERT   O! yea, I know it well.
SIR PETER   There! They were wrong, as wrong as men could be;
    For, as I think, they found it such delight
    To see fair Helen going through their town: 195
    Yea, any little common thing she did
    (As stooping to pick a flower) seem'd so strange,
    So new in its great beauty, that they said;
    'Here we will keep her living in this town,
    Till all burns up together.' And so, fought,   200
    In a mad whirl of knowing they were wrong;
    Yea, they fought well, and ever, like a man
    That hangs legs off the ground by both his hands,
    Over some great height, did they struggle sore,
    Quite sure to slip at last; wherefore, take note   205
    How almost all men, reading that sad siege,
    Hold for the Trojans; as I did at least,
    Thought Hector the best knight a long way:
                                        Now
    Why should I not do this thing that I think,
    For even when I come to count the gains,   210

I have them my side: men will talk, you know,
(We talk of Hector, dead so long agone,)
When I am dead, of how this Peter clung
To what he thought the right; of how he died,
Perchance, at last, doing some desperate deed   215
Few men would care do now, and this is gain
To me, as ease and money is to you.
Moreover, too, I like the straining game
Of striving well to hold up things that fall;
So one becomes great. See you; in good times   220
All men live well together, and you, too,
Live dull and happy—happy? not so quick,
Suppose sharp thoughts begin to burn you up.
Why then, but just to fight as I do now,
A halter round my neck, would be great bliss.   225
O! I am well off.   *Aside.*
        Talk, and talk, and talk,
I know this man has come to murder me,
And yet I talk still.
SIR LAMBERT   If your side were right,
You might be, though you lost; but if I said:
'You are a traitor, being, as you are,   230
Born Frenchman.' What are Edwards unto you,
Or Richards?
SIR PETER   Nay, hold there, my Lambert, hold!
For fear your zeal should bring you to some harm,
Don't call me traitor.
SIR LAMBERT   Furthermore, my knight,
Men call you slippery on your losing side,   235
When at Bordeaux I was ambassador,
I heard them say so, and could scarce say 'Nay.'
    He takes hold of something in his sleeve, and rises.

SIR PETER,   *Rising.*
They lied—and you lie, not for the first time.
What have you got there, fumbling up your sleeve,
A stolen purse?
SIR LAMBERT   Nay, liar in your teeth!   240
Dead liar too; St. Denis and St. Lambert!
    Strikes at SIR PETER *with a dagger.*

SIR PETER,   *Striking him flatlings with his axe.*
How thief! thief! thief! so there, fair thief, so there,

St. George Guienne! glaives for the castellan!
You French, you are but dead, unless you lay
Your spears upon the earth. St. George Guienne!   245
Well done, John Curzon, how he has them now.

In the Castle

JOHN CURZON What shall we do with all these prisoners, sir?
SIR PETER Why, put them all to ransom, those that can
    Pay anything, but not too light though, John,
    Seeing we have them on the hip: for those   250
    That have no money, that being certified,
    Why turn them out of doors before they spy;
    But bring Sir Lambert guarded unto me.
JOHN CURZON I will, fair sir.   *He goes.*
SIR PETER   I do not wish to kill him,
    Although I think I ought; he shall go mark'd,   255
    By all the saints, though!

                                Enter LAMBERT *guarded.*

                   Now, Sir Lambert, now!
    What sort of death do you expect to get,
    Being taken this way?
SIR LAMBERT   Cousin! cousin! think!
    I am your own blood; may God pardon me!
    I am not fit to die; if you knew all,   260
    All I have done since I was young and good,
    O! you would give me yet another chance,
    As God would, that I might wash all clear out,
    By serving you and Him. Let me go now!
    And I will pay you down more golden crowns   265
    Of ransom than the king would!
SIR PETER   Well, stand back,
    And do not touch me! No, you shall not die,
    Nor yet pay ransom. You, John Curzon, cause
    Some carpenters to build a scaffold, high,
    Outside the gate; when it is built, sound out   270
    To all good folks, 'Come, see a traitor punish'd!'
    Take me my knight, and set him up thereon,
    And let the hangman shave his head quite clean,
    And cut his ears off close up to the head;
    And cause the minstrels all the while to play   275
    Soft music, and good singing; for this day
    Is my high day of triumph; is it not,

Sir Lambert?

SIR LAMBERT　　Ah! on your own blood,
　　Own name, you heap this foul disgrace? you dare,
　　With hands and fame thus sullied, to go back　　　　　　280
　　And take the lady Alice—
SIR PETER　　　　　　　　Say her name
　　Again, and you are dead, slain here by me.
　　Why should I talk with you, I'm master here,
　　And do not want your schooling; is it not
　　My mercy that you are not dangling dead　　　　　　285
　　There in the gateway with a broken neck?
SIR LAMBERT　Such mercy! why not kill me then outright?
　　To die is nothing; but to live that all
　　May point their fingers! yea, I'd rather die.
JOHN CURZON　Why, will it make you any uglier man　　　290
　　To lose your ears? they're much too big for you,
　　You ugly Judas!
SIR PETER　　　Hold, John!　　　　　　　　*To* LAMBERT.
　　　　　　　　　That's your choice,
　　To die, mind! Then you shall die—Lambert mine,
　　I thank you now for choosing this so well,
　　It saves me much perplexity and doubt;　　　　　　295
　　Perchance an ill deed too, for half I count
　　This sparing traitors is an ill deed.
　　　　　　　　　　　Well,
　　Lambert, die bravely, and we're almost friends.
SIR LAMBERT,　　　　　　　　　　*Grovelling.*
　　O God! this is a fiend and not a man;
　　Will some one save me from him? help, help, help!　　　300
　　I will not die.
SIR PETER　　Why, what is this I see?
　　A man who is a knight, and bandied words
　　So well just now with me, is lying down,
　　Gone mad for fear like this! So, so, you thought
　　You knew the worst and might say what you pleased.　　　305
　　I should have guess'd this from a man like you.
　　Eh! righteous Job would give up skin for skin,
　　Yea, all a man can have for simple life,
　　And we talk fine, yea, even a hound like this,
　　Who needs must know when he dies, deep hell　　　310
　　Will hold him fast for ever—so fine we talk,
　　'Would rather die'—all that. Now sir, get up!

And choose again: shall it be head sans ears
Or trunk sans head?
     John Curzon, pull him up!
What, life then? Go and build the scaffold, John.   315
Lambert, I hope that never on this earth
We meet again; that you'll turn out a monk,
And mend the life I gave you, so farewell,
I'm sorry you're a rascal. John, despatch.

   In the French camp before the Castle.

  SIR PETER *prisoner*, GUESCLIN, CLISSON, SIR LAMBERT.

SIR PETER So now is come the ending of my life;   320
 If I could clear this sickening lump away
 That sticks in my dry throat, and say a word,
 Guesclin might listen.
GUESCLIN   Tell me, fair sir knight,
 If you have been clean liver before God,
 And then you need not fear much; as for me,   325
 I cannot say I hate you, yet my oath,
 And cousin Lambert's ears here clench the thing.
SIR PETER I knew you could not hate me, therefore I
 Am bold to pray for life; 'twill harm your cause
 To hang knights of good name, harm here in France 330
 I have small doubt, at any rate hereafter
 Men will remember you another way
 Than I should care to be remember'd, ah!
 Although hot lead runs through me for my blood,
 All this falls cold as though I said, 'Sweet lords, 335
 Give back my falcon!'
     See how young I am,
 Do you care altogether more for France,
 Say rather one French faction, than for all
 The state of Christendom? a gallant knight,
 As (yea, by God!) I have been, is more worth 340
 Than many castles; will you bring this death,
 For a mere act of justice, on my head?

 Think how it ends all, death! all other things
 Can somehow be retrieved, yea, send me forth
 Naked and maimed, rather than slay me here; 345
 Then somehow will I get me other clothes,
 And somehow will I get me some poor horse,
 And, somehow clad in poor old rusty arms,

Will ride and smite among the serried glaives,
Fear not death so; for I can tilt right well,   350
Let me not say 'I could;' I know all tricks,
That sway the sharp sword cunningly; ah you,
You, my Lord Clisson, in the other days
Have seen me learning these, yea, call to mind,
How in the trodden corn by Chartres town,   355
When you were nearly swooning from the back
Of your black horse, those three blades slid at once
From off my sword's edge; pray for me, my lord!
CLISSON Nay, this is pitiful, to see him die.
My Lord the Constable, I pray you note   360
That you are losing some few thousand crowns
By slaying this man; also think: his lands
Along the Garonne river lie for leagues,
And are right rich, a many mills he has,
Three abbeys of grey monks do hold of him,   365
Though wishing well for Clement, as we do;
I know the next heir, his old uncle, well,
Who does not care two deniers for the knight
As things go now, but slay him, and then see
How he will bristle up like any perch,   370
With curves of spears. What! do not doubt, my lord,
You'll get the money, this man saved my life,
And I will buy him for two thousand crowns;
Well, five then—eh! what! 'No' again? well then,
Ten thousand crowns?
GUESCLIN   My sweet lord, much I grieve   375
I cannot please you, yea, good sooth, I grieve
This knight must die, as verily he must;
For I have sworn it, so men, take him out,
Use him not roughly.
SIR LAMBERT,   *Coming forward.*
                    Music, do you know,
Music will suit you well, I think, because   380
You look so mild, like Laurence being grill'd;
Or perhaps music soft and slow, because
This is high day of triumph unto me,
Is it not, Peter?
                You are frighten'd, though,
Eh! You are pale, because this hurts you much,   385
Whose life was pleasant to you, not like mine,
You ruin'd wretch! Men mock me in the streets,

Only in whispers loud, because I am
Friend of the constable; will this please you,
Unhappy Peter? once a-going home,   390
Without my servants, and a little drunk,
At midnight through the lone dim lamp-lit streets,
A whore came up and spat into my eyes,
(Rather to blind me than to make me see,)
But she was very drunk, and tottering back,   395
Even in the middle of her laughter, fell
And cut her head against the pointed stones,
While I lean'd on my staff, and look'd at her,
And cried, being drunk.

                     Girls would not spit at you,
You are so handsome, I think verily   400
Most ladies would be glad to kiss your eyes,
And yet you will be hung like a cur dog
Five minutes hence, and grow black in the face,
And curl your toes up. Therefore I am glad.

    Guess why I stand and talk this nonsense now,   405
With Guesclin getting ready to play chess,
And Clisson doing something with his sword,
I can't see what, talking to Guesclin though,
I don't know what about, perhaps of you.
But, cousin Peter, while I stroke your beard,   410
Let me say this, I'd like to tell you now
That your life hung upon a game of chess,
That if, say, my squire Robert here should beat,
Why, you should live, but hang if I beat him;
Then guess, clever Peter, what I should do then: 415
Well, give it up? why, Peter, I should let
My squire Robert beat me, then you would think
That you were safe, you know; Eh? not at all,
But I should keep you three days in some hold,
Giving you salt to eat, which would be kind,   420
Considering the tax there is on salt;
And afterwards let you go, perhaps?
No, I should not, but I should hang you, sir,
With a red rope in lieu of mere grey rope.

But I forgot, you have not told me yet   425
If you can guess why I talk nonsense thus,
Instead of drinking wine while you are hang'd?

You are not quick at guessing, give it up.
This is the reason; here I hold your hand,
And watch you growing paler, see you writhe,　430
And this, my Peter, is a joy so dear,
I cannot by all striving tell you how
I love it, nor I think, good man, would you
Quite understand my great delight therein;
You, when you had me underneath you once,　435
Spat as it were, and said, 'Go take him out,'
(That they might do that thing to me whereat
E'en now this long time off I could well shriek,)
And then you tried forget I ever lived,
And sunk your hating into other things;　440
While I—St. Denis! though, I think you'll faint,
Your lips are grey so; yes, you will, unless
You let it out and weep like a hurt child;
Hurrah! you do now. Do not go just yet,
For I am Alice, am right like her now;　445
Will you not kiss me on the lips, my love?—
CLISSON　You filthy beast, stand back and let him go,
Or by God's eyes I'll choke you.

Kneeling to SIR PETER.

Fair sir knight,
I kneel upon my knees and pray to you
That you would pardon me for this your death;　450
God knows how much I wish you still alive,
Also how heartily I strove to save
Your life at this time; yea, he knows quite well,
(I swear it, so forgive me!) how I would,
If it were possible, give up my life　455
Upon this grass for yours; fair knight, although,
He knowing all things knows this thing too, well,
Yet when you see his face some short time hence,
Tell him I tried to save you.
SIR PETER　　　　　　　　O! my lord,
I cannot say this is as good as life,　460
But yet it makes me feel far happier now,
And if at all, after a thousand years,
I see God's face, I will speak loud and bold,
And tell Him you were kind, and like Himself;
Sir, may God bless you!
　　　　　　　　Did you note how I　465

Fell weeping just now? pray you, do not think
That Lambert's taunts did this, I hardly heard
The base things that he said, being deep in thought
Of all things that have happen'd since I was
A little child; and so at last I thought　　　　　　　470
Of my true lady: truly, sir, it seem'd
No longer gone than yesterday, that this
Was the sole reason God let me be born
Twenty-five years ago, that I might love
Her, my sweet lady, and be loved by her;　　　　　475
This seem'd so yesterday, to-day death comes,
And is so bitter strong, I cannot see
Why I was born.
　　　　　　　　But as a last request,
I pray you, O kind Clisson, send some man,
Some good man, mind you, to say how I died,　　　480
And take my last love to her: fare-you-well,
And may God keep you; I must go now, lest
I grow too sick with thinking on these things;
Likewise my feet are wearied of the earth,
From whence I shall be lifted upright soon.　　　485
　　　　　　　　　　　　　　　As he goes.

Ah me! shamed too, I wept at fear of death;
And yet not so, I only wept because
There was no beautiful lady to kiss me
Before I died, and sweetly wish good speed
From her dear lips. O for some lady, though　　　490
I saw her ne'er before; Alice, my love,
I do not ask for; Clisson was right kind,
If he had been a woman, I should die
Without this sickness: but I am all wrong,
So wrong and hopelessly afraid to die.　　　　　495
There, I will go.
　　　　　　　　My God! how sick I am,
If only she could come and kiss me now.

　　　　　The Hotel de la Barde, Bordeaux.

　The LADY ALICE DE LA BARDE *looking out of a window into the street.*

No news yet! surely, still he holds his own;
That garde stands well; I mind me passing it
Some months ago; God grant the walls are strong!　　500
I heard some knights say something yestereve,
I tried hard to forget: words far apart

Struck on my heart; something like this; one said,
'What eh! a Gascon with an English name,
Harpdon?' then nought, but afterwards: 'Poictou.'   505
As one who answers to a question ask'd;
Then carelessly regretful came: 'No, no.'
Whereto in answer loud and eagerly,
One said, 'Impossible? Christ, what foul play!'
And went off angrily; and while thenceforth   510
I hurried gaspingly afraid, I heard,
'Guesclin;' 'Five thousand men-at-arms;' 'Clisson.'
My heart misgives me it is all in vain
I send these succours; and in good time there!
Their trumpet sounds, ah! here they are; good knights,   515
God up in Heaven keep you.
                              If they come
And find him prisoner—for I can't believe
Guesclin will slay him, even though they storm—
(The last horse turns the corner.)
                              God in Heaven!
What have I got to thinking of at last!   520
That thief I will not name is with Guesclin,
Who loves him for his lands. My love! my love!
O, if I lose you after all the past,
What shall I do?
                    I cannot bear the noise
And light street out there, with this thought alive,   525
Like any curling snake within my brain;
Let me just hide my head within these soft
Deep cushions, there to try and think it out.

                              Lying in the window-seat.

I cannot hear much noise now, and I think
That I shall go to sleep: it all sounds dim   530
And faint, and I shall soon forget most things;
Yea, almost that I am alive and here;
It goes slow, comes slow, like a big mill-wheel
On some broad stream, with long green weeds a-sway,
And soft and slow it rises and it falls,   535
Still going onward.
                    Lying so, one kiss,
And I should be in Avalon asleep,
Among the poppies, and the yellow flowers;
And they should brush my cheek, my hair being spread
Far out among the stems; soft mice and small   540

Eating and creeping all about my feet,
Red shod and tired; and the flies should come
Creeping o'er my broad eyelids unafraid;
And there should be a noise of water going,
Clear blue, fresh water breaking on the slates, 545
Likewise the flies should creep—God's eyes! God help!
A trumpet? I will run fast, leap adown
The slippery sea-stairs, where the crabs fight.
                                        Ah!
I was half dreaming, but the trumpet's true,
He stops here at our house. The Clisson arms? 550
Ah, now for news. But I must hold my heart,
And be quite gentle till he is gone out;
And afterwards,—but he is still alive,
He must be still alive.

Enter a SQUIRE *of* CLISSON's.

                Good day, fair sir,
I give you welcome, knowing whence you come. 555
SQUIRE My Lady Alice de la Barde, I come
From Oliver Clisson, knight and mighty lord,
Bringing you tidings: I make bold to hope
You will not count me villain, even if
They wring your heart; nor hold me still in hate. 560
For I am but a mouthpiece after all,
A mouthpiece, too, of one who wishes well
To you and your's.
ALICE   Can you talk faster, sir,
Get all this over quicker? fix your eyes
On mine, I pray you, and whate'er you see, 565
Still go on talking fast, unless I fall,
Or bid you stop.
SQUIRE   I pray your pardon then,
And, looking in your eyes, fair lady, say
I am unhappy that your knight is dead.
Take heart, and listen! Let me tell you all. 570
We were five thousand goodly men-at-arms,
And scant five hundred had he in that hold;
His rotten sand-stone walls were wet with rain,
And fell in lumps wherever a stone hit;
Yet for three days about the barrier there 575
The deadly glaives were gather'd, laid across,
And push'd and pull'd; the fourth our engines came;

But still amid the crash of falling walls,
And roar of lombards, rattle of hard bolts,
The steady bow-strings flash'd, and still stream'd out   580
St. George's banner, and the seven swords,
And still they cried, 'St. George Guienne,' until
Their walls were flat as Jericho's of old,
And our rush came, and cut them from the keep.

ALICE   Stop, sir, and tell me if you slew him then,   585
And where he died, if you can really mean
That Peter Harpdon, the good knight, is dead?

SQUIRE   Fair lady, in the base-court—
ALICE   What base-court?
What do you talk of? Nay, go on, go on;
'Twas only something gone within my head: 590
Do you not know, one turns one's head round quick,
And something cracks there with sore pain? go on,
And still look at my eyes.

SQUIRE   Almost alone,
There in the base-court fought he with his sword,
Using his left hand much, more than the wont   595
Of most knights now-a-days; our men gave back,
For wheresoever he hit a downright blow,
Some one fell bleeding, for no plate could hold
Against the sway of body and great arm;
Till he grew tired, and some man (no! not I,   600
I swear not I, fair lady, as I live!)
Thrust at him with a glaive between the knees,
And threw him; down he fell, sword undermost;
Many fell on him, crying out their cries,
Tore his sword from him, tore his helm off, and—   605

ALICE   Yea, slew him; I am much too young to live,
Fair God, so let me die.
                         You have done well,
Done all your message gently, pray you go,
Our knights will make you cheer; moreover, take
This bag of franks for your expenses.

                                   The SQUIRE *kneels.*

                         But   610
You do not go; still looking at my face,
You kneel! what, squire, do you mock me then?
You need not tell me who has set you on,
But tell me only, 'tis a made-up tale.

You are some lover may-be, or his friend; 615
Sir, if you loved me once, or your friend loved,
Think, is it not enough that I kneel down
And kiss your feet? your jest will be right good
If you give in now, carry it too far,
And 'twill be cruel; not yet? but you weep 620
Almost, as though you loved me; love me then,
And go to Heaven by telling all your sport,
And I will kiss you then with all my heart,
Upon the mouth; O! what can I do then
To move you?

SQUIRE   Lady fair, forgive me still! 625
You know I am so sorry, but my tale
Is not yet finish'd:
                So they bound his hands,
And brought him tall and pale to Guesclin's tent,
Who, seeing him, leant his head upon his hand,
And ponder'd somewhile, afterwards, looking up— 630
Fair dame, what shall I say?

ALICE   Yea, I know now,
Good squire, you may go now with my thanks.

SQUIRE Yet, lady, for your own sake I say this,
Yea, for my own sake, too, and Clisson's sake.
When Guesclin told him he must be hanged soon, 635
Within a while he lifted up his head
And spoke for his own life; not crouching, though,
As abjectly afraid to die, nor yet
Sullenly brave as many a thief will die;
Nor yet as one that plays at japes with God: 640
Few words he spoke; not so much what he said
Moved us, I think, as, saying it, there played
Strange tenderness from that big soldier there
About his pleading; eagerness to live
Because folk loved him, and he loved them back, 645
And many gallant plans unfinish'd now
For ever. Clisson's heart, which may God bless!
Was moved to pray for him, but all in vain;
Wherefore I bring this message:
                            That he waits,
Still loving you, within the little church 650
Whose windows, with the one eye of the light
Over the altar, every night behold
The great dim broken walls he strove to keep!

There my Lord Clisson did his burial well.
Now, lady, I will go; God give you rest!   655
ALICE Thank Clisson from me, squire, and farewell!
And now to keep myself from going mad.
Christ! I have been a many times to church,
And, ever since my mother taught me prayers,
Have used them daily, but to-day I wish   660
To pray another way; come face to face,
O Christ, that I may clasp your knees and pray,
I know not what, at any rate come now,
From one of many places where you are;
Either in Heaven amid thick angel wings,   665
Or sitting on the altar strange with gems,
Or high up in the dustiness of the apse;
Let us go, You and I, a long way off,
To the little damp, dark, Poitevin church;
While you sit on the coffin in the dark,   670
Will I lie down, my face on the bare stone
Between your feet, and chatter anything
I have heard long ago, what matters it
So I may keep you there, your solemn face
And long hair even-flowing on each side,   675
Until you love me well enough to speak,
And give me comfort; yea, till o'er your chin
And cloven red beard the great tears roll down
In pity for my misery, and I die,
Kissed over by you.
              Eh Guesclin! if I were   680
Like Countess Mountfort now, that kiss'd the knight,
Across the salt sea come to fight for her;
Ah! just to go about with many knights,
Wherever you went, and somehow on one day,
In a thick wood to catch you off your guard,   685
Let you find, you and your some fifty friends,
Nothing but arrows wheresoe'er you turn'd,
Yea, and red crosses, great spears over them;
And so, between a lane of my true men,
To walk up pale and stern and tall, and with   690
My arms on my surcoat, and his therewith,
And then to make you kneel, O knight Guesclin;
And then—alas! alas! when all is said,
What could I do but let you go again,
Being pitiful woman? I get no revenge,   695

Whatever happens; and I get no comfort,
I am but weak, and cannot move my feet,
But as men bid me.
                         Strange I do not die.
Suppose this has not happen'd after all;
I will lean out again and watch for news.   700

I wonder how long I can still feel thus,
As though I watch'd for news, feel as I did
Just half-an-hour ago, before this news.
How all the street is humming, some men sing,
And some men talk; some look up at the house,   705
Then lay their heads together and look grave;
Their laughter pains me sorely in the heart,
Their thoughtful talking makes my head turn round,
Yea, some men sing, what is it then they sing?
Eh Launcelot, and love and fate and death;   710
They ought to sing of him who was as wight
As Launcelot or Wade, and yet avail'd
Just nothing, but to fail and fail and fail,
And so at last to die and leave me here,
Alone and wretched; yea, perhaps they will,   715
When many years are past, make songs of us;
God help me, though, truly I never thought
That I should make a story in this way,
A story that his eyes can never see.

                                        One sings from outside.

              Therefore be it believed   720
              Whatsoever he grieved,
              Whan his horse was relieved,
                    This Launcelot,

              Beat down on his knee,
              Right valiant was he   725
              God's body to see,
                    Though he saw it not.

              Right valiant to move,
              But for his sad love
              The high God above   730
                    Stinted his praise.

Yet so he was glad
That his son Lord Galahad
That high joyaunce had
    All his life-days.   735

Sing we therefore then
Launcelot's praise again,
For he wan crownes ten,
    If he wan not twelve.

To his death from his birth   740
He was muckle of worth,
Lay him in the cold earth,
    A long grave ye may delve.

Omnes homines benedicite!
This last fitte ye may see   745
All men pray for me,
Who made this history
Cunning and fairly.

Concerning Geffray Teste Noire

And if you meet the Canon of Chimay,
    As going to Ortaise you may well do,
Greet him from John of Castel Neuf, and say,
    All that I tell you, for all this is true.

This Geffray Teste Noire was a Gascon thief,   5
    Who, under shadow of the English name,
Pilled all such towns and countries as were lief
    To King Charles and St. Denis; thought it blame

If anything escaped him; so my lord,
    The Duke of Berry, sent Sir John Bonne Lance,   10
And other knights, good players with the sword,
    To check this thief and give the land a chance.

Therefore we set our bastides round the tower
    That Geffray held, the strong thief! like a king,
High perch'd upon the rock of Ventadour,   15
    Hopelessly strong by Christ! It was mid spring,

When first I joined the little army there
    With ten good spears; Auvergne is hot, each day
We sweated armed before the barrier;
    Good feats of arms were done there often—eh?   20

Your brother was slain there? I mind me now,
    A right, good man-at-arms, God pardon him!
I think 'twas Geffray smote him on the brow
    With some spiked axe, and while he totter'd, dim

About the eyes, the spear of Alleyne Roux   25
    Slipped through his camaille and his throat; well well!
Alleyne is paid now; your name is Alleyne too?
    Mary! how strange—but this tale I would tell—

For spite of all our bastides, damned blackhead
    Would ride abroad whene'er he chose to ride,   30
We could not stop him; many a burgher bled
    Dear gold all round his girdle; far and wide

The villaynes dwelt in utter misery
    'Twixt us and thief Sir Geffray; hauled this way
By Sir Bonne Lance at one time, he gone by,   35
    Down comes this Teste Noire on another day.

And therefore they dig up the stone, grind corn,
   Hew wood, draw water, yea, they lived, in short,
As I said just now, utterly forlorn,
   Till this our knave and blackhead was out-fought.   40

So Bonne Lance fretted, thinking of some trap
   Day after day, till on a time he said;
'John of Newcastle, if we have good hap,
   We catch our thief in two days.' 'How?' I said.

'Why, Sir, to-day he rideth out again,   45
   Hoping to take well certain sumpter mules
From Carcassone, going with little train,
   Because, forsooth, he thinketh us mere fools;

'But if we set an ambush in some wood,
   He is but dead: so, Sir, take thirty spears   50
To Verville forest, if it seem you good.'
   Then I felt like the horse in Job, who hears

The dancing trumpet sound, and we went forth;
   And my red lion on the spear-head flapped,
As faster than the cool wind we rode North,   55
   Towards the wood of Verville; thus it happed.

We rode a soft pace on that day while spies
   Got news about Sir Geffray; the red wine
Under the road-side bush was clear; the flies,
   The dragon-flies I mind me most, did shine   60

In brighter arms than ever I put on;
   So—'Geffray,' said our spies, 'would pass that way
Next day at sundown:' then he must be won;
   And so we enter'd Verville wood next day,

In the afternoon; through it the highway runs,   65
   'Twixt copses of green hazel, very thick,
And underneath, with glimmering of suns,
   The primroses are happy; the dews lick

The soft green moss. 'Put cloths about your arms,
   Lest they should glitter; surely they will go   70
In a long thin line, watchful for alarms,
   With all their carriages of booty, so—

'Lay down my pennon in the grass—Lord God!
   What have we lying here? will they be cold,

I wonder, being so bare, above the sod,   75
   Instead of under? This was a knight too, fold

'Lying on fold of ancient rusted mail;
   No plate at all, gold rowels to the spurs,
And see the quiet gleam of turquoise pale
   Along the ceinture; but the long time blurs   80

'Even the tinder of his coat to nought,
   Except these scraps of leather; see how white
The skull is, loose with the coif! He fought
   A good fight, maybe, ere he was slain quite.

'No armour on the legs too; strange in faith—   85
   A little skeleton for a knight, though—ah!
This one is bigger, truly without scathe
   His enemies escaped not—ribs driven out far,—

'That must have reach'd the heart, I doubt— how now,
   What say you Aldovrand—a woman? why?'   90
'Under the coif a golden wreath on the brow,
   Yea, see the hair not gone to powder, lie,

'Golden, no doubt, once—yea, and very small,
   This for a knight; but for a dame, my lord,
These loose-hung bones seem shapely still, and tall,—   95
   Didst ever see a woman's bones, my lord?'

Often, God help me! I remember when
   I was a simple boy, fifteen years old,
The Jacquerie froze up the blood of men
   With their fell deeds, not fit now to be told: 100

God help again! we enter'd Beauvais town,
   Slaying them fast, whereto I help'd, mere boy
As I was then; we gentles cut them down,
   These burners and defilers, with great joy.

Reason for that, too, in the great church there   105
   These fiends had lit a fire, that soon went out,
The church at Beauvais being so great and fair—
   My father, who was by me, gave a shout

Between a beast's howl and a woman's scream,
   Then, panting, chuckled to me: 'John, look! look!   110
Count the dames' skeletons!' From some bad dream
   Like a man just awaked, my father shook;

And I, being faint with smelling the burnt bones,
   And very hot with fighting down the street,
And sick of such a life, fell down, with groans   115
   My head went weakly nodding to my feet.—

—An arrow had gone through her tender throat,
   And her right wrist was broken; then I saw
The reason why she had on that war-coat,
   Their story came out clear without a flaw;   120

For when he knew that they were being waylaid,
   He threw it over her, yea, hood and all;
Whereby he was much hack'd, while they were stay'd
   By those their murderers; many an one did fall

Beneath his arm, no doubt, so that he clear'd   125
   Their circle, bore his death-wound out of it;
But as they rode, some archer least afear'd
   Drew a strong bow, and thereby she was hit.

Still as he rode he knew not she was dead,
   Thought her but fainted from her broken wrist,   130
He bound with his great leathern belt—she bled?
   Who knows! he bled too, neither was there miss'd

The beating of her heart, his heart beat well
   For both of them, till here, within this wood,
He died scarce sorry; easy this to tell;   135
   After these years the flowers forget their blood.—

How could it be? Never before that day,
   However much a soldier I might be,
Could I look on a skeleton and say
   I care not for it, shudder not—now see,   140

Over those bones I sat and pored for hours,
   And thought, and dream'd, and still I scarce could see
The small white bones that lay upon the flowers,
   But evermore I saw the lady; she

With her dear gentle walking leading in,   145
   By a chain of silver twined about her wrists,
Her loving knight, mounted and arm'd to win
   Great honour for her, fighting in the lists.

O most pale face, that brings such joy and sorrow
   Into men's hearts—yea, too, so piercing sharp   150

That joy is, that it marcheth night to sorrow
    For ever—like an overwinded harp.

Your face must hurt me always; pray you now,
    Doth it not hurt you too? seemeth some pain
To hold you always, pain to hold your brow   155
    So smooth, unwrinkled ever; yea again,

Your long eyes where the lids seem like to drop,
    Would you not, lady, were they shut fast, feel
Far merrier? there so high they will not stop,
    They are most sly to glide forth and to steal   160

Into my heart; *I kiss their soft lids there,*
    And in green gardens scarce can stop my lips
From wandering on your face, but that your hair
    Falls down and tangles me, back my face slips.

Or say your mouth—I saw you drink red wine   165
    Once at a feast; how slowly it sank in,
As though you fear'd that some wild fate might twine
    Within that cup, and slay you for a sin.

And when you talk your lips do arch and move
    In such wise that a language new I know   170
Besides their sound; they quiver, too, with love
    When you are standing silent; know this, too,

I saw you kissing once, like a curved sword
    That bites with all its edge, did your lips lie,
Curled gently, slowly, long time could afford   175
    For caught-up breathings; like a dying sigh

They gather'd up their lines and went away,
    And still kept twitching with a sort of smile,
As likely to be weeping presently,—
    Your hands too—how I watch'd them all the while!   180

'Cry out St Peter now,' quoth Aldovrand;
    I cried, 'St Peter,' broke out from the wood
With all my spears; we met them hand to hand,
    And shortly slew them; natheless, by the rood,

We caught not blackhead then, or any day;   185
    Months after that he died at last in bed,
From a wound pick'd up at a barrier-fray;
    That same year's end a steel bolt in the head,

And much bad living kill'd Teste Noire at last;
　John Froissart knoweth he is dead by now,　　　190
No doubt, but knoweth not this tale just past;
　Perchance then you can tell him what I show.

In my new castle, down beside the Eure,
　There is a little chapel of squared stone,
Painted inside and out; in green nook pure　　　195
　There did I lay them, every wearied bone;

And over it they lay, with stone-white hands
　Clasped fast together, hair made bright with gold;
This Jacques Picard, known through many lands,
　Wrought cunningly; he's dead now—I am old.　　200

The Eve of Crecy

Gold on her head, and gold on her feet,
And gold where the hems of her kirtle meet,
And a golden girdle round my sweet;—
    Ah! qu'elle est belle La Marguerite.

Margaret's maids are fair to see,   5
Freshly dress'd and pleasantly;
Margaret's hair falls down to her knee;—
    Ah! qu'elle est belle La Marguerite.

If I were rich I would kiss her feet,
I would kiss the place where the gold hems meet,   10
And the golden girdle round my sweet—
    Ah! qu'elle est belle La Marguerite.

Ah me! I have never touch'd her hand;
When the arriere-ban goes through the land,
Six basnets under my pennon stand;—   15
    Ah! qu'elle est belle La Marguerite.

And many an one grins under his hood:
'Sir Lambert du Bois, with all his men good,
Has neither food nor firewood;'—
    Ah! qu'elle est belle La Marguerite.   20

If I were rich I would kiss her feet,
And the golden girdle of my sweet,
And thereabouts where the gold hems meet;—
    Ah! qu'elle est belle La Marguerite!

Yet even now it is good to think,   25
While my few poor varlets grumble and drink
In my desolate hall, where the fires sink,—
    Ah! qu'elle est belle La Marguerite.

Of Margaret sitting glorious there,
In glory of gold and glory of hair,   30
And glory of glorious face most fair;—
    Ah! qu'elle est belle La Marguerite.

Likewise to-night I make good cheer,
Because this battle draweth near:
For what have I to lose or fear?—   35
    Ah! qu'elle est belle La Marguerite.

For, look you, my horse is good to prance
A right fair measure in this war-dance,
Before the eyes of Philip of France;—
    Ah! qu'elle est belle La Marguerite.   40

And sometimes it may hap, perdie,
While my new towers stand up three and three,
And my hall gets painted fair to see—
    Ah! qu'elle est belle La Marguerite—

That folks may say: 'Times change, by the rood,   45
For Lambert, banneret of the wood,
Has heaps of food and firewood;—
    Ah! qu'elle est belle La Marguerite;—

And wonderful eyes, too, under the hood
Of a damsel of right noble blood:'   50
St. Ives, for Lambert of the wood!—
    Ah! qu'elle est belle La Marguerite.

Near Avalon

A ship with six shields before the sun,
Six maidens round the mast,
A red-gold crown on every one,
A green gown on the last.

The fluttering green banners there   5
Are wrought with ladies' heads most fair,
And a portrait of Guenevere
The middle of each sail doth bear.

A ship with sails before the wind,
And round the helm six knights,   10
Their heaumes are on, whereby, half-blind,
They pass by many sights.

The tatter'd scarlet banners there
Right soon will leave the spear-heads bare.
Those six knights sorrowfully bear   15
In all their heaumes some yellow hair.

In Prison

Wearily, drearily,
Half the day long,
Flap the great banners
High over the stone;
Strangely and eerily   5
Sounds the wind's song,
Bending the banner-poles.

While, all alone,
Watching the loophole's spark,
Lie I, with life all dark,   10
Feet tether'd, hands fetter'd
Fast to the stone,
The grim walls, square letter'd
With prison'd men's groan.

Still strain the banner-poles   15
Through the wind's song,
Westward the banner rolls
Over my wrong.

From *The Earthly Paradise*

Apology

Of Heaven or Hell I have no power to sing,
I cannot ease the burden of your fears,
Or make quick-coming death a little thing,
Or bring again the pleasure of past years,
Nor for my words shall ye forget your tears,   5
Or hope again for aught that I can say,
The idle singer of an empty day.

But rather, when aweary of your mirth,
From full hearts still unsatisfied ye sigh,
And, feeling kindly unto all the earth,   10
Grudge every minute as it passes by,
Made the more mindful that the sweet days die—
—Remember me a little then I pray,
The idle singer of an empty day.

The heavy trouble, the bewildering care   15
That weighs us down who live and earn our bread,
These idle verses have no power to bear;
So let me sing of names remembered,
Because they, living not, can ne'er be dead,
Or long time take their memory quite away   20
From us poor singers of an empty day.

Dreamer of dreams, born out of my due time,
Why should I strive to set the crooked straight?
Let it suffice me that my murmuring rhyme
Beats with light wing against the ivory gate,   25
Telling a tale not too importunate
To those who in the sleepy region stay,
Lulled by the singer of an empty day.

Folk say, a wizard to a northern king
At Christmas-tide such wondrous things did show,   30
That through one window men beheld the spring,
And through another saw the summer glow,
And through a third the fruited vines a-row,
While still, unheard, but in its wonted way,
Piped the drear wind of that December day.   35

So with this Earthly Paradise it is,
If ye will read aright, and pardon me,
Who strive to build a shadowy isle of bliss
Midmost the beating of the steely sea,
Where tossed about all hearts of men must be;   40
Whose ravening monsters mighty men shall slay,
Not the poor singer of an empty day.

From *the Prologue—the Wanderers*

ARGUMENT

Certain gentlemen and mariners of Norway, having considered all that they had heard of the Earthly Paradise, set sail to find it, and after many troubles and the lapse of many years came old men to some Western land, of which they had never before heard: there they died, when they had dwelt there certain years, much honoured of the strange people.

Forget six counties overhung with smoke,
Forget the snorting steam and piston stroke,
Forget the spreading of the hideous town;
Think rather of the pack-horse on the down,
And dream of London, small, and white, and clean,   5
The clear Thames bordered by its gardens green;
Think, that below bridge the green lapping waves
Smite some few keels that bear Levantine staves,
Cut from the yew wood on the burnt-up hill,
And pointed jars that Greek hands toiled to fill,   10
And treasured scanty spice from some far sea,
Florence gold cloth, and Ypres napery,
And cloth of Bruges, and hogsheads of Guienne;
While nigh the thronged wharf Geoffrey Chaucer's pen
Moves over bills of lading—mid such times   15
Shall dwell the hollow puppets of my rhymes.

A nameless city in a distant sea,
White as the changing walls of faërie,
Thronged with much people clad in ancient guise
I now am fain to set before your eyes;   20
There, leave the clear green water and the quays,
And pass betwixt its marble palaces,
Until ye come unto the chiefest square;
A bubbling conduit is set midmost there,
And round about it now the maidens throng,   25
With jest and laughter, and sweet broken song,
Making but light of labour new begun
While in their vessels gleams the morning sun.
      On one side of the square a temple stands,
Wherein the gods worshipped in ancient lands   30
Still have their altars, a great market-place
Upon two other sides fills all the space,

And thence the busy hum of men comes forth;
But on the cold side looking toward the north
A pillared council-house may you behold,   35
Within whose porch are images of gold,
Gods of the nations who dwelt anciently
About the borders of the Grecian sea.

Pass now between them, push the brazen door,
And standing on the polished marble floor   40
Leave all the noises of the square behind;
Most calm that reverent chamber shall ye find,
Silent at first, but for the noise you made
When on the brazen door your hand you laid
To shut it after you—but now behold   45
The city rulers on their thrones of gold,
Clad in most fair attire, and in their hands
Long carven silver-banded ebony wands;
Then from the daïs drop your eyes and see
Soldiers and peasants standing reverently   50
Before those elders, round a little band
Who bear such arms as guard the English land,
But battered, rent, and rusted sore, and they,
The men themselves, are shrivelled, bent, and grey;
And as they lean with pain upon their spears   55
Their brows seem furrowed deep with more than years;
For sorrow dulls their heavy sunken eyes,
Bent are they less with time than miseries.

Pondering on them the city grey-beards gaze
Through kindly eyes, midst thoughts of other days,   60
And pity for poor souls, and vague regret
For all the things that might have happened yet,
Until, their wonder gathering to a head,
The wisest man, who long that land has led,
Breaks the deep silence, unto whom again   65
A wanderer answers. Slowly as in pain,
And with a hollow voice as from a tomb
At first he tells the story of his doom,
But as it grows and once more hopes and fears,
Both measureless, are ringing round his ears,   70
His eyes grow bright, his seeming days decrease,
For grief once told brings somewhat back of peace.

The Elder of the City

From what unheard-of world, in what strange keel,
Have ye come hither to our commonweal?
No barbarous race, as these our peasants say,   75
But learned in memories of a long-past day,
Speaking, some few at least, the ancient tongue
That through the lapse of ages still has clung
To us, the seed of the Ionian race.
    Speak out and fear not; if ye need a place   80
Wherein to pass the end of life away,
That shall ye gain from us from this same day,
Unless the enemies of God ye are;
We fear not you and yours to bear us war,
And scarce can think that ye will try again   85
Across the perils of the shifting plain
To seek your own land whereso that may be:
For folk of ours bearing the memory
Of our old land, in days past oft have striven
To reach it, unto none of whom was given   90
To come again and tell us of the tale,
Therefore our ships are now content to sail,
About these happy islands that we know.

The Wanderer

    Masters, I have to tell a tale of woe,
A tale of folly and of wasted life,   95
Hope against hope, the bitter dregs of strife,
Ending, where all things end, in death at last:
So if I tell the story of the past,
Let it be worth some little rest, I pray,
A little slumber ere the end of day.   100

    No wonder if the Grecian tongue I know,
Since at Byzantium many a year ago
My father bore the twibil valiantly;
There did he marry, and get me, and die,
And I went back to Norway to my kin,   105
Long ere this beard ye see did first begin
To shade my mouth, but nathless not before

Among the Greeks I gathered some small lore,
And standing midst the Væringers, still heard
From this or that man many a wondrous word;   110
For ye shall know that though we worshipped God,
And heard mass duly, still of Swithiod
The Greater, Odin and his house of gold,
The noble stories ceased not to be told;
These moved me more than words of mine can say   115
E'en while at Micklegarth my folks did stay;
But when I reached one dying autumn-tide
My uncle's dwelling near the forest side,
And saw the land so scanty and so bare,
And all the hard things men contend with there,   120
A little and unworthy land it seemed,
And yet the more of Asagard I dreamed,
And worthier seemed the ancient faith of praise.

But now, but now—when one of all those days
Like Lazarus' finger on my heart should be   125
Breaking the fiery fixed eternity,
But for one moment—could I see once more
The grey-roofed sea-port sloping towards the shore,
Or note the brown boats standing in from sea,
Or the great dromond swinging from the quay,   130
Or in the beech-woods watch the screaming jay
Shoot up betwixt the tall trunks, smooth and grey—
Yea, could I see the days before distress
When very longing was but happiness.

Within our house there was a Breton squire   135
Well learned, who fail'd not to fan the fire
That evermore unholpen burned in me
Strange lands and things beyond belief to see;
Much lore of many lands this Breton knew;
And for one tale I told, he told me two.   140
He, counting Asagard a new-told thing,
Yet spoke of gardens ever blossoming
Across the western sea where none grew old,
E'en as the books at Micklegarth had told,
And said moreover that an English knight   145
Had had the Earthly Paradise in sight,
And heard the songs of those that dwelt therein,
But entered not, being hindered by his sin.

Shortly, so much of this and that he said
That in my heart the sharp barb entered,   150
And like real life would empty stories seem,
And life from day to day an empty dream.

    Another man there was, a Swabian priest,
Who knew the maladies of man and beast,
And what things helped them; he the stone still sought   155
Whereby base metal into gold is brought,
And strove to gain the precious draught, whereby
Men live midst mortal men yet never die;
Tales of the Kaiser Redbeard could he tell
Who neither went to Heaven nor yet to Hell,   160
When from that fight upon the Asian plain
He vanished, but still lives to come again
Men know not how or when; but I listening
Unto this tale thought it a certain thing
That in some hidden vale of Swithiod   165
Across the golden pavement still he trod.

    But while our longing for such things so grew,
And ever more and more we deemed them true,
Upon the land a pestilence there fell
Unheard-of yet in any chronicle,   170
And, as the people died full fast of it,
With these two men it chanced me once to sit,
This learned squire whose name was Nicholas,
And Swabian Laurence, as our manner was;
For could we help it scarcely did we part   175
From dawn to dusk: so heavy, sad at heart,
We from the castle yard beheld the bay
Upon that ne'er-to-be-forgotten day;
Little we said amidst that dreary mood
And certes nought that we could say was good.   180

    It was a bright September afternoon,
The parched-up beech trees would be yellowing soon;
The yellow flowers grown deeper with the sun
Were letting fall their petals one by one;
No wind there was, a haze was gathering o'er   185
The furthest bound of the faint yellow shore;
And in the oily waters of the bay
Scarce moving aught some fisher-cobles lay,
And all seemed peace; and had been peace indeed

But that we young men of our life had need,   190
And to our listening ears a sound was borne
That made the sunlight wretched and forlorn—
—The heavy tolling of the minster bell—
And nigher yet a tinkling sound did tell
That through the streets they bore our Saviour Christ   195
By dying lips in anguish to be kissed.

   At last spoke Nicholas, 'How long shall we
Abide here, looking forth into the sea
Expecting when our turn shall come to die?
Fair fellows, will ye come with me and try   200
Now at our worst that long desired quest,
Now—when our worst is death, and life our best.'

March

Slayer of the winter, art thou here again?
O welcome, thou that bring'st the summer nigh!
The bitter wind makes not thy victory vain,
Nor will we mock thee for thy faint blue sky.
Welcome, O March! whose kindly days and dry   5
Make April ready for the throstle's song,
Thou first redresser of the winter's wrong!

    Yea, welcome March! and though I die ere June,
Yet for the hope of life I give thee praise,
Striving to swell the burden of the tune   10
That even now I hear thy brown birds raise,
Unmindful of the past or coming days;
Who sing: 'O joy! A new year is begun:
What happiness to look upon the sun!'

    Ah, what begetteth all this storm of bliss   15
But Death himself, who crying solemnly,
E'en from the heart of sweet Forgetfulness,
Bids us 'Rejoice, lest pleasureless ye die.
Within a little time must ye go by.
Stretch forth your open hands, and while ye live   20
Take all the gifts that Death and Life may give.'

Behold once more within a quiet land
The remnant of that once aspiring band,
With all hopes fallen away, but such as light
The sons of men to that unfailing night,   25
That death they needs must look on face to face.
    Time passed, and ever fell the days apace
From off the new-strung chaplet of their life;
Yet though the time with no bright deeds was rife,
Though no fulfilled desire now made them glad,   30
They were not quite unhappy, rest they had,
And with their hope their fear had passed away;
New things and strange they saw from day to day,
Honoured they were and had no lack of things
For which men crouch before the feet of kings,   35
And, stripped of honour, yet may fail to have.
    Therefore their latter journey to the grave
Was like those days of later autumn-tide,

When he who in some town may chance to bide
Opens the window for the balmy air, 40
And seeing the golden hazy sky so fair,
And from some city garden hearing still
The wheeling rooks the air with music fill,
Sweet hopeful music, thinketh, is this spring,
Surely the year can scarce be perishing? 45
But then he leaves the clamour of the town,
And sees the withered scanty leaves fall down,
The half-ploughed field, the flowerless garden plot,
The dark full stream by summer long forgot,
The tangled hedges where, relaxed and dead, 50
The twining plants their withered berries shed,
And feels therewith the treachery of the sun,
And knows the pleasant time is well-nigh done.

    In such St. Luke's short summer lived these men,
Nearing the goal of threescore years and ten; 55
The elders of the town their comrades were,
And they to them were waxen now as dear
As ancient men to ancient men can be;
Grave matters of belief and polity
They spoke of oft, but not alone of these; 60
For in their times of idleness and ease
They told of poets' vain imaginings,
And memories vague of half-forgotten things,
Not true or false, but sweet to think upon.

    For nigh the time when first that land they won, 65
When new-born March made fresh the hopeful air,
The wanderers sat within a chamber fair,
Guests of that city's rulers, when the day
Far from the sunny noon had fallen away;
The sky grew dark, and on the window pane 70
They heard the beating of the sudden rain.
Then, all being satisfied with plenteous feast,
There spoke an ancient man, the land's chief priest,
Who said, 'Dear guests, the year begins to-day,
And fain are we, before it pass away, 75
To hear some tales of that now altered world,
Wherefrom our fathers in old time were hurled
By the hard hands of fate and destiny.
Nor would ye hear perchance unwillingly
How we have dealt with stories of the land 80

Wherein the tombs of our forefathers stand:
Wherefore henceforth two solemn feasts shall be
In every month, at which some history
Shall crown our joyance; and this day, indeed,
I have a story ready for our need,   85
If ye will hear it, though perchance it is
That many things therein are writ amiss,
This part forgotten, that part grown too great,
For these things, too, are in the hands of fate.'
    They cried aloud for joy to hear him speak,   90
And as again the sinking sun did break
Through the dark clouds and blazed adown the hall,
His clear thin voice upon their ears did fall,
Telling a tale of times long passed away,
When men might cross a kingdom in a day,   95
And kings remembered they should one day die,
And all folk dwelt in great simplicity.

November

Are thine eyes weary? Is thy heart too sick
To struggle any more with doubt and thought,
Whose formless veil draws darkening now and thick
Across thee e'en as smoke-tinged mist-wreaths brought
Down a fair dale to make it blind and nought?   5
Art thou so weary that no world there seems
Beyond these four walls, hung with pain and dreams?

Look out upon the real world, where the moon,
Half-way 'twixt root and crown of these high trees,
Turns the dead midnight into dreamy noon,   10
Silent and full of wonders, for the breeze
Died at the sunset, and no images,
No hopes of day, are left in sky or earth—
Is it not fair, and of most wondrous worth?

Yea, I have looked and seen November there;   15
The changeless seal of change it seemed to be,
Fair death of things that, living once, were fair;
Bright sign of loneliness too great for me,
Strange image of the dread eternity,
In whose void patience how can these have part,   20
These outstretched feverish hands, this restless heart?

On a clear eve when the November sky
Grew red with promise of the hoar-frost nigh,
These ancient men turned from the outside cold,
With something like content that they, grown old,   25
Needed but little now to help the ease
Of those last days before the final peace.
The empty month for them left no regret
For sweet things gained and lost, and longed for yet,
'Twixt spring-tide and this dying of the year.   30
Few things of small account the whole did bear,
Nor like a long lifetime of misery
Those few days seemed, as oft to such may be
As, seeing the patience of the world, whereby
Midst all its strife it falls not utterly   35
Into a wild, confused mass of pain,
Yet note it not, and have no will to gain,
Since they are young, a little time of rest,
Midst their vain raging for the hopeless best.

   Such thought, perchance, was in his heart, who broke   40
The silence of the fireside now, and spoke;
'This eve my tale tells of a fair maid born
Within a peaceful land, that peace to scorn,
In turn to scorn the deeds of mighty kings,
The council of the wise, and far-famed things,   45
And envied lives; so, born for discontent
She through the eager world of base folk went,
Still gaining nought but heavier weariness.
God grant that somewhere now content may bless
Her yearning heart; that she may look and smile   50
On the strange earth that wearied her awhile,
And now forgets her! Yet do not we,
Though some of us have lived full happily!'

February

Noon—and the north-west sweeps the empty road,
The rain-washed fields from hedge to hedge are bare;
Beneath the leafless elms some hind's abode
Looks small and void, and no smoke meets the air
From its poor hearth: one lonely rook doth dare   5
The gale, and beats above the unseen corn,
Then turns, and whirling down the wind is borne.

Shall it not hap that on some dawn of May
Thou shalt awake, and thinking of days dead,
See nothing clear but this same dreary day,   10
Of all the days that have passed o'er thine head?
Shalt thou not wonder, looking from thy bed,
Through green leaves on the windless east a-fire,
That this day too thine heart doth still desire?

Shalt thou not wonder that it liveth yet,   15
The useless hope, the useless craving pain,
That made thy face, that lonely noontide, wet
With more than beating of the chilly rain?
Shalt thou not hope for joy new born again,
Since no grief ever born can ever die   20
Through changeless change of seasons passing by?

The change has come at last, and from the west
Drives on the wind, and gives the clouds no rest,
And rustles up the water thin that lies
Over the surface of the thawing ice;   25
Sunrise and sunset with no glorious show
Are seen, as late they were across the snow;
The wet-lipped west wind chilleth to the bone
More than the light and flickering east hath done.
Full soberly the earth's fresh hope begins,   30
Nor stays to think of what each new day wins:
And still it seems to bid us turn away
From this chill thaw to dream of blossomed May:
E'en as some hapless lover's dull shame sinks
Away sometimes in day-dreams, and he thinks   35
No more of yesterday's disgrace and foil,
No more he thinks of all the sickening toil
Of piling straw on straw to reach the sky;

But rather now a pitying face draws nigh,
Mid tears and prayers for pardon; and a tale 40
To make love tenderer now is all the bale
Love brought him erst.
                   But on this chill dank tide
Still are the old men by the fireside,
And all things cheerful round the day just done 45
Shut out the memory of the cloud-drowned sun.
And dripping bough and blotched and snow-soaked earth;
And little as the tide seemed made for mirth,
Scarcely they lacked it less than months agone,
When on their wrinkles bright the great sun shone; 50
Rather, perchance, less pensive now they were,
And meeter for that cause old tales to hear
Of stirring deeds long dead:
               So, as it fell,
Preluding nought, an elder 'gan to tell 55
The story promised in mid-winter days
Of all that latter end of bliss and praise
That erst befell Bellerophon the bright,
Ere all except his name sank into night.

From *The Watching of the Falcon*

Across the sea a land there is,
Where, if fate will, may men have bliss,
For it is fair as any land:
There hath the reaper a full hand,
While in the orchard hangs aloft   5
The purple fig, a-growing soft;
And fair the trellised vine-bunches
Are swung across the high elm-trees;
And in the rivers great fish play,
While over them pass day by day   10
The laden barges to their place.
There maids are straight, and fair of face,
And men are stout for husbandry,
And all is well as it can be
Upon this earth where all has end.   15
    For on them God is pleased to send
The gift of Death down from above.
That envy, hatred, and hot love,
Knowledge with hunger by his side,
And avarice and deadly pride,   20
There may have end like everything
Both to the shepherd and the king:
Lest this green earth become but hell
If folk thereon should ever dwell.
    Full little most men think of this,   25
But half in woe and half in bliss
They pass their lives, and die at last
Unwilling, though their lot be cast
In wretched places of the earth,
Where men have little joy from birth   30
Until they die; in no such case
Were those who tilled this pleasant place.
    There soothly men were loth to die,
Though sometimes in his misery
A man would say 'Would I were dead!'   35
Alas! full little likelihead
That he should live for ever there.
    So folk within that country fair
Lived on unable to forget
The longed-for things they could not get,   40

And without need tormenting still
Each other with some bitter ill;
Yea, and themselves too, growing grey
With dread of some long-lingering day,
That never came ere they were dead   45
With green sods growing on the head;
Nowise content with what they had,
But falling still from good to bad
While hard they sought the hopeless best
And seldom happy or at rest   50
Until at last with lessening blood
One foot within the grave they stood.

Now so it chanced that in this land
There did a certain castle stand,
Set all alone deep in the hills,   55
Amid the sound of falling rills
Within a valley of sweet grass,
To which there went one narrow pass
Through the dark hills, but seldom trod.
Rarely did horse-hoof press the sod   60
About the quiet weedy moat,
Where unscared did the great fish float;
Because men dreaded there to see
The uncouth things of faërie;
Nathless by some few fathers old   65
These tales about the place were told
    That neither squire nor seneschal
Or varlet came in bower or hall,
Yet all things were in order due,
Hangings of gold and red and blue,   70
And tables with fair service set;
Cups that had paid the Cæsar's debt
Could he have laid his hands on them;
Dorsars, with pearls in every hem,
And fair embroidered gold-wrought things,   75
Fit for a company of kings;
And in the chambers dainty beds,
With pillows dight for fair young heads;
And horses in the stables were,
And in the cellars wine full clear   80
And strong, and casks of ale and mead;
Yea, all things a great lord could need.

For whom these things were ready there
None knew; but if one chanced to fare
Into that place at Easter-tide,   85
There would he find a falcon tied
Unto a pillar of the Hall;
And such a fate to him would fall,
That if unto the seventh night,
He watched the bird from dark to light,   90
And light to dark unceasingly,
On the last evening he should see
A lady beautiful past words;
Then, were he come of clowns or lords,
Son of a swineherd or a king,   95
There must she grant him anything
Perforce, that he might dare to ask,
And do his very hardest task

    But if he slumbered, ne'er again
The wretch would wake for he was slain   100
Helpless, by hands he could not see,
And his corpse mangled wretchedly.

Now said these elders—Ere this tide
Full many folk this thing have tried,
But few have got much good thereby;   105
For first, a many came to die
By slumbering ere their watch was done;
Or else they saw that lovely one,
And mazed, they knew not what to say;
Or asked for some small thing that day,   110
That easily they might have won,
Nor staked their lives and souls thereon;
Or asking, asked for some great thing
That was their bane; as to be king
One asked, and died the morrow morn   115
That he was crowned, of all forlorn.
Yet thither came a certain man,
Who from being poor great riches wan
Past telling, whose grandsons now are
Great lords thereby in peace and war.   120
And in their coat-of-arms they bear,
Upon a field of azure fair,
A castle and a falcon, set
Below a chief of golden fret.

And in our day a certain knight   125
Prayed to be worsted in no fight,
And so it happed to him: yet he
Died none the less most wretchedly,
And all his prowess was in vain,
For by a losel was he slain,   130
As on the highway side he slept
One summer night, of no man kept.

Such tales as these the fathers old
About that lonely castle told;
And in their day the king must try   135
Himself to prove that mystery,
Although, unless the fay could give
For ever on the earth to live,
Nought could he ask that he had not:
For boundless riches had he got,   140
Fair children, and a faithful wife;
And happily had passed his life,
And all fulfilled of victory,
Yet was he fain this thing to see.
    So towards the mountains he set out   145
One noontide, with a gallant rout
Of knights and lords, and as the day
Began to fail came to the way
Where he must enter all alone,
Between the dreary walls of stone.   150
Thereon to that fair company
He bade farewell, who wistfully
Looked backward oft as home they rode.
But in the entry he abode
Of that rough unknown narrowing pass,   155
Where twilight at the high noon was.
    Then onward he began to ride:
Smooth rose the rocks on every side,
And seemed as they were cut by man;
Adown them ever water ran,   160
But they of living things were bare,
Yea, not a blade of grass grew there;
And underfoot rough was the way,
For scattered all about there lay
Great jagged pieces of black stone.   165
Throughout the pass the wind did moan,

With such wild noises, that the King
Could almost think he heard something
Spoken of men; as one might hear
The voices of folk standing near   170
One's chamber wall: yet saw he nought
Except those high walls strangely wrought,
And overhead the strip of sky.
    So, going onward painfully,
He met therein no evil thing,   175
But came about the sunsetting
Unto the opening of the pass,
And thence beheld a vale of grass
Bright with the yellow daffodil;
And all the vale the sun did fill   180
With his last glory. Midmost there
Rose up a stronghold, built four-square,
Upon a flowery grassy mound,
That moat and high wall ran around.
    Thereby he saw a walled pleasance,   185
With walks and sward fit for the dance
Of Arthur's court in its best time,
That seemed to feel some magic clime;
For though through all the vale outside
Things were as in the April-tide,   190
And daffodils and cowslips grew
And hidden the March violets blew,
Within the bounds of that sweet close
Was trellised the bewildering rose;
There was the lily over-sweet,   195
And starry pinks for garlands meet;
And apricots hung on the wall
And midst the flowers did peaches fall,
And nought had blemish there or spot.
For in that place decay was not.   200

LETTER TO CHARLES ELIOT NORTON

26 Queen Sq:
Bloomsbury London
October 19, 1871

My dear Norton

How very kind it was of you to write to me at Reykjavik: I was delighted that you should form one of the packet I looked over, trembling lest anybody should be dead after having heard no news for nearly 8 weeks: as for you; you must have thought I was either dead or had forgotten how to write. I can make no excuse for not having done so, and can only say that I had by no means forgotten you—Georgie would say I fancy that that was the reason why I hadn't, in order viz. that the prick of conscience might keep you always in my mind.

Am I to defend myself for going to Iceland instead of Italy? I can only say in these matters one must follow ones instincts & mine drove me there: you see the change of life was complete: we were six weeks in the saddle: on 24 nights I slept in a tent: I got quite knowing about horses: I acquired a competent knowledge of the useful art of *cookery*—under difficulties too, I can tell you—for I was master-cook to the company. —don't you remember our argument about servants, at the Grange one night, & how I thought them immoral? (the use of them, I mean)—well here we were without them: for though our guides Gisti and Eyrvidr were engaged to serve us by the day yet they worked no harder than we, except where their knowledge was special, and they paid us no sort of defference except that of good-fellowship, for they were very good-tempered agreable men—now wasn't that delightful?—Then the people: lazy, dreamy, without enterprise or hope: awfully poor, and used to all kinds of privations—and with all that, gentle, kind, intensely curious, full of their old lore, living in their stirring past you would say, among dreams of the 'Furor Norsmanorum' and so contented and merry that one was quite ashamed of ones grumbling life—wasn't there something delightful & new about that also? Truly it would all have been nothing but for the memory of the old story-tellers; nay I think without them the people would have long ago sunk into stolidity and brutality—yet as it was all was enjoyment—or nearly all—almost every day's ride was a pleasure: I never got used to weariness of that starting in the morning, especially if the road was good and the day fair; the rattle and clatter of the horses (we had 30 of them) were got together and fairly set off: the anticipation of the unknown quarters we were coming to at night: then as to the look of the country, there is at least nothing commonplace about it; <the> its influence on the old story-tellers is obvious enough: often indeed the blank, barreness of some historical place, and the feebleness of the life that has taken the place of the old tragedies would depress one for a while, till one remembered the lapse of years, and the courage and hope that had been there.

Rewards I had at times too; as the sunny afternoon, when we mounted from a valley of black sand into a narrow shady pass, and presently as I looked up from my poney's head as we came to the brow of the pass, there lay before me the great valley of the Thing-meads bounded by great hills intensely blue in the clear sunny air: or the strangest ride we had up a dreadful valley close to Lithend, where the noble Gunnar of Njal's Saga lived & died, on a bright hot day, when we rode through a great plain of stones that the outrageously strange-shaped cliffs rose from: and crossing 9 streams of the terrible-looking Markfleet came to a birch-wood in a little valley and lay there for an hour in a place that looked the very end of the world—it is an indescribable and miraculous looking country—the hills almost always rise from quite flat plains: they are grey with moss-grown lava; or black with scorial sand; or burnt red; or striped green with the pastures on their sides. You always know when you are coming to a stead, for you see, a bright green patch about it, which is its túni or homefield. Sometimes though we would ride all day in the wastes: nothing with grey & black lava and sand, dotted over with tufts of sea-pink and Campion, and the grey roots of dwarf willow: the distant hills dark inky purple on a dull day; or blue from indigo to ultramarine on a sunny one.

Here is a sketch of where we went in the island in case you have a map by you. We started from Reykjavik and rode east first into the country of the Njal's Saga, thence we turned north about the feet of Hecla to the Geysirs: then N. still into the great wastes, sleeping a night close by the big lake of Eyne-water (Grettir) & so into Vatusdal. (Waterdale) (In gimnud the Old). Then S.W. through Willowdale to Midfirth and Biarg there, where Grettir was born & buried: thence west still through Ramfirth into Laxdale, and Herdholt there, the scene of my poem; we stayed 3 days there, making excursions to Soelingsdale the home of Gudrun, and went S.W. thence to Holy-fell, where she died, and where Snorri the Priest lived before her: this is also head quarters of the Eyrbiggia Saga. Thence we went right out to the end of the promontory dominated by the great mountain of Surfells-Jokul: then E. (having turned the corner) with the sea always on our right till we came to Hitdale (Grettir again). Thence to Burgfirth and White-river-side, the scene of many stories but most notably of Gunnlaug the Worm-tongue's love and troubles. Thence S. to Reykholt where Snorri the historian lived and was slain: then S. to the wonderful Thing meads—and so S. again to Reykjavik, having been away 6 weeks to the minute. Then on board ship in 3 days and home—and so glad to be there—in 9 weeks in all—

There—it was worth doing and has been of great service to me: I was getting nervous & depressed and very much wanted a rest, and I don't think anything would have given me so complete a one—I came back extremely well and tough, and set to work at once on a new poem (which has nothing whatever to do with Iceland) You will see it someday I hope with illustrations by Ned thereto—we are both very much excited about it. I have to thank you for kindly sending me the photograph of the beautiful picture of Lippi's— what a lovely work it must be. I hope I shall one day see Italy—next year perhaps—I think I can sympathise with that as well as Iceland—

Please give my kindest remembrances to Mrs Norton and the rest of your party. My wife is on the whole in much better health than she has been: we have taken a little house deep in the country where she and the children are to spend some months every year, as they did this— a beautiful and strangely naif house, Elizabethan in appearance though <not> much later in date, as in that out of the way corner people built gothic till the beginning or middle of last century: it is on the S.W. extremity of Oxfordshire within a stone's throw of the baby Thames: in the most beautiful grey little hamlet called Kelmscott.

I hope, but don't expect that you will enjoy Berlin—

I am
Yours affectionately
William Morris

From *The Story of Sigurd the Volsung and the Fall of the Niblungs*, Books 1 and 2, 1876

Book 1. Sigmund

In this book is told of the earlier days of the Volsungs, and of
Sigmund the father of Sigurd, and of his deeds, and of how he
died while Sigurd was yet unborn in his mother's womb.

Of the dwelling of King Volsung, and the wedding of Signy his Daughter.

There was a dwelling of Kings ere the world was waxen old;
Dukes were the door-wards there, and the roofs were thatched with gold;
Earls were the wrights that wrought it, and silver nailed its doors;
Earls' wives were the weaving-women, queens' daughters strewed its floors,
And the masters of its song-craft were the mightiest men that cast   5
The sails of the storm of battle adown the bickering blast.
There dwelt men merry-hearted, and in hope exceeding great
Met the good days and the evil as they went the way of fate:
There the Gods were unforgotten, yea whiles they walked with men,
Though e'en in that world's beginning rose a murmur now and again   10
Of the midward time and the fading and the last of the latter days,
And the entering in of the terror, and the death of the People's Praise.

Thus was the dwelling of Volsung, the King of the Midworld's Mark,
As a rose in the winter season, a candle in the dark;
And as in all other matters 'twas all earthly houses' crown,   15
And the least of its wall-hung shields was a battle-world's renown,
So therein withal was a marvel and a glorious thing to see,
For amidst of its midmost hall-floor sprang up a mighty tree,
That reared its blessings roofward, and wreathed the roof-tree dear
With the glory of the summer and the garland of the year.   20
I know not how they called it ere Volsung changed his life,
But his dawning of fair promise, and his noontide of the strife,
His eve of the battle-reaping and the garnering of his fame
Have bred us many a story and named us many a name;
And when men tell of Volsung, they call that war-duke's tree,   25
That crownèd stem, the Branstock; and so was it told unto me.

So there was the throne of Volsung beneath its blossoming bower,
But high o'er the roof crest red it rose 'twixt tower and tower,
And therein were the wild hawks dwelling, abiding the dole of their lord;
And they wailed high over the wine, and laughed to the waking sword.   30

Still were its boughs but for them, when lo on an even of May
Comes a man from Siggeir the King with a word for his mouth to say:

'All hail to thee King Volsung, from the King of the Goths I come:
He hath heard of thy sword victorious and thine abundant home;
He hath heard of thy sons in the battle, the fillers of Odin's hall;   35
And a word hath the west-wind blown him (full fruitful be its fall!)
A word of thy daughter Signy the crown of womanhood:
Now he deems thy friendship goodly, and thine help in the battle good,
And for these will he give his friendship and his battle-aid again:
But if thou wouldst grant his asking, and make his heart full fain,   40
Then shalt thou give him a matter, saith he, without a price,
—Signy the fairer than fair, Signy the wiser than wise.'

Such words in the hall of the Volsungs spake the Earl of Siggeir the Goth,
Bearing the gifts and the gold, the ring, and the tokens of troth.
But the King's heart laughed within him and the King's sons deemed it
     good;   45
For they dreamed how they fared with the Goths o'er ocean and acre and
     wood,
Till all the north was theirs, and the utmost southern lands.

But nought said the snow-white Signy as she sat with folded hands
And gazed at the Goth-king's Earl till his heart grew heavy and cold,
As one that half remembers a tale that the elders have told,   50
A story of weird and of woe: then spake King Volsung and said:

'A great king woos thee, daughter; wilt thou lie in a great king's bed,
And bear earth's kings on thy bosom, that our name may never die?'

A fire lit up her face, and her voice was e'en as a cry:
'I will sleep in a great king's bed, I will bear the lords of the earth,   55
And the wrack and the grief of my youth-days shall be held for nothing worth.'

Then would he question her kindly, as one who loved her sore,
But she put forth her hand and smiled, and her face was flushed no more:
'Would God it might otherwise be! but wert thou to will it not,
Yet should I will it and wed him, and rue my life and my lot.'   60

Lowly and soft she said it; but spake out louder now:
'Be of good cheer, King Volsung! for such a man art thou,
That what thou dost well-counselled, goodly and fair it is,
And what thou dost unwitting, the Gods have bidden thee this:
So work all things together for the fame of thee and thine.   65
And now meseems at my wedding shall be a hallowed sign,
That shall give thine heart a joyance, whate'er shall follow after.'

She spake, and the feast sped on, and the speech and the song and the
     laughter

Went over the words of boding as the tide of the norland main
Sweeps over the hidden skerry, the home of the shipman's bane.   70

So wendeth his way on the morrow that Earl of the Gothland King,
Bearing the gifts and the gold, and King Volsung's tokening,
And a word in his mouth moreover, a word of blessing and hail,
And a bidding to King Siggeir to come ere the June-tide fail
And wed him to white-hand Signy and bear away his bride,   75
While sleepeth the field of the fishes amidst the summer-tide.

So on Mid-Summer Even ere the undark night began
Siggeir the King of the Goth-folk went up from the bath of the swan
Unto the Volsung dwelling with many an Earl about;
There through the glimmering thicket the linkèd mail rang out,   80
And sang as mid the woodways sings the summer-hidden ford:
There were gold-rings God-fashioned, and many a Dwarf-wrought
     sword,
And many a Queen-wrought kirtle and many a written spear;
So came they to the acres, and drew the threshold near,
And amidst of the garden blossoms, on the grassy, fruit-grown land,   85
Was Volsung the King of the Wood-world with his sons on either hand;
Therewith down lighted Siggeir the lord of a mighty folk,
Yet showed he by King Volsung as the bramble by the oak,
Nor reached his helm to the shoulder of the least of Volsung's sons.
And so into the hall they wended, the Kings and their mighty ones;   90
And they dight the feast full glorious, and drank through the death
     of the day,
Till the shadowless moon rose upward, till it wended white away;
Then they went to the gold-hung beds, and at last for an hour or twain
Were all things still and silent, save a flaw of the summer rain.

But on the morrow noontide when the sun was high and bare,   95
More glorious was the banquet, and now was Signy there,
And she sat beside King Siggeir, a glorious bride forsooth;
Ruddy and white was she wrought as the fair-stained sea-beast's tooth,
But she neither laughed nor spake, and her eyes were hard and cold,
And with wandering side-long looks her lord would she behold.   100
That saw Sigmund her brother, the eldest Volsung son,
And oft he looked upon her, and their eyes met now and anon,
And ruth arose in his heart, and hate of Siggeir the Goth,
And there had he broken the wedding, but for plighted promise and troth.
But those twain were beheld of Siggeir, and he deemed of the Volsung kin,   105
That amid their might and their malice small honour should he win;
Yet thereof made he no semblance, but abided times to be

And laughed out with the loudest, amid the hope and the glee.
And nought of all saw Volsung, as he dreamed of the coming glory,
And how the Kings of his kindred should fashion the round world's story.   110

So round about the Branstock they feast in the gleam of the gold;
And though the deeds of man-folk were not yet waxen old,
Yet had they tales for songcraft, and the blossomed garth of rhyme;
Tales of the framing of all things and the entering in of time
From the halls of the outer heaven; so near they knew the door.   115
Wherefore uprose a sea-king, and his hands that loved the oar
Now dealt with the rippling harp-gold, and he sang of the shaping of
     earth,
And how the stars were lighted, and where the winds had birth,
And the gleam of the first of summers on the yet untrodden grass.
But e'en as men's hearts were hearkening some heard the thunder pass   120
O'er the cloudless noontide heaven; and some men turned about
And deemed that in the doorway they heard a man laugh out.
Then into the Volsung dwelling a mighty man there strode,
One-eyed and seeming ancient, yet bright his visage glowed:
Cloud-blue was the hood upon him, and his kirtle gleaming-grey   125
As the latter morning sundog when the storm is on the way:
A bill he bore on his shoulder, whose mighty ashen beam
Burnt bright with the flame of the sea and the blended silver's gleam.
And such was the guise of his raiment as the Volsung elders had told
Was borne by their fathers' fathers, and the first that warred in the wold.   130

So strode he to the Branstock nor greeted any lord,
But forth from his cloudy raiment he drew a gleaming sword,
And smote it deep in the tree-bole, and the wild hawks overhead
Laughed 'neath the naked heaven as at last he spake and said:
'Earls of the Goths, and Volsungs, abiders on the earth,   135
Lo there amid the Branstock a blade of plenteous worth!
The folk of the war-wand's forgers wrought never better steel
Since first the burg of heaven uprose for man-folk's weal.
Now let the man among you whose heart and hand may shift
To pluck it from the oakwood e'en take it for my gift.   140
Then ne'er, but his own heart falter, its point and edge shall fail
Until the night's beginning and the ending of the tale.
Be merry Earls of the Goth-folk, O Volsung Sons be wise,
And reap the battle-acre that ripening for you lies:
For they told me in the wild wood, I heard on the mountain side,   145
That the shining house of heaven is wrought exceeding wide,
And that there the Early-comers shall have abundant rest
While Earth grows scant of great ones, and fadeth from its best,

And fadeth from its midward and groweth poor and vile:—
All hail to thee King Volsung! farewell for a little while!'   150

So sweet his speaking sounded, so wise his words did seem,
That moveless all men sat there, as in a happy dream
We stir not lest we waken; but there his speech had end,
And slowly down the hall-floor, and outward did he wend;
And none would cast him a question or follow on his ways,   155
For they knew that the gift was Odin's, a sword for the world to praise.

But now spake Volsung the King: 'Why sit ye silent and still?
Is the Battle-Father's visage a token of terror and ill?
Arise O Volsung Children, Earls of the Goths arise,
And set your hands to the hilts as mighty men and wise!   160
Yet deem it not too easy; for belike a fateful blade
Lies there in the heart of the Branstock for a fated warrior made.'

Now therewith spake King Siggeir: 'King Volsung give me a grace
To try it the first of all men, lest another win my place
And mere chance-hap steal my glory and the gain that I might win.'   165
Then somewhat laughed King Volsung, and he said: 'O Guest, begin;
Though herein is the first as the last, for the Gods have long to live,
Nor hath Odin yet forgotten unto whom the gift he would give.'

Then forth to the tree went Siggeir, the Goth-folk's mighty lord,
And laid his hand on the gemstones, and strained at the glorious sword   170
Till his heart grew black with anger; and never a word he said
As he wended back to the high-seat: but Signy waxed blood-red
When he sat him adown beside her; and her heart was nigh to break
For the shame and the fateful boding: and therewith King Volsung spake:

'Thus comes back empty-handed the mightiest King of Earth,   175
And how shall the feeble venture? yet each man knows his worth;
And today may a great beginning from a little seed upspring
To o'erpass many a great one that hath the name of King:
So stand forth free and unfree; stand forth both most and least,
But first ye Earls of the Goth-folk, ye lovely lords we feast.'   180

Upstood the Earls of Siggeir, and each man drew anigh
And deemed his time was coming for a glorious gain and high;
But for all their mighty shaping and their deeds in the battle-wood,
No looser in the Branstock that gift of Odin stood.
Then uprose Volsung's homemen, and the fell-abiding folk;   185
And the yellow-headed shepherds came gathering round the Oak,
And the searchers of the thicket and the dealers with the oar:
And the least and the worst of them all was a mighty man of war.

But for all their mighty shaping, and the struggle and the strain
Of their hands, the deft in labour, they tugged thereat in vain;   190
And still as the shouting and jeers, and the names of men and the laughter
Beat backward from gable to gable, and rattled o'er roof-tree and rafter,
Moody and still sat Siggeir; for he said: 'They have trained me here
As a mock for their woodland bondsmen; and yet shall they buy it dear.'

Now the tumult sank a little, and men cried on Volsung the King   195
And his sons, the hedge of battle, to try the fateful thing.
So Volsung laughed, and answered: 'I will set me to the toil,
Lest these my guests of the Goth-folk should deem I fear the foil.
Yet nought am I ill-sworded, and the oldest friend is best;
And this, my hand's first fellow, will I bear to the grave-mound's rest,   200
Nor wield meanwhile another: Yea this shall I have in hand
When mid the host of Odin in the Day of Doom I stand.'

Therewith from his belt of battle he raised the golden sheath,
And showed the peace-strings glittering about the hidden death:
Then he laid his hand on the Branstock, and cried: 'O tree beloved,   205
I thank thee of thy good-heart that so little thou art moved:
Abide thou thus, green bower, when I am dead and gone
And the best of all my kindred a better day hath won!'

Then as a young man laughed he, and on the hilts of gold
His hand, the battle-breaker, took fast and certain hold,   210
And long he drew and strained him, but mended not the tale,
Yet none the more thereover his mirth of heart did fail;
But he wended to the high-seat and thence began to cry:

'Sons I have gotten and cherished, now stand ye forth to try;
Lest Odin tell in God-home how from the way he strayed,   215
And how to the man he would not he gave away his blade.'
So therewithal rose Rerir, and wasted might and main;
Then Gunthiof, and then Hunthiof, they wearied them in vain;
Nought was the might of Agnar; nought Helgi could avail;
Sigi the tall and Solar no further brought the tale,   220
Nor Geirmund the priest of the temple, nor Gylfi of the wood.

At last by the side of the Branstock Sigmund the Volsung stood,
And with right hand wise in battle the precious sword-hilt caught,
Yet in a careless fashion, as he deemed it all for nought:
When lo, from floor to rafter went up a shattering shout,   225
For aloft in the hand of Sigmund the naked blade shone out
As high o'er his head he shook it: for the sword had come away
From the grip of the heart of the Branstock, as though all loose it lay.

A little while he stood there mid the glory of the hall,
Like the best of the trees of the garden, when the April sunbeams fall   230
On its blossomed boughs in the morning, and tell of the days to be;
Then back unto the high-seat he wended soberly;
For this was the thought within him: Belike the day shall come
When I shall bide here lonely amid the Volsung home,
Its glory and sole avenger, its after-summer seed.   235
Yea, I am the hired of Odin, his workday will to speed,
And the harvest-tide shall be heavy.—What then, were it come and past
And I laid by the last of the sheaves with my wages earned at the last?

He lifted his eyes as he thought it, for now was he come to his place,
And there he stood by his father and met Siggeir face to face,   240
And he saw him blithe and smiling, and heard him how he spake:
'O best of the sons of Volsung, I am merry for thy sake
And the glory that thou hast gained us; but whereas thine hand and heart
Are e'en now the lords of the battle, how lack'st thou for thy part
A matter to better the best? Wilt thou overgild fine gold   245
Or dye the red rose redder? So I prithee let me hold
This sword that comes to thine hand on the day I wed thy kin.
For at home have I a store-house; there is mountain-gold therein
The weight of a war-king's harness; there is silver plenteous store;
There is iron, and huge-wrought amber, that the southern men love sore,   250
When they sell me the woven wonder, the purple born of the sea;
And it hangeth up in that bower; and all this is a gift for thee:
But the sword that came to my wedding, methinketh it meet and right,
That it lie on my knees in the council and stead me in the fight.'

But Sigmund laughed and answered, and he spake a scornful word: 255
'And if I take twice that treasure, will it buy me Odin's sword,
And the gift that the Gods have given? will it buy me again to stand
Betwixt two mightiest world-kings with a longed-for thing in mine hand
That all their might hath missed of? when the purple-selling men
Come buying thine iron and amber, dost thou sell thine honour then?   260
Do they wrap it in bast of the linden, or run it in moulds of earth?
And shalt thou account mine honour as a matter of lesser worth?
Came the sword to thy wedding, Goth-king, to thine hand it never came,
And thence is thine envy whetted to deal me this word of shame.'

Black then was the heart of Siggeir, but his face grew pale and red,   265
Till he drew a smile thereover, and spake the word and said:
'Nay, pardon me, Signy's kinsman! when the heart desires o'ermuch
It teacheth the tongue ill speaking, and my word belike was such.
But the honour of thee and thy kindred, I hold it even as mine,

And I love you as my heart-blood, and take ye this for a sign.   270
I bid thee now King Volsung, and these thy glorious sons,
And thine earls and thy dukes of battle and all thy mighty ones,
To come to the house of the Goth-kings as honoured guests and dear
And abide the winter over; that the dusky days and drear
May be glorious with thy presence, that all folk may praise my life,   275
And the friends that my fame hath gotten; and that this my new-wed wife
Thine eyes may make the merrier till she bear my eldest born.'

Then speedily answered Volsung: 'No king of the earth might scorn
Such noble bidding, Siggeir; and surely will I come
To look upon thy glory and the Goths' abundant home.   280
But let two months wear over, for I have many a thing
To shape and shear in the Woodland, as befits a people's king:
And thou meanwhile here abiding of all my goods shalt be free,
And then shall we twain together roof over the glass-green sea
With the sides of our golden dragons; and our war-hosts' blended
     shields   285
Shall fright the sea-abiders and the folk of the fishy fields.'

Answered the smooth-speeched Siggeir: 'I thank thee well for this,
And thy bidding is most kingly; yet take it not amiss
That I wend my ways in the morning; for we Goth-folk know indeed
That the sea is a foe full deadly, and a friend that fails at need,   290
And that Ran who dwells thereunder will many a man beguile:
And I bear a woman with me; nor would I for a while
Behold that sea-queen's dwelling; for glad at heart am I
Of the realm of the Goths and the Volsungs, and I look for long to lie
In the arms of the fairest woman that ever a king may kiss.   295
So I go mine house to order for the increase of thy bliss,
That there in nought but joyance all we may wear the days
And that men of the time hereafter the more our lives may praise.'

And for all the words of Volsung e'en so must the matter be,
And Siggeir the Goth and Signy on the morn shall sail the sea.   300
But the feast sped on the fairer, and the more they waxed in disport
And the glee that all men love, as they knew that the hours were short.
Yet a boding heart bare Sigmund amid his singing and laughter;
And somewhat Signy wotted of the deeds that were coming after;
For the wisest of women she was, and many a thing she knew;   305
She would hearken the voice of the midnight till she heard what the Gods
     would do,
And her feet fared oft on the wild, and deep was her communing
With the heart of the glimmering woodland, where never a fowl may sing.

So fair sped on the feasting amid the gleam of the gold,
Amid the wine and the joyance; and many a tale was told   310
To the harp-strings of that wedding, whereof the latter days
Yet hold a little glimmer to wonder at and praise.
Then the undark night drew over, and faint the high stars shone,
And there on the beds blue-woven the slumber-tide they won;
Yea while on the brightening mountain the herd-boy watched his sheep.   315
Yet soft on the breast of Signy King Siggeir lay asleep.

How the Volsungs fared to the Land of the Goths, and of the fall of King Volsung.

Now or ever the sun shone houseward, unto King Volsung's bed
Came Signy stealing barefoot, and she spake the word and said:
'Awake and hearken, my father, for though the wedding be done,
And I am the wife of the Goth-king, yet the Volsungs are not gone.   320
So I come as a dream of the night, with a word that the Gods would say,
And think thou thereof in the day-tide, and let Siggeir go on his way
With me and the gifts and the gold, but do ye abide in the land,
Nor trust in the guileful heart and the murder-loving hand,
Lest the kin of the Volsungs perish, and the world be nothing worth.'   325

So came the word unto Volsung, and wit in his heart had birth;
And he sat upright in the bed and kissed her on the lips;
But he said: 'My word is given, it is gone like the spring-tide ships:
To death or to life must I journey when the months are come to an end.
Yet my sons my words shall hearken, and shall nowise with me wend.'   330

Then she answered, speaking swiftly: 'Nay, have thy sons with thee;
Gather an host together and a mighty company,
And meet the guile and the death-snare with battle and with wrack.'

He said: 'Nay, my troth-word plighted e'en so should I draw aback:
I shall go a guest, as my word was; of whom shall I be afraid?   335
For an outworn elder's ending shall no mighty moan be made.'

Then answered Signy, weeping: 'I shall see thee yet again
When the battle thou arrayest on the Goth-folks' strand in vain.
Heavy and hard are the Norns: but each man his burden bears;
And what am I to fashion the fate of the coming years?'   340

She wept and she wended back to the Goth-king's bolster blue,
And Volsung pondered awhile till slumber over him drew;
But when once more he wakened, the kingly house was up,

And the homemen gathered together to drink the parting cup:
And grand amid the hall-floor was the Goth-king in his gear,   345
And Signy clad for faring stood by the Branstock dear
With the earls of the Goths about her: so queenly did she seem,
So calm and ruddy coloured, that Volsung well might deem
That her words were a fashion of slumber, a vision of the night.
But they drank the wine of departing, and brought the horses dight,   350
And forth abroad the Goth-folk and the Volsung Children rode
Nor ever once would Signy look back to that abode.

So down over acre and heath they rode to the side of the sea,
And there by the long-ships' bridges was the ship-host's company.
Then Signy kissed her brethren with ruddy mouth and warm   355
Nor was there one of the Goth-folk but blessed her from all harm;
Then sweet she kissed her father and hung about his neck,
And sure she whispered him somewhat ere she passed forth toward
     the deck,
Though nought I know to tell it: then Siggeir hailed them fair,
And called forth many a blessing on the hearts that bode his snare.   360
Then were the gangways shipped, and blown was the parting horn,
And the striped sails drew with the wind, and away was Signy borne
White on the shielded long-ship, a grief in the heart of the gold;
Nor once would she turn her about the strand of her folk to behold.

Thenceforward dwelt the Volsungs in exceeding glorious state,   365
And merry lived King Volsung, abiding the day of his fate;
But when the months aforesaid were well-nigh worn away
To his sons and his folk of counsel he fell these words to say:
'Ye mind you of Signy's wedding and of my plighted troth
To go in two months' wearing to the house of Siggeir the Goth: 370
Nor will I hide how Signy then spake a warning word
And did me to wit that her husband was a grim and guileful lord,
And would draw us to our undoing for envy and despite
Concerning the Sword of Odin, and for dread of the Volsung might.
Now wise is Signy my daughter and knoweth nought but sooth: 375
Yet are there seasons and times when for longing and self-ruth
The hearts of women wander, and this maybe is such;
Nor for her word of Siggeir, will I trow it overmuch,
Nor altogether doubt it, since the woman is wrought so wise;
Nor much might my heart love Siggeir for all his kingly guise.   380
Yet, shall a king hear murder when a king's mouth blessing saith?
So maybe he is bidding me honour, and maybe he is bidding me death
Let him do after his fashion, and I will do no less.
In peace will I go to his bidding let the spae-wrights ban or bless;

And no man now or hereafter of Volsung's blenching shall tell.   385
But ye, sons, in the land shall tarry, and heed the realm right well,
Lest the Volsung Children fade, and the wide world worser grow.'

But with one voice cried all men, that they one and all would go
To gather the Goth-king's honour, or let one fate go over all
If he bade them to battle and murder, till each by each should fall.   390
So spake the sons of his body, and the wise in wisdom and war.
Nor yet might it otherwise be, though Volsung bade full sore
That he go in some ship of the merchants with his life alone in his hand
With such love he loved his kindred, and the people of his land.
But at last he said:
                        'So be it; for in vain I war with fate,   395
Who can raise up a king from the dunghill and make the feeble great.
We will go, a band of friends, and be merry whatever shall come,
And the Gods, mine own forefathers, shall take counsel of our home.'

So now, when all things were ready, in the first of the autumn tide
Adown unto the swan-bath the Volsung Children ride;   400
And lightly go a shipboard, a goodly company,
Though the tale thereof be scanty and their ships no more than three:
But kings' sons dealt with the sail-sheets and earls and dukes of war
Were the halers of the hawsers and the tuggers at the oar.
So they drew the bridges shipward, and left the land behind,   405
And fair astern of the longships sprang up a following wind;
So swift o'er Ægir's acre those mighty sailors ran,
And speedier than all other ploughed down the furrows wan.
And they came to the land of the Goth-folk on the even of a day;
And lo by the inmost skerry a skiff with a sail of grey   410
That as they neared the foreshore ran Volsung's ship aboard,
And there was come white-hand Signy with her latest warning word.

'O strange,' she said, 'meseemeth, O sweet, your gear to see,
And the well-loved Volsung faces, and the hands that cherished me.
But short is the time that is left me for the work I have to win   415
Though nought it be but the speaking of a word ere the worst begin.
For that which I spake aforetime, the seed of a boding drear,
It hath sprung, it hath blossomed and born rank harvest of the spear:
Siggeir hath dight the death-snare; he hath spread the shielded net.
But ye come ere the hour appointed, and he looks not to meet you yet.   420
Now blest be the wind that wafted your sails here over-soon,
For thus have I won me seaward 'twixt the twilight and the moon,
To pray you for all the world's sake turn back from the murderous shore.
—Ah take me hence, my father, to see my land once more!'

Then sweetly Volsung kissed her: 'Woe am I for thy sake,   425
But Earth the word hath hearkened, that yet unborn I spake;
How I ne'er would turn me backward from the sword or the fire of bale;
—I have held that word till today, and today shall I change the tale?
And look on these thy brethren, how goodly and great are they,
Wouldst thou have the maidens mock them, when this pain hath
    past away   430
And they sit at the feast hereafter, that they feared the deadly stroke?
Let us do our day's work deftly for the praise and the glory of folk;
And if the Norns will have it that the Volsung kin shall fail,
Yet I know of the deed that dies not, and the name that shall ever avail.'

But she wept as one sick-hearted: 'Woe's me for the hope of the morn!   435
Yet send me not back unto Siggeir and the evil days and the scorn:
Let me bide the death as ye bide it, and let a woman feel
That hope of the death of battle and the rest of the foeman's steel.'

'Nay nay,' he said, 'go backward; this too thy fate will have;
For thou art the wife of a king, and many a matter mayst save.   440
Farewell! as the days win over, as sweet as a tale shall it grow,
This day when our hearts were hardened; and our glory thou shalt
    know,
And the love wherewith we loved thee mid the battle and the wrack.'

She kissed them and departed, and mid the dusk fared back,
And she sat that eve in the high-seat; and I deem that Siggeir knew   445
The way that her feet had wended, and the deed she went to do:
For the man was grim and guileful, and he knew that the snare was laid
For the mountain bull unblenching and the lion unafraid.

But when the sun on the morrow shone over earth and sea
Ashore went the Volsung Children a goodly company,   450
And toward King Siggeir's dwelling o'er heath and holt they went
But when they came to the topmost of a certain grassy bent,
Lo there lay the land before them as thick with shield and spear
As the rich man's wealthiest acre with the harvest of the year.
There bade King Volsung tarry and dight the wedge-array;   455
'For duly,' he said, 'doeth Siggeir to meet his guests by the way.'
So shield by shield they serried, nor ever hath been told
Of any host of battle more glorious with the gold;
And there stood the high King Volsung in the very front of war;
And lovelier was his visage than ever heretofore,   460
As he rent apart the peace-strings that his brand of battle bound
And the bright blade gleamed to the heavens, and he cast the sheath
    to the ground.

Then up the steep came the Goth-folk, and the spear-wood drew anigh,
And earth's face shook beneath them, yet cried they never a cry;
And the Volsungs stood all silent, although forsooth at whiles   465
O'er the faces grown earth-weary would play the flickering smiles,
And swords would clink and rattle: not long had they to bide,
For soon that flood of murder flowed round the hillock-side;
Then at last the edges mingled, and if men forebore the shout,
Yet the din of steel and iron in the grey clouds rang about;   470
But how to tell of King Volsung, and the valour of his folk!
Three times the wood of battle before their edges broke;
And the shield-wall, sorely dwindled and reft of the ruddy gold,
Against the drift of the war-blast for the fourth time yet did hold.
But men's shields were waxen heavy with the weight of shafts they bore   475
And the fifth time many a champion cast earthward Odin's door
And gripped the sword two-handed; and in sheaves the spears came on.
And at last the host of the Goth-folk within the shield-wall won,
And wild was the work within it, and oft and o'er again
Forth brake the sons of Volsung, and drave the foe in vain;   480
For the driven throng still thickened, till it might not give aback.
But fast abode King Volsung amid the shifting wrack
In the place where once was the forefront: for he said: 'My feet are old,
And if I wend on further there is nought more to behold
Than this that I see about me.'—Whiles drew his foes away   485
And stared across the corpses that before his sword-edge lay.
But nought he followed after: then needs must they in front
Thrust on by the thickening spear-throng come up to bear the brunt,
Till all his limbs were weary and his body rent and torn:
Then he cried: 'Lo now, Allfather, is not the swathe well shorn?   490
Wouldst thou have me toil for ever, nor win the wages due?'

And mid the hedge of foemen his blunted sword he threw,
And, laid like the oars of a longship the level war-shafts pressed
On 'gainst the unshielded elder, and clashed amidst his breast,
And dead he fell, thrust backward, and rang on the dead men's gear: 495
But still for a certain season durst no man draw anear.
For 'twas e'en as a great God's slaying, and they feared the wrath of the sky;
And they deemed their hearts might harden if awhile they should let him lie.

Lo, now as the plotting was long, so short is the tale to tell
How a mighty people's leaders in the field of murder fell.   500
For but feebly burned the battle when Volsung fell to field,
And all who yet were living were borne down before the shield:
So sinketh the din and the tumult; and the earls of the Goths ring round
That crown of the Kings of battle laid low upon the ground,

Looking up to the noon-tide heavens from the place where first he stood: 505
But the songful sing above him and they tell how his end is as good
As the best of the days of his life-tide; and well as he was loved
By his friends ere the time of his changing, so now are his foemen moved
With a love that may never be worsened, since all the strife is o'er,
And the warders look for his coming by Odin's open door.   510

But his sons, the stay of battle, alive with many a wound,
Borne down to the earth by the shield-rush amid the dead lie bound,
And belike a wearier journey must those lords of battle bide
Ere once more in the hall of Odin they sit by their father's side.
Woe's me for the boughs of the Branstock and the hawks that cried
   on the fight!   515
Woe's me for the fireless hearthstones and the hangings of delight,
That the women dare not look on, lest they see them sweat with blood!
Woe's me for the carven pillars where the spears of the Volsungs stood!
And who next shall shake the locks, or the silver door-rings meet?
Who shall pace the floor beloved, worn down by the Volsung feet?   520
Who shall fill the gold with the wine, or cry for the triumphing?
Shall it be kindred or foes, or thief, or thrall, or king?

Of the ending of all Volsung's sons save Sigmund only, and of how he abideth in the wild wood.

So there the earls of the Goth-folk lay Volsung 'neath the grass
On the last earth he had trodden; but his children bound must pass,
When the host is gathered together, amidst of their array   525
To the high-built dwelling of Siggeir; for sooth it is to say,
That he came not into the battle, nor faced the Volsung sword.
So now as he sat in his high-seat there came his chiefest lord,
And he said: 'I bear thee tidings of the death of the best of the brave,
For thy foes are slain or bondsmen; and have thou Sigmund's glaive,   530
If a token thou desirest; and that shall be surely enough.
And I do thee to wit, King Siggeir, that the road was exceeding rough,
And that many an earl there stumbled, who shall evermore lie down.
And indeed I deem King Volsung for all earthly kingship's crown.'

Then never a word spake Siggeir, save: 'Where be Volsung's sons?'   535
And he said: 'Without are they fettered, those battle-glorious ones:
And methinks 'twere a deed for a king, and a noble deed for thee,
To break their bonds and heal them, and send them back o'er the sea,
And abide their wrath and the bloodfeud for this matter of Volsung's slaying.'

'Witless thou waxest,' said Siggeir, 'nor heedest the wise man's saying;   540
"Slay thou the wolf by the house-door, lest he slay thee in the wood."

Yet since I am the overcomer, and my days henceforth shall be good,
I will quell them with no death-pains; let the young men smite them down,
But let me not behold them when my heart is angrier grown.'

E'en as he uttered the word was Signy at the door   545
And with hurrying feet she gat her apace to the high-seat floor,
As wan as the dawning-hour, though never a tear she had:
And she cried: 'I pray thee, Siggeir, now thine heart is merry and glad
With the death and the bonds of my kinsmen, to grant me this one prayer,
This one time and no other; let them breathe the earthly air   550
For a day, for a day or twain, ere they wend the way of death,
For "sweet to eye while seen," the elders' saying saith.'

Quoth he: 'Thou art mad with sorrow; wilt thou work thy friends this woe?
When swift and untormented e'en I would let them go:
Yet now shalt thou have thine asking, if it verily is thy will: 555
Nor forsooth do I begrudge them a longer tide of ill.'

She said: 'I will it, I will it—O sweet to eye while seen!'

Then to his earl spake Siggeir: 'There lies a wood-lawn green
In the first mile of the forest; there fetter these Volsung men
To the mightiest beam of the wild-wood, till Queen Signy come again   560
And pray me a boon for her brethren, the end of their latter life.'

So the Goth-folk led to the woodland those gleanings of the strife,
And smote down a great-boled oak-tree, the mightiest they might find,
And thereto with bonds of iron the Volsungs did they bind,
And left them there on the wood-lawn, mid the yew-trees' compassing,   565
And went back by the light of the moon to the dwelling of the king.

But he sent on the morn of the morrow to see how his foemen fared,
For now as he thought thereover, o'ermuch he deemed it dared
That he saw not the last of the Volsungs laid dead before his feet.
Back came his men ere the noontide, and he deemed their tidings sweet; 570
For they said: 'We tell thee, King Siggeir, that Geirmund and Gylfi are
    gone.
And we deem that a beast of the wild-wood this murder grim hath done,
For the bones yet lie in the fetters gnawed fleshless now and white;
But we deemed the eight abiding sore minished of their might.'

So wore the morn and the noontide, and the even 'gan to fall,   575
And watchful eyes held Signy at home in bower and hall.
And again came the men in the morning, and spake: 'The hopples hold
The bare white bones of Helgi, and the bones of Solar the bold:
And the six that abide seem feebler than they were a while ago.'

Still all the day and the night-tide must Signy nurse her woe   580
About the house of King Siggeir, nor any might she send:
And again came the tale on the morrow: 'Now are two more come to
    an end.
For Hunthiof dead and Gunthiof, their bones lie side by side,
And the four that are left, us seemeth, no long while will abide.'

O woe for the well-watched Signy, how often on that day   585
Must she send her helpless eyen adown the woodland way!
Yet silent in her bosom she held her heart of flame.
And again on the morrow morning the tale was still the same:

'We tell thee now, King Siggeir, that all will soon be done;
For the two last men of the Volsungs, they sit there one by one,   590
And Sigi's head is drooping, but somewhat Sigmund sings;
For the man was a mighty warrior and a beater down of kings.
But for Rerir and for Agnar, the last of them is said,
Their bones in the bonds are abiding, but their souls and lives are sped.'

That day from the eyes of the watchers nought Signy strove to depart,   595
But ever she sat in the high-seat and nursed the flame in her heart.
In the sight of all people she sat, with unmoved face and wan,
And to no man gave she a word, nor looked on any man.
Then the dusk and the dark drew over, but stirred she never a whit,
And the word of Siggeir's sending, she gave no heed to it.   600
And there on the morrow morning must he sit him down by her side,
When unto the council of elders folk came from far and wide.
And there came Siggeir's woodmen, and their voice in the hall arose:

'There is no man left on the tree-beam: some beast hath devoured thy foes;
There is nought left there but the bones, and the bonds that the
    Volsungs bound.'   605
No word spake the earls of the Goth-folk, but the hall rang out with
    a sound,
With the wail and the cry of Signy, as she stood upright on her feet,
And thrust all people from her, and fled to her bower as fleet
As the hind when she first is smitten; and her maidens fled away,
Fearing her face and her eyen: no less at the death of the day   610
She rose up amid the silence, and went her ways alone,
And no man watched her or hindered, for they deemed the story done.
So she went 'twixt the yellow acres, and the green meads of the sheep,
And or ever she reached the wild-wood the night was waxen deep.
No man she had to lead her, but the path was trodden well   615
By those messengers of murder, the men with the tale to tell;
And the beams of the high white moon gave a glimmering day through night

Till she came where that lawn of the woods lay wide in the flood of light.
Then she looked, and lo, in its midmost a mighty man there stood,
And laboured the earth of the green-sward with a truncheon torn
    from the wood;   620
And behold, it was Sigmund the Volsung: but she cried and had no fear:

'If thou art living, Sigmund, what day's work dost thou here
In the midnight and the forest? but if thou art nought but a ghost,
Then where are those Volsung brethren, of whom thou wert best
    and most?'

Then he turned about unto her, and his raiment was fouled and torn,   625
And his eyen were great and hollow, as a famished man forlorn;
But he cried: 'Hail, Sister Signy! I looked for thee before,
Though what should a woman compass, she one alone and no more,
When all we shielded Volsungs did nought in Siggeir's land?
O yea, I am living indeed, and this labour of mine hand   630
Is to bury the bones of the Volsungs; and lo, it is well-nigh done.
So draw near, Volsung's daughter, and pile we many a stone
Where lie the grey wolf's gleanings of what was once so good.'

So she set her hand to the labour, and they toiled, they twain in
    the wood
And when the work was over, dead night was beginning to fail: 635
Then spake the white-hand Signy: 'Now shalt thou tell the tale
Of the death of the Volsung brethren ere the wood thy wrath shall hide,
Ere I wend me back sick-hearted in the dwelling of kings to abide.'

He said: 'We sat on the tree, and well ye may wot indeed
That we had some hope from thy good-will amidst that bitter need.   640
Now none had 'scaped the sword-edge in the battle utterly,
And so hurt were Agnar and Helgi, that, unhelped, they were like to die;
Though for that we deemed them happier: but now when the moon
    shone bright,
And when by a doomed man's deeming 'twas the midmost of the night,
Lo, forth from yonder thicket were two mighty wood-wolves come,   645
Far huger wrought to my deeming than the beasts I knew at home:
Forthright on Gylfi and Geirmund those dogs of the forest fell,
And what of men so hoppled should be the tale to tell?
They tore them midst the irons, and slew them then and there,
And long we heard them snarling o'er that abundant cheer.   650
Night after night, O my sister, the story was the same,
And still from the dark and the thicket the wild-wood were-wolves came
And slew two men of the Volsungs whom the sword edge might not end.
And every day in the dawning did the King's own woodmen wend

To behold those craftsmen's carving and rejoice King Siggeir's heart.   655
And so was come last midnight, when I must play my part:
Forsooth when those first were murdered my heart was as blood and fire;
And I deemed that my bonds must burst with my uttermost desire
To free my naked hands, that the vengeance might be wrought;
But now was I wroth with the Gods, that had made the Volsungs
    for nought;   660
And I said: in the Day of their Doom a man's help shall they miss;
I will be as a wolf of the forest, if their kings must come to this;
Or if Siggeir indeed be their king, and their envy has brought it about
That dead in the dust lies Volsung, while the last of his seed dies out.
Therewith from out the thicket the grey wolves drew anigh,   665
And the he-wolf fell on Sigi, but he gave forth never a cry,
And I saw his lips that they smiled, and his steady eyes for a space:
And therewith was the she-wolf's muzzle thrust into my very face.
The Gods helped not, but I helped; and I too grew wolfish then;
Yea I, who have borne the sword-hilt high mid the kings of men,   670
I, lord of the golden harness, the flame of the Glittering Heath,
Must snarl to the she-wolf's snarling, and snap with greedy teeth
While my hands with the hand-bonds struggled; my teeth took hold
    the first
And amid her mighty writhing the bonds that bound me burst,
As with Fenrir's Wolf it shall be: then the beast with the hopples I smote,   675
When my left hand stiff with the bonds had got her by the throat.
But I turned when I had slain her, and there lay Sigi dead,
And once more to the night of the forest the fretting wolf had fled.
In the thicket I hid till the dawning, and thence I saw the men,
E'en Siggeir's heart-rejoicers, come back to the place again   680
To gather the well-loved tidings: I looked and I knew for sooth
How hate had grown in my bosom and the death of my days of ruth:
Though unslain they departed from me, lest Siggeir come to doubt.
But hereafter, yea hereafter, they that turned the world about,
And raised Hell's abode o'er God-home, and mocked all men-folk's
    worth—   685
Shall my hand turn back or falter, while these abide on earth,
Because I once was a child, and sat on my father's knees?
But long methinks shall Siggeir bide merrily at ease
In the high-built house of the Goths, with his shielded earls around,
His warders of day and of night-tide, and his world of peopled
    ground,   690
While his foe is a swordless outcast, a hunted beast of the wood,
A wolf of the holy places, where men-folk gather for good.

And didst thou think, my sister, when we sat in our summer bliss
Beneath the boughs of the Branstock, that the world was like to this?'

As the moon and the twilight mingled, she stood with kindling eyes,   695
And answered and said: 'My brother, thou art strong, and thou shalt
    be wise:
I am nothing so wroth as thou art with the ways of death and hell,
For thereof had I a deeming when all things were seeming well.
In sooth overlong it may linger; the children of murder shall thrive,
While thy work is a weight for thine heart, and a toil for thy hand to drive;   700
But I wot that the King of the Goth-folk for his deeds shall surely pay,
And that I shall live to see it: but thy wrath shall pass away,
And long shalt thou live on the earth an exceeding glorious king,
And thy words shall be told in the market, and all men of thy deeds
    shall sing:
Fresh shall thy memory be, and thine eyes like mine shall gaze   705
On the day unborn in the darkness, the last of all earthly days,
The last of the days of battle, when the host of the Gods is arrayed
And there is an end for ever of all who were once afraid.
There as thou drawest thy sword, thou shalt think of the days that were,
And the foul shall still seem foul, and the fair shall still seem fair;   710
But thy wit shall then be awakened, and thou shalt know indeed
Why the brave man's spear is broken, and his war-shield fails at need;
Why the loving is unbelovèd; why the just man falls from his state;
Why the liar gains in a day what the soothfast strives for late.
Yea, and thy deeds shalt thou know, and great shall thy gladness be;   715
As a picture all of gold thy life-days shalt thou see,
And know that thou too wert a God to abide through the hurry and
    haste;
A God in the golden hall, a God on the rain-swept waste,
A God in the battle triumphant, a God on the heap of the slain:
And thine hope shall arise and blossom, and thy love shall be quickened
    again: 720
And then shalt thou see before thee the face of all earthly ill;
Thou shalt drink of the cup of awakening that thine hand hath holpen
    to fill;
By the side of the sons of Odin shalt thou fashion a tale to be told
In the hall of the happy Baldur: nor there shall the tale grow old
Of the days before the changing, e'en those that over us pass.   725
So harden thine heart, O brother, and set thy brow as the brass!
Thou shalt do, and thy deeds shall be goodly, and the day's work
    shall be done,
Though nought but the wild deer see it. Nor yet shalt thou be alone

For ever-more in thy waiting; for belike a fearful friend
The long days for thee may fashion, to help thee ere the end.   730
But now shalt thou bide in the wild-wood, and make thee a lair therein:
Thou art here in the midst of thy foemen, and from them thou well
    mayst win
Whatso thine heart desireth; yet be thou not too bold,
Lest the tale of the wood-abider too oft to the king be told.
Ere many days are departed again shall I see thy face,   735
That I may wot full surely of thine abiding-place
To send thee help and comfort; but when that hour is o'er
It were good, O last of the Volsungs, that I see thy face no more,
If so indeed it may be: but the Norns must fashion all,
And what the dawn hath fated on the hour of noon shall fall.'   740

Then she kissed him and departed, for the day was nigh at hand,
And by then she had left the woodways green lay the horse-fed land
Beneath the new-born daylight, and as she brushed the dew
Betwixt the yellowing acres, all heaven o'erhead was blue.
And at last on that dwelling of Kings the golden sunlight lay,   745
And the morn and the noon and the even built up another day.

Of the birth and fostering of Sinfiotli, Signy's son.

So wrought is the will of King Siggeir, and he weareth Odin's sword,
And it lies on his knees in the council and hath no other lord:
And he sendeth earls o'er the sea-flood to take King Volsung's land,
And those scattered and shepherdless sheep must come beneath
    his hand.   750
And he holdeth the milk-white Signy as his handmaid and his wife,
And nought but his will she doeth, nor raiseth a word of strife;
So his heart is praising his wisdom, and he deems him of most avail
Of all the lords of the cunning that teacheth how to prevail.

Now again in a half-month's wearing goes Signy into the wild,   755
And findeth her way by her wisdom to the dwelling of Volsung's child.
It was e'en as a house of the Dwarfs, a rock, and a stony cave,
In the heart of the midmost thicket by the hidden river's wave.
There Signy found him watching how the white-head waters ran,
And she said in her heart as she saw him that once more she had
    seen a man.   760
His words were few and heavy, for seldom his sorrow slept,
Yet ever his love went with them; and men say that Signy wept
When she left that last of her kindred: yet wept she never more
Amid the earls of Siggeir, and as lovely as before

Was her face to all men's deeming: nor aught it changed for ruth,   765
Nor for fear nor any longing; and no man said for sooth
That she ever laughed thereafter till the day of her death was come.

So is Volsung's seed abiding in a rough and narrow home;
And wargear he gat him enough from the slaying of earls of men,
And gold as much as he would; though indeed but now and again   770
He fell on the men of the merchants, lest, wax he overbold,
The tale of the wood-abider too oft to the king should be told.
Alone in the woods he abided, and a master of masters was he
In the craft of the smithying folk; and whiles would the hunter see,
Belated amid the thicket, his forge's glimmering light,   775
And the boldest of all the fishers would hear his hammer benight.
Then dim waxed the tale of the Volsungs, and the word mid the wood-folk rose
That a King of the Giants had wakened from amidst the stone-hedged
    close
Where they slept in the heart of the mountains, and had come adown
    to dwell
In the cave whence the Dwarfs were departed, and they said: It is
    aught but well   780
To come anigh to his house-door, or wander wide in his woods,
For a tyrannous lord he is, and a lover of gold and of goods.

So win the long years over, and still sitteth Signy there
Beside the King of the Goth-folk, and is waxen no less fair,
And men and maids hath she gotten who are ready to work her will,   785
For the worship of her fairness, and remembrance of her ill.

So it fell on a morn of springtide, as Sigmund sat on the sward
By that ancient house of the Dwarf-kind and fashioned a golden sword,
By the side of the hidden river he saw a damsel stand,
And a manchild of ten summers was holding by her hand.   790
And she cried:
         'O Forest-dweller! harm not the child nor me,
For I bear a word of Signy's, and thus she saith to thee:
"I send thee a man to foster; if his heart be good at need
Then may he help thy workday; but hearken my words and heed;
If thou deem that his heart shall avail not, thy work is overgreat   795
That thou weary thy heart with such-like: let him wend the ways
    of his fate." '

And no more word spake the maiden, but turned and gat her gone,
And there by the side of the river the child abode alone:
But Sigmund stood on his feet, and across the river he went.
For he knew how the child was Siggeir's, and of Signy's fell intent.   800

So he took the lad on his shoulder, and bade him hold his sword,
And waded back to his dwelling across the rushing ford:
But the youngling fell a-prattling, and asked of this and that,
As above the rattle of waters on Sigmund's shoulder he sat;
And Sigmund deemed in his heart that the boy would be bold enough,   805
So he fostered him there in the woodland in life full hard and rough
For the space of three months' wearing; and the lad was deft and strong,
Yet his sight was a grief to Sigmund because of his father's wrong.

On a morn to the son of King Siggeir Sigmund the Volsung said:
'I go to the hunting of deer, bide thou and bake our bread   810
Against I bring the venison.'
                            So forth he fared on his way,
And came again with the quarry about the noon of day;
Quoth he: 'Is the morn's work done?' But the boy said nought for a space,
And all white he was and quaking as he looked on Sigmund's face.

'Tell me, O Son of the Goth-king,' quoth Sigmund, 'how thou hast fared?   815
Forsooth, is the baking of bread so mighty a thing to be dared?'

Quoth the lad: 'I went to the meal-sack, and therein was something quick,
And it moved, and I feared for the serpent, like a winter ashen stick
That I saw on the stone last even: so I durst not deal with the thing.'

Loud Sigmund laughed, and answered: 'I have heard of that son of a king,   820
Who might not be scared from his bread for all the worms of the land.'
And therewith he went to the meal-sack and thrust therein his hand,
And drew forth an ash-grey adder, and a deadly worm it was:
Then he went to the door of the cave and set it down in the grass,
While the King's son quaked and quivered: then he drew forth his
     sword from the sheath,   825
And said:
            'Now fearest thou this, that men call the serpent of death?'
Then said the son of King Siggeir: 'I am young as yet for the war,
Yet e'en such a blade shall I carry ere many a month be o'er.'

Then abroad went the King in the wind, and leaned on his naked sword
And stood there many an hour, and mused on Signy's word.   830
But at last when the moon was arisen, and the undark night begun,
He sheathed the sword and cried: 'Come forth, King Siggeir's son,
Thou shalt wend from out of the wild-wood and no more will I foster
     thee.'

Forth came the son of Siggeir, and quaked his face to see,
But thereof nought Sigmund noted, but bade him wend with him.   835

So they went through the summer night-tide by many a wood-way dim,
Till they came to a certain wood-lawn, and Sigmund lingered there,
And spake as his feet brushed o'er it: 'The June flowers blossom fair.'
So they came to the skirts of the forest, and the meadows of the neat,
And the earliest wind of dawning blew over them soft and sweet: 840
There stayed Sigmund the Volsung, and said:
                                           'King Siggeir's son,
Bide here till the birds are singing, and the day is well begun;
Then go to the house of the Goth-king, and find thou Signy the Queen,
And tell unto no man else the things thou hast heard and seen:
But to her shalt thou tell what thou wilt, and say this word withal: 845
"Mother, I come from the wild-wood, and he saith, whatever befal
Alone will I abide there, nor have such fosterlings;
For the sons of the Gods may help me, but never the sons of Kings."
Go, then, with this word in thy mouth—or do thou after thy fate,
And, if thou wilt, betray me!—and repent it early and late.'   850

Then he turned his back on the acres, and away to the woodland
      strode;
But the boy scarce bided the sunrise ere he went the homeward road;
So he came to the house of the Goth-kings, and spake with Signy the
      Queen,
Nor told he to any other the things he had heard and seen,
For the heart of a king's son had he.
                                        But Signy hearkened his word;   855
And long she pondered and said: 'What is it my heart hath feared?
And how shall it be with earth's people if the kin of the Volsungs die,
And King Volsung unavenged in his mound by the sea-strand lie?
I have given my best and bravest, as my heart's blood I would give,
And my heart and my fame and my body, that the name of Volsung
      might live.   860
Lo the first gift cast aback: and how shall it be with the last,—
—If I find out the gift for the giving before the hour be passed?'

Long while she mused and pondered while day was thrust on day,
Till the king and the earls of the strangers seemed shades of the
      dreamtide grey,
And gone seemed all earth's people, save that woman mid the gold   865
And that man in the depths of the forest in the cave of the Dwarfs of old.
And once in the dark she murmured: 'Where then was the ancient song
That the Gods were but twin-born once, and deemed it nothing wrong
To mingle for the world's sake, whence had the Æsir birth,
And the Vanir and the Dwarf-kind, and all the folk of earth?'   870

Now amidst those days that she pondered came a wife of the witch-folk
    there,
A woman young and lovesome, and shaped exceeding fair,
And she spake with Signy the Queen, and told her of deeds of her craft,
And how the might was with her her soul from her body to waft
And to take the shape of another and give her fashion in turn.   875
Fierce then in the heart of Signy a sudden flame 'gan burn,
And the eyes of her soul saw all things, like the blind, whom the world's
    last fire
Hath healed in one passing moment 'twixt his death and his desire.
And she thought: 'Alone I will bear it; alone I will take the crime;
On me alone be the shaming, and the cry of the coming time.   880
Yea, and he for the life is fated and the help of many a folk,
And I for the death and the rest, and deliverance from the yoke.'

Then wan as the midnight moon she answered the woman and spake:
'Thou art come to the Goth-queen's dwelling, wilt thou do so much for
    my sake,
And for many a pound of silver and for rings of the ruddy gold,   885
As to change thy body for mine ere the night is waxen old?'

Nought the witch-wife fair gainsaid it, and they went to the bower aloft
And hand in hand and alone they sung the spell-song soft:
Till Signy looked on her guest, and, lo, the face of a queen
With the steadfast eyes of grey, that so many a grief had seen: 890
But the guest held forth a mirror, and Signy shrank aback
From the laughing lips and the eyes, and the hair of crispy black,
But though she shuddered and sickened, the false face changed no whit;
But ruddy and white it blossomed and the smiles played over it;
And the hands were ready to cling, and beckoning lamps were the eyes,   895
And the light feet longed for the dance, and the lips for laughter and lies.

So that eve in the mid-hall's high-seat was the shape of Signy the Queen,
While swiftly the feet of the witch-wife brushed over the moonlit green,
But the soul mid the gleam of the torches, her thought was of gain and
    of gold;
And the soul of the wind-driven woman, swift-foot in the moonlight
    cold,   900
Her thoughts were of men's lives' changing, and the uttermost ending
    of earth,
And the day when death should be dead, and the new sun's nightless
    birth.

Men say that about that midnight King Sigmund wakened and heard
The voice of a soft-speeched woman, shrill-sweet as a dawning bird:

So he rose, and a woman indeed he saw by the door of the cave   905
With her raiment wet to her midmost, as though with the river-wave:
And he cried: 'What wilt thou, what wilt thou? be thou womankind or fay,
Here is no good abiding, wend forth upon thy way!'

She said: 'I am nought but a woman, a maid of the earl-folk's kin:
And I went by the skirts of the woodland to the house of my sister
    to win,   910
And have strayed from the way benighted: and I fear the wolves and the wild:
By the glimmering of thy torchlight from afar was I beguiled.
Ah, slay me not on thy threshold, nor send me back again
Through the rattling waves of thy ford, that I crossed in terror and pain;
Drive me not to the night and the darkness, for the wolves of the
    wood to devour.   915
I am weak and thou art mighty: I will go at the dawning hour.'

So Sigmund looked in her face and saw that she was fair;
And he said: 'Nay nought will I harm thee, and thou mayst harbour here,
God wot if thou fear'st not me, I have nought to fear thy face:
Though this house be the terror of men-folk, thou shalt find it as safe
    a place   920
As though I were nought but thy brother; and then mayst thou tell, if
    thou wilt,
Where dwelleth the dread of the woodland, the bearer of many a guilt,
Though meseems for so goodly a woman it were all too ill a deed
In reward for the wood-wight's guesting to betray him in his need.'

So he took the hand of the woman and straightway led her in   925
Where days agone the Dwarf-kind would their deeds of smithying win:
And he kindled the half-slaked embers, and gave her of his cheer
Amid the gold and the silver, and the fight-won raiment dear;
And soft was her voice, and she sung him sweet tales of yore agone,
Till all his heart was softened; and the man was all alone,   930
And in many wise she wooed him; so they parted not that night,
Nor slept till the morrow morning, when the woods were waxen bright:
And high above the tree-boughs shone the sister of the moon,
And hushed were the water-ouzels with the coming of the noon
When she stepped from the bed of Sigmund, and left the Dwarf's abode; 935
And turned to the dwellings of men, and the ways where the earl-folk rode.
But next morn from the house of the Goth-king the witch-wife went
    her ways
With gold and goods and silver, such store as a queen might praise.

But no long while with Sigmund dwelt remembrance of that night;
Amid his kingly longings and his many deeds of might   940

It fled like the dove in the forest or the down upon the blast:
Yet heavy and sad were the years, that even in suchwise passed,
As here it is written aforetime.
                              Thence were ten years worn by
When unto that hidden river a man-child drew anigh,
And he looked and beheld how Sigmund wrought on a helm of gold   945
By the crag and the stony dwelling where the Dwarf-kin wrought of old.
Then the boy cried: 'Thou art the wood-wight of whom my mother spake;
Now will I come to thy dwelling.'
                              So the rough stream did he take,
And the welter of the waters rose up to his chin and more;
But so stark and strong he waded that he won the further shore: 950
And he came and gazed on Sigmund: but the Volsung laughed, and said:
'As fast thou runnest toward me as others in their dread
Run over the land and the water: what wilt thou, son of a king?'

But the lad still gazed on Sigmund, and he said: 'A wondrous thing!
Here is the cave and the river, and all tokens of the place: 955
But my mother Signy told me none might behold that face,
And keep his flesh from quaking: but at thee I quake not aught:
Sure I must journey further, lest her errand come to nought:
Yet I would that my foster-father should be such a man as thou.'

But Sigmund answered and said: 'Thou shalt bide in my dwelling now;   960
And thou mayst wot full surely that thy mother's will is done
By this token and no other, that thou lookedst on Volsung's son
And smiledst fair in his face: but tell me thy name and thy years;
And what are the words of Signy that the son of the Goth-king bears?'

'Sinfiotli they call me,' he said, 'and ten summers have I seen;   965
And this is the only word that I bear from Signy the Queen,
That once more a man she sendeth the work of thine hands to speed,
If he be of the Kings or the Gods thyself shalt know in thy need.'

So Sigmund looked on the youngling and his heart unto him yearned;
But he thought; 'Shall I pay the hire ere the worth of the work be earned?   970
And what hath my heart to do to cherish Siggeir's son;
A brand belike for the burning when the last of its work is done?'

But there in the wild and the thicket those twain awhile abode,
And on the lad laid Sigmund full many a weary load,
And thrust him mid all dangers, and he bore all passing well,   975
Where hardihood might help him; but his heart was fierce and fell;
And ever said Sigmund the Volsung: The lad hath plenteous part
In the guile and malice of Siggeir, and in Signy's hardy heart:
But why should I cherish and love him, since the end must come at last?'

Now a summer and winter and spring o'er those men of the wilds had   980
    pass'd.
And summer was there again, when the Volsung spake on a day:
'I will wend to the wood-deer's hunting, but thou at home shalt stay,
And deal with the baking of bread against the even come.'

So he went and came on the hunting and brought the venison home,
And the child, as ever his wont was, was glad of his coming back,   985
And said: 'Thou hast gotten us venison, and the bread shall nowise lack.'
'Yea,' quoth Sigmund the Volsung, 'hast thou kneaded the meal that was
    yonder?'

'Yea, and what other?' he said; 'though therein forsooth was a wonder:
For when I would handle the meal-sack therein was something quick,
As if the life of an eel-grig were set in an ashen stick: 990
But the meal must into the oven, since we were lacking bread,
And all that is kneaded together, and the wonder is baked and dead.'

Then Sigmund laughed and answered: 'Thou hast kneaded up therein
The deadliest of all adders that is of the creeping kin:
So tonight from the bread refrain thee, lest thy bane should come of it.'   995

For here, the tale of the elders doth men a marvel to wit,
That such was the shaping of Sigmund among all earthly kings,
That unhurt he handled adders and other deadly things,
And might drink unscathed of venom: but Sinfiotli so was wrought,
That no sting of creeping creatures would harm his body aught.   1000

But now full glad was Sigmund, and he let his love arise
For the huge-limbed son of Signy with the fierce and eager eyes;
And all deeds of the sword he learned him, and showed him feats of war
Where sea and forest mingle, and up from the ocean's shore
The highway leads to the market, and men go up and down,   1005
And the spear-hedged wains of the merchants fare oft to the Goth-folk's
    town.
Sweet then Sinfiotli deemed it to look on the bale-fires' light,
And the bickering blood-reeds' tangle, and the fallow blades of fight.
And in three years' space were his war-deeds far more than the deeds of
    a man:
But dread was his face to behold ere the battle-play began,   1010
And grey and dreadful his face when the last of the battle sank.
And so the years won over, and the joy of the woods they drank,
And they gathered gold and silver, and plenteous outland goods.

But they came to a house on a day in the uttermost part of the woods
And smote on the door and entered, when a long while no man bade;   1015

And lo, a gold-hung hall, and two men on the benches laid
In slumber as deep as the death; and gold-rings great and fair
Those sleepers bore on their bodies, and broidered southland gear,
And over the head of each there hung a wolf-skin grey.

Then the drift of a cloudy dream rapt Sigmund's soul away,   1020
And his eyes were set on the wolf-skin, and long he gazed thereat,
And remembered the words he uttered when erst on the beam he sat,
That the Gods should miss a man in the utmost Day of Doom,
And win a wolf in his stead; and unto his heart came home
That thought, as he gazed on the wolf-skin and the other days
    waxed dim,   1025
And he gathered the thing in his hand, and did it over him;
And in likewise did Sinfiotli as he saw his fosterer do.
Then lo, a fearful wonder, for as very wolves they grew
In outward shape and semblance, and they howled out wolfish things,
Like the grey dogs of the forest; though somewhat the hearts of kings   1030
Abode in their bodies of beasts. Now sooth is the tale to tell,
That the men in the fair-wrought raiment were kings' sons bound
    by a spell
To wend as wolves of the wild-wood, for each nine days of the ten,
And to lie all spent for a season when they gat their shapes of men.

So Sigmund and his fellow rush forth from the golden place;   1035
And though their kings' hearts bade them the backward way to trace
Unto their Dwarf-wrought dwelling, and there abide the change,
Yet their wolfish habit drave them wide through the wood to range,
And draw nigh to the dwellings of men and fly upon the prey.

And lo now, a band of hunters on the uttermost woodland way,   1040
And they spy those dogs of the forest, and fall on with the spear,
Nor deemed that any other but woodland beasts they were,
And that easy would be the battle: short is the tale to tell;
For every man of the hunters amid the thicket fell.

Then onwards fare those were-wolves, and unto the sea they turn,   1045
And their ravening hearts are heavy, and sore for the prey they yearn:
And lo, in the last of the thicket a score of the chaffering men,
And Sinfiotli was wild for the onset, but Sigmund was wearying then
For the glimmering gold of his Dwarf-house, and he bade refrain
    from the folk,
But wrath burned in the eyes of Sinfiotli, and forth from the thicket
    he broke;   1050
Then rose the axes aloft, and the swords flashed bright in the sun,
And but little more it needed that the race of the Volsungs was done,

And the folk of the Gods' begetting: but at last they quelled the war,
And no man again of the sea-folk should ever sit by the oar.

Now Sinfiotli lay weary and faint, but Sigmund howled over the dead,   1055
And wrath in his heart there gathered, and a dim thought wearied
    his head
And his tangled wolfish wit, that might never understand;
As though some God in his dreaming had wasted the work of his hand,
And forgotten his craft of creation; then his wrath swelled up amain
And he turned and fell on Sinfiotli, who had wrought the wrack
    and the bane   1060
And across the throat he tore him as his very mortal foe
Till a cold dead corpse by the sea-strand his fosterling lay alow:
Then wearier yet grew Sigmund, and the dim wit seemed to pass
From his heart grown cold and feeble: when lo, amid the grass
There came two weazles bickering, and one bit his mate by the head,   1065
Till she lay there dead before him: then he sorrowed over her dead;
But no long while he abode there, but into the thicket he went,
And the wolfish heart of Sigmund knew somewhat his intent:
So he came again with a herb-leaf and laid it on his mate,
And she rose up whole and living and no worser of estate   1070
Than ever she was aforetime, and the twain went merry away.

Then swiftly rose up Sigmund from where his fosterling lay,
And a long while searched the thicket, till that three-leaved herb
    he found,
And he laid it on Sinfiotli, who rose up hale and sound
As ever he was in his life-days. But now in hate they had   1075
That hapless work of the witch-folk, and the skins that their
    bodies clad.
So they turn their faces homeward and a weary way they go,
Till they come to the hidden river, and the glimmering house they know.

There now they abide in peace, and wend abroad no more
Till the last of the nine days perished, and the spell for a space was o'er,   1080
And they might cast their wolf-shapes: so they stood on their
    feet upright
Great men again as aforetime, and they came forth into the light
And looked in each other's faces, and belike a change was there
Since they did on the bodies of wolves, and lay in the wood-wolves' lair,
And they looked, and sore they wondered, and they both for speech
    did yearn.   1085

First then spake out Sinfiotli: 'Sure I had a craft to learn,
And thou hadst a lesson to teach, that I left the dwelling of kings,

And came to the wood-wolves' dwelling; thou hast taught me many
   things
But the Gods have taught me more, and at last have abased us both,
That of nought that lieth before us our hearts and our hands may be loth.   1090
Come then, how long shall I tarry till I fashion something great?
Come, Master, and make me a master that I do the deeds of fate.'

Heavy was Sigmund's visage but fierce did his eyen glow,
'This is the deed of thy mastery;—we twain shall slay my foe—
And how if the foe were thy father?'
                       —Then he telleth him Siggeir's tale: 1095
And saith: 'Now think upon it; how shall thine heart avail
To bear the curse that cometh if thy life endureth long—
The man that slew his father and amended wrong with wrong?
Yet if the Gods have made thee a man unlike all men,
(For thou startest not, nor palest), can I forbear it then,   1100
To use the thing they have fashioned lest the Volsung seed should die
And unavenged King Volsung in his mound by the sea-strand lie?'

Then loud laughed out Sinfiotli, and he said: 'I wot indeed
That Signy is my mother, and her will I help at need:
Is the fox of the King-folk my father, that adder of the brake,   1105
Who gave me never a blessing, and many a cursing spake?
Yea, have I in sooth a father, save him that cherished my life,
The Lord of the Helm of Terror, the King of the Flame of Strife?
Lo now my hand is ready to strike what stroke thou wilt,
For I am the sword of the Gods: and thine hand shall hold the hilt.'   1110

Fierce glowed the eyes of King Sigmund, for he knew the time
   was come
When the curse King Siggeir fashioned at last shall seek him home:
And of what shall follow after, be it evil days, or bliss,
Or praise, or the cursing of all men,—the Gods shall see to this.

Of the slaying of Siggeir the Goth-king.

So there are those kings abiding, and they think of nought but the day   1115
When the time at last shall serve them, to wend on the perilous way.
And so in the first of winter, when nights grow long and mirk,
They fare unto Siggeir's dwelling and seek wherein to lurk.
And by hap 'twas the tide of twilight, ere the watch of the night was set
And the watch of the day was departed, as Sinfiotli minded yet.   1120
So now by a passage he wotted they gat them into the bower
Where lay the biggest wine-tuns, and there they abode the hour:
Anigh to the hall it was, but no man came thereto,

But now and again the cup-lord when King Siggeir's wine he drew:
Yea and so nigh to the feast-hall, that they saw the torches shine   1125
When the cup-lord was departed with King Siggeir's dear-bought wine,
And they heard the glee of the people, and the horns and the beakers' din,
When the feast was dight in the hall and the earls were merry therein.
Calm was the face of Sigmund, and clear were his eyes and bright;
But Sinfiotli gnawed on his shield-rim, and his face was haggard
     and white: 1130
For he deemed the time full long, ere the fallow blades should leap
In the hush of the midnight feast-hall o'er King Siggeir's golden sleep.

Now it fell that two little children, Queen Signy's youngest-born,
Were about the hall that even, and amid the glee of the horn
They played with a golden toy, and trundled it here and there,   1135
And thus to that lurking-bower they drew exceeding near,
When there fell a ring from their toy, and swiftly rolled away
And into the place of the wine-tuns, and by Sigmund's feet made stay;
Then the little ones followed after, and came to the lurking-place
Where lay those night-abiders, and met them face to face,   1140
And fled, ere they might hold them, aback to the thronging hall.

Then leapt those twain to their feet lest the sword and the murder fall
On their hearts in their narrow lair and they die without a stroke;
But e'en as they met the torch-light and the din and tumult of folk
Lo there on the very threshold did Signy the Volsung stand,   1145
And one of her last-born children she had on either hand:
For the children had cried: 'We have seen them—those two among the wine,
And their hats are wide and white, and their garments tinkle and shine.'
So while men ran to their weapons, those children Signy took
And went to meet her kinsmen: then once more did Sigmund look   1150
On the face of his father's daughter, and kind of heart he grew,
As the clash of the coming battle anigh the doomed men drew:
But wan and fell was Signy; and she cried:
                                   'The end is near!
—And thou with the smile on thy face and the joyful eyes and clear!
But with these thy two betrayers first stain the edge of fight,   1155
For why should the fruit of my body outlive my soul tonight?'

But he cried in the front of the spear-hedge: 'Nay this shall be far from me
To slay thy children sackless, though my death belike they be.
Now men will be dealing, sister, and old the night is grown,
And fair in the house of my fathers the benches are bestrown.'   1160

So she stood aside and gazed: but Sinfiotli taketh them up
And breaketh each tender body as a drunkard breaketh a cup;

With a dreadful voice he crieth, and casteth them down the hall,
And the Goth-folk sunder before them, and at Siggeir's feet they fall.

But the fallow blades leapt naked, and on the battle came,   1165
As the tide of the winter ocean sweeps up to the beaconing flame.
But firm in the midst of onset Sigmund the Volsung stood,
And stirred no more for the sword-strokes than the oldest oak of
    the wood
Shall shake to the herd-boys' whittles: white danced his war-flame's
    gleam,
And oft to men's beholding his eyes of God would beam   1170
Clear from the sword-blades' tangle, and often for a space
Amazed the garth of murder stared deedless on his face;
Nor back nor forward moved he: but fierce Sinfiotli went
Where the spears were set the thickest, and sword with sword was blent;
And great was the death before him, till he slipped in the blood and fell: 1175
Then the shield-garth compassed Sigmund, and short is the tale to tell;
For they bore him down unwounded, and bonds about him cast:
Nor sore hurt is Sinfiotli, but is hoppled strait and fast.

Then the Goth-folk went to slumber when the hall was washed
    from blood:
But a long while wakened Siggeir, for fell and fierce was his mood,   1180
And all the days of his kingship seemed nothing worth as then
While fared the son of Volsung as well as the worst of men,
While yet that son of Signy lay untormented there:
Yea the past days of his kingship seemed blossomless and bare
Since all their might had failed him to quench the Volsung kin.   1185

So when the first grey dawning a new day did begin,
King Siggeir bade his bondsmen to dight an earthen mound
Anigh to the house of the Goth-kings amid the fruit-grown ground:
And that house of death was twofold, for 'twas sundered by a stone
Into two woeful chambers: alone and not alone   1190
Those vanquished thralls of battle therein should bide their hour,
That each might hear the tidings of the other's baleful bower,
Yet have no might to help him. So now the twain they brought
And weary-dull was Sinfiotli, with eyes that looked at nought.
But Sigmund fresh and clear-eyed went to the deadly hall,   1195
And the song arose within him as he sat within its wall;
Nor aught durst Siggeir mock him, as he had good will to do,
But went his ways when the bondmen brought the roofing turfs thereto.

And that was at eve of the day; and lo now, Signy the white
Wan-faced and eager-eyed stole through the beginning of night   1200

To the place where the builders built, and the thralls with lingering hands
Had roofed in the grave of Sigmund and hidden the glory of lands,
But over the head of Sinfiotli for a space were the rafters bare.
Gold then to the thralls she gave, and promised them days full fair
If they held their peace for ever of the deed that then she did: 1205
And nothing they gainsayed it; so she drew forth something hid,
In wrappings of wheat-straw winded, and into Sinfiotli's place
She cast it all down swiftly; then she covereth up her face
And beneath the winter starlight she wendeth swift away.
But her gift do the thralls deem victual, and the thatch on the hall they lay,   1210
And depart, they too, to their slumber, now dight was the dwelling
    of death.

Then Sigmund hears Sinfiotli, how he cries through the stone and saith:
'Best unto babe is mother, well sayeth the elder's saw;
Here hath Signy sent me swine's-flesh in windings of wheaten straw.'

And again he held him silent of bitter words or of sweet;   1215
And quoth Sigmund, 'What hath betided? is an adder in the meat?'
Then loud his fosterling laughed: 'Yea, a worm of bitter tooth,
The serpent of the Branstock, the sword of thy days of youth!
I have felt the hilts aforetime; I have felt how the letters run
On each side of the trench of blood and the point of that glorious one.   1220
O mother, O mother of kings! we shall live and our days shall be sweet.
I have loved thee well aforetime, I shall love thee more when we meet.'

Then Sigmund heard the sword-point smite on the stone wall's side,
And slowly mid the darkness therethrough he heard it gride
As against it bore Sinfiotli: but he cried out at the last: 1225
'It biteth, O my fosterer! It cleaves the earth-bone fast!
Now learn we the craft of the masons that another day may come
When we build a house for King Siggeir, a strait unlovely home.'

Then in the grave-mound's darkness did Sigmund the king upstand;
And unto that saw of battle he set his naked hand;   1230
And hard the gift of Odin home to their breasts they drew;
Sawed Sigmund, sawed Sinfiotli, till the stone was cleft atwo,
And they met and kissed together: then they hewed and heaved full hard
Till lo, through the bursten rafters the winter heavens bestarred!
And they leap out merry-hearted; nor is there need to say   1235
A many words between them of whither was the way.

For they took the night-watch sleeping, and slew them one and all
And then on the winter fagots they made them haste to fall,
They pile the oak-trees cloven, and when the oak-beams fail
They bear the ash and the rowan, and build a mighty bale   1240

About the dwelling of Siggeir, and lay the torch therein.
Then they drew their swords and watched it till the flames began to win
Hard on to the mid-hall's rafters, and those feasters of the folk,
As the fire-flakes fell among them, to their last of days awoke.
By the gable-door stood Sigmund, and fierce Sinfiotli stood   1245
Red-lit by the door of the women in the lane of blazing wood:
To death each doorway opened, and death was in the hall.

Then amid the gathered Goth-folk 'gan Siggeir the king to call:
'Who lit the fire I burn in, and what shall buy me peace?
Will ye take my heaped-up treasure, or ten years of my fields'
     increase,   1250
Or half of my father's kingdom? O toilers at the oar,
O wasters of the sea-plain, now labour ye no more!
But take the gifts I bid you, and lie upon the gold,
And clothe your limbs in purple and the silken women hold!'

But a great voice cried o'er the fire: 'Nay no such men are we,   1255
No tuggers at the hawser, no wasters of the sea:
We will have the gold and the purple when we list such things to win;
But now we think on our fathers, and avenging of our kin.
Not all King Siggeir's kingdom, and not all the world's increase
For ever and for ever, shall buy thee life and peace.   1260
For now is the tree-bough blossomed that sprang from murder's seed;
And the death-doomed and the buried are they that do the deed;
Now when the dead shall ask thee by whom thy days were done,
Thou shalt say by Sigmund the Volsung, and Sinfiotli, Signy's son.'

Then stark fear fell on the earl-folk, and silent they abide   1265
Amid the flaming penfold; and again the great voice cried,
As the Goth-king's golden pillars grew red amidst the blaze:
'Ye women of the Goth-folk, come forth upon your ways;
And thou, Signy, O my sister, come forth from death and hell,
That beneath the boughs of the Branstock once more we twain may dwell.'   1270

Forth came the white-faced women and passed Sinfiotli's sword,
Free by the glaive of Odin the trembling pale ones poured,
But amid their hurrying terror came never Signy's feet;
And the pearls of the throne of Siggeir shrunk in the fervent heat.

Then the men of war surged outward to the twofold doors of bane,   1275
But there played the sword of Sigmund amidst the fiery lane
Before the gable door-way, and by the woman's door
Sinfiotli sang to the sword-edge amid the bale-fire's roar,
And back again to the burning the earls of the Goth-folk shrank:
And the light low licked the tables, and the wine of Siggeir drank.   1280

Lo now to the woman's doorway, the steel-watched bower of flame,
Clad in her queenly raiment King Volsung's daughter came
Before Sinfiotli's sword-point; and she said: 'O mightiest son,
Best now is our departing in the day my grief hath won,
And the many days of toiling, and the travail of my womb,   1285
And the hate, and the fire of longing: thou, son, and this day of
    the doom
Have long been as one to my heart; and now shall I leave you both,
And well ye may wot of the slumber my heart is nothing loth;
And all the more, as, meseemeth, thy day shall not be long
To weary thee with labour and mingle wrong with wrong.   1290
Yea, and I wot that the daylight thine eyes had never seen
Save for a great king's murder and the shame of a mighty queen.
But let thy soul, I charge thee, o'er all these things prevail
To make thy short day glorious and leave a goodly tale.'

She kissed him and departed, and unto Sigmund went   1295
As now against the dawning grey grew the winter bent
As the night and the morning mingled he saw her face once more,
And he deemed it fair and ruddy as in the days of yore;
Yet fast the tears fell from her, and the sobs upheaved her breast:
And she said: 'My youth was happy; but this hour belike is best   1300
Of all the days of my life-tide, that soon shall have an end.
I have come to greet thee, Sigmund, then back again must I wend,
For his bed the Goth-king dighteth: I have lain therein, time was,
And loathed the sleep I won there: but lo, how all things pass,
And hearts are changed and softened, for lovely now it seems.   1305
Yet fear not my forgetting: I shall see thee in my dreams
A mighty king of the world 'neath the boughs of the Branstock green,
With thine earls and thy lords about thee as the Volsung fashion
    hath been:
And there shall all ye remember how I loved the Volsung name,
Nor spared to spend for its blooming my joy, and my life, and my fame.   1310
For hear thou: that Sinfiotli, who hath wrought out our desire,
Who hath compassed about King Siggeir with this sea of a deadly fire,
Who brake thy grave asunder—my child and thine he is,
Begot in that house of the Dwarf-kind for no other end than this;
The son of Volsung's daughter, the son of Volsung's son.   1315
Look, look! might another helper this deed with thee have done?'

And indeed as the word she uttereth, high up the red flames flare
To the nether floor of the heavens: and yet men see them there,
The golden roofs of Siggeir, the hall of the silver door
That the Goths and the Gods had builded to last for evermore.   1320

She said: 'Farewell, my brother, for the earls my candles light,
And I must wend me bedward lest I lose the flower of night.'

And soft and sweet she kissed him, ere she turned about again,
And a little while was Signy beheld of the eyes of men;
And as she crossed the threshold, day brightened at her back   1325
Nor once did she turn her earthward from the reek and the whirling
    wrack,
But fair in the fashion of Queens passed on to the heart of the hall.

And then King Siggeir's roof-tree upheaved for its utmost fall,
And its huge walls clashed together, and its mean and lowly things
The fire of death confounded with the tokens of the kings.   1330
A sign for many people on the land of the Goths it lay,
A lamp of the earth none needed, for the bright sun brought the day.

How Sigmund cometh to the land of the Volsungs again, and of the death of Sinfiotli his son.

Now Sigmund the king bestirs him, and Sinfiotli, Sigmund's son,
And they gather a host together, and many a mighty one;
Then they set the ships in the sea-flood and sail from the stranger's shore,   1335
And the beaks of the golden dragons see the Volsungs' land once more:
And men's hearts are fulfilled of joyance; and they cry, The sun
    shines now
With never a curse to hide it, and they shall reap that sow!
Then for many a day sits Sigmund 'neath the boughs of the Branstock
    green,
With his earls and lords about him as the Volsung wont hath been.   1340
And oft he thinketh on Signy and oft he nameth her name,
And tells how she spent her joyance and her lifedays and her fame
That the Volsung kin might blossom and bear the fruit of worth
For the hope of unborn people and the harvest of the earth.
And again he thinks of the word that he spake that other day   1345
How he should abide there lonely when his kin was passed away,
Their glory and sole avenger, their after-summer seed.

And now for their fame's advancement, and the latter days to speed,
He weddeth a wife of the King-folk; Borghild she had to name;
And the woman was fair and lovely and bore him sons of fame;   1350
Men called them Hamond and Helgi, and when Helgi first saw light,
There came the Norns to his cradle and gave him life full bright,
And called him Sunlit Hill, Sharp Sword, and Land of Rings,
And bade him be lovely and great, and a joy in the tale of kings.
And he waxed up fair and mighty, and no worser than their word,   1355

And sweet are the tales of his life-days, and the wonders of his sword,
And the Maid of the Shield that he wedded, and how he changed his
    life,
And of marvels wrought in the gravemound where he rested from the
    strife.

But the tale of Sinfiotli telleth, that wide in the world he went,
And many a wall of ravens the edge of his warflame rent;   1360
And oft he drave the war-prey and wasted many a land:
Amidst King Hunding's battle he strengthened Helgi's hand;
And he went before the banners amidst the steel-grown wood,
When the sons of Hunding gathered and Helgi's hope withstood:
Nor less he mowed the war-swathe in Helgi's glorious day   1365
When the kings of the hosts at the Wolf-crag set the battle in array.
Then at home by his father's high-seat he wore the winter through;
And the marvel of all men he was for the deeds whereof they knew,
And the deeds whereof none wotted, and the deeds to follow after.

And yet but a little while he loved the song and the laughter,   1370
And the wine that was drunk in peace, and the swordless lying down,
And the deedless day's uprising and the ungirt golden gown.
And he thought of the word of his mother, that his day should not be
    long
To weary his soul with labour or mingle wrong with wrong;
And his heart was exceeding hungry o'er all men to prevail,   1375
And make his short day glorious and leave a goodly tale.

So when green leaves were lengthening and the spring was come again
He set his ships in the sea-flood and sailed across the main;
And the brother of Queen Borghild was his fellow in the war,
A king of hosts hight Gudrod; and each to each they swore,   1380
And plighted troth for the helping, and the parting of the prey.

Now a long way over the sea-flood they went ashore on a day
And fought with a mighty folk-king, and overcame at last:
Then wide about his kingdom the net of steel they cast,
And the prey was great and goodly that they drave unto the strand.   1385
But a greedy heart is Gudrod, and a king of griping hand,
Though nought he blench from the battle; so he speaks on a morning
    fair,
And saith:
        'Upon the foreshore the booty will we share
If thou wilt help me, fellow, before we sail our ways.'

Sinfiotli laughed, and answered: 'O'ershort methinks the days   1390
That two kings of war should chaffer like merchants of the men:

I will come again in the even and look on thy dealings then,
And take the share thou givest.'
                                        Then he went his ways withal,
And drank day-long in his warship as in his father's hall;
And came again in the even: now hath Gudrod shared the spoil,   1395
And throughout that day of summer not light had been his toil:
Forsooth his heap was the lesser; but Sinfiotli looked thereon,
And saw that a goodly getting had Borghild's brother won.
Clean-limbed and stark were the horses, and the neat were fat and sleek
And the men-thralls young and stalwart, and the women young
    and meek;   1400
Fair-gilt was the harness of battle, and the raiment fresh and bright,
And the household stuff new-fashioned for lords' and earls' delight.
On his own then looked Sinfiotli, and great it was forsooth,
But half-foundered were the horses, and a sight for all men's ruth
Were the thin-ribbed hungry cow-kind; and the thralls both carle   1405
    and queen
Were the wilful, the weak, and the witless, and the old and the ill-beseen;
Spoilt was the harness and house-gear, and the raiment rags of cloth.

Now Sinfiotli's men beheld it and grew exceeding wroth,
But Sinfiotli laughed and answered: 'The day's work hath been meet:
Thou hast done well, war-brother, to sift the chaff from the wheat;   1410
Nought have kings' sons to meddle with the refuse of the earth,
Nor shall warriors burden their long-ships with things of nothing worth.'

Then he cried across the sea-strand in a voice exceeding great:
'Depart, ye thralls of the battle; ye have nought to do to wait!
Old, young, and good, and evil, depart and share the spoil,   1415
That burden of the battle, that spring and seed of toil.
—But thou king of the greedy heart, thou king of the thievish grip,
What now wilt thou bear to the sea-strand and set within my ship
To buy thy life from the slaying? Unmeet for kings to hear
Of a king the breaker of troth, of a king the stealer of gear.'   1420

Then mad-wroth waxed King Gudrod, and he cried: 'Stand up, my men!
And slay this wood-abider lest he slay his brothers again!'

But no sword leapt from its sheath, and his men shrank back in dread:
Then Sinfiotli's brow grew smoother, and at last he spake and said:
'Indeed thou art very brother of my father Sigmund's wife: 1425
Wilt thou do so much for thine honour, wilt thou do so much for thy life,
As to bide my sword on the island in the pale of the hazel wands?
For I know thee no battle-blencher, but a valiant man of thine hands.'

Now nought King Gudrod gainsayeth, and men dight the hazelled field,
And there on the morrow morning they clash the sword and shield,   1430

And the fallow blades are leaping: short is the tale to tell,
For with the third stroke stricken to field King Gudrod fell.
So there in the holm they lay him; and plenteous store of gold
Sinfiotli lays beside him amid that hall of mould;
'For he gripped,' saith the son of Sigmund, 'and gathered for such a day.'   1435

Then Sinfiotli and his fellows o'er the sea-flood sail away,
And come to the land of the Volsungs: but Borghild heareth the tale,
And into the hall she cometh with eager face and pale
As the kings were feasting together, and glad was Sigmund grown
Of the words of Sinfiotli's battle, and the tale of his great renown: 1440
And there sat the sons of Borghild, and they hearkened and were glad
Of their brother born in the wild-wood, and the crown of fame he had.

So she stood before King Sigmund, and spread her hands abroad:
'I charge thee now, King Sigmund, as thou art the Volsungs' lord,
To tell me of my brother, why cometh he not from the sea?'   1445

Quoth Sinfiotli: 'Well thou wottest and the tale hath come to thee:
The white swords met in the island; bright there did the war-
    shields shine,
And there thy brother abideth, for his hand was worser than mine.'

But she heeded him never a whit, but cried on Sigmund and said:
'I charge thee now, King Sigmund, as thou art the lord of my bed,   1450
To drive this wolf of the King-folk from out thy guarded land;
Lest all we of thine house and kindred should fall beneath his hand.'

Then spake King Sigmund the Volsung: 'When thou hast heard the tale,
Thou shalt know that somewhat thy brother of his oath to my son
    did fail;
Nor fell the man all sackless: nor yet need Sigmund's son   1455
For any slain in sword-field to any soul atone.
Yet for the love I bear thee, and because thy love I know,
And because the man was mighty, and far afield would go,
I will lay down a mighty weregild, a heap of the ruddy gold.'

But no word answered Borghild, for her heart was grim and cold;   1460
And she went from the hall of the feasting, and lay in her bower a
    while;
Nor speech she took, nor gave it, but brooded deadly guile.
And now again on the morrow to Sigmund the king she went,
And she saith that her wrath hath failed her, and that well is she content
To take the king's atonement; and she kissed him soft and sweet,   1465
And she kissed Sinfiotli his son, and sat down in the golden seat
All merry and glad by seeming, and blithe to most and least.

And again she biddeth King Sigmund that he hold a funeral feast
For her brother slain on the island; and nought he gainsayeth her will.

And so on an eve of the autumn do men the beakers fill,   1470
And the earls are gathered together 'neath the boughs of the Branstock
   green;
There gold-clad mid the feasting went Borghild, Sigmund's Queen,
And she poured the wine for Sinfiotli, and smiled in his face and said:
'Drink now of this cup from mine hand, and bury we hate that is dead.'

So he took the cup from her fingers, nor drank but pondered long   1475
O'er the gathering days of his labour, and the intermingled wrong.

Now he sat by the side of his father; and Sigmund spake a word:
'O son, why sittest thou silent mid the glee of earl and lord?'

'I look in the cup,' quoth Sinfiotli, 'and hate therein I see.'

'Well looked it is,' said Sigmund; 'give thou the cup to me,'   1480
And he drained it dry to the bottom; for ye mind how it was writ
That this king might drink of venom, and have no hurt of it.
But the song sprang up in the hall, and merry was Sigmund's heart,
And he drank of the wine of King-folk and thrust all care apart.

Then the second time came Borghild and stood before the twain,   1485
And she said: 'O valiant step-son, how oft shall I say it in vain,
That my hate for thee hath perished, and the love hath sprouted green?
Wilt thou thrust my gift away, and shame the hand of a queen?'

So he took the cup from her fingers, and pondered over it long,
And thought on the labour that should be, and the wrong that amendeth
   wrong.   1490

Then spake Sigmund the King: 'O son what aileth thine heart,
When the earls of men are merry, and thrust all care apart?'

But he said: 'I have looked in the cup, and I see the deadly snare.'

'Well seen it is,' quoth Sigmund, 'but thy burden I may bear.'
And he took the beaker and drained it, and the song rose up in the hall;   1495
And fair bethought King Sigmund his latter days befall.

But again came Borghild the Queen and stood with the cup in her hand,
And said: 'They are idle liars, those singers of every land
Who sing how thou fearest nothing; for thou losest valour and might,
And art fain to live for ever.'
                   Then she stretched forth her fingers white,   1500
And he took the cup from her hand, nor drank, but pondered long
Of the toil that begetteth toil, and the wrong that beareth wrong.

But Sigmund turned him about, and he said: 'What aileth thee, son?
Shall our life-days never be merry, and our labour never be done?'

But Sinfiotli said: 'I have looked, and lo there is death in the cup.'   1505

And the song, and the tinkling of harp-strings to the roof-tree winded
   up:
And Sigmund was dreamy with wine and the wearing of many a year;
And the noise and the glee of the people as the sound of the wild woods
   were
And the blossoming boughs of the Branstock were the wild trees waving
   about;
So he said: 'Well seen, my fosterling; let the lip then strain it out.'   1510
Then Sinfiotli laughed and answered: 'I drink unto Odin then,
And the Dwellers up in God-home, the lords of the lives of men.'

He drank as he spake the word, and forthwith the venom ran
In a chill flood over his heart, and down fell the mighty man
With never an uttered death-word and never a death-changed look,   1515
And the floor of the hall of the Volsungs beneath his falling shook.
Then up rose the elder of days with a great and bitter cry
And lifted the head of the fallen, and none durst come anigh
To hearken the words of his sorrow, if any words he said,
But such as the Father of all men might speak over Baldur dead.   1520
And again, as before the death-stroke, waxed the hall of the Volsungs dim
And once more he seemed in the forest, where he spake with nought
   but him.

Then he lifted him up from the hall-floor and bore him on his breast,
And men who saw Sinfiotli deemed his heart had gotten rest,
And his eyes were no more dreadful. Forth fared the Volsung child   1525
With Signy's son through the doorway; and the wind was great and wild,
And the moon rode high in the heavens, and whiles it shone out bright,
And whiles the clouds drew over. So went he through the night,
Until the dwellings of man-folk were a long while left behind.
Then came he unto the thicket and the houses of the wind,   1530
And the feet of the hoary mountains, and the dwellings of the deer,
And the heaths without a shepherd, and the houseless dales and drear.
Then lo, a mighty water, a rushing flood and wide,
And no ferry for the shipless; so he went along its side,
As a man that seeketh somewhat: but it widened toward the sea,   1535
And the moon sank down in the west, and he went o'er a desert lea.

But lo, in that dusk ere the dawning a glimmering over the flood,
And the sound of the cleaving of waters, and Sigmund the Volsung stood

By the edge of the swirling eddy, and a white-sailed boat he saw,
And its keel ran light on the strand with the last of the dying flaw.   1540
But therein was a man most mighty, grey-clad like the mountain-cloud,
One-eyed and seeming ancient, and he spake and hailed him aloud:

'Now whither away, King Sigmund, for thou farest far to-night?'

Spake the King: 'I would cross this water, for my life hath lost its light,
And mayhap there be deeds for a king to be found on the further shore.'   1545

'My senders,' quoth the shipman, 'bade me waft a great king o'er,
So set thy burden a ship-board, for the night's face looks towards day.'

So betwixt the earth and the water his son did Sigmund lay;
But lo, when he fain would follow, there was neither ship nor man,
Nor aught but his empty bosom beside that water wan,   1550
That whitened by little and little as the night's face looked to the day.
So he stood a long while gazing and then turned and gat him away;
And ere the sun of the noon-tide across the meadows shone
Sigmund the King of the Volsungs was set in his father's throne,
And he hearkened and doomed and portioned, and did all the deeds
  of a king.   1555
So the autumn waned and perished, and the winter brought the spring.

Of the last battle of King Sigmund, and the death of him.

Now is Queen Borghild driven from the Volsung's bed and board,
And unwedded sitteth Sigmund an exceeding mighty lord,
And fareth oft to the war-field, and addeth fame to fame:
And where'er are the great ones told of his sons shall the people name;   1560
But short was their day of harvest and their reaping of renown,
And while men stood by to marvel they gained their latest crown.
So Sigmund alone abideth of all the Volsung seed,
And the folk that the Gods had fashioned lest the earth should lack
  a deed.
And he said: 'The tree was stalwart, but its boughs are old and worn.   1565
Where now are the children departed, that amidst my life were born?
I know not the men about me, and they know not of my ways:
I am nought but a picture of battle, and a song for the people to praise.
I must strive with the deeds of my kingship, and yet when mine hour is come
It shall meet me as glad as the goodman when he bringeth the last load
  home.'   1570

Now there was a king of the Islands, whom the tale doth Eylimi call,
And saith he was wise and valiant, though his kingdom were but small:

He had one only daughter that Hiordis had to name,
A woman wise and shapely beyond the praise of fame.
And now saith the son of King Volsung that his time is short enow   1575
To labour the Volsung garden, and the hand must be set to the plough:

So he sendeth an earl of the people to King Eylimi's high-built hall
Bearing the gifts and the tokens, and this word in his mouth withal:

'King Sigmund the son of Volsung hath sent me here with a word
That plenteous good of thy daughter among all folk he hath heard,   1580
And he wooeth that wisest of women that she may sit on his throne,
And lie in the bed of the Volsungs, and be his wife alone.
And he saith that he thinketh surely she shall bear the kings of the earth,
And maybe the best and the greatest of all who are deemed of worth.
Now hereof would he have an answer within a half-month's space,   1585
And these gifts meanwhile he giveth for the increase of thy grace.'

So King Eylimi hearkeneth the message, and hath no word to say,
For an earl of King Lyngi the mighty is come that very day,
He too for the wooing of Hiordis: and Lyngi's realm is at hand,
But afar King Sigmund abideth o'er many a sea and land: 1590
And the man is young and eager, and grim and guileful of mood.

At last he sayeth: 'Abide here such space as thou deemest good,
But tomorn shalt thou have thine answer that thine heart may the
    lighter be
For the hearkening of harp and songcraft, and the dealing with game
    and glee.'
Then he went to Queen Hiordis' bower, where she worked in the
    silk and the gold   1595
The deeds of the world that should be, and the deeds that were of old.
And he stood before her and said:
                                'I have spoken a word, time was,
That thy will should rule thy wedding; and now hath it come to pass
That again two kings of the people will woo thy body to bed.'

So she rose to her feet and hearkened: 'And which be they?' she said.   1600

He spake: 'The first is Lyngi, a valiant man and a fair,
A neighbour ill for thy father, if a foe's name he must bear:
And the next is King Sigmund the Volsung of a land far over sea,
And well thou knowest his kindred, and his might and his valiancy,
And the tales of his heart of a God; and though old he be waxen now,   1605
Yet men deem that the wide world's blossom from Sigmund's loins shall
    grow.'

Said Hiordis: 'I wot, my father, that hereof may strife arise;
Yet soon spoken is mine answer; for I, who am called the wise,
Shall I thrust by the praise of the people, and the tale that no ending hath,
And the love and the heart of the godlike, and the heavenward-
    leading path,   1610
For the rose and the stem of the lily, and the smooth-lipped
    youngling's kiss,
And the eyes' desire that passeth, and the frail unstable bliss?
Now shalt thou tell King Sigmund, that I deem it the crown of my life
To dwell in the house of his fathers amidst all peace and strife,
And to bear the sons of his body: and indeed full well I know   1615
That fair from the loins of Sigmund shall such a stem out-grow
That all folk of the earth shall be praising the womb where once he lay
And the paps that his lips have cherished, and shall bless my happy day.'

Now the king's heart sore misgave him, but herewith must he be content,
And great gifts to the earl of Lyngi and a word withal he sent,   1620
That the woman's troth was plighted to another people's king.
But King Sigmund's earl on the morrow hath joyful yea-saying,
And ere two moons be perished he shall fetch his bride away.
'And bid him,' King Eylimi sayeth, 'to come with no small array,
But with sword and shield and war-shaft, lest aught of ill betide.'   1625

So forth goes the earl of Sigmund across the sea-flood wide,
And comes to the land of the Volsungs, and meeteth Sigmund the king,
And tells how he sped on his errand, and the joyful yea-saying.
So King Sigmund maketh him ready, and they ride adown to the sea
All glorious of gear and raiment, and a goodly company.   1630
Yet hath Sigmund thought of his father, and the deed he wrought before,
And hath scorn to gather his people and all his hosts of war
To wend to the feast and the wedding: yet are their long-ships ten,
And the shielded folk aboard them are the mightiest men of men.
So Sigmund goeth a shipboard, and they hoist their sails to the wind,   1635
And the beaks of the golden dragons leave the Volsungs' land behind.
Then come they to Eylimi's kingdom, and good welcome have they
    there,
And when Sigmund looked on Hiordis, he deemed her wise and fair.
But her heart was exceeding fain when she saw the glorious king,
And it told her of times that should be full many a noble thing.   1640

So there is Sigmund wedded at a great and goodly feast,
And day by day on Hiordis the joy of her heart increased;
And her father joyed in Sigmund and his might and majesty,
And dead in the heart of the isle-king his ancient fear did lie.

Yet, forsooth, had men looked seaward, they had seen the gathering cloud,   1645
And the little wind arising, that should one day pipe so loud.
For well may ye wot indeed that King Lyngi the Mighty is wroth,
When he getteth the gifts and the answer, and that tale of the woman's
    troth:
And he saith he will have the gifts and the woman herself withal,
Either for loving or hating, and that both those heads shall fall.   1650
So now when Sigmund and Hiordis are wedded a month or more,
And the Volsung bids men dight them to cross the sea-flood o'er,
Lo, how there cometh the tidings of measureless mighty hosts
Who are gotten ashore from their long-ships on the skirts of King
    Eylimi's coasts.

Sore boded the heart of the Isle-king of what the end should be.   1655
But Sigmund long beheld him, and he said: 'Thou deem'st of me
That my coming hath brought thee evil; but put aside such things;
For long have I lived, and I know it, that the lives of mighty kings
Are not cast away, nor drifted like the down before the wind;
And surely I know, who say it, that never would Hiordis' mind   1660
Have been turned to wed King Lyngi or aught but the Volsung seed.
Come, go we forth to the battle, that shall be the latest deed
Of thee and me meseemeth: yea, whether thou live or die,
No more shall the brand of Odin at peace in his scabbard lie.'

And therewith he brake the peace-strings and drew the blade of bale,   1665
And Death on the point abided, Fear sat on the edges pale.

So men ride adown to the sea-strand, and the kings their hosts array
When the high noon flooded heaven; and the men of the Volsungs lay
With King Eylimi's shielded champions mid Lyngi's hosts of war
As the brown pips lie in the apple when ye cut it through the core.   1670

But now when the kings were departed, from the King's house Hiordis
    went,
And before men joined the battle she came to a woody bent,
Where she lay with one of her maidens the death and the deeds to behold.

In the noon sun shone King Sigmund as an image all of gold,
And he stood before the foremost and the banner of his fame,   1675
And many a thing he remembered, and he called on each earl by his name
To do well for the house of the Volsungs, and the ages yet unborn.
Then he tossed up the sword of the Branstock, and blew on his father's
    horn,
Dread of so many a battle, doom-song of so many a man.
Then all the earth seemed moving as the hosts of Lyngi ran   1680

On the Volsung men and the Isle-folk like wolves upon the prey;
But sore was their labour and toil ere the end of their harvesting day.

On went the Volsung banners, and on went Sigmund before,
And his sword was the flail of the tiller on the wheat of the
 wheat-thrashing floor,
And his shield was rent from his arm, and his helm was sheared
 from his head: 1685
But who may draw nigh him to smite for the heap and the rampart
 of dead?
White went his hair on the wind like the ragged drift of the cloud,
And his dust-driven, blood-beaten harness was the death-storm's angry
 shroud,
When the summer sun is departing in the first of the night of wrack;
And his sword was the cleaving lightning, that smites and is hurried aback 1690
Ere the hand may rise against it; and his voice was the following thunder.

Then cold grew the battle before him, dead-chilled with the fear and the
 wonder:
For again in his ancient eyes the light of victory gleamed;
From his mouth grown tuneful and sweet the song of his kindred streamed;
And no more was he worn and weary, and no more his life seemed spent: 1695
And with all the hope of his childhood was his wrath of battle blent;
And he thought: A little further, and the river of strife is passed,
And I shall sit triumphant the king of the world at last.

But lo, through the hedge of the war-shafts a mighty man there came,
One-eyed and seeming ancient, but his visage shone like flame: 1700
Gleaming-grey was his kirtle, and his hood was cloudy blue;
And he bore a mighty twi-bill, as he waded the fight-sheaves through,
And stood face to face with Sigmund, and upheaved the bill to smite.
Once more round the head of the Volsung fierce glittered the Branstock's
 light,
The sword that came from Odin; and Sigmund's cry once more   1705
Rang out to the very heavens above the din of war.
Then clashed the meeting edges with Sigmund's latest stroke,
And in shivering shards fell earthward that fear of worldly folk.
But changed were the eyes of Sigmund, and the war-wrath left his face;
For that grey-clad mighty helper was gone, and in his place   1710
Drave on the unbroken spear-wood 'gainst the Volsung's empty hands:
And there they smote down Sigmund, the wonder of all lands,
On the foemen, on the death-heap his deeds had piled that day.

Ill hour for Sigmund's fellows! they fall like the seeded hay
Before the brown scythes' sweeping, and there the Isle-king fell   1715

In the fore-front of his battle, wherein he wrought right well,
And soon they were nought but foemen who stand upon their feet
On the isle-strand by the ocean where the grass and the sea-sand meet.

And now hath the conquering War-king another deed to do,
And he saith: 'Who now gainsayeth King Lyngi come to woo,   1720
The lord and the overcomer and the bane of the Volsung kin?'
So he fares to the Isle-king's dwelling a wife of the kings to win;
And the host is gathered together, and they leave the field of the dead;
And round as a targe of the Goth-folk the moon ariseth red.

And so when the last is departed, and she deems they will come not aback   1725
Fares Hiordis forth from the thicket to the field of the fateful wrack,
And half-dead was her heart for sorrow as she waded the swathes of the
    sword.
Not far did she search the death-field ere she found her king and lord
On the heap that his glaive had fashioned: not yet was his spirit past,
Though his hurts were many and grievous, and his life-blood ebbing fast;   1730
And glad were his eyes and open as her wan face over him hung,
And he spake:
                    'Thou art sick with sorrow, and I would thou wert not
    so young:
Yet as my days passed shall thine pass; and a short while now it seems
Since my hand first gripped the sword-hilt, and my glory was but in
    dreams.'

She said: 'Thou livest, thou livest! the leeches shall heal thee still.'   1735

'Nay,' said he, 'my heart hath hearkened to Odin's bidding and will;
For today have mine eyes beheld him: nay, he needed not to speak:
Forsooth I knew of his message and the thing he came to seek.
And now do I live but to tell thee of the days that are yet to come:
And perchance to solace thy sorrow; and then will I get me home   1740
To my kin that are gone before me. Lo, yonder where I stood
The shards of a glaive of battle that was once the best of the good:
Take them and keep them surely. I have lived no empty days;
The Norns were my nursing mothers; I have won the people's praise.
When the Gods for one deed asked me I ever gave them twain;   1745
Spendthrift of glory I was, and great was my life-days' gain;
Now these shards have been my fellow in the work the Gods would have,
But today hath Odin taken the gift that once he gave.
I have wrought for the Volsungs truly, and yet have I known full well
That a better one than I am shall bear the tale to tell: 1750
And for him shall these shards be smithied; and he shall be my son
To remember what I have forgotten and to do what I left undone.

Under thy girdle he lieth, and how shall I say unto thee,
Unto thee, the wise of women, to cherish him heedfully.
Now, wife, put by thy sorrow for the little day we have had;   1755
For in sooth I deem thou weepest: The days have been fair and glad:
And our valour and wisdom have met, and thou knowest they shall
    not die:
Sweet and good were the days, nor yet to the Fates did we cry
For a little longer yet, and a little longer to live:
But we took, we twain in our meeting, all gifts that they had to give: 1760
Our wisdom and valour have kissed, and thine eyes shall see the fruit,
And the joy for his days that shall be hath pierced mine heart to the
    root.
Grieve not for me; for thou weepest that thou canst not see my face
How its beauty is not departed, nor the hope of mine eyes grown base.
Indeed I am waxen weary; but who heedeth weariness   1765
That hath been day-long on the mountain in the winter weather's stress,
And now stands in the lighted doorway and seeth the king draw nigh
And heareth men dighting the banquet, and the bed wherein he shall lie?'

Then failed the voice of Sigmund; but so mighty was the man,
That a long while yet he lingered till the dusky night grew wan,   1770
And she sat and sorrowed o'er him, but no more a word he spake.
Then a long way over the sea-flood the day began to break;
And when the sun was arisen a little he turned his head
Till the low beams bathed his eyen, and there lay Sigmund dead.
And the sun rose up on the earth; but where was the Volsung kin   1775
And the folk that the Gods had begotten the praise of all people to win?

How King Sigmund the Volsung was laid in mound on the sea-side of the isle-realm.

Now Hiordis looked from the dead, and her eyes strayed down to the sea,
And a shielded ship she saw, and a war-dight company,
Who beached the ship for the landing: so swift she fled away,
And once more to the depth of the thicket, wherein her handmaid lay: 1780
And she said: 'I have left my lord, and my lord is dead and gone,
And he gave me a charge full heavy, and here are we twain alone,
And earls from the sea are landing: give me thy blue attire,
And take my purple and gold and my crown of the sea-flood's fire,
And be thou the wife of King Volsung when men of our names shall ask,   1785
And I will be the handmaid: now I bid thee to this task,
And I pray thee not to fail me, because of thy faith and truth,
And because I have ever loved thee, and thy mother fostered my youth.

Yea, because my womb is wealthy with a gift for the days to be.
Now do this deed for mine asking and the tale shall be told of thee.'   1790

So the other nought gainsaith it and they shift their raiment there:
But well-spoken was the maiden, and a woman tall and fair.

Now the lord of those new-coming men was a king and the son of a king,
King Elf the son of the Helper, and he sailed from war-faring
And drew anigh to the Isle-realm and sailed along the strand;   1795
For the shipmen needed water and fain would go a-land;
And King Elf stood hard by the tiller while the world was yet a-cold:
Then the red sun lit the dawning, and they looked, and lo, behold!
The wrack of a mighty battle, and heaps of the shielded dead,
And a woman alive amidst them, a queen with crownèd head,   1800
And her eyes strayed down to the sea-strand, and she saw that
   weaponed folk,
And turned and fled to the thicket: then the lord of the shipmen spoke:
'Lo, here shall we lack for water, for the brooks with blood shall run,
Yet wend we ashore to behold it and to wot of the deeds late done.'

So they turned their faces to Sigmund, and waded the swathes
   of the sword.   1805
'O, look ye long,' said the Sea-king, 'for here lieth a mighty lord:
And all these are the deeds of his war-flame, yet hardy hearts, be sure,
That they once durst look in his face or the wrath of his eyen endure;
Though his lips be glad and smiling as a God that dreameth of mirth.
Would God I were one of his kindred, for none such are left upon earth.   1810
Now fare we into the thicket, for thereto is the woman fled,
And belike she shall tell us the story of this field of the mighty dead.'

So they wend and find the women, and bespeak them kind and fair:
Then spake the gold-crowned handmaid: 'Of the Isle-king's house we were,
And I am the Queen called Hiordis; and the man that lies on the field   1815
Was mine own lord Sigmund the Volsung, the mightiest under shield.'

Then all amazed were the sea-folk when they hearkened to that word,
And great and heavy tidings they deem their ears have heard:
But again spake out the Sea-king: 'And this blue-clad one beside,
So pale, and as tall as a Goddess, and white and lovely-eyed?'   1820

'In sooth and in troth,' said the woman, 'my serving-maid is this;
She hath wept long over the battle, and sore afraid she is.'

Now the king looks hard upon her, but he saith no word thereto,
And down again to the death-field with the women-folk they go.
There they set their hands to the labour, and amidst the deadly mead   1825

They raise a mound for Sigmund, a mighty house indeed;
And therein they set that folk-king, and goodly was his throne,
And dight with gold and scarlet: and the walls of the house were done
With the cloven shields of the foemen, and banners borne to field;
But none might find his war-helm or the splinters of his shield,   1830
And clenched and fast was his right hand, but no sword therein he had:
For Hiordis spake to the shipmen:
                              'Our lord and master bade
That the shards of his glaive of battle should go with our lady the Queen:
And by them that lie a-dying a many things are seen.'

So there lies Sigmund the Volsung, and far away, forlorn   1835
Are the blossomed boughs of the Branstock, and the house where he was
     born.
To what end was wrought that roof-ridge, and the rings of the silver door,
And the fair-carved golden high-seat, and the many-pictured floor
Worn down by the feet of the Volsungs? or the hangings of delight,
Or the marvel of its harp-strings, or the Dwarf-wrought beakers bright?   1840
Then the Gods have fashioned a folk who have fashioned a house in vain:
It is nought, and for nought they battled, and nought was their joy and
     their pain.

Lo, the noble oak of the forest with his feet in the flowers and grass,
How the winds that bear the summer o'er its topmost branches pass,
And the wood-deer dwell beneath it, and the fowl in its fair twigs sing,   1845
And there it stands in the forest, an exceeding glorious thing:
Then come the axes of men, and low it lies on the ground,
And the crane comes out of the southland, and its nest is nowhere found,
And bare and shorn of its blossoms is the house of the deer of the wood.
But the tree is a golden dragon; and fair it floats on the flood,   1850
And beareth the kings and the earl-folk, and is shield-hung all without:
And it seeth the blaze of the beacons, and heareth the war-God's shout.
There are tidings wherever it cometh, and the tale of its time shall be told.
A dear name it hath got like a king, and a fame that groweth not old.

Lo, such is the Volsung dwelling; lo, such is the deed he hath wrought   1855
Who laboured all his life-days, and had rest but little or nought,
Who died in the broken battle; who lies with swordless hand
In the realm that the foe hath conquered on the edge of a stranger-land.

How Queen Hiordis is known; and how she abideth
in the house of Elf the son of the Helper.

Now asketh the king of those women where now in the world they will go,
And Hiordis speaks for the twain: 'This is now but a land of the foe   1860

And our lady and Queen beseecheth that unto thine house we wend
And that there thou serve her kingly that her woes may have an end.'

Fain then was the heart of the folk-king, and he bade aboard forth-right,
And they hoist the sails to the wind and sail by day and by night
Till they come to a land of the people, and a goodly land it is,   1865
Where folk may dwell unharried and win abundant bliss,
The land of King Elf and the Helper; and there he bids them abide
In his house that is goodly shapen, and wrought full high and wide:
And he biddeth the Queen be merry, and set aside her woe,
And he doth by them better and better, as day on day doth go.   1870

Now there was the mother of Elf, and a woman wise was she,
And she spake to her son of a morning: 'I have noted them heedfully.
Those women thou broughtst from the outlands, and fain now would
    I wot
Why the worser of the women the goodlier gear hath got.'

He said: 'She hath named her Hiordis, the wife of the mightiest king,   1875
E'en Sigmund the son of Volsung with whose name the world
    doth ring.'

Then the old queen laughed and answered: 'Is it not so, my son,
That the handmaid still gave counsel when aught of deeds was done?'

He said: 'Yea, she spake mostly; and her words were exceeding wise,
And measureless sweet I deem her, and dear she is to mine eyes.'   1880

But she said: 'Do after my counsel, and win thee a goodly queen:
Speak ye to the twain unwary, and the truth shall soon be seen,
And again shall they shift their raiment, if I am aught but a fool.'

He said: 'Thou sayst well, mother, and settest me well to school.'
So he spake on a day to the women, and said to the gold-clad one: 1885
'How wottest thou in the winter of the coming of the sun
When yet the world is darkling?'
                              She said: 'In the days of my youth
I dwelt in the house of my father, and fair was the tide forsooth,
And ever I woke at the dawning, for folk betimes must stir,
Be the meadows bright or darksome; and I drank of the whey-tub
    there   1890
As much as the heart desired; and now, though changed be the days,
I wake athirst in the dawning, because of my wonted ways.'

Then laughed King Elf and answered: 'A fashion strange enow,
That the feet of the fair queen's-daughter must forth to follow the plough,
Be the acres bright or darkling! But thou with the eyes of grey,   1895

What sign hast thou to tell thee, that the night wears into day
When the heavens are mirk as the midnight?'

                          Said she, 'In the days
   that were
My father gave me this gold-ring ye see on my finger here,
And a marvel goeth with it: for when night waxeth old
I feel it on my finger grown most exceeding cold,   1900
And I know day comes through the darkness; and such is my dawning sign.'

Then laughed King Elf and answered: 'Thy father's house was fine;
There was gold enough meseemeth—But come now, say the word
And tell me the speech thou spakest awrong mine ears have heard,
And that thou wert the wife of Sigmund, the wife of the mightiest King.'   1905

No whit she smiled, but answered. 'Indeed thou sayst the thing:
Such a wealth I had in my storehouse that I feared the Kings of men.'

He said: 'Yet for nought didst thou hide thee; had I known of the matter
   then,
As the daughter of my father had I held thee in good sooth,
For dear to mine eyes wert thou waxen, and my heart of thy woe
   was ruth.   1910
But now shall I deal with thee better than thy dealings to me have been:
For my wife I will bid thee to be, and the people's very queen.'

She said: 'When the son of King Sigmund is brought forth to the light
   of day
And the world a man hath gotten, thy will shall I nought gainsay.
And I thank thee for thy goodness, and I know the love of thine heart;   1915
And I see thy goodly kingdom, thy country set apart,
With the day of peace begirdled from the change and the battle's wrack:
'Tis enough, and more than enough since none prayeth the past aback.'

Then the King is fain and merry, and he deems his errand sped,
And that night she sits on the high-seat with the crown on
   her shapely head: 1920
And amidst the song and the joyance, and the sound of the people's
   praise,
She thinks of the days that have been, and she dreams of the coming
   days.

So passeth the summer season, and the harvest of the year,
And the latter days of the winter on toward the springtide wear.

Book 2. Regin

NOW THIS IS THE FIRST BOOK OF THE LIFE AND DEATH OF SIGURD THE
VOLSUNG, AND THEREIN IS TOLD OF THE BIRTH OF HIM, AND OF HIS
DEALINGS WITH REGIN THE MASTER OF MASTERS, AND OF HIS DEEDS IN
THE WASTE PLACES OF THE EARTH.

Of the birth of Sigurd the son of Sigmund.

Peace lay on the land of the Helper and the house of Elf his son;   1925
There merry men went bedward when their tide of toil was done,
And glad was the dawn's awakening, and the noon-tide fair and glad:
There no great store had the franklin, and enough the hireling had;
And a child might go unguarded the length and breadth of the land
With a purse of gold at his girdle and gold rings on his hand.   1930
'Twas a country of cunning craftsmen, and many a thing they wrought,
That the lands of storm desired, and the homes of warfare sought.
But men deemed it o'er-well warded by more than its stems of fight,
And told how its earth-born watchers yet lived of plenteous might.
So hidden was that country, and few men sailed its sea,   1935
And none came o'er its mountains of men-folk's company.
But fair-fruited, many-peopled, it lies a goodly strip,
'Twixt the mountains cloudy-headed and the sea-flood's surging lip,
And a perilous flood is its ocean, and its mountains, who shall tell
What things in their dales deserted and their wind-swept heaths may
    dwell.   1940

Now a man of the Kings, called Gripir, in this land of peace abode:
The son of the Helper's father, though never lay his load
In the womb of the mother of Kings that the Helper's brethren bore;
But of Giant kin was his mother, of the folk that are seen no more;
Though whiles as ye ride some fell-road across the heath there comes   1945
The voice of their lone lamenting o'er their changed and conquered
    homes.
A long way off from the sea-strand and beneath the mountains' feet
Is the high-built hall of Gripir, where the waste and the tillage meet;
A noble and plentiful house, that a little men-folk fear,
But beloved of the crag-dwelling eagles and the kin of the woodland
    deer.   1950
A man of few words was Gripir, but he knew of all deeds that had been,
And times there came upon him, when the deeds to be were seen:
No sword had he held in his hand since his father fell to field,
And against the life of the slayer he bore undinted shield:

Yet no fear in his heart abided, nor desired he aught at all,   1955
But he noted the deeds that had been, and looked for what should
  befall.

Again, in the house of the Helper there dwelt a certain man
Beardless and low of stature, of visage pinched and wan:
So exceeding old was Regin, that no son of man could tell
In what year of the days passed over he came to that land to dwell: 1960
But the youth of King Elf had he fostered, and the Helper's youth
  thereto,
Yea and his father's father's: the lore of all men he knew,
And was deft in every cunning, save the dealings of the sword:
So sweet was his tongue-speech fashioned, that men trowed his every
  word;
His hand with the harp-strings blended was the mingler of delight   1965
With the latter days of sorrow; all tales he told aright;
The Master of the Masters in the smithying craft was he;
And he dealt with the wind and the weather and the stilling of the sea;
Nor might any learn him leech-craft, for before that race was made,
And that man-folk's generation, all their life-days had he weighed.   1970

In this land abideth Hiordis amid all people's praise
Till cometh the time appointed: in the fulness of the days
Through the dark and the dusk she travailed, till at last in the dawning
  hour
Have the deeds of the Volsungs blossomed, and borne their latest
  flower;
In the bed there lieth a man-child, and his eyes look straight on the
  sun,
And lo, the hope of the people, and the days of a king are begun.   1975

Men say of the serving-women, when they cried on the joy of the
  morn,
When they handled the linen raiment, and washed the king new-born,
When they bore him back unto Hiordis, and the weary and happy
  breast,
And bade her be glad to behold it, how the best was sprung from the
  best,   1980
Yet they shrank in their rejoicing before the eyes of the child,
So bright and dreadful were they; yea though the spring morn smiled,
And a thousand birds were singing round the fair familiar home,
And still as on other mornings they saw folk go and come,
Yet the hour seemed awful to them, and the hearts within them burned   1985
As though of fateful matters their souls were newly learned.

But Hiordis looked on the Volsung, on her grief and her fond desire,
And the hope of her heart was quickened, and her joy was a living
      fire;
And she said: 'Now one of the earthly on the eyes of my child hath gazed
Nor shrunk before their glory, nor stayed her love amazed: 1990
I behold thee as Sigmund beholdeth,—and I was the home of thine
      heart—
Woe's me for the day when thou wert not, and the hour when we shall
      part!'

Then she held him a little season on her weary and happy breast,
And she told him of Sigmund and Volsung and the best sprung forth
      from the best:
She spake to the new-born baby as one who might understand,   1995
And told him of Sigmund's battle, and the dead by the sea-flood's
      strand,
And of all the wars passed over, and the light with darkness blent.

So she spake, and the sun rose higher, and her speech at last was spent,
And she gave him back to the women to bear forth to the people's
      kings,
That they too may rejoice in her glory and her day of happy things.   2000

But there sat the Helper of Men with King Elf and his Earls in the hall,
And they spake of the deeds that had been, and told of the times to
      befall,
And they hearkened and heard sweet voices and the sound of harps
      draw nigh,
Till their hearts were exceeding merry and they knew not wherefore or
      why:
Then, lo, in the hall white raiment, as thither the damsels came,   2005
And amid the hands of the foremost was the woven gold aflame.

'O daughters of earls,' said the Helper, 'what tidings then do ye bear?
Is it grief in the merry morning, or joy or wonder or fear?'

Quoth the first: 'It is grief for the foemen that the Masters of God-
      home would grieve.'
Said the next: ''Tis a wonder of wonders, that the hearkening world
      shall believe.'   2010
'A fear of all fears,' said the third, 'for the sword is uplifted on men.'
'A joy of all joys,' said the fourth, 'once come, and it comes not again!'

'Lo, son,' said the ancient Helper, 'glad sit the earls and the lords!
Lookst thou not for a token of tidings to follow such-like words?'

Saith King Elf: 'Great words of women! or great hath our dwelling
    become.'   2015
Said the women: 'Words shall be greater, when all folk shall praise our
    home.'
'What then hath betid,' said King Elf, 'do the high Gods stand in our
    gate?'
'Nay,' said they, 'else were we silent, and they should be telling
    of fate.'
'Is the bidding come,' said the Helper, 'that we wend the Gods
    to see?'
'Many summers and winters,' they said, 'ye shall live on the earth, it
    may be.'   2020
Said a young man: 'Will ye be telling that all we shall die no more?'
'Nay,' they answered, 'nay, who knoweth but the change may be hard at
    the door?'
'Come ships from the sea,' said an elder, 'with all gifts of the Eastland
    gold?'
'Was there less than enough,' said the women, 'when last our treasure
    was told?'
'Speak then,' said the ancient Helper, 'let the worst and the best be
    said.'   2025
Quoth they: ''Tis the Queen of the Isle-folk, she is weary-sick on her
    bed.'
Said King Elf: 'Yet ye come rejoicing; what more lieth under the
    tongue?'

They said: 'The earth is weary: but the tender blade hath sprung,
That shall wax till beneath its branches fair bloom the meadows green;
For the Gods and they that were mighty were glad erewhile with the
    Queen.'   2030

Said King Elf: 'How say ye, women? Of a King new-born do ye tell,
By a God of the Heavens begotten in our fathers' house to dwell?'

'By a God of the Earth,' they answered; 'but greater yet is the son,
Though long were the days of Sigmund, and great are the deeds he
    hath done.'

Then she with the golden burden to the kingly high-seat stepped   2035
And away from the new-born baby the purple cloths she swept,
And cried: 'O King of the people, long mayst thou live in bliss,
As our hearts today are happy! Queen Hiordis sends thee this,
And she saith that the world shall call it by the name that thou shalt
    name;
Now the gift to thee is given, and to thee is brought the fame.'   2040

Then e'en as a man astonied King Elf the Volsung took,
While his feast-hall's ancient timbers with the cry of the earl-folk
　　shook;
For the eyes of the child gleamed on him till he was as one who sees
The very Gods arising mid their carven images:
To his ears there came a murmur of far seas beneath the wind   2045
And the tramp of fierce-eyed warriors through the outland forest
　　blind;
The sound of hosts of battle, cries round the hoisted shield,
Low talk of the gathered wise-ones in the Goth-folk's holy field:
So the thought in a little moment through King Elf the mighty ran
Of the years and their building and burden, and toil of the sons of
　　man,   2050
The joy of folk and their sorrow, and the hope of deeds to do:
With the love of many peoples was the wise king smitten through,
As he hung o'er the new-born Volsung: but at last he raised his head,
And looked forth kind o'er his people, and spake aloud and said:

'O Sigmund King of Battle; O man of many days,   2055
Whom I saw mid the shields of the fallen and the dead men's silent
　　praise,
Lo, how hath the dark tide perished and the dawn of day begun!
And now, O mighty Sigmund, wherewith shall we name thy son?'

But there rose up a man most ancient, and he cried: 'Hail Dawn
　　of the Day!
How many things shalt thou quicken, how many shalt thou slay!   2060
How many things shalt thou waken, how many lull to sleep!
How many things shalt thou scatter, how many gather and keep!
O me, how thy love shall cherish, how thine hate shall wither and burn!
How the hope shall be sped from thy right hand, nor the fear to thy left
　　return!
O thy deeds that men shall sing of! O thy deeds that the Gods shall see!   2065
O SIGURD, Son of the Volsungs, O Victory yet to be!'

Men heard the name and they knew it, and they caught it up in the air,
And it went abroad by the windows and the doors of the feast-hall fair,
It went through street and market; o'er meadow and acre it went,
And over the wind-stirred forest and the dearth of the sea-beat bent,   2070
And over the sea-flood's welter, till the folk of the fishers heard,
And the hearts of the isle-abiders on the sun-scorched rocks were
　　stirred.

But the Queen in her golden chamber, the name she hearkened and knew;
And she heard the flock of the women, as back to the chamber they drew,

And the name of Sigurd entered, and the body of Sigurd was come,   2075
And it was as if Sigmund were living and she still in her lovely home;
Of all folk of the world was she well, and a soul fulfilled of rest
As alone in the chamber she wakened and Sigurd cherished her breast.

But men feast in the merry noontide, and glad is the April green
That a Volsung looks on the sunlight and the night and the darkness
  have been.   2080
Earls think of marvellous stories, and along the golden strings
Flit words of banded brethren and names of war-fain Kings:
All the days of the deeds of Sigmund who was born so long ago;
All deeds of the glorious Signy, and her tarrying-tide of woe;
Men tell of the years of Volsung, and how long agone it was   2085
That he changed his life in battle, and brought the tale to pass:
Then goeth the word of the Giants, and the world seems waxen old
For the dimness of King Rerir and the tale of his warfare told:
Yet unhushed are the singers' voices, nor yet the harp-strings cease
While yet is left a rumour of the mirk-wood's broken peace,   2090
And of Sigi the very ancient, and the unnamed Sons of God,
Of the days when the Lords of Heaven full oft the world-ways trod.

So stilleth the wind in the even and the sun sinks down in the sea,
And men abide the morrow and the Victory yet to be.

Sigurd getteth to him the horse that is called Greyfell.

Now waxeth the son of Sigmund in might and goodliness,   2095
And soft the days win over, and all men his beauty bless.
But amidst the summer season was the Isle-queen Hiordis wed
To King Elf the son of the Helper, and fair their life-days sped.
Peace lay on the land for ever, and the fields gave good increase,
And there was Sigurd waxing mid the plenty and the peace.   2100

Now hath the child grown greater, and is keen and eager of wit
And full of understanding, and oft hath he joy to sit
Amid talk of weighty matters when the wise men meet for speech;
And joyous he is moreover and blithe and kind with each.
But Regin the wise craftsmaster heedeth the youngling well,   2105
And before the Kings he cometh, and saith such words to tell.

'I have fostered thy youth, King Elf, and thine O Helper of men,
And ye wot that such a master no king shall see again;
And now would I foster Sigurd; for, though he be none of thy blood,
Mine heart of his days that shall be speaketh abundant good.'   2110

Then spake the Helper of men-folk: 'Yea, do herein thy will:
For thou art the Master of Masters, and hast learned me all my skill:
But think how bright is this youngling, and thy guile from him withhold;
For this craft of thine hath shown me that thy heart is grim and cold,
Though three men's lives thrice over thy wisdom might not learn;   2115
And I love this son of Sigmund, and mine heart to him doth yearn.'

Then Regin laughed, and answered: 'I doled out cunning to thee;
But nought with him will I measure: yet no cold-heart shall he be,
Nor grim, nor evil-natured: for whate'er my will might frame,
Gone forth is the word of the Norns, that abideth ever the same.   2120
And now, despite my cunning, how deem ye I shall die?'

And they said he would live as he listed, and at last in peace should lie
When he listed to live no longer; so mighty and wise he was.

But again he laughed and answered: 'One day it shall come to pass,
That a beardless youth shall slay me: I know the fateful doom;   2125
But nought may I withstand it, as it heaves up dim through the gloom.'

So is Sigurd now with Regin, and he learns him many things;
Yea, all save the craft of battle, that men learned the sons of kings:
The smithying sword and war-coat; the carving runes aright;
The tongues of many countries, and soft speech for men's delight;   2130
The dealing with the harp-strings, and the winding ways of song.
So wise of heart waxed Sigurd, and of body wondrous strong:
And he chased the deer of the forest, and many a wood-wolf slew,
And many a bull of the mountains: and the desert dales he knew,
And the heaths that the wind sweeps over; and seaward would he fare,   2135
Far out from the outer skerries, and alone the sea-wights dare.

On a day he sat with Regin amidst the unfashioned gold,
And the silver grey from the furnace; and Regin spake and told
Sweet tales of the days that have been, and the Kings of the bold
    and wise;
Till the lad's heart swelled with longing and lit his sunbright eyes.   2140

Then Regin looked upon him: 'Thou too shalt one day ride
As the Volsung Kings went faring through the noble world and wide.
For this land is nought and narrow, and Kings of the carles are these,
And their earls are acre-biders, and their hearts are dull with peace.'

But Sigurd knit his brows, and in wrathful wise he said: 2145
'Ill words of those thou speakest that my youth have cherished.
And the friends that have made me merry, and the land that is fair and
    good.'

Then Regin laughed and answered: 'Nay, well I see by thy mood
That wide wilt thou ride in the world like thy kin of the earlier days:
And wilt thou be wroth with thy master that he longs for thy winning
    the praise? 2150
And now if the sooth thou sayest, that these King-folk cherish thee
    well,
Then let them give thee a gift whereof the world shall tell:
Yea hearken to this my counsel, and crave for a battle-steed.'

Yet wroth was the lad and answered: 'I have many a horse to my need,
And all that the heart desireth, and what wouldst thou wish me more?' 2155

Then Regin answered and said: 'Thy kin of the Kings of yore
Were the noblest men of men-folk; and their hearts would never rest
Whatso of good they had gotten, if their hands held not the best.
Now do thou after my counsel, and crave of thy fosterers here
That thou choose of the horses of Gripir whichso thine heart holds
    dear.' 2160

He spake and his harp was with him, and he smote the strings full
    sweet,
And sang of the host of the Valkyrs, how they ride the battle to meet,
And the dew from the dear manes drippeth as they ride in the first of
    the sun,
And the tree-boughs open to meet it when the wind of the dawning is
    done:
And the deep dales drink its sweetness and spring into blossoming
    grass, 2165
And the earth groweth fruitful of men, and bringeth their glory to
    pass.

Then the wrath ran off from Sigurd, and he left the smithying stead
While the song yet rang in the doorway: and that eve to the Kings he
    said:
'Will ye do so much for mine asking as to give me a horse to my will?
For belike the days shall come, that shall all my heart fulfill, 2170
And teach me the deeds of a king.'
                    Then answered King Elf and spake:
'The stalls of the Kings are before thee to set aside or to take,
And nought we begrudge thee the best.'
                      Yet answered Sigurd again;
For his heart of the mountains aloft and the windy drift was fain:
'Fair seats for the knees of Kings! but now do I ask for a gift 2175
Such as all the world shall be praising, the best of the strong and the
    swift.

Ye shall give me a token for Gripir, and bid him to let me choose
From out of the noble stud-beasts that run in his meadow loose.
But if overmuch I have asked you, forget this prayer of mine,
And deem the word unspoken, and get ye to the wine.'   2180

Then smiled King Elf, and answered: 'A long way wilt thou ride,
To where unpeace and troubles and the griefs of the soul abide,
Yea unto the death at the last: yet surely shalt thou win
The praise of many a people: so have thy way herein.
Forsooth no more may we hold thee than the hazel copse may hold   2185
The sun of the early dawning, that turneth it all unto gold.'

Then sweetly Sigurd thanked them; and through the night he lay
Mid dreams of many a matter till the dawn was on the way;
Then he shook the sleep from off him, and that dwelling of Kings he
left
And wended his ways unto Gripir. On a crag from the mountain reft   2190
Was the house of the old King builded; and a mighty house it was,
Though few were the sons of men that over its threshold would pass:
But the wild ernes cried about it, and the vultures toward it flew,
And the winds from the heart of the mountains searched every
chamber through,
And about were meads wide-spreading; and many a beast thereon,   2195
Yea some that are men-folk's terror, their sport and pasture won.

So into the hall went Sigurd; and amidst was Gripir set
In a chair of the sea-beast's tooth; and his sweeping beard nigh met
The floor that was green as the ocean, and his gown was of mountain-
gold,
And the kingly staff in his hand was knobbed with the crystal cold.   2200

Now the first of the twain spake Gripir: 'Hail King with the eyen
bright!
Nought needest thou show the token, for I know of thy life and thy
light.
And no need to tell of thy message; it was wafted here on the wind,
That thou wouldst be coming today a horse in my meadow to find:
And strong must he be for the bearing of those deeds of thine that
shall be.   2205
Now choose thou of all the way-wearers that are running loose in my lea,
And be glad as thine heart will have thee and the fate that leadeth thee
on,
And I bid thee again come hither when the sword of worth is won,
And thy loins are girt for thy going on the road that before thee lies;
For a glimmering over its darkness is come before mine eyes.'   2210

Then again gat Sigurd outward, and adown the steep he ran
And unto the horse-fed meadow: but lo, a grey-clad man,
One-eyed and seeming-ancient, there met him by the way:
And he spake: 'Thou hastest, Sigurd; yet tarry till I say
A word that shall well bestead thee: for I know of these mountains well   2215
And all the lea of Gripir, and the beasts that thereon dwell.'

'Wouldst thou have red gold for thy tidings? art thou Gripir's horse-
    herd then?
Nay sure, for thy face is shining like the battle-eager men
My master Regin tells of: and I love thy cloud-grey gown.
And thy visage gleams above it like a thing my dreams have known.'   2220

'Nay whiles have I heeded the horse-kind,' then spake that elder of days,
'And sooth do the sages say, when the beasts of my breeding they
    praise.'

There is one thereof in the meadow, and, wouldst thou cull him out,
Thou shalt follow an elder's counsel, who hath brought strange things
    about,
Who hath known thy father aforetime, and other kings of thy kin.'   2225

So Sigurd said, 'I am ready; and what is the deed to win?'

He said: 'We shall drive the horses adown to the water-side,
That cometh forth from the mountains, and note what next shall
    betide.'

Then the twain sped on together, and they drave the horses on
Till they came to a rushing river, a water wide and wan;   2230
And the white mews hovered o'er it; but none might hear their cry
For the rush and the rattle of waters, as the downlong flood swept by.
So the whole herd took the river and strove the stream to stem,
And many a brave steed was there; but the flood o'ermastered them:
And some, it swept them down-ward, and some won back to bank,   2235
Some, caught by the net of the eddies, in the swirling hubbub sank;
But one of all swam over, and they saw his mane of grey
Toss over the flowery meadows, a bright thing far away:
Wide then he wheeled about them, then took the stream again
And with the waves' white horses mingled his cloudy mane.   2240

Then spake the elder of days: 'Hearken now, Sigurd, and hear;
Time was when I gave thy father a gift thou shalt yet deem dear,
And this horse is a gift of my giving:—heed nought where thou mayst ride:
For I have seen thy fathers in a shining house abide,
And on earth they thought of its threshold, and the gifts I had to give;   2245
Nor prayed for a little longer, and a little longer to live.'

Then forth he strode to the mountains, and fain was Sigurd now
To ask him many a matter: but dim did his bright shape grow,
As a man from the litten doorway fades into the dusk of night;
And the sun in the high-noon shone, and the world was exceeding
   bright.   2250

So Sigurd turned to the river and stood by the wave-wet strand,
And the grey horse swims to his feet and lightly leaps aland,
And the youngling looks upon him, and deems none beside him good.
And indeed, as tells the story, he was come of Sleipnir's blood,
The tireless horse of Odin: cloud-grey he was of hue,   2255
And it seemed as Sigurd backed him that Sigmund's son he knew,
So glad he went beneath him. Then the youngling's song arose
As he brushed through the noon-tide blossoms of Gripir's mighty
   close,
Then he singeth the song of Greyfell, the horse that Odin gave,
Who swam through the sweeping river, and back through the toppling
   wave.   2260

Regin telleth Sigurd of his kindred, and of the gold that was accursed from ancient days.

Now yet the days pass over, and more than words may tell
Grows Sigurd strong and lovely, and all children love him well.
But oft he looks on the mountains and many a time is fain
To know of what lies beyond them, and learn of the wide world's
   gain.
And he saith: 'I dwell in a land that is ruled by none of my blood;   2265
And my mother's sons are waxing, and fair kings shall they be
   and good;
And their servant or their betrayer—not one of these will I be.
Yet needs must I wait for a little till Odin calls for me.'

Now again it happed on a day that he sat in Regin's hall
And hearkened many tidings of what had chanced to fall,   2270
And of kings that sought their kingdoms o'er many a waste and wild,
And at last saith the crafty master:
                         'Thou art King Sigmund's child:
Wilt thou wait till these kings of the carles shall die in a little land,
Or wilt thou serve their sons and carry the cup to their hand;
Or abide in vain for the day that never shall come about,   2275
When their banners shall dance in the wind and shake to the war-gods'
   shout?'

Then Sigurd answered and said: 'Nought such do I look to be.
But thou, a deedless man, too much thou eggest me:
And these folk are good and trusty, and the land is lovely and sweet,
And in rest and in peace it lieth as the floor of Odin's feet: 2280
Yet I know that the world is wide, and filled with deeds unwrought;
And for e'en such work was I fashioned, lest the songcraft come to
     nought,
When the harps of God-home tinkle, and the Gods are at stretch to
     hearken:
Lest the hosts of the Gods be scanty when their day hath begun to
     darken,
When the bonds of the Wolf wax thin, and Loki fretteth his chain.   2285
And sure for the house of my fathers full oft my heart is fain,
And meseemeth I hear them talking of the day when I shall come,
And of all the burden of deeds, that my hand shall bear them home.
And so when the deed is ready, nowise the man shall lack:
But the wary foot is the surest, and the hasty oft turns back.'   2290

Then answered Regin the guileful: 'The deed is ready to hand,
Yet holding my peace is the best, for well thou lovest the land;
And thou lovest thy life moreover, and the peace of thy youthful days,
And why should the full-fed feaster his hand to the rye-bread raise?
Yet they say that Sigmund begat thee and he looked to fashion a man.   2295
Fear nought; he lieth quiet in his mound by the sea-waves wan.'

So shone the eyes of Sigurd, that the shield against him hung
Cast back their light as the sunbeams; but his voice to the roof-tree rung:
'Tell me, thou Master of Masters, what deed is the deed I shall do?
Nor mock thou the son of Sigmund lest the day of his birth thou rue.'   2300

Then answered the Master of Sleight: 'The deed is the righting of
     wrong,
And the quelling a bale and a sorrow that the world hath endured
     o'erlong,
And the winning a treasure untold, that shall make thee more than the
     kings;
Thereof is the Helm of Aweing, the wonder of earthly things,
And thereof is its very fellow, the War-coat all of gold,   2305
That has not its like in the heavens, nor has earth of its fellow told.'

Then answered Sigurd the Volsung: 'How long hereof hast thou
     known?
And what unto thee is this treasure, that thou seemest to give as thine
     own?'

'Alas!' quoth the smithying master, 'it is mine, yet none of mine,
Since my heart herein avails not, and my hand is frail and fine—   2310
It is long since I first came hither to seek a man for my need;
For I saw by a glimmering light that hence would spring the deed,
And many a deed of the world: but the generations passed,
And the first of the days was as near to the end that I sought as the last;
Till I looked on thine eyes in the cradle: and now I deem through
     thee,   2315
That the end of my days of waiting, and the end of my woes shall be.'

Then Sigurd awhile was silent; but at last he answered and said:
'Thou shalt have thy will and the treasure, and shalt take the curse on
     thine head
If a curse the gold enwrappeth: but the deed will I surely do,
For today the dreams of my childhood have bloomed in my heart anew: 2320
And I long to look on the world and the glory of the earth,
And to deal in the dealings of men, and garner the harvest of worth.
But tell me, thou Master of Masters, where lieth this measureless
     wealth;
Is it guarded by swords of the earl-folk, or kept by cunning and
     stealth?
Is it over the main sea's darkness, or beyond the mountain wall?   2325
Or e'en in these peaceful acres anigh to the hands of all?'

Then Regin answered sweetly: 'Hereof must a tale be told:
Bide sitting, thou son of Sigmund, on the heap of unwrought gold,
And hearken of wondrous matters, and of things unheard, unsaid,
And deeds of my beholding ere the first of Kings was made.   2330

'And first ye shall know of a sooth, that I never was born of the race
Which the masters of God-home have made to cover the fair earth's face;
But I come of the Dwarfs departed; and fair was the earth whileome
Ere the short-lived thralls of the Gods amidst its dales were come:—
And how were we worse than the Gods, though maybe we lived not as
     long?   2335
Yet no weight of memory maimed us; nor aught we knew of wrong.
What felt our souls of shaming, what knew our hearts of love?
We did and undid at pleasure, and repented nought thereof.
—Yea we were exceeding mighty—bear with me yet, my son;
For whiles can I scarcely think it that our days are wholly done.   2340
And trust not thy life in my hands in the day when most I seem
Like the Dwarfs that are long departed, and most of my kindred
     I dream.

'So as we dwelt came tidings that the Gods amongst us were,
And the people come from Asgard: then rose up hope and fear,
And strange shapes of things went flitting betwixt the night and the
    eve,   2345
And our sons waxed wild and wrathful, and our daughters learned to
    grieve.
Then we fell to the working of metal, and the deeps of the earth would
    know,
And we dealt with venom and leechcraft, and we fashioned spear and
    bow,
And we set the ribs to the oak-keel, and looked on the landless sea;
And the world began to be such-like as the Gods would have it to be.   2350
In the womb of the woeful Earth had they quickened the grief and the
    gold.

'It was Reidmar the Ancient begat me; and now was he waxen old,
And a covetous man and a king; and he bade, and I built him a hall,
And a golden glorious house; and thereto his sons did he call,
And he bade them be evil and wise, that his will through them might
    be wrought.   2355
Then he gave unto Fafnir my brother the soul that feareth nought,
And the brow of the hardened iron, and the hand that may never fail,
And the greedy heart of a king, and the ear that hears no wail.

'But next unto Otter my brother he gave the snare and the net,
And the longing to wend through the wild-wood, and wade the
    highways wet: 2360
And the foot that never resteth, while aught be left alive
That hath cunning to match man's cunning or might with his might to
    strive.

'And to me, the least and the youngest, what gift for the slaying of ease?
Save the grief that remembers the past, and the fear that the future
    sees;
And the hammer and fashioning-iron, and the living coal of fire;   2365
And the craft that createth a semblance, and fails of the heart's desire;
And the toil that each dawning quickens and the task that is never
    done;
And the heart that longeth ever, nor will look to the deed that is won.

'Thus gave my father the gifts that might never be taken again;
Far worse were we now than the Gods, and but little better than men.   2370
But yet of our ancient might one thing had we left us still:
We had craft to change our semblance, and could shift us at our will

Into bodies of the beast-kind, or fowl, or fishes cold;
For belike no fixèd semblance we had in the days of old,
Till the Gods were waxen busy, and all things their form must take   2375
That knew of good and evil, and longed to gather and make.

'So dwelt we, brethren and father; and Fafnir my brother fared
As the scourge and compeller of all things, and left no wrong undared;
But for me, I toiled and I toiled; and fair grew my father's house;
But writhen and foul were the hands that had made it glorious;   2380
And the love of women left me, and the fame of sword and shield:
And the sun and the winds of heaven, and the fowl and the grass of the
     field
Were grown as the tools of my smithy; and all the world I knew,
And the glories that lie beyond it, and whitherward all things drew;
And myself a little fragment amidst it all I saw,   2385
Grim, cold-heart, and unmighty as the tempest-driven straw.
—Let be.—For Otter my brother saw seldom field or fold,
And he oftenest used that custom, whereof e'en now I told,
And would shift his shape with the wood-beasts and the things of land
     and sea;
And he knew what joy their hearts had, and what they longed to be,   2390
And their dim-eyed understanding, and his wood-craft waxed so great,
That he seemed the king of the creatures and their very mortal fate.

'Now as the years won over three folk of the heavenly halls
Grew aweary of sleepless sloth, and the day that nought befalls;
And they fain would look on the earth, and their latest handiwork,   2395
And turn the fine gold over, lest a flaw therein should lurk.
And the three were the heart-wise Odin, the Father of the Slain,
And Loki, the World's Begrudger, who maketh all labour vain,
And Hænir, the Utter-Blameless, who wrought the hope of man,
And his heart and inmost yearnings, when first the work began;—   2400
—The God that was aforetime, and hereafter yet shall be,
When the new light yet undreamed of shall shine o'er earth and sea.

'Thus about the world they wended and deemed it fair and good,
And they loved their life-days dearly: so came they to the wood,
And the lea without a shepherd and the dwellings of the deer,   2405
And unto a mighty water that ran from a fathomless mere.
Now that flood my brother Otter had haunted many a day
For its plenteous fruit of fishes; and there on the bank he lay
As the Gods came wandering thither; and he slept, and in his dreams

He saw the downlong river, and its fishy-peopled streams,   2410
And the swift smooth heads of its forces, and its swirling wells and deep,
Where hang the poisèd fishes, and their watch in the rock-halls keep.
And so, as he thought of it all, and its deeds and its wanderings,
Whereby it ran to the sea down the road of scaly things,
His body was changed with his thought, as yet was the wont of our
     kind,   2415
And he grew but an Otter indeed; and his eyes were sleeping and blind
The while he devoured the prey, a golden red-flecked trout.
Then passed by Odin and Hænir, nor cumbered their souls with
     doubt;
But Loki lingered a little, and guile in his heart arose,
And he saw through the shape of the Otter, and beheld a chief of
     his foes,   2420
A king of the free and the careless: so he called up his baleful might,
And gathered his godhead together, and tore a shard outright
From the rock-wall of the river, and across its green wells cast;
And roaring over the waters that bolt of evil passed,
And smote my brother Otter that his heart's life fled away,   2425
And bore his man's shape with it, and beast-like there he lay,
Stark dead on the sun-lit blossoms: but the Evil God rejoiced,
And because of the sound of his singing the wild grew many-voiced.

'Then the three Gods waded the river, and no word Hænir spake,
For his thoughts were set on God-home, and the day that is ever
     awake.   2430
But Odin laughed in his wrath, and murmured: "Ah, how long,
Till the iron shall ring on the anvil for the shackles of thy wrong!"

'Then Loki takes up the quarry, and is e'en as a man again;
And the three wend on through the wild-wood till they come to a
     grassy plain
Beneath the untrodden mountains; and lo a noble house,   2435
And a hall with great craft fashioned, and made full glorious;
But night on the earth was falling; so scantly might they see
The wealth of its smooth-wrought stonework and its world of imagery:
Then Loki bade turn thither since day was at an end,
And into that noble dwelling the lords of God-home wend;   2440
And the porch was fair and mighty, and so smooth-wrought was its
     gold,
That the mirrored stars of heaven therein might ye behold:
But the hall, what words shall tell it, how fair it rose aloft,
And the marvels of its windows, and its golden hangings soft,
And the forest of its pillars! and each like the wave's heart shone   2445

And the mirrored boughs of the garden were dancing fair thereon.
—Long years agone was it builded, and where are its wonders now?

'Now the men of God-home marvelled, and gazed through the
    golden glow,
And a man like a covetous king amidst of the hall they saw;
And his chair was the tooth of the whale, wrought smooth with
    never a flaw;   2450
And his gown was the sea-born purple, and he bore a crown on his
    head,
But never a sword was before him: kind-seeming words he said,
And bade rest to the weary feet that had worn the wild so long.
So they sat, and were men by seeming; and there rose up music and
    song,
And they ate and drank and were merry: but amidst the glee of
    the cup   2455
They felt themselves tangled and caught, as when the net cometh up
Before the folk of the firth, and the main sea lieth far off;
And the laughter of lips they hearkened, and that hall-abider's scoff,
As his face and his mocking eyes anigh to their faces drew,
And their godhead was caught in the net, and no shift of creation they
    knew   2460
To escape from their man-like bodies; so great that day was the Earth.

'Then spake the hall-abider: "Where then is thy guileful mirth,
And thy hall-glee gone, O Loki? Come, Hænir, fashion now
My heart for love and for hope, that the fear in my body may grow,
That I may grieve and be sorry, that the ruth may arise in me,   2465
As thou dealtst with the first of men-folk, when a master-smith thou
    wouldst be.
And thou, Allfather Odin, hast thou come on a bastard brood?
Or hadst thou belike a brother, thy twin for evil and good,
That waked amidst thy slumber, and slumbered midst thy work?
Nay, Wise-one, art thou silent as a child amidst the mirk?   2470
Ah, I know ye are called the Gods, and are mighty men at home,
But now with a guilt on your heads to no feeble folk are ye come,
To a folk that need you nothing: time was when we knew you not:
Yet e'en then fresh was the winter, and the summer sun was hot,
And the wood-meats stayed our hunger, and the water quenched our
    thirst,   2475
Ere the good and the evil wedded and begat the best and the worst.
And how if today I undo it, that work of your fashioning,
If the web of the world run backward, and the high heavens lack a
    King?

—Woe's me! for your ancient mastery shall help you at your need:
If ye fill up the gulf of my longing and my empty heart of greed,   2480
And slake the flame ye have quickened, then may ye go your ways
And get ye back to your kingship and the driving on of the days
To the day of the gathered war-hosts, and the tide of your Fateful
    Gloom.
Now nought may ye gainsay it that my mouth must speak the doom,
For ye wot well I am Reidmar, and that there ye lie red-hand   2485
From the slaughtering of my offspring, and the spoiling of my land;
For his death of my wold hath bereft me and every highway wet.
—Nay, Loki, naught avails it, well-fashioned is the net.
Come forth, my son, my war-god, and show the Gods their work,
And thou who mightst learn e'en Loki, if need were to lie or lurk!"   2490

'And there was I, I Regin, the smithier of the snare,
And high up Fafnir towered with the brow that knew no fear,
With the wrathful and pitiless heart that was born of my father's will,
And the greed that the Gods had fashioned the fate of the earth to
    fulfill.

'Then spake the Father of Men: "We have wrought thee wrong indeed,   2495
And, wouldst thou amend it with wrong, thine errand must we speed;
For I know of thine heart's desire, and the gold thou shalt nowise lack,
—Nor all the works of the gold. But best were thy word drawn back,
If indeed the doom of the Norns be not utterly now gone forth."

'Then Reidmar laughed and answered: "So much is thy word of worth!   2500
And they call thee Odin for this, and stretch forth hands in vain,
And pray for the gifts of a God who giveth and taketh again!
It was better in times past over, when we prayed for nought at all,
When no love taught us beseeching, and we had no troth to recall.
Ye have changed the world, and it bindeth with the right and the wrong
    ye have made,   2505
Nor may ye be Gods henceforward save the rightful ransom be paid.
But perchance ye are weary of kingship, and will deal no more with the
    earth?
Then curse the world, and depart, and sit in your changeless mirth;
And there shall be no more kings, and battle and murder shall fail,
And the world shall laugh and long not, nor weep, nor fashion the
    tale."   2510

'So spake Reidmar the Wise; but the wrath burned through his word,
And wasted his heart of wisdom; and there was Fafnir the Lord,
And there was Regin the Wright, and they raged at their father's back:

And all these cried out together with the voice of the sea-storm's
　　wrack;
"O hearken, Gods of the Goths! ye shall die, and we shall be Gods,   2515
And rule your men belovèd with bitter-heavy rods,
And make them beasts beneath us, save today ye do our will,
And pay us the ransom of blood, and our hearts with the gold fulfill."

'But Odin spake in answer, and his voice was awful and cold:
"Give righteous doom, O Reidmar! say what ye will of the Gold!"   2520

'Then Reidmar laughed in his heart, and his wrath and his wisdom fled,
And nought but his greed abided; and he spake from his throne and
　　said:

' "Now hearken the doom I shall speak! Ye stranger-folk shall be free
When ye give me the Flame of the Waters, the gathered Gold of the
　　Sea,
That Andvari hideth rejoicing in the wan realm pale as the grave;   2525
And the Master of Sleight shall fetch it, and the hand that never gave,
And the heart that begrudgeth for ever shall gather and give and rue.
—Lo this is the doom of the wise, and no doom shall be spoken anew."

'Then Odin spake: "It is well; the Curser shall seek for the curse;
And the Greedy shall cherish the evil—and the seed of the Great they
　　shall nurse."   2530
'No word spake Reidmar the great, for the eyes of his heart were
　　turned

'To the edge of the outer desert, so sore for the gold he yearned.
But Loki I loosed from the toils, and he goeth his way abroad;
And the heart of Odin he knoweth, and where he shall seek the Hoard.

'There is a desert of dread in the uttermost part of the world,   2535
Where over a wall of mountains is a mighty water hurled,
Whose hidden head none knoweth, nor where it meeteth the sea;
And that force is the Force of Andvari, and an Elf of the Dark is he.
In the cloud and the desert he dwelleth amid that land alone;
And his work is the storing of treasure within his house of stone.   2540
Time was when he knew of wisdom, and had many a tale to tell
Of the days before the Dwarf-age, and of what in that world befell:
And he knew of the stars and the sun, and the worlds that come and go
On the nether rim of heaven, and whence the wind doth blow,
And how the sea hangs balanced betwixt the curving lands,   2545
And how all drew together for the first Gods' fashioning hands.
But now is all gone from him, save the craft of gathering gold,
And he heedeth nought of the summer, nor knoweth the winter cold,

Nor looks to the sun nor the snowfall, nor ever dreams of the sea,
Nor hath heard of the making of men-folk, nor of where the high
    Gods be: 2550
But ever he gripeth and gathereth, and he toileth hour by hour,
Nor knoweth the noon from the midnight as he looks on his stony
    bower,
And saith: "It is short, it is narrow for all I shall gather and get;
For the world is but newly fashioned, and long shall its years be yet."

'There Loki fareth, and seeth in a land of nothing good,   2555
Far off o'er the empty desert, the reek of the falling flood
Go up to the floor of heaven, and thither turn his feet
As he weaveth the unseen meshes and the snare of strong deceit;
So he cometh his ways to the water, where the glittering foam-bow
    glows,
And the huge flood leaps the rock-wall and a green arch over it throws.   2560
There under the roof of water he treads the quivering floor,
And the hush of the desert is felt amid the water's roar,
And the bleak sun lighteth the wave-vault, and tells of the fruitless plain,
And the showers that nourish nothing, and the summer come in vain.

'There did the great Guile-master his toils and his tangles set,   2565
And as wide as was the water, so wide was woven the net;
And as dim as the Elf's remembrance did the meshes of it show;
And he had no thought of sorrow, nor spared to come and go
On his errands of griping and getting till he felt himself tangled and
    caught:
Then back to his blinded soul was his ancient wisdom brought,   2570
And he saw his fall and his ruin, as a man by the lightning's flame
Sees the garth all flooded by foemen; and again he remembered his
    name;
And e'en as a book well written the tale of the Gods he knew,
And the tale of the making of men, and much of the deeds they
    should do.

'But Loki took his man-shape, and laughed aloud and cried: 2575
"What fish of the ends of the earth is so strong and so feeble-eyed,

That he draweth the pouch of my net on his road to the dwelling of
    Hell?
What Elf that hath heard the gold growing, but hath heard not the
    light winds tell
That the Gods with the world have been dealing and have fashioned
    men for the earth?

Where is he that hath ridden the cloud-horse and measured the ocean's
    girth,   2580
But seen nought of the building of God-home nor the forging of the
    sword:
Where then is the maker of nothing, the earless and eyeless lord?
In the pouch of my net he lieth, with his head on the threshold of
    Hell!"

'Then the Elf lamented, and said: "Thou knowst of my name full well:
Andvari begotten of Oinn, whom the Dwarf-kind called the Wise,   2585
By the worst of the Gods is taken, the forge and the father of lies."

'Said Loki: "How of the Elf-kind, do they love their latter life,
When their weal is all departed, and they lie alow in the strife?"

'Then Andvari groaned and answered: "I know what thou wouldst
    have,
The wealth mine own hands gathered, the gold that no man gave."   2590

' "Come forth," said Loki, "and give it, and dwell in peace
    henceforth—
Or die in the toils if thou listest, if thy life be nothing worth." '

'Full sore the Elf lamented, but he came before the God,
And the twain went into the rock-house and on fine gold they trod,
And the walls shone bright, and brighter than the sun of the upper air.   2595
How great was that treasure of treasures: and the Helm of Dread was
    there;
The world but in dreams had seen it; and there was the hauberk of
    gold;
None other is in the heavens, nor has earth of its fellow told.

'Then Loki bade the Elf-king bring all to the upper day,
And he dight himself with his Godhead to bear the treasure away: 2600
So there in the dim grey desert before the God of Guile,
Great heaps of the hid-world's treasure the weary Elf must pile,
And Loki looked on laughing: but, when it all was done,
And the Elf was hurrying homeward, his finger gleamed in the sun:
Then Loki cried: "Thou art guileful: thou hast not learned the tale   2605
Of the wisdom that Gods hath gotten and their might of all avail.
Hither to me! that I learn thee of a many things to come;
Or despite of all wilt thou journey to the dead man's deedless home.
Come hither again to thy master, and give the ring to me;
For meseems it is Loki's portion, and the Bale of Men shall it be."   2610

'Then the Elf drew off the gold-ring and stood with empty hand
E'en where the flood fell over 'twixt the water and the land,
And he gazed on the great Guile-master, and huge and grim he grew;
And his anguish swelled within him, and the word of the Norns he
    knew;
How that gold was the seed of gold to the wise and the shapers of
    things,   2615
The hoarders of hidden treasure, and the unseen glory of rings;
But the seed of woe to the world and the foolish wasters of men,
And grief to the generations that die and spring again:
Then he cried:
           "There farest thou Loki, and might I load thee worse
Than with what thine ill heart beareth, then shouldst thou bear my
    curse: 2620
But for men a curse thou bearest: entangled in my gold,
Amid my woe abideth another woe untold.
Two brethren and a father, eight kings my grief shall slay;
And the hearts of queens shall be broken, and their eyes shall loathe
    the day.
Lo, how the wilderness blossoms! Lo, how the lonely lands   2625
Are waving with the harvest that fell from my gathering hands!"

'But Loki laughed in silence, and swift in Godhead went,
To the golden hall of Reidmar and the house of our content.
But when that world of treasure was laid within our hall
'Twas as if the sun were minded to live 'twixt wall and wall,   2630
And all we stood by and panted. Then Odin spake and said:

"O Kings, O folk of the Dwarf-kind, lo, the ransom duly paid!
Will ye have this sun of the ocean, and reap the fruitful field,
And garner up the harvest that earth therefrom shall yield?"

'So he spake; but a little season nought answered Reidmar the wise   2635
But turned his face from the Treasure, and peered with eager eyes
Endlong the hall and athwart it, as a man may chase about
A ray of the sun of the morning that a naked sword throws out;
And lo from Loki's right-hand came the flash of the fruitful ring,
And at last spake Reidmar scowling:
                    "Ye wait for my yea-saying   2640
That your feet may go free on the earth, and the fear of my toils may
    be done;
That then ye may say in your laughter: The fools of the time agone!
The purblind eyes of the Dwarf-kind! they have gotten the garnered
    sheaf

And have let their Masters depart with the Seed of Gold and of Grief:
O Loki, friend of Allfather, cast down Andvari's ring,   2645
Or the world shall yet turn backward and the high heavens lack a king."

'Then Loki drew off the Elf-ring and cast it down on the heap,
And forth as the gold met gold did the light of its glory leap:
But he spake: "It rejoiceth my heart that no whit of all ye shall lack,
Lest the curse of the Elf-king cleave not, and ye 'scape the utter
    wrack."   2650

'Then laughed and answered Reidmar: "I shall have it while I live,
And that shall be long, meseemeth: for who is there may strive
With my sword, the war-wise Fafnir, and my shield that is Regin the
    Smith?
But if indeed I should die, then let men-folk deal therewith,
And ride to the golden glitter through evil deeds and good.   2655
I will have my heart's desire, and do as the high Gods would."

'Then I loosed the Gods from their shackles, and great they grew on
    the floor
And into the night they gat them; but Odin turned by the door,
And we looked not, little we heeded, for we grudged his mastery;
Then he spake, and his voice was waxen as the voice of the winter sea: 2660

'"O Kings, O folk of the Dwarfs, why then will ye covet and rue?
I have seen your fathers' fathers and the dust wherefrom they grew;
But who hath heard of my father or the land where first I sprung?
Who knoweth my day of repentance, or the year when I was young?
Who hath learned the names of the Wise-one or measured out his will?   2665
Who hath gone before to teach him, and the doom of days fulfill?
Lo, I look on the Curse of the Gold, and wrong amended by wrong,
And love by love confounded, and the strong abased by the strong;
And I order it all and amend it, and the deeds that are done I see,
And none other beholdeth or knoweth; and who shall be wise unto me?   2670
For myself to myself I offered, that all wisdom I might know,
And fruitful I waxed of works, and good and fair did they grow;
And I knew, and I wrought and fore-ordered; and evil sat by my side,
And myself by myself hath been doomed, and I look for the fateful
    tide;
And I deal with the generations, and the men mine hand hath made,   2675
And myself by myself shall be grieved, lest the world and its fashioning
    fade."

'They went and the Gold abided: but the words Allfather spake,
I call them back full often for that golden even's sake,

Yet little that hour I heard them, save as wind across the lea;
For the gold shone up on Reidmar and on Fafnir's face and on me.   2680
And sore I loved that treasure: so I wrapped my heart in guile,
And sleeked my tongue with sweetness, and set my face in a smile,
And I bade my father keep it, the more part of the gold,
Yet give good store to Fafnir for his goodly help and bold,
And deal me a little handful for my smithying-help that day.   2685
But no little I desired, though for little I might pray;
And prayed I for much or for little, he answered me no more
Than the shepherd answers the wood-wolf who howls at the yule-tide
     door:
But good he ever deemed it to sit on his ivory throne,
And stare on the red rings' glory, and deem he was ever alone: 2690
And never a word spake Fafnir, but his eyes waxed red and grim
As he looked upon our father, and noted the ways of him.

'The night waned into the morning, and still above the Hoard
Sat Reidmar clad in purple; but Fafnir took his sword,
And I took my smithying-hammer, and apart in the world we went;   2695
But I came aback in the even, and my heart was heavy and spent;
And I longed, but fear was upon me and I durst not go to the Gold;
So I lay in the house of my toil mid the things I had fashioned of old;
And methought as I lay in my bed 'twixt waking and slumber of night
That I heard the tinkling metal and beheld the hall alight,   2700
But I slept and dreamed of the Gods, and the things that never have
     slept,
Till I woke to a cry and a clashing and forth from the bed I leapt,
And there by the heaped-up Elf-gold my brother Fafnir stood,
And there at his feet lay Reidmar and reddened the Treasure with
     blood;
And e'en as I looked on his eyen they glazed and whitened with death,   2705
And forth on the torch-litten hall he shed his latest breath.

'But I looked on Fafnir and trembled for he wore the Helm of Dread,
And his sword was bare in his hand, and the sword and the hand were red
With the blood of our father Reidmar, and his body was wrapped in
     gold,
With the ruddy-gleaming mailcoat of whose fellow hath nought been
     told,   2710
And it seemed as I looked upon him that he grew beneath mine eyes:
And then in the mid-hall's silence did his dreadful voice arise:

' "I have slain my father Reidmar, that I alone might keep
The Gold of the darksome places, the Candle of the Deep.

I am such as the Gods have made me, lest the Dwarf-kind people the
    earth,   2715
Or mingle their ancient wisdom with its short-lived latest birth.
I shall dwell alone henceforward, and the Gold and its waxing curse,
I shall brood on them both together, let my life grow better or worse.
And I am a King henceforward and long shall be my life,
And the Gold shall grow with my longing, for I shall hide it from strife, 2720
And hoard up the Ring of Andvari in the house thine hand hath built.
O thou, wilt thou tarry and tarry, till I cast thy blood on the guilt?
Lo, I am a King for ever, and alone on the Gold shall I dwell
And do no deed to repent of and leave no tale to tell."

'More awful grew his visage as he spake the word of dread   2725
And no more durst I behold him, but with heart a-cold I fled;
I fled from the glorious house my hands had made so fair,
As poor as the new-born baby with nought of raiment or gear:
I fled from the heaps of gold, and my goods were the eager will,
And the heart that remembereth all, and the hand that may never be
    still.   2730

'Then unto this land I came, and that was long ago
As men-folk count the years; and I taught them to reap and to sow,
And a famous man I became: but that generation died,
And they said that Frey had taught them, and a God my name did
    hide.
Then I taught them the craft of metals, and the sailing of the sea, 2735
And the taming of the horse-kind, and the yoke-beasts' husbandry,
And the building up of houses; and that race of men went by,
And they said that Thor had taught them; and a smithying-carle was I.
Then I gave their maidens the needle and I bade them hold the rock,
And the shuttle-race gaped for them as they sat at the weaving-stock. 2740
But by then these were waxen crones to sit dim-eyed by the door,
It was Freyia had come among them to teach the weaving-lore.
Then I taught them the tales of old, and fair songs fashioned and true,
And their speech grew into music of measured time and due,
And they smote the harp to my bidding, and the land grew soft and
    sweet: 2745
But ere the grass of their grave-mounds rose up above my feet,
It was Bragi had made them sweet-mouthed, and I was the wandering
    scald;
Yet green did my cunning flourish by whatso name I was called,
And I grew the master of masters—Think thou how strange it is
That the sword in the hands of a stripling shall one day end all this! 2750

'Yet oft mid all my wisdom did I long for my brother's part,
And Fafnir's mighty kingship weighed heavy on my heart
When the Kings of the earthly kingdoms would give me golden gifts
From out of their scanty treasures, due pay for my cunning shifts.
And once—didst thou number the years thou wouldst think it long
 ago—   2755
I wandered away to the country from whence our stem did grow.
There methought the fells grown greater, but waste did the meadows
 lie,
And the house was rent and ragged and open to the sky.
But lo, when I came to the doorway, great silence brooded there,
Nor bat nor owl would haunt it, nor the wood-wolves drew anear.   2760
Then I went to the pillared hall-stead, and lo, huge heaps of gold,
And to and fro amidst them a mighty Serpent rolled:
Then my heart grew chill with terror, for I thought on the wont of our
 race,
And I, who had lost their cunning, was a man in a deadly place,
A feeble man and a swordless in the lone destroyer's fold;   2765
For I knew that the Worm was Fafnir, the Wallower on the Gold.

'So I gathered my strength and fled, and hid my shame again
Mid the foolish sons of men-folk; and the more my hope was vain,
The more I longed for the Treasure, and deliv'rance from the yoke:
And yet passed the generations, and I dwelt with the short-lived folk. 2770

'Long years, and long years after the tale of men-folk told
How up on the Glittering Heath was the house and the dwelling of
 gold,
And within that house was the Serpent, and the Lord of the Fearful
 Face:
Then I wondered sore of the desert; for I thought of the golden place
My hands of old had builded; for I knew by many a sign   2775
That the Fearful Face was my brother, that the blood of the Worm was
 mine.
This was ages long ago, and yet in that desert he dwells,
Betwixt him and men death lieth, and no man of his semblance tells;
But the tale of the great Gold-wallower is never the more outworn.
Then came thy kin, O Sigurd, and thy father's father was born,   2780
And I fell to the dreaming of dreams, and I saw thine eyes therein,
And I looked and beheld thy glory and all that thy sword should win;
And I thought that thou shouldst be he, who should bring my heart its
 rest,
That of all the gifts of the Kings thy sword should give me the best.

'Ah, I fell to the dreaming of dreams; and oft the gold I saw,   2785
And the golden-fashioned Hauberk, clean-wrought without a flaw,
And the Helm that aweth the world; and I knew of Fafnir's heart
That his wisdom was greater than mine, because he had held him
    apart,
Nor spilt on the sons of men-folk our knowledge of ancient days,
Nor bartered one whit for their love, nor craved for the
    people's praise.   2790

'And some day I shall have it all, his gold and his craft and his heart
And the gathered and garnered wisdom he guards in the mountains
    apart.
And then when my hand is upon it, my hand shall be as the spring
To thaw his winter away and the fruitful tide to bring.
It shall grow, it shall grow into summer, and I shall be he that wrought,   2795
And my deeds shall be remembered, and my name that once was
    nought.
Yea I shall be Frey, and Thor, and Freyia, and Bragi in one:
Yea the God of all that is,—and no deed in the wide world done,
But the deed that my heart would fashion: and the songs of the freed
    from the yoke
Shall bear to my house in the heavens the love and the longing of folk;   2800
And there shall be no more dying, and the sea shall be as the land,
And the world for ever and ever shall be young beneath my hand.'

Then his eyelids fell, and he slumbered, and it seemed as Sigurd gazed
That the flames leapt up in the stithy and about the Master blazed,
And his hand in the harp-strings wandered and the sweetness from
    them poured.   2805
Then unto his feet leapt Sigurd and drew his stripling's sword,
And he cried: 'Awake, O Master, for, lo, the day goes by,
And this too is an ancient story, that the sons of men-folk die,
And all save fame departeth. Awake! for the day grows late,
And deeds by the door are passing, nor the Norns will have them wait.'   2810

Then Regin groaned and wakened, sad-eyed and heavy-browed,
And weary and worn was he waxen, as a man by a burden bowed:
And he spake: 'Hast thou hearkened, Sigurd, wilt thou help a man that
    is old
To avenge him for his father? Wilt thou win that Treasure of Gold
And be more than the Kings of the earth? Wilt thou rid the earth of a
    wrong   2815
And heal the woe and the sorrow my heart hath endured o'erlong?'

Then Sigurd looked upon him with steadfast eyes and clear,
And Regin drooped and trembled as he stood the doom to hear:
But the bright child spake as aforetime, and answered the Master and said:
'Thou shalt have thy will, and the Treasure, and take the curse on thine
  head.'   2820

Of the forging of the sword that is called The Wrath of Sigurd.

Now again came Sigurd to Regin, and said: 'Thou hast taught me a task
Whereof none knoweth the ending: and a gift at thine hands I ask.'

Then answered Regin the Master: 'The world must be wide indeed
If my hand may not reach across it for aught thine heart may need.'

'Yea wide is the world,' said Sigurd, 'and soon spoken is thy word;   2825
But this gift thou shalt nought gainsay me: for I bid thee forge me a
  sword.'

Then spake the Master of Masters, and his voice was sweet and soft:
'Look forth abroad, O Sigurd, and note in the heavens aloft
How the dim white moon of the daylight hangs round as the Goth-
  God's shield:
Now for thee first rang mine anvil when she walked the heavenly field   2830
A slim and lovely lady, and the old moon lay on her arm:
Lo, here is a sword I have wrought thee with many a spell and charm
And all the craft of the Dwarf-kind; be glad thereof and sure;
'Mid many a storm of battle full well shall it endure.'

Then Sigurd looked on the slayer, and never a word would speak: 2835
Gemmed were the hilts and golden, and the blade was blue and bleak,
And runes of the Dwarf-kind's cunning each side the trench were
  scored:
But soft and sweet spake Regin: 'How likest thou the sword?'
Then Sigurd laughed and answered: 'The work is proved by the deed;
See now if this be a traitor to fail me in my need.'   2840

Then Regin trembled and shrank, so bright his eyes outshone
As he turned about to the anvil, and smote the sword thereon;
But the shards fell shivering earthward, and Sigurd's heart grew
  wroth
As the steel-flakes tinkled about him: 'Lo, there the right-hand's
  troth!
Lo, there the golden glitter, and the word that soon is spilt.'   2845
And down amongst the ashes he cast the glittering hilt,
And turned his back on Regin and strode out through the door,
And for many a day of spring-tide came back again no more.

But at last he came to the stithy and again took up the word:
'What hast thou done, O Master, in the forging of the sword?'   2850

Then sweetly Regin answered: 'Hard task-master art thou,
But lo, a blade of battle that shall surely please thee now!
Two moons are clean departed since thou lookedst toward the sky
And sawest the dim white circle amid the cloud-flecks lie;
And night and day have I laboured; and the cunning of old days   2855
Hath surely left my right-hand if this sword thou shalt not praise.'

And indeed the hilts gleamed glorious with many a dear-bought stone,
And down the fallow edges the light of battle shone;
Yet Sigurd's eyes shone brighter, nor yet might Regin face
Those eyes of the heart of the Volsungs; but trembled in his place   2860
As Sigurd cried: 'O Regin, thy kin of the days of old
Were an evil and treacherous folk, and they lied and murdered for gold;
And now if thou wouldst bewray me, of the ancient curse beware,
And set thy face as the flint the bale and the shame to bear:
For he that would win to the heavens, and be as the Gods on high,   2865
Must tremble nought at the road, and the place where men-folk die.'

White leaps the blade in his hand and gleams in the gear of the wall,
And he smites, and the oft-smitten edges on the beaten anvil fall:
But the life of the sword departed, and dull and broken it lay
On the ashes and flaked-off iron, and no word did Sigurd say,   2870
But strode off through the door of the stithy and went to the Hall of
     Kings,
And was merry and blithe that even mid all imaginings.

But when the morrow was come he went to his mother and spake:
'The shards, the shards of the sword, that thou gleanedst for my sake
In the night on the field of slaughter, in the tide when my father fell,   2875
Hast thou kept them through sorrow and joyance? hast thou warded
     them trusty and well?
Where hast thou laid them, my mother?
               Then she looked upon him and said:
'Art thou wroth, O Sigurd my son, that such eyes are in thine head?
And wilt thou be wroth with thy mother? do I withstand thee at all?'

'Nay,' said he, 'nought am I wrathful, but the days rise up like a wall   2880
Betwixt my soul and the deeds, and I strive to rend them through.
And why wilt thou fear mine eyen? as the sword lies baleful and blue
E'en 'twixt the lips of lovers, when they swear their troth thereon,
So keen are the eyes ye have fashioned, ye folk of the days agone;
For therein is the light of battle, though whiles it lieth asleep.   2885
Now give me the sword, my mother, that Sigmund gave thee to keep.'

She said: 'I shall give it thee gladly, for fain shall I be of thy praise
When thou knowest my careful keeping of that hope of the earlier
  days.'

So she took his hand in her hand, and they went their ways, they twain,
Till they came to the treasure of queen-folk, the guarded chamber of
  gain: 2890
They were all alone with its riches, and she turned the key in the gold,
And lifted the sea-born purple, and the silken web unrolled,
And lo, 'twixt her hands and her bosom the shards of Sigmund's
  sword;
No rust-fleck stained its edges, and the gems of the ocean's hoard
Were as bright in the hilts and glorious, as when in the Volsungs' hall   2895
It shone in the eyes of the earl-folk and flashed from the shielded wall.

But Sigurd smiled upon it, and he said: 'O Mother of Kings,
Well hast thou warded the war-glaive for a mirror of many things,
And a hope of much fulfilment: well hast thou given to me
The message of my fathers, and the word of things to be: 2900
Trusty hath been thy warding, but its hour is over now:
These shards shall be knit together, and shall hear the war-wind blow.
They shall shine through the rain of Odin, as the sun come back to the
  world,
When the heaviest bolt of the thunder amidst the storm is hurled:
They shall shake the thrones of Kings, and shear the walls of war,   2905
And undo the knot of treason when the world is darkening o'er.
They have shone in the dusk and the night-tide, they shall shine in the
  dawn and the day;
They have gathered the storm together, they shall chase the clouds
  away;
They have sheared red gold asunder, they shall gleam o'er the garnered
  gold;
They have ended many a story, they shall fashion a tale to be told: 2910
They have lived in the wrack of the people; they shall live in the glory
  of folk:
They have stricken the Gods in battle, for the Gods shall they strike
  the stroke.'

Then she felt his hands about her as he took the fateful sword,
And he kissed her soft and sweetly; but she answered never a word:
So great and fair was he waxen, so glorious was his face,   2915
So young, as the deathless Gods are, that long in the golden place
She stood when he was departed: as some for-travailed one
Comes over the dark fell-ridges on the birth-tide of the sun,

And his gathering sleep falls from him mid the glory and the blaze;
And he sees the world grow merry and looks on the lightened ways,   2920
While the ruddy streaks are melting in the day-flood broad and white;
Then the morn-dusk he forgetteth, and the moon-lit waste of night,
And the hall whence he departed with its yellow candles' flare:
So stood the Isle-king's daughter in that treasure-chamber fair.

But swift on his ways went Sigurd, and to Regin's house he came,   2925
Where the Master stood in the doorway and behind him leapt the flame,
And dark he looked and little: no more his speech was sweet,
No words on his lip were gathered the Volsung child to greet,
Till he took the sword from Sigurd and the shards of the days of old;
Then he spake:
                    'Will nothing serve thee save this blue steel and cold,   2930
The bane of thy father's father, the fate of all his kin,
The baleful blade I fashioned, the Wrath that the Gods would win?'

Then answered the eye-bright Sigurd: 'If thou thy craft wilt do
Nought save these battle-gleanings shall be my helper true:
And what if thou begrudgest, and my battle-blade be dull,   2935
Yet the hand of the Norns is lifted and the cup is over-full.
Repentst thou ne'er so sorely that thy kin must lie alow,
How much soe'er thou longest the world to overthrow,
And, doubting the gold and the wisdom, wouldst even now appease
Blind hate and eyeless murder, and win the world with these,   2940
O'er-late is the time for repenting the word thy lips have said:
Thou shalt have the Gold and the wisdom and take its curse on thine
    head.
I say that thy lips have spoken, and no more with thee it lies
To do the deed or leave it: since thou hast shown mine eyes
The world that was aforetime, I see the world to be;   2945
And woe to the tangling thicket, or the wall that hindereth me!
And short is the space I will tarry; for how if the Worm should die
Ere the first of my strokes be stricken? Wilt thou get to thy mastery
And knit these shards together that once in the Branstock stood?
But if not and a smith's hands fail me, a king's hand yet shall be good;   2950
And the Norns have doomed thy brother. And yet I deem this sword
Is the slayer of the Serpent, and the scatterer of the Hoard.'

Great waxed the gloom of Regin, and he said: 'Thou sayest sooth,
For none may turn him backward: the sword of a very youth
Shall one day end my cunning, as the Gods my joyance slew,   2955
When nought thereof they were deeming, and another thing would do.
But this sword shall slay the Serpent; and do another deed,

And many an one thereafter till it fail thee in thy need.
But as fair and great as thou standest, yet get thee from mine house,
For in me too might ariseth, and the place is perilous   2960
With the craft that was aforetime, and shall never be again,
When the hands that have taught thee cunning have failed from the
    world of men.
Thou art wroth; but thy wrath must slumber till fate its blossom bear;
Not thus were the eyes of Odin when I held him in the snare.
Depart! lest the end overtake us ere thy work and mine be done,   2965
But come again in the night-tide and the slumber of the sun,
When the sharded moon of April hangs round in the undark May.'

Hither and thither a while did the heart of Sigurd sway;
For he feared no craft of the Dwarf-kind, nor heeded the ways of Fate,
But his hand wrought e'en as his heart would: and now was he weary   2970
    with hate
Of the hatred and scorn of the Gods, and the greed of gold and of gain,
And the weaponless hands of the stripling of the wrath and the rending
    were fain.
But there stood Regin the Master, and his eyes were on Sigurd's eyes,
Though nought belike they beheld him, and his brow was sad and wise;
And the greed died out of his visage and he stood like an image of old.   2975

So the Norns drew Sigurd away, and the tide was an even of gold,
And sweet in the April even were the fowl-kind singing their best;
And the light of life smote Sigurd, and the joy that knows no rest,
And the fond unnamed desire, and the hope of hidden things;
And he wended fair and lovely to the house of the feasting Kings.   2980

But now when the moon was at full and the undark May begun,
Went Sigurd unto Regin mid the slumber of the sun,
And amidst the fire-hall's pavement the King of the Dwarf-kind stood
Like an image of deeds departed and days that once were good;
And he seemed but faint and weary, and his eyes were dim and dazed   2985
As they met the glory of Sigurd where the fitful candles blazed.
Then he spake:
        'Hail, Son of the Volsungs, the corner-stone is laid,
I have toiled and thou hast desired, and, lo, the fateful blade!'

Then Sigurd saw it lying on the ashes slaked and pale,
Like the sun and the lightning mingled mid the even's cloudy bale;   2990
For ruddy and great were the hilts, and the edges fine and wan,
And all adown to the blood-point a very flame there ran
That swallowed the runes of wisdom wherewith its sides were scored.
No sound did Sigurd utter as he stooped adown for his sword,

But it seemed as his lips were moving with speech of strong desire.   2995
White leapt the blade o'er his head, and he stood in the ring of its fire
As hither and thither it played, till it fell on the anvil's strength,
And he cried aloud in his glory, and held out the sword full length,
As one who would show it the world; for the edges were dulled no whit,
And the anvil was cleft to the pavement with the dreadful dint of it.   3000

But Regin cried to his harp-strings: 'Before the days of men
I smithied the Wrath of Sigurd, and now is it smithied again:
And my hand alone hath done it, and my heart alone hath dared
To bid that man to the mountain, and behold his glory bared.
Ah, if the son of Sigmund might wot of the thing I would,   3005
Then how were the ages bettered, and the world all waxen good!
Then how were the past forgotten and the weary days of yore,
And the hope of man that dieth and the waste that never bore!
How should this one live through the winter and know of all increase!
How should that one spring to the sunlight and bear the blossom of
     peace!   3010
No more should the long-lived wisdom o'er the waste of the wilderness
     stray;
Nor the clear-eyed hero hasten to the deedless ending of day.
And what if the hearts of the Volsungs for this deed of deeds were
     born,
How then were their life-days evil and the end of their lives forlorn?'

There stood Sigurd the Volsung, and heard how the harp-strings rang,   3015
But of other things they told him than the hope that the Master sang;
And his world lay far away from the Dwarf-king's eyeless realm
And the road that leadeth nowhere, and the ship without a helm
But he spake: 'How oft shall I say it, that I shall work thy will?
If my father hath made me mighty, thine heart shall I fulfill   3020
With the wisdom and gold thou wouldest, before I wend on my ways;
For now hast thou failed me nought, and the sword is the wonder of
     days.'

No word for a while spake Regin; but he hung his head adown
As a man that pondereth sorely, and his voice once more was grown
As the voice of the smithying-master as he spake: 'This Wrath of thine   3025
Hath cleft the hard and the heavy; it shall shear the soft and the fine:
Come forth to the night and prove it.'
                              So they twain went forth abroad,
And the moon lay white on the river and lit the sleepless ford,
And down to its pools they wended, and the stream was swift and full;
Then Regin cast against it a lock of fine-spun wool,   3030

And it whirled about on the eddy till it met the edges bared,
And as clean as the careless water the laboured fleece was sheared.

Then Regin spake: 'It is good, what the smithying-carle hath wrought:
Now the work of the King beginneth, and the end that my soul hath
    sought.
Thou shalt toil and I shall desire, and the deed shall be surely done: 3035
For thy Wrath is alive and awake and the story of bale is begun.'

Therewith was the Wrath of Sigurd laid soft in a golden sheath
And the peace-strings knit around it; for that blade was fain of death;
And 'tis ill to show such edges to the broad blue light of day,
Or to let the hall-glare light them, if ye list not play the play.   3040

Of Gripir's foretelling.

Now Sigurd backeth Greyfell on the first of the morrow morn,
And he rideth fair and softly through the acres of the corn;
The Wrath to his side is girded, but hid are the edges blue,
As he wendeth his ways to the mountains, and rideth the horse-mead
    through.
His wide grey eyes are happy, and his voice is sweet and soft,   3045
As amid the mead-lark's singing he casteth song aloft:
Lo, lo, the horse and the rider! So once maybe it was,
When over the Earth unpeopled the youngest God would pass;
But never again meseemeth shall such a sight betide,
Till over a world unwrongful new-born shall Baldur ride.   3050

So he comes to that ness of the mountains, and Gripir's garden steep,
That bravely Greyfell breasteth, and adown by the door doth he leap
And his war-gear rattleth upon him; there is none to ask or forbid
As he wendeth the house clear-lighted, where no mote of the dust is hid,
Though the sunlight hath not entered: the walls are clear and bright,   3055
For they cast back each to other the golden Sigurd's light;
Through the echoing ways of the house bright-eyed he wendeth along,
And the mountain-wind is with him, and the hovering eagles' song;
But no sound of the children of men may the ears of the Volsung hear,
And no sign of their ways in the world, or their will, or their hope or
    their fear.   3060

So he comes to the hall of Gripir, and gleaming-green is it built
As the house of under-ocean where the wealth of the greedy is spilt;
Gleaming and green as the sea, and rich as its rock-strewn floor,
And fresh as the autumn morning when the burning of summer is o'er.
There he looks and beholdeth the high-seat, and he sees it strangely
    wrought,   3065

Of the tooth of the sea-beast fashioned ere the Dwarf-kind came to
    nought;
And he looks, and thereon is Gripir, the King exceeding old,
With the sword of his fathers girded, and his raiment wrought of gold;
With the ivory rod in his right-hand, with his left on the crystal laid,
That is round as the world of men-folk, and after its image made,   3070
And clear is it wrought to the eyen that may read therein of Fate,
Though little indeed be its sea, and its earth not wondrous great.

There Sigurd stands in the hall, on the sheathèd Wrath doth he lean.
All his golden light is mirrored in the gleaming floor and green;
But the smile in his face upriseth as he looks on the ancient King,   3075
And their glad eyes meet and their laughter, and sweet is the
    welcoming:
And Gripir saith: 'Hail Sigurd! for my bidding hast thou done,
And here in the mountain-dwelling are two Kings of men alone.'

But Sigurd spake: 'Hail father! I am girt with the fateful sword
And my face is set to the highway, and I come for thy latest word.'   3080
Said Gripir: 'What wouldst thou hearken ere we sit and drink the
    wine?'
'Thy word and the Norns',' said Sigurd, 'but never a word of mine.'

'What sights wouldst thou see,' said Gripir, ''ere mine hand shall take
    thine hand?'
'As the Gods would I see,' said Sigurd, 'though Death light up the land.'

'What hope wouldst thou hope, O Sigurd, ere we kiss, we twain, and
    depart?'   3085
'Thy hope and the Gods',' said Sigurd, 'though the grief lie hard on
    my heart.'

Nought answered the ancient wise-one, and not a whit had he
    stirred
Since the clash of Sigurd's raiment in his mountain-hall he heard;
But the ball that imaged the earth was set in his hand grown old;
And belike it was to his vision, as the wide-world's ocean rolled,   3090
And the forests waved with the wind, and the corn was gay with the
    lark,
And the gold in its nether places grew up in the dusk and the dark,
And its children built and departed, and its King-folk conquered and
    went,
As over the crystal image his all-wise face was bent:
For all his desire was dead, and he lived as a God shall live,   3095
Whom the prayers of the world hath forgotten, and to whom no hand
    may give.

But there stood the mighty Volsung, and leaned on the hidden Wrath;
As the earliest sun's uprising o'er the sea-plain draws a path
Whereby men sail to the Eastward and the dawn of another day,
So the image of King Sigurd on the gleaming pavement lay.   3100

Then great in the hall fair-pillared the voice of Gripir arose,
And it ran through the glimmering house-ways, and forth to the sunny
     close;
There mid the birds' rejoicing went the voice of an o'er-wise King
Like a wind of midmost winter come back to talk with spring.

But the voice cried: 'Sigurd, Sigurd! O great, O early born!   3105
O hope of the Kings first fashioned! O blossom of the morn!
Short day and long remembrance, fair summer of the North!
One day shall the worn world wonder how first thou wentest forth!

'Arise, O Sigurd, Sigurd! In the night arise and go,
Thou shalt smite when the day-dawn glimmers through the folds of
     God-home's foe: 3110

'There the child in the noon-tide smiteth; the young King rendeth
     apart,
The old guile by the guile encompassed, the heart made wise by the
     heart.

'Bind the red rings, O Sigurd; bind up to cast abroad!
That the earth may laugh before thee rejoiced by the Waters' Hoard.

'Ride on, O Sigurd, Sigurd! for God's word goes forth on the wind,   3115
And he speaketh not twice over; nor shall they loose that bind:
But the Day and the Day shall loosen, and the Day shall awake and
     arise,
And the Day shall rejoice with the Dawning, and the wise heart learn
     of the wise.

'O fair, O fearless, O mighty, how green are the garths of Kings,
How soft are the ways before thee to the heart of their war-farings!   3120

'How green are the garths of King-folk, how fair is the lily and rose
In the house of the Cloudy People, 'neath the towers of kings and foes!

'Smite now, smite now in the noontide! ride on through the hosts of men!
Lest the dear remembrance perish, and today come not again.

'Is it day?—But the house is darkling—But the hand would gather and
     hold,   3125
And the lips have kissed the cloud-wreath, and a cloud the arms enfold.

'In the dusk hath the Sower arisen; in the dark hath he cast the seed,
And the ear is the sorrow of Odin and the wrong, and the nameless
   need!

'Ah the hand hath gathered and garnered, and empty is the hand,
Though the day be full and fruitful mid the drift of the Cloudy Land!   3130

'Look, look on the drift of the clouds, how the day and the even doth
   grow
As the long-forgotten dawning that was a while ago!

'Dawn, dawn, O mighty of men! and why wilt thou never awake,
When the holy field of the Goth-folk cries out for thy love and thy
   sake?

'Dawn, now; but the house is silent, and dark is the purple blood   3135
On the breast of the Queen fair-fashioned; and it riseth up as a flood
Round the posts of the door belovèd; and a deed there lieth therein:
The last of the deeds of Sigurd; the worst of the Cloudy Kin—
The slayer slain by the slain within the door and without.
—O dawn as the eve of the birth-day! O dark world cumbered with
   doubt!   3140

'Shall it never be day any more, nor the sun's uprising and growth?
Shall the kings of earth lie sleeping and the war-dukes wander in sloth
Through the last of the winter twilight? is the word of the wise-ones
   said
Till the five-fold winter be ended and the trumpet waken the dead?

'Short day and long remembrance! great glory for the earth!   3145
O deeds of the Day triumphant! O word of Sigurd's worth!
It is done, and who shall undo it of all who were ever alive?
May the Gods or the high Gods' masters 'gainst the tale of the
   righteous strive,
And the deeds to follow after, and all their deeds increase,
Till the uttermost field is foughten, and Baldur riseth in peace!   3150

'Cry out, O waste, before him! O rocks of the wilderness, cry!
For tomorn shalt thou see the glory, and the man not made to die!
Cry out, O upper heavens! O clouds beneath the lift
For the golden King shall be riding high-headed midst the drift:
The mountain waits and the fire; there waiteth the heart of the wise   3155
Till the earthly toil is accomplished, and again shall the fire arise;
And none shall be nigh in the ending and none by his heart shall be laid,
Save the world that he cherished and quickened, and the Day that he
   wakened and made.'

So died the voice of Gripir from amidst the sunny close,
And the sound of hastening eagles from the mountain's feet arose,   3160
But the hall was silent a little, for still stood Sigmund's son,
And he heard the words and remembered, and knew them one by one.
Then he turned on the ancient Gripir with eyes that knew no guile
And smiled on the wise of King-folk as the first of men might smile
On the God that hath fashioned him happy; and he spake:
                                        'Hast thou spoken and known   3165
How there standeth a child before thee and a stripling scarcely grown?
Or hast thou told of the Volsungs, and the gathered heart of these,
And their still unquenched desire for garnering fame's increase?
E'en so do I hearken thy words: for I wot how they deem it long
Till a man from their seed be arisen to deal with the cumber and wrong.   3170
Bid me therefore to sit by thy side, for behold I wend on my way,
And the gates swing to behind me, and each day of mine is a day
With deeds in the eve and the morning, nor deeds shall the noontide
    lack;
To the right and the left none calleth, and no voice crieth aback.'

'Come, kin of the Gods,' said Gripir, 'come up and sit by my side   3175
That we twain may be glad as the fearless, and they that have nothing
    to hide:
I have wrought out my will and abide it, and I sit ungrieved and alone,
I look upon men and I help not; to me are the deeds long done
As those of today and tomorrow: for these and for those am I glad;
But the Gods and men are the framers, and the days of my life I have
    had.'   3180

Then Sigurd came unto Gripir, and he kissed the wise-one's face,
And they sat in the high-seat together, the child and the elder of days;
And they drank of the wine of King-folk, and were joyful each of each,
And spake for a while of matters that are meet for King-folk's speech;
The deeds of men that have been and Kin of the Kings of the earth;   3185
And Gripir told of the outlands, and the mid-world's billowy girth,
And tales of the upper heaven were mingled with his talk,
And the halls where the Sea-Queen's kindred o'er the gem-strewn
    pavement walk,
And the innermost parts of the earth, where they lie, the green and the
    blue,
And the red and the glittering gem-stones that of old the Dwarf-kind
    knew.   3190

Long Sigurd sat and marvelled at the mouth that might not lie,
And the eyes no God had blinded, and the lone heart raised on high,

Then he rose from the gleaming high-seat, and the rings of battle rang
And the sheathèd Wrath was hearkening and a song of war it sang,
But Sigurd spake unto Gripir:

       'Long and lovely are thy days,   3195
And thy years fulfilled of wisdom, and thy feet on the unhid ways,
And the guileless heart of the great that knoweth not anger nor pain:
So once hath a man been fashioned and shall not be again.
But for me hath been foaled the war-horse, the grey steed swift as the
 cloud,
And for me were the edges smithied, and the Wrath cries out aloud; 3200
And a voice hath called from the darkness, and I ride to the Glittering
 Heath;
To smite on the door of Destruction, and waken the warder of Death.'

So they kissed, the wise and the wise, and the child from the elder turned;
And again in the glimmering house-ways the golden Sigurd burned;
He stood outside in the sunlight, and tarried never a deal,   3205
But leapt on the cloudy Greyfell with the clank of gold and steel,
And he rode through the sinking day to the walls of the kingly stead,
And came to Regin's dwelling when the wind was fallen dead,
And the great sun just departing: then blood-red grew the west,
And the fowl flew home from the sea-mead, and all things sank to rest. 3210

Sigurd rideth to the Glittering Heath.

Again on the morrow morning doth Sigurd the Volsung ride,
And Regin, the Master of Masters, is faring by his side,
And they leave the dwelling of kings and ride the summer land,
Until at the eve of the day the hills are on either hand:
Then they wend up higher and higher, and over the heaths they fare 3215
Till the moon shines broad on the midnight, and they sleep 'neath the
 heavens bare;
And they waken and look behind them, and lo, the dawning of day
And the little land of the Helper and its valleys far away;
But the mountains rise before them, a wall exceeding great.

Then spake the Master of Masters: 'We have come to the garth and the
 gate: 3220
There is youth and rest behind thee and many a thing to do,
There is many a fond desire, and each day born anew;
And the land of the Volsungs to conquer, and many a people's praise:
And for me there is rest it maybe, and the peaceful end of days.
We have come to the garth and the gate; to the hall-door now shall we
 win,   3225
Shall we go to look on the high-seat and see what sitteth therein?'

'Yea, and what else?' said Sigurd, 'was thy tale but mockeries,
And have I been drifted hither on a wind of empty lies?'

'It was sooth, it was sooth,' said Regin, 'and more might I have told
Had I heart and space to remember the deeds of the days of old.'　3230

And he hung down his head as he spake it, and was silent a little space;
And when it was lifted again there was fear in the Dwarf-king's face.
And he said: 'Thou knowest my thought, and wise-hearted art thou
　　grown:
It were well if thine eyes were blinder, and we each were faring alone,
And I with my eld and my wisdom, and thou with thy youth and thy
　　might;　3235
Yet whiles I dream I have wrought thee, a beam of the morning bright,
A fatherless motherless glory, to work out my desire;
Then high my hope ariseth, and my heart is all afire
For the world I behold from afar, and the day that yet shall be;
Then I wake and all things I remember and a youth of the Kings
　　I see—　3240
—The child of the Wood-abider, the seed of a conquered King,
The sword that the Gods have fashioned, the fate that men shall
　　sing:—
Ah might the world run backward to the days of the Dwarfs of old,
When I hewed out the pillars of crystal, and smoothed the walls of
　　gold!'

Nought answered the Son of Sigmund; nay he heard him nought at all,　3245
Save as though the wind were speaking in the bights of the mountain-
　　hall:
But he leapt aback of Greyfell, and the glorious sun rose up,
And the heavens glowed above him like the bowl of Baldur's cup,
And a golden man was he waxen; as the heart of the sun he seemed,
While over the feet of the mountains like blood the new light streamed;　3250
Then Sigurd cried to Greyfell and swift for the pass he rode,
And Regin followed after as a man bowed down by a load.

Day-long they fared through the mountains, and that highway's
　　fashioner
Forsooth was a fearful craftsman, and his hands the waters were,
And the heaped-up ice was his mattock, and the fire-blast was his man,　3255
And never a whit he heeded though his walls were waste and wan,
And the guest-halls of that wayside great heaps of the ashes spent
But, each as a man alone, through the sun-bright day they went,
And they rode till the moon rose upward, and the stars were small and
　　fair,

Then they slept on the long-slaked ashes beneath the heavens bare;   3260
And the cold dawn came and they wakened, and the King of the
    Dwarf-kind seemed
As a thing of that wan land fashioned; but Sigurd glowed and gleamed
Amid the shadowless twilight by Greyfell's cloudy flank,
As a little space they abided while the latest star-world shrank;
On the backward road looked Regin and heard how Sigurd drew   3265
The girths of Greyfell's saddle, and the voice of his sword he knew,
And he feared to look on the Volsung, as thus he fell to speak:

'I have seen the Dwarf-folk mighty, I have seen the God-folk weak;
And now, though our might be minished, yet have we gifts to give.
When men desire and conquer, most sweet is their life to live;   3270
When men are young and lovely there is many a thing to do.
And sweet is their fond desire and the dawn that springs anew.'

'This gift,' said the Son of Sigmund, 'the Norns shall give me yet,
And no blossom slain by the sunshine while the leaves with dew are wet.'

Then Regin turned and beheld him: 'Thou shalt deem it hard and
    strange,   3275
When the hand hath encompassed it all, and yet thy life must change.
Ah, long were the lives of men-folk, if betwixt the Gods and them
Were mighty warders watching mid the earth's and the heaven's hem!
Is there any man so mighty he would cast this gift away,—
The heart's desire accomplished, and life so long a day,   3280
That the dawn should be forgotten ere the even was begun?'

Then Sigurd laughed and answered: 'Fare forth O glorious sun;
Bright end from bright beginning, and the mid-way good to tell,
And death, and deeds accomplished, and all remembered well!
Shall the day go past and leave us, and we be left with night,   3285
To tread the endless circle, and strive in vain to smite?
But thou—wilt thou still look backward? thou sayst I know thy
    thought:
Thou hast whetted the sword for the slaying, it shall turn aside for
    nought.
Fear not! with the Gold and the wisdom thou shalt deem thee God
    alone,
And mayst do and undo at pleasure, nor be bound by right nor
    wrong;   3290
And then, if no God I be waxen, I shall be the weak with the strong.'

And his war-gear clanged and tinkled as he leapt to the saddle-stead:
And the sun rose up at their backs and the grey world changed to red,
And away to the west went Sigurd by the glory wreathed about,

But little and black was Regin as a fire that dieth out.   3295
Day-long they rode the mountains by the crags exceeding old,
And the ash that the first of the Dwarf-kind found dull and quenched
   and cold.
Then the moon in the mid-sky swam, and the stars were fair and pale,
And beneath the naked heaven they slept in an ash-grey dale;
And again at the dawn-dusk's ending they stood upon their feet,   3300
And Sigurd donned his war-gear nor his eyes would Regin meet.

A clear streak widened in heaven low down above the earth;
And above it lay the cloud-flecks, and the sun, anigh its birth,
Unseen, their hosts was staining with the very hue of blood,
And ruddy by Greyfell's shoulder the Son of Sigmund stood.   3305

Then spake the Master of Masters: 'What is thine hope this morn
That thou dightest thee, O Sigurd, to ride this world forlorn?'

'What needeth hope,' said Sigurd, 'when the heart of the Volsungs
   turns
To the light of the Glittering Heath, and the house where the Waster
   burns?
I shall slay the Foe of the Gods, as thou badst me a while agone,   3310
And then with the Gold and its wisdom shalt thou be left alone.'

'O Child,' said the King of the Dwarf-kind, 'when the day at last
   comes round
For the dread and the Dusk of the Gods, and the kin of the Wolf is
   unbound,
When thy sword shall hew the fire, and the wildfire beateth thy shield,
Shalt thou praise the wages of hope and the Gods that pitched the
   field?'   3315

'O Foe of the Gods,' said Sigurd, 'wouldst thou hide the evil thing,
And the curse that is greater than thou, lest death end thy labouring,
Lest the night should come upon thee amidst thy toil for nought?
It is me, it is me that thou fearest, if indeed I know thy thought;
Yea me, who would utterly light the face of all good and ill,   3320
If not with the fruitful beams that the summer shall fulfill,
Then at least with the world a-blazing, and the glare of the grinded
   sword.'

And he sprang aloft to the saddle as he spake the latest word,
And the Wrath sang loud in the sheath as it ne'er had sung before,
And the cloudy flecks were scattered like flames on the heaven's floor,   3325
And all was kindled at once, and that trench of the mountains grey
Was filled with the living light as the low sun lit the way:

But Regin turned from the glory with blinded eyes and dazed,
And lo, on the cloudy war-steed how another light there blazed,
And a great voice came from amidst it:
'O Regin, in good sooth,   3330
I have hearkened not nor heeded the words of thy fear and thy ruth:
Thou hast told thy tale and thy longing, and thereto I hearkened
    well:—
Let it lead thee up to heaven, let it lead thee down to hell,
The deed shall be done tomorrow: thou shalt have that measureless
    Gold,
And devour the garnered wisdom that blessed thy realm of old,   3335
That hath lain unspent and begrudged in the very heart of hate:
With the blood and the might of thy brother thine hunger shalt thou
    sate;
And this deed shall be mine and thine; but take heed for what followeth
    then!
Let each do after his kind! I shall do the deeds of men;
I shall harvest the field of their sowing, in the bed of their strewing
    shall sleep;   3340
To them shall I give my life-days, to the Gods my glory to keep.
But thou with the wealth and the wisdom that the best of the Gods
    might praise,
If thou shalt indeed excel them and become the hope of the days,
Then me in turn hast thou conquered, and I shall be in turn
Thy fashioned brand of the battle through good and evil to burn,   3345
Or the flame that sleeps in thy stithy for the gathered winds to blow,
When thou listest to do and undo and thine uttermost cunning to
    show.
But indeed I wot full surely that thou shalt follow thy kind;
And for all that cometh after, the Norns shall loose and bind.'

Then his bridle-reins rang sweetly, and the warding-walls of death,   3350
And Regin drew up to him, and the Wrath sang loud in the sheath,
And forth from that trench in the mountains by the westward way they
    ride;
And little and black goes Regin by the golden Volsung's side;
But no more his head is drooping, for he seeth the Elf-king's Gold;
The garnered might and the wisdom e'en now his eyes behold.   3355

So up and up they journeyed, and ever as they went
About the cold-slaked forges, o'er many a cloud-swept bent,
Betwixt the walls of blackness, by shores of the fishless meres,
And the fathomless desert waters, did Regin cast his fears,
And wrap him in desire; and all alone he seemed   3360

As a God to his heirship wending, and forgotten and undreamed
Was all the tale of Sigurd, and the folk he had toiled among,
And the Volsungs, Odin's children, and the men-folk fair and young.

So on they ride to the westward; and huge were the mountains grown
And the floor of heaven was mingled with that tossing world of stone: 3365
And they rode till the noon was forgotten and the sun was waxen low,
And they tarried not, though he perished, and the world grew dark
   below.
Then they rode a mighty desert, a glimmering place and wide,
And into a narrow pass high-walled on either side
By the blackness of the mountains, and barred aback and in face   3370
By the empty night of the shadow; a windless silent place:
But the white moon shone o'erhead mid the small sharp stars and pale,
And each as a man alone they rode on the highway of bale.

So ever they wended upward, and the midnight hour was o'er,
And the stars grew pale and paler, and failed from the heaven's floor,   3375
And the moon was a long while dead, but where was the promise of
   day?
No change came over the darkness, no streak of the dawning grey;
No sound of the wind's uprising adown the night there ran:
It was blind as the Gaping Gulf ere the first of the worlds began.

Then athwart and athwart rode Sigurd and sought the walls of the
   pass,   3380
But found no wall before him; and the road rang hard as brass
Beneath the hoofs of Greyfell, as up and up he trod:
—Was it the daylight of Hell, or the night of the doorway of God?

But lo, at the last a glimmer, and a light from the west there came,
And another and another, like points of far-off flame;   3385
And they grew and brightened and gathered; and whiles together they
   ran
Like the moonwake over the waters; and whiles they were scant and
   wan,
Some greater and some lesser, like the boats of fishers laid
About the sea of midnight; and a dusky dawn they made,
A faint and glimmering twilight: So Sigurd strains his eyes,   3390
And he sees how a land deserted all round about him lies
More changeless than mid-ocean, as fruitless as its floor:
Then the heart leaps up within him, for he knows that his journey is
   o'er,
And there he draweth bridle on the first of the Glittering Heath:

And the Wrath is waxen merry and sings in the golden sheath   3395
As he leaps adown from Greyfell, and stands upon his feet,
And wends his ways through the twilight the Foe of the Gods to meet.

Sigurd slayeth Fafnir the serpent.

Nought Sigurd seeth of Regin, and nought he heeds of him,
As in watchful might and glory he strides the desert dim,
And behind him paceth Greyfell; but he deems the time o'erlong   3400
Till he meet the great gold-warden, the over-lord of wrong.

So he wendeth midst the silence through the measureless desert place,
And beholds the countless glitter with wise and steadfast face,
Till him-seems in a little season that the flames grown somewhat wan,
And a grey thing glimmers before him, and becomes a mighty man.   3405
One-eyed and ancient-seeming, in cloud-grey raiment clad;
A friendly man and glorious, and of visage smiling-glad:
Then content in Sigurd groweth because of his majesty,
And he heareth him speak in the desert as the wind of the winter sea:

'Hail Sigurd! Give me thy greeting ere thy ways alone thou wend!'   3410
Said Sigurd: 'Hail! I greet thee, my friend and my fathers' friend.'
'Now whither away,' said the elder, 'with the Steed and the ancient
    Sword?'
'To the greedy house,' said Sigurd, 'and the King of the Heavy
    Hoard.'
'Wilt thou smite, O Sigurd, Sigurd?' said the ancient mighty-one.
'Yea, yea, I shall smite,' said the Volsung, 'save the Gods have slain the
    sun.'   3415
'What wise wilt thou smite,' said the elder, 'lest the dark devour thy
    day?'
'Thou hast praised the sword,' said the child, 'and the sword shall find
    a way.'
'Be learned of me,' said the Wise-one, 'for I was the first of thy folk.'
Said the child: 'I shall do thy bidding, and for thee shall I strike the
    stroke.'

Spake the Wise-one: 'Thus shalt thou do when thou wendest hence
    alone: 3420
Thou shalt find a path in the desert, and a road in the world of stone;
It is smooth and deep and hollow, but the rain hath riven it not,
And the wild wind hath not worn it, for it is but Fafnir's slot,
Whereby he wends to the water and the fathomless pool of old,
When his heart in the dawn is weary, and he loathes the Ancient Gold: 3425

There think of the great and the fathers, and bare the whetted Wrath,
And dig a pit in the highway, and a grave in the Serpent's path:
Lie thou therein, O Sigurd, and thine hope from the glooming hide,
And be as the dead for a season, and the living light abide!
And so shall thine heart avail thee, and thy mighty fateful hand,   3430
And the Light that lay in the Branstock, the well-belovèd brand.'

Said the child: 'I shall do thy bidding, and for thee shall I strike the
    stroke;
For I love thee, friend of my fathers, Wise Heart of the holy folk.'

So spake the Son of Sigmund, and beheld no man anear,
And again was the night the midnight, and the twinkling flames shone
    clear   3435
In the hush of the Glittering Heath; and alone went Sigmund's son
Till he came to the road of Fafnir, and the highway worn by one,
By the drift of the rain unfurrowed, by the windy years unrent,
And forth from the dark it came, and into the dark it went.

Great then was the heart of Sigurd, for there in the midmost he stayed,   3440
And thought of the ancient fathers, and bared the bright blue blade,
That shone as a fleck of the day-light, and the night was all around.
Fair then was the Son of Sigmund as he toiled and laboured the
    ground;
Great, mighty he was in his working, and the Glittering Heath he clave,
And the sword shone blue before him as he dug the pit and the grave: 3445
There he hid his hope from the night-tide and lay like one of the dead,
And wise and wary he bided; and the heavens hung over his head.

Now the night wanes over Sigurd, and the ruddy rings he sees,
And his war-gear's fair adornment, and the God-folk's images;
But a voice in the desert ariseth, a sound in the waste has birth,   3450
A changing tinkle and clatter, as of gold dragged over the earth:
O'er Sigurd widens the day-light, and the sound is drawing close,
And speedier than the trample of speedy feet it goes;
But ever deemeth Sigurd that the sun brings back the day,
For the grave grows lighter and lighter and heaven o'erhead is grey.   3455

But now, how the rattling waxeth till he may not heed nor hark!
And the day and the heavens are hidden, and o'er Sigurd rolls the
    dark,
As the flood of a pitchy river, and heavy-thick is the air
With the venom of hate long hoarded, and lies once fashioned fair:
Then a wan face comes from the darkness, and is wrought in manlike
    wise,   3460

And the lips are writhed with laughter and bleared are the blinded
    eyes;
And it wandereth hither and thither, and searcheth through the grave
And departeth, leaving nothing, save the dark, rolled wave on wave
O'er the golden head of Sigurd and the edges of the sword,
And the world weighs heavy on Sigurd, and the weary curse of the
    Hoard: 3465
Him-seemed the grave grew straiter, and his hope of life grew chill,
And his heart by the Worm was enfolded, and the bonds of the Ancient
    Ill.

Then was Sigurd stirred by his glory, and he strove with the swaddling
    of Death;
He turned in the pit on the highway, and the grave of the Glittering
    Heath;
He laughed and smote with the laughter and thrust up over his head,   3470
And smote the venom asunder, and clave the heart of Dread;
Then he leapt from the pit and the grave, and the rushing river of
    blood,
And fulfilled with the joy of the War-God on the face of earth he stood
With red sword high uplifted, with wrathful glittering eyes;
And he laughed at the heavens above him for he saw the sun arise,   3475
And Sigurd gleamed on the desert, and shone in the new-born light,
And the wind in his raiment wavered, and all the world was bright.

But there was the ancient Fafnir, and the Face of Terror lay
On the huddled folds of the Serpent, that were black and ashen-grey
In the desert lit by the sun; and those twain looked each on each,   3480
And forth from the Face of Terror went a sound of dreadful speech:

'Child, child, who art thou that hast smitten? bright child, of whence is
    thy birth?'
'I am called the Wild-thing Glorious, and alone I wend on the earth.'
'Fierce child, and who was thy father?—Thou hast cleft the heart of
    the Foe!'
'Am I like to the sons of men-folk, that my father I should know?'   3485
'Wert thou born of a nameless wonder? shall the lies to my death-day
    cling?'
'How lieth Sigurd the Volsung, and the Son of Sigmund the King?'
'O bitter father of Sigurd!—thou hast cleft mine heart atwain!'
'I arose, and I wondered and wended, and I smote, and I smote not in
    vain.'
'What master hath taught thee of murder?—Thou hast wasted Fafnir's
    day.'   3490

'I, Sigurd, knew and desired, and the bright sword learned the way.'
'Thee, thee shall the rattling Gold and the red rings bring to the bane.'
'Yet mine hand shall cast them abroad, and the earth shall gather
    again.'
'I see thee great in thine anger, and the Norns thou heedest not.'
'O Fafnir, speak of the Norns and the wisdom unforgot!'   3495
'Let the death-doomed flee from the ocean, him the wind and the
    weather shall drown.'
'O Fafnir, tell of the Norns ere thy life thou layest adown!'
'O manifold is their kindred, and who shall tell them all?

There are they that rule o'er men-folk and the stars that rise and fall:
—I knew of the folk of the Dwarfs, and I knew their Norns of old;   3500
And I fought, and I fell in the morning, and I die afar from the gold:
—I have seen the Gods of heaven, and their Norns withal I know:
They love and withhold their helping, they hate and refrain the blow;
They curse and they may not sunder, they bless and they shall not blend;
They have fashioned the good and the evil; they abide the change and
    the end.'   3505

'O Fafnir, what of the Isle, and what hast thou known of its name,
Where the Gods shall mingle edges with Surt and the Sons of the
    Flame?'

'O child, O Strong Compeller! Unshapen is it hight;
There the fallow blades shall be shaken and the Dark & the Day shall
    smite,
When the Bridge of the Gods is broken, and their white steeds swim
    the sea,   3510
And the uttermost field is stricken, last strife of thee and me.'

'What then shall endure, O Fafnir, the tale of the battle to tell?'

'I am blind, O Strong Compeller, in the bonds of Death and Hell.
But thee shall the rattling Gold and the red rings bring unto bane.'

'Yet the rings mine hand shall scatter, and the earth shall gather again.'   3515

'Woe, woe! in the days passed over I bore the Helm of Dread,
I reared the Face of Terror, and the hoarded hate of the Dead:
I overcame and was mighty; I was wise and cherished my heart
In the waste where no man wandered, and the high house builded apart:
Till I met thine hand, O Sigurd, and thy might ordained from of old;   3520
And I fought and fell in the morning, and I die far off from the Gold.'

Then Sigurd leaned on his sword, and a dreadful voice went by
Like the wail of a God departing and the War-God's misery;

And strong words of ancient wisdom went by on the desert wind,
The words that mar and fashion, the words that loose and bind;   3525
And sounds of a strange lamenting, and such strange things bewailed,
That words to tell their meaning the tongue of man hath failed.

Then all sank into silence, and the Son of Sigmund stood
On the torn and furrowed desert by the pool of Fafnir's blood,
And the Serpent lay before him, dead, chilly, dull, and grey;   3530
And over the Glittering Heath fair shone the sun and the day,
And a light wind followed the sun and breathed o'er the fateful place,
As fresh as it furrows the sea-plain or bows the acres' face.

Sigurd slayeth Regin the Master of Masters on the Glittering Heath.

There standeth Sigurd the Volsung, and leaneth on his sword,
And beside him now is Greyfell and looks on his golden lord,   3535
And the world is awake and living; and whither now shall they wend,
Who have come to the Glittering Heath, and wrought that deed to its end?
For hither comes Regin the Master from the skirts of the field of death,
And he shadeth his eyes from the sunlight as afoot he goeth and saith:
'Ah, let me live for a while! for a while and all shall be well,   3540
When passed is the house of murder and I creep from the prison of
    hell.'

Afoot he went o'er the desert, and he came unto Sigurd and stared
At the golden gear of the man, and the Wrath yet bloody and bared,
And the light locks raised by the wind, and the eyes beginning to smile,
And the lovely lips of the Volsung, and the brow that knew no guile;   3545
And he murmured under his breath while his eyes grew white with
    wrath:

'O who art thou, and wherefore, and why art thou in the path?'

Then he turned to the ash-grey Serpent, and grovelled low on the
    ground,
And he drank of that pool of the blood where the stones of the wild
    were drowned,
And long he lapped as a dog; but when he arose again,   3550
Lo, a flock of the mountain-eagles that drew to the feastful plain;
And he turned and looked on Sigurd, as bright in the sun he stood,
A stripling fair and slender, and wiped the Wrath of the blood.

But Regin cried: 'O Dwarf-kind, O many-shifting folk,
O shapes of might and wonder, am I too freed from the yoke,   3555

That binds my soul to my body a withered thing forlorn,
While the short-lived fools of man-folk so fair and oft are born?
Now swift in the air shall I be, and young in the concourse of kings,
If my heart shall come to desire the gain of earthly things.'

And he looked and saw how Sigurd was sheathing the Flame of War,   3560
And the eagles screamed in the wind, but their voice came faint from
    afar:
Then he scowled, and crouched and darkened, and came to Sigurd and
    spake:
'O child, thou hast slain my brother, and the Wrath is alive and awake.'

'Thou sayest sooth,' said Sigurd, 'thy deed and mine is done:
But now our ways shall sunder, for here, meseemeth, the sun   3565
Hath but little of deeds to do, and no love to win aback.'

Then Regin crouched before him, and he spake: 'Fare on to the wrack!
Fare on to the murder of men, and the deeds of thy kindred of old!
And surely of thee as of them shall the tale be speedily told.
Thou hast slain thy Master's brother, and what wouldst thou say
    thereto,   3570
Were the judges met for the judging and the doom-ring hallowed due?'

Then Sigurd spake as aforetime: 'Thy deed and mine it was,
And now our ways shall sunder, and into the world will I pass.'

But Regin darkened before him, and exceeding grim was he grown,
And he spake: 'Thou hast slain my brother, and wherewith wilt thou
    atone?'   3575

'Stand up, O Master,' said Sigurd, 'O Singer of ancient days,
And take the wealth I have won thee, ere we wend on the sundering
    ways.
I have toiled and thou hast desired, and the Treasure is surely anear,
And thou hast wisdom to find it, and I have slain thy fear.'

But Regin crouched and darkened: 'Thou hast slain my brother,' he
    said.   3580

'Take thou the Gold,' quoth Sigurd, 'for the ransom of my head!'

Then Regin crouched and darkened, and over the earth he hung;
And he said: 'Thou hast slain my brother, and the Gods are yet but
    young.'

Bright Sigurd towered above him, and the Wrath cried out in the
    sheath,
And Regin writhed against it as the adder turns on death;   3585

And he spake: 'Thou hast slain my brother, and today shalt thou be my
    thrall:
Yea a King shall be my cook-boy and this heath my cooking-hall.'

Then he crept to the ash-grey coils where the life of his brother had lain.
And he drew a glaive from his side and smote the smitten and slain,
And tore the heart from Fafnir, while the eagles cried o'erhead,   3590
And sharp and shrill was their voice o'er the entrails of the dead.

Then Regin spake to Sigurd: 'Of this slaying wilt thou be free?
Then gather thou fire together and roast the heart for me,
That I may eat it and live, and be thy master and more;
For therein was might and wisdom, and the grudged and hoarded
    lore:—   3595
—Or else, depart on thy ways afraid from the Glittering Heath.'

Then he fell abackward and slept, nor set his sword in the sheath,
But his hand was red on the hilts and blue were the edges bared,
Ash-grey was his visage waxen, and with open eyes he stared
On the height of heaven above him, and a fearful thing he seemed,   3600
As his soul went wide in the world, and of rule and kingship he
    dreamed.

But Sigurd took the Heart, and wood on the waste he found,
The wood that grew and died, as it crept on the niggard ground,
And grew and died again, and lay like whitened bones;
And the ernes cried over his head, as he builded his hearth of stones,   3605
And kindled the fire for cooking, and sat and sang o'er the roast
The song of his fathers of old, and the Wolflings' gathering host:
So there on the Glittering Heath rose up the little flame,
And the dry sticks crackled amidst it, and alow the eagles came,
And seven they were by tale, and they pitched all round about   3610
The cooking-fire of Sigurd, and sent their song-speech out:
But nought he knoweth its wisdom, or the word that they would speak:
And hot grew the Heart of Fafnir and sang amid the reek.

Then Sigurd looketh on Regin, and he deemeth it overlong
That he dighteth the dear-bought morsel, and the might for the
    Master of wrong,   3615
So he reacheth his hand to the roast to see if the cooking be o'er;
But the blood and the fat seethed from it and scalded his finger sore,
And he set his hand to his mouth to quench the fleshly smart,
And he tasted the flesh of the Serpent and the blood of Fafnir's Heart:
Then there came a change upon him, for the speech of fowl he knew,   3620
And wise in the ways of the beast-kind as the Dwarfs of old he grew;

And he knitted his brows and hearkened, and wrath in his heart arose;
For he felt beset of evil in a world of many foes.
But the hilts of the Wrath he handled, and Regin's heart he saw,
And how that the Foe of the Gods the net of death would draw;   3625
And his bright eyes flashed and sparkled, and his mouth grew set and
   stern
As he hearkened the voice of the eagles, and their song began to learn.

For the first cried out in the desert: 'O mighty Sigmund's son,
How long wilt thou sit and tarry now the dear-bought roast is done?'

And the second: 'Volsung, arise! for the horns blow up to the hall,   3630
And dight are the purple hangings, and the King to the feasting should
   fall.'

And the third: 'How great is the feast if the eater eat aright
The Heart of the wisdom of old and the after-world's delight!'

And the fourth: 'Yea what of Regin? shall he scatter wrack o'er the
   world?
Shall the father be slain by the son, and the brother 'gainst brother be
   hurled?'   3635

And the fifth: 'He hath taught a stripling the gifts of a God to give:
He hath reared up a King for the slaying, that he alone might live.'

And the sixth: 'He shall waken mighty as a God that scorneth at truth;
He hath drunk of the blood of the Serpent, and drowned all hope and
   ruth.'

And the seventh: 'Arise, O Sigurd, lest the hour be overlate!   3640
For the sun in the mid-noon shineth, and swift is the hand of Fate:
Arise! lest the world run backward and the blind heart have its will,
And once again be tangled the sundered good and ill;
Lest love and hatred perish, lest the world forget its tale,
And the Gods sit deedless, dreaming, in the high-walled heavenly
   vale.'   3645

Then swift ariseth Sigurd, and the Wrath in his hand is bare,
And he looketh, and Regin sleepeth, and his eyes wide-open glare;
But his lips smile false in his dreaming, and his hand is on the
   sword;
For he dreams himself the Master and the new world's fashioning-
   lord.
And his dream hath forgotten Sigurd, and the King's life lies in the pit;   3650
He is nought; Death gnaweth upon him, while the Dwarfs in mastery
   sit.

But lo, how the eyes of Sigurd the heart of the guileful behold,
And great is Allfather Odin, and upriseth the Curse of the Gold,
And the Branstock bloometh to heaven from the ancient wondrous root;
The summer hath shone on its blossoms, and Sigurd's Wrath is the
    fruit: 3655
Dread then he cried in the desert: 'Guile-master, lo thy deed!
Hast thou nurst my life for destruction, and my death to serve thy
    need?
Hast thou kept me here for the net and the death that tame things die?
Hast thou feared me overmuch, thou Foe of the Gods on high?
Lest the sword thine hand was wielding should turn about and cleave   3660
The tangled web of nothing thou hadst wearied thyself to weave.
Lo here the sword and the stroke! judge the Norns betwixt us twain!
But for me, I will live and die not, nor shall all my hope be vain.'

Then his second stroke struck Sigurd, for the Wrath flashed thin and
    white,
And 'twixt head and trunk of Regin fierce ran the fateful light;   3665
And there lay brother by brother a faded thing and wan.
But Sigurd cried in the desert: 'So far have I wended on!
Dead are the foes of God-home that would blend the good and the ill;
And the World shall yet be famous, and the Gods shall have their will.
Nor shall I be dead and forgotten, while the earth grows worse and
    worse,   3670
With the blind heart king o'er the people, and binding curse with
    curse.'

How Sigurd took to him the treasure
of the Elf Andvari.

Now Sigurd eats of the heart that once in the Dwarf-king lay,
The hoard of the wisdom begrudged, the might of the earlier day.
Then wise of heart was he waxen, but longing in him grew
To sow the seed he had gotten, and till the field he knew.   3675
So he leapeth aback of Greyfell, and rideth the desert bare,
And the hollow slot of Fafnir, that led to the Serpent's lair.
Then long he rode adown it, and the ernes flew overhead,
And tidings great and glorious of that Treasure of old they said.
So far o'er the waste he wended, and when the night was come   3680
He saw the earth-old dwelling, the dread Gold-wallower's home:
On the skirts of the Heath it was builded by a tumbled stony bent;
High went that house to the heavens, down 'neath the earth it went,
Of unwrought iron fashioned for the heart of a greedy king:
'Twas a mountain, blind without, and within was its plenishing   3685

But the Hoard of Andvari the ancient, and the sleeping Curse unseen,
The Gold of the Gods that spared not and the greedy that have been.

Through the door strode Sigurd the Volsung, and the grey moon and
    the sword
Fell in on the tawny gold-heaps of the ancient hapless Hoard:
Gold gear of hosts unburied, and the coin of cities dead,   3690
Great spoil of the ages of battle, lay there on the Serpent's bed:
Huge blocks from mid-earth quarried, where none but the Dwarfs
    have mined,
Wide sands of the golden rivers no foot of man may find
Lay 'neath the spoils of the mighty and the ruddy rings of yore:
But amidst was the Helm of Aweing that the Fear of earth-folk bore,   3695
And there gleamed a wonder beside it, the Hauberk all of gold,
Whose like is not in the heavens nor has earth of its fellow told:
There Sigurd seeth moreover Andvari's Ring of Gain,
The hope of Loki's finger, the Ransom's utmost grain;
For it shone on the midmost gold-heap like the first star set in the sky   3700
In the yellow space of even when moon-rise draweth anigh.
Then laughed the Son of Sigmund, and stooped to the golden land,
And gathered that first of the harvest and set it on his hand;
And he did on the Helm of Aweing, and the Hauberk all of gold,
Whose like is not in the heavens nor has earth of its fellow told: 3705
Then he praised the day of the Volsungs amid the yellow light,
And he set his hand to the labour and put forth his kingly might;
He dragged forth gold to the moon, on the desert's face he laid
The innermost earth's adornment, and rings for the nameless made;
He toiled and loaded Greyfell, and the cloudy war-steed shone   3710
And the gear of Sigurd rattled in the flood of moonlight wan;
There he toiled and loaded Greyfell, and the Volsung's armour rang
Mid the yellow bed of the Serpent: but without the eagles sang:

'Bind the red rings, O Sigurd! let the gold shine free and clear!
For what hath the Son of the Volsungs the ancient Curse to fear?'   3715

'Bind the red rings, O Sigurd! for thy tale is well begun,
And the world shall be good and gladdened by the Gold lit up by the
    sun.'

'Bind the red rings, O Sigurd! and gladden all thine heart!
For the world shall make thee merry ere thou and she depart.'

'Bind the red rings, O Sigurd! for the ways go green below,   3720
Go green to the dwelling of Kings, and the halls that the Queen-folk
    know.'

'Bind the red rings, O Sigurd! for what is there bides by the way,
Save the joy of folk to awaken, and the dawn of the merry day?'

'Bind the red rings, O Sigurd! for the strife awaits thine hand,
And a plenteous war-field's reaping, and the praise of many a land.'   3725

'Bind the red rings, O Sigurd! But how shall storehouse hold
That glory of thy winning and the tidings to be told?'

Now the moon was dead, and the star-worlds were great on the
 heavenly plain,
When the steed was fully laden; then Sigurd taketh the rein
And turns to the ruined rock-wall that the lair was built beneath,   3730
For there he deemed was the gate and the door of the Glittering Heath,
But not a whit moved Greyfell for aught that the King might do;
Then Sigurd pondered a while, till the heart of the beast he knew,
And clad in all his war-gear he leaped to the saddle-stead,
And with pride and mirth neighed Greyfell and tossed aloft his head,   3735
And sprang unspurred o'er the waste, and light and swift he went,
And breasted the broken rampart, the stony tumbled bent;
And over the brow he clomb, and there beyond was the world,
A place of many mountains and great crags together hurled.
So down to the west he wendeth, and goeth swift and light,   3740
And the stars are beginning to wane, and the day is mingled with
 night;
For full fain was the sun to arise and look on the Gold set free,
And the Dwarf-wrought rings of the Treasure and the gifts from the
 floor of the sea.

How Sigurd awoke Brynhild upon Hindfell.

By long roads rideth Sigurd amidst that world of stone,
And somewhat south he turneth; for he would not be alone,   3745
But longs for the dwellings of man-folk, and the kingly people's
 speech,
And the days of the glee and the joyance, where men laugh each to each.
But still the desert endureth, and afar must Greyfell fare
From the wrack of the Glittering Heath, and Fafnir's golden lair.
Long Sigurd rideth the waste, when, lo, on a morning of day   3750
From out of the tangled crag-walls, amidst the cloud-land grey
Comes up a mighty mountain, and it is as though there burns
A torch amidst of its cloud-wreath; so thither Sigurd turns,
For he deems indeed from its topmost to look on the best of the earth;
And Greyfell neigheth beneath him, and his heart is full of mirth.   3755

So he rideth higher and higher, and the light grows great and strange,
And forth from the clouds it flickers, till at noon they gather and
   change,
And settle thick on the mountain, and hide its head from sight;
But the winds in a while are awakened, and day bettereth ere the night,
And, lifted a measureless mass o'er the desert crag-walls high,   3760
Cloudless the mountain riseth against the sunset sky,
The sea of the sun grown golden, as it ebbs from the day's desire;
And the light that afar was a torch is grown a river of fire,
And the mountain is black above it, and below is it dark and dun;
And there is the head of Hindfell as an island in the sun.   3765

Night falls, but yet rides Sigurd, and hath no thought of rest,
For he longs to climb that rock-world and behold the earth at its best;
But now mid the maze of the foot-hills he seeth the light no more,
And the stars are lovely and gleaming on the lightless heavenly
   floor.
So up and up he wendeth till the night is wearing thin;   3770
And he rideth a rift of the mountain, and all is dark therein,
Till the stars are dimmed by dawning and the wakening world is cold;
Then afar in the upper rock-wall a breach doth he behold,
And a flood of light poured inward the doubtful dawning blinds:
So swift he rideth thither and the mouth of the breach he finds,   3775
And sitteth awhile on Greyfell on the marvellous thing to gaze:
For lo, the side of Hindfell enwrapped by the fervent blaze,
And nought 'twixt earth and heaven save a world of flickering flame,
And a hurrying shifting tangle, where the dark rents went and came.

Great groweth the heart of Sigurd with uttermost desire,   3780
And he crieth kind to Greyfell, and they hasten up, and nigher,
Till he draweth rein in the dawning on the face of Hindfell's steep:
But who shall heed the dawning where the tongues of that wildfire
   leap?
For they weave a wavering wall, that driveth over the heaven
The wind that is born within it; nor ever aside is it driven   3785
By the mightiest wind of the waste, and the rain-flood amidst it is
   nought;
And no wayfarer's door and no window the hand of its builder hath
   wrought
But thereon is the Volsung smiling as its breath uplifteth his hair,
And his eyes shine bright with its image, and his mail gleams white and
   fair,
And his war-helm pictures the heavens and the waning stars behind: 3790

But his neck is Greyfell stretching to snuff at the flame-wall blind,
And his cloudy flank upheaveth, and tinkleth the knitted mail,
And the gold of the uttermost waters is waxen wan and pale.

Now Sigurd turns in his saddle, and the hilt of the Wrath he shifts,
And draws a girth the tighter; then the gathered reins he lifts,   3795
And crieth aloud to Greyfell, and rides at the wildfire's heart;
But the white wall wavers before him and the flame-flood rusheth
    apart,
And high o'er his head it riseth, and wide and wild is its roar
As it beareth the mighty tidings to the very heavenly floor:
But he rideth through its roaring as the warrior rides the rye,   3800
When it bows with the wind of the summer and the hid spears draw
    anigh
The white flame licks his raiment and sweeps through Greyfell's mane,
And bathes both hands of Sigurd and the hilts of Fafnir's bane,
And winds about his war-helm and mingles with his hair,
But nought his raiment dusketh or dims his glittering gear;   3805
Then it fails and fades and darkens till all seems left behind,
And dawn and the blaze is swallowed in mid-mirk stark and blind.

But forth a little further and a little further on
And all is calm about him, and he sees the scorched earth wan
Beneath a glimmering twilight, and he turns his conquering eyes,   3810
And a ring of pale slaked ashes on the side of Hindfell lies;
And the world of the waste is beyond it; and all is hushed and grey,
And the new-risen moon is a-paleing, and the stars grow faint with day.

Then Sigurd looked before him and a Shield-burg there he saw,
A wall of the tiles of Odin wrought clear without a flaw,   3815
The gold by the silver gleaming, and the ruddy by the white;
And the blazonings of their glory were done upon them bright,
As of dear things wrought for the war-lords new come to Odin's hall.
Piled high aloft to the heavens uprose that battle-wall,
And far o'er the topmost shield-rim for a banner of fame there hung   3820
A glorious golden buckler; and against the staff it rung
As the earliest wind of dawning uprose on Hindfell's face
And the light from the yellowing east beamed soft on the shielded
    place.

But the Wrath cried out in answer as Sigurd leapt adown
To the wasted soil of the desert by that rampart of renown;   3825
He looked but little beneath it, and the dwelling of God it seemed,
As against its gleaming silence the eager Sigurd gleamed:

He draweth not sword from scabbard, as the wall he wendeth around,
And it is but the wind and Sigurd that wakeneth any sound:
But, lo, to the gate he cometh, and the doors are open wide,   3830
And no warder the way withstandeth, and no earls by the threshold
    abide;
So he stands awhile and marvels; then the baleful light of the Wrath
Gleams bare in his ready hand as he wendeth the inward path:
For he doubteth some guile of the Gods, or perchance some Dwarf-
    king's snare,
Or a mock of the Giant people that shall fade in the morning air: 3835
But he getteth him in and gazeth; and a wall doth he behold,
And the ruddy set by the white, and the silver by the gold;
But within the garth that it girdeth no work of man is set,
But the utmost head of Hindfell ariseth higher yet;
And below in the very midmost is a Giant-fashioned mound,   3840
Piled high as the rims of the Shield-burg above the level ground;
And there, on that mound of the Giants, o'er the wilderness forlorn,
A pale grey image lieth, and gleameth in the morn.

So there was Sigurd alone; and he went from the shielded door,
And aloft in the desert of wonder the Light of the Branstock he bore;   3845
And he set his face to the earth-mound, and beheld the image wan,
And the dawn was growing about it; and, lo, the shape of a man
Set forth to the eyeless desert on the tower-top of the world,
High over the cloud-wrought castle whence the windy bolts are hurled.

Now he comes to the mound and climbs it, and will see if the man
    be dead;   3850
Some King of the days forgotten laid there with crownèd head,
Or the frame of a God, it may be, that in heaven hath changed his life,
Or some glorious heart belovèd, God-rapt from the earthly strife:
Now over the body he standeth, and seeth it shapen fair,
And clad from head to foot-sole in pale grey-glittering gear,   3855
In a hauberk wrought as straitly as though to the flesh it were grown:
But a great helm hideth the head and is girt with a glittering crown.

So thereby he stoopeth and kneeleth, for he deems it were good
    indeed
If the breath of life abide there and the speech to help at need;
And as sweet as the summer wind from a garden under the sun   3860
Cometh forth on the topmost Hindfell the breath of that sleeping-one.
Then he saith he will look on the face, if it bear him love or hate,
Or the bonds for his life's constraining, or the sundering doom of fate.
So he draweth the helm from the head, and, lo, the brow snow-white,

And the smooth unfurrowed cheeks, and the wise lips breathing light;   3865
And the face of a woman it is, and the fairest that ever was born,
Shown forth to the empty heavens and the desert world forlorn:
But he looketh, and loveth her sore, and he longeth her spirit to move,
And awaken her heart to the world, that she may behold him and love.
And he toucheth her breast and her hands, and he loveth her passing
     sore;   3870
And he saith: 'Awake! I am Sigurd;' but she moveth never the more.

Then he looked on his bare bright blade, and he said: 'Thou—what
     wilt thou do?
For indeed as I came by the war-garth thy voice of desire I knew.'
Bright burnt the pale blue edges for the sunrise drew anear,
And the rims of the Shield-burg glittered, and the east was exceeding
     clear: 3875
So the eager edges he setteth to the Dwarf-wrought battle-coat
Where the hammered ring-knit collar constraineth the woman's throat;
But the sharp Wrath biteth and rendeth, and before it fail the rings,
And, lo, the gleam of the linen, and the light of golden things:
Then he driveth the blue steel onward, and through the skirt, and out,   3880
Till nought but the rippling linen is wrapping her about;
Then he deems her breath comes quicker and her breast begins to
     heave,
So he turns about the War-Flame and rends down either sleeve,
Till her arms lie white in her raiment, and a river of sun-bright hair
Flows free o'er bosom and shoulder and floods the desert bare.   3885

Then a flush cometh over her visage and a sigh up-heaveth her breast,
And her eyelids quiver and open, and she wakeneth into rest;
Wide-eyed on the dawning she gazeth, too glad to change or smile,
And but little moveth her body, nor speaketh she yet for a while;
And yet kneels Sigurd moveless her wakening speech to heed,   3890
While soft the waves of the daylight o'er the starless heavens speed,
And the gleaming rims of the Shield-burg yet bright and brighter
     grow,
And the thin moon hangeth her horns dead-white in the golden-glow.

Then she turned and gazed on Sigurd, and her eyes met the Volsung's
     eyes.
And mighty and measureless now did the tide of his love arise,   3895
For their longing had met and mingled, and he knew of her heart that
     she loved,
As she spake unto nothing but him and her lips with the speech-flood
     moved:

'O, what is the thing so mighty that my weary sleep hath torn,
And rent the fallow bondage, and the wan woe over-worn?'

He said: 'The hand of Sigurd and the Sword of Sigmund's son,   3900
And the heart that the Volsungs fashioned this deed for thee have
    done.'

But she said: 'Where then is Odin that laid me here alow?
Long lasteth the grief of the world, and man-folk's tangled woe!'

'He dwelleth above,' said Sigurd, 'but I on the earth abide,
And I came from the Glittering Heath the waves of thy fire to ride.'   3905

But therewith the sun rose upward and lightened all the earth,
And the light flashed up to the heavens from the rims of the glorious
    girth;
But they twain arose together, and with both her palms outspread,
And bathed in the light returning, she cried aloud and said:

'All hail O Day and thy Sons, and thy kin of the coloured things!   3910
Hail, following Night, and thy Daughter that leadeth thy wavering
    wings!
Look down with unangry eyes on us today alive,
And give us the hearts victorious, and the gain for which we strive!
All hail, ye Lords of God-home, and ye Queens of the House of Gold!
Hail, thou dear Earth that bearest, and thou Wealth of field and fold!   3915
Give us, your noble children, the glory of wisdom and speech,
And the hearts and the hands of healing, and the mouths and hands
    that teach!'

Then they turned and were knit together; and oft and o'er again
They craved, and kissed rejoicing, and their hearts were full and fain.

Then Sigurd looketh upon her, and the words from his heart arise: 3920
'Thou art the fairest of earth, and the wisest of the wise;
O who art thou that lovest? I am Sigurd, e'en as I told;
I have slain the Foe of the Gods, and gotten the Ancient Gold;
And great were the gain of thy love, and the gift of mine earthly days,
If we twain should never sunder as we wend on the changing ways.   3925
O who art thou that lovest, thou fairest of all things born?
And what meaneth thy sleep and thy slumber in the wilderness
    forlorn?'

She said: 'I am she that loveth: I was born of the earthly folk,
But of old Allfather took me from the Kings and their wedding yoke:
And he called me the Victory-Wafter, and I went and came as he would,   3930

And I chose the slain for his war-host, and the days were glorious and
    good,
Till the thoughts of my heart overcame me, and the pride of my
    wisdom and speech,
And I scorned the earth-folk's Framer and the Lord of the world
    I must teach:
For the death-doomed I caught from the sword, and the fated life
    I slew,
And I deemed that my deeds were goodly, and that long I should do
    and undo.   3935
But Allfather came against me and the God in his wrath arose;
And he cried: 'Thou hast thought in thy folly that the Gods have
    friends and foes,
That they wake, and the world wends onward, that they sleep, and the
    world slips back,
That they laugh, and the world's weal waxeth, that they frown and
    fashion the wrack:
Thou hast cast up the curse against me; it shall fall aback on thine
    head;   3940
Go back to the sons of repentance, with the children of sorrow wed!
For the Gods are great unholpen, and their grief is seldom seen,
And the wrong that they will and must be is soon as it had not been.'

'Yet I thought: 'Shall I wed in the world, shall I gather grief on the
    earth?
Then the fearless heart shall I wed, and bring the best to birth,   3945
And fashion such tales for the telling, that Earth shall be holpen at
    least,
If the Gods think scorn of its fairness, as they sit at the changeless
    feast.'
'Then somewhat smiled Allfather; and he spake: 'So let it be!
The doom thereof abideth; the doom of me and thee.
Yet long shall the time pass over ere thy waking-day be born: 3950
Fare forth, and forget and be weary 'neath the Sting of the Sleepful
    Thorn!'

'So I came to the head of Hindfell and the ruddy shields and white,
And the wall of the wildfire wavering around the isle of night;
And there the Sleep-thorn pierced me, and the slumber on me fell,
And the night of nameless sorrows that hath no tale to tell.   3955
Now I am she that loveth; and the day is nigh at hand
When I, who have ridden the sea-realm and the regions of the land,
And dwelt in the measureless mountains and the forge of stormy days,

Shall dwell in the house of my fathers and the land of the people's
    praise;
And there shall hand meet hand, and heart by heart shall beat,   3960
And the lying-down shall be joyous, and the morn's uprising sweet.
Lo now, I look on thine heart and behold of thine inmost will,
That thou of the days wouldst hearken that our portion shall fulfill;
But O, be wise of man-folk, and the hope of thine heart refrain!
As oft in the battle's beginning ye vex the steed with the rein,   3965
Lest at last in its latter ending, when the sword hath hushed the horn,
His limbs should be weary and fail, and his might be over-worn.
O be wise, lest thy love constrain me, and my vision wax o'er-clear,
And thou ask of the thing that thou shouldst not, and the thing that
    thou wouldst not hear.

'Know thou, most mighty of men, that the Norns shall order all,   3970
And yet without thine helping shall no whit of their will befall;
Be wise! 'tis a marvel of words, and a mock for the fool and the blind;
But I saw it writ in the heavens, and its fashioning there did I find:
And the night of the Norns and their slumber, and the tide when the
    world runs back,
And the way of the sun is tangled, it is wrought of the dastard's lack.   3975
But the day when the fair earth blossoms, and the sun is bright above,
Of the daring deeds is it fashioned and the eager hearts of love.

'Be wise, and cherish thine hope in the freshness of the days,
And scatter its seed from thine hand in the field of the people's praise;
Then fair shall it fall in the furrow, and some the earth shall speed,   3980
And the sons of men shall marvel at the blossom of the deed:
But some the earth shall speed not; nay rather, the wind of the heaven
Shall waft it away from thy longing—and a gift to the Gods hast thou
    given,
And a tree for the roof and the wall in the house of the hope that
    shall be,
Though it seemeth our very sorrow, and the grief of thee and me.   3985

'Strive not with the fools of man-folk: for belike thou shalt overcome;
And what then is the gain of thine hunting when thou bearest the
    quarry home?
Or else shall the fool overcome thee, and what deed thereof shall grow?
Nay, strive with the wise man rather, and increase thy woe and his woe;
Yet thereof a gain hast thou gotten; and the half of thine heart hast
    thou won   3990
If thou may'st prevail against him, and his deeds are the deeds thou
    hast done:

Yea, and if thou fall before him, in him shalt thou live again,
And thy deeds in his hand shall blossom, and his heart of thine heart
  shall be fain.

'When thou hearest the fool rejoicing, and he saith, 'It is over and past,
And the wrong was better than right, and hate turns into love at the
  last,   3995
And we strove for nothing at all, and the Gods are fallen asleep;
For so good is the world a growing that the evil good shall reap:'
Then loosen thy sword in the scabbard and settle the helm on thine
  head,
For men betrayed are mighty, and great are the wrongfully dead.

'Wilt thou do the deed and repent it? thou hadst better never been
  born: 4000
Wilt thou do the deed and exalt it? then thy fame shall be outworn:
Thou shalt do the deed and abide it, and sit on thy throne on high,
And look on today and tomorrow as those that never die.

'Love thou the Gods—and withstand them, lest thy fame should fail in
  the end,
And thou be but their thrall and their bondsmen, who wert born for
  their very friend: 4005
For few things from the Gods are hidden, and the hearts of men they
  know,
And how that none rejoiceth to quail and crouch alow.

'I have spoken the words, belovèd, to thy matchless glory and worth;
But thy heart to my heart hath been speaking, though my tongue hath
  set it forth:
For I am she that loveth, and I know what thou wouldst teach   4010
From the heart of thine unlearned wisdom, and I needs must speak thy
  speech.'

Then words were weary and silent, but oft and o'er again
They craved and kissed rejoicing, and their hearts were full and fain.

Then spake the Son of Sigmund: 'Fairest, and most of worth,
Hast thou seen the ways of man-folk and the regions of the earth?   4015
Then speak yet more of wisdom; for most meet meseems it is
That my soul to thy soul be shapen, and that I should know thy bliss.'

So she took his right hand meekly, nor any word would say,
Not e'en of love or praising, his longing to delay;
And they sat on the side of Hindfell, and their fain eyes looked and
  loved,   4020
As she told of the hidden matters whereby the world is moved:

And she told of the framing of all things, and the houses of the heaven;
And she told of the star-worlds' courses, and how the winds be driven;
And she told of the Norns and their names, and the fate that abideth
　　the earth;
And she told of the ways of King-folk in their anger and their mirth; 4025
And she spake of the love of women, and told of the flame that burns,
And the fall of mighty houses, and the friend that falters and turns,
And the lurking blinded vengeance, and the wrong that amendeth
　　wrong,
And the hand that repenteth its stroke, and the grief that endureth for
　　long:
And how man shall bear and forbear, and be master of all that is; 4030
And how man shall measure it all, the wrath, and the grief, and the
　　bliss.

'I saw the body of Wisdom, and of shifting guise was she wrought,
And I stretched out my hands to hold her, and a mote of the dust they
　　caught;
And I prayed her to come for my teaching, and she came in the
　　midnight dream—
And I woke and might not remember, nor betwixt her tangle deem: 4035
She spake, and how might I hearken; I heard, and how might I know;
I knew, and how might I fashion, or her hidden glory show?
All things I have told thee of Wisdom are but fleeting images
Of her hosts that abide in the heavens, and her light that Allfather sees:
Yet wise is the sower that sows, and wise is the reaper that reaps, 4040
And wise is the smith in his smiting, and wise is the warder that keeps:
And wise shalt thou be to deliver, and I shall be wise to desire;
—And lo, the tale that is told, and the sword and the wakening fire!
Lo now, I am she that loveth, and hark how Greyfell neighs,
And Fafnir's Bed is gleaming, and green go the downward ways, 4045
The road to the children of men and the deeds that thou shalt do
In the joy of thy life-days' morning, when thine hope is fashioned
　　anew.
Come now, O Bane of the Serpent, for now is the high-noon come,
And the sun hangeth over Hindfell and looks on the earth-folk's home;
But the soul is so great within thee, and so glorious are thine eyes, 4050
And me so love constraineth, and mine heart that was called the wise,
That we twain may see men's dwellings and the house where we shall
　　dwell,
And the place of our life's beginning, where the tale shall be to tell.'

So they climb the burg of Hindfell, and hand in hand they fare,
Till all about and above them is nought but the sunlit air, 4055

And there close they cling together rejoicing in their mirth;
For far away beneath them lie the kingdoms of the earth,
And the garths of men-folk's dwellings and the streams that water them,
And the rich and plenteous acres, and the silver ocean's hem,
And the woodland wastes and the mountains, and all that holdeth all;   4060
The house and the ship and the island, the loom and the mine and the
    stall,
The beds of bane and healing, the crafts that slay and save,
The temple of God and the Doom-ring, the cradle and the grave.

Then spake the Victory-Wafter: 'O King of the Earthly Age,
As a God thou beholdest the treasure and the joy of thine heritage,   4065
And where on the wings of his hope is the spirit of Sigurd borne?
Yet I bid thee hover awhile as a lark alow on the corn;
Yet I bid thee look on the land 'twixt the wood and the silver sea
In the bight of the swirling river, and the house that cherished me!
There dwelleth mine earthly sister and the king that she hath wed;   4070
There morn by morn aforetime I woke on the golden bed;
There eve by eve I tarried mid the speech and the lays of kings;
There noon by noon I wandered and plucked the blossoming things;
The little land of Lymdale by the swirling river's side,
Where Brynhild once was I called in the days ere my father died;   4075
The little land of Lymdale 'twixt the woodland and the sea,
Where on thee mine eyes shall brighten and thine eyes shall beam
    on me.'

'I shall seek thee there,' said Sigurd, 'when the day-spring is begun,
Ere we wend the world together in the season of the sun.'

'I shall bide thee there,' said Brynhild, 'till the fulness of the days,   4080
And the time for the glory appointed, and the springing-tide of praise.'

From his hand then draweth Sigurd Andvari's ancient Gold;
There is nought but the sky above them as the ring together they hold,
The shapen ancient token, that hath no change nor end,
No change, and no beginning, no flaw for God to mend: 4085
Then Sigurd cries: 'O Brynhild, now hearken while I swear,
That the sun shall die in the heavens and the day no more be fair,
If I seek not love in Lymdale and the house that fostered thee,
And the land where thou awakedst 'twixt the woodland and the sea!'

And she cried: 'O Sigurd, Sigurd, now hearken while I swear   4090
That the day shall die for ever and the sun to blackness wear,
Ere I forget thee, Sigurd, as I lie 'twixt wood and sea
In the little land of Lymdale and the house that fostered me!'

Then he set the ring on her finger and once, if ne'er again,
They kissed and clung together, and their hearts were full and fain.   4095

So the day grew old about them and the joy of their desire,
And eve and the sunset came, and faint grew the sunset fire,
And the shadowless death of the day was sweet in the golden tide;
But the stars shone forth on the world, and the twilight changed and
    died;
And sure if the first of man-folk had been born to that starry night,   4100
And had heard no tale of the sunrise, he had never longed for the light:
But Earth longed amidst her slumber, as 'neath the night she lay,
And fresh and all abundant abode the deeds of Day.

From THE LESSER ARTS

Hereafter I hope in another lecture to have the pleasure of laying before you an historical survey of the lesser, or, as they are called, the Decorative Arts, and I must confess it would have been pleasanter to me to have begun my talk with you by entering at once upon the subject of the history of this great industry; but, as I have something to say in a third lecture about various matters connected with the practice of Decoration among ourselves in these days, I feel that I should be in a false position before you, and one that might lead to confusion, or overmuch explanation, if I did not let you know what I think on the nature and scope of these arts, on their condition at the present time, and their outlook in times to come. In doing this it is like enough that I shall say things with which you will very much disagree; I must ask you therefore from the outset to believe that whatever I may blame or whatever I may praise, I neither, when I think of what history has been, am inclined to lament the past, to despise the present, or despair of the future; that I believe all the change and stir about us is a sign of the world's life, and that it will lead—by ways, indeed, of which we have no guess—to the bettering of all mankind.

Now as to the scope and nature of these Arts I have to say, that though when I come more into the details of my subject I shall not meddle much with the great art of Architecture, and less still with the great arts commonly called Sculpture and Painting, yet I cannot in my own mind quite sever them from those lesser so-called Decorative Arts, which I have to speak about: it is only in latter times, and under the most intricate conditions of life, that they have fallen apart from one another; and I hold that, when they are so parted, it is ill for the Arts altogether: the lesser ones become trivial, mechanical, unintelligent, incapable of resisting the changes pressed upon them by fashion or dishonesty; while the greater, however they may be practised for a while by men of great minds and wonder-working hands, unhelped by the lesser, unhelped by each other, are sure to lose their dignity of popular arts, and become nothing but dull adjuncts to unmeaning pomp, or ingenious toys for a few rich and idle men.

However, I have not undertaken to talk to you of Architecture, Sculpture, and Painting, in the narrower sense of those words, since, most unhappily as I think, these master-arts, these arts more specially of the intellect, are at the present day divorced from decoration in its narrower sense. Our subject is that great body of art, by means of which men have at all times more or less striven to beautify the familiar matters of everyday life: a wide subject, a great industry; both a great part of the history of the world, and a most helpful instrument to the study of that history.

A very great industry indeed, comprising the crafts of house-building, painting, joinery and carpentry, smiths' work, pottery and glass-making, weaving, and many others: a body of art most important to the public in general, but still more so to us handicraftsmen; since there is scarce anything that they use, and that we fashion, but it has always been thought to be unfinished till it has had some touch or other of decoration about it. True it is that in many or most cases we have got so used to this ornament, that we look upon it as if it had grown of itself, and note it no more than the mosses on the dry sticks with which we light our fires. So much the worse! for there *is* the decoration, or some pretence of it, and it has, or ought to have, a use and a meaning. For, and this is at the root of the whole matter, everything made by man's hands has a form, which must be either beautiful or ugly; beautiful if it is in accord with Nature, and helps her; ugly if it is discordant with Nature, and thwarts her; it cannot be indifferent: we, for our parts, are busy or sluggish, eager or unhappy, and our eyes are apt to get dulled to this eventfulness of form in those things which we are always looking at. Now it is one of the chief uses of decoration, the chief part of its alliance with nature, that it has to sharpen our dulled senses in this matter: for this end are those wonders of intricate patterns interwoven, those strange forms invented, which men have so long delighted in: forms and intricacies that do not necessarily imitate nature, but in which the hand of the craftsman is guided to work in the way that she does, till the web, the cup, or the knife, look as natural, nay as lovely, as the green field, the river bank, or the mountain flint.

To give people pleasure in the things they must perforce *use*, that is one great office of decoration; to give people pleasure in the things they must perforce *make*, that is the other use of it.

Does not our subject look important enough now? I say that without these arts, our rest would be vacant and uninteresting, our labour mere endurance, mere wearing away of body and mind.

As for that last use of these arts, the giving us pleasure in our work, I scarcely know how to speak strongly enough of it; and yet if I did not know the value of repeating a truth again and again, I should have to excuse myself to you for saying any more about this, when I remember how a great man now living has spoken of it: I mean my friend Professor John Ruskin: if you read the chapter in the 2nd vol. of his 'Stones of Venice' entitled, 'On the Nature of Gothic, and the Office of the Workman therein,' you will read at once the truest and the most eloquent words that can possibly be said on the subject. What I have to say upon it can scarcely be more than an echo of his words, yet I repeat there is some use in reiterating a truth, lest it be forgotten; so I will say this much further: we all know what people have said about the curse of labour, and what heavy and grievous nonsense are the more part of their words thereupon; whereas indeed the real curses of craftsmen have been the curse of stupidity, and the curse of injustice from within and from without: no, I cannot suppose there is anybody here who would think it either a good life, or an amusing one, to sit with one's hands before one doing nothing—to live like a gentleman, as fools call it.

Nevertheless there *is* dull work to be done, and a weary business it is setting men about such work, and seeing them through it, and I would rather do the work twice over with my own hands than have such a job: but now only let the arts which we are talking of beautify our labour, and be widely spread, intelligent, well understood both by the maker and the user, let them grow in one word *popular*, and there will be pretty much an end of dull work and its wearing slavery; and no man will any longer have an excuse for talking about the curse of labour, no man will any longer have an excuse for evading the blessing of labour. I believe there is nothing that will aid the world's progress so much as the attainment of this; I protest there is nothing in the world that I desire so much as this, wrapped up, as I am sure it is, with changes political and social, that in one way or another we all desire.

Now if the objection be made, that these arts have been the handmaids of luxury, of tyranny, and of superstition, I must needs say that it is true in a sense; they have been so used, as many other excellent things have been. But it is also true that, among some nations, their most vigorous and freest times have been the very blossoming times of art: while at the same time, I must allow that these decorative arts have flourished among oppressed peoples, who have seemed to have no hope of freedom: yet I do not think that we shall be wrong in thinking that at such times, among such peoples, art, at least, was free; when it has not been, when it has really been gripped by superstition, or by luxury, it has straightway begun to sicken under that grip. Nor must you forget that when men say popes, kings, and emperors built such and such buildings, it is a mere way of speaking. You look in your history-books to see who built Westminster Abbey, who built St. Sophia at Constantinople, and they tell you Henry III, Justinian the Emperor. Did they? or, rather, men like you and me, handicraftsmen, who have left no names behind them, nothing but their work?

Now as these arts call people's attention and interest to the matters of everyday life in the present, so also, and that I think is no little matter, they call our attention at every step to that history, of which, I said before, they are so great a part; for no nation, no state of society, however rude, has been wholly without them: nay, there are peoples not a few, of whom we know scarce anything, save that they thought such and such forms beautiful. So strong is the bond between history and decoration, that in the practice of the latter we cannot, if we would, wholly shake off the influence of past times over what we do at present. I do not think it is too much to say that no man, however original he may be, can sit down to-day and draw the ornament of a cloth, or the form of an ordinary vessel or piece of furniture, that will be other than a development or a degradation of forms used hundreds of years ago; and these, too, very often, forms that once had a serious meaning, though they are now become little more than a habit of the hand; forms that were once perhaps the mysterious symbols of worships and beliefs now little remembered or wholly forgotten. Those who have diligently followed the delightful study of these arts are able as if through windows to look upon the life of the past— the very first beginnings of thought among nations whom we cannot even name; the terrible empires of the ancient East; the free vigour and glory of Greece; the heavy weight, the firm grasp of Rome; the fall of her temporal Empire which spread so wide about the world all that good and evil which men can never forget, and never cease to feel; the clashing of East and West, South and North, about her rich and fruitful daughter Byzantium; the rise, the dissensions, and the waning of Islam; the wanderings of Scandinavia; the Crusades; the foundation of the States of modern Europe; the struggles of free thought with ancient dying system—with all these events and their meaning is the history of popular art interwoven; with all this, I say, the careful student of decoration as an historical industry must be familiar. When I think of this, and the usefulness of all this knowledge, at a time when history has become so earnest a study amongst us as to have given us, as it were, a new sense: at a time when we so long to know the reality of all that has happened, and are to be put off no longer with the dull records of the battles and intrigues of kings and scoundrels,—I say when I think of all this, I hardly know how to say that this interweaving of the Decorative Arts with the history of the past is of less importance than their dealings with the life of the present: for should not these memories also be a part of our daily life?

[...]

For your teachers, they must be Nature and History: as for the first, that you must learn of it is so obvious that I need not dwell upon that now: hereafter, when I have to speak more of matters of detail, I may have to speak of the manner in which you must learn of Nature. As to the second, I do not think that any man but one of the highest genius, could do anything in these days without much study of ancient art, and even he would be much hindered if he lacked it. If you think that this contradicts what I said about the death of that ancient art, and the necessity I implied for an art that should be characteristic of the present day, I can only say that, in these times of plenteous knowledge and meagre performance, if we do not study the ancient work directly and learn to understand it, we shall find ourselves influenced by the feeble work all round us, and shall be copying the better work through the copyists and *without* understanding it, which will by no means bring about intelligent art. Let us therefore study it wisely, be taught by it, kindled by it; all the while determining not to imitate or repeat it; to have either no art at all, or an art which we have made our own.

Yet I am almost brought to a stand-still when bidding you to study nature and the history of art, by remembering that this is London, and what it is like: how can I ask working-men passing up and down these hideous streets day by day to care about beauty? If it were politics, we must care about that; or science, you could wrap yourselves up in the study of facts, no doubt, without much caring what goes on about you—but beauty! do you not see what terrible difficulties beset art, owing to a long neglect of art—and neglect of reason, too, in this matter? It is such a heavy question by what effort, by what dead-lift, you can thrust this difficulty from you, that I must perforce set it aside for the present, and must at least hope that the study of history and its monuments will help you somewhat herein. If you can really fill your minds with memories of great works of art, and great times of art, you will, I think, be able to a certain extent to look through the aforesaid ugly surroundings, and will be moved to discontent of what is careless and brutal now, and will, I hope, at last be so much discontented with what is bad, that you will determine to bear no longer that short-sighted, reckless brutality of squalor that so disgraces our intricate civilisation.

Well, at any rate, London is good for this, that it is well off for museums,—which I heartily wish were to be got at seven days in the week instead of six, or at least on the only day on which an ordinarily busy man, one of the taxpayers who support them, can as a rule see them quietly,—and certainly any of us who may have any natural turn for art must get more help from frequenting them than one can well say. It is true, however, that people need some preliminary instruction before they can get all the good possible to be got from the prodigious treasures of art possessed by the country in that form: there also one sees things in a piecemeal way: nor can I deny that there is something melancholy about a museum, such a tale of violence, destruction, and carelessness, as its treasured scraps tell us.

But moreover you may sometimes have an opportunity of studying ancient art in a narrower but a more intimate, a more kindly form, the monuments of our own land. Sometimes only, since we live in the middle of this world of brick and mortar, and there is little else left us amidst it, except the ghost of the great church at Westminster, ruined as its exterior is by the stupidity of the restoring architect, and insulted as its glorious interior is by the pompous undertakers' lies, by the vainglory and ignorance of the last two centuries and a half—little besides that and the matchless Hall near it: but when we can get beyond that smoky world, there, out in the country, we may still see the works of our fathers yet alive amidst the very nature they were wrought into, and of which they are so completely a part. For there indeed if anywhere, in the English country, in the days when people cared about such things, was there a full sympathy between the works of man, and the land they were made for:—the land is a little land; too much shut up within the narrow seas, as it seems, to have much space for swelling into hugeness: there are no great wastes overwhelming in their dreariness, no great solitudes of forests, no terrible untrodden mountain-walls: all is measured, mingled, varied, gliding easily one thing into another: little rivers, little plains, swelling, speedily-changing uplands, all beset with handsome orderly trees; little hills, little mountains, netted over with the walls of sheep-walks: all is little; yet not foolish and blank, but serious rather, and abundant of meaning for such as choose to seek it: it is neither prison nor palace, but a decent home.

All which I neither praise nor blame, but say that so it is: some people praise this homeliness overmuch, as if the land were the very axle-tree of the world; so do not I, nor any unblinded by pride in themselves and all that belongs to them: others there are who scorn it and the tameness of it: not I any the more: though it would indeed be hard if there were nothing else in the world, no wonders, no terrors, no unspeakable beauties: yet when we think what a small part of the world's history, past, present, and to come, is this land we live in, and how much smaller still in the history of the arts, and yet how our forefathers clung to it, and with what care and pains they adorned it, this unromantic, uneventful-looking land of England, surely by this too our hearts may be touched, and our hope quickened.

For as was the land, such was the art of it while folk yet troubled themselves about such things; it strove little to impress people either by pomp or ingenuity: not unseldom it fell into commonplace, rarely it rose into majesty; yet was it never oppressive, never a slave's nightmare nor an insolent boast: and at its best it had an inventiveness, an individuality that grander styles have never overpassed: its best too, and that was in its very heart, was given as freely to the yeoman's house, and the humble village church, as to the lord's palace or the mighty cathedral: never coarse, though often rude enough, sweet, natural and unaffected, an art of peasants rather than of merchant-princes or courtiers, it must be a hard heart, I think, that does not love it: whether a man has been born among it like ourselves, or has come wonderingly on its simplicity from all the grandeur over-seas. A peasant art, I say, and it clung fast to the life of the people, and still lived among the cottagers and yeomen in many parts of the country while the big houses were being built 'French and fine': still lived also in many a quaint pattern of loom and printing-block, and embroiderer's needle, while over-seas stupid pomp had extinguished all nature and freedom, and art was become, in France especially, the mere expression of that successful and exultant rascality, which in the flesh no long time afterwards went down into the pit for ever.

Such was the English art, whose history is in a sense at your doors, grown scarce indeed, and growing scarcer year by year, not only through greedy destruction, of which there is certainly less than there used to be, but also through the attacks of another foe, called now-a-days 'restoration.'

I must not make a long story about this, but also I cannot quite pass it over, since I have pressed on you the study of these ancient monuments. Thus the matter stands: these old buildings have been altered and added to century after century, often beautifully, always historically; their very value, a great part of it, lay in that: they have suffered almost always from neglect also, often from violence (that latter a piece of history often far from uninteresting), but ordinary obvious mending would almost always have kept them standing, pieces of nature and of history.

But of late years a great uprising of ecclesiastical zeal, coinciding with a great increase of study, and consequently of knowledge of mediæval architecture, has driven people into spending their money on these buildings, not merely with the purpose of repairing them, of keeping them safe, clean, and wind and water-tight, but also of 'restoring' them to some ideal state of perfection; sweeping away if possible all signs of what has befallen them at least since the Reformation, and often since dates much earlier: this has sometimes been done with much disregard of art and entirely from ecclesiastical zeal, but oftener it has been well meant enough as regards art: yet you will not have listened to what I have said to-night if you do not see that from my point of view this restoration must be as impossible to bring about, as the attempt at it is destructive to the buildings so dealt with: I scarcely like to think what a great part of them have been made nearly useless to students of art and history: unless you knew a great deal about architecture you perhaps would scarce understand what terrible damage has been done by that dangerous 'little knowledge' in this matter: but at least it is easy to be understood, that to deal recklessly with valuable (and national) monuments which, when once gone, can never be replaced by any splendour of modern art, is doing a very sorry service to the State.

You will see by all that I have said on this study of ancient art that I mean by education herein something much wider than the teaching of a definite art in schools of design, and that it must be something that we must do more or less for ourselves: I mean by it a systematic concentration of our thoughts on the matter, a studying of it in all ways, careful and laborious practice of it, and a determination to do nothing but what is known to be good in workmanship and design.

Of course, however, both as an instrument of that study we have been speaking of, as well as of the practice of the arts, all handicraftsmen should be taught to draw very carefully; as indeed all people should be taught drawing who are not physically incapable of learning it: but the art of drawing so taught would not be the art of designing, but only a means towards *this* end, *general capability in dealing with the arts.*

For I wish specially to impress this upon you, that *designing* cannot be taught at all in a school: continued practice will help a man who is naturally a designer, continual notice of nature and of art: no doubt those who have some faculty for designing are still numerous, and they want from a school certain technical teaching, just as they want tools: in these days also, when the best school, the school of successful practice going on around you, is at such a low ebb, they do undoubtedly want instruction in the history of the arts: these two things schools of design can give: but the royal road of a set of rules deduced from a sham science of design, that is itself not a science but another set of rules, will lead nowhere;—or, let us rather say, to beginning again.

As to the kind of drawing that should be taught to men engaged in ornamental work, there is only *one best* way of teaching drawing, and that is teaching the scholar to draw the human figure: both because the lines of a man's body are much more subtle than anything else, and because you can more surely be found out and set right if you go wrong. I do think that such teaching as this, given to all people who care for it, would help the revival of the arts very much: the habit of discriminating between right and wrong, the sense of pleasure in drawing a good line, would really, I think, be education in the due sense of the word for all such people as had the germs of invention in them; yet as aforesaid, in this age of the world it would be mere affectation to pretend to shut one's eyes to the art of past ages: that also we must study. If other circumstances, social and economical, do not stand in our way, that is to say, if the world is not too busy to allow us to have Decorative Arts at all, these two are the *direct* means by which we shall get them; that is, general cultivation of the powers of the mind, general cultivation of the powers of the eye and hand.

Perhaps that seems to you very commonplace advice and a very roundabout road; nevertheless 'tis a certain one, if by any road you desire to come to the new art, which is my subject to-night: if you do not, and if those germs of invention, which, as I said just now, are no doubt still common enough among men, are left neglected and undeveloped, the laws of Nature will assert themselves in this as in other matters, and the faculty of design itself will gradually fade from the race of man. Sirs, shall we approach nearer to perfection by casting away so large a part of that intelligence which makes us *men*?

And now before I make an end, I want to call your attention to certain things, that, owing to our neglect of the arts for other business, bar that good road to us and are such an hindrance, that, till they are dealt with, it is hard even to make a beginning of our endeavour. And if my talk should seem to grow too serious for our subject, as indeed I think it cannot do, I beg you to remember what I said earlier, of how the arts all hang together. Now there is one art of which the old architect of Edward the Third's time was thinking—he who founded New College at Oxford, I mean—when he took this for his motto: 'Manners maketh man:' he meant by manners the art of morals, the art of living worthily, and like a man. I must needs claim this art also as dealing with my subject.

There is a great deal of sham work in the world, hurtful to the buyer, more hurtful to the seller, if he only knew it, most hurtful to the maker: how good a foundation it would be toward getting good Decorative Art, that is ornamental workmanship, if we craftsmen were to resolve to turn out nothing but excellent workmanship in all things, instead of having, as we too often have now, a very low average standard of work, which we often fall below.

I do not blame either one class or another in this matter, I blame all: to set aside our own class of handicraftsmen, of whose shortcomings you and I know so much that we need talk no more about it, I know that the public in general are set on having things cheap, being so ignorant that they do not know when they get them nasty also; so ignorant that they neither know nor care whether they give a man his due: I know that the manufacturers (so called) are so set on carrying out competition to its utmost, competition of cheapness, not of excellence, that they meet the bargain-hunters half way, and cheerfully furnish them with nasty wares at the cheap rate they are asked for, by means of what can be called by no prettier name than fraud. England has of late been too much busied with the counting-house and not enough with the workshop: with the result that the counting-house at the present moment is rather barren of orders.

I say all classes are to blame in this matter, but also I say that the remedy lies with the handicraftsmen, who are not ignorant of these things like the public, and who have no call to be greedy and isolated like the manufacturers or middlemen; the duty and honour of educating the public lies with them, and they have in them the seeds of order and organisation which make that duty the easier.

When will they see to this and help to make men of us all by insisting on this most weighty piece of manners: so that we may adorn life with the pleasure of cheerfully *buying* goods at their due price; with the pleasure of *selling* goods that we could be proud of both for fair price and fair workmanship: with the pleasure of working soundly and without haste at *making* goods that we could be proud of?—much the greatest pleasure of the three is that last, such a pleasure as, I think, the world has none like it.

You must not say that this piece of manners lies out of my subject: it is essentially a part of it and most important: for I am bidding you learn to be artists, if art is not to come to an end amongst us: and what is an artist but a workman who is determined that, whatever else happens, his work shall be excellent? or, to put it in another way: the decoration of workmanship, what is it but the expression of man's pleasure in successful labour? But what pleasure can there be in *bad* work, in *un*successful labour; why should we decorate *that*? and how can we bear to be always unsuccessful in our labour?

As greed of unfair gain, wanting to be paid for what we have not earned, cumbers our path with this tangle of bad work, of sham work, so the heaped-up money which this greed has brought us (for greed will have its way, like all other strong passions), this money, I say, gathered into heaps little and big, with all the false distinction which so unhappily it yet commands amongst us, has raised up against the arts a barrier of the love of luxury and show, which is of all obvious hindrances the worst to overpass: the highest and most cultivated classes are not free from the vulgarity of it, the lower are not free from its pretence. I beg you to remember both as a remedy against this, and as explaining exactly what I mean, that nothing can be a work of art which is not useful; that is to say, which does not minister to the body when well under command of the mind, or which does not amuse, soothe, or elevate the mind in a healthy state. What tons upon tons of unutterable rubbish pretending to be works of art in some degree would this maxim clear out of our London houses, if it were understood and acted upon! To my mind it is only here and there (out of the kitchen) that you can find in a well-to-do house things that are of any use at all: as a rule all the decoration (so called) that has got there is there for the sake of show, not because anybody likes it. I repeat, this stupidity goes through all classes of society: the silk curtains in my Lord's drawing-room are no more a matter of art to him than the powder in his footman's hair; the kitchen in a country farmhouse is most commonly a pleasant and homelike place, the parlour dreary and useless.

Simplicity of life, begetting simplicity of taste, that is, a love for sweet and lofty things, is of all matters most necessary for the birth of the new and better art we crave for; simplicity everywhere, in the palace as well as in the cottage.

Still more is this necessary, cleanliness and decency everywhere, in the cottage as well as in the palace: the lack of that is a serious piece of *manners* for us to correct: that lack and all the inequalities of life, and the heaped-up thoughtlessness and disorder of so many centuries that cause it: and as yet it is only a very few men who have begun to think about a remedy for it in its widest range: even in its narrower aspect, in the defacements of our big towns by all that commerce brings with it, who heeds it? who tries to control their squalor and hideousness? there is nothing but thoughtlessness and recklessness in the matter: the helplessness of people who don't live long enough to do a thing themselves, and have not manliness and foresight enough to begin the work, and pass it on to those that shall come after them.

Is money to be gathered? cut down the pleasant trees among the houses, pull down ancient and venerable buildings for the money that a few square yards of London dirt will fetch; blacken rivers, hide the sun and poison the air with smoke and worse, and it's nobody's business to see to it or mend it: that is all that modern commerce, the counting-house forgetful of the workshop, will do for us herein.

And Science—we have loved her well, and followed her diligently, what will she do? I fear she is so much in the pay of the counting-house—the counting-house and the drill-sergeant—that she is too busy, and will for the present do nothing. Yet there are matters which I should have thought easy for her; say for example teaching Manchester how to consume its own smoke, or Leeds how to get rid of its superfluous black dye without turning it into the river, which would be as much worth her attention as the production of the heaviest of heavy black silks, or the biggest of useless guns. Anyhow, however it be done, unless people care about carrying on their business without making the world hideous, how can they care about Art? I know it will cost much both of time and money to better these things even a little; but I do not see how these can be better spent than in making life cheerful and honourable for others and for ourselves; and the gain of good life to the country at large that would result from men seriously setting about the bettering of the decency of our big towns would be priceless, even if nothing specially good befell the arts in consequence: I do not know that it would; but I should begin to think matters hopeful if men turned their attention to such things, and I repeat that, unless they do so, we can scarcely even begin with any hope our endeavours for the bettering of the Arts.

Unless something or other is done to give all men some pleasure for the eyes and rest for the mind in the aspect of their own and their neighbours' houses, until the contrast is less disgraceful between the fields where beasts live and the streets where men live, I suppose that the practice of the arts must be mainly kept in the hands of a few highly cultivated men, who can go often to beautiful places, whose education enables them, in the contemplation of the past glories of the world, to shut out from their view the everyday squalors that the most of men move in. Sirs, I believe that art has such sympathy with cheerful freedom, open-heartedness and reality, so much she sickens under selfishness and luxury, that she will not live thus isolated and exclusive. I will go further than this and say that on such terms I do not wish her to live. I protest that it would be a shame to an honest artist to enjoy what he had huddled up to himself of such art, as it would be for a rich man to sit and eat dainty food amongst starving soldiers in a beleaguered fort.

I do not want art for a few, any more than education for a few, or freedom for a few.

No, rather than art should live this poor thin life among a few exceptional men, despising those beneath them for an ignorance for which they themselves are responsible, for a brutality that they will not struggle with,—rather than this, I would that the world should indeed sweep away all art for awhile, as I said before I thought it possible she might do: rather than the wheat should rot in the miser's granary, I would that the earth had it, that it might yet have a chance to quicken in the dark.

I have a sort of faith, though, that this clearing away of all art will not happen, that men will get wiser, as well as more learned; that many of the intricacies of life, on which we now pride ourselves more than enough, partly because they are new, partly because they have come with the gain of better things, will be cast aside as having played their part, and being useful no longer. I hope that we shall have leisure from war,—war commercial, as well as war of the bullet and the bayonet; leisure from the knowledge that darkens counsel; leisure above all from the greed of money, and the craving for that overwhelming distinction that money now brings: I believe that as we have even now partly achieved LIBERTY, so we shall one day achieve EQUALITY, which, and which only, means FRATERNITY, and so have leisure from poverty and all its griping, sordid cares.

Then, having leisure from all these things, amidst renewed simplicity of life we shall have leisure to think about our work, that faithful daily companion, which no man any longer will venture to call the Curse of labour: for surely then we shall be happy in it, each in his place, no man grudging at another; no one bidden to be any man's *servant*, every one scorning to be any man's *master*: men will then assuredly be happy in their work, and that happiness will assuredly bring forth decorative, noble, *popular* art.

That art will make our streets as beautiful as the woods, as elevating as the mountain-sides: it will be a pleasure and a rest, and not a weight upon the spirits to come from the open country into a town; every man's house will be fair and decent, soothing to his mind and helpful to his work: all the works of man that we live amongst and handle will be in harmony with nature, will be reasonable and beautiful: yet all will be simple and inspiriting, not childish nor enervating; for as nothing of beauty and splendour that man's mind and hand may compass shall be wanting from our public buildings, so in no private dwelling will there be any signs of waste, pomp, or insolence, and every man will have his share of the *best*.

It is a dream, you may say, of what has never been and never will be: true, it has never been, and therefore, since the world is alive and moving yet, my hope is the greater that it one day will be: true, it is a dream; but dreams have before now come about of things so good and necessary to us, that we scarcely think of them more than of the daylight, though once people had to live without them, without even the hope of them.

Anyhow, dream as it is, I pray you to pardon my setting it before you, for it lies at the bottom of all my work in the Decorative Arts, nor will it ever be out of my thoughts: and I am here with you to-night to ask you to help me in realising this dream, this *hope*.

THE BEAUTY OF LIFE

'—propter vitam vivendi perdere causas.'—
Juvenal

I stand before you this evening weighted with a disadvantage that I did not feel last year;—I have little fresh to tell you; I can somewhat enlarge on what I said then; here and there I may make bold to give you a practical suggestion, or I may put what I have to say in a way which will be clearer to some of you perhaps; but my message is really the same as it was when I first had the pleasure of meeting you.

It is true that if all were going smoothly with art, or at all events so smoothly that there were but a few malcontents in the world, you might listen with some pleasure, and perhaps advantage, to the talk of an old hand in the craft concerning ways of work, the snares that beset success, and the shortest road to it, to a tale of workshop receipts and the like: that would be a pleasant talk surely between friends and fellow-workmen; but it seems to me as if it were not for us as yet; nay, maybe we may live long and find no time fit for such restful talk as the cheerful histories of the hopes and fears of our workshops: anyhow to-night I cannot do it, but must once again call the faithful of art to a battle wider and more distracting than that kindly struggle with nature, to which all true craftsmen are born; which is both the building-up and the wearing-away of their lives.

As I look round on this assemblage, and think of all that it represents, I cannot choose but be moved to the soul by the troubles of the life of civilised man, and the hope that thrusts itself through them; I cannot refrain from giving you once again the message with which, as it seems, some chance-hap has charged me: that message is, in short, to call on you to face the latest danger which civilisation is threatened with, a danger of her own breeding: that men in struggling towards the complete attainment of all the luxuries of life for the strongest portion of their race should deprive their whole race of all the beauty of life: a danger that the strongest and wisest of mankind, in striving to attain to a complete mastery over nature, should destroy her simplest and widest-spread gifts, and thereby enslave simple people to them, and themselves to themselves, and so at last drag the world into a second barbarism more ignoble, and a thousandfold more hopeless, than the first.

Now of you who are listening to me, there are some, I feel sure, who have received this message, and taken it to heart, and are day by day fighting the battle that it calls on you to fight: to you I can say nothing but that if any word

I speak discourage you, I shall heartily wish I had never spoken at all: but to be shown the enemy, and the castle we have got to storm, is not to be bidden to run from him; nor am I telling you to sit down deedless in the desert because between you and the promised land lies many a trouble, and death itself maybe: the hope before you you know, and nothing that I can say can take it away from you; but friend may with advantage cry out to friend in the battle that a stroke is coming from this side or that: take my hasty words in that sense, I beg of you.

But I think there will be others of you in whom vague discontent is stirring: who are oppressed by the life that surrounds you; confused and troubled by that oppression, and not knowing on which side to seek a remedy, though you are fain to do so: well, we, who have gone further into those troubles, believe that we can help you: true we cannot at once take your trouble from you; nay, we may at first rather add to it; but we can tell you what we think of the way out of it; and then amidst the many things you will have to do to set yourselves and others fairly on that way, you will many days, nay most days, forget your trouble in thinking of the good that lies beyond it, for which you are working.

But, again, there are others amongst you (and to speak plainly, I daresay they are the majority), who are not by any means troubled by doubt of the road the world is going, nor excited by any hope of its bettering that road: to them the cause of civilisation is simple and even commonplace: wonder, hope, and fear no longer hang about it; it has become to us like the rising and setting of the sun; it cannot err, and we have no call to meddle with it, either to complain of its course, or to try to direct it.

There is a ground of reason and wisdom in that way of looking at the matter: surely the world will go on its ways, thrust forward by impulses which we cannot understand or sway: but as it grows in strength for the journey, its necessary food is the life and aspirations of *all* of us: and we discontented strugglers with what at times seems the hurrying blindness of civilisation, no less than those who see nothing but smooth, unvarying progress in it, are bred of civilisation also, and shall be used up to further it in some way or other, I doubt not: and it may be of some service to those who think themselves the only loyal subjects of progress to hear of our existence, since their not hearing of it would not make an end of it: it may set them a-thinking not unprofitably to hear of burdens that they do not help to bear, but which are nevertheless real and weighty enough to some of their fellow-men, who are helping, even as they are, to form the civilisation that is to be.

The danger that the present course of civilisation will destroy the beauty of life—these are hard words, and I wish I could mend them, but I cannot, while I speak what I believe to be the truth.

That the beauty of life is a thing of no moment, I suppose few people would venture to assert, and yet most civilised people act as if it were of none, and in so doing are wronging both themselves and those that are to come after them; for that beauty, which is what is meant by *art*, using the word in its widest sense, is, I contend, no mere accident to human life, which people can take or leave as they choose, but a positive necessity of life, if we are to live as nature meant us to; that is, unless we are content to be less than men.

Now I ask you, as I have been asking myself this long while, what proportion of the population in civilised countries has any share at all in that necessity of life?

I say that the answer which must be made to that question justifies my fear that modern civilisation is on the road to trample out all the beauty of life, and to make us less than men.

Now if there should be any here who will say: It was always so; there always was a mass of rough ignorance that knew and cared nothing about art; I answer first, that if that be the case, then it was always wrong, and we, as soon as we have become conscious of that wrong, are bound to set it right if we can.

But moreover, strange to say, and in spite of all the suffering that the world has wantonly made for itself, and has in all ages so persistently clung to, as if it were a good and holy thing, this wrong of the mass of men being regardless of art was *not* always so.

So much is now known of the periods of art that have left abundant examples of their work behind them, that we can judge of the art of all periods by comparing these with the remains of times of which less has been left us; and we cannot fail to come to the conclusion that down to very recent days everything that the hand of man touched was more or less beautiful: so that in those days all people who made anything shared in art, as well as all people who used the things so made: that is, *all* people shared in art.

But some people may say: And was that to be wished for? would not this universal spreading of art stop progress in other matters, hinder the work of the world? Would it not make us unmanly? or if not that, would it not be intrusive, and push out other things necessary also for men to study?

Well, I have claimed a necessary place for art, a natural place, and it would be in the very essence of it, that it would apply its own rules of order and fitness to the general ways of life: it seems to me, therefore, that people who are over-anxious of the outward expression of beauty becoming too great a force among the other forces of life, would, if they had had the making of the external world, have been afraid of making an ear of wheat beautiful, lest it should not have been good to eat.

But indeed there seems no chance of art becoming universal, unless on the terms that it shall have little self-consciousness, and for the most part be done with little effort; so that the rough work of the world would be as little hindered by it, as the work of external nature is by the beauty of all her forms and moods: this was the case in the times that I have been speaking of: of art which was made by conscious effort, the result of the individual striving towards perfect expression of their thoughts by men very specially gifted, there was perhaps no more than there is now, except in very wonderful and short periods; though I believe that even for such men the struggle to produce beauty was not so bitter as it now is. But if there were not more great thinkers than there are now, there was a countless multitude of happy workers whose work did express, and could not choose but express, some original thought, and was consequently both interesting and beautiful: now there is certainly no chance of the more individual art becoming common, and either wearying us by its over-abundance, or by noisy self-assertion preventing highly cultivated men taking their due part in the other work of the world; it is too difficult to do: it will be always but the blossom of all the half-conscious work below it, the fulfilment of the shortcomings of less complete minds: but it will waste much of its power, and have much less influence on men's minds, unless it be surrounded by abundance of that commoner work, in which all men once shared, and which, I say, will, when art has really awakened, be done so easily and constantly, that it will stand in no man's way to hinder him from doing what he will, good or evil. And as, on the one hand, I believe that art made by the people and for the people as a joy both to the maker and the user would further progress in other matters rather than hinder it, so also I firmly believe that that higher art produced only by great brains and miraculously gifted hands cannot exist without it: I believe that the present state of things in which it does exist, while popular art is, let us say, asleep or sick, is a transitional state, which must end at last either in utter defeat or utter victory for the arts.

For whereas all works of craftsmanship were once beautiful, unwittingly or not, they are now divided into two kinds, works of art and non-works of art: now nothing made by man's hand can be indifferent: it must be either beautiful and elevating, or ugly and degrading; and those things that are without art are so aggressively; they wound it by their existence, and they are now so much in the majority that the works of art we are obliged to set ourselves to seek for, whereas the other things are the ordinary companions of our everyday life; so that if those who cultivate art intellectually were inclined never so much to wrap themselves in their special gifts and their high cultivation, and so live happily, apart from other men, and despising them, they could not do so: they are as it were living in an enemy's country; at every turn there is something lying in wait to offend and vex their nicer sense and educated eyes: they must share in the general discomfort—and I am glad of it.

So the matter stands: from the first dawn of history till quite modern times, art, which nature meant to solace all, fulfilled its purpose; all men shared in it; that was what made life romantic, as people call it, in those days; that and not robber-barons and inaccessible kings with their hierarchy of serving-nobles and other such rubbish: but art grew and grew, saw empires sicken and sickened with them; grew hale again, and haler, and grew so great at last, that she seemed in good truth to have conquered everything, and laid the material world under foot. Then came a change at a period of the greatest life and hope in many ways that Europe had known till then: a time of so much and such varied hope that people call it the time of the New Birth: as far as the arts are concerned I deny it that title; rather it seems to me that the great men who lived and glorified the practice of art in those days, were the fruit of the old, not the seed of the new order of things: but a stirring and hopeful time it was, and many things were newborn then which have since brought forth fruit enough: and it is strange and perplexing that from those days forward the lapse of time, which, through plenteous confusion and failure, has on the whole been steadily destroying privilege and exclusiveness in other matters, has delivered up art to be the exclusive privilege of a few, and has taken from the people their birthright; while both wronged and wrongers have been wholly unconscious of what they were doing.

Wholly unconscious—yes, but we are no longer so: there lies the sting of it, and there also the hope.

When the brightness of the so-called Renaissance faded, and it faded very suddenly, a deadly chill fell upon the arts: that New-birth mostly meant looking back to past times, wherein the men of those days thought they saw a perfection of art, which to their minds was different in kind, and not in degree only, from the ruder suggestive art of their own fathers: this perfection they were ambitious to imitate, this alone seemed to be art to them, the rest was childishness: so wonderful was their energy, their success so great, that no doubt to commonplace minds among them, though surely not to the great masters, that perfection seemed to be gained: and, perfection being gained, what are you to do?—you can go no further, you must aim at standing still— which you cannot do.

Art by no means stood still in those latter days of the Renaissance, but took the downward road with terrible swiftness, and tumbled down at the bottom of the hill, where as if bewitched it lay long in great content, believing itself to be the art of Michael Angelo, while it was the art of men whom nobody remembers but those who want to sell their pictures.

Thus it fared with the more individual forms of art. As to the art of the people; in countries and places where the greater art had flourished most, it went step by step on the downward path with that: in more out-of-the-way places, England for instance, it still felt the influence of the life of its earlier and happy days, and in a way lived on a while; but its life was so feeble, and, so to say, illogical, that it could not resist any change in external circumstances, still less could it give birth to anything new; and before this century began, its last flicker had died out. Still, while it was living, in whatever dotage, it did imply something going on in those matters of daily use that we have been thinking of, and doubtless satisfied some cravings for beauty: and when it was dead, for a long time people did not know it, or what had taken its place, crept so to say into its dead body—that pretence of art, to wit, which is done with machines, though sometimes the machines are called men, and doubtless are so out of working hours: nevertheless long before it was quite dead it had fallen so low that the whole subject was usually treated with the utmost contempt by every one who had any pretence of being a sensible man, and in short the whole civilised world had forgotten that there had ever been an art *made by the people for the people as a joy for the maker and the user.*

But now it seems to me that the very suddenness of the change ought to comfort us, to make us look upon this break in the continuity of the golden chain as an accident only, that itself cannot last: for think how many thousand years it may be since that primeval man graved with a flint splinter on a bone the story of the mammoth he had seen, or told us of the slow uplifting of the heavily-horned heads of the reindeer that he stalked: think I say of the space of time from then till the dimming of the brightness of the Italian Renaissance! whereas from that time till popular art died unnoticed and despised among ourselves is just but two hundred years.

Strange too, that very death is contemporaneous with new-birth of something at all events; for out of all despair sprang a new time of hope lighted by the torch of the French Revolution: and things that have languished with the languishing of art, rose afresh and surely heralded its new birth: in good earnest poetry was born again, and the English Language, which under the hands of sycophantic verse-makers had been reduced to a miserable jargon, whose meaning, if it have a meaning, cannot be made out without translation, flowed clear, pure, and simple, along with the music of Blake and Coleridge: take those names, the earliest in date among ourselves, as a type of the change that has happened in literature since the time of George II.

With that literature in which romance, that is to say humanity, was re-born, there sprang up also a feeling for the romance of external nature, which is surely strong in us now, joined with a longing to know something real of the lives of those who have gone before us; of these feelings united you will find the broadest expression in the pages of Walter Scott: it is curious as showing how sometimes one art will lag behind another in a revival, that the man who wrote the exquisite and wholly unfettered naturalism of the Heart of Midlothian, for instance, thought himself continually bound to seem to feel ashamed of, and to excuse himself for, his love of Gothic Architecture: he felt that it was romantic, and he knew that it gave him pleasure, but somehow he had not found out that it was art, having been taught in many ways that nothing could be art that was not done by a named man under academical rules.

I need not perhaps dwell much on what of change has been since: you know well that one of the master-arts, the art of painting, has been revolutionised. I have a genuine difficulty in speaking to you of men who are my own personal friends, nay my masters: still, since I cannot quite say nothing of them I must say the plain truth, which is this; never in the whole history of art did any set of men come nearer to the feat of making something out of nothing than that little knot of painters who have raised English art from what it was, when as a boy I used to go to the Royal Academy Exhibition, to what it is now.

It would be ungracious indeed for me who have been so much taught by him that I cannot help feeling continually as I speak that I am echoing his words, to leave out the name of John Ruskin from an account of what has happened since the tide, as we hope, began to turn in the direction of art. True it is, that his unequalled style of English and his wonderful eloquence would, whatever its subject-matter, have gained him some sort of a hearing in a time that has not lost its relish for literature; but surely the influence that he has exercised over cultivated people must be the result of that style and that eloquence expressing what was already stirring in men's minds; he could not have written what he has done unless people were in some sort ready for it; any more than those painters could have begun their crusade against the dulness and incompetency that was the rule in their art thirty years ago unless they had some hope that they would one day move people to understand them.

Well, we find that the gains since the turning-point of the tide are these: that there are some few artists who have, as it were, caught up the golden chain dropped two hundred years ago, and that there are a few highly cultivated people who can understand them; and that beyond these there is a vague feeling abroad among people of the same degree, of discontent at the ignoble ugliness that surrounds them.

That seems to me to mark the advance that we have made since the last of popular art came to an end amongst us, and I do not say, considering where we then were, that it is not a great advance, for it comes to this, that though the battle is still to win, there are those who are ready for the battle.

Indeed it would be a strange shame for this age if it were not so: for as every age of the world has its own troubles to confuse it, and its own follies to cumber it, so has each its own work to do, pointed out to it by unfailing signs of the times; and it is unmanly and stupid for the children of any age to say: we will not set our hands to the work; we did not make the troubles, we will not weary ourselves seeking a remedy for them: so heaping up for their sons a heavier load than they can lift without such struggles as will wound and cripple them sorely. Not thus our fathers served us, who, working late and early, left us at last that seething mass of people so terribly alive and energetic, that we call modern Europe; not thus those served us, who have made for us these present days, so fruitful of change and wondering expectation.

The century that is now beginning to draw to an end, if people were to take to nicknaming centuries, would be called the Century of Commerce; and I do not think I undervalue the work that it has done: it has broken down many a prejudice and taught many a lesson that the world has been hitherto slow to learn: it has made it possible for many a man to live free, who would in other times have been a slave, body or soul, or both: if it has not quite spread peace and justice through the world, as at the end of its first half we fondly hoped it would, it has at least stirred up in many fresh cravings for peace and justice: its work has been good and plenteous, but much of it was roughly done, as needs was; recklessness has commonly gone with its energy, blindness too often with its haste: so that perhaps it may be work enough for the next century to repair the blunders of that recklessness, to clear away the rubbish which that hurried work has piled up; nay even we in the second half of its last quarter may do something towards setting its house in order.

You, of this great and famous town, for instance, which has had so much to do with the Century of Commerce, your gains are obvious to all men, but the price you have paid for them is obvious to many—surely to yourselves most of all: I do not say that they are not worth the price; I know that England and the world could very ill afford to exchange the Birmingham of to-day for the Birmingham of the year 1700: but surely if what you have gained be more than a mockery, you cannot stop at those gains, or even go on always piling up similar ones. Nothing can make me believe that the present condition of your Black Country yonder is an unchangeable necessity of your life and position: such miseries as this were begun and carried on in pure thoughtlessness, and a hundredth part of the energy that was spent in creating them would get rid of them: I do think if we were not all of us too prone to acquiesce in the base byword 'after me the deluge,' it would soon be something more than an idle dream to hope that your pleasant midland hills and fields might begin to become pleasant again in some way or other, even without depopulating them; or that those once lovely valleys of Yorkshire in the 'heavy woollen district,' with their sweeping hill-sides and noble rivers, should not need the stroke of ruin to make them once more delightful abodes of men, instead of the dog-holes that the Century of Commerce has made them.

Well, people will not take the trouble or spend the money necessary to beginning this sort of reforms, because they do not feel the evils they live amongst, because they have degraded themselves into something less than men; they are unmanly because they have ceased to have their due share of art.

For again I say that herein rich people have defrauded themselves as well as the poor: you will see a refined and highly educated man nowadays, who has been to Italy and Egypt, and where not, who can talk learnedly enough (and fantastically enough sometimes) about art, and who has at his fingers' ends abundant lore concerning the art and literature of past days, sitting down without signs of discomfort in a house, that with all its surroundings is just brutally vulgar and hideous: all his education has not done more for him than that.

The truth is, that in art, and in other things besides, the laboured education of a few will not raise even those few above the reach of the evils that beset the ignorance of the great mass of the population: the brutality, of which such a huge stock has been accumulated lower down, will often show without much peeling through the selfish refinement of those who have let it accumulate.

The lack of art, or rather the murder of art, that curses our streets from the sordidness of the surroundings of the lower classes, has its exact counterpart in the dulness and vulgarity of those of the middle classes, and the double-distilled dulness, and scarcely less vulgarity of those of the upper classes.

I say this is as it should be; it is just and fair as far as it goes; and moreover the rich with their leisure are the more like to move if they feel the pinch themselves.

But how shall they and we, and all of us, move? What is the remedy?

What remedy can there be for the blunders of civilisation but further civilisation? You do not by any accident think that we have gone as far in that direction as it is possible to go, do you?—even in England, I mean?

When some changes have come to pass, that perhaps will be speedier than most people think, doubtless education will both grow in quality and in quantity; so that it may be, that as the nineteenth century is to be called the Century of Commerce, the twentieth may be called the Century of Education. But that education does not end when people leave school is now a mere commonplace; and how then can you really educate men who lead the life of machines, who only think for the few hours during which they are not at work, who in short spend almost their whole lives in doing work which is not proper for developing them body and mind in some worthy way? You cannot educate, you cannot civilise men, unless you can give them a share in art.

Yes, and it is hard indeed as things go to give most men that share; for they do not miss it, or ask for it, and it is impossible as things are that they should either miss or ask for it. Nevertheless everything has a beginning, and many great things have had very small ones; and since, as I have said, these ideas are already abroad in more than one form, we must not be too much discouraged at the seemingly boundless weight we have to lift.

After all, we are only bound to play our own parts, and do our own share of the lifting; and as in no case that share can be great, so also in all cases it is called for, it is necessary. Therefore let us work and faint not; remembering that though it be natural, and therefore excusable, amidst doubtful times to feel doubts of success oppress us at whiles, yet not to crush those doubts, and work as if we had them not, is simple cowardice, which is unforgivable. No man has any right to say that all has been done for nothing, that all the faithful unwearying strife of those that have gone before us shall lead us nowhither; that mankind will but go round and round in a circle for ever: no man has a right to say that, and then get up morning after morning to eat his victuals and sleep a-nights, all the while making other people toil to keep his worthless life a-going.

Be sure that some way or other will be found out of the tangle, even when things seem most tangled, and be no less sure that some use will then have come of our work, if it has been faithful, and therefore unsparingly careful and thoughtful.

So once more I say, if in any matters civilisation has gone astray, the remedy lies not in standing still, but in more complete civilisation.

Now whatever discussion there may be about that often used and often misused word, I believe all who hear me will agree with me in believing from their hearts, and not merely in saying in conventional phrase, that the civilisation which does not carry the whole people with it, is doomed to fall, and give place to one which at least aims at doing so.

We talk of the civilisation of the ancient peoples, of the classical times, well, civilised they were no doubt, some of their folk at least: an Athenian citizen for instance led a simple, dignified, almost perfect life; but there were drawbacks to happiness perhaps in the life of his slaves: and the civilisation of the ancients was founded on slavery.

Indeed that ancient society did give a model to the world, and showed us for ever what blessings are freedom of life and thought, self-restraint and a generous education: all those blessings the ancient free peoples set forth to the world—and kept them to themselves.

Therefore no tyrant was too base, no pretext too hollow, for enslaving the grandsons of the men of Salamis and Thermopylæ: therefore did the descendants of those stern and self-restrained Romans, who were ready to give up everything, and life as the least of things, to the glory of their commonweal, produce monsters of license and reckless folly. Therefore did a little knot of Galilean peasants overthrow the Roman Empire.

Ancient civilisation was chained to slavery and exclusiveness, and it fell; the barbarism that took its place has delivered us from slavery and grown into modern civilisation: and that in its turn has before it the choice of never-ceasing growth, or destruction by that which has in it the seeds of higher growth.

There is an ugly word for a dreadful fact, which I must make bold to use—the residuum: that word since the time I first saw it used, has had a terrible significance to me, and I have felt from my heart that if this residuum were a necessary part of modern civilisation, as some people openly, and many more tacitly, assume that it is, then this civilisation carries with it the poison that shall one day destroy it, even as its elder sister did: if civilisation is to go no further than this, it had better not have gone so far: if it does not aim at getting rid of this misery and giving some share in the happiness and dignity of life to *all* the people that it has created, and which it spends such unwearying energy in creating, it is simply an organised injustice, a mere instrument for oppression, so much the worse than that which has gone before it, as its pretensions are higher, its slavery subtler, its mastery harder to overthrow, because supported by such a dense mass of commonplace well-being and comfort.

Surely this cannot be: surely there is a distinct feeling abroad of this injustice: so that if the residuum still clogs all the efforts of modern civilisation to rise above mere population-breeding and money-making, the difficulty of dealing with it is the legacy, first of the ages of violence and almost conscious brutal injustice, and next of the ages of thoughtlessness, of hurry and blindness; surely all those who think at all of the future of the world are at work in one way or other in striving to rid it of this shame.

That to my mind is the meaning of what we call National Education, which we have begun, and which is doubtless already bearing its fruits, and will bear greater, when all people are educated, not according to the money which they or their parents possess, but according to the capacity of their minds.

What effect that will have upon the future of the arts, I cannot say, but one would surely think a very great effect; for it will enable people to see clearly many things which are now as completely hidden from them as if they were blind in body and idiotic in mind: and this, I say, will act not only upon those who most directly feel the evils of ignorance, but also upon those who feel them indirectly,—upon us, the educated: the great wave of rising intelligence, rife with so many natural desires and aspirations, will carry all classes along with it, and force us all to see that many things which we have been used to look upon as necessary and eternal evils are merely the accidental and temporary growths of past stupidity, and can be escaped from by due effort, and the exercise of courage, goodwill, and forethought.

And among those evils, I do, and must always, believe will fall that one which last year I told you that I accounted the greatest of all evils, the heaviest of all slaveries; that evil of the greater part of the population being engaged for by far the most part of their lives in work, which at the best cannot interest them, or develop their best faculties, and at the worst (and that is the commonest, too) is mere unmitigated slavish toil, only to be wrung out of them by the sternest compulsion, a toil which they shirk all they can—small blame to them. And this toil degrades them into less than men: and they will some day come to know it, and cry out to be made men again, and art only can do it, and redeem them from this slavery; and I say once more that this is her highest and most glorious end and aim; and it is in her struggle to attain to it that she will most surely purify herself, and quicken her own aspirations towards perfection.

But we—in the meantime we must not sit waiting for obvious signs of these later and glorious days to show themselves on earth, and in the heavens, but rather turn to the commonplace, and maybe often dull work of fitting ourselves in detail to take part in them if we should live to see one of them; or in doing our best to make the path smooth for their coming, if we are to die before they are here.

What, therefore, can we do, to guard traditions of time past that we may not one day have to begin anew from the beginning with none to teach us? What are we to do, that we may take heed to, and spread the decencies of life, so that at the least we may have a field where it will be possible for art to grow when men begin to long for it: what finally can we do, each of us, to cherish some germ of art, so that it may meet with others, and spread and grow little by little into the thing that we need?

Now I cannot pretend to think that the first of these duties is a matter of indifference to you, after my experience of the enthusiastic meeting that I had the honour of addressing here last autumn on the subject of the (so called) restoration of St. Mark's at Venice; you thought, and most justly thought, it seems to me, that the subject was of such moment to art in general, that it was a simple and obvious thing for men who were anxious on the matter to address themselves to those who had the decision of it in their hands; even though the former were called Englishmen, and the latter Italians; for you felt that the name of lovers of art would cover those differences: if you had any misgivings, you remembered that there was but one such building in the world, and that it was worth while risking a breach of etiquette, if any words of ours could do anything towards saving it; well, the Italians were, some of them, very naturally, though surely unreasonably, irritated, for a time, and in some of their prints they bade us, look at home! that was no argument in favour of the wisdom of wantonly rebuilding St. Mark's façade: but certainly those of us who have not yet looked at home in this matter had better do so speedily, late and over late though it be: for though we have no golden-pictured interiors like St. Mark's Church at home, we still have many buildings which are both works of ancient art and monuments of history: and just think what is happening to them, and note, since we profess to recognise their value, how helpless art is in the Century of Commerce!

In the first place, many and many a beautiful and ancient building is being destroyed all over civilised Europe as well as in England, because it is supposed to interfere with the convenience of the citizens, while a little forethought might save it without trenching on that convenience;* but even apart from that, I say that if we are not prepared to put up with a little inconvenience in our lifetimes for the sake of preserving a monument of art which will elevate and educate, not only ourselves, but our sons, and our sons' sons, it is vain and idle of us to talk about art—or education either. Brutality must be bred of such brutality.

The same thing may be said about enlarging, or otherwise altering for convenience' sake, old buildings still in use for something like their original purposes: in almost all such cases it is really nothing more than a question of a little money for a new site: and then a new building can be built exactly

---

* As I correct these sheets for the press, the case of two such pieces of destruction is forced upon me: first, the remains of the Refectory of Westminster Abbey, with the adjacent Ashburnam House, a beautiful work, probably by Inigo Jones; and second, Magdalen Bridge at Oxford. Certainly this seems to mock my hope of the influence of education on the Beauty of Life; since the first scheme of destruction is eagerly pressed forward by the authorities of Westminster School, the second scarcely opposed by the resident members of the University of Oxford.

fitted for the uses it is needed for, with such art about it as our own days can furnish; while the old monument is left to tell its tale of change and progress, to hold out example and warning to us in the practice of the arts: and thus the convenience of the public, the progress of modern art, and the cause of education, are all furthered at once at the cost of a little money.

Surely if it be worth while troubling ourselves about the works of art of to-day, of which any amount almost can be done, since we are yet alive, it is worth while spending a little care, forethought, and money in preserving the art of bygone ages, of which (woe worth the while!) so little is left, and of which we can never have any more, whatever good-hap the world may attain to.

No man who consents to the destruction or the mutilation of an ancient building has any right to pretend that he cares about art; or has any excuse to plead in defence of his crime against civilisation and progress, save sheer brutal ignorance.

But before I leave this subject I must say a word or two about the curious invention of our own days called Restoration, a method of dealing with works of bygone days which, though not so degrading in its spirit as downright destruction, is nevertheless little better in its results on the condition of those works of art; it is obvious that I have no time to argue the question out to-night, so I will only make these assertions:

That ancient buildings, being both works of art and monuments of history, must obviously be treated with great care and delicacy: that the imitative art of to-day is not, and cannot be the same thing as ancient art, and cannot replace it; and that therefore if we superimpose this work on the old, we destroy it both as art and as a record of history: lastly, that the natural weathering of the surface of a building is beautiful, and its loss disastrous.

Now the restorers hold the exact contrary of all this: they think that any clever architect to-day can deal off-hand successfully with the ancient work; that while all things else have changed about us since (say) the thirteenth century, art has not changed, and that our workmen can turn out work identical with that of the thirteenth century; and, lastly, that the weather-beaten surface of an ancient building is worthless, and to be got rid of wherever possible.

You see the question is difficult to argue, because there seem to be no common grounds between the restorers and the anti-restorers: I appeal therefore to the public, and bid them note, that though our opinions may be wrong, the action we advise is not rash: let the question be shelved awhile: if, as we are always pressing on people, due care be taken of these monuments, so that they shall not fall into disrepair, they will be always there to 'restore' whenever people think proper and when we are proved wrong; but if it should turn out that we are right, how can the 'restored' buildings be restored? I beg of you therefore to let the question be shelved, till art has so advanced among us, that we can deal authoritatively with it, till there is no longer any doubt about the matter.

Surely these monuments of our art and history, which, whatever the lawyers may say, belong not to a coterie, or to a rich man here and there, but to the nation at large, are worth this delay: surely the last relics of the life of the 'famous men and our fathers that begat us' may justly claim of us the exercise of a little patience.

It will give us trouble no doubt, all this care of our possessions: but there is more trouble to come; for I must now speak of something else, of possessions which should be common to all of us, of the green grass, and the leaves, and the waters, of the very light and air of heaven, which the Century of Commerce has been too busy to pay any heed to. And first let me remind you that I am supposing every one here present professes to care about art.

Well, there are some rich men among us whom we oddly enough call manufacturers, by which we mean capitalists who pay other men to organise manufacturers; these gentlemen, many of whom buy pictures and profess to care about art, burn a deal of coal: there is an Act in existence which was passed to prevent them sometimes and in some places from pouring a dense cloud of smoke over the world, and, to my thinking, a very lame and partial Act it is: but nothing hinders these lovers of art from being a law to themselves, and making it a point of honour with them to minimise the smoke nuisance as far as their own works are concerned; and if they don't do so, when mere money, and even a very little of that, is what it will cost them, I say that their love of art is a mere pretence: how can you care about the image of a landscape when you show by your deeds that you don't care for the landscape itself? or what right have you to shut yourself up with beautiful form and colour when you make it impossible for other people to have any share in these things?

Well, and as to the smoke Act itself: I don't know what heed you pay to it in Birmingham,* but I have seen myself what heed is paid to it in other places; Bradford for instance: though close by them at Saltaire they have an example which I should have thought might have shamed them; for the huge chimney there which serves the acres of weaving and spinning sheds of Sir Titus Salt and his brothers is as guiltless of smoke as an ordinary kitchen chimney. Or Manchester: a gentleman of that city told me that the smoke Act was a mere dead letter there: well, they buy pictures in Manchester and profess to wish to further the arts: but you see it must be idle pretence as far as their rich people are concerned: they only want to talk about it, and have themselves talked of.

I don't know what you are doing about this matter here; but you must forgive my saying, that unless you are beginning to think of some way of dealing with it, you are not beginning yet to pave your way to success in the arts.

---

* Since perhaps some people may read these words who are not of Birmingham, I ought to say that it was authoritatively explained at the meeting to which I addressed these words, that in Birmingham the law is strictly enforced.

Well, I have spoken of a huge nuisance, which is a type of the worst nuisances of what an ill-tempered man might be excused for calling the Century of Nuisances, rather than the Century of Commerce. I will now leave it to the consciences of the rich and influential among us, and speak of a minor nuisance which it is in the power of every one of us to abate, and which, small as it is, is so vexatious, that if I can prevail on a score of you to take heed to it by what I am saying, I shall think my evening's work a good one. Sandwich-papers I mean—of course you laugh: but come now, don't you, civilised as you are in Birmingham, leave them all about the Lickey hills and your public gardens and the like? If you don't, I really scarcely know with what words to praise you. When we Londoners go to enjoy ourselves at Hampton Court, for instance, we take special good care to let everybody know that we have had something to eat: so that the park just outside the gates (and a beautiful place it is) looks as if it had been snowing dirty paper. I really think you might promise me one and all who are here present to have done with this sluttish habit, which is the type of many another in its way, just as the smoke nuisance is. I mean such things as scrawling one's name on monuments, tearing down tree boughs, and the like.

I suppose 'tis early days in the revival of the arts to express one's disgust at the daily increasing hideousness of the posters with which all our towns are daubed. Still we ought to be disgusted at such horrors, and I think make up our minds never to buy any of the articles so advertised. I can't believe they can be worth much if they need all that shouting to sell them.

Again, I must ask what do you do with the trees on a site that is going to be built over? do you try to save them, to adapt your houses at all to them? do you understand what treasures they are in a town or a suburb? or what a relief they will be to the hideous dog-holes which (forgive me!) you are probably going to build in their places? I ask this anxiously, and with grief in my soul, for in London and its suburbs we always* begin by clearing a site till it is as bare as the pavement: I really think that almost anybody would have been shocked, if I could have shown him some of the trees that have been wantonly murdered in the suburb in which I live (Hammersmith to wit), amongst them some of those magnificent cedars, for which we along the river used to be famous once.

But here again see how helpless those are who care about art or nature amidst the hurry of the Century of Commerce.

Pray do not forget, that any one who cuts down a tree wantonly or carelessly, especially in a great town or its suburbs, need make no pretence of caring about art.

---

* Not *quite* always: in the little colony at Bedford Park, Chiswick, as many trees have been left as possible, to the boundless advantage of its quaint and pretty architecture.

What else can we do to help to educate ourselves and others in the path of art, to be on the road to attaining an *Art made by the people and for the people as a joy to the maker and the user?*

Why, having got to understand something of what art was, having got to look upon its ancient monuments as friends that can tell us something of times bygone, and whose faces we do not wish to alter, even though they be worn by time and grief: having got to spend money and trouble upon matters of decency, great and little; having made it clear that we really do care about nature even in the suburbs of a big town—having got so far, we shall begin to think of the houses in which we live.

For I must tell you that unless you are resolved to have good and rational architecture, it is, once again, useless your thinking about art at all.

I have spoken of the popular arts, but they might all be summed up in that one word Architecture; they are all parts of that great whole, and the art of house-building begins it all: if we did not know how to dye or to weave; if we had neither gold, nor silver, nor silk; and no pigments to paint with, but half-a-dozen

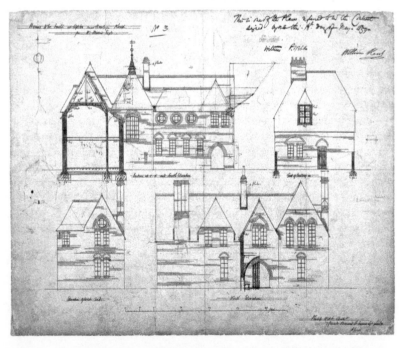

FIGURE 2. Architectural designs for the Red House. Image ©Victoria and Albert Museum, London. Drawings by Philip Speakman Webb to Morris's specifications, for Morris's first family home, built 1859–60.

ochres and umbers, we might yet frame a worthy art that would lead to everything, if we had but timber, stone, and lime, and a few cutting tools to make these common things not only shelter us from wind and weather, but also express the thoughts and aspirations that stir in us.

Architecture would lead us to all the arts, as it did with earlier men: but if we despise it and take no note of how we are housed, the other arts will have a hard time of it indeed.

Now I do not think the greatest of optimists would deny that, taking us one and all, we are at present housed in a perfectly shameful way, and since the greatest part of us have to live in houses already built for us, it must be admitted that it is rather hard to know what to do, beyond waiting till they tumble about our ears.

Only we must not lay the fault upon the builders, as some people seem inclined to do: they are our very humble servants, and will build what we ask for; remember, that rich men are not obliged to live in ugly houses, and yet you see they do; which the builders may be well excused for taking as a sign of what is wanted.

Well, the point is we must do what we can, and make people understand what we want them to do for us, by letting them see what we do for ourselves.

Hitherto, judging us by that standard, the builders may well say, that we want the pretence of a thing rather than the thing itself; that we want a show of petty luxury if we are unrich, a show of insulting stupidity if we are rich: and they are quite clear that as a rule we want to get something that shall look as if it cost twice as much as it really did.

You cannot have Architecture on those terms: simplicity and solidity are the very first requisites of it: just think if it is not so: How we please ourselves with an old building by thinking of all the generations of men that have passed through it! do we not remember how it has received their joy, and borne their sorrow, and not even their folly has left sourness upon it? it still looks as kind to us, as it did to them. And the converse of this we ought to feel when we look at a newly-built house if it were as it should be: we should feel a pleasure in thinking how he who had built it had left a piece of his soul behind him to greet the new-comers one after another long and long after he was gone:—but what sentiment can an ordinary modern house move in us, or what thought—save a hope that we may speedily forget its base ugliness?

But if you ask me how we are to pay for this solidity and extra expense, that seems to me a reasonable question; for you must dismiss at once as a delusion the hope that has been sometimes cherished, that you can have a building which is a work of art, and is therefore above all things properly built, at the same price as a building which only pretends to be this: never forget when people talk about cheap art in general, by the way, that all art costs time, trouble, and thought, and that money is only a counter to represent these things.

However, I must try to answer the question I have supposed put, how are we to pay for decent houses?

It seems to me that by a great piece of good luck, the way to pay for them is by doing that which alone can produce popular art among us: living a simple life, I mean. Once more I say that the greatest foe to art is luxury, art cannot live in its atmosphere.

When you hear of the luxuries of the ancients, you must remember that they were not like our luxuries, they were rather indulgence in pieces of extravagant folly than what we to-day call luxury; which perhaps you would rather call comfort: well, I accept the word, and say that a Greek or Roman of the luxurious time would stare astonished could he be brought back again, and shown the comforts of a well-to-do middle-class house.

But some, I know, think that the attainment of these very comforts is what makes the difference between civilisation and uncivilisation, that they are the essence of civilisation. Is it so indeed? Farewell my hope then!—I had thought that civilisation meant the attainment of peace and order and freedom, of goodwill between man and man, of the love of truth and the hatred of injustice, and by consequence the attainment of the good life which these things breed, a life free from craven fear, but full of incident: that was what I thought it meant, not more stuffed chairs and more cushions, and more carpets and gas, and more dainty meat and drink—and therewithal more and sharper differences between class and class.

If that be what it is, I for my part wish I were well out of it, and living in a tent in the Persian desert, or a turf hut on the Iceland hill-side. But however it be, and I think my view is the true view, I tell you that art abhors that side of civilisation, she cannot breathe in the houses that lie under its stuffy slavery.

Believe me, if we want art to begin at home, as it must, we must clear our houses of troublesome superfluities that are for ever in our way: conventional comforts that are no real comforts, and do but make work for servants and doctors: if you want a golden rule that will fit everybody, this is it:

Have nothing in your houses that you do not know to be useful, or believe to be beautiful.

And if we apply that rule strictly, we shall in the first place show the builders and such-like servants of the public what we really want, we shall create a demand for real art, as the phrase goes; and in the second place, we shall surely have more money to pay for decent houses.

Perhaps it will not try your patience too much if I lay before you my idea of the fittings necessary to the sitting-room of a healthy person: a room, I mean, which he would not have to cook in much, or sleep in generally, or in which he would not have to do any very litter-making manual work.

First a book-case with a great many books in it: next a table that will keep steady when you write or work at it: then several chairs that you can move, and

FIGURE 3. Settle in the drawing room at Red House. 1270427. NTPL Commissioned (NTPL) ©National Trust Images/Andreas von Einsiedel. Settle designed by Morris, with the addition of ladder and canopy by Philip Webb. The walls behind are decorated by Morris and his friends with murals, his preferred decoration for walls.

a bench that you can sit or lie upon: next a cupboard with drawers: next, unless either the book-case or the cupboard be very beautiful with painting or carving, you will want pictures or engravings, such as you can afford, only not stop-gaps, but real works of art on the wall; or else the wall itself must be ornamented with some beautiful and restful pattern: we shall also want a vase or two to put flowers in, which latter you must have sometimes, especially if you live in a town. Then there will be the fireplace of course, which in our climate is bound to be the chief object in the room.

That is all we shall want, especially if the floor be good; if it be not, as, by the way, in a modern house it is pretty certain not to be, I admit that a small carpet which can be bundled out of the room in two minutes will be useful, and we must also take care that it is beautiful, or it will annoy us terribly.

Now unless we are musical, and need a piano (in which case, as far as beauty is concerned, we are in a bad way), that is quite all we want: and we can add very little to these necessaries without troubling ourselves, and hindering our work, our thought, and our rest.

If these things were done at the least cost for which they could be done well and solidly, they ought not to cost much; and they are so few, that those that could afford to have them at all, could afford to spend some trouble to get

FIGURE 4. Detail from Redcar carpet. Design: 1881. Image ©Victoria and Albert Museum, London.

them fitting and beautiful: and all those who care about art ought to take great trouble to do so, and to take care that there be no sham art amongst them, nothing that it has degraded a man to make or sell. And I feel sure, that if all who care about art were to take this pains, it would make a great impression upon the public.

This simplicity you may make as costly as you please or can, on the other hand: you may hang your walls with tapestry instead of whitewash or paper; or you may cover them with mosaic, or have them frescoed by a great painter: all this is not luxury, if it be done for beauty's sake, and not for show: it does not break our golden rule: *Have nothing in your houses which you do not know to be useful or believe to be beautiful.*

All art starts from this simplicity; and the higher the art rises, the greater the simplicity. I have been speaking of the fittings of a dwelling-house—a place in which we eat and drink, and pass familiar hours; but when you come to places which people want to make more specially beautiful because of the solemnity or dignity of their uses, they will be simpler still, and have little in them save the bare walls made as beautiful as may be. St. Mark's at Venice has very little furniture in it, much less than most Roman Catholic churches: its lovely and stately mother St. Sophia of Constantinople had less still, even when it was a Christian church: but we need not go either to Venice or Stamboul to take note of that: go into one of our own mighty Gothic naves (do any of you remember the first time you did so?) and note how the huge free space satisfies and elevates you, even now when window and wall are stripped of ornament: then think of the meaning of simplicity, and absence of encumbering gew-gaws.

Now after all, for us who are learning art, it is not far to seek what is the surest way to further it; that which most breeds art is art; every piece of work that we do which is well done, is so much help to the cause; every piece of pretence and half-heartedness is so much hurt to it. Most of you who take to the practice of art can find out in no very long time whether you have any gifts for it or not: if you have not, throw the thing up, or you will have a wretched time of it yourselves, and will be damaging the cause by laborious pretence: but if you have gifts of any kind, you are happy indeed beyond most men; for your pleasure is always with you, nor can you be intemperate in the enjoyment of it, and as you use it, it does not lessen, but grows: if you are by chance weary of it at night, you get up in the morning eager for it; or if perhaps in the morning it seems folly to you for a while, yet presently, when your hand has been moving a little in its wonted way, fresh hope has sprung up beneath it and you are happy again. While others are getting through the day like plants thrust into the earth, which cannot turn this way or that but as the wind blows them, you know what you want, and your will is on the alert to find it, and you, whatever happens, whether it be joy or grief, are at least alive.

Now when I spoke to you last year, after I had sat down I was half afraid that I had on some points said too much, that I had spoken too bitterly in my eagerness; that a rash word might have discouraged some of you; I was very far from meaning that: what I wanted to do, what I want to do to-night is to put definitely before you a cause for which to strive.

That cause is the Democracy of Art, the ennobling of daily and common work, which will one day put hope and pleasure in the place of fear and pain, as the forces which move men to labour and keep the world a-going.

If I have enlisted any one in that cause, rash as my words may have been, or feeble as they may have been, they have done more good than harm; nor do I believe that any words of mine can discourage any who have joined that cause or are ready to do so: their way is too clear before them for that, and every one of us can help the cause whether he be great or little.

I know indeed that men, wearied by the pettiness of the details of the strife, their patience tried by hope deferred, will at whiles, excusably enough, turn back in their hearts to other days, when, if the issues were not clearer, the means of trying them were simpler; when, so stirring were the times, one might even have atoned for many a blunder and backsliding by visibly dying for the cause: to have breasted the Spanish pikes at Leyden, to have drawn sword with Oliver: that may well seem to us at times amidst the tangles of to-day a happy fate: for a man to be able to say, I have lived like a fool, but now I will cast away fooling for an hour, and die like a man—there is something in that certainly: and yet 'tis clear that few men can be so lucky as to die for a cause, without having first of all lived for it. And as this is the most that can be asked from the greatest man that follows a cause, so it is the least that can be taken from the smallest.

So to us who have a Cause at heart, our highest ambition and our simplest duty are one and the same thing: for the most part we shall be too busy doing the work that lies ready to our hands, to let impatience for visibly great progress vex us much; but surely since we are servants of a Cause, hope must be ever with us, and sometimes perhaps it will so quicken our vision that it will outrun the slow lapse of time, and show us the victorious days when millions of those who now sit in darkness will be enlightened by an *Art made by the people and for the people, a joy to the maker and the user.*

From SOME HINTS ON PATTERN-DESIGNING

A Lecture Delivered at the Working Men's College,
London, on December 10 [1881]

By the word pattern-design, of which I have undertaken to speak to you
to-night, I mean the ornamentation of a surface by work that is not imitative or
historical—at any rate not principally or essentially so. Such work is often not
literally flat, for it may be carving or moulded work in plaster or pottery; but
whatever material relief it may have is given to it for the sake of beauty and
richness, and not for the sake of imitation, or to tell a fact directly; so that people
have called this art ornamental art, though indeed all real art is ornamental.

Now, before we go further, we may as well ask ourselves what reason or
right this so-called ornamental art has to existence? We might answer the
question shortly by saying that it seems clear that mankind has hitherto
determined to have it even at the cost of a good deal of labour and trouble: an
answer good enough to satisfy our consciences that we are not necessarily
wasting our time in meeting here to consider it; but we may furthermore try
to get at the reasons that have forced men in the mass always to expect to have
what to some of them doubtless seems an absurd superfluity of life.

I do not know a better way of getting at these reasons than for each of us to
suppose himself to be in the room in which he will have to pass a good part of
his life, the said room being quite bare of ornament, and to be there that he
may consider what he can do to make the bare walls pleasant and helpful to
him; I say the walls, because, after all, the widest use of pattern-designing is
the clothing of the walls of a room, hall, church, or what building you will.
Doubtless there will be some, in these days at least, who will say, "'Tis most
helpful to me to let the bare walls alone.' So also there would be some who,
when asked with what manner of books they will furnish their room, would
answer, 'With none.' So I think you will agree with me in thinking that both
these sets of people would be in an unhealthy state of mind, and probably of
body also, in which case we need not trouble ourselves about their whims,
since it is with healthy and sane people only that art has dealings.

Again, a healthy and sane person being asked with what kind of art he
would clothe his walls, might well answer, 'With the best art,' and so end the
question. Yet, out on it! so complex is human life, that even this seemingly
most reasonable answer may turn out to be little better than an evasion.

For I suppose the best art to be the pictured representation of men's imaginings; what they have thought has happened to the world before their time, or what they deem they have seen with the eyes of the body or the soul: and the imaginings thus represented are always beautiful indeed, but oftenest stirring to men's passions and aspirations, and not seldom sorrowful or even terrible.

Stories that tell of men's aspirations for more than material life can give them, their struggles for the future welfare of their race, their unselfish love, their unrequited service—things like this are the subjects for the best art; in such subjects there is hope surely, yet the aspect of them is likely to be sorrowful enough: defeat the seed of victory, and death the seed of life, will be shown on the face of most of them.

Take note, too, that in the best art all of these solemn and awful things are expressed clearly and without any vagueness, with such life and power that they impress the beholder so deeply that he is brought face to face with the very scenes, and lives among them for a time; so raising his life above the daily tangle of small things that wearies him, to the level of the heroism which they represent.

This is the best art; and who can deny that it is good for us all that it should be at hand to stir our emotions: yet its very greatness makes it a thing to be handled carefully, for we cannot always be having our emotions deeply stirred: that wearies us body and soul; and man, an animal that longs for rest like other animals, defends himself against the weariness by hardening his heart, and refusing to be moved every hour of the day by tragic emotions; nay, even by beauty that claims his attention over-much.

Such callousness is bad, both for the arts and our own selves; and therefore it is not so good to have the best art for ever under our eyes, though it is abundantly good that we should be able to get at it from time to time.

Meantime, I cannot allow that it is good for any hour of the day to be wholly stripped of life and beauty; therefore we must provide ourselves with lesser (I will not say worse) art with which to surround our common workaday or restful times; and for those times, I think, it will be enough for us to clothe our daily and domestic walls with ornament that reminds us of the outward face of the earth, of the innocent love of animals, or of man passing his days between work and rest as he does. I say, with ornament that reminds us of these things, and sets our minds and memories at work easily creating them; because scientific representation of them would again involve us in the problems of hard fact and the troubles of life, and so once more destroy our rest for us.

If this lesser art will really be enough to content us, it is a good thing; for as to the higher art there never can be very much of it going on, since but few people can be found to do it; also few can find money enough to possess themselves of any portion of it, and, if they could, it would be a piece of

FIGURE 5. Brer Rabbit textile. William Morris Society. Design: *c*.1881. May Morris records her father reading aloud from the African American Uncle Remus tales of the trickster Brer Rabbit, and enjoying 'the fascinating drolleries of Brer Rabbit and Brer Fox'. *CW*, XXII, xviii.

preposterous selfishness to shut it up from other people's eyes; while of the secondary art there ought to be abundance for all men—so much that you need but call in the neighbours, and not all the world, to see your pretty new wall when it is finished.

But this kind of art must be suggestive rather than imitative; because, in order to have plenty of it, it must be a kind of work that is not too difficult for ordinary men with imaginations capable of development; men from whom you cannot expect miracles of skill, and from whose hands you must not ask too much, lest you lose what their intelligence has to give you, by over-wearying them. Withal, the representation of this lower kind of life is pretty sure to become soulless and tiresome unless it have a soul given to it by the efforts of men forced by the limits of order and the necessities of art to think of these things for themselves, and so to give you some part of the infinite variety which abides in the mind of man.

Of course you understand that it is impossible to imitate nature literally; the utmost realism of the most realistic painter falls a long way short of that; and as to the work which must be done by ordinary men, not unskilled or dull to beauty, the attempt to attain to realism would be sure to result in obscuring their intelligence, and in starving you of all the beauty which you desire in your hearts, but which you have not learned to express by means of art.

Let us get back to our wall again, and think of it. If you are to put nothing on it but what strives to be a literal imitation of nature, all you can do is to have a few cut flowers or bits of boughs nailed to it, with perhaps a blue-bottle fly or a butterfly here and there. Well, I don't deny that this may make good decoration now and then, but if all decoration had to take that form I think weariness of it would drive you to a white-washed wall; and at the best it is a very limited view to take of nature.

Is it not better to be reminded, however simply, of the close vine-trellis that keeps out the sun by the Nile side; or of the wild-woods and their streams, with the dogs panting beside them; or of the swallows sweeping above the garden boughs toward the house-eaves where their nestlings are, while the sun breaks the clouds on them; or of the many-flowered summer meadows of Picardy? Is not all this better than having to count day after day a few sham-real boughs and flowers, casting sham-real shadows on your walls with little hint of anything beyond Covent Garden in them?

You may be sure that any decoration is futile, and has fallen into at least the first stage of degradation, when it does not remind you of something beyond itself—of something of which it is but a visible symbol.

Now, to sum up, what we want to clothe our walls with is (1) something that it is possible for us to get; (2) something that is beautiful; (3) something which will not drive us either into unrest or into callousness; (4) something which reminds us of life beyond itself, and which has the impress of human imagination strong on it; and (5) something which can be done by a great many people without too much difficulty and with pleasure.

These conditions I believe to have been fulfilled by the pattern-designers in all times when art has been healthy, and to have been all more or less violated when art has been unhealthy and unreal. In such evil times beauty has given place to whim, imagination to extravagance, nature to sick nightmare fancies, and finally workmanlike considerate skill, which refuses to allow either the brain or the hand to be over-taxed—which, without sparing labour when necessary, refuses sternly to waste it—has given place to commercial trickery sustained by laborious botching.

Now, I have been speaking of what may be called the moral qualities of the art we are thinking of; let us try, therefore, to shorten their names, and have one last word on them before we deal with the material or technical part.

Ornamental pattern-work, to be raised above the contempt of reasonable men, must possess three qualities—beauty, imagination, and order.

'Tis clear I need not waste many words on the first of these. You will be drawing water with a sieve with a vengeance if you cannot manage to make ornamental work beautiful.

As for the second quality—imagination—the necessity for that may not be so clear to you, considering the humble nature of our art; yet you will probably admit, when you come to think of it, that every work of man which has beauty in it must have some meaning in it also; that the presence of any beauty in a piece of handicraft implies that the mind of the man who made it was more or less excited at the time, was lifted somewhat above the commonplace; that he had something to communicate to his fellows which they did not know or feel before, and which they would never have known or felt if he had not been there to force them to it.

I want you to think of this when you see, as, unfortunately, you are only too likely often to see, some lifeless imitation of a piece of bygone art, and are puzzled to know why it does not satisfy you. The reason is that the imitator has not entered into the soul of the dead artist; nay, has supposed that he had but a hand and no soul, and so has not known what he meant to do. I dwell on this, because it forces on us the conclusion that if we cannot have an ornamental art of our own, we cannot have one at all. Every real work of art, even the humblest, is inimitable. I am most sure that all the heaped-up knowledge of modern science, all the energy of modern commerce, all the depth and spirituality of modern thought, cannot reproduce so much as the handiwork of an ignorant, superstitious Berkshire peasant of the fourteenth century; nay, of a wandering Kurdish shepherd, or of a skin-and-bone oppressed Indian ryot. This, I say, I am sure of; and to me the certainty is not depressing, but inspiriting, for it bids us remember that the world has been noteworthy for more than one century and one place—a fact which we are pretty much apt to forget.

Now as to the third of the essential qualities of our art—order. I have to say of it, that without it neither the beauty nor the imagination could be made visible; it is the bond of their life, and as good as creates them, if they are to be of any use to people in general. Let us see, therefore, with what instruments it works, how it brings together the material and spiritual sides of the craft.

I have already said something of the way in which it deals with the materials which Nature gives it, and how, as it were, it both builds a wall against vagueness and opens a door therein for imagination to come in by. Now, this is done by means of treatment which is called, as one may say technically, the conventionalizing of nature. That is to say, order invents certain beautiful and natural forms, which, appealing to a reasonable and imaginative person, will

FIGURE 6. Strawberry Thief plain weave cotton. Design: 1883. Cleveland Museum of Art. On 14 May 1883 Morris writes to his daughter Jenny, 'I was a great deal at Merton last week, [...] anxiously superintending the first printing of the Strawberry thief, which I think we shall manage this time'. *CL*, II, 190. May Morris notes: 'the first many-coloured print. It is a net pattern, but so concealed that you scarcely see the construction'. *AWS*, I, 44.

remind him not only of the part of nature which, to his mind at least, they represent, but also of much that lies beyond that part. I have already hinted at some reasons for this treatment of natural objects. You can't bring a whole country-side, or a whole field, into your room, nor even a whole bush; and, moreover, only a very specially skilled craftsman can make any approach to what might pass with us in moments of excitement for an imitation of such-like things.

These are limitations which are common to every form of the lesser arts; but, besides these, every material in which household goods are fashioned imposes certain special limitations within which the craftsman must work.

Here, again, is the wall of order against vagueness, and the door of order for imagination. For you must understand from the first that these limitations are as far as possible from being hindrances to beauty in the several crafts. On the contrary, they are incitements and helps to its attainment; those who find them irksome are not born craftsmen, and the periods of art that try to get rid of them are declining periods.

Now this must be clear to you, if you come to think of it. Give an artist a piece of paper, and say to him, 'I want a design,' and he must ask of you, 'What for? What's to be done with it?' And if you can't tell him, well, I dare not venture to tell you the name which his irritation will give you. But if you say, I want this queer space filled with ornament, I want you to make such and such a pretty thing out of these intractable materials, straightway his invention will be quickened, and he will set to work with a will; for, indeed, delight in skill lies at the root of all art.

Now, further, this working in materials, which is the *raison d'être* of all pattern-work, still further limits it in the direct imitation of nature, drives it still more decidedly to appeal to the imagination. For example: you have a heap of little coloured cubes of glass to make your picture of, or you have some coloured thrums of worsted wherewith to build up at once a picture and a piece of cloth; well, there is a wrong and a right way of setting to work about this: if you please you may set to work with your cubes and your thrums to imitate a brush-painted picture, a work of art done in a material wherein the limitations are as few and pliable as they are many and rigid in the one you are working in; with almost invisible squares or shuttle-strokes, you may build up, square by square, or line by line, an imitation of an oil-painter's rapid stroke of the brush, and so at last produce your imitation, which doubtless people will wonder at, and say, 'How *was* it done?—we can see neither cubes nor thrums in it.' And so also would they have wondered if you had made a portrait of the Lord Mayor in burnt sugar, or of Mr. Parnell in fireworks. But the wonder being over, 'tis like that some reasonable person will say, 'This is not specially beautiful; and as to its skill, after all, you have taken a year to do what a second-rate painter could have done in three days. Why have you done it at all?' An unanswerable question, I fear.

Well, such materials may be used thus, so clever are men; nay, they *have* been used thus, so perverse and dull are men!

On the other hand, if you will, you may thoroughly consider your glass cubes or your worsted thrums, and think what can best be done with them; but they need not fetter your imagination, for you may, with them, tell a story in a new way, even if it be not a new story; you may conquer the obstinacy of your material and make it obey you as far as the needs of beauty go, and the telling of your tale; you will be pleased with the victory of your skill, but you will not have forgotten your subject amidst mere laboriousness, and you will know that your victory has been no barren one, but has produced a beautiful thing, which nothing but your struggle with difficulties could have brought forth, and when people look at it they will be forced to say: 'Well, though it is rough, yet, in spite of the material, the workman has shown that he knows what a good line is; it is beautiful, certainly, after its fashion, and the workman has looked at things with his own eyes: and then how the tesseræ gleam in this indestructible picture, how the gold glitters!' Or, 'What wealth of colour and softness of gradation there is in these interwoven thrums of worsted, that have drunk the dye so deeply! No other material conceivable could have done it just like this. And the wages are not so high; we can have plenty of this sort of work. Yes, the man *is* worth his keep.'

In this way, also, your materials can be used, so simple and trustful may men be that they may venture to make a work of art thus: nay, so helpful and joyous have they been, that they have so ventured—for the pleasure of many people, their own not least of all.

Now, I have tried to point out to you that the nature of the craft of pattern-designing imposes certain limitations within which it has to work, and also that each branch of it has further limitations of its own. Before saying a few words that relate to these special limitations, I will, by your leave, narrow our subject by dwelling a little on what is one of the most important parts of pattern-designing: the making of a recurring pattern for a flat surface. Let us first look a little on the construction of these, at the lines on which they are built. Now, the beauty and imagination which I have spoken of as necessary to all patterns may be, and often have been, of the very simplest kind, and their order the most obvious. So, to begin with, let us take one of these: our wall may be ornamented with mere horizontal stripes of colour; what beauty there may be in these will be limited to the beauty of very simple proportion, and in the tints and contrast of tints used, while the meaning of them will be confined to the calling people's attention to the charm of material, and due orderly construction of a wall.

After this simplest form comes that of chequers and squares of unfoliated diaper, so to call it, which still is but a hint at the possible construction of the wall, when it is not in itself constructional. From that we get to diapers made by lines, either rectilinear or taking the form of circles touching one another.

We have now left the idea of constructional blocks or curves, and are probably suggesting scoring of lines on the surface of the wall joined to inlaying, perhaps; or else there is an idea in it of some sort of hangings, at first as in much of the ancient Egyptian work, woven of reeds or grass, but later on suggesting weaving of finer materials that do not call attention to the crossing of warp and weft.

This next becomes a floriated diaper. The lines are formed by shapes of stems, and leaves or flowers fill the spaces between the lines. This kind of ornamentation has got a long way from the original stripes and squares, and even from the cross-barred matting diapers. The first of these (when used quite simply) is commonly external work, and is used to enrich further what sunlight and shadow already enrich. The second either implies an early stage of civilisation, or a persistent memory of its rudeness.

But as to this more elaborate diaper—for, simple as its construction is, it has never been superseded—in its richer forms it is intimately connected with the stately and vast shapes of Roman architecture; and until the great change took place, when the once-despised East began to mingle with the old, decaying Western civilisation, and even to dominate it, it was really the only form taken by recurring patterns, except mere chequer and scalework, though certain complications of the circle and the square were used to gain greater richness.

Now the next change, so far as mere construction goes, takes us into what is practically the last stage that recurring patterns can get to, and the change is greater than at first sight it may seem to you: it is part of that change in the master-art from late and decaying Classical art into Byzantine, or, as I would rather call it, newborn Gothic art. The first places where it is seen are a few buildings of the early part of the sixth century, when architecture seems to have taken a sudden leap, and, in fact, to have passed from death to new birth. As to the construction of patterns the change was simply this—continuous growth of curved lines took the place of mere contiguity, or of the interlacement of straight lines.

All the recurring patterns of the ancient and classical world were, I repeat, founded on the diaper, square or round. All their borders or friezes were formed either by tufts of flowers growing side by side, with their tendrils sometimes touching or interlacing, or by scrolls wherein there was no continuous growth, but only a masking of the repeat by some spreading member of the pattern. But when young Gothic took the place of old Classic, the change was marked in pattern-designing by the universal acceptance of continuous growth as a necessity of borders and friezes; and in square pattern-work, as I should call it, this growth was the general rule in all the more important designs.

Of this square continuous pattern-work there are two principal forms of construction.—1. The branch formed on a diagonal line, and (2) the net framed on variously-proportioned diamonds. These main constructions were, as time went on, varied in all sorts of ways, more or less beautiful and ingenious; and they are of course only bounding or leading lines, and are to be filled up in all sorts of ways. Nay, sometimes these leading lines are not drawn, and we have left us a sort of powdering in the devices which fill up the spaces between the imaginary lines. Our Sicilian pattern of the thirteenth century gives us an example of this; and this Italian one of the fourteenth century gives us another of the leading lines of the diagonal branch being broken, and so leaving a powdering on those lines; but in all cases the net or branch lines—that is, the simple diagonal or crossing diagonal—are really there.

For clearness' sake, I will run through the different kinds of construction that I have named:—1. Horizontal stripes; 2. Block diaper or chequer; 3. Matting diaper, very various in form; 4. Square line diaper; 5. Floriated square diaper; 6. Round diaper formed by contiguous circles; 7. The diagonal branch; 8. The net; 9 (which is supplementary), powderings on the lines of the diagonal branch, or of the net.

These are all the elementary forms of construction for a recurring pattern, but of course there may be many varieties of each of them. Elaborate patterns may be wrought on the stripes or chequers; the foliated diaper may be wrought interlocking; the net may be complicated by net within net; the diagonal bough may be crossed variously, or the alternate boughs may be slipped down so as to form a kind of untied and dislocated net; the circles may intersect each other instead of touching, or polygonal figures may be built on them, as in the strange star patterns which are the differentia of Arab art.

Of course, also, these constructional lines may be masked in an infinite number of ways, and in certain periods it was most usual to do this, and much ingenuity was spent, and not a little wasted, in doing it.

Before I pass to the use to which these forms of pattern may be put, I will say a little on the subject of the relief of patterns, which may be considered as the other side of their mechanism. We have, you see, been talking about the skeletons of them, and those skeletons must be clothed with flesh—that is, their members must have tangible superficial area; and by the word relief I understand the method of bringing this out.

Of course this part of the subject is intimately connected with the colour of designs, but of that I shall only say so much as is necessary for dealing with their relief.

To put the matter as shortly as possible, one may say that there are two ways of relief for a recurring surface-pattern—either that the figure shall show light upon a dark, or dark upon a light ground; or that the whole pattern, member by member, should be outlined by a line of colour which both serves to relieve it from its ground, which is not necessarily either lighter or darker than the figure, and also prevents the colour from being inharmonious or hard.

FIGURE 7. Willow Bough wallpaper. Design: 1887. Image ©Victoria and Albert Museum, London. May Morris notes that, walking by the Thames at Kelmscott, 'my father pointed out the detail and variety in the leaf-forms, and soon afterwards this paper was done'. *AWS*, I, 36.

Now, to speak broadly, the first of these methods of relief is used by those who are chiefly thinking about form, the second by those whose minds are most set on colour; and you will easily see, if you come to think of it, how widely different the two methods are. Those who have been used to the first method of dark upon light, or light upon dark, often get confused and troubled when they have to deal with many colours, and wonder why it is that, in spite of all their attempts at refinement of colour, their designs still look wrong. The fact is, that when you have many colours, when you are making up your design by contrast of hues and variety of shades, you must use the bounding line to some extent, if not through and through.

Of these two methods of relief, you must think of the first as being the relief of one plane from another; in it there is always an idea of at least more than one plane of surface, and often of several planes. The second you must think of as the relief of colour from colour, and designs treated thus both should look, and do look, perfectly flat. Again, to speak broadly, the first method is that of the West, the second that of the East; but of the later and (excuse the 'bull') the Gothic East. The idea of plane relieved on plane was always present in all the patterns of the ancient and classical world.

Now, as to the use to be made of these recurring surface patterns, the simpler of them, such as mere stripes and simple diapers, have been, and doubtless will always be used for external decoration of walls, and also for subsidiary decoration where the scale is large and where historical art plays the chief part. On the other hand, some people may doubt as to what share, if any, the more elaborate forms of pattern-work should have in internal wall decoration. True it is that the principle of the continuous line, which led up to all that elaboration, was an invention of the later East, just as the system of relieving colour from colour was; and I believe the two things are closely connected, and sprang from this cause, that these peoples were for various reasons not much driven towards the higher pictorial art, and did not reach any great excellence in it; therefore they felt a need for developing their pattern art to the highest degree possible, till it became something more than a little-noticed accompaniment to historical art, which was all that it used to be in the ancient or the classical world.

Perhaps the fact that the barbarians invented what the elder civilisation, the great nurse of the higher arts, despised, may seem to some of you a condemnation of this more elaborate pattern-work; but before you make up your minds to that, I would ask you to remember within what narrow limits that perfection of Greece moved. It seems to me that unless you can have the whole of that severe system of theirs, you will not be bettered by taking to a minor part of it; nor, indeed, do I think that you can have that system now, for it was the servant of a perfection which is no longer attainable. The whole art of the classical ancients, while it was alive and growing, was the art of a society made up of a narrow aristocracy of citizens, waited upon by a large body of slaves, and surrounded by a world of barbarism which was always despised and never noticed till it threatened to overwhelm the self-sufficient aristocracy that called itself the civilised world.

No, I think that the barbarians who invented modern Europe invented also several other things which we, their children, cannot decently disregard, or

FIGURE 8. Kennet plain weave cotton. Design: 1883. Cleveland Museum of Art.
This is one of many river-based designs Morris used for fabrics and wallpapers.
The Kennet is a tributary of the Thames.

pass by wrapped up in a cloak of sham classical disguise; and that one of these
things—the smallest of them if you will—was this invention of the continuous
line that led to elaborate and independent pattern-work; and I believe that
this was one of those things which, once invented, cannot be dropped, but
must always remain a part of architecture, like the arch—like the pointed
arch. Properly subordinated to architecture on the one hand, and to historic
art on the other, it ought yet, I think, to play a great part in the making our
houses at once beautiful and restful; an end which is one of the chief reasons
for existence of all art.

As to its subordination to the greater arts, all we can say about that is that
we should not have too much of it. I don't think there is any danger of its
thrusting the more intellectual and historic arts out of their due place; rather,
perhaps, it is like to be neglected in comparison with them. But if it makes any
advance, as it may do, I can see that counsels of despair may sometimes drive

us into excess in the use of surface ornament. I mean that our houses are so base and ugly, and it is so hard to alter this bad condition of life, that people may be driven out of all hope of getting good architecture, and try to forget their troubles in that respect by overdoing their internal decoration. Well, you must not suppose that I object to people making the best of their ugly houses; indeed, you probably know that I personally should be finely landed if they did not. Nevertheless, noble building is the first and best and least selfish of the arts, and unless we can manage to get it somehow, we shall soon have no decoration—or, indeed, art of any kind—to put into the dog-hutches which we now think good enough for refined and educated people, to say nothing about other buildings lesser and greater.

[…]

I must ask your patience for a few minutes yet while I say a word or two on these matters, for I have made a compact with myself that I will never address my countrymen on the subject of art without speaking as briefly, but also as plainly as I can, on the degradation of labour which I believe to be the great danger of civilisation, as it has certainly proved itself to be the very bane of art.

Foresight and goodwill have set on foot many schemes for educating people before they come to working years: for tending them when misfortune or sickness prevents them from working, for amusing them reasonably when they are at leisure from their work—aims that are all good and some necessary to the well-being of our race.

But can they alone touch the heart of the matter—to be sedulous about what people do with their time till they are growing out of childhood into youth, to take pains to add to the pleasure of their few hours of rest, and at the same time never to give a thought to the way in which they spend their working hours (ten hours a day, and a long time it is to spend in wishing we were come to the end of it) between the ages of thirteen and seventy? This, I say, does seem to me a strange shutting of the eyes to one of the main difficulties of life, a strange turning from the great question which all well-wishers to their neighbours ought to ask—how can men gain hope and pleasure in their daily work?

I do not profess to foretell what will happen to the world if we persist in keeping our eyes shut on this point; but one thing I know will happen—the extinction of all art. I say I know it will happen, and indeed it is happening now, and unless we take the other turn before long it will soon be all done. You would not believe me if I professed to think that a light matter even by itself—the thrusting out of all beauty from the life of man; but when one knows what lies at the bottom of it, how much heavier it seems, the thrusting out of all pleasure and self-respect from man's daily work, the helplessly letting that daily work become a mere blind instrument for the over-peopling of the world, for the ceaseless multiplication of causeless and miserable lives.

Surely I am speaking to some whose lives, like mine, are blessed with pleasurable and honourable work, who cannot bear the thought that we are to go on shutting our eyes to this, and to do nothing because our time on earth is not long. Can we not face the evil and do our best to amend it our very selves? If it be a necessary evil, let us at least do our share of proving that it is so by withstanding it to the utmost. The worst that can happen to us rebels in that case is to be swept away before the flood of that necessity, which will happen to us no less if we do not struggle against it—if we are flunkies, not rebels. Indeed, you may think that the metaphor is all too true, and that we are but mere straws in that resistless flood. But don't let us strain a metaphor; for we are no straws, but men, with each one of us a will and aspirations, and with duties to fulfil; so let us see after all what we can do to prove whether it is necessary that art should perish—that is, whether men should live in an ugly world, with no work to do in it but wearisome work.

Well, first we must be conscious of the evil, as I believe some are who do not dare to acknowledge it. And next we must dare to acknowledge it, as some do who dare not act further in the matter.

And next—why, a good deal next, though it may be put into few words, for steady rebellion is a heavyish matter to take in hand; and I tell you that every one who loves art in these days and dares pursue it to the uttermost is a dangerous rebel enough; and I will finish by speaking of one or two things that we must do to fit ourselves for our troublous life of rebellion.

We ought to get to understand the value of intelligent work, the work of men's hands guided by their brains, and to take that, though it be rough, rather than the unintelligent work of machines or slaves, though it be delicate; to refuse altogether to use machine-made work unless where the nature of the thing made compels it, or where the machine does what mere human suffering would otherwise have to do: to have a high standard of excellence in wares and not to accept makeshifts for the real thing, but rather to go without; to have no ornament merely for fashion's sake, but only because we really think it beautiful, otherwise to go without it; not to live in an ugly and squalid place (such as London) for the sake of mere excitement or the like, but only because our duties bind us to it; to treat with the utmost care whatever of architecture and the like is left us of the times of art. I deny that it can ever be our own to do as we like with; it is the property of the world, that we hold in trust for those that come after us.

Here is a set of things not easy to do (as it seems), which I believe to be the duty of all men taking some trouble in the art of life, and not giving in to the barbarous and cumbrous luxury—or comfort as you may please to call it—which I sometimes think is really fated to stifle all art, and in the long run all intelligence, unless we grow wise in time and look to it.

I dare say that nobody but men who consciously or unconsciously care about art would strive to bind themselves by these rules, but perhaps some others may join them in trying to act on these that follow. To have as little as possible to do with middlemen, but to bring together the makers and the buyers of goods as closely as possible. To do our best to further the independence and reasonable leisure of all handicraftsmen. To eschew all bargains, real or imaginary (they are mostly the latter), and to be anxious to pay and to get what a piece of goods is really worth. To that end to try to understand the difference between good and bad in wares, which will also give you an insight into the craftsman's troubles, and will tend to do away with an ignorant impatience and ill-temper which is much too common in our dealings with them nowadays.

In short, as I have said before that we must strive against barbarous luxury, so here I must say that we must strive against barbarous waste. What we have to do is to strive to put co-operation in the place of competition in the dealings of men; that is, in place of commercial war, with all the waste and injustice of war—which, since men are foolish rather than malicious, has to be softened ever and anon by weak compliance and contemptuous good-nature—we must strive to put commercial peace with justice and thrift beside it.

I ask you not to think that I have been wandering from my point in saying all this: I have had to talk to you tonight about popular art, the foundation on which all art stands. I could not go through the dreary task of speaking to you of a phantom of bygone times, of a thing with no life in it; I must speak of a living thing with hope in it, or hold my peace; and most deeply am I convinced that popular art cannot live if labour is to be for ever the thrall of muddle, dishonesty, and disunion. Cheerfully I admit that I see signs about us of a coming time of order, goodwill, and union, and it is that which has given me the courage to say to you these few last words, and to hint to you what in my poor judgment we each and all of us who have the cause at heart may do to further the cause.

LETTER TO ROBERT THOMSON

Kelmscott House,
Upper Mall,
Hammersmith,
24 July 1884

Dear Mr Thomson

I write to you in a hurry, as 'tis my best chance of answering your letter to do so at once. You must understand 1st that though I have a great respect for Ruskin and his works (beside personal friendship) he is not a socialist, that is not a *practical* one. he does not expect to see any general scheme even begun: he mingles with certain sound ideas which he seems to have acquired instinctively, a great deal of mere whims, deduced probably from that early training of which he gives an amusing account: anyhow his idea of national workshops is one which could only be realized in a state (that is a society) already socialised: nor could it ever take effect in the way that he thinks it could. You mustn't attach too much importance to what I said about the present Government doing something towards humanizing its own establishments; that together with the 'organization of labour' of our handbill or manifesto are merely transitional remedies for the present poverty. Neither could these two quite incomplete measures be taken unless the state, ie the people (for the 'Government' must abdicate its present position of a class government first) unless the state, or people rather, has made up its mind to take over for the good of the community *all the means of production*: ie *credit*, railways, mines, factories, shipping, land, machinery, which at present are in the hands of private monopolists: this determination once come to by the people its execution will be easy, and the details of it will clear up one after the other; and the thing may be done gradually: but any partial scheme *elaborated as a scheme* which implies the existence <by> with it side by side of the ordinary commercial competition is doomed to fail just as the co-operative scheme is failing: it will be sucked into the tremendous stream of commercial production and vanish into it, after having played its part as a red-herring to spoil the scent of revolution.

I believe (and have always done so) on the other hand that the most important thing to press upon the notice of the people at present is the legal reduction of the working day: every working man can see the immediate advantage to him of this: the Trades Unions *may* be got to take it up; and I doubt if the Government dare resist a strong cry for it: it is of all our

'Stepping Stones' at once the most possible to carry within a reasonable time, and the most important: much more important than at first sight appears; all the more because it would at once become an international affair. I am glad to say that my colleagues quite agree with me in this view, as do the foreign socialists.

As to the 'programme', I suppose you mean the political programme: I should think that this would in all probability be much shortened & simplified. But you must remember that though you may make a formula or maxim which carries Socialism with it, & which may be useful to impress our aims on people's minds, the subject is a difficult & intricate one, and to understand really requires a great deal of reading: I dont mean to say that everybody who joins our ranks must understand it in this way; but some must, & everybody must know something of its elements.

Petitions to Parliament, I must tell you, have long been considered by all parties as very poor instruments of agitation; although they are used in default of better sometimes: you see the fact is that Parliament is a dying thing.

We will by all means have a mass meeting in Hyde Park of employed and unemployed, when we can: but it would be a great mistake to be in a hurry with such a demonstration; a fact which the Liberals may find out even about Monday's if they dont take care: that is, if they don't work hard at it now. <We m> A great demonstration by us must be nothing but the sign of our having a great and closely-knit *organization*. Otherwise even its apparent success would bring about languor & reaction. To make really convinced converts if only one by one: to show even the most ignorant of the 'poor' that we are on their side, and that we are striving to make them gain a better condition of life for themselves—themselves now living, you understand, not the generations a thousand years to come: to infuse hope into the oppressed in fact—that is our business; and I don't think it is possible for us to fail in it, in spite of our own mistakes & weaknesses.

You see what we Socialists aim at is to remove from people the weight of overwork and anxiety which now crushes them: we know that a condition of poverty has not always meant overwork and anxiety, but under modern civilisation it does, and with modern civilisation we have to deal: we cannot turn our people back into Catholic English peasants and guild craftsmen, or into heathen Norse bonders, much as may be said for such conditions of life: we have no choice but to accept the task which the centuries have laid on us of using the corruption of 300 years of profit-mongering for the overthrow of that very corruption: commerce has bred the Proletariat and used it quite blindly, and is still blind to the next move <in the next move> in the game; which will be that the Proletariat will say: We will be *used* no longer, you have organized us for *our own* use. Again it is our business to make people hope that they can be organized into saying this as if they meant it: in the course of their gathering that hope, it may well be that rough things may befall: but I say plainly that I shrink from no consequences of that gathering hope: for when it begins to realize itself (as it will) there will be an end of overwork and anxiety—and *then* people will find out what kind of education and morals they need and will have them: not unlikely that they may be somewhat different from our preconceptions of them. Meantime to try to settle amidst our present corruption what that education, those morals shall be, except in the most general way seems to me a putting of the cart before the horse.

Summa—Whatever Socialism may lead to, our aim, to be always steadily kept in view, is, to obtain for the whole people, duly organized, the possession & controul of all the means of production & <controul> exchange, destroying at the same time all national rivalries.

The means whereby this is to be brought about is first, educating people into desiring it, next organizing them into claiming it effectually. Whatever happens in the course of this education and organization must be accepted coolly & as a necessary incident, and not discussed as a matter of essential principle, even if those incidents should mean ruin and war. I mean that we must not say 'we must drop <our aim object> our purpose rather than carry it across this river of violence'. To say that means casting the whole thing into the hands of chance: and we cant do that; we *cant* say, If this is the evolution of history, let it evolve itself, we won't help. The evolution will force us to help; will breed in us passionate desire for action, which will quench the dread of consequences.

You see you have drawn a long, and I fear rambling letter from me: you had better join us in any case, since you can learn while working with us; & feeling as strongly as you seem to do will help to keep us straight.

I am
Yours faithfully
William Morris

USEFUL WORK *VERSUS* USELESS TOIL

The above title may strike some of my readers as strange. It is assumed by most people nowadays that all work is useful, and by most *well-to-do* people that all work is desirable. Most people, well-to-do or not, believe that, even when a man is doing work which appears to be useless, he is earning his livelihood by it—he is 'employed', as the phrase goes; and most of those who are well-to-do cheer on the happy worker with congratulations and praises, if he is only 'industrious' enough and deprives himself of all pleasure and holidays in the sacred cause of labour. In short, it has become an article of the creed of modern morality that all labour is good in itself—a convenient belief to those who live on the labour of others. But as to those on whom they live, I recommend them not to take it on trust, but to look into the matter a little deeper.

Let us grant, first, that the race of man must either labour or perish. Nature does not give us our livelihood gratis; we must win it by toil of some sort or degree. Let us see, then, if she does not give us some compensation for this compulsion to labour, since certainly in other matters she takes care to make the acts necessary to the continuance of life in the individual and the race not only endurable, but even pleasurable.

You may be sure that she does so, that it is of the nature of man, when he is not diseased, to take pleasure in his work under certain conditions. And, yet, we must say in the teeth of the hypocritical praise of all labour, whatsoever it may be, of which I have made mention, that there is some labour which is so far from being a blessing that it is a curse; that it would be better for the community and for the worker if the latter were to fold his hands and refuse to work, and either die or let us pack him off to the workhouse or prison—which you will.

Here, you see, are two kinds of work—one good, the other bad; one not far removed from a blessing, a lightening of life; the other a mere curse, a burden to life.

What is the difference between them, then? This: one has hope in it, the other has not. It is manly to do the one kind of work, and manly also to refuse to do the other.

What is the nature of the hope which, when it is present in work, makes it worth doing?

It is threefold, I think—hope of rest, hope of product, hope of pleasure in the work itself; and hope of these also in some abundance and of good quality;

rest enough and good enough to be worth having; product worth having by one who is neither a fool nor an ascetic; pleasure enough for all for us to be conscious of it while we are at work; not a mere habit, the loss of which we shall feel as a fidgety man feels the loss of the bit of string he fidgets with.

I have put the hope of rest first because it is the simplest and most natural part of our hope. Whatever pleasure there is in some work, there is certainly some pain in all work, the beast-like pain of stirring up our slumbering energies to action, the beast-like dread of change when things are pretty well with us; and the compensation for this animal pain is animal rest. We must feel while we are working that the time will come when we shall not have to work. Also the rest, when it comes, must be long enough to allow us to enjoy it; it must be longer than is merely necessary for us to recover the strength we have expended in working, and it must be animal rest also in this, that it must not be disturbed by anxiety, else we shall not be able to enjoy it. If we have this amount and kind of rest we shall, so far, be no worse off than the beasts.

As to the hope of product, I have said that Nature compels us to work for that. It remains for *us* to look to it that we *do* really produce something, and not nothing, or at least nothing that we want or are allowed to use. If we look to this and use our wills we shall, so far, be better than machines.

The hope of pleasure in the work itself: how strange that hope must seem to some of my readers—to most of them! Yet I think that to all living things there is a pleasure in the exercise of their energies, and that even beasts rejoice in being lithe and swift and strong. But a man at work, making something which he feels will exist because he is working at it and wills it, is exercising the energies of his mind and soul as well as of his body. Memory and imagination help him as he works. Not only his own thoughts, but the thoughts of the men of past ages guide his hands; and, as a part of the human race, he creates. If we work thus we shall be men, and our days will be happy and eventful.

Thus worthy work carries with it the hope of pleasure in rest, the hope of the pleasure in our using what it makes, and the hope of pleasure in our daily creative skill.

All other work but this is worthless; it is slaves' work—mere toiling to live, that we may live to toil.

Therefore, since we have, as it were, a pair of scales in which to weigh the work now done in the world, let us use them. Let us estimate the worthiness of the work we do, after so many thousand years of toil, so many promises of hope deferred, such boundless exultation over the progress of civilization and the gain of liberty.

Now, the first thing as to the work done in civilization and the easiest to notice is that it is portioned out very unequally amongst the different classes of society. First, there are people—not a few—who do no work, and make no pretence of doing any. Next, there are people, and very many of them, who work fairly hard, though with abundant easements and holidays, claimed and allowed; and lastly, there are people who work so hard that they may be said to do nothing else than work, and are accordingly called 'the working classes,' as distinguished from the middle classes and the rich, or aristocracy, whom I have mentioned above.

It is clear that this inequality presses heavily upon the 'working' class, and must visibly tend to destroy their hope of rest at least, and so, in that particular, make them worse off than mere beasts of the field; but that is not the sum and end of our folly of turning useful work into useless toil, but only the beginning of it.

For first, as to the class of rich people doing no work, we all know that they consume a great deal while they produce nothing. Therefore, clearly, they have to be kept at the expense of those who do work, just as paupers have, and are a mere burden on the community. In these days there are many who have learned to see this, though they can see no further into the evils of our present system, and have formed no idea of any scheme for getting rid of this burden; though perhaps they have a vague hope that changes in the system of voting for members of the House of Commons may, as if by magic, tend in that direction. With such hopes or superstitions we need not trouble ourselves. Moreover, this class, the aristocracy, once thought most necessary to the State, is scant of numbers, and has now no power of its own, but depends on the support of the class next below it—the middle class. In fact, it is really composed either of the most successful men of that class, or of their immediate descendants.

As to the middle class, including the trading, manufacturing, and professional people of our society, they do, as a rule, seem to work quite hard enough, and so at first sight might be thought to help the community, and not burden it. But by far the greater part of them, though they work, do not produce, and even when they do produce, as in the case of those engaged (wastefully indeed) in the distribution of goods, or doctors, or (genuine) artists and literary men, they consume out of all proportion to their due share. The commercial and manufacturing part of them, the most powerful part, spend their lives and energies in fighting amongst themselves for their respective shares of the wealth which they *force* the genuine workers to provide for them; the others are almost wholly the hangers-on of these; they do not work for the public, but a privileged class: they are the parasites of property, sometimes, as in the case of lawyers, undisguisedly so; sometimes, as the doctors and others above mentioned, professing to be useful, but too often of no use save as supporters of the system of folly, fraud, and tyranny of which they form a part. And all these we must remember have, as a rule, one aim in view; not the production of utilities, but the gaining of a position either for themselves or their children in which they will not have to work at all. It is their ambition and the end of their whole lives to gain, if not for themselves yet at least for their children, the proud position of being obvious burdens on the community. For their work itself, in spite of the sham dignity with which they surround it, they care nothing: save a few enthusiasts, men of science, art, or letters, who, if they are not the salt of the earth, are at least (and oh, the pity of it!) the salt of the miserable system of which they are the slaves, which hinders and thwarts them at every turn, and even sometimes corrupts them.

Here then is another class, this time very numerous and all-powerful, which produces very little and consumes enormously, and is therefore in the main supported, as paupers are, by the real producers. The class that remains to be considered produces all that is produced, and supports both itself and the other classes, though it is placed in a position of inferiority to them; real inferiority, mind you, involving a degradation both of mind and body. But it is a necessary consequence of this tyranny and folly that again many of these workers are not producers. A vast number of them once more are merely parasites of property, some of them openly so, as the soldiers by land and sea who are kept on foot for the perpetuating of national rivalries and enmities, and for the purposes of the national struggle for the share of the product of unpaid labour. But besides this obvious burden on the producers and the scarcely less obvious one of domestic servants, there is first the army of clerks, shop-assistants, and so forth, who are engaged in the service of the private war for wealth, which, as above said, is the real occupation of the well-to-do middle class. This is a larger body of workers than might be supposed, for it includes amongst others all those engaged in what I should call competitive salesmanship, or, to use a less dignified word, the puffery of wares, which has now got to such a pitch that there are many things which cost far more to sell than they do to make.

Next there is the mass of people employed in making all those articles of folly and luxury, the demand for which is the outcome of the existence of the rich non-producing classes; things which people leading a manly and uncorrupted life would not ask for or dream of. These things, whoever may gainsay me, I will for ever refuse to call wealth: they are not wealth, but waste. Wealth is what Nature gives us and what a reasonable man can make out of the gifts of Nature for his reasonable use. The sunlight, the fresh air, the unspoiled face of the earth, food, raiment and housing necessary and decent; the storing up of knowledge of all kinds, and the power of disseminating it; means of free communication between man and man; works of art, the beauty which man creates when he is most a man, most aspiring and thoughtful—all things which serve the pleasure of people, free, manly, and uncorrupted. This is wealth. Nor can I think of anything worth having which does not come under one or other of these heads. But think, I beseech you, of the product of England, the workshop of the world, and will you not be bewildered, as I am, at the thought of the mass of things which no sane man could desire, but which our useless toil makes—and sells?

Now, further, there is even a sadder industry yet, which is forced on many, very many, of our workers—the making of wares which are necessary to them and their brethren, *because they are an inferior class*. For if many men live without producing, nay, must live lives so empty and foolish that they *force* a great part of the workers to produce wares which no one needs, not even the rich, it follows that most men must be poor; and, living as they do on wages from those whom they support, cannot get for their use the *goods* which men naturally desire, but must put up with miserable makeshifts for them, with coarse food that does not nourish, with rotten raiment which does not shelter, with wretched houses which may well make a town-dweller in civilization look back with regret to the tent of the nomad tribe, or the cave of the pre-historic savage. Nay, the workers must even lend a hand to the great industrial invention of the age—adulteration, and by its help produce for their own use shams and mockeries of the luxury of the rich; for the wage-earners must always live as the wage-payers bid them, and their very habits of life are *forced* on them by their masters.

But it is waste of time to try to express in words due contempt of the productions of the much-praised cheapness of our epoch. It must be enough to say that this cheapness is necessary to the system of exploiting on which modern manufacture rests. In other words, our society includes a great mass of slaves, who must be fed, clothed, housed and amused as slaves, and that their daily necessity compels them to make the slave-wares whose use is the perpetuation of their slavery.

To sum up, then, concerning the manner of work in civilized States, these States are composed of three classes—a class which does not even pretend to work, a class which pretends to work but which produces nothing, and a class which works, but is compelled by the other two classes to do work which is often unproductive.

Civilization therefore wastes its own resources, and will do so as long as the present system lasts. These are cold words with which to describe the tyranny under which we suffer; try then to consider what they mean.

There is a certain amount of natural material and of natural forces in the world, and a certain amount of labour-power inherent in the persons of the men that inhabit it. Men urged by their necessities and desires have laboured for many thousands of years at the task of subjugating the forces of Nature and of making the natural material useful to them. To our eyes, since we cannot see into the future, that struggle with Nature seems nearly over, and the victory of the human race over her nearly complete. And, looking backwards to the time when history first began, we note that the progress of that victory has been far swifter and more startling within the last two hundred years than ever before. Surely, therefore, we moderns ought to be in all ways vastly better off than any who have gone before us. Surely we ought, one and all of us, to be wealthy, to be well furnished with the good things which our victory over Nature has won for us.

But what is the real fact? Who will dare to deny that the great mass of civilized men are poor? So poor are they that it is mere childishness troubling ourselves to discuss whether perhaps they are in some ways a little better off than their forefathers. They are poor; nor can their poverty be measured by the poverty of a resourceless savage, for he knows of nothing else than his poverty; that he should be cold, hungry, houseless, dirty, ignorant, all that is to him as natural as that he should have a skin. But for us, for the most of us, civilization has bred desires which she forbids us to satisfy, and so is not merely a niggard but a torturer also.

Thus then have the fruits of our victory over Nature been stolen from us, thus has compulsion by Nature to labour in hope of rest, gain, and pleasure been turned into compulsion by man to labour in hope—of living to labour!

What shall we do then, can we mend it?

Well, remember once more that it is not our remote ancestors who achieved the victory over Nature, but our fathers, nay, our very selves. For us to sit hopeless and helpless then would be a strange folly indeed: be sure that we can amend it. What, then, is the first thing to be done?

We have seen that modern society is divided into two classes, one of which is *privileged* to be kept by the labour of the other—that is, it forces the other to work for it and takes from this inferior class everything that it *can* take from it, and uses the wealth so taken to keep its own members in a superior position, to make them beings of a higher order than the others: longer lived, more beautiful, more honoured, more refined than those of the other class. I do not say that it troubles itself about its members being *positively* long lived, beautiful or refined, but merely insists that they shall be so *relatively* to the inferior class. As also it cannot use the labour-power of the inferior class fairly in producing real wealth, it wastes it wholesale in the production of rubbish.

It is this robbery and waste on the part of the minority which keeps the majority poor; if it could be shown that it is necessary for the preservation of society that this should be submitted to, little more could be said on the matter, save that the despair of the oppressed majority would probably at some time or other destroy Society. But it has been shown, on the contrary, even by such incomplete experiments, for instance, as Co-operation (so-called), that the existence of a privileged class is by no means necessary for the production of wealth, but rather for the 'government' of the producers of wealth, or, in other words, for the upholding of privilege.

The first step to be taken then is to abolish a class of men privileged to shirk their duties as men, thus forcing others to do the work which they refuse to do. All must work according to their ability, and so produce what they consume—that is, each man should work as well as he can for his own livelihood, and his livelihood should be assured to him; that is to say, all the advantages which society would provide for each and all of its members.

Thus, at last, would true Society be founded. It would rest on equality of condition. No man would be tormented for the benefit of another—nay, no one man would be tormented for the benefit of Society. Nor, indeed, can that order be called Society which is not upheld for the benefit of every one of its members.

But since men live now, badly as they live, when so many people do not produce at all, and when so much work is wasted, it is clear that, under conditions where all produced and no work was wasted, not only would every one work with the certain hope of gaining a due share of wealth by his work, but also he could not miss his due share of rest. Here, then, are two out of the three kinds of hope mentioned above as an essential part of worthy work assured to the worker. When class robbery is abolished, every man will reap the fruits of his labour, every man will have due rest—leisure, that is. Some Socialists might say we need not go any further than this; it is enough that the worker should get the full produce of his work, and that his rest should be abundant. But though the compulsion of man's tyranny is thus abolished, I yet demand compensation for the compulsion of Nature's necessity. As long as the work is repulsive it will still be a burden which must be taken up daily, and even so would mar our life, even though the hours of labour were short. What we want to do is to add to our wealth without diminishing our pleasure. Nature will not be finally conquered till our work becomes a part of the pleasure of our lives.

That first step of freeing people from the compulsion to labour needlessly will at least put us on the way towards this happy end; for we shall then have time and opportunities for bringing it about. As things are now, between the waste of labour-power in mere idleness and its waste in unproductive work, it is clear that the world of civilization is supported by a small part of its people; when *all* were working *usefully* for its support, the share of work which each would have to do would be but small, if our standard of life were about on the footing of what well-to-do and refined people now think desirable. We shall have labour-power to spare, and shall, in short, be as wealthy as we please. It will be easy to live. If we were to wake up some morning now, under our present system, and find it 'easy to live,' that system would force us to set to work at once and make it hard to live; we should call that 'developing our resources,' or some such fine name. The multiplication of labour has become a necessity for us, and as long as that goes on no ingenuity in the invention of machines will be of any real use to us. Each new machine will cause a certain amount of misery among the workers whose special industry it may disturb; so many of them will be reduced from skilled to unskilled workmen, and then gradually matters will slip into their due grooves, and all will work apparently smoothly again; and if it were not that all this is preparing revolution, things would be, for the greater part of men, just as they were before the new wonderful invention.

But when revolution has made it 'easy to live,' when all are working harmoniously together and there is no one to rob the worker of his time, that is to say, his life; in those coming days there will be no compulsion on us to go on producing things we do not want, no compulsion on us to labour for nothing; we shall be able calmly and thoughtfully to consider what we shall do with our wealth of labour-power. Now, for my part, I think the first use we ought to make of that wealth, of that freedom, should be to make all our labour, even the commonest and most necessary, pleasant to everybody; for thinking over the matter carefully I can see that the one course which will certainly make life happy in the face of all accidents and troubles is to take a pleasurable interest in all the details of life. And lest perchance you think that an assertion too universally accepted to be worth making, let me remind you how entirely modern civilization forbids it; with what sordid, and even terrible, details it surrounds the life of the poor, what a mechanical and empty life she forces on the rich; and how rare a holiday it is for any of us to feel ourselves a part of Nature, and unhurriedly, thoughtfully, and happily to note the course of our lives amidst all the little links of events which connect them with the lives of others, and build up the great whole of humanity.

But such a holiday our whole lives might be, if we were resolute to make all our labour reasonable and pleasant. But we must be resolute indeed; for no half measures will help us here. It has been said already that our present joyless labour, and our lives scared and anxious as the life of a hunted beast, are forced upon us by the present system of producing for the profit of the privileged classes. It is necessary to state what this means. Under the present system of wages and capital the 'manufacturer' (most absurdly so called, since a manufacturer means a person who makes with his hands) having a monopoly of the means whereby the power to labour inherent in every man's body can be used for production, is the master of those who are not so privileged; he, and he alone, is able to make use of this labour-power, which, on the other hand, is the only commodity by means of which his 'capital,' that is to say, the accumulated product of past labour, can be made productive to him. He therefore buys the labour-power of those who are bare of capital and can only live by selling it to him; his purpose in this transaction is to increase his capital, to make it breed. It is clear that if he paid those with whom he makes his bargain the full value of their labour, that is to say, all that they produced, he would fail in his purpose. But since he is the monopolist of the means of productive labour, he can *compel* them to make a bargain better for him and worse for them than that; which bargain is that after they have earned their livelihood, estimated according to a standard high enough to ensure their peaceable submission to his mastership, the rest (and by far the larger part as a matter of fact) of what they produce shall belong to him, shall be his *property* to do as he likes with, to use or abuse at his pleasure; which property is, as we all know, jealously guarded by army and navy, police and prison; in short, by that huge mass of physical force which superstition, habit, fear of death by starvation—IGNORANCE, in one word, among the propertyless masses enables the propertied classes to use for the subjection of—their slaves.

Now, at other times, other evils resulting from this system may be put forward. What I want to point out now is the impossibility of our attaining to attractive labour under this system, and to repeat that it is this robbery (there is no other word for it) which wastes the available labour-power of the civilized world, forcing many men to do nothing, and many, very many more to do nothing useful; and forcing those who carry on really useful labour to most burdensome over-work. For understand once for all that the 'manufacturer' aims primarily at producing, by means of the labour he has stolen from others, not goods but profits, that is, the 'wealth' that is produced over and above the livelihood of his workmen, and the wear and tear of his machinery. Whether that 'wealth' is real or sham matters nothing to him. If it sells and yields him a 'profit' it is all right. I have said that, owing to there being rich people who have more money than they can spend reasonably, and who therefore buy sham wealth, there is waste on that side; and also that, owing to there being poor people who cannot afford to buy things which are worth making, there is waste on that side. So that the 'demand' which the capitalist 'supplies' is a false demand. The market in which he sells is 'rigged' by the miserable inequalities produced by the robbery of the system of Capital and Wages.

It is this system, therefore, which we must be resolute in getting rid of, if we are to attain to happy and useful work for all. The first step towards making labour attractive is to get the means of making labour fruitful, the Capital, including the land, machinery, factories, &c., into the hands of the community, to be used for the good of all alike, so that we might all work at 'supplying' the real 'demands' of each and all—that is to say, work for livelihood, instead of working to supply the demand of the profit market—instead of working for profit—*i.e.*, the power of compelling other men to work against their will.

When this first step has been taken and men begin to understand that Nature wills all men either to work or starve, and when they are no longer such fools as to allow some the alternative of stealing, when this happy day is come, we shall then be relieved from the tax of waste, and consequently shall find that we have, as aforesaid, a mass of labour-power available, which will enable us to live as we please within reasonable limits. We shall no longer be hurried and driven by the fear of starvation, which at present presses no less on the greater part of men in civilised communities than it does on mere savages. The first and most obvious necessities will be so easily provided for in a community in which there is no waste of labour, that we shall have time to look round and consider what we really do want, that can be obtained without over-taxing our energies; for the often-expressed fear of mere idleness falling upon us when the force supplied by the present hierarchy of compulsion is withdrawn, is a fear which is but generated by the burden of excessive and repulsive labour, which we most of us have to bear at present.

I say once more that, in my belief, the first thing which we shall think so necessary as to be worth sacrificing some idle time for, will be the attractiveness of labour. No very heavy sacrifice will be required for attaining this object, but some *will* be required. For we may hope that men who have just waded through a period of strife and revolution will be the last to put up long with a life of mere utilitarianism, though Socialists are sometimes accused by ignorant persons of aiming at such a life. On the other hand, the ornamental part of modern life is already rotten to the core, and must be utterly swept away before the new order of things is realized. There is nothing of it—there is nothing which could come of it that could satisfy the aspirations of men set free from the tyranny of commercialism.

We must begin to build up the ornamental part of life—its pleasures, bodily and mental, scientific and artistic, social and individual—on the basis of work undertaken willingly and cheerfully, with the consciousness of benefiting ourselves and our neighbours by it. Such absolutely necessary work as we should have to do would in the first place take up but a small part of each day, and so far would not be burdensome; but it would be a task of daily recurrence, and therefore would spoil our day's pleasure unless it were made at least endurable while it lasted. In other words, all labour, even the commonest, must be made attractive.

How can this be done?—is the question the answer to which will take up the rest of this paper. In giving some hints on this question, I know that, while all Socialists will agree with many of the suggestions made, some of them may seem to some strange and venturesome. These must be considered as being given without any intention of dogmatizing, and as merely expressing my own personal opinion.

From all that has been said already it follows that labour, to be attractive, must be directed towards some obviously useful end, unless in cases where it is undertaken voluntarily by each individual as a pastime. This element of obvious usefulness is all the more to be counted on in sweetening tasks otherwise irksome, since social morality, the responsibility of man towards the life of man, will, in the new order of things, take the place of theological morality, or the responsibility of man to some abstract idea. Next, the day's work will be short. This need not be insisted on. It is clear that with work unwasted it *can* be short. It is clear also that much work which is now a torment, would be easily endurable if it were much shortened.

Variety of work is the next point, and a most important one. To compel a man to do day after day the same task, without any hope of escape or change, means nothing short of turning his life into a prison-torment. Nothing but the tyranny of profit-grinding makes this necessary. A man might easily learn and practise at least three crafts, varying sedentary occupation with outdoor—occupation calling for the exercise of strong bodily energy for work in which the mind had more to do. There are few men, for instance, who would not wish to spend part of their lives in the most necessary and pleasantest of all work—cultivating the earth. One thing which will make this variety of employment possible will be the form that education will take in a socially ordered community. At present all education is directed towards the end of fitting people to take their places in the hierarchy of commerce—these as masters, those as workmen. The education of the masters is more ornamental than that of the workmen, but it is commercial still; and even at the ancient universities learning is but little regarded, unless it can in the long run be made *to pay*. Due education is a totally different thing from this, and concerns itself in finding out what different people are fit for, and helping them along the road which they are inclined to take. In a duly ordered society, therefore, young people would be taught such handicrafts as they had a turn for as a part of their education, the discipline of their minds and bodies; and adults would also have opportunities of learning in the same schools, for the development of individual capacities would be of all things chiefly aimed at by education, instead, as now, the subordination of all capacities to the great end of 'money-making' for oneself—or one's master. The amount of talent, and even genius, which the present system crushes, and which would be drawn out by such a system, would make our daily work easy and interesting.

Under this head of variety I will note one product of industry which has suffered so much from commercialism that it can scarcely be said to exist, and is, indeed, so foreign from our epoch that I fear there are some who will find it difficult to understand what I have to say on the subject, which I nevertheless must say, since it is really a most important one. I mean that side of art which is, or ought to be, done by the ordinary workman while he is about his ordinary work, and which has got to be called, very properly, Popular Art. This art, I repeat, no longer exists now, having been killed by commercialism. But from the beginning of man's contest with Nature till the rise of the present capitalistic system, it was alive, and generally flourished. While it lasted, everything that was made by man was adorned by man, just as everything made by Nature is adorned by her. The craftsman, as he fashioned the thing he had under his hand, ornamented it so naturally and so entirely without conscious effort, that it is often difficult to distinguish where the mere utilitarian part of his work ended and the ornamental began. Now the origin of this art was the necessity that the workman felt for variety in his work, and though the beauty produced by this desire was a great gift to the world, yet the obtaining variety and pleasure in the work by the workman was a matter of more importance still, for it stamped all labour with the impress of pleasure. All this has now quite disappeared from the work of civilization. If you wish to have ornament, you must pay specially for it, and the workman is compelled to produce ornament, as he is to produce other wares. He is compelled to pretend happiness in his work, so that the beauty produced by man's hand, which was once a solace to his labour, has now become an extra burden to him, and ornament is now but one of the follies of useless toil, and perhaps not the least irksome of its fetters.

Besides the short duration of labour, its conscious usefulness, and the variety which should go with it, there is another thing needed to make it attractive, and that is pleasant surroundings. The misery and squalor which we people of civilization bear with so much complacency as a necessary part of the manufacturing system, is just as necessary to the community at large as a proportionate amount of filth would be in the house of a private rich man. If such a man were to allow the cinders to be raked all over his drawing-room, and a privy to be established in each corner of his dining-room, if he habitually made a dust and refuse heap of his once beautiful garden, never washed his sheets or changed his tablecloth, and made his family sleep five in a bed, he would surely find himself in the claws of a commission *de lunatico*. But such acts of miserly folly are just what our present society is doing daily under the compulsion of a supposed necessity, which is nothing short of madness. I beg you to bring your commission of lunacy against civilization without more delay.

For all our crowded towns and bewildering factories are simply the outcome of the profit system. Capitalistic manufacture, capitalistic land-owning, and capitalistic exchange force men into big cities in order to manipulate them in the interests of capital; the same tyranny contracts the due space of the factory so much that (for instance) the interior of a great weaving-shed is almost as ridiculous a spectacle as it is a horrible one. There is no other necessity for all this, save the necessity for grinding profits out of men's lives, and of producing cheap goods for the use (and subjection) of the slaves who grind. All labour is not yet driven into factories; often where it is there is no necessity for it, save again the profit-tyranny. People engaged in all such labour need by no means be compelled to pig together in close city quarters. There is no reason why they should not follow their occupations in quiet country homes, in industrial colleges, in small towns, or, in short, where they find it happiest for them to live.

As to that part of labour which must be associated on a large scale, this very factory system, under a reasonable order of things (though to my mind there might still be drawbacks to it), would at least offer opportunities for a full and eager social life surrounded by many pleasures. The factories might be centres of intellectual activity also, and work in them might well be varied very much: the tending of the necessary machinery might to each individual be but a short part of the day's work. The other work might vary from raising food from the surrounding country to the study and practice of art and science. It is a matter of course that people engaged in such work, and being the masters of their own lives, would not allow any hurry or want of foresight to force them into enduring dirt, disorder, or want of room. Science duly applied would enable them to get rid of refuse, to minimize, if not wholly to destroy, all the inconveniences which at present attend the use of elaborate machinery, such as smoke, stench and noise; nor would they endure that the buildings in which they worked or lived should be ugly blots on the fair face of the earth. Beginning by making their factories, buildings, and sheds decent and convenient like their homes, they would infallibly go on to make them not merely negatively good, inoffensive merely, but even beautiful, so that the glorious art of architecture, now for some time slain by commercial greed, would be born again and flourish.

So, you see, I claim that work in a duly ordered community should be made attractive by the consciousness of usefulness, by its being carried on with intelligent interest, by variety, and by its being exercised amidst pleasurable surroundings. But I have also claimed, as we all do, that the day's work should not be wearisomely long. It may be said, 'How can you make this last claim square with the others? If the work is to be so refined, will not the goods made be very expensive?'

I do admit, as I have said before, that some sacrifice will be necessary in order to make labour attractive. I mean that, if we *could* be contented in a free community to work in the same hurried, dirty, disorderly, heartless way as we do now, we might shorten our day's labour very much more than I suppose we shall do, taking all kinds of labour into account. But if we did, it would mean that our new-won freedom of condition would leave us listless and wretched, if not anxious, as we are now, which I hold is simply impossible. We should be contented to make the sacrifices necessary for raising our condition to the standard called out for as desirable by the whole community. Nor only so. We should, individually, be emulous to sacrifice quite freely still more of our time and our ease towards the raising of the standard of life. Persons, either by themselves or associated for such purposes, would freely, and for the love of the work and for its results—stimulated by the hope of the pleasure of creation—produce those ornaments of life for the service of all, which they are now bribed to produce (or pretend to produce) for the service of a few rich men. The experiment of a civilized community living wholly without art or literature has not yet been tried. The past degradation and corruption of civilization may force this denial of pleasure upon the society which will arise from its ashes. If that must be, we will accept the passing phase of utilitarianism as a foundation for the art which is to be. If the cripple and the starveling disappear from our streets, if the earth nourish us all alike, if the sun shine for all of us alike, if to one and all of us the glorious drama of the earth—day and night, summer and winter—can be presented as a thing to understand and love, we can afford to wait awhile till we are purified from the shame of the past corruption, and till art arises again amongst people freed from the terror of the slave and the shame of the robber.

Meantime, in any case, the refinement, thoughtfulness, and deliberation of labour must indeed be paid for, but not by compulsion to labour long hours.

Our epoch has invented machines which would have appeared wild dreams to the men of past ages, and of those machines we have as yet *made no use*.

They are called 'labour-saving' machines—a commonly used phrase which implies what we expect of them; but we do not get what we expect. What they really do is to reduce the skilled labourer to the ranks of the unskilled, to increase the number of the 'reserve army of labour'—that is, to increase the precariousness of life among the workers and to intensify the labour of those who serve the machines (as slaves their masters). All this they do by the way, while they pile up the profits of the employers of labour, or force them to expend those profits in bitter commercial war with each other. In a true society these miracles of ingenuity would be for the first time used for minimizing the amount of time spent in unattractive labour, which by their means might be so reduced as to be but a very light burden on each individual. All the more as these machines would most certainly be very much improved when it was no longer a question as to whether their improvement would 'pay' the individual, but rather whether it would benefit the community.

So much for the ordinary use of machinery, which would probably, after a time, be somewhat restricted when men found out that there was no need for anxiety as to mere subsistence, and learned to take an interest and pleasure in handiwork which, done deliberately and thoughtfully, could be made more attractive than machine work.

Again, as people freed from the daily terror of starvation find out what they really wanted, being no longer compelled by anything but their own needs, they would refuse to produce the mere inanities which are now called luxuries, or the poison and trash now called cheap wares. No one would make plush breeches when there were no flunkies to wear them, nor would anybody waste his time over making oleo-margarine when no one was *compelled* to abstain from real butter. Adulteration laws are only needed in a society of thieves— and in such a society they are a dead letter.

Socialists are often asked how work of the rougher and more repulsive kind could be carried out in the new condition of things. To attempt to answer such questions fully or authoritatively would be attempting the impossibility of constructing a scheme of a new society out of the materials of the old, before we knew which of those materials would disappear and which endure through the evolution which is leading us to the great change. Yet it is not difficult to conceive of some arrangement whereby those who did the roughest work should work for the shortest spells. And again, what is said above of the variety of work applies specially here. Once more I say, that for a man to be the whole of his life hopelessly engaged in performing one repulsive and never-ending task, is an arrangement fit enough for the hell imagined by theologians, but scarcely fit for any other form of society. Lastly, if this rougher work were of any special kind, we may suppose that special volunteers would be called on to perform it, who would surely be forthcoming, unless men in a state of freedom should lose the sparks of manliness which they possessed as slaves.

And yet if there be any work which cannot be made other than repulsive, either by the shortness of its duration or the intermittency of its recurrence, or by the sense of special and peculiar usefulness (and therefore honour) in the mind of the man who performs it freely—if there be any work which cannot be but a torment to the worker, what then? Well, then, let us see if the heavens will fall on us if we leave it undone, for it were better that they should. The produce of such work cannot be worth the price of it.

Now we have seen that the semi-theological dogma that all labour, under any circumstances, is a blessing to the labourer, is hypocritical and false; that, on the other hand, labour is good when due hope of rest and pleasure accompanies it. We have weighed the work of civilization in the balance and found it wanting, since hope is mostly lacking to it, and therefore we see that civilization has bred a dire curse for men. But we have seen also that the work of the world might be carried on in hope and with pleasure if it were not wasted by folly and tyranny, by the perpetual strife of opposing classes.

It is Peace, therefore, which we need in order that we may live and work in hope and with pleasure. Peace so much desired, if we may trust men's words, but which has been so continually and steadily rejected by them in deeds. But for us, let us set our hearts on it and win it at whatever cost.

What the cost may be, who can tell? Will it be possible to win peace peaceably? Alas, how can it be? We are so hemmed in by wrong and folly, that in one way or other we must always be fighting against them: our own lives may see no end to the struggle, perhaps no obvious hope of the end. It may be that the best we can hope to see is that struggle getting sharper and bitterer day by day, until it breaks out openly at last into the slaughter of men by actual warfare instead of by the slower and crueller methods of 'peaceful' commerce. If we live to see that, we shall live to see much; for it will mean the rich classes grown conscious of their own wrong and robbery, and consciously defending them by open violence; and then the end will be drawing near.

But in any case, and whatever the nature of our strife for peace may be, if we only aim at it steadily and with singleness of heart, and ever keep it in view, a reflection from that peace of the future will illumine the turmoil and trouble of our lives, whether the trouble be seemingly petty, or obviously tragic; and we shall, in our hopes at least, live the lives of men: nor can the present times give us any reward greater than that.

HOW WE LIVE AND HOW WE MIGHT LIVE

The word Revolution, which we Socialists are so often forced to use, has a terrible sound in most people's ears, even when we have explained to them that it does not necessarily mean a change accompanied by riot and all kinds of violence, and cannot mean a change made mechanically and in the teeth of opinion by a group of men who have somehow managed to seize on the executive power for the moment. Even when we explain that we use the word revolution in its etymological sense, and mean by it a change in the basis of society, people are scared at the idea of such a vast change, and beg that you will speak of reform and not revolution. As, however, we Socialists do not at all mean by our word revolution what these worthy people mean by their word reform, I can't help thinking that it would be a mistake to use it, whatever projects we might conceal beneath its harmless envelope. So we will stick to our word, which means a change of the basis of society; it may frighten people, but it will at least warn them that there is something to be frightened about, which will be no less dangerous for being ignored; and also it may encourage some people, and will mean to them at least not a fear, but a hope.

Fear and Hope—those are the names of the two great passions which rule the race of man, and with which revolutionists have to deal; to give hope to the many oppressed and fear to the few oppressors, that is our business; if we do the first and give hope to the many, the few *must* be frightened by their hope; otherwise we do not want to frighten them; it is not revenge we want for poor people, but happiness; indeed, what revenge can be taken for all the thousands of years of the sufferings of the poor?

However, many of the oppressors of the poor, most of them, we will say, are not conscious of their being oppressors (we shall see why presently); they live in an orderly, quiet way themselves, as far as possible removed from the feelings of a Roman slave-owner or a Legree; they know that the poor exist, but their sufferings do not present themselves to them in a trenchant and dramatic way; they themselves have troubles to bear, and they think doubtless that to bear trouble is the lot of humanity; nor have they any means of comparing the troubles of their lives with those of people lower in the social scale; and if ever the thought of those heavier troubles obtrudes itself upon them, they console themselves with the maxim that people do get used to the troubles they have to bear, whatever they may be.

Indeed, as far as regards individuals at least, that is but too true, so that we have as supporters of the present state of things, however bad it may be, first those comfortable unconscious oppressors who think that they have everything to fear from any change which would involve more than the softest and most gradual of reforms, and secondly those poor people who, living hard and anxiously as they do, can hardly conceive of any change for the better happening to them, and dare not risk one tittle of their poor possessions in taking any action towards a possible bettering of their condition; so that while we can do little with the rich save inspire them with fear, it is hard indeed to give the poor any hope. It is, then, no less than reasonable that those whom we try to involve in the great struggle for a better form of life than that which we now lead should call on us to give them at least some idea of what that life may be like.

A reasonable request, but hard to satisfy, since we are living under a system that makes conscious effort towards reconstruction almost impossible: it is not unreasonable on our part to answer, 'There are certain definite obstacles to the real progress of man; we can tell you what these are; take them away, and then you shall see.'

However, I purpose now to offer myself as a victim for the satisfaction of those who consider that as things now go we have at least got something, and are terrified at the idea of losing their hold of that, lest they should find they are worse off than before, and have nothing. Yet in the course of my endeavour to show how we might live, I must more or less deal in negatives. I mean to say I must point out where in my opinion we fall short in our present attempt at decent life. I must ask the rich and well-to-do what sort of a position it is which they are so anxious to preserve at any cost? and if, after all, it will be such a terrible loss to them to give it up? and I must point out to the poor that they, with capacities for living a dignified and generous life, are in a position which they cannot endure without continued degradation.

How do we live, then, under our present system? Let us look at it a little.

And first, please to understand that our present system of Society is based on a state of perpetual war. Do any of you think that this is as it should be? I know that you have often been told that the competition, which is at present the rule of all production, is a good thing, and stimulates the progress of the race; but the people who tell you this should call competition by its shorter name of *war* if they wish to be honest, and you would then be free to consider whether or no war stimulates progress, otherwise than as a mad bull chasing you over your own garden may do. War or competition, whichever you please to call it, means at the best pursuing your own advantage at the cost of someone else's loss, and in the process of it you must not be sparing of destruction even of your own possessions, or you will certainly come by the worse in the struggle. You understand that perfectly as to the kind of war in which people go out to kill and be killed; that sort of war in which ships are commissioned, for instance, 'to sink, burn, and destroy'; but it appears that you are not so conscious of this waste of goods when you are only carrying on that other war called *commerce*; observe, however, that the waste is there all the same.

Now let us look at this kind of war a little closer, run through some of the forms of it, that we may see how the 'burn, sink, and destroy' is carried on in it.

First, you have that form of it called national rivalry, which in good truth is nowadays the cause of all gunpowder and bayonet wars which civilized nations wage. For years past we English have been rather shy of them, except on those happy occasions when we could carry them on at no sort of risk to ourselves, when the killing was all on one side, or at all events when we hoped it would be. We have been shy of gunpowder war with a respectable enemy for a long while, and I will tell you why: It is because we have had the lion's share of the world-market; we didn't want to fight for it as a nation, for we had got it; but now this is changing in a most significant, and, to a Socialist, a most cheering way; we are losing or have lost that lion's share; it is now a desperate 'competition' between the great nations of civilization for the world-market, and tomorrow it may be a desperate war for that end. As a result, the furthering of war (if it be not on too large a scale) is no longer confined to the honour-and-glory kind of old Tories, who if they meant anything at all by it meant that a Tory war would be a good occasion for damping down democracy; we have changed all that, and now it is quite another kind of politician that is wont to urge us on to 'patriotism' as 'tis called. The leaders of the Progressive Liberals, as they would call themselves, longheaded persons who know well enough that social movements are going on, who are not blind to the fact that the world will move with their help or without it; these have been the Jingoes of these later days. I don't mean to say they know what they are doing: politicians, as you well know, take good care to shut their eyes to everything that may happen six months ahead; but what is being done is this: that the present system, which always must include national rivalry, is pushing us into a desperate scramble for the markets on more or less equal terms with other nations, because, once more, we have lost that command of them which we once had. Desperate is not too strong a word. We shall let this impulse to snatch markets carry us whither it will, whither it must. To-day it is successful burglary and disgrace, tomorrow it may be mere defeat and disgrace.

Now this is not a digression, although in saying this I am nearer to what is generally called politics than I shall be again. I only want to show you what commercial war comes to when it has to do with foreign nations, and that even the dullest can see how mere waste must go with it. That is how we live now with foreign nations, prepared to ruin them without war if possible, with it if necessary, let alone meantime the disgraceful exploiting of savage tribes and barbarous peoples on whom we force at once our shoddy wares and our hypocrisy at the cannon's mouth.

Well, surely Socialism can offer you something in the place of all that. It can; it can offer you peace and friendship instead of war. We might live utterly without national rivalries, acknowledging that while it is best for those who feel that they naturally form a community under one name to govern themselves, yet that no community in civilization should feel that it had interests opposed to any other, their economical condition being at any rate similar; so that any citizen of one community could fall to work and live without disturbance of his life when he was in a foreign country, and would fit into his place quite naturally; so that all civilized nations would form one great community, agreeing together as to the kind and amount of production and distribution needed; working at such and such production where it could be best produced; avoiding waste by all means. Please to think of the amount of waste which they would avoid, how much such a revolution would add to the wealth of the world! What creature on earth would be harmed by such a revolution? Nay, would not everybody be the better for it? And what hinders it? I will tell you presently.

Meantime let us pass from this 'competition' between nations to that between 'the organizers of labour,' great firms, joint-stock companies; capitalists in short, and see how competition 'stimulates production' among them: indeed it does do that; but what kind of production? Well, production of something to sell at a profit, or say production of profits: and note how war commercial stimulates that: a certain market is demanding goods; there are, say, a hundred manufacturers who make that kind of goods, and every one of them would if he could keep that market to himself, and struggles desperately to get as much of it as he can, with the obvious result that presently the thing is overdone, and the market is glutted, and all that fury of manufacture has to sink into cold ashes. Doesn't that seem something like war to you? Can't you see the waste of it—waste of labour, skill, cunning, waste of life in short? Well, you may say, but it cheapens the goods. In a sense it does; and yet only apparently, as wages have a tendency to sink for the ordinary worker in proportion as prices sink; and at what a cost do we gain this appearance of cheapness! Plainly speaking, at the cost of cheating the consumer and starving the real producer for the benefit of the gambler, who uses both consumer and producer as his milch cows. I needn't go at length into the subject of adulteration, for every one knows what kind of a part it plays in this sort of commerce; but remember that it is an absolutely necessary incident to the production of profit out of wares, which is the business of the so-called manufacturer; and this you must understand, that, taking him in the lump, the consumer is perfectly helpless against the gambler; the goods are forced on him by their cheapness, and with them a certain kind of life which that energetic, that aggressive cheapness determines for him: for so far-reaching is this curse of commercial war that no country is safe from its ravages; the traditions of a thousand years fall before it in a month; it overruns a weak or semi-barbarous country, and whatever romance or pleasure or art existed there, is trodden down into a mire of sordidness and ugliness; the Indian or Javanese craftsman may no longer ply his craft leisurely, working a few hours a day, in producing a maze of strange beauty on a piece of cloth: a steam-engine is set a-going at Manchester, and that victory over nature and a thousand stubborn difficulties is used for the base work of producing a sort of plaster of china-clay and shoddy, and the Asiatic worker, if he is not starved to death outright, as plentifully happens, is driven himself into a factory to lower the wages of his Manchester brother worker, and nothing of character is left him except, most like, an accumulation of fear and hatred of that to him most unaccountable evil, his English master. The South Sea Islander must leave his canoe-carving, his sweet rest, and his graceful dances, and become the slave of a slave: trousers, shoddy, rum, missionary, and fatal disease—he must swallow all this civilization in the lump, and neither himself nor we can help him now till social order displaces the hideous tyranny of gambling that has ruined him.

Let those be types of the consumer: but now for the producer; I mean the real producer, the worker; how does this scramble for the plunder of the market affect him? The manufacturer, in the eagerness of his war, has had to collect into one neighbourhood a vast army of workers, he has drilled them till they are as fit as may be for his special branch of production, that is, for making a profit out of it, and with the result of their being fit for nothing else: well, when the glut comes in that market he is supplying, what happens to this army, every private in which has been depending on the steady demand in that market, and acting, as he could not choose but act, as if it were to go on for ever? You know well what happens to these men: the factory door is shut on them; on a very large part of them often, and at the best on the reserve army of labour, so busily employed in the time of inflation. What becomes of them? Nay, we know that well enough just now. But what we don't know, or don't choose to know, is, that this reserve army of labour is an absolute necessity for commercial war: if *our* manufacturers had not got these poor devils whom they could draft on to their machines when the demand swelled, other manufacturers in France, or Germany, or America, would step in and take the market from them.

So you see, as we live now, it is necessary that a vast part of the industrial population should be exposed to the danger of periodical semi-starvation, and that, not for the advantage of the people in another part of the world, but for their degradation and enslavement.

Just let your minds run for a moment on the kind of waste which this means, this opening up of new markets among savage and barbarous countries which is the extreme type of the force of the profit-market on the world, and you will surely see what a hideous nightmare that profit-market is: it keeps us sweating and terrified for our livelihood, unable to read a book, or look at a picture, or have pleasant fields to walk in, or to lie in the sun, or to share in the knowledge of our time, to have in short either animal or intellectual pleasure, and for what? that we may go on living the same slavish life till we die, in order to provide for a rich man what is called a life of ease and luxury; that is to say, a life so empty, unwholesome, and degraded, that perhaps, on the whole, he is worse off than we the workers are: and as to the result of all this suffering, it is luckiest when it is nothing at all, when you can say that the wares have done nobody any good; for oftenest they have done many people harm, and we have toiled and groaned and died in making poison and destruction for our fellow-men.

Well, I say all this is war, and the results of war, the war this time, not of competing nations, but of competing firms or capitalist units: and it is this war of the firms which hinders the peace between nations which you surely have agreed with me in thinking is so necessary; for you must know that war is the very breath of the nostrils of these fighting firms, and they have now, in our times, got into their hands nearly all the political power, and they band together in each country in order to make their respective governments fulfil just two functions: the first is at home to act as a strong police force, to keep the ring in which the strong are beating down the weak; the second is to act as a piratical body-guard abroad, a petard to explode the doors which lead to the markets of the world: markets at any price abroad, uninterfered-with privilege, falsely called *laissez-faire*,* at any price at home, to provide these is the sole business of a government such as our industrial captains have been able to conceive of. I must now try to show you the reason of all this, and what it rests on, by trying to answer the question, Why have the profit-makers got all this power, or at least why are they able to keep it?

That takes us to the third form of war commercial: the last, and the one which all the rest is founded on. We have spoken first of the war of rival nations; next of that of rival firms: we have now to speak of rival men. As nations under the present system are driven to compete with one another for the markets of the world, and as firms or the captains of industry have to scramble for their share of the profits of the markets, so also have the workers to compete with each other—for livelihood; and it is this constant competition or war amongst them which enables the profit-grinders to make their profits, and by means of wealth so acquired to take all the executive power of the country into their hands. But here is the difference between the position of the workers and the profit-makers: to the latter, the profit-grinders, war is necessary; you cannot have profit-making without competition, individual,

---

* Falsely; because the privileged classes have at their back the force of the Executive by means of which to compel the unprivileged to accept the terms; if this is 'free competition' there is no meaning in words.

corporate, and national; but you may work for a livelihood without competing; you may combine instead of competing.

I have said war was the life-breath of the profit-makers; in like manner, combination is the life of the workers. The working classes or proletariat cannot even exist as a class without combination of some sort. The necessity which forced the profit-grinders to collect their men first into workshops working by the division of labour, and next into great factories worked by machinery, and so gradually to draw them into the great towns and centres of civilization, gave birth to a distinct working-class or proletariat: and this it was which gave them their *mechanical* existence, so to say. But note, that they are indeed combined into social groups for the production of wares, but only as yet mechanically; they do not know what they are working at, nor whom they are working for, because they are combining to produce wares of which the profit of a master forms an essential part, instead of goods for their own use: as long as they do this, and compete with each other for leave to do it, they will be, and will feel themselves to be, simply a part of those competing firms I have been speaking of; they will be in fact just a part of the machinery for the production of profit; and so long as this lasts it will be the aim of the masters or profit-makers to decrease the market value of this human part of the machinery; that is to say, since they already hold in their hands the labour of dead men in the form of capital and machinery, it is their interest, or we will say their necessity, to pay as little as they can help for the labour of living men which they have to buy from day to day: and since the workmen they employ have nothing but their labour-power, they are compelled to underbid one another for employment and wages, and so enable the capitalist to play his game.

I have said that, as things go, the workers are a part of the competing firms, an adjunct of capital. Nevertheless, they are only so by compulsion; and, even without their being conscious of it, they struggle against that compulsion and its immediate results, the lowering of their wages, of their standard of life: and this they do, and must do, both as a class and individually: just as the slave of the great Roman lord, though he distinctly felt himself to be a part of the household, yet collectively was a force in reserve for its destruction, and individually stole from his lord whenever he could safely do so. So, here, you see, is another form of war necessary to the way we live now, the war of class against class, which, when it rises to its height, and it seems to be rising at present, will destroy those other forms of war we have been speaking of; will make the position of the profit-makers, of perpetual commercial war, untenable; will destroy the present system of competitive privilege, or commercial war.

Now observe, I said that to the existence of the workers it was combination, not competition, that was necessary, while to that of the profit-makers combination was impossible, and war necessary. The present position of the workers is that of the machinery of commerce, or in plainer words its slaves; when they change that position and become free, the class of profit-makers must cease to exist; and what will then be the position of the workers? Even as it is they are the one necessary part of society, the life-giving part; the other classes are but hangers-on who live on them. But what should they be, what will they be, when they, once for all, come to know their real power, and cease competing with one another for livelihood? I will tell you: they will be society, they will be the community. And being society—that is, there being no class outside them to contend with—they can then regulate their labour in accordance with their own real needs.

There is much talk about supply and demand, but the supply and demand usually meant is an artificial one; it is under the sway of the gambling market; the demand is forced, as I hinted above, before it is supplied; nor, as each producer is working against all the rest, can the producers hold their hands, till the market is glutted and the workers, thrown out on the streets, hear that there has been over-production, amidst which over-plus of unsaleable goods they go ill supplied with even necessaries, because the wealth which they themselves have created is 'ill distributed,' as we call it—that is, unjustly taken away from them.

When the workers are society they will regulate their labour, so that the supply and demand shall be genuine, not gambling; the two will then be commensurate, for it is the same society which demands that also supplies; there will be no more artificial famines then, no more poverty amidst over-production, amidst too great a stock of the very things which should supply poverty and turn it into well-being. In short, there will be no waste and therefore no tyranny.

Well, now, what Socialism offers you in place of these artificial famines, with their so-called over-production, is, once more, regulation of the markets; supply and demand commensurate; no gambling, and consequently (once more) no waste; not overwork and weariness for the worker one month, and the next no work and terror of starvation, but steady work and plenty of leisure every month; not cheap market wares, that is to say, adulterated wares, with scarcely any *good* in them, mere scaffold-poles for building up profits; no labour would be spent on such things as these, which people would cease to want when they ceased to be slaves. Not these, but such goods as best fulfilled the real uses of the consumers would labour be set to make; for profit being abolished, people could have what they wanted, instead of what the profit-grinders at home and abroad forced them to take.

For what I want you to understand is this: that in every civilized country at least there is plenty for all—is, or at any rate might be. Even with labour so misdirected as it is at present, an equitable distribution of the wealth we have would make all people comparatively comfortable; but that is nothing to the wealth we might have if labour were not misdirected.

Observe, in the early days of the history of man he was the slave of his most immediate necessities; Nature was mighty and he was feeble, and he had to wage constant war with her for his daily food and such shelter as he could get. His life was bound down and limited by this constant struggle; all his morals, laws, religion, are in fact the outcome and the reflection of this ceaseless toil of earning his livelihood. Time passed, and little by little, step by step, he grew stronger, till now after all these ages he has almost completely conquered Nature, and one would think should now have leisure to turn his thoughts towards higher things than procuring to-morrow's dinner. But, alas! his progress has been broken and halting; and though he has indeed conquered Nature and has her forces under his control to do what he will with, he still has himself to conquer, he still has to think how he will best use those forces which he has mastered. At present he uses them blindly, foolishly, as one driven by mere fate. It would almost seem as if some phantom of the ceaseless pursuit of food which was once the master of the savage was still haunting the civilized man; who toils in a dream, as it were, haunted by mere dim unreal hopes, borne of vague recollections of the days gone by. Out of that dream he must wake, and face things as they really are. The conquest of Nature is complete, may we not say? and now our business is, and has for long been the organization of man, who wields the forces of Nature. Nor till this is attempted at least shall we ever be free of that terrible phantom of fear of starvation which, with its brother devil, desire of domination, drives us into injustice, cruelty, and dastardliness of all kinds: to cease to fear our fellows and learn to depend on them, to do away with competition and build up co-operation, is our one necessity.

Now, to get closer to details; you probably know that every man in civilization is worth, so to say, more than his skin; working, as he must work, socially, he can produce more than will keep himself alive and in fair condition; and this has been so for many centuries, from the time, in fact, when warring tribes began to make their conquered enemies slaves instead of killing them; and of course his capacity of producing these extras has gone on increasing faster and faster, till to-day one man will weave, for instance, as much cloth in a week as will clothe a whole village for years: and the real question of civilization has always been what are we to do with extra produce of labour— a question which the phantom, fear of starvation, and its fellow, desire of domination, has driven men to answer pretty badly always, and worst of all perhaps in these present days, when the extra produce has grown with such prodigious speed. The practical answer has always been for man to struggle with his fellow for private possession of undue shares of these extras, and all kinds of devices have been employed by those who found themselves in possession of the power of taking them from others to keep those whom they had robbed in perpetual subjection; and these latter, as I have already hinted, had no chance of resisting this fleecing as long as they were few and scattered, and consequently could have little sense of their common oppression. But now that, owing to the very pursuit of these undue shares of profit, or extra earnings, men have become more dependent on each other for production, and have been driven, as I said before, to combine together for that end more completely, the power of the workers—that is to say, of the robbed or fleeced class—has enormously increased, and it only remains for them to understand that they have this power. When they do that they will be able to give the right answer to the question what is to be done with the extra products of labour over and above what will keep the labourer alive to labour: which answer is, that the worker will have all that he produces, and not be fleeced at all: and remember that he produces collectively, and therefore he will do effectively what work is required of him according to his capacity, and of the produce of that work he will have what he needs; because, you see, he cannot *use* more than he needs—he can only *waste* it.

If this arrangement seems to you preposterously ideal, as it well may, looking at our present condition, I must back it up by saying that when men are organized so that their labour is not wasted, they will be relieved from the fear of starvation and the desire of domination, and will have freedom and leisure to look round and see what they really do need.

Now something of that I can conceive for my own self, and I will lay my ideas before you, so that you may compare them with your own, asking you always to remember that the very differences in men's capacities and desires, after the common need of food and shelter is satisfied, will make it easier to deal with their desires in a communal state of things.

What is it that I need, therefore, which my surrounding circumstances can give me—my dealings with my fellow-men—setting aside inevitable accidents which co-operation and forethought cannot control, if there be such?

Well, first of all I claim good health; and I say that a vast proportion of people in civilization scarcely even know what that means. To feel mere life a pleasure; to enjoy the moving one's limbs and exercising one's bodily powers; to play, as it were, with sun and wind and rain; to rejoice in satisfying the due bodily appetites of a human animal without fear of degradation or sense of wrong-doing; yes, and therewithal to be well-formed, straight-limbed, strongly knit, expressive of countenance—to be, in a word, beautiful—that also I claim. If we cannot have this claim satisfied, we are but poor creatures after all; and I claim it in the teeth of those terrible doctrines of asceticism, which, born of the despair of the oppressed and degraded, have been for so many ages used as instruments for the continuance of that oppression and degradation.

And I believe that this claim for a healthy body for all of us carries with it all other due claims: for who knows where the seeds of disease which even rich people suffer from were first sown: from the luxury of an ancestor, perhaps: yet often, I suspect, from his poverty. And for the poor: a distinguished physicist has said that the poor suffer always from one disease—hunger; and at least I know this, that if a man is overworked in any degree he cannot enjoy the sort of health I am speaking of; nor can he if he is continually chained to one dull round of mechanical work, with no hope at the other end of it; nor if he lives in continual sordid anxiety for his livelihood, nor if he is ill-housed, nor if he is deprived of all enjoyment of the natural beauty of the world, nor if he has no amusement to quicken the flow of his spirits from time to time: all these things, which touch more or less directly on his bodily condition, are born of the claim I make to live in good health; indeed, I suspect that these good conditions must have been in force for several generations before a population in general will be really healthy, as I have hinted above; but also I doubt not that in the course of time they would, joined to other conditions, of which more hereafter, gradually breed such a population, living in enjoyment of animal life at least, happy therefore, and beautiful according to the beauty of their race. On this point I may note that the very variations in the races of men are caused by the conditions under which they live, and though in these rougher parts of the world we lack some of the advantages of climate and surroundings, yet, if we were working for livelihood and not for profit, we might easily neutralize many of the disadvantages of our climate, at least enough to give due scope to the full development of our race.

Now the next thing I claim is education. And you must not say that every English child is educated now; that sort of education will not answer my claim, though I cheerfully admit it is something: something, and yet after all only class education. What I claim is liberal education; opportunity, that is, to have my share of whatever knowledge there is in the world according to my capacity or bent of mind, historical or scientific; and also to have my share of skill of hand which is about in the world, either in the industrial handicrafts or in the fine arts; picture-painting, sculpture, music, acting, or the like: I claim to be taught, if I can be taught, more than one craft to exercise for the benefit of the community. You may think this a large claim, but I am clear it is not too large a claim if the community is to have any gain out of my special capacities, if we are not all to be beaten down to a dull level of mediocrity as we are now, all but the very strongest and toughest of us.

But also I know that this claim for education involves one for public advantages in the shape of public libraries, schools, and the like, such as no private person, not even the richest, could command: but these I claim very confidently, being sure that no reasonable community could bear to be without such helps to a decent life.

Again, the claim for education involves a claim for abundant leisure, which once more I make with confidence; because when once we have shaken off the slavery of profit, labour would be organized so unwastefully that no heavy burden would be laid on the individual citizens; every one of whom as a matter of course would have to pay his toll of some obviously useful work.

At present you must note that all the amazing machinery which we have invented has served only to increase the amount of profit-bearing wares; in other words, to increase the amount of profit pouched by individuals for their own advantage, part of which profit they use as capital for the production of more profit, with ever the same waste attached to it; and part as private riches or means for luxurious living, which again is sheer waste—is in fact to be looked on as a kind of bonfire in which rich men burn up the product of the labour they have fleeced from the workers beyond what they themselves can use. So I say that, in spite of our inventions, no worker works under the present system an hour the less on account of those labour-saving machines, so-called. But under a happier state of things they would be used simply for saving labour, with the result of a vast amount of leisure gained for the community to be added to that gained by the avoidance of the waste of useless luxury, and the abolition of the service of commercial war.

And I may say that as to that leisure, as I should in no case do any harm to any one with it, so I should often do some direct good to the community with it, by practising arts or occupations for my hands or brain which would give pleasure to many of the citizens; in other words, a great deal of the best work done would be done in the leisure time of men relieved from any anxiety as to their livelihood, and eager to exercise their special talent, as all men, nay, all animals are.

Now, again, this leisure would enable me to please myself and expand my mind by travelling if I had a mind to it; because, say, for instance, that I were a shoemaker; if due social order were established, it by no means follows that I should always be obliged to make shoes in one place; a due amount of easily conceivable arrangement would enable me to make shoes in Rome, say, for three months, and to come back with new ideas of building, gathered from the sight of the works of past ages, amongst other things which would perhaps be of service in London.

But now, in order that my leisure might not degenerate into idleness and aimlessness, I must set up a claim for due work to do. Nothing to my mind is more important than this demand, and I must ask your leave to say something about it. I have mentioned that I should probably use my leisure for doing a good deal of what is now called work; but it is clear that if I am a member of a Socialist Community I must do my due share of rougher work than this—my due share of what my capacity enables me to do, that is; no fitting of me to a Procrustean bed; but even that share of work necessary to the existence of the simplest social life must, in the first place, whatever else it is, be reasonable work; that is, it must be such work as a good citizen can see the necessity for; as a member of the community, I must have agreed to do it.

To take two strong instances of the contrary, I won't submit to be dressed up in red and marched off to shoot at my French or German or Arab friend in a quarrel that I don't understand; I will rebel sooner than do that.

Nor will I submit to waste my time and energies in making some trifling toy which I know only a fool can desire; I will rebel sooner than do that.

However, you may be sure that in a state of social order I shall have no need to rebel against any such pieces of unreason; only I am forced to speak from the way we live to the way we might live.

Again, if the necessary reasonable work be of a mechanical kind, I must be helped to do it by a machine, not to cheapen my labour, but so that as little time as possible may be spent upon it, and that I may be able to think of other things while I am tending the machine. And if the work be specially rough or exhausting, you will, I am sure, agree with me in saying that I must take turns in doing it with other people; I mean I mustn't, for instance, be expected to spend my working hours always at the bottom of a coal-pit. I think such work as that ought to be largely volunteer work, and done, as I say, in spells. And what I say of very rough work I say also of nasty work. On the other hand, I should think very little of the manhood of a stout and healthy man who did not feel a pleasure in doing rough work; always supposing him to work under the conditions I have been speaking of—namely, feeling that it was useful (and consequently honoured), and that it was not continuous or hopeless, and that he was really doing it of his own free will.

The last claim I make for my work is that the places I worked in, factories or workshops, should be pleasant, just as the fields where our most necessary work is done are pleasant. Believe me there is nothing in the world to prevent this being done, save the necessity of making profits on all wares; in other words, the wares are cheapened at the expense of people being forced to work in crowded, unwholesome, squalid, noisy dens: that is to say, they are cheapened at the expense of the workman's life.

Well, so much for my claims as to my *necessary* work, my tribute to the community. I believe people would find, as they advanced in their capacity for carrying on social order, that life so lived was much less expensive than we now can have any idea of, and that, after a little, people would rather be anxious to seek work than to avoid it; that our working hours would rather be merry parties of men and maids, young men and old enjoying themselves over their work, than the grumpy weariness it mostly is now. Then would come the time for the new birth of art, so much talked of, so long deferred; people could not help showing their mirth and pleasure in their work, and would be always wishing to express it in a tangible and more or less enduring form, and the workshop would once more be a school of art, whose influence no one could escape from.

And, again, that word art leads me to my last claim, which is that the material surroundings of my life should be pleasant, generous, and beautiful; that I know is a large claim, but this I will say about it, that if it cannot be satisfied, if every civilized community cannot provide such surroundings for all its members, I do not want the world to go on; it is a mere misery that man has ever existed. I do not think it possible under the present circumstances to speak too strongly on this point. I feel sure that the time will come when people will find it difficult to believe that a rich community such as ours, having such command over external Nature, could have submitted to live such a mean, shabby, dirty life as we do.

And once for all, there is nothing in our circumstances save the hunting of profit that drives us into it. It is profit which draws men into enormous unmanageable aggregations called towns, for instance; profit which crowds them up when they are there into quarters without gardens or open spaces; profit which won't take the most ordinary precautions against wrapping a whole district in a cloud of sulphurous smoke; which turns beautiful rivers into filthy sewers, which condemns all but the rich to live in houses idiotically cramped and confined at the best, and at the worst in houses for whose wretchedness there is no name.

I say it is almost incredible that we should bear such crass stupidity as this; nor should we if we could help it. We shall not bear it when the workers get out of their heads that they are but an appendage to profit-grinding, that the more profits that are made the more employment at high wages there will be for them, and that therefore all the incredible filth, disorder, and degradation of modern civilization are signs of their prosperity. So far from that, they are signs of their slavery. When they are no longer slaves they will claim as a matter of course that every man and every family should be generously lodged; that every child should be able to play in a garden close to the place his parents live in; that the houses should by their obvious decency and order be ornaments to Nature, not disfigurements of it; for the decency and order above mentioned when carried to the due pitch would most assuredly lead to beauty in building. All this, of course, would mean the people—that is, all society—duly organized, having in its own hands the means of production, to be *owned* by no individual, but used by all as occasion called for its use, and can only be done on those terms; on any other terms people will be driven to accumulate private wealth for themselves, and thus, as we have seen, to waste the goods of the community and perpetuate the division into classes, which means continual war and waste.

As to what extent it may be necessary or desirable for people under social order to live in common, we may differ pretty much according to our tendencies towards social life. For my part I can't see why we should think it a hardship to eat with the people we work with; I am sure that as to many things, such as valuable books, pictures, and splendour of surroundings, we shall find it better to club our means together; and I must say that often when I have been sickened by the stupidity of the mean idiotic rabbit-warrens that rich men build for themselves in Bayswater and elsewhere, I console myself with visions of the noble communal hall of the future, unsparing of materials, generous in worthy ornament, alive with the noblest thoughts of our time, and the past, embodied in the best art which a free and manly people could produce; such an abode of man as no private enterprise could come anywhere near for beauty and fitness, because only collective thought and collective life could cherish the aspirations which would give birth to its beauty, or have the skill and leisure to carry them out. I for my part should think it much the reverse of a hardship if I had to read my books and meet my friends in such a place; nor do I think I am better off to live in a vulgar stuccoed house crowded with upholstery that I despise, in all respects degrading to the mind and enervating to the body to live in, simply because I call it my own, or my house.

It is not an original remark, but I make it here, that my home is where I meet people with whom I sympathize, whom I love.

Well, that is my opinion as a middle-class man. Whether a working-class man would think his family possession of his wretched little room better than his share of the palace of which I have spoken, I must leave to his opinion, and to the imagination of the middle class, who perhaps may sometimes conceive the fact that the said worker is cramped for space and comfort—say on washing-day.

Before I leave this matter of the surroundings of life, I wish to meet a possible objection. I have spoken of machinery being used freely for releasing people from the more mechanical and repulsive part of necessary labour; and I know that to some cultivated people, people of the artistic turn of mind, machinery is particularly distasteful, and they will be apt to say you will never get your surroundings pleasant so long as you are surrounded by machinery. I don't quite admit that; it is the allowing machines to be our masters and not our servants that so injures the beauty of life nowadays. In other words, it is the token of the terrible crime we have fallen into of using our control of the powers of Nature for the purpose of enslaving people, we care less meantime of how much happiness we rob their lives of.

Yet for the consolation of the artists I will say that I believe indeed that a state of social order would probably lead at first to a great development of machinery for really useful purposes, because people will still be anxious about getting through the work necessary to holding society together; but that after a while they will find that there is not so much work to do as they expected, and that then they will have leisure to reconsider the whole subject; and if it seems to them that a certain industry would be carried on more pleasantly as regards the worker, and more effectually as regards the goods, by using hand-work rather than machinery, they will certainly get rid of their machinery, because it will be possible for them to do so. It isn't possible now; we are not at liberty to do so; we are slaves to the monsters which we have created. And I have a kind of hope that the very elaboration of machinery in a society whose purpose is not the multiplication of labour, as it now is, but the carrying on of a pleasant life, as it would be under social order—that the elaboration of machinery, I say, will lead to the simplification of life, and so once more to the limitation of machinery.

Well, I will now let my claims for decent life stand as I have made them. To sum them up in brief, they are: First, a healthy body; second, an active mind in sympathy with the past, the present, and the future; thirdly, occupation fit for a healthy body and an active mind; and fourthly, a beautiful world to live in.

These are the conditions of life which the refined man of all ages has set before him as the thing above all others to be attained. Too often he has been so foiled in their pursuit that he has turned longing eyes backward to the days before civilization, when man's sole business was getting himself food from day to day, and hope was dormant in him, or at least could not be expressed by him.

Indeed, if civilization (as many think) forbids the realization of the hope to attain such conditions of life, then civilization forbids mankind to be happy; and if that be the case, then let us stifle all aspirations towards progress—nay, all feelings of mutual good-will and affection between men—and snatch each one of us what we can from the heap of wealth that fools create for rogues to grow fat on; or better still, let us as speedily as possible find some means of dying like men, since we are forbidden to live like men.

Rather, however, take courage, and believe that we of this age, in spite of all its torment and disorder, have been born to a wonderful heritage fashioned of the work of those that have gone before us; and that the day of the organization of man is dawning. It is not we who can build up the new social order; the past ages have done the most of that work for us; but we can clear our eyes to the signs of the times, and we shall then see that the attainment of a good condition of life is being made possible for us, and that it is now our business to stretch out our hands, to take it.

And how? Chiefly, I think, by educating people to a sense of their real capacities as men, so that they may be able to use to their own good the political power which is rapidly being thrust upon them; to get them to see that the old system of organizing labour for *individual profit* is becoming unmanageable, and that the whole people have now got to choose between the confusion resulting from the break up of that system and the determination to take in hand the labour now organized for profit, and use its organization for the livelihood of the community: to get people to see that individual profit-makers are not a necessity for labour but an obstruction to it, and that not only or chiefly because they are the perpetual pensioners of labour, as they are, but rather because of the waste which their existence as a class necessitates. All this we have to teach people, when we have taught ourselves; and I admit that the work is long and burdensome; as I began by saying, people have been made so timorous of change by the terror of starvation that even the unluckiest of them are stolid and hard to move. Hard as the work is, however, its reward is not doubtful. The mere fact that a body of men, however small, are banded together as Socialist missionaries shows that the change is going on. As the working-classes, the real organic part of society, take in these ideas, hope will arise in them, and they will claim changes in society, many of which doubtless will not tend directly towards their emancipation, because they will be claimed without due knowledge of the one thing necessary to claim, *equality of condition*; but which indirectly will help to break up our rotten sham society, while that claim for equality of condition will be made constantly and with growing loudness till it *must* be listened to, and then at last it will only be a step over the border, and the civilized world will be socialized; and, looking back on what has been, we shall be astonished to think of how long we submitted to live as we live now.

UNATTRACTIVE LABOUR

From 'Supplement to the *Commonweal*', May 1885

For our purpose of considering the relations of labour to industrial art, the wares made for the present day, the articles made for the market that is, may be divided into two classes—those that have some pretensions to be considered ornamental, and those that have not. The latter, I suppose, is much the larger class; but at any rate the important thing is to remember that there is this difference. Now it seems to me necessary to understand that everything made by man must be either ugly or beautiful. Neutrality is impossible in man's handiwork. But in times past, before the commercial age, it did not follow that a piece of handiwork was ugly because it did not aim at being ornamental; it had a certain use, which it fulfilled, and at the same time, without apparent effort of the maker, it was beautiful. *It grew so*, one may say exactly as a piece of Nature does. That is far from being the case now. In the wares which are made for utility only, it is rare that you find any beauty of form; they have a natural tendency to grow ugly, like a London starveling has. Even in the commonest things, such as fences in fields and other simple agricultural appliances, except for a few survivals, matters which have accidentally clung to old traditions, ugliness is the rule. An ordinary house, or piece of furniture or attire, is not only not beautiful, it is aggressively and actively ugly, and we assume as a matter of course that it must be so. And if we have a mind for any beauty (or pretence of it), we must make a definite effort; we must give our orders for an ornamental article to be made for us. And I may say, in passing, that, order as we please, we cannot always get our order executed. The sense of beauty and power of expressing it, under the present circumstances, is one of the rarest of gifts, so that the ordinary public have to put up with such pretence to beauty as the so-called ornamental class of wares can furnish to them. Therefore, while the rich man, by spending much money, can gather about him a certain amount of beauty, and while the man of moderate means may be able to attain the same end by taking an infinitude of trouble, the working man, who has no time to take trouble and no money to enable him to dispense with it, must put up with the lack of beauty altogether. Here, then, is a strange thing, that whereas in the pre-commercial ages we had beauty without paying for it, it has now become an article of the market, and, like most other market articles, is so shamefully adulterated that we can scarcely buy it even for our money.

I know that to many people this will seem a small matter, because only those (and how few they are!) who can make their surroundings decent can understand the full horror, the dullness and poverty of life which it involves. For my part, having regard to the general happiness of the race, I say without shrinking that the bloodiest of violent revolutions would be a light price to pay for the righting of this wrong.

For this is not a matter of accident, but springs from the form which the slavery of the many has taken in our days. It is but one of the consequences of wage-slavery. Until that wage-slavery was completed and crowned by the revolution of the great machine industries, there was some attractiveness in the work of the artisan. There is now none, or next to none; and the reason why the ornamental wares above-mentioned are so adulterated is because the very ornament itself is but a part of the machine labour, made to sell, and not for use, whether it be done by human machines or non-human ones. It is no exaggeration to say that our civilisation has destroyed the attractiveness of labour, and that by more means than one: by lengthening the hours of labour; by intensifying the labour during its continuance; by the forcing of the workmen into noisy, dirty, crowded factories; by the aggregation of the population into cities and manufacturing districts, and the consequent destruction of all beauty and decency of surroundings; by the levelling all intelligence and excellence of workmanship by means of machinery, and the consequent gradual extinction of the skilled craftsman. All this is the exact contrary of the conditions under which the spontaneous art of past ages was produced. Our forefathers of the Middle Ages worked shorter hours than we do (even since the passing of the Factory Acts) and had more holidays. They worked deliberately and thoughtfully as all artists do; they worked in their own homes and had plenty of elbow room; the unspoiled country came up to their very doors and, except in their dreams of hell—if even there—they could have had no conception of the glories of the Black Country or South Lancashire, which I heard a famous demagogue the other night enumerating among the blessings of peace, such peace as he could conceive of. Finally, all their work depended on their own skill of hand and invention, and never failed to show signs of that in its beauty and fitness; it was even thought wrong to cheat people by adulteration of goods, so that (strange to say) good work was creditable to the worker.

Thus the development of the commercial system crowned by the revolution of the great machine industries has deprived us of the attractiveness of labour, and as far as it could of the beauty of the earth. What, then, has it left us? The hope of revolution, of the transformation of civilisation, now become on the face of it a mere corruption and curse to the world, into Socialism, which will set free the hands and minds of men for the production and safe-guarding of the beauty of life.

I have said that our mediæval forefathers worked shorter hours than we do; but yet they worked far too long, and of course suffered from their special form of slavery, that is serfdom, and other arbitrary violence of the privileged classes, and their chances of successful rebellion were pretty much *nil*. It was necessary that they should struggle upwards till they formed a middle-class with its proletariat doomed to ceaseless unattractive dull labour, in place of the old yeoman and craftsguildsman with his pleasant easy-going work. Nevertheless, it is that proletariat only that can make good the claim of workmen to their share of art, without which no art can live long.

It is no real paradox to say that the unattractiveness of labour which is now the curse of the world will become the hope of the world. As long as the workman could sit at home, working easily and quietly, his long hours of labour mattered little to him, and other evils could be borne. Those evils, too, were visible and palpable to everyone and external to their lives; and the remedies were not far to seek. Peace instead of violence, equal rights before the law, these were things which people might hope their very masters would try to win for them.

But now that labour has become a mere burden, the disease of a class, that class will, by all means, try to throw it off, to lessen its weight, and in their efforts to do so they must of necessity destroy society, which is founded on the patient bearing of that burden. For there is no longer, as in the days of feudal violence, any means of relieving them of the burden while our present society exists. True, their masters, taught prudence by fear, will try, are trying, various means to make the workers bear their burden; but one after the other they will be found out and discredited. Philanthropy has had its day and is gone; thrift and self-help are going; participation in *profits*, parliamentarism and universal suffrage, State Socialism will have to go the same road, and the workers will be face to face at last with the fact that modern civilisation with its elaborate hierarchy and iron drill is founded on their intolerable burden, and then no shortening of the day's work which would leave profit to their employer will make their labour hours short enough. They will see that modern society can only exist as long as they bear their burden with some degree of patience, their patience will be worn out, and to pieces will modern society go.

And I repeat, that to my mind, the unattractiveness of labour, which has been the necessary outcome of commercial industry, will have played a great part in this revolution; the price which commercialism will have to pay for depriving the worker of his share of art will be its own death.

ATTRACTIVE LABOUR

From 'Supplement to the *Commonweal*', June 1885

In what I wrote last month I tried to make it clear that under the wages-system labour is bound to be unattractive as well as excessive in quantity and underpaid. The creation of surplus value being the one aim of the employers of labour, they cannot for a moment trouble themselves as to whether the work which creates the surplus value is pleasurable to the worker or not. In fact in order to get the greatest amount possible of surplus value out of the work, and to make a profit in the teeth of competition, it is absolutely necessary that it should be done under such conditions as make (as I wrote in my last) a mere burden which nobody would endure unless upon compulsion. This is admitted on all hands, nay is loudly insisted upon by anti-Socialists. The necessity for the existence of class distinctions as a means of compelling people to work is always present in their thoughts; and no wonder, since the only type of worker that they can conceive of is the worker of to-day, degraded by centuries of forced labour, wearisome and hopeless. To such a man, indeed, ever fresh and fresh compulsion must be applied at any cost, at any risk, until the string breaks with the strain. It is no wonder that the bare idea of the destruction of the hierarchy of compulsion terrifies those who rejoice in our modern civilisation. But for us whose business is leading people towards the destruction of that hierarchy, who believe that men's morals, aspirations, and what not, are made by their material surroundings, there is no room for fear of the consequences of revolution. We do not *fear* for the transformation of civilisation, we *hope* for it; nay it is an assured hope for us which consoles us for the disappointments and griefs of the passing day, which makes 'life worth living' for us; and my reason for writing this is to do my best to quicken that hope in the minds of our comrades. For that purpose I want if I can to give a very light sketch of attractive labour which, of course, I presuppose is to be done not for the profit of a master but for the production of wealth for the use of ourselves and our neighbours.

I can see, without much straining, labour going on under quite the reverse of the circumstances which surround it at present, and yet the world none the poorer for it. It would, one might think, be possible in the first place for a man to choose the work which he could do best; which if he were a healthily constituted man in mind and body, would mean from the outset that his work would be no longer a mere burden to him, since everyone likes to do what he can do well; there is at least some pleasure in such work. This choice of work would not be difficult; for though it may seem under our present profit-ridden conditions that people have little choice in such matters, are listless and don't care what they do, so they can but live by it pretty easily—this state of mind is artificially produced by commercial tyranny. People's innate capacities are pretty much as various as their faces are; but individual character and varied capacity are not cherished by the system which tends to get rid of skilled labour altogether. If a man would live now, as a part of industrial economy, he must submit to be the hundredth part of a machine and swallow any longings he may have to exercise any special faculty.

But in a reasonable community these various capacities would be looked out for and cultivated; the industrial arts would be an essential part of all education, and not only would they be taught gradually and easily to children, and as a part of their pastime, but grown men also would have opportunities for learning more than one craft. There would be no reason for forcing them to practice one craft only all their lives long. Nay many, or most, men would be carrying on more than one occupation from day to day. Surely almost everyone would wish to take some share in field or garden work besides his indoor occupation, even if it were no more than helping to get in the harvest or save the hay; and such occasions would become really the joyous and triumphant festivals which the poets have dreamed of them as being, and of which pleasure there is still some hint or, it may be, survival in *barbarous* countries. But besides such obvious change in work as this, there could certainly be found useful outdoor occupation whereby a person could vary his or her indoor work; helping, for instance, in the work which has to do with the transit of foods. It needs but people to turn their attention to life and not to profit-scraping to find such opportunities.

This matter of fitting people's work to their capacities and not, as now, their capacities to their work, would be the most important reversal of the present system of labour. And though my hint about it has been put in a few words, I beg our readers to consider what a difference it would make in labour if it were carried out. It is not too much to say that the difference would be immeasurable; labour so set about would not differ in degree from our present labour but in kind. But to complete the change, two other elements are necessary: leisure and pleasantness of external surroundings. I need not say much about the first, it may be thought, since among the better-off part of the workers the struggle with the employers about the length of the working-day has been going on so long, and in our own times, so obviously; though even with these it has been and is being fought on the assumption that the wages-system is to endure for ever—that the hierarchy of compulsion is necessary and the shortening of the day's labour has really meant a mere raising of the day's wages.

As for real leisure in work, I am afraid I must say that working men do not know what it means; their work being generally an anxious, strained hurry of drudgery, varied by what the natural repulsion to such slavery is sure to bring about as a reflection of it, a listless dawdling through the day, when owing to the due driver not being to the fore they are able to indulge in it. Both of these miseries are miles apart from the way of working when people are not working for wages but for the wealth of the community: the work would be done deliberately and thoughtfully for the good's sake and not for the profit's sake, but cleanly and briskly too, under the influence of hope and the looking, not to next day's drudgery, but to this day's further pleasure by men saying, 'Let us get through with this job, and then on to the next piece of our life.' In work so done there is no slavery; whereas ordinary work now is nothing but slavery. It is only a question whether the slaves shall be idle or industrious. Perhaps on the whole, looking at the effect on the community, they had better be idle.

Work so done, with variety and intelligently, not intensified to the bursting point of the human machine, and yet with real workmanlike or rather artistic eagerness, but an interest added to life quite apart from its necessity; with such work to do we might even bear with equanimity as a temporary evil, some of the discomforts of our town life, though surely not the dreadful squalor which the hierarchy of compulsion condemns us to to-day. But there is no reason why we should bear with the discomforts; it is, for instance, only the necessity for making a profit that compels us to the wretched and even ridiculous want of elbow-room, which is the universal rule in factories.

The crowding up of factories into towns, or congeries of towns, is a thing which we shall refuse to bear when we work voluntarily and for the purpose of leading happy lives. A great deal of work is done on the workshop rather than the factory system. There is no sort of need for these workshops being heaped together in the mass of disorder and misery which we call a big town. Centres of a manageable size would afford all the necessary elements of life and refinement and movement when all were educated and had the leisure which alone can make education valuable, and had the intelligence which, pretty equally distributed between every knot of men and women, would not be repressed by sordid misery. The only thing which makes huge centres desirable to the privileged few at present, is that fact that the lives of the greater part of men are wasted in drudgery. On the other hand, where associated labour on the large scale was necessary, and the factory system in its fullest organisation had to be used, each of those factories highly improved as to the means of production, as it would be, should be itself a town. It should be no mere phalangstery on a philanthropical basis, arranged for the passing an existence somewhat better indeed than our helpless wage-slaves of the mill now live, but bare of the real joys of life; but it should contain in itself all the resources for a refined and well-occupied life—at once manly, restful and eager. There is no reason why it should not be beautiful itself, and the country about it might well be a garden. When we were working for our own wealth, and not the waste of others, we should surely think it well in spending part of our work on housing ourselves decently, and on taking care that we left behind our work no signs of the haste, bred by the terror of ruin and starvation, in the shape of smoke and ash-heaps and all the unutterable filth which now disgrace our manufacturing districts and distinctly brand the work done there for what it is—work done by helpless slaves for helpless masters.

But work done under such conditions as I have been trying to sketch out would, I am sure, be attractive to all except the exceptions, the monsters of vagabondage and loafing who are now bred by the excessive overwork which is the general lot of the workers or by the privileged idleness of the rich, and whose descendants might last through a few generations, but would soon melt into the general body of people living in the happy exercise of energy.

By such work and such life we should be set free from intestine warfare among ourselves for the nobler contest with Nature, and should find that she also, when conquered, would be our friend, and not our enemy.

From TWO LETTERS TO GEORGIANA BURNE-JONES, 1885

Millthorpe, 28 April, 1885

I have been getting on pretty well in Scotland, but whether pock-pudding prejudice or not, I can't bring myself to love that country, 'tis so raw-boned. But I had my reward by the journey (the first time in daylight) from Carlisle to Settle: 'tis true that the day was most splendid, but at any rate 'tis the pick of all England for beauty. I fared to feel as if I must live there, say somewhere near Kirkby Stephen, for a year or two before I die: even the building there is not bad; necessitous and rude, but looking like shelter and quiet. There is a good deal of this lovely country; the railway goes right up into the mountains among the sheepwalks: there was a little snow lying in bights of the highest crags. I needn't enlarge on an entry into the Yorkshire manufacturing country after this; but I was so elated by the beauty we had passed through that I did not feel it as much as usual. I read a queer book called 'After London' coming down: I rather liked it: absurd hopes curled round my heart as I read it. I rather wish I were thirty years younger: I want to see the game played out.

13 May 1885

I am in low spirits about the prospects of our 'party', if I can dignify a little knot of men by such a word. Scheu is, I fear, leaving London again, which is a great disappointment to me, but he must get work where he can. You see we are such a few, and hard as we work we don't seem to pick up people to take out places when we demit. All this you understand is only said about the petty skirmish of outposts, the fight of a corporal's guard, in which I am immediately concerned; I have more faith than a grain of mustard seed in the future history of 'civilization', which I *know* now is doomed to destruction, and probably before very long: what a joy it is to think of! and how often it consoles me to think of barbarism once more flooding the world, and real feelings and passions, however rudimentary, taking the place of our wretched hypocrisies. With this thought in my mind all the history of the past is lighted up and lives again to me. I used really to despair once because I thought what the idiots of our day call progress would go on perfecting itself: happily I know now that all that will have a sudden check—sudden in appearance I mean—'as it was in the days of Noë'.

THE VULGARIZATION OF OXFORD

To the Editor of the *Daily News*, 20 November 1885

Sir, — I have just read your too true article on the vulgarisation of Oxford, and I wish to ask if it is too late to appeal to the mercy of the 'Dons' to spare the few specimens of ancient town architecture which they have not yet had time to destroy, such, for example, as the little plaster houses in front of Trinity College or the beautiful houses left on the north side of Holywell-street. These are in their way as important as the more majestic buildings to which all the world makes pilgrimage. Oxford thirty years ago, when I first knew it, was full of these treasures; but Oxford 'culture' cynically contemptuous of the knowledge which it does not know, and steeped to the lips in the commercialism of the day, has made a clean sweep of most of them; but those that are left are of infinite value, and still give some character above that of Victoria-street or Bayswater to modern Oxford. Is it impossible, Sir, to make the authorities of Oxford, town and gown, see this, and stop the destruction? The present theory of the use to which Oxford should be put appears to be that it should be used as a huge upper public school for fitting lads of the upper and middle class for their laborious future of living on other people's labour. For my part I do not think this a lofty conception of the function of a University; but if it be the only admissible one nowadays, it is at least clear that it does not need the history and art of our forefathers which Oxford still holds to develop it. London, Manchester, Birmingham, or perhaps a rising city of Australia, would be a fitter place for the experiment, which it seems to me is too rough a one for Oxford. In sober truth, what speciality has Oxford if it is not the genius loci which our modern commercial dons are doing their best to destroy? One word on the subject of Dr Hornby and Eton. Is there no appeal against a brutality of which I dare not trust myself to write further? Is it impossible that the opinions of distinguished men or all kinds might move him? Surely a memorial might be got up which would express those opinions.—I am, Sir, yours obediently,

William Morris.
Kelmscott House,
Upper Mall,
Hammersmith

CHANTS FOR SOCIALISTS

BY

WILLIAM MORRIS.

CONTENTS:

The Day is Coming. | No Master.
The Voice of Toil. | All for the Cause.
The Message of the March Wind. | The March of the Workers.
Down Among the Dead Men.

LONDON:
40, BERNER STREET, COMMERCIAL ROAD, E.

1892.

PRICE ONE PENNY.

FIGURE 9. *Chants for Socialists*. Image ©Working Class Movement Library. This collection of Morris's chants was designed to be used at socialist gatherings and demonstrations. The first edition was 1885, and new songs were added to later editions. The Socialist League logo was designed by Walter Crane.

The Day Is Coming

Come hither lads, and hearken, for a tale there is to tell
Of the wonderful days a-coming when all shall be better than well.

And the tale shall be told of a country, a land in the midst of the sea,
And folk shall call it England in the days that are going to be.

There more than one in a thousand in the days that are yet to come, 5
Shall have some hope of the morrow, some joy of the ancient home.

For then—laugh not, but listen, to this strange tale of mine—
All folk that are in England shall be better lodged than swine.

Then a man shall work and bethink him, and rejoice in the deeds of
    his hand,
Nor yet come home in the even too faint and weary to stand. 10

Men in that time a-coming shall work and have no fear
For to-morrow's lack of earning and the hunger-wolf anear.

I tell you this for a wonder, that no man then shall be glad
Of his fellow's fall and mishap to snatch at the work he had.

For that which the worker winneth shall then be his indeed, 15
Nor shall half be reaped for nothing by him that sowed no seed.

O strange new wonderful justice! But for whom shall we gather the gain?
For ourselves and for each of our fellows, and no hand shall labour in vain.

Then all *mine* and all *thine* shall be *ours*, and no more shall any man crave
For riches that serve for nothing but to fetter a friend for a slave. 20

And what wealth then shall be left us when none shall gather gold
To buy his friend in the market, and pinch and pine the sold?

Nay, what save the lovely city, and the little house on the hill,
And the wastes and the woodland beauty, and the happy fields we till.

And the homes of ancient stories, the tombs of the mighty dead; 25
And the wise men seeking out marvels, and the poet's teeming head;

And the painter's hand of wonder; and the marvellous fiddle-bow,
And the banded choirs of music:—all those that do and know.

For all these shall be ours and all men's, nor shall any lack a share
Of the toil and the gain of living in the days when the world grows fair. 30

Ah! such are the days that shall be! But what are the deeds of to-day,
In the days of the years we dwell in, that wear our lives away?

Why, then, and for what are we waiting? There are three words to speak.
WE WILL IT, and what is the foeman but the dream-strong wakened
    and weak?

O why and for what are we waiting? while our brothers droop and die,   35
And on every wind of the heavens a wasted life goes by.

How long shall they reproach us where crowd on crowd they dwell,
Poor ghosts of the wicked city, the gold-crushed hungry hell?

Through squalid life they laboured, in sordid grief they died,
Those sons of a mighty mother, those props of England's pride.   40

They are gone; there is none can undo it, nor save our souls from
    the curse;
But many a million cometh, and shall they be better or worse?

It is we must answer and hasten, and open wide the door
For the rich man's hurrying terror, and the slow-foot hope of the poor.

Yea, the voiceless wrath of the wretched, and their unlearned discontent,   45
We must give it voice and wisdom till the waiting-tide be spent.

Come, then, since all things call us, the living and the dead
And o'er the weltering tangle a glimmering light is shed.

Come, then, let us cast off fooling, and put by ease and rest
For the CAUSE alone is worthy till the good days bring the best.   50

Come, join in the only battle wherein no man can fail,
Where whoso fadeth and dieth, yet his deed shall still prevail.

Ah! come, cast off all fooling, for this, at least we know:
That the Dawn and the Day is coming, and forth the Banners go.

All for the Cause

Hear a word, a word in season, for the day is drawing nigh,
When the Cause shall call upon us, some to live and some to die!

He that dies shall not die lonely, many an one hath gone before,
He that lives shall bear no burden heavier than the life they bore.

Nothing ancient is their story, e'en but yesterday they bled,   5
Youngest they of earth's beloved, last of all the valiant dead.

E'en the tidings we are telling was the tale they had to tell,
E'en the hope that our hearts cherish, was the hope for which they fell.

In the grave where tyrants thrust them, lies their labour and their pain,
But undying from their sorrow springeth up the hope again.   10

Mourn not therefore, nor lament it, that the world outlives their life;
Voice and vision yet they give us, making strong our hands for strife.

Some had name, and fame, and honour, learn'd they were, and wise
    and strong;
Some were nameless, poor, unlettered, weak in all but grief and wrong.

Named and nameless all live in us; one and all they lead us yet   15
Every pain to count for nothing, every sorrow to forget.

Hearken how they cry, 'O happy, happy ye that ye were born
'In the sad slow night's departing, in the rising of the morn.

'Fair the crown the Cause hath for you well to die or well to live
'Through the battle, through the tangle, peace to gain or peace to give.'   20

Ah, it may be! Oft meseemeth, in the days that yet shall be,
When no slave of gold abideth 'twixt the breadth of sea to sea,

Oft, when men and maids are merry, ere the sunlight leaves the earth,
And they bless the day beloved, all too short for all their mirth,

Some shall pause awhile and ponder on the bitter days of old,   25
Ere the toil of strife and battle overthrew the curse of gold;

Then 'twixt lips of loved and lover solemn thoughts of us shall rise;
We who once were fools and dreamers, then shall be the brave and wise.

There amidst the world new-builded shall our earthly deeds abide,
Though our names be all forgotten, and the tale of how we died.   30

Life or death then, who shall heed it, what we gain or what we lose?
Fair flies life amid the struggle, and the Cause for each shall choose.

Hear a word, a word in season, for the day is drawing nigh,
When the Cause shall call upon us, some to live and some to die!

The March of the Workers

(AIR: 'John Brown')

What is this, the sound and rumour? What is this that all men hear,
Like the wind in hollow valleys when the storm is drawing near,
Like the rolling on of ocean in the eventide of fear?
'Tis the people marching on.

Whither go they, and whence come they? What are these of whom ye tell?   5
In what country are they dwelling 'twixt the gates of heaven and hell?
Are they mine or thine for money? Will they serve a master well?
Still the rumour's marching on.
Hark the rolling of the thunder!
Lo the sun! and lo thereunder   10
Riseth wrath, and hope, and wonder,
And the host comes marching on.

Forth they come from grief and torment; on they wend toward health
and mirth,
All the wide world is their dwelling, every corner of the earth.
Buy them, sell them for thy service! Try the bargain what 'tis worth   15
For the days are marching on.

These are they who build thy houses, weave thy raiment, win thy wheat,
Smooth the rugged, fill the barren, turn the bitter into sweet,
All for thee this day—and ever. What reward for them is meet?
Till the host comes marching on.   20
Hark the rolling, etc.

Many a hundred years passed over have they laboured deaf and blind;
Never tidings reached their sorrow, never hope their toil might find.
Now at last they've heard and hear it, and the cry comes down the wind,
And their feet are marching on.   25

O ye rich men hear and tremble! for with words the sound is rife:
'Once for you and death we laboured; changed henceforward is the strife.
We are men and we shall battle for the world of men and life;
And our host is marching on.'
Hark the rolling, etc.   30

'Is it war, then? Will ye perish as the dry wood in the fire?
Is it peace? Then be ye of us, let your hope be our desire.
Come and live! For life awaketh, and the world shall never tire;
And hope is marching on.'

'On we march then, we the workers, and the rumour that ye hear 35
Is the blended sound of battle and deliv'rance drawing near;
For the hope of every creature is the banner that we bear,
     And the world is marching on,
    Hark the rolling of the thunder!
    Lo the sun! And lo thereunder 40
    Riseth wrath, and hope, and wonder,
     And the host comes marching on.

A Dream of John Ball

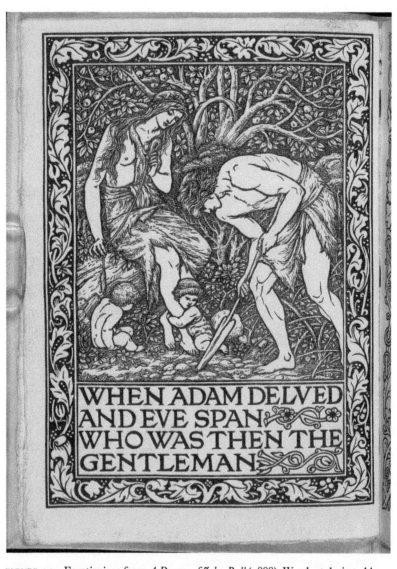

WHEN ADAM DELVED
AND EVE SPAN
WHO WAS THEN THE
GENTLEMAN

FIGURE 10. Frontispiece from *A Dream of John Ball* (1888). Woodcut designed by Edward Burne-Jones, engraved by W. H. Hooper.

Chapter I. The Men of Kent

Sometimes I am rewarded for fretting myself so much about present matters by a quite unasked-for pleasant dream. I mean when I am asleep. This dream is as it were a present of an architectural peep-show. I see some beautiful and noble building new made, as it were for the occasion, as clearly as if I were awake; not vaguely or absurdly, as often happens in dreams, but with all the detail clear and reasonable. Some Elizabethan house with its scrap of earlier fourteenth-century building, and its later degradations of Queen Anne and Silly Billy and Victoria, marring but not destroying it, in an old village once a clearing amid the sandy woodlands of Sussex. Or an old and unusually curious church, much churchwardened, and beside it a fragment of fifteenth-century domestic architecture amongst the not unpicturesque lath and plaster of an Essex farm, and looking natural enough among the sleepy elms and the meditative hens scratching about in the litter of the farmyard, whose trodden yellow straw comes up to the very jambs of the richly carved Norman doorway of the church. Or sometimes 'tis a splendid collegiate church, untouched by restoring parson and architect, standing amid an island of shapely trees and flower-beset cottages of thatched grey stone and cob, amidst the narrow stretch of bright green water-meadows that wind between the sweeping Wiltshire downs, so well beloved of William Cobbett. Or some new-seen and yet familiar cluster of houses in a grey village of the upper Thames overtopped by the delicate tracery of a fourteenth-century church; or even sometimes the very buildings of the past untouched by the degradation of the sordid utilitarianism that cares not and knows not of beauty and history: as once, when I was journeying (in a dream of the night) down the well-remembered reaches of the Thames betwixt Streatley and Wallingford, where the foothills of the White Horse fall back from the broad stream, I came upon a clear-seen mediæval town standing up with roof and tower and spire within its walls, grey and ancient, but untouched from the days of its builders of old. All this I have seen in the dreams of the night clearer than I can force myself to see them in dreams of the day. So that it would have been nothing new to me the other night to fall into an architectural dream if that were all, and yet I have to tell of things strange and new that befell me after I had fallen asleep. I had begun my sojourn in the Land of Nod by a very confused attempt to conclude that it was all right for me to have an engagement to lecture at Manchester and Mitcham Fair Green at half-past eleven at night on one and the same Sunday, and that I could manage pretty well. And then I had gone on to try to make the best of addressing a large open-air audience in the costume I was really then wearing—to wit, my night-shirt, reinforced for the dream occasion by a pair of braceless trousers. The consciousness of this fact so bothered me, that the earnest faces of my audience—who would *not* notice it, but were clearly preparing terrible anti-Socialist posers for me—began to fade away and my dream grew thin, and I awoke (as I thought) to find myself lying on a strip of wayside waste by an oak copse just outside a country village.

I got up and rubbed my eyes and looked about me, and the landscape seemed unfamiliar to me, though it was, as to the lie of the land, an ordinary English low-country, swelling into rising ground here and there. The road was narrow, and I was convinced that it was a piece of Roman road from its straightness. Copses were scattered over the country, and there were signs of two or three villages and hamlets in sight besides the one near me, between which and me there was some orchard-land, where the early apples were beginning to redden on the trees. Also, just on the other side of the road and the ditch which ran along it, was a small close of about a quarter of an acre, neatly hedged with quick, which was nearly full of white poppies, and, as far as I could see for the hedge, had also a good few rose-bushes of the bright-red nearly single kind, which I had heard are the ones from which rose-water used to be distilled. Otherwise the land was quite unhedged, but all under tillage of various kinds, mostly in small strips. From the other side of a copse not far off rose a tall spire white and brand-new, but at once bold in outline and unaffectedly graceful and also distinctly English in character. This, together with the unhedged tillage and a certain unwonted trimness and handiness about the enclosures of the garden and orchards, puzzled me for a minute or two, as I did not understand, new as the spire was, how it could have been designed by a modern architect; and I was of course used to the hedged tillage and tumble-down bankrupt-looking surroundings of our modern agriculture. So that the garden-like neatness and trimness of everything surprised me. But after a minute or two that surprise left me entirely; and if what I saw and heard afterwards seems strange to you, remember that it did not seem strange to me at the time, except where now and again I shall tell you of it. Also, once for all, if I were to give you the very words of those who spoke to me you would scarcely understand them, although their language was English too, and at the time I could understand them at once.

Well, as I stretched myself and turned my face toward the village, I heard horse-hoofs on the road, and presently a man and horse showed on the other end of the stretch of road and drew near at a swinging trot with plenty of clash of metal. The man soon came up to me, but paid me no more heed than throwing me a nod. He was clad in armour of mingled steel and leather, a sword girt to his side, and over his shoulder a long-handled bill-hook. His armour was fantastic in form and well wrought; but by this time I was quite used to the strangeness of him, and merely muttered to myself, 'He is coming to summon the squire to the leet'; so I turned toward the village in good earnest. Nor, again, was I surprised at my own garments, although I might well have been from their unwontedness. I was dressed in a black cloth gown reaching to my ankles, neatly embroidered about the collar and cuffs, with wide sleeves gathered in at the wrists; a hood with a sort of bag hanging down from it was on my head, a broad red leather girdle round my waist, on one side of which hung a pouch embroidered very prettily and a case made of hard leather chased with a hunting scene, which I knew to be a pen and ink case; on the other side a small sheath-knife, only an arm in case of dire necessity.

Well, I came into the village, where I did not see (nor by this time expected to see) a single modern building, although many of them were nearly new, notably the church, which was large, and quite ravished my heart with its extreme beauty, elegance, and fitness. The chancel of this was so new that the dust of the stone still lay white on the midsummer grass beneath the carvings of the windows. The houses were almost all built of oak frame-work filled with cob or plaster well whitewashed; though some had their lower stories of rubble-stone, with their windows and doors of well-moulded freestone. There was much curious and inventive carving about most of them; and though some were old and much worn, there was the same look of deftness and trimness, and even beauty, about every detail in them which I noticed before in the field-work. They were all roofed with oak shingles, mostly grown as grey as stone; but one was so newly built that its roof was yet pale and yellow. This was a corner house, and the corner post of it had a carved niche wherein stood a gaily painted figure holding an anchor—St. Clement to wit, as the dweller in the house was a blacksmith. Half a stone's throw from the east end of the churchyard wall was a tall cross of stone, new like the church, the head beautifully carved with a crucifix amidst leafage. It stood on a set of wide stone steps, octagonal in shape, where three roads from other villages met and formed a wide open space on which a thousand people or more could stand together with no great crowding.

All this I saw, and also that there was a goodish many people about, women and children, and a few old men at the doors, many of them somewhat gaily clad, and that men were coming into the village street by the other end to that by which I had entered, by twos and threes, most of them carrying what I could see were bows in cases of linen yellow with wax or oil; they had quivers at their backs, and most of them a short sword by their left side, and a pouch and knife on the right; they were mostly dressed in red or brightish green or blue cloth jerkins, with a hood on the head generally of another colour. As they came nearer I saw that the cloth of their garments was somewhat coarse, but stout and serviceable. I knew, somehow, that they had been shooting at the butts, and, indeed, I could still hear a noise of men thereabout, and even now and again when the wind set from that quarter the twang of the bowstring and the plump of the shaft in the target.

I leaned against the churchyard wall and watched these men, some of whom went straight into their houses and some loitered about still; they were rough-looking fellows, tall and stout, very black some of them, and some red-haired, but most had hair burnt by the sun into the colour of tow; and, indeed, they were all burned and tanned and freckled variously. Their arms and buckles and belts and the finishings and hems of their garments were all what we should now call beautiful, rough as the men were; nor in their speech was any of that drawling snarl or thick vulgarity which one is used to hear from labourers in civilisation; not that they talked like gentlemen either, but full and round and bold, and they were merry and good-tempered enough; I could see that, though I felt shy and timid amongst them.

One of them strode up to me across the road, a man some six feet high, with a short black beard and black eyes and berry-brown skin, with a huge bow in his hand bare of the case, a knife, a pouch, and a short hatchet, all clattering together at his girdle.

'Well, friend,' said he, 'thou lookest partly mazed; what tongue hast thou in thine head?'

'A tongue that can tell rhymes,' said I.

'So I thought,' said he. 'Thirstest thou any?'

'Yea, and hunger,' said I.

And therewith my hand went into my purse, and came out again with but a few small and thin silver coins with a cross stamped on each, and three pellets in each corner of the cross. The man grinned.

'Aha!' said he, 'is it so? Never heed it, mate. It shall be a song for a supper this fair Sunday evening. But first, whose man art thou?'

'No one's man,' said I, reddening angrily; 'I am my own master.'

He grinned again.

'Nay, that's not the custom of England, as one time belike it will be. Methinks thou comest from heaven down, and hast had a high place there too.'

He seemed to hesitate a moment, and then leant forward and whispered in my ear: '*John the Miller, that ground small, small, small,*' and stopped and winked at me, and from between my lips without my mind forming any meaning came the words, '*The king's son of heaven shall pay for all.*'

He let his bow fall on to his shoulder, caught my right hand in his and gave it a great grip, while his left hand fell among the gear at his belt, and I could see that he half drew his knife.

'Well, brother,' said he, 'stand not here hungry in the highway when there is flesh and bread in the "Rose" yonder. Come on.'

And with that he drew me along toward what was clearly a tavern door, outside which men were sitting on a couple of benches and drinking meditatively from curiously shaped earthen pots glazed green and yellow, some with quaint devices on them.

Chapter II. The Man from Essex

I entered the door and started at first with my old astonishment, with which I had woke up, so strange and beautiful did this interior seem to me, though it was but a pothouse parlour. A quaintly-carved side-board held an array of bright pewter pots and dishes and wooden and earthen bowls; a stout oak table went up and down the room, and a carved oak chair stood by the chimney-corner, now filled by a very old man dim-eyed and white-bearded. That, except the rough stools and benches on which the company sat, was all the furniture. The walls were panelled roughly enough with oak boards to about six feet from the floor, and about three feet of plaster above that was wrought in a pattern of a rose stem running all round the room, freely and roughly done, but with (as it seemed to my unused eyes) wonderful skill and spirit. On the hood of the great chimney a huge rose was wrought in the plaster and brightly painted in its proper colours. There were a dozen or more of the men I had seen coming along the street sitting there, some eating and all drinking; their cased bows leaned against the wall, their quivers hung on pegs in the panelling, and in a corner of the room I saw half-a-dozen bill-hooks that looked made more for war than for hedge-shearing, with ashen handles some seven foot long. Three or four children were running about among the legs of the men, heeding them mighty little in their bold play, and the men seemed little troubled by it, although they were talking earnestly and seriously too. A well-made comely girl leaned up against the chimney close to the gaffer's chair, and seemed to be in waiting on the company: she was clad in a close-fitting gown of bright blue cloth, with a broad silver girdle, daintily wrought, round her loins, a rose wreath was on her head and her hair hung down unbound; the gaffer grumbled a few words to her from time to time, so that I judged he was her grandfather.

The men all looked up as we came into the room, my mate leading me by the hand, and he called out in his rough, good-tempered voice, 'Here, my masters, I bring you tidings and a tale; give it meat and drink that it may be strong and sweet.'

'Whence are thy tidings, Will Green?' said one.

My mate grinned again with the pleasure of making his joke once more in a bigger company: 'It seemeth from heaven, since this good old lad hath no master,' said he.

'The more fool he to come here,' said a thin man with a grizzled beard, amidst the laughter that followed, 'unless he had the choice given him between hell and England.'

'Nay,' said I, 'I come not from heaven, but from Essex.'

As I said the word a great shout sprang from all mouths at once, as clear and sudden as a shot from a gun. For I must tell you that I knew somehow, but I know not how, that the men of Essex were gathering to rise against the poll-groat bailiffs and the lords that would turn them all into villeins again, as their grandfathers had been. And the people was weak and the lords were poor; for many a mother's son had fallen in the war in France in the old king's time, and the Black Death had slain a many; so that the lords had bethought them: 'We are growing poorer, and these upland-bred villeins are growing richer, and the Guilds of Craft are waxing in the towns, and soon what will there be left for us who cannot weave and will not dig? Good it were if we fell on all who are not guildsmen or men of free land, if we fell on soccage tenants and others, and brought both the law and the strong hand on them, and made them all villeins in deed as they are now in name; for now these rascals make more than their bellies need of bread, and their backs of homespun, and the overplus they keep to themselves; and we are more worthy of it than they. So let us get the collar on their necks again, and make their day's work longer and their bever-time shorter, as the good statute of the old king bade. And good it were if the Holy Church were to look to it (and the Lollards might help herein) that all these naughty and wearisome holidays were done away with; or that it should be unlawful for any man below the degree of a squire to keep the holy days of the church, except in the heart and the spirit only, and let the body labour meanwhile; for does not the Apostle say, "If a man work not, neither should he eat"? And if such things were done, and such an estate of noble rich men and worthy poor men upholden for ever, then would it be good times in England, and life were worth the living.'

All this were the lords at work on, and such talk I knew was common not only among the lords themselves, but also among their sergeants and very serving-men. But the people would not abide it; therefore, as I said, in Essex they were on the point of rising, and word had gone how that at St. Albans they were wellnigh at blows with the Lord Abbot's soldiers; that north away at Norwich John Litster was wiping the woad from his arms, as who would have to stain them red again, but not with grain or madder; and that the valiant tiler of Dartford had smitten a poll-groat bailiff to death with his lath-rending axe for mishandling a young maid, his daughter; and that the men of Kent were on the move.

Now, knowing all this I was not astonished that they shouted at the thought of their fellows the men of Essex, but rather that they said little more about it; only Will Green saying quietly, 'Well, the tidings shall be told when our fellowship is greater; fall-to now on the meat, brother, that we may the sooner have thy tale.' As he spoke the blue-clad damsel bestirred herself and brought me a clean trencher—that is, a square piece of thin oak board scraped clean—and a pewter pot of liquor. So without more ado, and as one used to it, I drew my knife out of my girdle and cut myself what I would of the flesh and bread on the table. But Will Green mocked at me as I cut, and said, 'Certes, brother, thou hast not been a lord's carver, though but for thy word thou mightest have been his reader. Hast thou seen Oxford, scholar?'

A vision of grey-roofed houses and a long winding street and the sound of many bells came over me at that word as I nodded 'Yes' to him, my mouth full of salt pork and rye-bread; and then I lifted my pot and we made the clattering mugs kiss and I drank, and the fire of the good Kentish mead ran through my veins and deepened my dream of things past, present, and to come, as I said: 'Now hearken a tale, since ye will have it so. For last autumn I was in Suffolk at the good town of Dunwich, and thither came the keels from Iceland, and on them were some men of Iceland, and many a tale they had on their tongues; and with these men I foregathered, for I am in sooth a gatherer of tales, and this that is now at my tongue's end is one of them.'

So such a tale I told them, long familiar to me; but as I told it the words seemed to quicken and grow, so that I knew not the sound of my own voice, and they ran almost into rhyme and measure as I told it; and when I had done there was silence awhile, till one man spake, but not loudly:

'Yea, in that land was the summer short and the winter long; but men lived both summer and winter; and if the trees grew ill and the corn throve not, yet did the plant called man thrive and do well. God send us such men even here.'

'Nay,' said another, 'such men have been and will be, and belike are not far from this same door even now.'

'Yea,' said a third, 'hearken a stave of Robin Hood; maybe that shall hasten the coming of one I wot of.' And he fell to singing in a clear voice, for he was a young man, and to a sweet wild melody, one of those ballads which in an incomplete and degraded form you have read perhaps. My heart rose high as I heard him, for it was concerning the struggle against tyranny for the freedom of life, how that the wild wood and the heath, despite of wind and weather, were better for a free man than the court and the cheaping-town; of the taking from the rich to give to the poor; of the life of a man doing his own will and not the will of another man commanding him for the commandment's sake. The men all listened eagerly, and at whiles took up as a refrain a couplet at the end of a stanza with their strong and rough, but not unmusical voices. As they sang, a picture of the wild-woods passed by me, as they were indeed, no park-like dainty glades and lawns, but rough and tangled thicket and bare waste and heath, solemn under the morning sun, and dreary with the rising of the evening wind and the drift of the night-long rain.

When he had done, another began in something of the same strain, but singing more of a song than a story ballad; and thus much I remember of it:

> The Sheriff is made a mighty lord,
>   Of goodly gold he hath enow,
> And many a sergeant girt with sword;
>   But forth will we and bend the bow.

> We shall bend the bow on the lily lea   5
>   Betwixt the thorn and the oaken tree.
>
> With stone and lime is the burg wall built,
>   And pit and prison are stark and strong,
>   And many a true man there is spilt,
> And many a right man doomed by wrong.   10
>   So forth shall we and bend the bow
>   And the king's writ never the road shall know.
>
> Now yeomen walk ye warily,
>   And heed ye the houses where ye go,
> For as fair and as fine as they may be,   15
>   Lest behind your heels the door clap to.
>   Fare forth with the bow to the lily lea
>   Betwixt the thorn and the oaken tree.
>
> Now bills and bows! and out a-gate!
>   And turn about on the lily lea!   20
> And though their company be great
>   The grey-goose wing shall set us free.
>   Now bent is the bow in the green abode
>   And the king's writ knoweth not the road.
>
> So over the mead and over the hithe,   25
>   And away to the wild-wood wend we forth;
> There dwell we yeomen bold and blithe
>   Where the Sheriff's word is nought of worth.
>   Bent is the bow on the lily lea
>   Betwixt the thorn and the oaken tree.   30

But here the song dropped suddenly, and one of the men held up his hand as who would say, Hist! Then through the open window came the sound of another song, gradually swelling as though sung by men on the march. This time the melody was a piece of the plain-song of the church, familiar enough to me to bring back to my mind the great arches of some cathedral in France and the canons singing in the choir.

All leapt up and hurried to take their bows from wall and corner; and some had bucklers withal, circles of leather, boiled and then moulded into shape and hardened: these were some two hand-breadths across, with iron or brass bosses in the centre. Will Green went to the corner where the bills leaned against the wall and handed them round to the first comers as far as they would go, and out we all went gravely and quietly into the village street and the fair sunlight of the calm afternoon, now beginning to turn towards evening. None had said anything since we first heard the new-come singing, save that as we went out of the door the ballad-singer clapped me on the shoulder and said:

'Was it not sooth that I said, brother, that Robin Hood should bring us John Ball?'

Chapter III. They Meet at the Cross

The street was pretty full of men by then we were out in it, and all faces turned toward the cross. The song still grew nearer and louder, and even as we looked we saw it turning the corner through the hedges of the orchards and closes, a good clump of men, more armed, as it would seem, than our villagers, as the low sun flashed back from many points of bright iron and steel. The words of the song could now be heard, and amidst them I could pick out Will Green's late challenge to me and my answer; but as I was bending all my mind to disentangle more words from the music, suddenly from the new white tower behind us clashed out the church bells, harsh and hurried at first, but presently falling into measured chime; and at the first sound of them a great shout went up from us and was echoed by the new-comers, 'John Ball hath rung our bell!' Then we pressed on, and presently we were all mingled together at the cross.

Will Green had good-naturedly thrust and pulled me forward, so that I found myself standing on the lowest step of the cross, his seventy-two inches of man on one side of me. He chuckled while I panted, and said:

'There's for thee a good hearing and seeing stead, old lad. Thou art tall across thy belly and not otherwise, and thy wind, belike, is none of the best, and but for me thou wouldst have been amidst the thickest of the throng, and have heard words muffled by Kentish bellies and seen little but swinky woollen elbows and greasy plates and jacks. Look no more on the ground, as though thou sawest a hare, but let thine eyes and thine ears be busy to gather tidings to bear back to Essex—or heaven!'

I grinned good-fellowship at him but said nothing, for in truth my eyes and ears were as busy as he would have them to be. A buzz of general talk went up from the throng amidst the regular cadence of the bells, which now seemed far away and as it were that they were not swayed by hands, but were living creatures making that noise of their own wills.

I looked around and saw that the newcomers mingled with us must have been a regular armed band; all had bucklers slung at their backs, few lacked a sword at the side. Some had bows, some 'staves'—that is, bills, pole-axes, or pikes. Moreover, unlike our villagers, they had defensive arms. Most had steel-caps on their heads, and some had body armour, generally a 'jack,' or coat into which pieces of iron or horn were quilted; some had also steel or steel-and-leather arm or thigh pieces. There were a few mounted men among them, their horses being big-boned hammer-headed beasts, that looked as if they had been taken from plough or waggon, but their riders were well armed with steel armour on their heads, legs, and arms. Amongst the horsemen I noted the man that had ridden past me when I first awoke; but he seemed to be a prisoner, as he had a woollen hood on his head instead of his helmet, and carried neither bill, sword, nor dagger. He seemed by no means ill-at-ease, however, but was laughing and talking with the men who stood near him.

Above the heads of the crowd, and now slowly working towards the cross, was a banner on a high-raised cross-pole, a picture of a man and woman half-clad in skins of beasts seen against a background of green trees, the man holding a spade and the woman a distaff and spindle rudely done enough, but yet with a certain spirit and much meaning; and underneath this symbol of the early world and man's first contest with nature were the written words:

> When Adam delved and Eve span
> Who was then the gentleman?

The banner came on and through the crowd, which at last opened where we stood for its passage, and the banner-bearer turned and faced the throng and stood on the first step of the cross beside me.

A man followed him, clad in a long dark-brown gown of coarse woollen, girt with a cord, to which hung a 'pair of beads' (or rosary, as we should call it to-day) and a book in a bag. The man was tall and big-boned, a ring of dark hair surrounded his priest's tonsure; his nose was big but clear cut and with wide nostrils; his shaven face showed a longish upper lip and a big but blunt chin; his mouth was big and the lips closed firmly; a face not very noteworthy but for his grey eyes well opened and wide apart, at whiles lighting up his whole face with a kindly smile, at whiles set and stern, at whiles resting in that look as if they were gazing at something a long way off, which is the wont of the eyes of the poet or enthusiast.

He went slowly up the steps of the cross and stood at the top with one hand laid on the shaft, and shout upon shout broke forth from the throng. When the shouting died away into a silence of the human voices, the bells were still quietly chiming with that far-away voice of theirs, and the long-winged dusky swifts, by no means scared by the concourse, swung round about the cross with their wild squeals; and the man stood still for a little, eyeing the throng, or rather looking first at one and then another man in it, as though he were trying to think what such an one was thinking of, or what he were fit for. Sometimes he caught the eye of one or other, and then that kindly smile spread over his face, but faded off it into the sternness and sadness of a man who has heavy and great thoughts hanging about him.

But when John Ball first mounted the steps of the cross a lad at some one's bidding had run off to stop the ringers, and so presently the voice of the bells fell dead, leaving on men's minds that sense of blankness or even disappointment which is always caused by the sudden stopping of a sound one has got used to and found pleasant. But a great expectation had fallen by now on all that throng, and no word was spoken even in a whisper, and all men's hearts and eyes were fixed upon the dark figure standing straight up now by the tall white shaft of the cross, his hands stretched out before him, one palm laid upon the other. And for me, as I made ready to hearken, I felt a joy in my soul that I had never yet felt.

Chapter IV. The Voice of John Ball

So now I heard John Ball; how he lifted up his voice and said:

'Ho, all ye good people! I am a priest of God, and in my day's work it cometh that I should tell you what ye should do, and what ye should forbear doing, and to that end I am come hither: yet first, if I myself have wronged any man here, let him say wherein my wrongdoing lieth, that I may ask his pardon and his pity.'

A great hum of good-will ran through the crowd as he spoke; then he smiled as in a kind of pride, and again he spoke:

'Wherefore did ye take me out of the archbishop's prison but three days agone, when ye lighted the archbishop's house for the candle of Canterbury, but that I might speak to you and pray you: therefore I will not keep silence, whether I have done ill, or whether I have done well. And herein, good fellows and my very brethren, I would have you to follow me; and if there be such here, as I know full well there be some, and may be a good many, who have been robbers of their neighbours ("And who is my neighbour?" quoth the rich man), or lechers, or despiteful haters, or talebearers, or fawners on rich men for the hurt of the poor (and that is the worst of all)—Ah, my poor brethren who have gone astray, I say not to you, go home and repent lest you mar our great deeds, but rather come afield and there repent. Many a day have ye been fools, but hearken unto me and I shall make you wise above the wisdom of the earth; and if ye die in your wisdom, as God wot ye well may, since the fields ye wend to bear swords for daisies, and spears for bents, then shall ye be, though men call you dead, a part and parcel of the living wisdom of all things, very stones of the pillars that uphold the joyful earth.

'Forsooth, ye have heard it said that ye shall do well in this world that in the world to come ye may live happily for ever; do ye well then, and have your reward both on earth and in heaven; for I say to you that earth and heaven are not two but one; and this one is that which ye know, and are each one of you a part of, to wit, the Holy Church, and in each one of you dwelleth the life of the church, unless ye slay it. Forsooth, brethren, will ye murder the church any one of you, and go forth a wandering man and lonely, even as Cain did who slew his brother? Ah, my brothers, what an evil doom is this, to be an outcast from the Church, to have none to love you and to speak with you, to be without fellowship! Forsooth, brothers, fellowship is heaven, and lack of fellowship is hell: fellowship is life, and lack of fellowship is death: and the deeds that ye do upon the earth, it is for fellowship's sake that ye do them, and the life that is in it, that shall live on and on for ever, and each one of you part of it, while many a man's life upon the earth from the earth shall wane.

'Therefore, I bid you not dwell in hell but in heaven, or while ye must, upon earth, which is a part of heaven, and forsooth no foul part.

'Forsooth, he that waketh in hell and feeleth his heart fail him, shall have memory of the merry days of earth, and how that when his heart failed him there, he cried on his fellow, were it his wife or his son or his brother or his gossip or his brother sworn in arms, and how that his fellow heard him and came and they mourned together under the sun, till again they laughed together and were but half sorry between them. This shall he think on in hell, and cry on his fellow to help him, and shall find that therein is no help because there is no fellowship, but every man for himself. Therefore, I tell you that the proud, despiteous rich man, though he knoweth it not, is in hell already, because he hath no fellow; and he that hath so hardy a heart that in sorrow he thinketh of fellowship, his sorrow is soon but a story of sorrow—a little change in the life that knows not ill.'

He left off for a little; and indeed for some time his voice had fallen, but it was so clear and the summer evening so soft and still, and the silence of the folk so complete, that every word told. His eyes fell down to the crowd as he stopped speaking, since for some little while they had been looking far away into the blue distance of summer; and the kind eyes of the man had a curious sight before him in that crowd, for amongst them were many who by this time were not dry-eyed, and some wept outright in spite of their black beards, while all had that look as if they were ashamed of themselves, and did not want others to see how deeply they were moved, after the fashion of their race when they are strongly stirred. I looked at Will Green beside me: his right hand clutched his bow so tight, that the knuckles whitened; he was staring straight before him, and the tears were running out of his eyes and down his big nose as though without his will, for his face was stolid and unmoved all the time, till he caught my eye, and then he screwed up the strangest face, of scowling brow, weeping eyes, and smiling mouth, while he dealt me a sounding thump in the ribs with his left elbow, which, though it would have knocked me down but for the crowd, I took as an esquire does the accolade which makes a knight of him.

But while I pondered all these things, and how men fight and lose the battle, and the thing that they fought for comes about in spite of their defeat, and when it comes turns out not to be what they meant, and other men have to fight for what they meant under another name—while I pondered all this, John Ball began to speak again in the same soft and clear voice with which he had left off.

'Good fellows, it was your fellowship and your kindness that took me out of the archbishop's prison three days agone, though God wot ye had nought to gain by it save outlawry and the gallows; yet lacked I not your fellowship before ye drew near me in the body, and when between me and Canterbury street was yet a strong wall, and the turnkeys and sergeants and bailiffs.

'For hearken, my friends and helpers; many days ago, when April was yet young, I lay there, and the heart that I had strung up to bear all things because of the fellowship of men and the blessed saints and the angels and those that are, and those that are to be, this heart, that I had strung up like a strong bow, fell into feebleness, so that I lay there a-longing for the green fields and the white-thorn bushes and the lark singing over the corn, and the talk of good fellows round the ale-house bench, and the babble of the little children, and the team on the road and the beasts afield, and all the life of earth; and I alone all the while, near my foes and afar from my friends, mocked and flouted and starved with cold and hunger; and so weak was my heart that though I longed for all these things yet I saw them not, nor knew them but as names; and I longed so sore to be gone that I chided myself that I had once done well; and I said to myself:

'Forsooth hadst thou kept thy tongue between thy teeth thou mightest have been something, if it had been but a parson of a town, and comfortable to many a poor man; and then mightest thou have clad here and there the naked back, and filled the empty belly, and holpen many, and men would have spoken well of thee, and of thyself thou hadst thought well; and all this hast thou lost for lack of a word here and there to some great man, and a little winking of the eyes amidst murder and wrong and unruth; and now thou art nought and helpless, and the hemp for thee is sown and grown and heckled and spun, and lo there, the rope for thy gallows-tree!—all for nought, for nought.

'Forsooth, my friends, thus I thought and sorrowed in my feebleness that I had not been a traitor to the Fellowship of the church, for e'en so evil was my foolish imagination.

'Yet, forsooth, as I fell a-pondering over all the comfort and help that I might have been and that I might have had, if I had been but a little of a trembling cur to creep and crawl before abbot and bishop and baron and bailiff, came the thought over me of the evil of the world wherewith I, John Ball, the rascal hedge-priest, had fought and striven in the Fellowship of the saints in heaven and poor men upon earth.

'Yea, forsooth, once again I saw as of old, the great treading down the little, and the strong beating down the weak, and cruel men fearing not, and kind men daring not, and wise men caring not; and the saints in heaven forbearing and yet bidding me not to forbear; forsooth, I knew once more that he who doeth well in fellowship, and because of fellowship, shall not fail though he seem to fail to-day, but in days hereafter shall he and his work yet be alive, and men be holpen by them to strive again and yet again; and yet indeed even that was little, since, forsooth, to strive was my pleasure and my life.

'So I became a man once more, and I rose up to my feet and went up and down my prison what I could for my hopples, and into my mouth came words of good cheer, even such as we to-day have sung, and stoutly I sang them, even as we now have sung them; and then did I rest me, and once more thought of those pleasant fields where I would be, and all the life of man and beast about them, and I said to myself that I should see them once more before I died, if but once it were.

'Forsooth, this was strange, that whereas before I longed for them and yet saw them not, now that my longing was slaked my vision was cleared, and I saw them as though the prison walls opened to me and I was out of Canterbury street and amidst the green meadows of April; and therewithal along with me folk that I have known and who are dead, and folk that are living; yea, and all those of the Fellowship on earth and in heaven; yea, and all that are here this day. Overlong were the tale to tell of them, and of the time that is gone.

'So thenceforward I wore through the days with no such faint heart, until one day the prison opened verily and in the daylight, and there were ye, my fellows, in the door—your faces glad, your hearts light with hope, and your hands heavy with wrath; then I saw and understood what was to do. Now, therefore, do ye understand it!'

His voice was changed, and grew louder than loud now, as he cast his hands abroad towards that company with those last words of his; and I could feel that all shame and fear was falling from those men, and that mere fiery manhood was shining through their wonted English shamefast stubbornness, and that they were moved indeed and saw the road before them. Yet no man spoke, rather the silence of the menfolk deepened, as the sun's rays grew more level and more golden, and the swifts wheeled about shriller and louder than before.

Then again John Ball spoke and said, 'In good sooth, I deem ye wot no worse than I do what is to do—and first that somewhat we shall do—since it is for him that is lonely or in prison to dream of fellowship, but for him that is of a fellowship to do and not to dream.

'And next, ye know who is the foeman, and that is the proud man, the oppressor, who scorneth fellowship, and himself is a world to himself and needeth no helper nor helpeth any, but, heeding no law, layeth law on other men because he is rich; and surely every one that is rich is such an one, nor may be other.

'Forsooth, in the belly of every rich man dwelleth a devil of hell, and when the man would give his goods to the poor, the devil within him gainsayeth it, and saith, "Wilt thou then be of the poor, and suffer cold and hunger and mocking as they suffer, then give thou thy goods to them, and keep them not." And when he would be compassionate, again saith the devil to him, "If thou heed these losels and turn on them a face like to their faces, and deem of them as men, then shall they scorn thee, and evil shall come of it, and even one day they shall fall on thee to slay thee when they have learned that thou art but as they be."

'Ah, woe worth the while! too oft he sayeth sooth, as the wont of the devil is, that lies may be born of the barren truth; and sooth it is that the poor deemeth the rich to be other than he, and meet to be his master, as though, forsooth, the poor were come of Adam, and the rich of him that made Adam, that is God; and thus the poor man oppresseth the poor man, because he feareth the oppressor. Nought such are ye, my brethren; or else why are ye gathered here in harness to bid all bear witness of you that ye are the sons of one man and one mother, begotten of the earth?'

As he said the words there came a stir among the weapons of the throng, and they pressed closer round the cross, yet withheld the shout as yet which seemed gathering in their bosoms.

And again he said:

'Forsooth, too many rich men there are in this realm; and yet if there were but one, there would be one too many, for all should be his thralls. Hearken, then, ye men of Kent. For overlong belike have I held you with words; but the love of you constrained me, and the joy that a man hath to babble to his friends and his fellows whom he hath not seen for a long season.

'Now, hearken, I bid you: To the rich men that eat up a realm there cometh a time when they whom they eat up, that is the poor, seem poorer than of wont, and their complaint goeth up louder to the heavens; yet it is no riddle to say that oft at such times the fellowship of the poor is waxing stronger, else would no man have heard his cry. Also at such times is the rich man become fearful, and so waxeth in cruelty, and of that cruelty do people misdeem that it is power and might waxing. Forsooth, ye are stronger than your fathers, because ye are more grieved than they, and ye should have been less grieved than they had ye been horses and swine; and then, forsooth, would ye have been stronger to bear; but ye, ye are not strong to bear, but to do.

'And wot ye why we are come to you this fair eve of holiday? and wot ye why I have been telling of fellowship to you? Yea, forsooth, I deem ye wot well, that it is for this cause, that ye might bethink you of your fellowship with the men of Essex.'

His last word let loose the shout that had been long on all men's lips, and great and fierce it was as it rang shattering through the quiet upland village. But John Ball held up his hand, and the shout was one and no more.

Then he spoke again:

'Men of Kent, I wot well that ye are not so hard bested as those of other shires, by the token of the day when behind the screen of leafy boughs ye met Duke William with bill and bow as he wended Londonward from that woeful field of Senlac; but I have told of fellowship, and ye have hearkened and understood what the Holy Church is, whereby ye know that ye are fellows of the saints in heaven and the poor men of Essex; and as one day the saints shall call you to the heavenly feast, so now do the poor men call you to the battle.

'Men of Kent, ye dwell fairly here, and your houses are framed of stout oak beams, and your own lands ye till; unless some accursed lawyer with his false lying sheepskin and forged custom of the Devil's Manor hath stolen it from you; but in Essex slaves they be and villeins, and worse they shall be, and the lords swear that ere a year be over ox and horse shall go free in Essex, and man and woman shall draw the team and the plough; and north away in the east countries dwell men in poor halls of wattled reeds and mud, and the north-east wind from off the fen whistles through them; and poor they be to the letter; and there him whom the lord spareth, the bailiff squeezeth, and him whom the bailiff forgetteth, the Easterling Chapman sheareth; yet be these stout men and valiant, and your very brethren.

'And yet if there be any man here so base as to think that a small matter, let him look to it that if these necks abide under the yoke, Kent shall sweat for it ere it be long; and ye shall lose acre and close and woodland, and be servants in your own houses, and your sons shall be the lords' lads, and your daughters their lemans, and ye shall buy a bold word with many stripes, and an honest deed with a leap from the gallows-tree.

'Bethink ye, too, that ye have no longer to deal with Duke William, who, if he were a thief and a cruel lord, was yet a prudent man and a wise warrior; but cruel are these, and headstrong, yea, thieves and fools in one—and ye shall lay their heads in the dust.'

A shout would have arisen again, but his eager voice rising higher yet, restrained it as he said:

'And how shall it be then when these are gone? What else shall ye lack when ye lack masters? Ye shall not lack for the fields ye have tilled, nor the houses ye have built, nor the cloth ye have woven; all these shall be yours, and whatso ye will of all that the earth beareth; then shall no man mow the deep grass for another, while his own kine lack cow-meat; and he that soweth shall reap, and the reaper shall eat in fellowship the harvest that in fellowship he hath won; and he that buildeth a house shall dwell in it with those that he biddeth of his free will; and the tithe barn shall garner the wheat for all men to eat of when the seasons are untoward, and the rain-drift hideth the sheaves in August; and all shall be without money and without price. Faithfully and merrily then shall all men keep the holidays of the Church in peace of body and joy of heart.

And man shall help man, and the saints in heaven shall be glad, because men no more fear each other; and the churl shall be ashamed, and shall hide his churlishness till it be gone, and he be no more a churl; and fellowship shall be established in heaven and on the earth.'

Chapter V. They Hear Tidings of Battle and Make Them Ready

He left off as one who had yet something else to say; and, indeed, I thought he would give us some word as to the trysting-place, and whither the army was to go from it; because it was now clear to me that this gathering was but a band of an army. But much happened before John Ball spoke again from the cross, and it was on this wise.

When there was silence after the last shout that the crowd had raised a while ago, I thought I heard a thin sharp noise far away, somewhat to the north of the cross, which I took rather for the sound of a trumpet or horn, than for the voice of a man or any beast. Will Green also seemed to have heard it, for he turned his head sharply and then back again, and looked keenly into the crowd as though seeking to catch some one's eye. There was a very tall man standing by the prisoner on the horse near the outskirts of the crowd, and holding his bridle. This man, who was well-armed, I saw look up and say something to the prisoner, who stooped down and seemed to whisper him in turn. The tall man nodded his head and the prisoner got off his horse, which was a cleaner-limbed, better-built beast than the others belonging to the band, and the tall man quietly led him a little way from the crowd, mounted him, and rode off northward at a smart pace.

Will Green looked on sharply at all this, and when the man rode off, smiled as one who is content, and deems that all is going well, and settled himself down again to listen to the priest.

But now when John Ball had ceased speaking, and after another shout, and a hum of excited pleasure and hope that followed it, there was silence again, and as the priest addressed himself to speaking once more, he paused and turned his head towards the wind, as if he heard something, which certainly I heard, and belike every one in the throng, though it was not over-loud, far as sounds carry in clear quiet evenings. It was the thump-a-thump of a horse drawing near at a hand-gallop along the grassy upland road; and I knew well it was the tall man coming back with tidings, the purport of which I could well guess.

I looked up at Will Green's face. He was smiling as one pleased, and said softly as he nodded to me, 'Yea, shall we see the grey-goose fly this eve?'

But John Ball said in a great voice from the cross, 'Hear ye the tidings on the way, fellows! Hold ye together and look to your gear; yet hurry not, for no great matter shall this be. I wot well there is little force between Canterbury and Kingston, for the lords are looking north of Thames toward Wat Tyler and his men. Yet well it is, well it is!'

The crowd opened and spread out a little, and the men moved about in it, some tightening a girdle, some getting their side arms more within reach of their right hands, and those who had bows stringing them.

Will Green set hand and foot to the great shapely piece of polished red yew, with its shining horn tips, which he carried, and bent it with no seeming effort; then he reached out his hand over his shoulder and drew out a long arrow, smooth, white, beautifully balanced, with a barbed iron head at one end, a horn nock and three strong goose feathers at the other. He held it loosely between the finger and thumb of his right hand, and there he stood with a thoughtful look on his face, and in his hands one of the most terrible weapons which a strong man has ever carried, the English long-bow and cloth-yard shaft.

But all this while the sound of the horse's hoofs was growing nearer, and presently from the corner of the road amidst the orchards broke out our long friend, his face red in the sun near sinking now. He waved his right hand as he came in sight of us, and sang out, 'Bills and bows! bills and bows!' and the whole throng turned towards him and raised a great shout.

He reined up at the edge of the throng, and spoke in a loud voice, so that all might hear him:

'Fellows, these are the tidings; even while our priest was speaking we heard a horn blow far off; so I bade the sergeant we have taken, and who is now our fellow-in-arms, to tell me where away it was that there would be folk a-gathering, and what they were; and he did me to wit that mayhappen Sir John Newton was stirring from Rochester Castle; or, maybe, it was the sheriff and Rafe Hopton with him; so I rode off what I might towards Hartlip, and I rode warily, and that was well, for as I came through a little wood between Hartlip and Guildstead, I saw beyond it a gleam of steel, and lo in the field there a company, and a pennon of Rafe Hopton's arms, and that is blue and thereon three silver fish: and a pennon of the sheriff's arms, and that is a green tree; and withal another pennon of three red kine, and whose they be I know not.*

'There tied I my horse in the middle of the wood, and myself I crept along the dyke to see more and to hear somewhat; and no talk I heard to tell of save at whiles a big knight talking to five or six others, and saying somewhat, wherein came the words London and Nicholas Bramber, and King Richard; but I saw that of men-at-arms and sergeants there might be a hundred, and of bows not many, but of those outland arbalests maybe a fifty; and so, what with one and another of servants and tipstaves and lads, some three hundred, well armed, and the men-at-arms of the best. Forsooth, my masters, there had I been but a minute, ere the big knight broke off his talk, and cried out to the music to blow up, "And let us go look on these villeins," said he; and withal the men began to gather in a due and ordered company, and their faces turned hitherward; forsooth, I got to my horse, and led him out of the wood on the other side, and so to saddle and away along the green roads; neither was I seen

---

* Probably one of the Calverlys, a Cheshire family, one of whom was a noted captain in the French wars.

or chased. So look ye to it, my masters, for these men will be coming to speak with us; nor is there need for haste, but rather for good speed; for in some twenty or thirty minutes will be more tidings to hand.'

By this time one of our best-armed men had got through the throng and was standing on the cross beside John Ball. When the long man had done, there was confused noise of talk for a while, and the throng spread itself out more and more, but not in a disorderly manner; the bowmen drawing together toward the outside, and the billmen forming behind them. Will Green was still standing beside me and had hold of my arm, as though he knew both where he and I were to go.

'Fellows,' quoth the captain from the cross, 'belike this stour shall not live to be older than the day, if ye get not into a plump together for their arbalestiers to shoot bolts into, and their men-at-arms to thrust spears into. Get you to the edge of the crofts and spread out there six feet between man and man, and shoot, ye bowmen, from the hedges, and ye with the staves keep your heads below the level of the hedges, or else for all they be thick a bolt may win its way in.'

He grinned as he said this, and there was laughter enough in the throng to have done honour to a better joke.

Then he sung out, 'Hob Wright, Rafe Wood, John Pargetter, and thou Will Green, bestir ye and marshal the bowshot; and thou Nicholas Woodyer shall be under me Jack Straw in ordering of the staves. Gregory Tailor and John Clerk, fair and fine are ye clad in the arms of the Canterbury bailiffs; ye shall shine from afar; go ye with the banner into the highway, and the bows on either side shall ward you; yet jump, lads, and over the hedge with you when the bolts begin to fly your way! Take heed, good fellows all, that our business is to bestride the highway, and not let them get in on our flank the while; so half to the right, half to the left of the highway. Shoot straight and strong, and waste no breath with noise; let the loose of the bow-string cry for you! and look you! think it no loss of manhood to cover your bodies with tree and bush; for one of us who know is worth a hundred of those proud fools. To it, lads, and let them see what the grey goose bears between his wings! Abide us here, brother John Ball, and pray for us if thou wilt; but for me, if God will not do for Jack Straw what Jack Straw would do for God were he in like case, I can see no help for it.'

'Yea, forsooth,' said the priest, 'here will I abide you my fellows if ye come back; or if ye come not back, here will I abide the foe. Depart, and the blessing of the Fellowship be with you.'

Down then leapt Jack Straw from the cross, and the whole throng set off without noise or hurry, soberly and steadily in outward seeming. Will Green led me by the hand as if I were a boy, yet nothing he said, being forsooth intent on his charge. We were some four hundred men in all; but I said to myself that without some advantage of the ground we were lost men before the men-at-arms that long Gregory Tailor had told us of; for I had not seen as yet the yard-long shaft at its work.

We and somewhat more than half of our band turned into the orchards on the left of the road, through which the level rays of the low sun shone brightly. The others took up their position on the right side of it. We kept pretty near to the road till we had got through all the closes save the last, where we were brought up by a hedge and a dyke, beyond which lay a wide-open nearly treeless space, not of tillage, as at the other side of the place, but of pasture, the common grazing ground of the township. A little stream wound about through the ground, with a few willows here and there; there was only a thread of water in it in this hot summer tide, but its course could easily be traced by the deep blue-green of the rushes that grew plenteously in the bed. Geese were lazily wandering about and near this brook, and a herd of cows, accompanied by the town bull, were feeding on quietly, their heads all turned one way; while half a dozen calves marched close together side by side like a plump of soldiers, their tails swinging in a kind of measure to keep off the flies, of which there was great plenty. Three or four lads and girls were sauntering about, heeding or not heeding the cattle. They looked up toward us as we crowded into the last close, and slowly loitered off toward the village. Nothing looked like battle; yet battle sounded in the air; for now we heard the beat of the horse-hoofs of the men-at-arms coming on towards us like the rolling of distant thunder, and growing louder and louder every minute; we were none too soon in turning to face them. Jack Straw was on our side of the road, and with a few gestures and a word or two he got his men into their places. Six archers lined the hedge along the road where the banner of Adam and Eve, rising above the grey leaves of the apple-trees, challenged the new-comers; and of the billmen also he kept a good few ready to guard the road in case the enemy should try to rush it with the horsemen. The road, not being a Roman one, was, you must remember, little like the firm smooth country roads that you are used to; it was a mere track between the hedges and fields, partly grass-grown, and cut up by the deep-sunk ruts hardened by the drought of summer. There was a stack of fagot and small wood on the other side, and our men threw themselves upon it and set to work to stake the road across for a rough defence against the horsemen.

What befell more on the road itself I had not much time to note, for our bowmen spread themselves out along the hedge that looked into the pasture-field, leaving some six feet between man and man; the rest of the billmen went along with the bowmen, and halted in clumps of some half-dozen along their line, holding themselves ready to help the bowmen if the enemy should run up under their shafts, or to run on to lengthen the line in case they should try to break in on our flank. The hedge in front of us was of quick. It had been strongly plashed in the past February, and was stiff and stout. It stood on a low bank; moreover, the level of the orchard was some thirty inches higher than that of the field, and the ditch some two foot deeper than the face of the field. The field went winding round to beyond the church, making a quarter of a circle about the village, and at the western end of it were the butts whence the folk were coming from shooting when I first came into the village street.

Altogether, to me who knew nothing of war the place seemed defensible enough. I have said that the road down which Long Gregory came with his tidings went north; and that was its general direction; but its first reach was nearly east, so that the low sun was not in the eyes of any of us, and where Will Green took his stand, and I with him, it was nearly at our backs.

Chapter VI. The Battle at the Township's End

Our men had got into their places leisurely and coolly enough, and with no lack of jesting and laughter. As we went along the hedge by the road, the leaders tore off leafy twigs from the low oak bushes therein, and set them for a rallying sign in their hats and headpieces, and two or three of them had horns for blowing.

Will Green, when he got into his place, which was some thirty yards from where Jack Straw and the billmen stood in the corner of the two hedges, the road hedge and the hedge between the close and field, looked to right and left of him a moment, then turned to the man on the left and said:

'Look you, mate, when you hear our horns blow ask no more questions, but shoot straight and strong at whatso cometh towards us, till ye hear more tidings from Jack Straw or from me. Pass that word onward.'

Then he looked at me and said:

'Now, lad from Essex, thou hadst best sit down out of the way at once: forsooth I wot not why I brought thee hither. Wilt thou not back to the cross, for thou art little of a fighting-man?'

'Nay,' said I, 'I would see the play. What shall come of it?'

'Little,' said he; 'we shall slay a horse or twain maybe. I will tell thee, since thou hast not seen a fight belike, as I have seen some, that these men-at-arms cannot run fast either to the play or from it, if they be a-foot; and if they come on a-horseback, what shall hinder me to put a shaft into the poor beast? But down with thee on the daisies, for some shot there will be first.'

As he spoke he was pulling off his belts and other gear, and his coat, which done, he laid his quiver on the ground, girt him again, did his axe and buckler on to his girdle, and hung up his other attire on the nearest tree behind us. Then he opened his quiver and took out of it some two dozen of arrows, which he stuck in the ground beside him ready to his hand. Most of the bowmen within sight were doing the like.

As I glanced toward the houses I saw three or four bright figures moving through the orchards, and presently noted that they were women, all clad more or less like the girl in the Rose, except that two of them wore white coifs on their heads. Their errand there was clear, for each carried a bundle of arrows under her arm.

One of them came straight up to Will Green, and I could see at once that she was his daughter. She was tall and strongly made, with black hair like her father, somewhat comely, though no great beauty; but as they met, her eyes smiled even more than her mouth, and made her face look very sweet and kind, and the smile was answered back in a way so quaintly like to her father's face, that I too smiled for goodwill and pleasure.

'Well, well, lass', said he, 'dost thou think that here is Crecy field toward, that ye bring all this artillery? Turn back, my girl, and set the pot on the fire; for that shall we need when we come home, I and this ballad-maker here.'

'Nay,' she said, nodding kindly at me, 'if this is to be no Crecy, then may I stop to see, as well as the ballad-maker, since he hath neither sword nor staff?'

'Sweetling,' he said, 'get thee home in haste. This play is but little, yet mightest thou be hurt in it; and trust me the time may come, sweetheart, when even thou and such as thou shalt hold a sword or a staff. Ere the moon throws a shadow we shall be back.'

She turned away lingering, not without tears on her face, laid the sheaf of arrows at the foot of the tree, and hastened off through the orchard. I was going to say something, when Will Green held up his hand as who would bid us hearken. The noise of the horsehoofs, after growing nearer and nearer, had ceased suddenly, and a confused murmur of voices had taken the place of it.

'Get thee down, and take cover, old lad,' said Will Green; 'the dance will soon begin, and ye shall hear the music presently.'

Sure enough as I slipped down by the hedge close to which I had been standing, I heard the harsh twang of the bowstrings, one, two, three, almost together, from the road, and even the whew of the shafts, though that was drowned in a moment by a confused but loud and threatening shout from the other side, and again the bowstrings twanged, and this time a far-off clash of arms followed, and therewithal that cry of a strong man that comes without his will, and is so different from his wonted voice that one has a guess thereby of the change that death is. Then for a while was almost silence; nor did our horns blow up, though some half-dozen of the bill-men had leapt into the road when the bows first shot. But presently came a great blare of trumpets and horns from the other side, and therewith as it were a river of steel and bright coats poured into the field before us, and still their horns blew as they spread out toward the left of our line; the cattle in the pasture-field, heretofore feeding quietly, seemed frightened silly by the sudden noise, and ran about tail in air and lowing loudly; the old bull with his head a little lowered, and his stubborn legs planted firmly, growling threateningly; while the geese about the brook waddled away gobbling and squeaking; all which seemed so strange to us along with the threat of sudden death that rang out from the bright array over against us, that we laughed outright, the most of us, and Will Green put down his head in mockery of the bull and grunted like him, whereat we laughed yet more. He turned round to me as he nocked his arrow, and said:

'I would they were just fifty paces nigher, and they move not. Ho! Jack Straw, shall we shoot?'

For the latter-named was nigh us now; he shook his head and said nothing as he stood looking at the enemy's line.

'Fear not but they are the right folk, Jack,' quoth Will Green.

'Yea, yea,' said he, 'but abide awhile; they could make nought of the highway, and two of their sergeants had a message from the grey goose feather. Abide, for they have not crossed the road to our right hand, and belike have not seen our fellows on the other side, who are now for a bushment to them.'

I looked hard at the man. He was a tall, wiry, and broad-shouldered fellow, clad in a handsome armour of bright steel that certainly had not been made for a yeoman, but over it he had a common linen smock-frock or gabardine, like our field workmen wear now or used to wear, and in his helmet he carried instead of a feather a wisp of wheaten straw. He bore a heavy axe in his hand besides the sword he was girt with, and round his neck hung a great horn for blowing. I should say that I knew that there were at least three 'Jack Straws' among the fellowship of the discontented, one of whom was over in Essex.

As we waited there, every bowman with his shaft nocked on the string, there was a movement in the line opposite, and presently came from it a little knot of three men, the middle one on horseback, the other two armed with long-handled glaives; all three well muffled up in armour. As they came nearer I could see that the horseman had a tabard over his armour, gaily embroidered with a green tree on a gold ground, and in his hand a trumpet.

'They are come to summon us. Wilt thou that he speak, Jack?' said Will Green.

'Nay,' said the other; 'yet shall he have warning first. Shoot when my horn blows!'

And therewith he came up to the hedge, climbed over, slowly because of his armour, and stood some dozen yards out in the field. The man on horseback put his trumpet to his mouth and blew a long blast, and then took a scroll into his hand and made as if he were going to read; but Jack Straw lifted up his voice and cried out:

'Do it not, or thou art but dead! We will have no accursed lawyers and their sheep-skins here! Go back to those that sent thee—'

But the man broke in in a loud harsh voice:

'Ho! YE PEOPLE! what will ye gathering in arms?'

Then cried Jack Straw:

'Sir Fool, hold your peace till ye have heard me, or else we shoot at once. Go back to those that sent thee, and tell them that we free men of Kent are on the way to London to speak with King Richard, and to tell him that which he wots not; to wit, that there is a certain sort of fools and traitors to the realm who would put collars on our necks and make beasts of us, and that it is his right and his devoir to do as he swore when he was crowned and anointed at Westminster on the Stone of Doom, and gainsay these thieves and traitors; and if he be too weak, then shall we help him; and if he will not be king, then shall we have one who will be, and that is the King's Son of Heaven. Now, therefore, if any withstand us on our lawful errand as we go to speak with our own king and lord, let him look to it. Bear back this word to them that sent thee. But for thee, hearken, thou bastard of an inky sheepskin! get thee gone and tarry not; three times shall I lift up my hand, and the third time look to thyself, for then shalt thou hear the loose of our bowstrings, and after that nought else till thou hearest the devil bidding thee welcome to hell!'

Our fellows shouted, but the summoner began again, yet in a quavering voice:

'Ho! YE PEOPLE! what will ye gathering in arms? Wot ye not that ye are doing or shall do great harm, loss, and hurt to the king's lieges—'

He stopped; Jack Straw's hand was lowered for the second time. He looked to his men right and left, and then turned rein and turned tail, and scuttled back to the main body at his swiftest. Huge laughter rattled out all along our line as Jack Straw climbed back into the orchard grinning also.

Then we noted more movement in the enemy's line. They were spreading the archers and arbalestiers to our left, and the men-at-arms and others also spread somewhat under the three pennons of which Long Gregory had told us, and which were plain enough to us in the clear evening. Presently the moving line faced us, and the archers set off at a smart pace toward us, the men-at-arms holding back a little behind them. I knew now that they had been within bow-shot all along, but our men were loth to shoot before their first shots would tell, like those half-dozen in the road when, as they told me afterwards, a plump of their men-at-arms had made a show of falling on.

But now as soon as those men began to move on us directly in face, Jack Straw put his horn to his lips and blew a loud rough blast that was echoed by five or six others along the orchard hedge. Every man had his shaft nocked on the string; I watched them, and Will Green specially; he and his bow and its string seemed all of a piece, so easily by seeming did he draw the nock of the arrow to his ear. A moment, as he took his aim, and then—O then did I understand the meaning of the awe with which the ancient poet speaks of the loose of the god Apollo's bow; for terrible indeed was the mingled sound of the twanging bowstring and the whirring shaft so close to me.

I was now on my knees right in front of Will and saw all clearly; the arbalestiers (for no long-bow men were over against our stead) had all of them bright head-pieces, and stout body-armour of boiled leather with metal studs, and as they came towards us, I could see over their shoulders great wooden shields hanging at their backs. Further to our left their long-bow men had shot almost as soon as ours, and I heard or seemed to hear the rush of the arrows through the apple-boughs and a man's cry therewith; but with us the long-bow had been before the cross-bow; one of the arbalestiers fell outright, his great shield clattering down on him, and moved no more; while three others were hit and were crawling to the rear. The rest had shouldered their bows and were aiming, but I thought unsteadily; and before the triggers were drawn again Will Green had nocked and loosed, and not a few others of our folk; then came the wooden hail of the bolts rattling through the boughs, but all overhead and no one hit.

The next time Will Green nocked his arrow he drew with a great shout, which all our fellows took up; for the arbalestiers instead of turning about in their places covered by their great shields and winding up their cross-bows for a second shot, as is the custom of such soldiers, ran huddling together toward their men-at-arms, our arrows driving thump-thump into their shields as they ran: I saw four lying on the field dead or sore wounded.

But our archers shouted again, and kept on each plucking the arrows from the ground, and nocking and loosing swiftly but deliberately at the line before them; indeed now was the time for these terrible bowmen, for as Will Green told me afterwards they always reckoned to kill through cloth or leather at five hundred yards, and they had let the cross-bow men come nearly within three hundred, and these were now all mingled and muddled up with the men-at-arms at scant five hundred yards' distance; and belike, too, the latter were not treating them too well, but seemed to be belabouring them with their spear-staves in their anger at the poorness of the play; so that as Will Green said it was like shooting at hay-ricks.

All this you must understand lasted but a few minutes, and when our men had been shooting quite coolly, like good workmen at peaceful work, for a few minutes more, the enemy's line seemed to clear somewhat; the pennon with the three red kine showed in front and three men armed from head to foot in gleaming steel, except for their short coats bright with heraldry, were with it. One of them (and he bore the three kine on his coat) turned round and gave some word of command, and an angry shout went up from them, and they came on steadily towards us, the man with the red kine on his coat leading them, a great naked sword in his hand: you must note that they were all on foot; but as they drew nearer I saw their horses led by grooms and pages coming on slowly behind them.

Sooth said Will Green that the men-at-arms run not fast either to or fro the fray; they came on no faster than a hasty walk, their arms clashing about them and the twang of the bows and whistle of the arrows never failing all the while, but going on like the push of the westerly gale, as from time to time the men-at-arms shouted, 'Ha! ha! out! out! Kentish thieves!'

But when they began to fall on, Jack Straw shouted out, 'Bills to the field! bills to the field!'

Then all our bill-men ran up and leapt over the hedge into the meadow and stood stoutly along the ditch under our bows, Jack Straw in the forefront handling his great axe. Then he cast it into his left hand, caught up his horn and winded it loudly. The men-at-arms drew near steadily, some fell under the arrow-storm, but not a many; for though the target was big, it was hard, since not even the cloth-yard shaft could pierce well-wrought armour of plate, and there was much armour among them. Withal the arbalestiers were shooting again, but high and at a venture, so they did us no hurt.

But as these soldiers made wise by the French war were now drawing near, and our bowmen were casting down their bows and drawing their short swords, or handling their axes, as did Will Green, muttering, 'Now must Hob Wright's gear end this play'— while this was a-doing, lo, on a sudden a flight of arrows from our right on the flank of the sergeants' array, which stayed them somewhat; not because it slew many men, but because they began to bethink them that their foes were many and all around them; then the road-hedge on the right seemed alive with armed men, for whatever could hold sword or staff amongst us was there; every bowman also leapt our orchard-hedge sword or axe in hand, and with a great shout, bill-men, archers, and all, ran in on them; half-armed, yea, and half-naked some of them; strong and stout and lithe and light withal, the wrath of battle and the hope of better times lifting up their hearts till nothing could withstand them. So was all mingled together, and for a minute or two was a confused clamour over which rose a clatter like the riveting of iron plates, or the noise of the street of the coppersmiths at Florence; then the throng burst open and the steel-clad sergeants and squires and knights ran huddling and shuffling towards their horses; but some cast down their weapons and threw up their hands and cried for peace and ransom; and some stood and fought desperately, and slew some till they were hammered down by many strokes, and of these were the bailiffs and tipstaves, and the lawyers and their men, who could not run and hoped for no mercy.

I looked as on a picture and wondered, and my mind was at strain to remember something forgotten, which yet had left its mark on it. I heard the noise of the horse-hoofs of the fleeing men-at-arms (the archers and arbalestiers had scattered before the last minutes of the play), I heard the confused sound of laughter and rejoicing down in the meadow, and close by me the evening wind lifting the lighter twigs of the trees, and far away the many noises of the quiet country, till light and sound both began to fade from me and I saw and heard nothing.

I leapt up to my feet presently and there was Will Green before me as I had first seen him in the street with coat and hood and the gear at his girdle and his unstrung bow in his hand; his face smiling and kind again, but maybe a thought sad.

'Well,' quoth I, 'what is the tale for the ballad-maker?'

'As Jack Straw said it would be,' said he, '"the end of the day and the end of the fray;"' and he pointed to the brave show of the sky over the sunken sun; 'the knights fled and the sheriff dead: two of the lawyer kind slain afield, and one hanged: and cruel was he to make them cruel: and three bailiffs knocked on the head—stout men, and so witless, that none found their brains in their skulls; and five arbalestiers and one archer slain, and a score and a half of others, mostly men come back from the French wars, men of the Companions there, knowing no other craft than fighting for gold; and this is the end they are paid for. Well, brother, saving the lawyers who belike had no souls, but only parchment deeds and libels of the same, God rest their souls!'

He fell a-musing; but I said, 'And of our Fellowship were any slain?'

'Two good men of the township,' he said, 'Hob Horner and Antony Webber, were slain outright, Hob with a shaft and Antony in the hand-play, and John Pargetter hurt very sore on the shoulder with a glaive; and five more men of the Fellowship slain in the hand-play, and some few hurt, but not sorely. And as to those slain, if God give their souls rest it is well; for little rest they had on the earth belike; but for me, I desire rest no more.'

I looked at him and our eyes met with no little love; and I wondered to see how wrath and grief within him were contending with the kindness of the man, and how clear the tokens of it were in his face.

'Come now, old lad,' said he, 'for I deem that John Ball and Jack Straw have a word to say to us at the cross yet, since these men broke off the telling of the tale; there shall we know what we are to take in hand to-morrow. And afterwards thou shalt eat and drink in my house this once, if never again.'

So we went through the orchard closes again; and others were about and anigh us, all turned toward the cross as we went over the dewy grass, whereon the moon was just beginning to throw shadows.

Chapter VII. More Words at the Cross

I got into my old place again on the steps of the cross, Will Green beside me, and above me John Ball and Jack Straw again. The moon was half-way up the heavens now, and the short summer night had begun, calm and fragrant, with just so much noise outside our quiet circle as made one feel the world alive and happy.

We waited silently until we had heard John Ball and the story of what was to do; and presently he began to speak.

'Good people, it is begun, but not ended. Which of you is hardy enough to wend the road to London to-morrow?'

'All! All!' they shouted.

'Yea,' said he, 'even so I deemed of you. Yet forsooth hearken! London is a great and grievous city; and mayhappen when ye come thither it shall seem to you over-great to deal with, when ye remember the little townships and the cots ye came from.

'Moreover, when ye dwell here in Kent ye think forsooth of your brethren in Essex or Suffolk, and there belike an end. But from London ye may have an inkling of all the world, and over-burdensome maybe shall that seem to you, a few and a feeble people.

'Nevertheless I say to you, remember the Fellowship, in the hope of which ye have this day conquered; and when ye come to London be wise and wary; and that is as much as to say, be bold and hardy; for in these days are ye building a house which shall not be overthrown, and the world shall not be too great or too little to hold it: for indeed it shall be the world itself, set free from evil-doers for friends to dwell in.'

He ceased awhile, but they hearkened still, as if something more was coming. Then he said:

'To-morrow we shall take the road for Rochester; and most like it were well to see what Sir John Newton in the castle may say to us: for the man is no ill man, and hath a tongue well-shapen for words; and it were well that we had him out of the castle and away with us, and that we put a word in his mouth to say to the King. And wot ye well, good fellows, that by then we come to Rochester we shall be a goodly company, and ere we come to Blackheath a very great company; and at London Bridge who shall stay our host?

'Therefore there is nought that can undo us except our own selves and our hearkening to soft words from those who would slay us. They shall bid us go home and abide peacefully with our wives and children while they, the lords and councillors and lawyers, imagine counsel and remedy for us; and even so shall our own folly bid us; and if we hearken thereto we are undone indeed; for they shall fall upon our peace with war, and our wives and children they shall take from us, and some of us they shall hang, and some they shall scourge, and the others shall be their yoke-beasts—yea, and worse, for they shall lack meat more.

'To fools hearken not, whether they be yourselves or your foemen, for either shall lead you astray.

'With the lords parley not, for ye know already what they would say to you, and that is, "Churl, let me bridle thee and saddle thee, and eat thy livelihood that thou winnest, and call thee hard names because I eat thee up; and for thee, speak not and do not, save as I bid thee."

'All that is the end of their parleying.

'Therefore be ye bold, and again bold, and thrice bold! Grip the bow, handle the staff, draw the sword, and set on in the name of the Fellowship!'

He ended amid loud shouts; but straightway answering shouts were heard, and a great noise of the winding of horns, and I misdoubted a new onslaught;

and some of those in the throng began to string their bows and handle their bills; but Will Green pulled me by the sleeve and said,

'Friends are these by the winding of their horns; thou art quit for this night, old lad.' And then Jack Straw cried out from the cross: 'Fair and softly, my masters! These be men of our Fellowship, and are for your guests this night; they are from the bents this side of Medway, and are with us here because of the pilgrimage road, and that is the best in these parts, and so the shortest to Rochester. And doubt ye nothing of our being taken unawares this night; for I have bidden and sent out watchers of the ways, and neither a man's son nor a mare's son may come in on us without espial. Now make we our friends welcome. Forsooth, I looked for them an hour later; and had they come an hour earlier yet, some heads would now lie on the cold grass which shall lie on a feather bed to-night. But let be, since all is well!

'Now get we home to our houses, and eat and drink and slumber this night, if never once again, amid the multitude of friends and fellows; and yet soberly and without riot, since so much work is to hand. Moreover the priest saith, bear ye the dead men, both friends and foes, into the chancel of the church, and there this night he will wake them: but after to-morrow let the dead abide to bury their dead!'

Therewith he leapt down from the cross, and Will and I bestirred ourselves and mingled with the new-comers. They were some three hundred strong, clad and armed in all ways like the people of our township, except some half-dozen whose armour shone cold like ice under the moonbeams. Will Green soon had a dozen of them by the sleeve to come home with him to board and bed, and then I lost him for some minutes, and turning about saw John Ball standing behind me, looking pensively on all the stir and merry humours of the joyous uplanders.

'Brother from Essex,' said he, 'shall I see thee again to-night? I were fain of speech with thee; for thou seemest like one that has seen more than most.'

'Yea,' said I, 'if ye come to Will Green's house, for thither am I bidden.'

'Thither shall I come,' said he, smiling kindly, 'or no man I know in field. Lo you, Will Green looking for something, and that is me. But in his house will be song and the talk of many friends; and forsooth I have words in me that crave to come out in a quiet place where they may have each one his own answer. If thou art not afraid of dead men who were alive and wicked this morning, come thou to the church when supper is done, and there we may talk all we will.'

Will Green was standing beside us before he had done, with his hand laid on the priest's shoulder, waiting till he had spoken out; and as I nodded Yea to John Ball he said:

'Now, master priest, thou hast spoken enough this two or three hours, and this my new brother must tell and talk in my house; and there my maid will hear his wisdom which lay still under the hedge e'en now when the bolts were abroad. So come ye, and ye good fellows, come!'

So we turned away together into the little street. But while John Ball had been speaking to me I felt strangely, as though I had more things to say than the words I knew could make clear: as if I wanted to get from other people a new set of words. Moreover, as we passed up the street again I was once again smitten with the great beauty of the scene; the houses, the church with its new chancel and tower, snow-white in the moonbeams now; the dresses and arms of the people, men and women (for the latter were now mixed up with the men); their grave sonorous language, and the quaint and measured forms of speech, were again become a wonder to me and affected me almost to tears.

Chapter VIII. Supper at Will Green's

I walked along with the others musing as if I did not belong to them, till we came to Will Green's house. He was one of the wealthier of the yeomen, and his house was one of those I told you of, the lower story of which was built of stone. It had not been built long, and was very trim and neat. The fit of wonder had worn off me again by then I reached it, or perhaps I should give you a closer description of it, for it was a handsome yeoman's dwelling of that day, which is as much as saying it was very beautiful. The house on the other side of it, the last house in the village, was old or even ancient; all built of stone, and except for a newer piece built on to it—a hall, it seemed—had round arches, some of them handsomely carved. I knew that this was the parson's house; but he was another sort of priest than John Ball, and what for fear, what for hatred, had gone back to his monastery with the two other chantrey priests who dwelt in that house: so that the men of the township, and more especially the women, were thinking gladly how John Ball should say mass in their new chancel on the morrow.

Will Green's daughter was waiting for him at the door and gave him a close and eager hug, and had a kiss to spare for each of us withal: a strong girl she was, as I have said, and sweet and wholesome also. She made merry with her father; yet it was easy to see that her heart was in her mouth all along. There was a younger girl some twelve summers old, and a lad of ten, who were easily to be known for his children; an old woman also, who had her livelihood there, and helped the household; and moreover three long young men, who came into the house after we had sat down, to whom Will nodded kindly. They were brisk lads and smart, but had been afield after the beasts that evening, and had not seen the fray.

The room we came into was indeed the house, for there was nothing but it on the ground floor, but a stair in the corner went up to the chamber or loft above. It was much like the room at the Rose, but bigger; the cupboard better wrought, and with more vessels on it, and handsomer. Also the walls, instead of being panelled, were hung with a coarse loosely-woven stuff of green worsted with birds and trees woven into it. There were flowers in plenty stuck about the room, mostly of the yellow blossoming flag or flower-de-luce, of which I had seen plenty in all the ditches, but in the window near the door was a pot full of those same white poppies I had seen when I first woke up; and the table was all set forth with meat and drink, a big salt-cellar of pewter in the middle, covered with a white cloth.

We sat down, the priest blessed the meat in the name of the Trinity, and we crossed ourselves and fell to. The victual was plentiful of broth and flesh-meat, and bread and cherries, so we ate and drank, and talked lightly together when we were full.

Yet was not the feast so gay as might have been. Will Green had me to sit next to him, and on the other side sat John Ball; but the priest had grown somewhat distraught, and sat as one thinking of somewhat that was like to escape his thought. Will Green looked at his daughter from time to time, and whiles his eyes glanced round the fair chamber as one who loved it, and his kind face grew sad, yet never sullen. When the herdsmen came into the hall they fell straightway to asking questions concerning those of the Fellowship who had been slain in the fray, and of their wives and children; so that for a while thereafter no man cared to jest, for they were a neighbourly and kind folk, and were sorry both for the dead, and also for the living that should suffer from that day's work.

So then we sat silent awhile. The unseen moon was bright over the roof of the house, so that outside all was gleaming bright save the black shadows, though the moon came not into the room, and the white wall of the tower was the whitest and the brightest thing we could see.

Wide open were the windows, and the scents of the fragrant night floated in upon us, and the sounds of the men at their meat or making merry about the township; and whiles we heard the gibber of an owl from the trees westward of the church, and the sharp cry of a blackbird made fearful by the prowling stoat, or the far-off lowing of a cow from the upland pastures; or the hoofs of a horse trotting on the pilgrimage road (and one of our watchers would that be).

Thus we sat awhile, and once again came that feeling over me of wonder and pleasure at the strange and beautiful sights, mingled with the sights and sounds and scents beautiful indeed, yet not strange, but rather long familiar to me.

But now Will Green started in his seat where he sat with his daughter hanging over his chair, her hand amidst his thick black curls, and she weeping softly I thought; and his rough strong voice broke the silence.

'Why, lads and neighbours, what ails us? If the knights who fled from us this eve were to creep back hither and look in at the window, they would deem that they had slain us after all, and that we were but the ghosts of the men who fought them. Yet, forsooth, fair it is at whiles to sit with friends and let the summer night speak for us and tell us its tales. But now, sweetling, fetch the mazer and the wine.'

'Forsooth,' said John Ball, 'if ye laugh not over-much now, ye shall laugh the more on the morrow of to-morrow, as ye draw nearer to the play of point and edge.'

'That is sooth,' said one of the upland guests. 'So it was seen in France when we fought there; and the eve of fight was sober and the morn was merry.'

'Yea,' said another, 'but there, forsooth, it was for nothing ye fought; and to-morrow it shall be for a fair reward.'

'It was for life we fought,' said the first.

'Yea,' said the second, 'for life; and leave to go home and find the lawyers at their fell game. Ho, Will Green, call a health over the cup!'

For now Will Green had a bowl of wine in his hand. He stood up and said: 'Here, now, I call a health to the wrights of Kent who be turning our plough-shares into swords and our pruning-hooks into spears! Drink around, my masters!'

Then he drank, and his daughter filled the bowl brimming again and he passed it to me. As I took it I saw that it was of light polished wood curiously speckled, with a band of silver round it, on which was cut the legend, 'In the name of the Trinity fill the cup and drink to me.' And before I drank, it came upon me to say, 'To-morrow, and the fair days afterwards!'

Then I drank a great draught of the strong red wine, and passed it on; and every man said something over it, as 'The road to London Bridge!' 'Hob Carter and his mate!' and so on, till last of all John Ball drank, saying:

'Ten years hence, and the freedom of the Fellowship!' Then he said to Will Green: 'Now, Will, must I needs depart to go and wake the dead, both friend and foe in the church yonder; and whoso of you will be shriven let him come to me thither in the morn, nor spare for as little after sunrise as it may be. And this our friend and brother from over the water of Thames, he hath will to talk with me and I with him; so now will I take him by the hand: and so God keep you, fellows!'

I rose to meet him as he came round the head of the table, and took his hand. Will Green turned round to me and said:

'Thou wilt come back again timely, old lad; for betimes on the morrow must we rise if we shall dine at Rochester.'

I stammered as I yea-said him; for John Ball was looking strangely at me with a half-smile, and my heart beat anxiously and fearfully: but we went quietly to the door and so out into the bright moonlight.

I lingered a little when we had passed the threshold, and looked back at the yellow-lighted window and the shapes of the men that I saw therein with a grief and longing that I could not give myself a reason for, since I was to come back so soon. John Ball did not press me to move forward, but held up his hand as if to bid me hearken. The folk and guests there had already shaken themselves down since our departure, and were gotten to be reasonably merry it seemed; for one of the guests, he who had spoken of France before, had fallen to singing a ballad of the war to a wild and melancholy tune. I remember the first rhymes of it, which I heard as I turned away my head and we moved on toward the church:

> On a fair field of France
> We fought on a morning
> So lovely as it lieth   35
> Along by the water.
> There was many a lord there
> Mowed men in the medley,
> 'Midst the banners of the barons
> And bold men of the knighthood,   40
> And spearmen and sergeants
> And shooters of the shaft.

Chapter IX. Betwixt the Living and the Dead

We entered the church through the south porch under a round-arched door carved very richly, and with a sculpture over the doorway and under the arch, which, as far as I could see by the moonlight, figured St. Michael and the Dragon. As I came into the rich gloom of the nave I noticed for the first time that I had one of those white poppies in my hand; I must have taken it out of the pot by the window as I passed out of Will Green's house.

The nave was not very large, but it looked spacious too; it was somewhat old, but well-built and handsome; the roof of curved wooden rafters with great tie-beams going from wall to wall. There was no light in it but that of the moon streaming through the windows, which were by no means large, and were glazed with white fretwork, with here and there a little figure in very deep rich colours. Two larger windows near the east end of each aisle had just been made so that the church grew lighter toward the east, and I could see all the work on the great screen between the nave and chancel which glittered bright in new paint and gilding: a candle glimmered in the loft above it, before the huge rood that filled up the whole space between the loft and the chancel-arch. There was an altar at the east end of each aisle, the one on the south side standing against the outside wall, the one on the north against a traceried gaily-painted screen, for that aisle ran on along the chancel. There were a few oak benches near this second altar, seemingly just made, and well carved and moulded; otherwise the floor of the nave, which was paved with a quaint pavement of glazed tiles like the crocks I had seen outside as to ware, was quite clear, and the shafts of the arches rose out of it white and beautiful under the moon as though out of a sea, dark but with gleams struck over it.

The priest let me linger and look round, when he had crossed himself and given me the holy water; and then I saw that the walls were figured all over with stories, a huge St. Christopher with his black beard looking like Will Green, being close to the porch by which we entered, and above the chancel arch the Doom of the last Day, in which the painter had not spared either kings or bishops, and in which a lawyer with his blue coif was one of the chief figures in the group which the Devil was hauling off to hell.

'Yea,' said John Ball, ''tis a goodly church and fair as you may see 'twixt Canterbury and London as for its kind; and yet do I misdoubt me where those who are dead are housed, and where those shall house them after they are dead, who built this house for God to dwell in. God grant they be cleansed at last; forsooth one of them who is now alive is a foul swine and a cruel wolf. Art thou all so sure, scholar, that all such have souls? and if it be so, was it well done of God to make them? I speak to thee thus, for I think thou art no delator; and if thou be, why should I heed it, since I think not to come back from this journey.'

I looked at him and, as it were, had some ado to answer him; but I said at last, 'Friend, I never saw a soul, save in the body; I cannot tell.'

He crossed himself and said, 'Yet do I intend that ere many days are gone by my soul shall be in bliss among the fellowship of the saints, and merry shall it be, even before my body rises from the dead; for wisely I have wrought in the world, and I wot well of friends that are long ago gone from the world, as St. Martin, and St. Francis, and St. Thomas of Canterbury, who shall speak well of me to the heavenly Fellowship, and I shall in no wise lose my reward.'

I looked shyly at him as he spoke; his face looked sweet and calm and happy, and I would have said no word to grieve him; and yet belike my eyes looked wonder on him: he seemed to note it and his face grew puzzled. 'How deemest thou of these things?' said he: 'why do men die else, if it be otherwise than this?'

I smiled: 'Why then do they live?' said I.

Even in the white moonlight I saw his face flush, and he cried out in a great voice, 'To do great deeds or to repent them that they ever were born.'

'Yea,' said I, 'they live to live because the world liveth.' He stretched out his hand to me and grasped mine, but said no more; and went on till we came to the door in the rood-screen; then he turned to me with his hand on the ring-latch, and said, 'Hast thou seen many dead men?'

'Nay, but few,' said I.

'And I a many,' said he; 'but come now and look on these, our friends first and then our foes, so that ye may not look to see them while we sit and talk of the days that are to be on the earth before the Day of Doom cometh.'

So he opened the door, and we went into the chancel; a light burned on the high altar before the host, and looked red and strange in the moonlight that came through the wide traceried windows unstained by the pictures and beflowerings of the glazing; there were new stalls for the priests and vicars where we entered, carved more abundantly and beautifully than any of the woodwork I had yet seen, and everywhere was rich and fair colour and delicate and dainty form. Our dead lay just before the high altar on low biers, their faces all covered with linen cloths, for some of them had been sore smitten and hacked in the fray. We went up to them and John Ball took the cloth from the face of one; he had been shot to the heart with a shaft and his face was calm and smooth. He had been a young man fair and comely, with hair flaxen almost to whiteness; he lay there in his clothes as he had fallen, the hands crossed over his breast and holding a rush cross. His bow lay on one side of him, his quiver of shafts and his sword on the other.

John Ball spake to me while he held the corner of the sheet: 'What sayest thou, scholar? feelest thou sorrow of heart when thou lookest on this, either for the man himself, or for thyself and the time when thou shalt be as he is?'

I said, 'Nay, I feel no sorrow for this; for the man is not here: this is an empty house, and the master has gone from it. Forsooth, this to me is but as a waxen image of a man; nay, not even that, for if it were an image, it would be an image of the man as he was when he was alive. But here is no life nor semblance of life, and I am not moved by it; nay, I am more moved by the man's clothes and war-gear—there is more life in them than in him.'

'Thou sayest sooth,' said he; 'but sorrowest thou not for thine own death when thou lookest on him?'

I said, 'And how can I sorrow for that which I cannot so much as think of? Bethink thee that while I am alive I cannot think that I shall die, or believe in death at all, although I know well that I shall die—I can but think of myself as living in some new way.'

Again he looked on me as if puzzled; then his face cleared as he said, 'Yea, forsooth, and that is what the Church meaneth by death, and even that I look for; and that hereafter I shall see all the deeds that I have done in the body, and what they really were, and what shall come of them; and ever shall I be a member of the Church, and that is the Fellowship; then, even as now.'

I sighed as he spoke; then I said, 'Yea, somewhat in this fashion have most of men thought, since no man that is can conceive of not being; and I mind me that in those stories of the old Danes, their common word for a man dying is to say, "He changed his life."'

'And so deemest thou?'

I shook my head and said nothing.

'What hast thou to say hereon?' said he, 'for there seemeth something betwixt us twain as it were a wall that parteth us.'

'This,' said I, 'that though I die and end, yet mankind yet liveth, therefore I end not, since I am a man; and even so thou deemest, good friend; or at the least even so thou doest, since now thou art ready to die in grief and torment rather than be unfaithful to the Fellowship, yea rather than fail to work thine utmost for it; whereas, as thou thyself saidst at the cross, with a few words spoken and a little huddling-up of the truth, with a few pennies paid, and a few masses sung, thou mightest have had a good place on this earth and in that heaven. And as thou doest, so now doth many a poor man unnamed and unknown, and shall do while the world lasteth: and they that do less than this, fail because of fear, and are ashamed of their cowardice, and make many tales to themselves to deceive themselves, lest they should grow too much ashamed to live. And trust me if this were not so, the world would not live, but would die, smothered by its own stink. Is the wall betwixt us gone, friend?'

He smiled as he looked at me, kindly, but sadly and shamefast, and shook his head.

Then in a while he said, 'Now ye have seen the images of those who were our friends, come and see the images of those who were once our foes.'

So he led the way through the side screen into the chancel aisle, and there on the pavement lay the bodies of the foemen, their weapons taken from them and they stripped of their armour, but not otherwise of their clothes, and their faces mostly, but not all, covered. At the east end of the aisle was another altar, covered with a rich cloth beautifully figured, and on the wall over it was a deal of tabernacle work, in the midmost niche of it an image painted and gilt of a gay knight on horseback, cutting his own cloak in two with his sword to give a cantle of it to a half-naked beggar.

'Knowest thou any of these men?' said I.

He said, 'Some I should know, could I see their faces; but let them be.'

'Were they evil men?' said I.

'Yea,' he said, 'some two or three. But I will not tell thee of them; let St. Martin, whose house this is, tell their story if he will. As for the rest they were hapless fools, or else men who must earn their bread somehow, and were driven to this bad way of earning it; God rest their souls! I will be no tale-bearer, not even to God.'

So we stood musing a little while, I gazing not on the dead men, but on the strange pictures on the wall, which were richer and deeper coloured than those in the nave; till at last John Ball turned to me and laid his hand on my shoulder. I started and said, 'Yea, brother; now must I get me back to Will Green's house, as I promised to do so timely.'

'Not yet, brother,' said he; 'I have still much to say to thee, and the night is yet young. Go we and sit in the stalls of the vicars, and let us ask and answer on matters concerning the fashion of this world of menfolk, and of this land

are dead, but few unfree men in England; so that your lives and your deaths both shall bear fruit.'

'Said I not,' quoth John Ball, 'that thou wert a sending from other times? Good is thy message, for the land shall be free. Tell on now.'

He spoke eagerly, and I went on somewhat sadly: 'The times shall better, though the king and lords shall worsen, the Guilds of Craft shall wax and become mightier; more recourse shall there be of foreign merchants. There shall be plenty in the land and not famine. Where a man now earneth two pennies he shall earn three.'

'Yea,' said he, 'then shall those that labour become strong and stronger, and so soon shall it come about that all men shall work and none make to work, and so shall none be robbed, and at last shall all men labour and live and be happy, and have the goods of the earth without money and without price.'

'Yea,' said I, 'that shall indeed come to pass, but not yet for a while, and belike a long while.'

And I sat for long without speaking, and the church grew darker as the moon waned yet more.

Then I said: 'Bethink thee that these men shall yet have masters over them, who have at hand many a law and custom for the behoof of masters, and being masters can make yet more laws in the same behoof; and they shall suffer poor people to thrive just so long as their thriving shall profit the mastership and no longer; and so shall it be in those days I tell of; for there shall be king and lords and knights and squires still, with servants to do their bidding, and make honest men afraid; and all these will make nothing and eat much as aforetime, and the more that is made in the land the more shall they crave.'

'Yea,' said he, 'that wot I well, that these are of the kin of the daughters of the horse-leech; but how shall they slake their greed, seeing that as thou sayest villeinage shall be gone? Belike their men shall pay them quit-rents and do them service, as free men may, but all this according to law and not beyond it; so that though the workers shall be richer than they now be, the lords shall be no richer, and so all shall be on the road to being free and equal.'

Said I, 'Look you, friend; aforetime the lords, for the most part, held the land and all that was on it, and the men that were on it worked for them as their horses worked, and after they were fed and housed all was the lords'; but in the time to come the lords shall see their men thriving on the land, and shall say once more, "These men have more than they need, why have we not the surplus since we are their lords?" Moreover, in those days shall betide much chaffering for wares between man and man, and country and country; and the lords shall note that if there were less corn and less men on their lands there would be more sheep, that is to say more wool for chaffer, and that thereof they should have abundantly more than aforetime; since all the land they own, and it pays them quit-rent or service, save here and there a croft or a close of a yeoman; and all this might grow wool for them to sell to the Easterlings. Then shall England see a new thing, for whereas hitherto men have lived on the land and by it, the land shall no longer need them, but many sheep and a few shepherds shall make wool grow to be sold for money to the Easterlings, and that money shall the lords pouch: for, look you, they shall set the lawyers a-work and the strong hand moreover, and the land they shall take to themselves and their sheep; and except for these lords of land few shall be the free men that shall hold a rood of land whom the word of their lord may not turn adrift straightway.'

'How mean you?' said John Ball: 'shall all men be villeins again?'

'Nay,' said I, 'there shall be no villeins in England.'

'Surely then,' said he, 'it shall be worse, and all men save a few shall be thralls to be bought and sold at the cross.'

'Good friend,' said I, 'it shall not be so; all men shall be free even as ye would have it; yet, as I say, few indeed shall have so much land as they can stand upon save by buying such a grace of their masters.'

'And now,' said he, 'I wot not what thou sayest. I know a thrall, and he is his master's every hour, and never his own; and a villein I know, and whiles he is his own and whiles his lord's; and I know a free man, and he is his own always; but how shall he be his own if he have nought whereby to make his livelihood? Or shall he be a thief and take from others? Then is he an outlaw. Wonderful is this thou tellest of a free man with nought whereby to live!'

'Yet so it shall be,' said I, 'and by such free men shall all wares be made.'

'Nay, that cannot be; thou art talking riddles,' said he; 'for how shall a wood-wright make a chest without the wood and the tools?'

Said I, 'He must needs buy leave to labour of them that own all things except himself and such as himself.'

'Yea, but wherewith shall he buy it?' said John Ball. 'What hath he except himself?'

'With himself then shall he buy it,' quoth I, 'with his body and the power of labour that lieth therein; with the price of his labour shall he buy leave to labour.'

'Riddles again!' said he; 'how can he sell his labour for aught else but his daily bread? He must win by his labour meat and drink and clothing and housing! Can he sell his labour twice over?'

'Not so,' said I, 'but this shall he do belike; he shall sell himself, that is the labour that is in him, to the master that suffers him to work, and that master shall give to him from out of the wares he maketh enough to keep him alive, and to beget children and nourish them till they be old enough to be sold like himself, and the residue shall the rich man keep to himself.'

John Ball laughed aloud, and said: 'Well, I perceive we are not yet out of the land of riddles. The man may well do what thou sayest and live, but he may not do it and live a free man.'

'Thou sayest sooth,' said I.

Chapter XI. Hard It Is for the Old World to See the New

He held his peace awhile, and then he said: 'But no man selleth himself and his children into thraldom uncompelled; nor is any fool so great a fool as willingly to take the name of freeman and the life of a thrall as payment for the very life of a freeman. Now would I ask thee somewhat else; and I am the readier to do so since I perceive that thou art a wondrous seer; for surely no man could of his own wit have imagined a tale of such follies as thou hast told me. Now well I wot that men having once shaken themselves clear of the burden of villeinage, as thou sayest we shall do (and I bless thee for the word), shall never bow down to this worser tyranny without sore strife in the world; and surely so sore shall it be, before our valiant sons give way, that maids and little lads shall take the sword and the spear, and in many a field men's blood and not water shall turn the grist-mills of England. But when all this is over, and the tyranny is established, because there are but few men in the land after the great war, how shall it be with you then? Will there not be many soldiers and sergeants and few workers? Surely in every parish ye shall have the constables to see that the men work; and they shall be saying every day, "Such an one, hast thou yet sold thyself for this day or this week or this year? Go to now, and get thy bargain done, or it shall be the worse for thee." And wheresoever work is going on there shall be constables again, and those that labour shall labour under the whip like the Hebrews in the land of Egypt. And every man that may, will steal as a dog snatches at a bone; and there again shall ye need more soldiers and more constables till the land is eaten up by them; nor shall the lords and the masters even be able to bear the burden of it; nor will their gains be so great, since that which each man may do in a day is not right great when all is said.'

'Friend,' said I, 'from thine own valiancy and high heart thou speakest, when thou sayest that they who fall under this tyranny shall fight to the death against it. Wars indeed there shall be in the world, great and grievous, and yet few on this score; rather shall men fight as they have been fighting in France at the bidding of some lord of the manor, or some king, or at last at the bidding of some usurer and forestaller of the market. Valiant men, forsooth, shall arise in the beginning of these evil times, but though they shall die as ye shall, yet shall not their deaths be fruitful as yours shall be; because ye, forsooth, are fighting against villeinage which is waning, but they shall fight against usury which is waxing. And, moreover, I have been telling thee how it shall be when the measure of the time is full; and we, looking at these things from afar, can see them as they are indeed; but they who live at the beginning of those times and amidst them, shall not know what is doing around them; they shall indeed feel the plague and yet not know the remedy; by little and by little they shall fall from their better livelihood, and weak and helpless shall they grow, and have no might to withstand the evil of this tyranny; and then again when the times mend somewhat and they have but a little more ease, then shall it be to them like the kingdom of heaven, and they shall have no will to withstand any tyranny, but shall think themselves happy that they be pinched somewhat less. Also whereas thou sayest that there shall be for ever constables and sergeants going to and fro to drive men to work, and that they will not work save under the lash, thou art wrong and it shall not be so; for there shall ever be more workers than the masters may set to work, so that men shall strive eagerly for leave to work; and when one says, I will sell my hours at such and such a price, then another will say, and I for so much less; so that never shall the lords lack slaves willing to work, but often the slaves shall lack lords to buy them.'

'Thou tellest marvels indeed,' said he; 'but how then? if all the churls work not, shall there not be famine and lack of wares?'

'Famine enough,' said I, 'yet not from lack of wares; it shall be clean contrary. What wilt thou say when I tell thee that in the latter days there shall be such traffic and such speedy travel across the seas that most wares shall be good cheap, and bread of all things the cheapest?'

Quoth he: 'I should say that then there would be better livelihood for men, for in times of plenty it is well; for then men eat that which their own hands have harvested, and need not to spend of their substance in buying of others. Truly, it is well for honest men, but not so well for forestallers and regraters;* but who heeds what befalls such foul swine, who filch the money from people's purses, and do not one hair's turn of work to help them?'

'Yea, friend,' I said, 'but in those latter days all power shall be in the hands of these foul swine, and they shall be the rulers of all; therefore, hearken, for I tell thee that times of plenty shall in those days be the times of famine, and all shall pray for the prices of wares to rise, so that the forestallers and regraters may thrive, and that some of their well-doing may overflow on to those on whom they live.'

'I am weary of thy riddles,' he said. 'Yet at least I hope that there may be fewer and fewer folk in the land; as may well be, if life is then so foul and wretched.'

'Alas, poor man!' I said; 'nor mayst thou imagine how foul and wretched it may be for many of the folk; and yet I tell thee that men shall increase and multiply, till where there is one man in the land now, there shall be twenty in those days—yea, in some places ten times twenty.'

---

* Forestaller, one who buys up goods when they are cheap, and so raises the price for his own benefit; forestalls the due and real demand. Regrater, one who both buys and sells in the same market, or within five miles thereof; buys, say a ton of cheese at 10 a.m. and sells it at 5 p.m. a penny a pound dearer without moving from his chair. The word 'monopolist' will cover both species of thief.

'I have but little heart to ask thee more questions,' said he; 'and when thou answerest, thy words are plain, but the things they tell of I may scarce understand. But tell me this: in those days will men deem that so it must be for ever, as great men even now tell us of our ills, or will they think of some remedy?'

I looked about me. There was but a glimmer of light in the church now, but what there was, was no longer the strange light of the moon, but the first coming of the kindly day.

'Yea,' said John Ball, ''tis the twilight of the dawn. God and St. Christopher send us a good day!'

'John Ball,' said I, 'I have told thee that thy death will bring about that which thy life has striven for: thinkest thou that the thing which thou strivest for is worth the labour? or dost thou believe in the tale I have told thee of the days to come?'

He said: 'I tell thee once again that I trust thee for a seer; because no man could make up such a tale as thou; the things which thou tellest are too wonderful for a minstrel, the tale too grievous. And whereas thou askest as to whether I count my labour lost, I say nay; if so be that in those latter times (and worser than ours they will be) men shall yet seek a remedy: therefore again I ask thee, is it so that they shall?'

'Yea,' said I, 'and their remedy shall be the same as thine, although the days be different: for if the folk be enthralled, what remedy save that they be set free? and if they have tried many roads towards freedom, and found that they led nowhither, then shall they try yet another. Yet in the days to come they shall be slothful to try it, because their masters shall be so much mightier than thine, that they shall not need to show the high hand, and until the days get to their evilest, men shall be cozened into thinking that it is of their own free will that they must needs buy leave to labour by pawning their labour that is to be. Moreover, your lords and masters seem very mighty to you, each one of them, and so they are, but they are few; and the masters of the days to come shall not each one of them seem very mighty to the men of those days, but they shall be very many, and they shall be of one intent in these matters without knowing it; like as one sees the oars of a galley when the rowers are hidden, that rise and fall as it were with one will.'

'And yet,' he said, 'shall it not be the same with those that these men devour? shall not they also have one will?'

'Friend,' I said, 'they shall have the will to live, as the wretchedest thing living has: therefore shall they sell themselves that they may live, as I told thee; and their hard need shall be their lord's easy livelihood, and because of it he shall sleep without fear, since their need compelleth them not to loiter by the way to lament with friend or brother that they are pinched in their servitude, or to devise means for ending it. And yet indeed thou sayest it: they also shall have one will if they but knew it; but for a long while they shall have but a glimmer of knowledge of it: yet doubt it not that in the end they shall come to know it clearly, and then shall they bring about the remedy; and in those days shall it be seen that thou hast not wrought for nothing, because thou hast seen beforehand what the remedy should be, even as those of later days have seen it.'

We both sat silent a little while. The twilight was gaining on the night, though slowly. I looked at the poppy which I still held in my hand, and bethought me of Will Green, and said:

'Lo, how the light is spreading: now must I get me back to Will Green's house as I promised.'

'Go, then,' said he, 'if thou wilt. Yet meseems before long he shall come to us; and then mayst thou sleep among the trees on the green grass till the sun is high, for the host shall not be on foot very early; and sweet it is to sleep in shadow by the sun in the full morning when one has been awake and troubled through the night-tide.'

'Yet I will go now,' said I; 'I bid thee good-night, or rather good-morrow.'

Therewith I half rose up; but as I did so the will to depart left me as though I had never had it, and I sat down again, and heard the voice of John Ball, at first as one speaking from far away, but little by little growing nearer and more familiar to me, and as if once more it were coming from the man himself whom I had got to know.

Chapter XII. Ill Would Change Be at Whiles Were It Not for the Change beyond the Change

He said: 'Many strange things hast thou told me that I could not understand; yea, some my wit so failed to compass, that I cannot so much as ask thee questions concerning them; but of some matters would I ask thee, and I must hasten, for in very sooth the night is worn old and grey. Whereas thou sayest that in the days to come, when there shall be no labouring men who are not thralls after their new fashion, that their lords shall be many and very many, it seemeth to me that these same lords, if they be many, shall hardly be rich, or but very few of them, since they must verily feed and clothe and house their thralls, so that that which they take from them, since it will have to be dealt out amongst many, will not be enough to make many rich; since out of one man ye may get but one man's work; and pinch him never so sorely, still as aforesaid ye may not pinch him so sorely as not to feed him. Therefore, though the eyes of my mind may see a few lords and many slaves, yet can they not see many lords as well as many slaves; and if the slaves be many and the lords few, then some day shall the slaves make an end of that mastery by the force of their bodies. How then shall thy mastership of the latter days endure?'

'John Ball,' said I, 'mastership hath many shifts whereby it striveth to keep itself alive in the world. And now hear a marvel: whereas thou sayest these two times that out of one man ye may get but one man's work, in days to come one man shall do the work of a hundred men—yea, of a thousand or more: and this is the shift of mastership that shall make many masters and many rich men.'

John Ball laughed. 'Great is my harvest of riddles to-night,' said he; 'for even if a man sleep not, and eat and drink while he is a-working, ye shall but make two men, or three at the most, out of him.'

Said I: 'Sawest thou ever a weaver at his loom?'

'Yea,' said he, 'many a time.'

He was silent a little, and then said: 'Yet I marvelled not at it; but now I marvel, because I know what thou wouldst say. Time was when the shuttle was thrust in and out of all the thousand threads of the warp, and it was long to do; but now the spring-staves go up and down as the man's feet move, and this and that leaf of the warp cometh forward and the shuttle goeth in one shot through all the thousand warps. Yea, so it is that this multiplieth a man many times. But look you, he is so multiplied already; and so hath he been, meseemeth, for many hundred years.'

'Yea,' said I, 'but what hitherto needed the masters to multiply him more? For many hundred years the workman was a thrall bought and sold at the cross; and for other hundreds of years he hath been a villein—that is, a working-beast and a part of the stock of the manor on which he liveth; but then thou and the like of thee shall free him, and then is mastership put to its shifts; for what should avail the mastery then, when the master no longer owneth the man by law as his chattel, nor any longer by law owneth him as stock of his land, if the master hath not that which he on whom he liveth may not lack and live withal, and cannot have without selling himself?'

He said nothing, but I saw his brow knitted and his lips pressed together as though in anger; and again I said:

'Thou hast seen the weaver at his loom: think how it should be if he sit no longer before the web and cast the shuttle and draw home the sley, but if the shed open of itself and the shuttle of itself speed through it as swift as the eye can follow, and the sley come home of itself; and the weaver standing by and whistling *The Hunt's Up!* the while, or looking to half-a-dozen looms and bidding them what to do. And as with the weaver so with the potter, and the smith, and every worker in metals, and all other crafts, that it shall be for them looking on and tending, as with the man that sitteth in the cart while the horse draws. Yea, at last so shall it be even with those who are mere husbandmen; and no longer shall the reaper fare afield in the morning with his hook over his shoulder, and smite and bind and smite again till the sun is down and the moon is up; but he shall draw a thing made by men into the field with one or two horses, and shall say the word and the horses shall go up and down, and the thing shall reap and gather and bind, and do the work of many men. Imagine all this in thy mind if thou canst, at least as ye may imagine a tale of enchantment told by a minstrel, and then tell me what shouldst thou deem that the life of men would be amidst all this, men such as these men of the township here, or the men of the Canterbury guilds.'

'Yea,' said he; 'but before I tell thee my thoughts of thy tale of wonder, I would ask thee this: In those days when men work so easily, surely they shall make more wares than they can use in one country-side, or one good town, whereas in another, where things have not gone as well, they shall have less than they need; and even so it is with us now, and thereof cometh scarcity and famine; and if people may not come at each other's goods, it availeth the whole land little that one country-side hath more than enough while another hath less; for the goods shall abide there in the storehouses of the rich place till they perish. So if that be so in the days of wonder ye tell of (and I see not how it can be otherwise), then shall men be but little holpen by making all their wares so easily and with so little labour.'

I smiled again and said: 'Yea, but it shall not be so; not only shall men be multiplied a hundred and a thousand fold, but the distance of one place from another shall be as nothing; so that the wares which lie ready for market in Durham in the evening may be in London on the morrow morning; and the men of Wales may eat corn of Essex and the men of Essex wear wool of Wales; so that, so far as the flitting of goods to market goes, all the land shall be as one parish. Nay, what say I? Not as to this land only shall it be so, but even the Indies, and far countries of which thou knowest not, shall be, so to say, at every man's door, and wares which now ye account precious and dear-bought, shall then be common things bought and sold for little price at every huckster's stall. Say then, John, shall not those days be merry, and plentiful of ease and contentment for all men?'

'Brother,' said he, 'meseemeth some doleful mockery lieth under these joyful tidings of thine; since thou hast already partly told me to my sad bewilderment what the life of man shall be in those days. Yet will I now for a little set all that aside to consider thy strange tale as of a minstrel from over sea, even as thou biddest me. Therefore I say, that if men still abide men as I have known them, and unless these folk of England change as the land changeth—and forsooth of the men, for good and for evil, I can think no other than I think now, or behold them other than I have known them and loved them—I say if the men be still men, what will happen except that there should be all plenty in the land, and not one poor man therein, unless of his own free will he choose to lack and be poor, as a man in religion or such like; for there would then be such abundance of all good things, that, as greedy as the lords might be, there would be enough to satisfy their greed and yet leave good living for all who laboured with their hands; so that these should labour far less than now, and they would have time to learn knowledge, so that there should be no learned or unlearned, for all should be learned; and they would have time also to learn how to order the matters of the parish and the hundred, and of the parliament of the realm, so that the king should take no more than his own; and to order the rule of the realm, so that all men, rich and unrich, should have part therein; and so by undoing of evil laws and making of good ones, that fashion would come to an end whereof thou speakest, that rich men make laws for their own behoof; for they should no longer be able to do thus when all had part in making the laws; whereby it would soon come about that there would be no men rich and tyrannous, but all should have enough and to spare of the increase of the earth and the work of their own hands. Yea surely, brother, if ever it cometh about that men shall be able to make things, and not men, work for their superfluities, and that the length of travel from one place to another be made of no account, and all the world be a market for all the world, then all shall live in health and wealth; and envy and grudging shall perish. For then shall we have conquered the earth and it shall be enough; and then shall the kingdom of heaven be come down to the earth in very deed. Why lookest thou so sad and sorry? what sayest thou?'

I said: 'Hast thou forgotten already what I told thee, that in those latter days a man who hath nought save his own body (and such men shall be far the most of men) must needs pawn his labour for leave to labour? Can such a man be wealthy? Hast thou not called him a thrall?'

'Yea,' he said; 'but how could I deem that such things could be when those days should be come wherein men could make things work for them?'

'Poor man!' said I. 'Learn that in those very days, when it shall be with the making of things as with the carter in the cart, that there he sitteth and shaketh the reins and the horse draweth and the cart goeth; in those days, I tell thee, many men shall be as poor and wretched always, year by year, as they are with thee when there is famine in the land; nor shall any have plenty and surety of livelihood save those that shall sit by and look on while others labour; and these, I tell thee, shall be a many, so that they shall see to the making of all laws, and in their hands shall be all power, and the labourers shall think that they cannot do without these men that live by robbing them, and shall praise them and wellnigh pray to them as ye pray to the saints, and the best worshipped man in the land shall be he who by forestalling and regrating hath gotten to him the most money.'

'Yea,' said he, 'and shall they who see themselves robbed worship the robber? Then indeed shall men be changed from what they are now, and they shall be sluggards, dolts, and cowards beyond all the earth hath yet borne. Such are not the men I have known in my life-days, and that now I love in my death.'

'Nay,' I said, 'but the robbery shall they not see; for have I not told thee that they shall hold themselves to be free men? And for why? I will tell thee: but first tell me how it fares with men now; may the labouring man become a lord?'

He said: 'The thing hath been seen that churls have risen from the dortoir of the monastery to the abbot's chair and the bishop's throne; yet not often; and whiles hath a bold sergeant become a wise captain, and they have made him squire and knight; and yet but very seldom. And now I suppose thou wilt tell me that the Church will open her arms wider to this poor people, and that many through her shall rise into lordship. But what availeth that? Nought were it to me if the Abbot of St. Alban's with his golden mitre sitting guarded by his knights and sergeants, or the Prior of Merton with his hawks and his hounds, had once been poor men, if they were now tyrants of poor men; nor would it better the matter if there were ten times as many Houses of Religion in the land than now are, and each with a churl's son for abbot or prior over it.'

I smiled and said: 'Comfort thyself; for in those days shall there be neither abbey nor priory in the land, nor monks nor friars, nor any religious.' (He started as I spoke.) 'But thou hast told me that hardly in these days may a poor man rise to be a lord: now I tell thee that in the days to come poor men shall be able to become lords and masters and do-nothings; and oft will it be seen that they shall do so; and it shall be even for that cause that their eyes shall be blinded to the robbing of themselves by others, because they shall hope in their souls that they may each live to rob others: and this shall be the very safeguard of all rule and law in those days.'

'Now am I sorrier than thou hast yet made me,' said he; 'for when once this is established, how then can it be changed? Strong shall be the tyranny of thy latter days. And now meseems, if thou sayest sooth, this time of the conquest of the earth shall not bring heaven down to the earth, as erst I deemed it would, but rather that it shall bring hell up on to the earth. Woe's me, brother, for thy sad and weary foretelling! And yet saidst thou that the men of those days would seek a remedy. Canst thou yet tell me, brother, what that remedy shall be, lest the sun rise upon me made hopeless by thy tale of what is to be? And, lo you, soon shall she rise upon the earth.'

In truth the dawn was widening now, and the colours coming into the pictures on wall and in window; and as well as I could see through the varied glazing of these last (and one window before me had as yet nothing but white glass in it), the ruddy glow, which had but so little a while quite died out in the west, was now beginning to gather in the east—the new day was beginning. I looked at the poppy that I still carried in my hand, and it seemed to me to have withered and dwindled. I felt anxious to speak to my companion and tell him much, and withal I felt that I must hasten, or for some reason or other I should be too late; so I spoke at last loud and hurriedly:

'John Ball, be of good cheer; for once more thou knowest, as I know, that the Fellowship of Men shall endure, however many tribulations it may have to wear through. Look you, a while ago was the light bright about us; but it was because of the moon, and the night was deep notwithstanding, and when the moonlight waned and died, and there was but a little glimmer in place of the bright light, yet was the world glad because all things knew that the glimmer was of day and not of night. Lo you, an image of the times to betide the hope of the Fellowship of Men. Yet forsooth, it may well be that this bright day of summer which is now dawning upon us is no image of the beginning of the day that shall be; but rather shall that day-dawn be cold and grey and surly; and yet by its light shall men see things as they verily are, and no longer enchanted by the gleam of the moon, and the glamour of the dreamtide. By such grey light shall wise men and valiant souls see the remedy, and deal with it, a real thing that may be touched and handled, and no glory of the heavens to be worshipped from afar off. And what shall it be, as I told thee before, save that men shall be determined to be free; yea, free as thou wouldst have them, when thine hope rises the highest, and thou art thinking not of the king's uncles, and poll-groat bailiffs, and the villeinage of Essex, but of the end of all, when men shall have the fruits of the earth and the fruits of their toil thereon, without money and without price. The time shall come, John Ball, when that dream of thine that this shall one day be, shall be a thing that men shall talk of soberly, and as a thing soon to come about, as even with thee they talk of the villeins becoming tenants paying their lord quit-rent; therefore, hast thou done well to hope it; and, if thou heedest this also, as I suppose thou heedest it little, thy name shall abide by thy hope in those days to come, and thou shalt not be forgotten.'

I heard his voice come out of the twilight, scarcely seeing him, though now the light was growing fast, as he said:

'Brother, thou givest me heart again; yet since now I wot well that thou art a sending from far-off times and far-off things: tell thou, if thou mayest, to a man who is going to his death how this shall come about.'

'Only this may I tell thee,' said I; 'to thee, when thou didst try to conceive of them, the ways of the days to come seemed follies scarce to be thought of; yet shall they come to be familiar things, and an order by which every man liveth, ill as he liveth, so that men shall deem of them, that thus it hath been since the beginning of the world, and that thus it shall be while the world endureth; and in this wise so shall they be thought of a long while; and the complaint of the poor the rich man shall heed, even as much and no more as he who lieth in pleasure under the lime-trees in the summer heedeth the murmur of his toiling bees. Yet in time shall this also grow old, and doubt shall creep in, because men shall scarce be able to live by that order, and the complaint of the poor shall be hearkened, no longer as a tale not utterly grievous, but as a threat of ruin, and a fear. Then shall those things, which to thee seem follies, and to the men between thee and me mere wisdom and the bond of stability, seem follies once again; yet, whereas men have so long lived by them, they shall cling to them yet from blindness and from fear; and those that see, and that have thus much conquered fear that they are furthering the real time that cometh and not the dream that faileth, these men shall the blind and the fearful mock and missay, and torment and murder; and great and grievous shall be the strife in those days, and many the failures of the wise, and too oft sore shall be the despair of the valiant; and back-sliding, and doubt, and contest between friends and fellows lacking time in the hubbub to understand each other, shall grieve many hearts and hinder the Host of the Fellowship: yet shall all bring about the end, till thy deeming of folly and ours shall be one, and thy hope and our hope; and then—the Day will have come.'

Once more I heard the voice of John Ball: 'Now, brother, I say farewell; for now verily hath the Day of the Earth come, and thou and I are lonely of each other again; thou hast been a dream to me as I to thee, and sorry and glad have we made each other, as tales of old time and the longing of times to come shall ever make men to be. I go to life and to death, and leave thee; and scarce do I know whether to wish thee some dream of the days beyond thine to tell what shall be, as thou hast told me, for I know not if that shall help or hinder thee; but since we have been kind and very friends, I will not leave thee without a wish of good-will, so at least I wish thee what thou thyself wishest for thyself, and that is hopeful strife, and blameless peace, which is to say in one word, life. Farewell, friend.'

For some little time, although I had known that the daylight was growing and what was around me, I had scarce seen the things I had before noted so keenly; but now in a flash I saw all—the east crimson with sunrise through the white window on my right hand; the richly-carved stalls, and gilded screen work, the pictures on the walls, the loveliness of the faultless colour of the mosaic window lights, the altar and the red light over it looking strange in the daylight, and the biers with the hidden dead men upon them that lay before the high altar. A great pain filled my heart at the sight of all that beauty, and withal I heard quick steps coming up the paved church-path to the porch, and the loud whistle of a sweet old tune therewith; then the footsteps stopped at the door; I heard the latch rattle, and knew that Will Green's hand was on the ring of it.

Then I strove to rise up, but fell back again; a white light, empty of all sights, broke upon me for a moment, and lo! behold, I was lying in my familiar bed, the south-westerly gale rattling the Venetian blinds and making their hold-fasts squeak.

I got up presently, and going to the window looked out on the winter morning; the river was before me broad between outer bank and bank, but it was nearly dead ebb, and there was a wide space of mud on each side of the hurrying stream, driven on the faster as it seemed by the push of the south-west wind. On the other side of the water the few willow-trees left us by the Thames Conservancy looked doubtfully alive against the bleak sky and the row of wretched-looking blue-slated houses, although, by the way, the latter were the backs of a sort of street of 'villas' and not a slum; the road in front of the house was sooty and muddy at once, and in the air was that sense of dirty discomfort which one is never quit of in London. The morning was harsh too, and though the wind was from the south-west it was as cold as a north wind: and yet amidst it all, I thought of the corner of the next bight of the river which I could not quite see from where I was, but over which one can see clear of houses and into Richmond Park, looking like the open country; and dirty as the river was, and harsh as was the January wind, they seemed to woo me toward the countryside, where away from the miseries of the 'Great Wen' I might of my own will carry on a daydream of the friends I had made in the dream of the night and against my will.

But as I turned away shivering and downhearted, on a sudden came the frightful noise of the 'hooters,' one after the other, that call the workmen to the factories, this one the after-breakfast one, more by token. So I grinned surlily, and dressed and got ready for my day's 'work' as I call it, but which many a man besides John Ruskin (though not many in his position) would call 'play.'

From A TALE OF THE HOUSE OF THE WOLFINGS AND ALL THE KINDREDS OF THE MARK WRITTEN IN PROSE AND IN VERSE BY WILLIAM MORRIS

WHILES IN THE EARLY WINTER EVE
WE PASS AMID THE GATHERING NIGHT
SOME HOMESTEAD THAT WE HAD TO LEAVE
YEARS PAST; AND SEE ITS CANDLES BRIGHT
SHINE IN THE ROOM BESIDE THE DOOR   5
WHERE WE WERE MERRY YEARS AGONE
BUT NOW MUST NEVER ENTER MORE,
AS STILL THE DARK ROAD DRIVES US ON.
E'EN SO THE WORLD OF MEN MAY TURN
AT EVEN OF SOME HURRIED DAY   10
AND SEE THE ANCIENT GLIMMER BURN
ACROSS THE WASTE THAT HATH NO WAY;
THEN WITH THAT FAINT LIGHT IN ITS EYES
A WHILE I BID IT LINGER NEAR
AND NURSE IN WAVERING MEMORIES   15
THE BITTER-SWEET OF DAYS THAT WERE.

Chapter I. The Dwellings of Mid-mark

The tale tells that in times long past there was a dwelling of men beside a great wood. Before it lay a plain, not very great, but which was, as it were, an isle in the sea of woodland, since even when you stood on the flat ground, you could see trees everywhere in the offing, though as for hills, you could scarce say that there were any; only swellings-up of the earth here and there, like the upheavings of the water that one sees at whiles going on amidst the eddies of a swift but deep stream.

On either side, to right and left the tree-girdle reached out toward the blue distance, thick close and unsundered, save where it and the plain which it begirdled was cleft amidmost by a river about as wide as the Thames at Sheene when the flood-tide is at its highest, but so swift and full of eddies, that it gave token of mountains not so far distant, though they were hidden. On each side moreover of the stream of this river was a wide space of stones, great and little, and in most places above this stony waste were banks of a few feet high, showing where the yearly winter flood was most commonly stayed.

You must know that this great clearing in the woodland was not a matter of haphazard; though the river had driven a road whereby men might fare on each side of its hurrying stream. It was men who had made that isle in the woodland.

For many generations the folk that now dwelt there had learned the craft of iron-founding, so that they had no lack of wares of iron and steel, whether they were tools of handicraft or weapons for hunting and for war. It was the men of the Folk, who coming adown by the river-side had made that clearing. The tale tells not whence they came, but belike from the dales of the distant mountains, and from dales and mountains and plains further aloof and yet further.

Anyhow they came adown the river; on its waters on rafts, by its shores in wains or bestriding their horses or their kine, or afoot, till they had a mind to abide; and there as it fell they stayed their travel, and spread from each side of the river, and fought with the wood and its wild things, that they might make to themselves a dwelling-place on the face of the earth.

So they cut down the trees, and burned their stumps that the grass might grow sweet for their kine and sheep and horses; and they diked the river where need was all through the plain, and far up into the wild-wood to bridle the winter floods: and they made them boats to ferry them over, and to float down stream and track up-stream: they fished the river's eddies also with net and with line; and drew drift from out of it of far-travelled wood and other matters; and the gravel of its shallows they washed for gold; and it became their friend, and they loved it, and gave it a name, and called it the Dusky, and the Glassy, and the Mirkwood-water; for the names of it changed with the generations of man.

There then in the clearing of the wood that for many years grew greater yearly they drave their beasts to pasture in the new-made meadows, where year by year the grass grew sweeter as the sun shone on it and the standing waters went from it; and now in the year whereof the tale telleth it was a fair and smiling plain, and no folk might have a better meadow.

But long before that had they learned the craft of tillage and taken heed to the acres and begun to grow wheat and rye thereon round about their roofs; the spade came into their hands, and they bethought them of the plough-share, and the tillage spread and grew, and there was no lack of bread.

In such wise that Folk had made an island amidst of the Mirkwood, and established a home there, and upheld it with manifold toil too long to tell of. And from the beginning this clearing in the wood they called the Mid-mark: for you shall know that men might journey up and down the Mirkwood-water, and half a day's ride up or down they would come on another clearing or island in the woods, and these were the Upper-mark and the Nether-mark: and all these were inhabited by men of one folk and one kindred, which was called the Mark-men, though of many branches was that stem of folk, who bore divers signs in battle and at the council whereby they might be known.

Now in the Mid-mark itself were many Houses of men; for by that word had they called for generations those who dwelt together under one token of kinship. The river ran from South to North, and both on the East side and on the West were there Houses of the Folk, and their habitations were shouldered up nigh unto the wood, so that ever betwixt them and the river was there a space of tillage and pasture.

Tells the tale of one such House, whose habitations were on the west side of the water, on a gentle slope of land, so that no flood higher than common might reach them. It was straight down to the river mostly that the land fell off, and on its downward-reaching slopes was the tillage, 'the Acres,' as the men of that time always called tilled land; and beyond that was the meadow going fair and smooth, though with here and there a rising in it, down to the lips of the stony waste of the winter river.

Now the name of this House was the Wolfings, and they bore a Wolf on their banners, and their warriors were marked on the breast with the image of the Wolf, that they might be known for what they were if they fell in battle, and were stripped.

The house, that is to say the Roof, of the Wolfings of the Mid-mark stood on the topmost of the slope aforesaid with its back to the wild-wood and its face to the acres and the water. But you must know that in those days the men of one branch of kindred dwelt under one roof together, and had therein their place and dignity; nor were there many degrees amongst them as hath befallen afterwards, but all they of one blood were brethren and of equal dignity. Howbeit they had servants or thralls, men taken in battle, men of alien blood, though true it is that from time to time were some of such men taken into the House, and hailed as brethren of the blood.

Also (to make an end at once of these matters of kinship and affinity) the men of one House might not wed the women of their own House: to the Wolfing men all Wolfing women were as sisters: they must needs wed with the Hartings or the Elkings or the Bearings, or other such Houses of the Mark as were not so close akin to the blood of the Wolf; and this was a law that none dreamed of breaking. Thus then dwelt this folk and such was their Custom.

As to the Roof of the Wolfings, it was a great hall and goodly, after the fashion of their folk and their day; not built of stone and lime, but framed of the goodliest trees of the wild-wood squared with the adze, and betwixt the framing filled with clay wattled with reeds. Long was that house, and at one end anigh the gable was the Man's-door, not so high that a man might stand on the threshold and his helmcrest clear the lintel; for such was the custom, that a tall man must bow himself as he came into the hall; which custom maybe was a memory of the days of onslaught when the foemen were mostly wont to beset the hall; whereas in the days whereof the tale tells they drew out into the fields and fought unfenced; unless at whiles when the odds were over great, and then they drew their wains about them and were fenced by the wainburg. At least it was from no niggardry that the door was made thus low, as might be seen by the fair and manifold carving of knots and dragons that was wrought above the lintel of the door for some three foot's space. But a like door was there anigh the other gable-end, whereby the women entered, and it was called the Woman's-door.

Near to the house on all sides except toward the wood were there many bowers and cots round about the penfolds and the byres: and these were booths for the stowage of wares, and for crafts and smithying that were unhandy to do in the house; and withal they were the dwelling-places of the thralls. And the lads and young men often abode there many days and were cherished there of the thralls that loved them, since at whiles they shunned the Great Roof that they might be the freer to come and go at their pleasure, and deal as they would. Thus was there a clustering on the slopes and bents betwixt the acres of the Wolfings and the wild-wood wherein dwelt the wolves.

As to the house within, two rows of pillars went down it endlong, fashioned of the mightiest trees that might be found, and each one fairly wrought with base and chapiter, and wreaths and knots, and fighting men and dragons; so that it was like a church of later days that has a nave and aisles; windows there were above the aisles, and a passage underneath the said windows in their roofs. In the aisles were the sleeping-places of the Folk, and down the nave under the crown of the roof were three hearths for the fires, and above each hearth a luffer or smoke-bearer to draw the smoke up when the fires were lighted. Forsooth on a bright winter afternoon it was strange to see the three columns of smoke going wavering up to the dimness of the mighty roof, and one maybe smitten athwart by the sunbeams. As for the timber of the roof itself and its framing, so exceeding great and high it was, that the tale tells how that none might see the fashion of it from the hall-floor unless he were to raise aloft a blazing faggot on a long pole: since no lack of timber was there among the men of the Mark.

At the end of the hall anigh the Man's-door was the daïs, and a table thereon set thwartwise of the hall; and in front of the daïs was the noblest and greatest of the hearths; (but of the others one was in the very midmost, and another in the Woman's-Chamber) and round about the daïs, along the gable-wall, and hung from pillar to pillar were woven cloths pictured with images of ancient tales and the deeds of the Wolfings, and the deeds of the Gods from whence they came. And this was the fairest place of all the house and the best-beloved of the Folk, and especially of the older and the mightier men: and there were tales told, and songs sung, especially if they were new: and thereto also were messengers brought if any tidings were abroad: there also would the elders talk together about matters concerning the House or the Mid-mark or the whole Folk of the Markmen.

Yet you must not think that their solemn councils were held there, the folk-motes whereat it must be determined what to do and what to forbear doing; for according as such councils (which they called Things) were of the House or of the Mid-mark or of the whole Folk, were they held each at the due Thing-steads in the Wood aloof from either acre or meadow, (as was the custom of our forefathers for long after) and at such Things would all the men of the House or the Mid-mark or the Folk be present man by man. And in each of these steads was there a Doomring wherein Doom was given by the neighbours chosen, (whom now we call the Jury) in matters between man and man; and no such doom of neighbours was given, and no such voice of the Folk proclaimed in any house or under any roof, nor even as aforesaid on the tilled acres or the depastured meadows. This was the custom of our forefathers, in memory, belike, of the days when as yet there was neither house nor tillage, nor flocks and herds, but the Earth's face only and what freely grew thereon.

But over the daïs there hung by chains and pulleys fastened to a tie-beam of the roof high aloft a wondrous lamp fashioned of glass; yet of no such glass as the folk made them then and there, but of a fair and clear green like an emerald, and all done with figures and knots in gold, and strange beasts, and a warrior slaying a dragon, and the sun rising on the earth: nor did any tale tell whence this lamp came, but it was held as an ancient and holy thing by all the Mark-men, and the kindred of the Wolf had it in charge to keep a light burning in it night and day for ever; and they appointed a maiden of their own kindred to that office; which damsel must needs be unwedded, since no wedded woman dwelling under that roof could be a Wolfing woman, but would needs be of the houses wherein the Wolfings wedded.

This lamp which burned ever was called the Hall-Sun, and the woman who had charge of it, and who was the fairest that might be found was called after it the Hall-Sun also.

At the other end of the hall was the Woman's-Chamber, and therein were the looms and other gear for the carding and spinning of wool and the weaving of cloth.

Such was the Roof under which dwelt the kindred of the Wolfings; and the other kindreds of the Mid-mark had roofs like to it; and of these the chiefest were the Elkings, the Vallings, the Alftings, the Beamings, the Galtings, and the Bearings; who bore on their banners the Elk, the Falcon, the Swan, the Tree, the Boar, and the Bear. But other lesser and newer kindreds there were than these: as for the Hartings above named, they were a kindred of the Upper-mark.

Chapter II. The Flitting of the War-Arrow

Tells the tale that it was an evening of summer, when the wheat was in the ear, but yet green; and the neat-herds were done driving the milch-kine to the byre, and the horseherds and the shepherds had made the night-shift, and the out-goers were riding two by two and one by one through the lanes between the wheat and the rye towards the meadow. Round the cots of the thralls were gathered knots of men and women both thralls and freemen, some talking together, some hearkening a song or a tale, some singing and some dancing together; and the children gambolling about from group to group with their shrill and tuneless voices, like young throstles who have not yet learned the song of their race. With these were mingled dogs, dun of colour, long of limb, sharp-nosed, gaunt and great; they took little heed of the children as they pulled them about in their play, but lay down, or loitered about, as though they had forgotten the chase and the wild-wood.

Merry was the folk with that fair tide, and the promise of the harvest, and the joy of life, and there was no weapon among them so close to the houses, save here and there the boar-spear of some herdman or herdwoman lately come from the meadow.

Tall and for the most part comely were both men and women; the most of them light-haired and grey-eyed, with cheek-bones somewhat high; white of skin but for the sun's burning, and the wind's parching, and whereas they were tanned of a very ruddy and cheerful hue. But the thralls were some of them of a shorter and darker breed, black-haired also and dark-eyed, lighter of limb; sometimes better knit but sometimes crookeder of leg and knottier of arm. But some also were of build and hue not much unlike to the freemen; and these doubtless came of some other folk of the Goths which had given way in battle before the Men of the Mark, either they or their fathers.

Moreover, some of the freemen were unlike their fellows and kindred, being slenderer and closer-knit, and black-haired, but grey-eyed withal; and amongst these were one or two who exceeded in beauty all others of the House.

Now the sun was set and the glooming was at point to begin and the shadowless twilight lay upon the earth. The nightingales on the borders of the wood sang ceaselessly from the scattered hazel-trees above the greensward where the grass was cropped down close by the nibbling of the rabbits; but in spite of their song and the divers voices of the men-folk about the houses, it was an evening on which sounds from aloof can be well heard, since noises carry far at such tides.

Suddenly they who were on the edges of those throngs and were the less noisy, held themselves as if to listen; and a group that had gathered about a minstrel to hear his story fell hearkening also round about the silenced and hearkening tale-teller: some of the dancers and singers noted them and in their turn stayed the dance and kept silence to hearken; and so from group to group spread the change, till all were straining their ears to hearken the tidings.

Already the men of the night-shift had heard it, and the shepherds of them had turned about, and were trotting smartly back through the lanes of the tall wheat: but the horseherds were now scarce seen on the darkening meadow, as they galloped on fast toward their herds to drive home the stallions. For what they had heard was the tidings of war.

There was a sound in the air as of a humble-bee close to the ear of one lying on a grassy bank; or whiles as of a cow afar in the meadow lowing in the afternoon when milking-time draws nigh: but it was ever shriller than the one, and fuller than the other; for it changed at whiles, though after the first sound of it, it did not rise or fall, because the eve was windless. You might hear at once for all that it was afar, it was a great and mighty sound; nor did any that hearkened doubt what it was, but all knew it for the blast of the great war-horn of the Elkings, whose Roof lay up Mirkwood-water next to the Roof of the Wolfings.

So those little throngs broke up at once; and all the freemen, and of the thralls a good many, flocked, both men and women, to the Man's-door of the hall, and streamed in quietly and with little talk, as men knowing that they should hear all in due season.

Within under the Hall-Sun, amidst the woven stories of time past, sat the elders and chief warriors on the daïs, and amidst of all a big strong man of forty winters, his dark beard a little grizzled, his eyes big and grey. Before him on the board lay the great War-horn of the Wolfings carved out of the tusk of a sea-whale of the North and with many devices on it and the Wolf amidst them all; its golden mouth-piece and rim wrought finely with flowers. There it abode the blowing, until the spoken word of some messenger should set forth the tidings borne on the air by the horn of the Elkings.

But the name of the dark-haired chief was Thiodolf (to wit Folkwolf) and he was deemed the wisest man of the Wolfings, and the best man of his hands, and of heart most dauntless. Beside him sat the fair woman called the Hall-Sun; for she was his foster-daughter before men's eyes; and she was black-haired and grey-eyed like to her fosterer, and never was woman fashioned fairer: she was young of years, scarce twenty winters old.

There sat the chiefs and elders on the daïs, and round about stood the kindred intermingled with the thralls, and no man spake, for they were awaiting sure and certain tidings: and when all were come in who had a mind to, there was so great a silence in the hall, that the song of the nightingales on the wood-edge sounded clear and loud therein, and even the chink of the bats about the upper windows could be heard. Then amidst the hush of men-folk, and the sounds of the life of the earth came another sound that made all turn their eyes toward the door; and this was the pad-pad of one running on the trodden and summer-dried ground anigh the hall: it stopped for a moment at the Man's-door, and the door opened, and the throng parted, making way for the man that entered and came hastily up to the midst of the table that stood on the daïs athwart the hall, and stood there panting, holding forth in his outstretched hand something which not all could see in the dimness of the hall-twilight, but which all knew nevertheless. The man was young, lithe and slender, and had no raiment but linen breeches round his middle, and skin shoes on his feet. As he stood there gathering his breath for speech, Thiodolf stood up, and poured mead into a drinking horn and held it out towards the new-comer, and spake, but in rhyme and measure:

'Welcome, thou evening-farer, and holy be thine head,
Since thou hast sought unto us in the heart of the Wolfings' stead;
Drink now of the horn of the mighty, and call a health if thou wilt
O'er the eddies of the mead-horn to the washing out of guilt.   20
For thou com'st to the peace of the Wolfings, and our very guest thou art,
And meseems as I behold thee, that I look on a child of the Hart.'

But the man put the horn from him with a hasty hand, and none said another word to him until he had gotten his breath again; and then he said:

'All hail ye Wood-Wolfs' children! nought may I drink the wine,
For the mouth and the maw that I carry this eve are nought of mine;
And my feet are the feet of the people, since the word went forth that tide,   25
"O Elfhere of the Hartings, no longer shalt thou bide
In any house of the Markmen than to speak the word and wend,
Till all men know the tidings and thine errand hath an end."
Behold, O Wolves, the token and say if it be true!
I bear the shaft of battle that is four-wise cloven through,   30
And its each end dipped in the blood-stream, both the iron and the horn,

And its midmost scathed with the fire; and the word that I have borne
Along with this war-token is "Wolfings of the Mark
Whenso ye see the war-shaft, by the daylight or the dark,
Busk ye to battle faring, and leave all work undone   35
Save the gathering for the handplay at the rising of the sun
Three days hence is the hosting, and thither bear along
Your wains and your kine for the slaughter lest the journey should be long.
For great is the Folk, saith the tidings, that against the Markmen come;
In a far off land is their dwelling, whenso they sit at home,   40
And Welsh* is their tongue, and we wot not of the word that is in their
    mouth,
As they march a many together from the cities of the South."'

Therewith he held up yet for a minute the token of the war-arrow ragged and
burnt and bloody; and turning about with it in his hand went his ways through
the open door, none hindering; and when he was gone, it was as if the token
were still in the air there against the heads of the living men, and the heads of
the woven warriors, so intently had all gazed at it; and none doubted the
tidings or the token. Then said Thiodolf:

'Forth will we Wolfing children, and cast a sound abroad:
The mouth of the sea-beast's weapon shall speak the battle-word;
And ye warriors harken and hasten, and dight the weed of war,   45
And then to acre and meadow wend ye adown no more,
For this work shall be for the women to drive our neat from the mead,
And to yoke the wains, and to load them as the men of war have need.'

Out then they streamed from the hall, and no man was left therein save the
fair Hall-Sun sitting under the lamp whose name she bore. But to the highest
of the slope they went, where was a mound made higher by man's handiwork;
thereon stood Thiodolf and handled the horn, turning his face toward the
downward course of Mirkwood-water; and he set the horn to his lips, and
blew a long blast, and then again, and yet again a third time; and all the sounds
of the gathering night were hushed under the sound of the roaring of the war-
horn of the Wolfings; and the Kin of the Beamings heard it as they sat in their
hall, and they gat them ready to hearken to the bearer of the tidings who
should follow on the sound of the war-blast.

But when the last sound of the horn had died away, then said Thiodolf:

'Now Wolfing children hearken, what the splintered War-shaft saith,
The fire scathed blood-stained aspen! we shall ride for life or death,   50
We warriors, a long journey with the herd and with the wain;

---

* Welsh with these men means Foreign, and is used for all people of Europe who are not of
Gothic or Teutonic blood.

But unto this our homestead shall we wend us back again,
All the gleanings of the battle; and here for them that live
Shall stand the Roof of the Wolfings, and for them shall the meadow
    thrive,
And the acres give their increase in the harvest of the year;   55
Now is no long departing since the Hall-Sun bideth here
'Neath the holy Roof of the Fathers, and the place of the Wolfing kin,
And the feast of our glad returning shall yet be held therein.
Hear the bidding of the War-shaft! All men, both thralls and free,
'Twixt twenty winters and sixty, beneath the shield shall be,   60
And the hosting is at the Thingstead, the Upper-mark anigh;
And we wend away to-morrow ere the Sun is noon-tide high.'

Therewith he stepped down from the mound, and went his way back to the hall; and manifold talk arose among the folk; and of the warriors some were already dight for the journey, but most not, and a many went their ways to see to their weapons and horses, and the rest back again into the hall.

By this time night had fallen, and between then and the dawning would be no darker hour, for the moon was just rising; a many of the horseherds had done their business, and were now making their way back again through the lanes of the wheat, driving the stallions before them, who played together kicking, biting and squealing, paying but little heed to the standing corn on either side. Lights began to glitter now in the cots of the thralls, and brighter still in the stithies where already you might hear the hammers clinking on the anvils, as men fell to looking to their battle gear.

But the chief men and the women sat under their Roof on the eve of departure: and the tuns of mead were broached, and the horns filled and borne round by young maidens, and men ate and drank and were merry; and from time to time as some one of the warriors had done with giving heed to his weapons, he entered into the hall and fell into the company of those whom he loved most and by whom he was best beloved; and whiles they talked, and whiles they sang to the harp up and down that long house; and the moon risen high shone in at the windows, and there was much laughter and merriment, and talk of deeds of arms of the old days on the eve of that departure: till little by little weariness fell on them, and they went their ways to slumber, and the hall was fallen silent.

MR SHAW LEFEVRE'S
MONUMENTAL CHAPEL

Letter to the Editor of the *Daily News*, 30 January 1889

Sir,—

I do not quite understand whether Mr Shaw Lefevre's scheme implies any meddling with either the Abbey Church, or the interesting remains of the ancient buildings near it; if it does, it cannot be too severely condemned; but your own article (of Jan 26th) on this subject gives a dangerous hint, which I hope will not be taken, for 'beautifying, at a comparatively small expense, the cloisters which form part of the ancient chapel.' I must say that part of the 'expense' would be the destruction of the cloisters themselves, and such an expense is not easily measured in money. As to the general question of monuments in Westminster Abbey, you say with truth that it is one of the most beautiful of ancient fanes. I do not think that it is an exaggeration to say that at the beginning of the 16th century it was the most beautiful of Gothic buildings. Everything which has been either taken away from or added to it since then has done more or less to destroy this beauty, until to-day the exterior no longer exists as a work of art, and even in the matchless interior we are forced if we are to receive any impression of beauty from it, to abstract our thoughts from a mass of monuments which, even apart from their incongruity with the delicate loveliness of the ancient architecture, are for the most part the most hideous specimens of false art that can be found in the whole world; mere Cockney nightmares and aberrations of the human intellect. I do not think, Sir, that I am saying too much in asserting that this is generally acknowledged. For what has been done in the past I fear that there is no remedy possible; or at least only a very partial one; since most of these abortions have been built into the very structure of the Church. It is true that if we had any common sense we might at once set to work and remove whatever of these idiocies is removable without interfering with the structure; but with a sinking heart I must admit that we lack the due amount of common sense for that simple purging, that demonstration against a national disgrace. There remains, however, the future: surely, Sir, we might close Westminster Abbey once for all to any more memorials, whatever their form might be: it appears to me a poor reward for a man's past services to privilege him to share in the degradation of a true monument of bygone ages, a record of men who, to judge by the works which they left behind them, were not unworthy, though they have chanced to be nameless to us. If some evil fate does compel us to continue the series of conventional undertakers' lies, of which the above-mentioned brutalities, in all their loathsomeness, are but too fitting an expression, surely now that we have learned that if they are necessary they are still ugly, we need not defile a beautiful building with them. Therefore, Sir, I most cordially agree with your suggestion that St Paul's should be utilised for the stowage of such fatuities; and that all the more as it was clearly meant to fulfil that function. Also, properly speaking, it is a modern building, the product of an architect's office, a work conceived and carried out under much the same conditions as a building would be now, and expressing much the same aspirations and ideas as ours. Whereas between us and the mournful but beautiful ruins of Westminster Abbey, once built by the hands of the people for the hearts of the people, lies a gulf wide, deep, unbridgeable, at least at present.

I am, Sir, yours obediently,
William Morris
Kelmscott House,
Upper Mall,
Hammersmith

LOOKING BACKWARD

Commonweal, 22 June 1889

We often hear it said that the signs of the spread of Socialism among English-speaking people are both abundant and striking. This is true; six or seven years ago the word Socialism was known in this country, but few even among the 'educated' classes knew more about its meaning than Mr Bradlaugh, Mr Gladstone, or Admiral Maxse know now—*i.e.*, nothing. Whereas at present it is fashionable for even West-end dinner-parties to affect an interest in and knowledge of it, which indicates a wide and deep public interest. This interest is more obvious in literature perhaps than in anything else, quite outside the propagandist tracts issued by definitely Socialist societies. A certain tincture of Socialism, for instance (generally very watery), is almost a necessary ingredient nowadays in a novel which aims at being at once serious and life-like, while more serious treatment of the subject at the hands of non-Socialists is common enough. In short the golden haze of self-satisfaction and content with the best of all possible societies is rolling away before the sun-heat bred of misery and aspiration, and all people above the lowest level of intelligence (which I take to be low gambling and statesmanship) are looking towards the new development, some timorously, some anxiously, some hopefully.

It seems clear to me that the reception which Mr Bellamy's 'Looking Backward' has received that there are a great many people who are hopeful in regard to Socialism. I am sure that ten years ago it would have been very little noticed, if at all; whereas now several editions have been sold in America, and it is attracting general attention in England, and to anyone not deeply interested in the social question it could not be at all an attractive book. It is true that it is cast into the form of a romance, but the author states very frankly in his preface that he has only given it this form as a sugar-coating to the pill, and the device of making a man wake up in a new world has now grown so common, and has been done with so much more care and art than Mr Bellamy has used, that by itself this would have done little for it: it is the serious essay and not the slight envelope of romance which people have found interesting to them.

Since, therefore, both Socialists and non Socialists have been so much impressed with the book, it seems to me necessary that the *Commonweal* should notice it. For it is a 'Utopia'. It purports to be written in the year 2000, and to describe the state of society at that period after a gradual and peaceable revolution has realised the Socialism which to us is but in the beginning of its militant period. It requires notice all the more because there is a certain danger in such books as this: a twofold danger; for there will be some temperaments to whom the answer given to the question 'How shall we live then?' will be pleasing and satisfactory, others to whom it will be displeasing and unsatisfactory. The danger to the first is that they will accept it with all its necessary errors and fallacies (which such a book *must* abound in) as conclusive statements of facts and rules of action, which will warp their efforts into futile directions. The danger to the second, if they are but enquirers or very young Socialists, is that they also accepting its speculations as facts, will be inclined to say, 'If *that is* Socialism, we won't help its advent, as it holds out no hope to us'.

The only safe way of reading a utopia is to consider it as the expression of the temperament of its author. So looked at, Mr Bellamy's utopia must be still called very interesting, as it is constructed with due economical knowledge, and with much adroitness; and of course his temperament is that of many thousands of people. This temperament may be called the unmixed modern one, unhistoric and unartistic; it makes its owner (if a Socialist) perfectly satisfied with modern civilisation, if only the injustice, misery, and waste of class society could be got rid of; which half-change seems possible to him. The only ideal of life which such a man can see is that of the industrious *professional* middle-class men of to-day purified from their crime of complicity with the monopolist class, and become independent instead of being, as they now are, parasitical. It is not to be denied that if such an ideal could be realised, it would be a great improvement on the present society. But can it be realised? It means in fact the alteration of the machinery of life in such a way that all men shall be allowed to share in the fulness of that life, for the production and upholding of which the machinery was instituted. There are clear signs to show us that that very group whose life is thus put forward as an ideal for the future are condemning it in the present, and that they also demand a revolution. The pessimistic revolt of the latter end of this century led by John Ruskin against the philistinism of the triumphant bourgeois, halting and stumbling as it necessarily was, shows that the change in the life of civilisation had begun, before any one seriously believed in the possibility of altering its machinery.

It follows naturally from the author's satisfaction with the best part of modern life that he conceives of the change to Socialism as taking place without any breakdown of that life, or indeed disturbance of it, by means of the final development of the great private monopolies which are such a noteworthy feature of the present day. He supposes that these must necessarily be absorbed into one great monopoly which will include the whole people and be worked for its benefit by the whole people. It may be noted in passing that by this use of the word monopoly he shows unconsciously that he has his mind fixed firmly on the mere *machinery* of life: for clearly the only part of their system which the people would or could take over from the monopolists would be the machinery of organisation, which monopoly is forced to use, but which is not an essential part of it. The essential of monopoly is, 'I warm myself by the fire which you have made, and you (very much the plural) stay outside in the cold'.

To go on. This hope of the development of the trusts and rings to which the competition for privilege has driven commerce, especially in America, is the distinctive part of Mr Bellamy's book; and it seems to me to be a somewhat dangerous hope to rest upon, too uncertain to be made a sheet-anchor of. It may be indeed the logical outcome of the most modern side of commercialism—*i.e.*, the outcome that *ought* to be; but then there is its historical outcome to be dealt with—*i.e.*, what *will* be; which I cannot help thinking may be after all, as far as this commercial development is concerned, the recurrence of breaks-up and re-formations of this kind of monopoly, under the influence of competition for privilege, or war for the division of plunder, till the flood comes and destroys them all. A far better hope to trust to is that men having once got it into their heads that true life implies free and equal life, and that is now possible of attainment, they will consciously strive for its attainment at any cost. The economical semi-fatalism of some Socialists is a deadening and discouraging view, and may easily become more so, if events at present unforeseen bring back the full tide of 'commercial prosperity'; which is by no means unlikely to happen.

The great change having thus peaceably and fatalistically taken place, the author has to put forward his scheme of the organisation of life; which is organised with a vengeance. His scheme may be described as State Communism, worked by the very extreme of national centralisation. The underlying vice in it is that the author cannot conceive, as aforesaid, of anything else than the *machinery* of society, and that, doubtless naturally, he reads in to the future of society, which he tells us is unwastefully conducted, that terror of starvation which is the necessary accompaniment of a society in which two-thirds or more of its labour-power is wasted: the result is that though he *tells* us that every man is free to choose his occupation and that work is no burden to anyone, the *impression* which he produces is that of a huge standing army, tightly drilled, compelled by some mysterious fate to unceasing anxiety for the production of wares to satisfy every caprice, however wasteful and absurd, that may cast up amongst them.

As an illustration it may be mentioned that everybody is to begin the serious work of production at the age of twenty-one, work three years as a labourer, and then choose his skilled occupation and work till he is forty-five, when he is to knock off his work and amuse himself (improve his mind, if he has one left him). Heavens! think of a man of forty-five changing all his habits suddenly and by compulsion! It is a small matter after this that the said persons past work should form a kind of aristocracy (how curiously old ideas cling) for the performance of certain judicial and political functions.

Mr Bellamy's ideas of life are curiously limited; he has no idea beyond existence in a great city; his dwelling of man in the future is Boston (U.S.A.) beautified. In one passage, indeed, he mentions villages, but with unconscious simplicity shows that they do not come into his scheme of economical equality, but are mere servants of the great centres of civilisation. This seems strange to some of us, who cannot help thinking that our experience ought to have taught us that such aggregations of population afford the worst possible form of dwelling-place, whatever the second-worst might be.

In short, a machine-life is the best which Mr Bellamy can imagine for us on all sides; it is not to be wondered at then that his only idea of making labour tolerable is to decrease the amount of it by means of fresh and ever fresh developments of machinery. This view I know he will share with many Socialists with whom I might otherwise agree more than I can with him; but I think a word or two is due to this important side of the subject. Now surely this ideal of the great reduction of the hours of labour by the mere means of machinery is a futility. The human race has always put forth about as much energy as it could in given conditions of climate and the like, though that energy has had to struggle against the natural laziness of mankind: and the development of man's resources, which has given him greater power over nature, has driven him also into fresh desires and fresh demands on nature, and thus made his expenditure of energy much what it was before. I believe that this will be always so, and the multiplication of machinery will just— multiply machinery; I believe that the ideal of the future does not point to the lessening of men's energy by the reduction of *labour* to a minimum, but rather to the reduction of *pain in labour* to a minimum, so small that it will cease to be a pain; a gain to humanity which can only be dreamed of till men are even more completely equal than Mr Bellamy's utopia would allow them to be, but which will most assuredly come about when men are really equal in condition; although it is probable that much of our so-called 'refinement', our luxury—in short, our civilisation—will have to be sacrificed to it. In this part of his scheme, therefore, Mr Bellamy worries himself unnecessarily in seeking (with obvious failure) some incentive to labour to replace the fear of starvation, which is at present our only one, whereas it cannot be too often repeated that the true incentive to useful and happy labour is and must be pleasure in the work itself.

I think it necessary to state these objections to Mr Bellamy's utopia, not because there is any need to quarrel with a man's vision of the future of society, which, as above said, must always be more or less personal to himself; but because this book, having produced a great impression on people who are really enquiring into Socialism, will be sure to be quoted as an authority for what Socialists believe, and that, therefore, it is necessary to point out that there are some Socialists who do not think that the problem of the organisation of life and necessary labour can be dealt with by a huge national centralisation, working by a kind of magic for which no one feels himself responsible; that on the contrary it will be necessary for the unit of administration to be small enough for every citizen to feel himself responsible for its details, and be interested in them; that individual men cannot shuffle off the business of life on to the shoulders of an abstraction called the State, but must deal with it in conscious association with each other. That variety of life is as much an aim of true Communism as equality of condition, and that nothing but an union of these two will bring about real freedom. That modern nationalities are mere artificial devices for the commercial war that we seek to put an end to, and will disappear with it. And, finally, that art, using that word in its widest and due signification, is not a mere adjunct of life which free and happy men can do without, but the necessary expression and indispensable instrument of human happiness.

On the other hand, it must be said that Mr Bellamy has faced the difficulty of economical reconstruction with courage, though he does not see any other sides to the problem, such, *e.g.*, as the future of the family; that at any rate he sees the necessity for the equality of the reward of labour, which is such a stumbling block for incomplete Socialists; and his criticism of the present monopolist system is forcible and fervid. Also up and down his pages there will be found satisfactory answers to many ordinary objections. The book is one to be read and considered seriously, but it should not be taken as the Socialist bible of reconstruction; a danger which perhaps it will not altogether escape, as incomplete systems impossible to be carried out but plausible on the surface are always attractive to people ripe for change, but not knowing clearly what their aim is.

News from Nowhere
or An Epoch of Rest
Being Some Chapters from a Utopian Romance

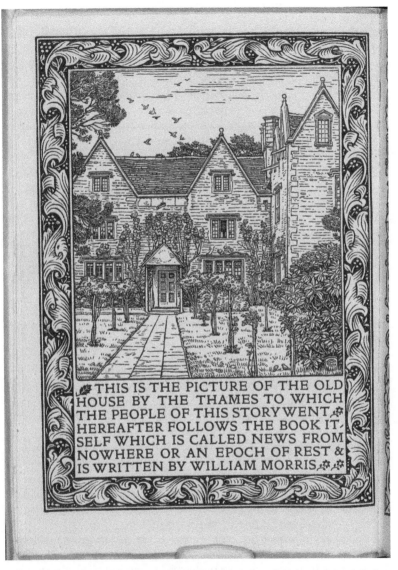

THIS IS THE PICTURE OF THE OLD HOUSE BY THE THAMES TO WHICH THE PEOPLE OF THIS STORY WENT. HEREAFTER FOLLOWS THE BOOK IT SELF WHICH IS CALLED NEWS FROM NOWHERE OR AN EPOCH OF REST & IS WRITTEN BY WILLIAM MORRIS.

FIGURE 11. Frontispiece from *News from Nowhere* (1891). The house is modelled on Morris's own Oxfordshire home, Kelmscott Manor. Woodcut designed by Charles Gere, engraved by W. H. Hooper.

Chapter I. Discussion and Bed

Up at the League, says a friend, there had been one night a brisk conversational discussion, as to what would happen on the Morrow of the Revolution, finally shading off into a vigorous statement by various friends of their views on the future of the fully-developed new society.

Says our friend: Considering the subject, the discussion was good-tempered; for those present being used to public meetings and after-lecture debates, if they did not listen to each other's opinions (which could scarcely be expected of them), at all events did not always attempt to speak all together, as is the custom of people in ordinary polite society when conversing on a subject which interests them. For the rest, there were six persons present, and consequently six sections of the party were represented, four of which had strong but divergent Anarchist opinions. One of the sections, says our friend, a man whom he knows very well indeed, sat almost silent at the beginning of the discussion, but at last got drawn into it, and finished by roaring out very loud, and damning all the rest for fools; after which befel a period of noise, and then a lull, during which the aforesaid section, having said good-night very amicably, took his way home by himself to a western suburb, using the means of travelling which civilisation has forced upon us like a habit. As he sat in that vapour-bath of hurried and discontented humanity, a carriage of the underground railway, he, like others, stewed discontentedly, while in self-reproachful mood he turned over the many excellent and conclusive arguments which, though they lay at his fingers' ends, he had forgotten in the just past discussion. But this frame of mind he was so used to, that it didn't last him long, and after a brief discomfort, caused by disgust with himself for having lost his temper (which he was also well used to), he found himself musing on the subject-matter of discussion, but still discontentedly and unhappily. 'If I could but see a day of it,' he said to himself; 'if I could but see it!'

As he formed the words, the train stopped at his station, five minutes' walk from his own house, which stood on the banks of the Thames, a little way above an ugly suspension bridge. He went out of the station, still discontented and unhappy, muttering 'If I could but see it! if I could but see it!' but had not gone many steps towards the river before (says our friend who tells the story) all that discontent and trouble seemed to slip off him.

It was a beautiful night of early winter, the air just sharp enough to be refreshing after the hot room and the stinking railway carriage. The wind, which had lately turned a point or two north of west, had blown the sky clear of all cloud save a light fleck or two which went swiftly down the heavens. There was a young moon halfway up the sky, and as the home-farer caught sight of it, tangled in the branches of a tall old elm, he could scarce bring to his mind the shabby London suburb where he was, and he felt as if he were in a pleasant country place—pleasanter, indeed, than the deep country was as he had known it.

He came right down to the river-side, and lingered a little, looking over the low wall to note the moonlit river, near upon high water, go swirling and glittering up to Chiswick Eyot: as for the ugly bridge below, he did not notice it or think of it, except when for a moment (says our friend) it struck him that he missed the row of lights down stream. Then he turned to his house door and let himself in; and even as he shut the door to, disappeared all remembrance of that brilliant logic and foresight which had so illuminated the recent discussion; and of the discussion itself there remained no trace, save a vague hope, that was now become a pleasure, for days of peace and rest, and cleanness and smiling goodwill.

In this mood he tumbled into bed, and fell asleep after his wont, in two minutes' time; but (contrary to his wont) woke up again not long after in that curiously wide-awake condition which sometimes surprises even good sleepers; a condition under which we feel all our wits preternaturally sharpened, while all the miserable muddles we have ever got into, all the disgraces and losses of our lives, will insist on thrusting themselves forward for the consideration of those sharpened wits.

In this state he lay (says our friend) till he had almost begun to enjoy it: till the tale of his stupidities amused him, and the entanglements before him, which he saw so clearly, began to shape themselves into an amusing story for him.

He heard one o'clock strike, then two and then three; after which he fell asleep again. Our friend says that from that sleep he awoke once more, and afterwards went through such surprising adventures that he thinks that they should be told to our comrades, and indeed the public in general, and therefore proposes to tell them now. But, says he, I think it would be better if I told them in the first person, as if it were myself who had gone through them; which, indeed, will be the easier and more natural to me, since I understand the feelings and desires of the comrade of whom I am telling better than any one else in the world does.

Chapter II. A Morning Bath

Well, I awoke, and found that I had kicked my bed-clothes off; and no wonder, for it was hot and the sun shining brightly. I jumped up and washed and hurried on my clothes, but in a hazy and half-awake condition, as if I had slept for a long, long while, and could not shake off the weight of slumber. In fact, I rather took it for granted that I was at home in my own room than saw that it was so.

When I was dressed, I felt the place so hot that I made haste to get out of the room and out of the house; and my first feeling was a delicious relief caused by the fresh air and pleasant breeze; my second, as I began to gather my wits together, mere measureless wonder: for it was winter when I went to bed the last night, and now, by witness of the river-side trees, it was summer, a beautiful bright morning seemingly of early June. However, there was still the Thames sparkling under the sun, and near high water, as last night I had seen it gleaming under the moon.

I had by no means shaken off the feeling of oppression, and wherever I might have been should scarce have been quite conscious of the place; so it was no wonder that I felt rather puzzled in despite of the familiar face of the Thames. Withal I felt dizzy and queer; and remembering that people often got a boat and had a swim in mid-stream, I thought I would do no less. It seems very early, quoth I to myself, but I daresay I shall find someone at Biffin's to take me. However, I didn't get as far as Biffin's, or even turn to my left thitherward, because just then I began to see that there was a landing-stage right before me in front of my house: in fact, on the place where my next-door neighbour had rigged one up, though somehow it didn't look like that either. Down I went on to it, and sure enough among the empty boats moored to it lay a man on his sculls in a solid-looking tub of a boat clearly meant for bathers. He nodded to me, and bade me good-morning as if he expected me, so I jumped in without any words and he paddled away quietly as I peeled for my swim. As we went, I looked down in the water, and couldn't help saying—

'How clear the water is this morning!'

'Is it?' said he; 'I didn't notice it. You know the flood-tide always thickens it a bit.'

'H'm,' said I, 'I have seen it pretty muddy even at half-ebb.'

He said nothing in answer, but seemed rather astonished; and as he now lay just stemming the tide, and I had my clothes off, I jumped in without more ado. Of course when I had my head above water again I turned towards the tide, and my eyes naturally sought for the bridge, and so utterly astonished was I by what I saw, that I forgot to strike out, and went spluttering under water again, and when I came up made straight for the boat; for I felt I that I must ask some questions of my waterman, so bewildering had been the half-sight I had seen from the face of the river with the water hardly out of my eyes; though by this time I was quit of the slumbrous and dizzy feeling, and was wide-awake and clear-headed.

As I got in up the steps which he had lowered, and he held out his hand to help me, we went drifting speedily up towards Chiswick; but now he caught up the sculls and brought her head round again, and said—

'A short swim, neighbour; but perhaps you find the water cold this morning, after your journey. Shall I put you ashore at once, or would you like to go down to Putney before breakfast?'

He spoke in a way so unlike what I should have expected from a Hammersmith waterman, that I stared at him, as I answered, 'Please to hold her a little; I want to look about me a bit.'

'All right,' he said; 'it's no less pretty in its way here than it is off Barn Elms; it's jolly everywhere this time in the morning. I'm glad you got up early; it's barely five o'clock yet.' If I was astonished with my sight of the river banks, I was no less astonished at my waterman, now that I had time to look at him and see him with my head and eyes clear.

He was a handsome young fellow, with a peculiarly pleasant and friendly look about his eyes,—an expression which was quite new to me then, though I soon became familiar with it. For the rest, he was dark-haired and berry-brown of skin, well-knit and strong, and obviously used to exercising his muscles, but with nothing rough or coarse about him, and clean as might be. His dress was not like any modern work-a-day clothes I had seen, but would have served very well as a costume for a picture of fourteenth-century life: it was of dark blue cloth, simple enough, but of fine web, and without a stain on it. He had a brown leather belt around his waist, and I noticed that its clasp was of damascened steel beautifully wrought. In short, he seemed to be like some specially manly and refined young gentleman, playing waterman for a spree, and I concluded that this was the case.

I felt that I must make some conversation; so I pointed to the Surrey bank, where I noticed some light plank stages running down the foreshore, with windlasses at the landward end of them, and said, 'What are they doing with those things here? If we were on the Tay, I should have said that they were for drawing the salmon nets; but here—'

'Well,' said he, smiling, 'of course that is what they *are* for. Where there are salmon, there are likely to be salmon-nets, Tay or Thames; but of course they are not always in use; we don't want salmon *every* day of the season.'

I was going to say, 'But is this the Thames?' but held my peace in my wonder, and turned my bewildered eyes eastward to look at the bridge again, and thence to the shores of the London river; and surely there was enough to astonish me. For though there was a bridge across the stream and houses on its banks, how all was changed from last night! The soap-works with their smoke-vomiting chimneys were gone; the engineer's works gone; the lead-works gone; and no sound of riveting and hammering came down the west wind from Thorneycroft's. Then the bridge! I had perhaps dreamed of such a bridge, but never seen such an one out of an illuminated manuscript; for not even the Ponte Vecchio at Florence came anywhere near it. It was of stone arches, splendidly solid, and as graceful as they were strong; high enough also to let ordinary river traffic through easily. Over the parapet showed quaint and fanciful little buildings, which I supposed to be booths or shops, beset with painted and gilded vanes and spirelets. The stone was a little weathered but showed no marks of the grimy sootiness which I was used to on every London building more than a year old. In short, to me a wonder of a bridge.

The sculler noted my eager astonished look, and said, as if in answer to my thoughts—

'Yes, it *is* a pretty bridge, isn't it? Even the up-stream bridges, which are so much smaller, are scarcely daintier, and the down-stream ones are scarcely more dignified and stately.'

I found myself saying, almost against my will, 'How old is it?'

'Oh, not very old', he said; 'it was built or at least opened, in 2003. There used to be a rather plain timber bridge before then.'

The date shut my mouth as if a key had been turned in a padlock fixed to my lips; for I saw that something inexplicable had happened, and that if I said much, I should be mixed up in a game of cross questions and crooked answers. So I tried to look unconcerned, and to glance in a matter-of-course way at the banks of the river, though this is what I saw up to the bridge and a little beyond; say as far as the site of the soap-works. Both shores had a line of very pretty houses, low and not large, standing back a little way from the river; they were mostly built of red brick and roofed with tiles, and looked, above all, comfortable, and as if they were, so to say, alive, and sympathetic with the life of the dwellers in them. There was a continuous garden in front of them, going down to the water's edge, in which the flowers were now blooming luxuriantly, and sending delicious waves of summer scent over the eddying stream. Behind the houses, I could see great trees rising, mostly planes, and looking down the water there were the reaches towards Putney almost as if they were a lake with a forest shore, so thick were the big trees; and I said aloud, but as if to myself—

'Well, I'm glad that they have not built over Barn Elms.'

I blushed for my fatuity as the words slipped out of my mouth, and my companion looked at me with a half smile which I thought I understood; so to hide my confusion I said, 'Please take me ashore now: I want to get my breakfast.'

He nodded, and brought her head round with a sharp stroke, and in a trice we were at the landing-stage again. He jumped out and I followed him; and of course I was not surprised to see him wait, as if for the inevitable after-piece that follows the doing of a service to a fellow-citizen. So I put my hand into my waistcoat-pocket, and said, 'How much?' though still with the uncomfortable feeling that perhaps I was offering money to a gentleman.

He looked puzzled, and said, 'How much? I don't quite understand what you are asking about. Do you mean the tide? If so, it is close on the turn now.'

I blushed, and said, stammering, 'Please don't take it amiss if I ask you; I mean no offence: but what ought I to pay you? You see I am a stranger, and don't know your customs—or your coins.'

And therewith I took a handful of money out of my pocket, as one does in a foreign country. And by the way, I saw that the silver had oxydised, and was like a blackleaded stove in colour.

He still seemed puzzled, but not at all offended; and he looked at the coins with some curiosity. I thought, Well after all, he *is* a waterman, and is considering what he may venture to take. He seems such a nice fellow that I'm sure I don't grudge him a little over-payment. I wonder, by the way, whether I couldn't hire him as a guide for a day or two, since he is so intelligent.

Therewith my new friend said thoughtfully:

'I think I know what you mean. You think that I have done you a service; so you feel yourself bound to give me something which I am not to give to a neighbour, unless he has done something special for me. I have heard of this kind of thing; but pardon me for saying, that it seems to us a troublesome and roundabout custom; and we don't know how to manage it. And you see this ferrying and giving people casts about the water is my *business*, which I would do for anybody; so to take gifts in connection with it would look very queer. Besides, if one person gave me something, then another might, and another, and so on; and I hope you won't think me rude if I say that I shouldn't know where to stow away so many mementos of friendship.'

And he laughed loud and merrily, as if the idea of being paid for his work was a very funny joke. I confess I began to be afraid that the man was mad, though he looked sane enough; and I was rather glad to think that I was a good swimmer, since we were so close to a deep swift stream. However, he went on by no means like a madman:

'As to your coins, they are curious, but not very old; they seem to be all of the reign of Victoria; you might give them to some scantily-furnished museum. Ours has enough of such coins, besides a fair number of earlier ones, many of which are beautiful, whereas these nineteenth century ones are so beastly ugly, ain't they? We have a piece of Edward III, with the king in a ship, and little leopards and fleurs-de-lys all along the gunwale, so delicately worked. You see,' he said, with something of a smirk, 'I am fond of working in gold and fine metals; this buckle here is an early piece of mine.'

No doubt I looked a little shy of him under the influence of that doubt as to his sanity. So he broke off short, and said in a kind voice:

'But I see that I am boring you, and I ask your pardon. For, not to mince matters, I can tell that you *are* a stranger, and must come from a place very unlike England. But it also is clear that it won't do to overdose you with information about this place, and that you had best suck it in little by little. Further, I should take it as very kind in you if you would allow me to be the showman of our new world to you, since you have stumbled on me first. Though indeed it will be a mere kindness on your part, for almost anybody would make as good a guide, and many much better.'

There certainly seemed no flavour in him of Colney Hatch; and besides I thought I could easily shake him off if it turned out that he really was mad; so I said:

'It is a very kind offer, but it is difficult for me to accept it, unless—' I was going to say, Unless you will let me pay you properly; but fearing to stir up Colney Hatch again, I changed the sentence into, 'I fear I shall be taking you away from your work—or your amusement.'

'O,' he said, 'don't trouble about that, because it will give me an opportunity of doing a good turn to a friend of mine, who wants to take my work here. He is a weaver from Yorkshire, who has rather overdone himself between his weaving and his mathematics, both indoor work, you see; and being a great friend of mine, he naturally came to me to get him some outdoor work. If you think you can put up with me, pray take me as your guide.'

He added presently: 'It is true that I have promised to go up-stream to some special friends of mine, for the hay-harvest; but they won't be ready for us for more than a week: and besides, you might go with me, you know, and see some very nice people, besides making notes of our ways in Oxfordshire. You could hardly do better if you want to see the country.'

I felt myself obliged to thank him, whatever might come of it; and he added eagerly:

'Well, then, that's settled. I will give my friend a call; he is living in the Guest House like you, and if he isn't up yet, he ought to be this fine summer morning.'

Therewith he took a little silver bugle-horn from his girdle and blew two or three sharp but agreeable notes on it; and presently from the house which stood on the site of my old dwelling (of which more hereafter) another young man came sauntering towards us. He was not so well-looking or so strongly made as my sculler friend, being sandy-haired, rather pale, and not stout-built; but his face was not wanting in that happy and friendly expression which I had noticed in his friend. As he came up smiling towards us, I saw with pleasure that I must give up the Colney Hatch theory as to the waterman, for no two madmen ever behaved as they did before a sane man. His dress also was of the same cut as the first man's, though somewhat gayer, the surcoat being light green with a golden spray embroidered on the breast, and his belt being of filagree silver-work.

He gave me good-day very civilly, and greeting his friend joyously, said:

'Well, Dick, what is it this morning? Am I to have my work, or rather your work? I dreamed last night that we were off up the river fishing.'

'All right, Bob,' said my sculler; 'you will drop into my place, and if you find it too much, there is George Brightling on the look out for a stroke of work, and he lives close handy to you. But see, here is a stranger who is willing to amuse me to-day by taking me as his guide about our country-side, and you may imagine I don't want to lose the opportunity; so you had better take to the boat at once. But in any case I shouldn't have kept you out of it for long, since I am due in the hayfields in a few days.'

The newcomer rubbed his hands with glee, but turning to me, said in a friendly voice:

'Neighbour, both you and friend Dick are lucky, and will have a good time to-day, as indeed I shall too. But you had better both come in with me at once and get something to eat, lest you should forget your dinner in your amusement. I suppose you came into the Guest House after I had gone to bed last night?'

I nodded, not caring to enter into a long explanation which would have led to nothing, and which in truth by this time I should have begun to doubt myself. And we all three turned toward the door of the Guest House.

Chapter III. The Guest House and Breakfast therein

I lingered a little behind the others to have a stare at this house, which, as I have told you, stood on the site of my old dwelling.

It was a longish building with its gable ends turned away from the road, and long traceried windows coming rather low down set in the wall that faced us. It was very handsomely built of red brick with a lead roof; and high up above the windows there ran a frieze of figure subjects in baked clay, very well executed, and designed with a force and directness which I had never noticed in modern work before. The subjects I recognised at once, and indeed was very particularly familiar with them.

However, all this I took in in a minute; for we were presently within doors, and standing in a hall with a floor of marble mosaic and an open timber roof. There were no windows on the side opposite to the river, but arches below leading into chambers, one of which showed a glimpse of a garden beyond, and above them a long space of wall gaily painted (in fresco, I thought) with similar subjects to those of the frieze outside; everything about the place was handsome and generously solid as to material; and though it was not very large (somewhat smaller than Crosby Hall perhaps), one felt in it that exhilarating sense of space and freedom which satisfactory architecture always gives to an unanxious man who is in the habit of using his eyes.

In this pleasant place, which of course I knew to be the hall of the Guest House, three young women were flitting to and fro. As they were the first of the sex I had seen on this eventful morning, I naturally looked at them very attentively, and found them at least as good as the gardens, the architecture, and the male men. As to their dress, which of course I took note of, I should say that they were decently veiled with drapery, and not bundled up with millinery; that they were clothed like women, not upholstered like arm-chairs, as most women of our time are. In short, their dress was somewhat between that of the ancient classical costume and the simpler forms of the fourteenth century garments, though it was clearly not an imitation of either: the materials were light and gay to suit the season. As to the women themselves, it was pleasant indeed to see them, they were so kind and happy-looking in expression of face, so shapely and well-knit of body, and thoroughly healthy-looking and strong. All were at least comely, and one of them very handsome and regular of feature. They came up to us at once merrily and without the least affectation of shyness, and all three shook hands with me as if I were a friend newly come back from a long journey: though I could not help noticing that they looked askance at my garments; for I had on my clothes of last night, and at the best was never a dressy person.

A word or two from Robert the weaver, and they bustled about on our behoof, and presently came and took us by the hands and led us to a table in the pleasantest corner of the hall, where our breakfast was spread for us; and, as we sat down, one of them hurried out by the chambers aforesaid, and came back again in a little while with a great bunch of roses, very different in size and quality to what Hammersmith had been wont to grow, but very like the produce of an old country garden. She hurried back thence into the buttery, and came back once more with a delicately made glass, into which she put the flowers and set them down in the midst of our table. One of the others, who had run off also, then came back with a big cabbage-leaf filled with strawberries, some of them barely ripe, and said as she set them on the table, 'There, now; I thought of that before I got up this morning; but looking at the stranger here getting into your boat, Dick, put it out of my head; so that I was not before *all* the blackbirds: however, there are a few about as good as you will get them anywhere in Hammersmith this morning.'

Robert patted her on the head in a friendly manner; and we fell to on our breakfast, which was simple enough, but most delicately cooked, and set on the table with much daintiness. The bread was particularly good, and was of several different kinds, from the big, rather close, dark-coloured, sweet-tasting farmhouse loaf, which was most to my liking, to the thin pipe-stems of wheaten crust, such as I have eaten in Turin.

As I was putting the first mouthfuls into my mouth, my eye caught a carved and gilded inscription on the panelling, behind what we should have called the High Table in an Oxford college hall, and a familiar name in it forced me to read it through. Thus it ran:

Guests and neighbours, on the site of this Guest-hall once stood the lecture-room of the Hammersmith Socialists. Drink a glass to the memory! May 1962.

It is difficult to tell you how I felt as I read these words, and I suppose my face showed how much I was moved, for both my friends looked curiously at me, and there was silence between us for a little while.

Presently the weaver, who was scarcely so well mannered a man as the ferryman, said to me rather awkwardly:

'Guest, we don't know what to call you: is there any indiscretion in asking you your name?'

'Well,' said I, 'I have some doubts about it myself; so suppose you call me Guest, which is a family name, you know, and add William to it if you please.'

Dick nodded kindly to me; but a shade of anxiousness passed over the weaver's face, and he said—

'I hope you don't mind my asking, but would you tell me where you come from? I am curious about such things for good reasons, literary reasons.'

Dick was clearly kicking him underneath the table; but he was not much abashed, and awaited my answer somewhat eagerly. As for me, I was just going to blurt out 'Hammersmith', when I bethought me what an entanglement of cross purposes that would lead us into; so I took time to invent a lie with circumstance, guarded by a little truth, and said:

'You see, I have been such a long time away from Europe that things seem strange to me now; but I was born and bred on the edge of Epping Forest; Walthamstow and Woodford, to wit.'

'A pretty place too,' broke in Dick; 'a very jolly place, now that the trees have had time to grow again since the great clearing of houses in 1955.'

Quoth the irrepressible weaver: 'Dear neighbour, since you knew the Forest some time ago, could you tell me what truth there is in the rumour that in the nineteenth century the trees were all pollards?'

This was catching me on my archaeological natural-history side, and I fell into the trap without any thought of where and when I was; so I began on it, while one of the girls, the handsome one, who had been scattering little twigs of lavender and other sweet-smelling herbs about the floor, came near to listen, and stood behind me with her hand on my shoulder, in which she held some of the plant that I used to call balm: its strong sweet smell brought back to my mind my very early days in the kitchen-garden at Woodford, and the large blue plums which grew on the wall beyond the sweet-herb patch,—a connection of memories which all boys will see at once.

I started off: 'When I was a boy, and for long after, except for a piece about Queen Elizabeth's Lodge, and for the part about High Beech, the Forest was almost wholly made up of pollard hornbeams mixed with holly thickets. But when the Corporation of London took it over about twenty-five years ago, the topping and lopping, which was a part of the old commoners' rights, came to an end, and the trees were let to grow. But I have not seen the place now for many years except once, when we Leaguers went apleasuring to High Beech. I was very much shocked then to see how it was built-over and altered; and the other day we heard that the philistines were going to landscape-garden it. But what you were saying about the building being stopped and the trees growing is only too good news;—only you know—'

At that point I suddenly remembered Dick's date, and stopped short rather confused. The eager weaver didn't notice my confusion, but said hastily, as if he were almost aware of his breach of good manners, 'But, I say, how old are you?'

Dick and the pretty girl both burst out laughing, as if Robert's conduct were excusable on the grounds of eccentricity; and Dick said amidst his laughter:

'Hold hard, Bob; this questioning of guests won't do. Why, much learning is spoiling you. You remind me of the radical cobblers in the silly old novels, who, according to the authors, were prepared to trample down all good manners in the pursuit of utilitarian knowledge. The fact is, I begin to think that you have so muddled your head with mathematics, and with grubbing into those idiotic old books about political economy (he he!), that you scarcely know how to behave. Really, it is about time for you to take to some open-air work, so that you may clear away the cobwebs from your brain.'

The weaver only laughed good-humouredly; and the girl went up to him and patted his cheek and said laughingly, 'Poor fellow! he was born so.'

As for me, I was a little puzzled, but I laughed also, partly for company's sake, and partly with pleasure at their unanxious happiness and good temper; and before Robert could make the excuse to me which he was getting ready, I said:

'But neighbours' (I had caught up that word), 'I don't in the least mind answering questions, when I can do so: ask me as many as you please; it's fun for me. I will tell you all about Epping Forest when I was a boy, if you please; and as to my age, I'm not a fine lady, you know, so why shouldn't I tell you? I'm hard on fifty-six.'

In spite of the recent lecture on good manners, the weaver could not help giving a long 'whew' of astonishment, and the others were so amused by his *naïveté* that the merriment flitted all over their faces, though for courtesy's sake they forbore actual laughter; while I looked from one to the other in a puzzled manner, and at last said:

'Tell me, please, what is amiss: you know I want to learn from you. And please laugh; only tell me.'

Well, they *did* laugh, and I joined them again, for the above-stated reasons. But at last the pretty woman said coaxingly—

'Well, well, he *is* rude, poor fellow! but you see I may as well tell you what he is thinking about: he means that you look rather old for your age. But surely there need be no wonder in that, since you have been travelling; and clearly from all you have been saying, in unsocial countries. It has often been said, and no doubt truly, that one ages very quickly if one lives amongst unhappy people. Also they say that southern England is a good place for keeping good looks.' She blushed and said: 'How old am I, do you think?'

'Well,' quoth I, 'I have always been told that a woman is as old as she looks, so without offence or flattery, I should say that you were twenty.'

She laughed merrily, and said, 'I am well served out for fishing for compliments, since I have to tell you the truth, to wit, that I am forty-two.'

I stared at her, and drew musical laughter from her again; but I might well stare, for there was not a careful line on her face; her skin was as smooth as ivory, her cheeks full and round, her lips as red as the roses she had brought in; her beautiful arms, which she had bared for her work, firm and well-knit from shoulder to wrist. She blushed a little under my gaze, though it was clear that she had taken me for a man of eighty; so to pass it off I said—

'Well, you see, the old saw is proved right again, and I ought not to have let you tempt me into asking you a rude question.'

She laughed again, and said: 'Well, lads, old and young, I must get to my work now. We shall be rather busy here presently; and I want to clear it off soon, for I began to read a pretty old book yesterday, and I want to get on with it this morning; so good-bye for the present.'

She waved a hand to us, and stepped lightly down the hall, taking (as Scott says) at least part of the sun from our table as she went.

When she was gone, Dick said, 'Now guest, won't you ask a question or two of our friend here? It is only fair that you should have your turn.'

'I shall be very glad to answer them,' said the weaver.

'If I ask you any questions, sir,' said I, 'they will not be very severe; but since I hear that you are a weaver, I should like to ask you something about that craft, as I am—or was—interested in it.'

'Oh,' said he, 'I shall not be of much use to you there, I'm afraid. I only do the most mechanical kind of weaving, and am in fact but a poor craftsman, unlike Dick here. Then besides the weaving, I do a little with machine printing and composing, though I am little use at the finer kinds of printing; and moreover machine printing is beginning to die out, along with the waning of the plague of book-making; so I have had to turn to other things that I have a taste for, and have taken to mathematics; and also I am writing a sort of antiquarian book about the peaceable and private history, so to say, of the end of the nineteenth century,—more for the sake of giving a picture of the country before the fighting began than for anything else. That was why I asked you those questions about Epping Forest. You have rather puzzled me, I confess, though your information was so interesting. But later on, I hope, we may have some more talk together, when our friend Dick isn't here. I know he thinks me rather a grinder, and despises me for not being very deft with my hands: that's the way nowadays. From what I have read of the nineteenth century literature (and I have read a good deal), it is clear to me that this is a kind of revenge for the stupidity of that day, which despised everybody who *could* use his hands. But, Dick, old fellow, *Ne quid nimis!* Don't overdo it!'

'Come now,' said Dick, 'am I likely to? Am I not the most tolerant man in the world? Am I not quite contented so long as you don't make me learn mathematics, or go into your new science of aesthetics, and let me do a little practical aesthetics with my gold and steel, and the blowpipe and the nice little hammer? But, hillo! here comes another questioner for you, my poor guest. I say, Bob, you must help me to defend him now.'

'Here, Boffin,' he cried out, after a pause; 'here we are, if you must have it!'

I looked over my shoulder, and saw something flash and gleam in the sunlight that lay across the hall; so I turned round, and at my ease saw a splendid figure slowly sauntering over the pavement; a man whose surcoat was embroidered most copiously as well as elegantly, so that the sun flashed back from him as if he had been clad in golden armour. The man himself was tall, dark-haired, and exceedingly handsome, and though his face was no less kindly in expression than that of the others, he moved with that somewhat haughty mien which great beauty is apt to give to both men and women. He came and sat down at our table with a smiling face, stretching out his long legs and hanging his arm over the chair in the slowly graceful way which tall and well-built people may use without affectation. He was a man in the prime of life, but looked as happy as a child who has just got a new toy. He bowed gracefully to me and said—

'I see clearly that you are the guest, of whom Annie has just told me, who have come from some distant country that does not know of us, or our ways of life. So I daresay you would not mind answering me a few question; for you see—'

Here Dick broke in: 'No, please, Boffin! let it alone for the present. Of course you want the guest to be happy and comfortable; and how can that be if he has to trouble himself with answering all sorts of questions while he is still confused with the new customs and people about him? No, no: I am going to take him where he can ask questions himself, and have them answered; that is, to my great-grandfather in Bloomsbury: and I am sure you can't have anything to say against that. So instead of bothering, you had much better go out to James Allen's and get a carriage for me, as I shall drive him up myself; and please tell Jim to let me have the old grey, for I can drive a wherry much better than a carriage. Jump up, old fellow, and don't be disappointed; our guest will keep himself for you and your stories.'

I stared at Dick; for I wondered at his speaking to such a dignified-looking personage so familiarly, not to say curtly; for I thought that this Mr. Boffin, in spite of his well-known name out of Dickens, must be at the least a senator of these strange people. However, he got up and said, 'All right, old oar-wearer, whatever you like; this is not one of my busy days; and though' (with a condescending bow to me) 'my pleasure of a talk with this learned guest is put off, I admit that he ought to see your worthy kinsman as soon as possible. Besides, perhaps he will be the better able to answer *my* questions after his own have been answered.'

And therewith he turned and swung himself out of the hall.

When he was well gone, I said: 'Is it wrong to ask what Mr. Boffin is? whose name, by the way reminds me of many pleasant hours passed in reading Dickens.'

Dick laughed. 'Yes, yes,' said he: 'as it does us. I see you take the allusion. Of course his real name is not Boffin, but Henry Johnson; we only call him Boffin as a joke, partly because he is a dustman, and partly because he will dress so showily, and get as much gold on him as a baron of the Middle Ages. As why should he not if he likes? only we are his special friends, you know, so of course we jest with him.'

I held my tongue for some time after that; but Dick went on:

'He is a capital fellow, and you can't help liking him; but he has a weakness: he will spend his time in writing reactionary novels, and is very proud of getting the local colour right, as he calls it; and as he thinks you come from some forgotten corner of the earth, where people are unhappy, and consequently interesting to a story-teller, he thinks he might get some information out of you. O, he will be quite straightforward with you, for that matter. Only for your own comfort beware of him!'

'Well, Dick' said the weaver, doggedly, 'I think his novels are very good.'

'Of course you do,' said Dick; 'birds of a feather flock together; mathematics and antiquarian novels stand on much the same footing. But here he comes again.'

And in effect the Golden Dustman hailed us from the hall-door; so we all got up and went into the porch, before which, with a strong grey horse in the shafts, stood a carriage ready for us which I could not help noticing. It was light and handy, but had none of that sickening vulgarity which I had known as inseparable from the carriages of our time, especially the 'elegant' ones, but was as graceful and pleasant in line as a Wessex wagon. We got in, Dick and I. The girls, who had come into the porch to see us off, waved their hands to us; the weaver nodded kindly; the dustman bowed as gracefully as a troubadour; Dick shook the reins, and we were off.

Chapter IV. A Market by the Way

We turned away from the river at once, and were soon in the main road that runs through Hammersmith. But I should have had no guess as to where I was, if I had not started from the waterside; for King Street was gone, and the highway ran through wide sunny meadows and garden-like tillage. The Creek, which we crossed at once, had been rescued from its culvert, and as we went over its pretty bridge we saw its waters, yet swollen by the tide, covered with gay boats of different sizes. There were houses about, some on the road, some amongst the fields with pleasant lanes leading down to them, and each surrounded by a teeming garden. They were all pretty in design, and as solid as might be, but countryfied in appearance, like yeomen's dwellings; some of them of red brick like those by the river, but more of timber and plaster, which were by the necessity of their construction so like mediæval houses of the same materials that I fairly felt as if I were alive in the fourteenth century; a sensation helped out by the costume of the people that we met or passed, in whose dress there was nothing 'modern'. Almost everybody was gaily dressed, but especially the women, who were so well-looking, or even so handsome, that I could scarcely refrain my tongue from calling my companion's attention to the fact. Some faces I saw that were thoughtful, and in these I noticed great nobility of expression, but none that had a glimmer of unhappiness, and the greater part (we came upon a good many people) were frankly and openly joyous.

I thought I knew the Broadway by the lie of the roads that still met there. On the north side of the road was a range of buildings and courts, low, but very handsomely built and ornamented, and in that way forming a great contrast to the unpretentiousness of the houses round about; while above this lower building rose the steep lead-covered roof and the buttresses and higher part of the wall of a great hall, of a splendid and exuberant style of architecture, of which one can say little more than that it seemed to me to embrace the best qualities of the Gothic of northern Europe with those of the Saracenic and Byzantine, though there was no copying of any one of these styles. On the other, the south side, of the road was an octagonal building with a high roof, not unlike the Baptistry at Florence in outline, except that it was surrounded by a lean-to that clearly made an arcade or cloisters to it; it also was most delicately ornamented.

This whole mass of architecture which we had come upon so suddenly from amidst the pleasant fields was not only exquisitely beautiful in itself, but it bore upon it the expression of such generosity and abundance of life that I was exhilarated to a pitch that I had never yet reached. I fairly chuckled for pleasure. My friend seemed to understand it, and sat looking on me with a pleased and affectionate interest. We had pulled up amongst a crowd of carts, wherein sat handsome healthy-looking people, men, women, and children very gaily dressed, and which were clearly market carts, as they were full of very tempting-looking country produce.

I said, 'I need not ask if this is a market, for I see clearly that it is; but what market is it that it is so splendid? And what is the glorious hall there, and what is the building on the south side?'

'O,' said he, 'it is just our Hammersmith market; and I am glad you like it so much, for we are really proud of it. Of course the hall inside is our winter Mote-House; for in summer we mostly meet in the fields down by the river opposite Barn Elms. The building on our right hand is our theatre: I hope you like it.'

'I should be a fool if I didn't,' said I.

He blushed a little as he said: 'I am glad of that, too, because I had a hand in it; I made the great doors, which are of damascened bronze. We will look at them later in the day, perhaps: but we ought to be getting on now. As to the market, this is not one of our busy days; so we shall do better with it another time, because you will see more people.'

I thanked him, and said: 'Are these the regular country people? What very pretty girls there are amongst them.'

As I spoke, my eye caught the face of a beautiful woman, tall, dark-haired, and white-skinned, dressed in a pretty light-green dress in honour of the season and the hot day, who smiled kindly on me, and more kindly still, I thought, on Dick; so I stopped a minute, but presently went on:

'I ask because I do not see any of the country-looking people I should have expected to see at a market—I mean selling things there.'

'I don't understand,' said he, 'what kind of people you would expect to see; nor quite what you mean by "country" people. These are the neighbours and that like they run in the Thames valley. There are parts of these islands which are rougher and rainier than we are here, and there people are rougher in their dress; and they themselves are tougher and more hard-bitten than we are to look at. But some people like their looks better than ours; they say they have more character in them—that's the word. Well, it's a matter of taste.— Anyhow, the cross between us and them generally turns out well,' added he, thoughtfully.

I heard him, though my eyes were turned away from him, for that pretty girl was just disappearing through the gate with her big basket of early peas, and I felt that disappointed kind of feeling which overtakes one when one has seen an interesting or lovely face in the streets which one is never likely to see again; and I was silent a little. At last I said: 'What I mean is, that I haven't seen any poor people about—not one.'

He knit his brows, looked puzzled, and said: 'No, naturally; if anybody is poorly, he is likely to be within doors, or at best crawling about the garden: but I don't know of any one sick at present. Why should you expect to see poorly people on the road?'

'No, no,' I said; 'I don't mean sick people. I mean poor people, you know; rough people.'

'No,' said he, smiling merrily, 'I really do not know. The fact is, you must come along quick to my great-grandfather, who will understand you better than I do. Come on, Greylocks!' Therewith he shook the reins, and we jogged along merrily eastward.

Chapter V. Children on the Road

Past the Broadway there were fewer houses on either side. We presently crossed a pretty little brook that ran across a piece of land dotted over with trees, and awhile after came to another market and town-hall, as we should call it. Although there was nothing familiar to me in its surroundings, I knew pretty well where we were and was not surprised when my guide said briefly, 'Kensington Market.'

Just after this we came into a short street of houses; or rather, one long house on either side of the way, built of timber and plaster, and with a pretty arcade over the footway before it.

Quoth Dick: 'This is Kensington proper. People are apt to gather here rather thick, for they like the romance of the wood; and naturalists haunt it, too; for it is a wild spot even here, what there is of it; for it does not go far to the south: it goes from here northward and west right over Paddington and a little way down Notting Hill: thence it runs north-east to Primrose Hill, and so on; rather a narrow strip of it gets through Kingsland to Stoke-Newington and Clapton, where it spreads out along the heights above the Lea marshes; on the other side of which, as you know, is Epping Forest holding out a hand to it. This part we are just coming to is called Kensington Gardens; though why "gardens" I don't know.'

I rather longed to say, 'Well, *I* know;' but there were so many things about me which I did *not* know, in spite of his assumptions, that I thought it better to hold my tongue.

The road plunged at once into a beautiful wood spreading out on either side, but obviously much further on the north side, where even the oaks and sweet chestnuts were of a good growth; while the quicker-growing trees (amongst which I thought the planes and sycamores too numerous) were very big and fine-grown.

It was exceedingly pleasant in the dappled shadow, for the day was growing as hot as need be, and the coolness and shade soothed my excited mind into a condition of dreamy pleasure, so that I felt as if I should like to go on for ever through that balmy freshness. My companion seemed to share in my feelings, and let the horse go slower and slower as he sat inhaling the green forest scents, chief amongst which was the smell of the trodden bracken near the way-side.

Romantic as this Kensington wood was, however, it was not lonely. We came on many groups both coming and going, or wandering in the edges of the wood. Amongst these were many children from six or eight years old up to sixteen or seventeen. They seemed to me to be especially fine specimens of their race, and were clearly enjoying themselves to the utmost; some of them were hanging about little tents pitched on the greensward, and by some of these fires were burning, with pots hanging over them gipsy fashion. Dick explained to me that there were scattered houses in the forest, and indeed we caught a glimpse of one or two. He said they were mostly quite small, such as used to be called cottages when there were slaves in the land, but they were pleasant enough and fitting for the wood.

'They must be pretty well stocked with children,' said I, pointing to the many youngsters about the way.

'O,' said he, 'these children do not all come from the near houses, the woodland houses, but from the countryside generally. They often make up parties, and come to play in the woods for weeks together in summer-time, living in tents, as you see. We rather encourage them to it; they learn to do things for themselves, and get to notice the wild creatures; and, you see, the less they stew inside houses the better for them. Indeed, I must tell you that many grown people will go to live in the forests through the summer; though they for the most part go to the bigger ones, like Windsor, or the Forest of the Dean, or the northern wastes. Apart from the other pleasures of it, it gives them a little rough work, which I am sorry to say is getting somewhat scarce for the last fifty years.'

He broke off, and then said, 'I tell you all this because I see that if I talk I must be answering questions, which you are thinking, even if you are not speaking them out; but my kinsman will tell you more about it.'

I saw that I was likely to get out of my depth again, and so merely for the sake of tiding over an awkwardness and to say something, I said:

'Well, the youngsters here will be all the fresher for school when the summer gets over and they have to go back again.'

'School?' he said; 'yes, what do you mean by that word? I don't see how it can have anything to do with children. We talk, indeed, of a school of herring, and a school of painting, and in the former sense we might talk of a school of children—but otherwise,' said he, laughing, 'I must own myself beaten.'

Hang it! thought I, I can't open my mouth without digging up some new complexity. I wouldn't try to set my friend right in his etymology; and I thought I had best say nothing about the boy-farms which I had been used to call schools, as I saw pretty clearly that they had disappeared; and so I said after a little fumbling, 'I was using the word in the sense of a system of education.'

'Education?' said he, meditatively, 'I know enough Latin to know that the word must come from *educere*, to lead out; and I have heard it used; but I have never met anybody who could give me a clear explanation of what it means.'

You may imagine how my new friends fell in my esteem when I heard this frank avowal; and I said, rather contemptuously, 'Well, education means a system of teaching young people.'

'Why not old people also?' said he with a twinkle in his eye. 'But,' he went on, 'I can assure you our children learn, whether they go through a "system of teaching" or not. Why, you will not find one of these children about here, boy or girl, who cannot swim, and every one of them has been used to tumbling about the little forest ponies—there's one of them now! They all of them know how to cook; the bigger lads can mow; many can thatch and do odd jobs at carpentering; or they know how to keep shop. I can tell you they know plenty of things.

'Yes, but their mental education, the teaching of their minds,' said I, kindly translating my phrase.

'Guest,' said he, 'perhaps you have not learned to do these things I have been speaking about; and if that's the case, don't you run away with the idea that it doesn't take some skill to do them, and doesn't give plenty of work for one's mind: you would change your opinion if you saw a Dorsetshire lad thatching, for instance. But, however, I understand you to be speaking of book-learning; and as to that, it is a simple affair. Most children, seeing books lying about, manage to read by the time they are four years old; though I am told it has not always been so. As to writing, we do not encourage them to scrawl too early (though scrawl a little they will), because it gets them into a habit of ugly writing; and what's the use of a lot of ugly writing being done, when rough printing can be done so easily. You understand that handsome writing we like, and many people will write their books out when they make them, or get them written; I mean books of which only a few copies are needed—poems, and such like, you know. However, I am wandering from my lambs; but you must excuse me, for I am interested in this matter of writing, being myself a fair writer.'

'Well,' said I, 'about the children; when they know how to read and write, don't they learn something else—languages, for instance?'

'Of course,' he said; 'sometimes even before they can read, they can talk French, which is the nearest language talked on the other side of the water; and they soon get to know German also, which is talked by a huge number of communes and colleges on the mainland. These are the principal languages we speak in these islands, along with English or Welsh, or Irish, which is another form of Welsh; and children pick them up very quickly, because their elders all know them; and besides our guests from over sea often bring their children with them, and the little ones get together, and rub their speech into one another.'

'And the older languages?' said I.

'O, yes,' said he, 'they mostly learn Latin and Greek along with the modern ones, when they do anything more than merely pick up the latter.'

'And history?' said I; 'how do you teach history?'

'Well,' said he, 'when a person can read, of course he reads what he likes to; and he can easily get someone to tell him what are the best books to read on such or such a subject, or to explain what he doesn't understand in the books when he is reading them.'

'Well,' said I, 'what else do they learn? I suppose they don't all learn history?'

'No, no,' said he; 'some don't care about it; in fact, I don't think many do. I have heard my great-grandfather say that it is mostly in periods of turmoil and strife and confusion that people care so much about history; and you know,' said my friend, with an amiable smile, 'we are not like that now. No; many people study facts about the make of things and the matters of cause and effect, so that knowledge increases on us, if that be good; and some, as you heard about friend Bob yonder, will spend time over mathematics. 'Tis no use forcing people's tastes.'

Said I: 'But you don't mean that children learn all these things?'

Said he: 'That depends on what you mean by children; and also you must remember how much they differ. As a rule, they don't do much reading, except for a few story-books, till they are about fifteen years old; we don't encourage early bookishness; though you will find some children who *will* take to books very early; which perhaps is not good for them; but it's no use thwarting them; and very often it doesn't last long with them, and they find their level before they are twenty years old. You see, children are mostly given to imitating their elders, and when they see most people about them engaged in genuinely amusing work, like house-building and street-paving, and gardening and the like, that is what they want to be doing; so I don't think we need fear having too many book-learned men.'

What could I say? I sat and held my peace, for fear of fresh entanglements. Besides, I was using my eyes with all my might, wondering as the old horse jogged on, when I should come into London proper, and what it would be like now.

But my companion couldn't let his subject quite drop, and went on meditatively:

'After all, I don't know that it does them much harm, even if they do grow up book-students. Such people as that, 'tis a great pleasure seeing them so happy over work which is not much sought for. And besides, these students are generally such pleasant people; so kind and sweet tempered; so humble, and at the same time so anxious to teach everybody all that they know. Really, I like those that I have met prodigiously.'

This seemed to me such *very* queer talk that I was on the point of asking him another question; when just as we came to the top of a rising ground, down a long glade of the wood on my right I caught sight of a stately building whose outline was familiar to me, and I cried out, 'Westminster Abbey!'

'Yes,' said Dick, 'Westminster Abbey—what there is left of it.'

'Why, what have you done with it?' quoth I in terror.

'What have *we* done with it?' said he; 'nothing much, save clean it. But you know the whole outside was spoiled centuries ago: as to the inside, that remains in its beauty after the great clearance, which took place over a hundred years ago, of the beastly monuments to fools and knaves, which once blocked it up, as great-grandfather says.'

We went on a little further, and I looked to the right again, and said, in rather a doubtful tone of voice, 'Why, there are the Houses of Parliament! Do you still use them?'

He burst out laughing, and was some time before he could control himself; then he clapped me on the back and said:

'I take you, neighbour; you may well wonder at our keeping them standing, and I know something about that, and my old kinsman has given me books to read about the strange game that they played there. Use them! Well, yes, they are used for a sort of subsidiary market, and a storage place for manure, and they are handy for that, being on the water-side. I believe it was intended to pull them down quite at the beginning of our days; but there was, I am told, a queer antiquarian society which had done some service in past times, and which straightway set up its pipe against their destruction, as it has done with many other buildings, which most people looked on as worthless, and public nuisances; and it was so energetic, and had such good reasons to give, that it generally gained its point; and I must say that when all is said I am glad of it: because you know at the worst these silly old buildings serve as a kind of foil to the beautiful ones which we build now. You will see several others in these parts; the place my great-grandfather lives in, for instance, and a big building called St. Paul's. And you see, in this matter we need not grudge a few poorish buildings standing, because we can always build elsewhere; nor need we be anxious as to the breeding of pleasant work in such matters, for there is always room for more and more work in a new building, even without making it pretentious. For instance, elbow-room *within* doors is to me so delightful that if I were driven to it I would almost sacrifice out-door space to it. Then, of course, there is the ornament, which, as we must all allow, may easily be overdone in mere living houses, but can hardly be in mote-halls and markets, and so forth. I must tell you, though, that my great-grandfather sometimes tells me I am a little cracked on this subject of fine building; and indeed I *do* think that the energies of mankind are chiefly of use to them for such work; for in that direction I can see no end to the work, while in many others a limit does seem possible.'

Chapter VI. A Little Shopping

As he spoke, we came suddenly out of the woodland into a short street of handsomely built houses, which my companion named to me at once as Piccadilly: the lower part of these I should have called shops, if it had not been that, as far as I could see, the people were ignorant of the arts of buying and selling. Wares were displayed in their finely designed fronts, as if to tempt people in, and people stood and looked at them, or went in and came out with parcels under their arms, just like the real thing. On each side of the street ran an elegant arcade to protect foot-passengers, as in some of the old Italian cities. About half-way down, a huge building of the kind I was now prepared to expect told me that this was a centre of some kind, and had its special public buildings.

Said Dick: 'Here, you see, is another market on a different plan from most others: the upper stories of these houses are used for guest-houses; for people from all about the country are apt to drift up hither from time to time, as folk are very thick upon the ground, which you will see evidence of presently, and there are people who are fond of crowds, though I can't say that I am.'

I couldn't help smiling to see how long a tradition would last. Here was the ghost of London still asserting itself as a centre,—an intellectual centre, for aught I knew. However, I said nothing, except that I asked him to drive very slowly as the things in the booth looked exceedingly pretty.

'Yes,' said he, 'this is a very good market for pretty things, and is mostly kept for the handsomer goods, as the Houses-of-Parliament market, where they set out cabbages and turnips and such like things, along with beer and the rougher kind of wine, is so near.'

Then he looked at me curiously, and said, 'Perhaps you would like to do a little shopping, as 'tis called.'

I looked at what I could see of my rough blue duds, which I had plenty of opportunity of contrasting with the gay attire of the citizens we had come across; and I thought that if, as seemed likely, I should presently be shown about as a curiosity for the amusement of this most unbusinesslike people, I should like to look a little less like a discharged ship's purser. But in spite of all that had happened, my hand went down into my pocket again, where to my dismay it met nothing metallic except two rusty old keys, and I remembered that amidst our talk in the guest-hall at Hammersmith I had taken the cash out of my pocket to show to the pretty Annie, and had left it lying there. My face fell fifty per cent., and Dick, beholding me, said rather sharply:

'Hilloa, Guest! what's the matter now? Is it a wasp?'

'No,' said I, 'but I've left it behind.'

'Well,' said he, 'whatever you have left behind, you can get in this market again, so don't trouble yourself about it.'

I had come to my senses by this time, and remembering the astounding customs of this country, had no mind for another lecture on social economy and the Edwardian coinage; so I said only:

'My clothes—Couldn't I? You see—What do you think could be done about them?'

He didn't seem in the least inclined to laugh, but said quite gravely:

'O don't get new clothes yet. You see, my great-grandfather is an antiquarian, and he will want to see you just as you are. And, you know, I mustn't preach to you, but surely it wouldn't be right for you to take away people's pleasure of studying your attire, by just going and making yourself like everybody else. You feel that, don't you?' said he, earnestly.

I did *not* feel it my duty to set myself up for a scarecrow amidst this beauty-loving people but I saw I had got across some ineradicable prejudice, and that it wouldn't do to quarrel with my new friend. So I merely said, 'O certainly, certainly.'

'Well,' said he, pleasantly, 'you may as well see what the inside of these booths is like: think of something you want.'

Said I: 'Could I get some tobacco and a pipe?'

'Of course,' said he; 'what was I thinking of, not asking you before? Well, Bob is always telling me that we non-smokers are a selfish lot, and I'm afraid he is right. But come along; here is a place just handy.'

Therewith he drew rein and jumped down, and I followed. A very handsome woman, splendidly clad in figured silk, was slowly passing by, looking into the windows as she went. To her quoth Dick: 'Maiden, would you kindly hold our horse while we go in for a little while?' She nodded to us with a kind smile, and fell to patting the horse with her pretty hand.

'What a beautiful creature!' said I to Dick as we entered.

'What, old Greylocks?' said he, with a sly grin.

'No, no,' said I; 'Goldylocks,—the lady.'

'Well, so she is,' said he. ''Tis a good job there are so many of them that every Jack may have his Jill; else I fear that we should get fighting for them. Indeed,' said he, becoming very grave, 'I don't say that it does not happen even now, sometimes. For you know love is not a very reasonable thing, and perversity and self-will are commoner than some of our moralists think.' He added, in a still more sombre tone: 'Yes, only a month ago there was a mishap down by us, that in the end cost the lives of two men and a woman, and, as it were, put out the sunlight for us for a while. Don't ask me about it just now; I may tell you about it later on.'

By this time we were within the shop or booth, which had a counter, and shelves on the walls, all very neat, though without any pretence of showiness, but otherwise not very different to what I had been used to. Within were a couple of children—a brown-skinned boy of about twelve, who sat reading a book, and a pretty little girl of about a year older, who was sitting also reading behind the counter; they were obviously brother and sister.

'Good morning, little neighbours,' said Dick. 'My friend here wants tobacco and a pipe; can you help him?'

'O yes, certainly,' said the girl with a sort of demure alertness which was somewhat amusing. The boy looked up, and fell to staring at my outlandish attire, but presently reddened and turned his head, as if he knew that he was not behaving prettily.

'Dear neighbour,' said the girl, with the most solemn countenance of a child playing at keeping shop, 'what tobacco is it you would like?'

'Latakia,' quoth I, feeling as if I were assisting at a child's game, and wondering whether I should get anything but make-believe.

But the girl took a dainty little basket from a shelf beside her, went to a jar, and took out a lot of tobacco and put the filled basket down on the counter before me, where I could both smell and see that it was excellent Latakia.

'But you haven't weighed it,' said I, 'and—and how much am I to take?'

'Why,' she said, 'I advise you to cram your bag, because you may be going where you can't get Latakia. Where is your bag?'

I fumbled about, and at last pulled out my piece of cotton print which does duty with me for a tobacco pouch. But the girl looked at it with some disdain, and said:

'Dear neighbour, I can give you something much better than that cotton rag.' And she tripped up the shop and came back presently, and as she passed the boy whispered something in his ear, and he nodded and got up and went out. The girl held up in her finger and thumb a red morocco bag, gaily embroidered, and said, 'There, I have chosen one for you, and you are to have it: it is pretty, and will hold a lot.'

Therewith she fell to cramming it with the tobacco, and laid it down by me and said, 'Now for the pipe: that also you must let me choose for you; there are three pretty ones just come in.'

She disappeared again, and came back with a big-bowled pipe in her hand, carved out of some hard wood very elaborately, and mounted in gold sprinkled with little gems. It was, in short, as pretty and gay a toy as I had ever seen; something like the best kind of Japanese work, but better.

'Dear me!' said I, when I set eyes on it, 'this is altogether too grand for me, or for anybody but the Emperor of the World. Besides, I shall lose it: I always lose my pipes.'

The child seemed rather dashed, and said, 'Don't you like it, neighbour?'

'O yes,' I said, 'of course I like it.'

'Well, then, take it,' said she, 'and don't trouble about losing it. What will it matter if you do? Somebody is sure to find it, and he will use it, and you can get another.'

I took it out of her hand to look at it, and while I did so, forgot my caution, and said, 'But however am I to pay for such a thing as this?'

Dick laid his hand on my shoulder as I spoke, and turning I met his eyes with a comical expression in them, which warned me against another exhibition of extinct commercial morality; so I reddened and held my tongue, while the girl simply looked at me with the deepest gravity, as if I were a foreigner blundering in my speech, for she clearly didn't understand me a bit.

'Thank you so very much,' I said at last, effusively, as I put the pipe in my pocket, not without a qualm of doubt as to whether I shouldn't find myself before a magistrate presently.

'O, you are so very welcome,' said the little lass, with an affectation of grown-up manners at their best which was very quaint. 'It is such a pleasure to serve dear old gentlemen like you; specially when one can see at once that you have come from far over sea.'

'Yes, my dear,' quoth I, 'I have been a great traveller.'

As I told this lie from pure politeness, in came the lad again, with a tray in his hands, on which I saw a long flask and two beautiful glasses. 'Neighbours,' said the girl (who did all the talking, her brother being very shy, clearly), 'please to drink a glass to us before you go since we do not have guests like this every day.'

Therewith the boy put the tray on the counter and solemnly poured out a straw-coloured wine into the long bowls. Nothing loth, I drank, for I was thirsty with the hot day; and thinks I, I am yet in the world, and the grapes of the Rhine have not yet lost their flavour; for if ever I drank good Steinberg, I drank it that morning; and I made a mental note to ask Dick how they managed to make fine wine when there were no longer labourers compelled to drink rot-gut instead of the fine wine which they themselves made.

'Don't you drink a glass to us, dear little neighbours?' said I.

'I don't drink wine,' said the lass; 'I like lemonade better: but I wish your health!'

'And I like ginger-beer better,' said the little lad.

Well, well, thought I, neither have children's tastes changed much. And therewith we gave them good day and went out of the booth.

To my disappointment, like a change in a dream, a tall old man was holding our horse instead of the beautiful woman. He explained to us that the maiden could not wait, and that he had taken her place; and he winked at us and laughed when he saw how our faces fell so that we had nothing for it but to laugh also.

'Where are you going?' said he to Dick.

'To Bloomsbury,' said Dick.

'If you two don't want to be alone, I'll come with you,' said the old man.

'All right,' said Dick, 'tell me when you want to get down and I'll stop for you. Let's get on.'

So we got under way again; and I asked if children generally waited on people in the markets. 'Often enough,' said he, 'when it isn't a matter of dealing with heavy weights, but by no means always. The children like to amuse themselves with it, and it is good for them, because they handle a lot of diverse wares and get to learn about them, how they are made, and where they come from, and so on. Besides, it is such very easy work that anybody can do it. It is said that in the early days of our epoch there were a good many people who were hereditarily afflicted with a disease called Idleness, because they were the direct descendants of those who in the bad times used to force other people to work for them—the people, you know, who are called slave-holders or employers of labour in the history books. Well, these Idleness-stricken people used to serve booths *all* their time, because they were fit for so little. Indeed, I believe that at one time they were actually *compelled* to do some such work, because, they, especially the women, got so ugly and produced such ugly children if their disease was not treated sharply, that the neighbours couldn't stand it. However I am happy to say that all that is gone by now; the disease is either extinct, or exists in such a mild form that a short course of aperient medicine carries it off. It is sometimes called the Blue-devils now, or the Mulleygrubs. Queer names, ain't they?'

'Yes,' said I, pondering much. But the old man broke in:

'Yes, all that is true, neighbour; and I have seen some of those women grown old. But my father used to know some of them when they were young; and he said that they were as little like young women as might be: they had hands like bunches of skewers, and wretched little arms like sticks; and waists like hour-glasses, and thin lips and peaked noses and pale cheeks; and they were always pretending to be offended at anything you said or did to them. No wonder they bore ugly children, for no one except men like them could be in love with them—poor things!'

He stopped, and seemed to be musing on his past life, and then said:

'And do you know, neighbours, that once on a time people were still anxious about that disease of Idleness: at one time we gave ourselves a great deal of trouble in trying to cure people of it. Have you not read any of the medical books on the subject?'

'No,' said I; for the old man was speaking to me.

'Well,' said he, 'it was thought at the time that it was the survival of the old mediæval disease of leprosy: it seems it was very catching, for many of the people afflicted by it were much secluded, and were waited upon by a special class of diseased persons queerly dressed up, so that they might be known. They wore amongst other garments, breeches made of worsted velvet, that stuff which used to be called plush some years ago.'

All this seemed very interesting to me, and I should like to have made the old man talk more. But Dick got rather restive under so much ancient history: besides, I suspect he wanted to keep me as fresh as he could for his great-grandfather. So he burst out laughing at last, and said: 'Excuse me, neighbours, but I can't help it. Fancy people not liking to work!—it's too ridiculous. Why, even you like to work, old fellow—sometimes,' said he, affectionately patting the old horse with the whip. 'What a queer disease! it may well be called Mulleygrubs!'

And he laughed out again most boisterously; rather too much so, I thought, for his usual good manners; and I laughed with him for company's sake, but from the teeth outward only; for *I* saw nothing funny in people not liking to work, as you may well imagine.

Chapter VII. Trafalgar Square

And now again I was busy looking about me, for we were quite clear of Piccadilly Market, and were in a region of elegantly-built much ornamented houses, which I should have called villas if they had been ugly and pretentious, which was very far from being the case. Each house stood in a garden carefully cultivated, and running over with flowers. The blackbirds were singing their best amidst the garden-trees, which, except for a bay here and there, and occasional groups of limes, seemed to be all fruit-trees: there were a great many cherry-trees, now all laden with fruit; and several times as we passed by a garden we were offered baskets of fine fruit by children and young girls. Amidst all these gardens and houses it was of course impossible to trace the sites of the old streets: but it seemed to me that the main roadways were the same as of old.

We came presently into a large open space, sloping somewhat toward the south, the sunny site of which had been taken advantage of for planting an orchard, mainly, as I could see, of apricot trees, in the midst of which was a pretty gay little structure of wood, painted and gilded, that looked like a refreshment-stall. From the southern side of the said orchard ran a long road, chequered over with the shadow of tall old pear trees, at the end of which showed the high tower of the Parliament House, or Dung Market.

A strange sensation came over me; I shut my eyes to keep out the sight of the sun glittering on this fair abode of gardens, and for a moment there passed before them a phantasmagoria of another day. A great space surrounded by tall ugly houses, with an ugly church at the corner and a nondescript ugly cupolaed building at my back; the roadway thronged with a sweltering and excited crowd, dominated by omnibuses crowded with spectators. In the midst a paved be-fountained square, populated only by a few men dressed in blue and a good many singularly ugly bronze images (one on the top of a tall column). The said square guarded up to the edge of the roadway by a four-fold line of big men clad in blue, and across the southern roadway the helmets of a band of horse-soldiers, dead white in the greyness of the chilly November afternoon—

I opened my eyes to the sunlight again and looked round me, and cried out among the whispering trees and odorous blossoms, 'Trafalgar Square!'

'Yes,' said Dick, who had drawn rein again, 'so it is. I don't wonder at your finding the name ridiculous: but after all, it was nobody's business to alter it, since the name of a dead folly doesn't bite. Yet sometimes I think we might have given it a name which would have commemorated the great battle which was fought on the spot itself in 1952,—*that* was important enough, if the historians don't lie.'

'Which they generally do, or at least did,' said the old man. 'For instance what can you make of this, neighbours? I have read a muddled account in a book—O a stupid book!—called James' Social Democratic History, of a fight which took place here in or about the year 1887 (I am bad at dates). Some people, says this story, were going to hold a ward-mote here, or some such thing, and the Government of London, or the Council, or the Commission, or what not other barbarous half-hatched body of fools, fell upon these citizens (as they were then called) with the armed hand. That seems too ridiculous to be true; but according to this version of the story, nothing much came of it, which certainly *is* too ridiculous to be true.'

'Well,' quoth I, 'but after all your Mr. James is right so far, and it *is* true; except that there was no fighting, merely unarmed and peaceable people attacked by ruffians armed with bludgeons.'

'And they put up with that?' said Dick, with the first unpleasant expression I had seen on his good-tempered face.

Said I, reddening: 'We *had* to put up with it; we couldn't help it.'

The old man looked at me keenly, and said: 'You seem to know a great deal about it, neighbour! And is it really true that nothing came of it?'

'This came of it,' said I, 'that a good many people were sent to prison because of it.'

'What, of the bludgeoners?' said the old man. 'Poor devils!'

'No, no,' said I, 'of the bludgeoned.'

Said the old man rather severely: 'Friend, I expect that you have been reading some rotten collection of lies, and have been taken in by it too easily.'

'I assure you,' said I, 'what I have been saying is true.'

'Well, well, I am sure you think so, neighbour,' said the old man, 'but I don't see why you should be so cocksure.'

As I couldn't explain why, I held my tongue. Meanwhile Dick, who had been sitting with knit brows, cogitating, spoke at last, and said gently and rather sadly:

'How strange to think that there have been men like ourselves, and living in this beautiful and happy country, who I suppose had feelings and affections like ourselves, who could yet do such dreadful things.'

'Yes,' said I, in a didactic tone; 'yet after all, even those days were a great improvement on the days that had gone before them. Have you not read of the Mediæval period, and the ferocity of its criminal laws; and how in those days men fairly seemed to have enjoyed tormenting their fellow-men?—nay, for the matter of that, they made their God a tormenter and a jailer rather than anything else.'

'Yes,' said Dick, 'there are good books on the period also, some of which I have read. But as to the great improvement of the nineteenth century, I don't see it. After all, the Mediæval folk acted after their conscience, as your remark about their God (which is true) shows, and they were ready to bear what they inflicted on others; whereas the nineteenth century ones were hypocrites, and pretended to be humane, and yet went on tormenting those whom they dared to treat so by shutting them up in prison, for no reason at all, except that they were what they themselves, the prison-masters, had forced them to be. O, it's horrible to think of!'

'But perhaps,' said I, 'they did not know what the prisons were like.'

Dick seemed roused, and even angry. 'More shame for them,' said he, 'when you and I know it all these years afterwards. Look you, neighbour, they couldn't fail to know what a disgrace prison is to the Commonwealth at the best, and that their prisons were a good step on towards being at the worst.'

Quoth I: 'But have you no prisons at all now?'

As soon as the words were out of my mouth, I felt that I had made a mistake, for Dick flushed red and frowned, and the old man looked surprised and pained; and presently Dick said angrily, yet as if restraining himself somewhat—

'Man alive! how can you ask such a question? Have I not told you that we know what a prison means by the undoubted evidence of really trustworthy books, helped out by our own imaginations? And haven't you specially called me to notice that the people about the roads and streets look happy? and how could they look happy if they knew that their neighbours were shut up in prison, while they bore such things quietly? And if there were people in prison, you couldn't hide it from folk, like you may an occasional man-slaying; because that isn't done of set purpose with a lot of people backing up the slayer in cold blood, as this prison business is. Prisons, indeed! O no, no, no!'

He stopped, and began to cool down, and said in a kind voice: 'But forgive me! I needn't be so hot about it, since there are *not* any prisons: I'm afraid you will think the worse of me for losing my temper. Of course, you, coming from the outlands, cannot be expected to know about these things. And now I'm afraid I have made you feel uncomfortable.'

In a way he had; but he was so generous in his heat, that I liked him the better for it, and I said: 'No, really 'tis all my fault for being so stupid. Let me change the subject, and ask you what the stately building is on our left just showing at the end of that grove of plane-trees?'

'Ah,' he said, 'that is an old building built before the middle of the twentieth century, and as you see, in a queer fantastic style not over beautiful; but there are some fine things inside it, too, mostly pictures, some very old. It is called the National Gallery; I have sometimes puzzled as to what the name means: anyhow, nowadays wherever there is a place where pictures are kept as curiosities permanently it is called a National Gallery, perhaps after this one. Of course there are a good many of them up and down the country.'

I didn't try to enlighten him, feeling the task too heavy; but I pulled out my magnificent pipe and fell a-smoking, and the old horse jogged on again. As we went, I said:

'This pipe is a very elaborate toy, and you seem so reasonable in this country and your architecture is so good, that I rather wonder at your turning out such trivialities.'

It struck me as I spoke that this was rather ungrateful of me, after having received such a fine present; but Dick didn't seem to notice my bad manners, but said:

'Well, I don't know; it *is* a pretty thing, and since nobody need make such things unless they like, I don't see why they shouldn't make them, *if* they like. Of course, if carvers were scarce they would all be busy on the architecture, as you call it, and then these "toys" (a good word) would not be made; but since there are plenty of good people who can carve—in fact, almost everybody, and as work is somewhat scarce, or we are afraid it may be, folk do not discourage this kind of petty work.'

He mused a little, and seemed somewhat perturbed; but presently his face cleared, and he said: 'After all, you must admit that the pipe is a very pretty thing, with the little people under the trees all cut so clean and sweet;—too elaborate for a pipe, perhaps, but—well, it is very pretty.'

'Too valuable for its use, perhaps,' said I.

'What's that?' said he; 'I don't understand.'

I was just going on in a helpless way to try to make him understand, when we came by the gates of a big rambling building, in which work of some sort seemed going on. 'What building is that?' said I, eagerly; for it was a pleasure amidst all these strange things to see something a little like what I was used to: 'it seems to be a factory.'

'Yes, he said, 'I think I know what you mean, and that's what it is; but we don't call them factories now, but Banded-workshops: that is, places where people collect who want to work together.'

'I suppose,' said I, 'power of some sort is used there?'

'No, no,' said he. 'Why should people collect together to use power, when they can have it at the places where they live or hard by, any two or three of them; or any one, for the matter of that? No; folk collect in these Banded-workshops to do hand-work in which working together is necessary or convenient; such work is often very pleasant. In there for instance they make pottery and glass,—there, you can see the tops of the furnaces. Well, of course it's handy to have fair-sized ovens and kilns and glass-pots, and a good lot of things to use them for: though of course there are a good many such places, as it would be ridiculous if a man had a liking for pot-making or glass-blowing that he should have to live in one place or be obliged to forego the work he liked.'

'I see no smoke coming from the furnaces,' said I.

'Smoke?' said Dick; 'why should you see smoke?'

I held my tongue, and he went on: 'It's a nice place inside, though as plain as you see outside. As to the crafts, throwing clay must be jolly work: the glass-blowing is rather a sweltering job; but some folk like it very much indeed; and I don't much wonder: there is such a sense of power, when you have got deft in it, in dealing with the hot metal. It makes a lot of pleasant work,' said he, smiling, 'for however much care you take of such goods, break they will, one day or another, so there is always plenty to do.

I held my tongue and pondered.

We came just here on a gang of men road-mending, which delayed us a little; but I was not sorry for it; for all I had seen hitherto seemed a mere part of a summer holiday; and I wanted to see how this folk would set to on a piece of real necessary work. They had been resting, and had only just begun work again as we came up; so that the rattle of the picks was what woke me from my musing. There were about a dozen of them, strong young men, looking much like a boating party at Oxford would have looked in the days I remembered, and not more troubled with their work: their outer raiment lay on the road-side in an orderly pile under the guardianship of a six-year-old boy, who had his arm thrown over the neck of a big mastiff, who was as happily lazy as if the summer-day had been made for him alone. As I eyed the pile of clothes, I could see the gleam of gold and silk embroidery on it, and judged that some of these workmen had tastes akin to those of the Golden Dustman of Hammersmith. Beside them lay a good big basket that had hints about it of cold pie and wine: a half-dozen of young women stood by watching the work or the workers, both of which were worth watching, for the latter smote great strokes and were very deft in their labour, and as handsome clean-built fellows as you might find a dozen of in a summer day. They were laughing and talking merrily with each other and the women, but presently their foreman looked up and saw our way stopped. So he stayed his pick and sang out, 'Spell ho, mates! here are neighbours want to get past.' Whereon the others stopped also, and, drawing around us, helped the old horse by easing our wheels over the half undone road, and then, like men with a pleasant task on hand, hurried back to their work, only stopping to give us a smiling good-day; so that the sound of the picks broke out again before Greylocks had taken to his jog-trot. Dick looked back over his shoulder at them and said:

'They are in luck to-day: it's right down good sport trying how much pick-work one can get into an hour; and I can see those neighbours know their business well. It is not a mere matter of strength getting on quickly with such work; is it, guest?'

'I should think not,' said I, 'but to tell you the truth, I have never tried my hand at it.'

'Really?' said he gravely, 'that seems a pity; it is good work for hardening the muscles, and I like it; though I admit it is pleasanter the second week than the first. Not that I am a good hand at it; the fellows used to chaff me at one job where I was working, I remember, and sing out to me, "Well rowed, stroke!" "Put your back into it, bow!"'

'Not much of a joke,' quoth I.

'Well,' said Dick, 'everything seems like a joke when we have a pleasant spell of work on, and good fellows merry about us; we feel so happy, you know.' Again I pondered silently.

Chapter VIII. An Old Friend

We now turned into a pleasant lane where the branches of great plane-trees nearly met overhead, but behind them lay low houses standing rather close together.

'This is Long Acre,' quoth Dick; 'so there must once have been a cornfield here. How curious it is that places change so, and yet keep their old names! Just look how thick the houses stand! and they are still going on building, look you!'

'Yes,' said the old man, 'but I think the cornfields must have been built over before the middle of the nineteenth century. I have heard that about here was one of the thickest parts of the town. But I must get down here, neighbours; I have got to call on a friend who lives in the gardens behind this Long Acre. Good-bye and good luck, Guest!'

And he jumped down and strode away vigorously, like a young man.

'How old should you say that neighbour will be?' said I to Dick as we lost sight of him; for I saw that he was old, and yet he looked dry and sturdy like a piece of old oak; a type of old man I was not used to seeing.

'O, about ninety, I should say,' said Dick.

'How long-lived your people must be!' said I.

'Yes,' said Dick 'certainly we have beaten the three-score-and-ten of the old Jewish proverb-book. But then you see that was written of Syria, a hot dry country, where people live faster than in our temperate climate. However, I don't think it matters much, so long as a man is healthy and happy while he *is* alive. But now, Guest, we are so near to my old kinsman's dwelling-place that I think you had better keep all future questions for him.'

I nodded a yes; and therewith we turned to the left, and went down a gentle slope through some beautiful rose-gardens, laid out on what I took to be the site of Endell Street. We passed on, and Dick drew rein an instant as we came across a long straightish road with houses scantily scattered up and down it. He waved his hand right and left, and said, 'Holborn that side, Oxford Road that. This was once a very important part of the crowded city outside the ancient walls of the Roman and Mediæval burg: many of the feudal nobles of the Middle Ages, we are told, had big houses on either side of Holborn. I daresay you remember that the Bishop of Ely's house is mentioned in Shakespeare's play of King Richard III; and there are some remains of that still left. However, this road is not of the same importance, now that the ancient city is gone, walls and all.'

He drove on again, while I smiled faintly to think how the nineteenth century, of which such big words have been said, counted for nothing in the memory of this man, who read Shakespeare and had not forgotten the Middle Ages.

We crossed the road into a short narrow lane between the gardens, and came out again into a wide road, on one side of which was a great and long building, turning its gables away from the highway, which I saw at once was another public group. Opposite to it was a wide space of greenery, without any wall or fence of any kind. I looked through the trees and saw beyond them a pillared portico quite familiar to me—no less old a friend, in fact, than the British Museum. It rather took my breath away, amidst all the strange things I had seen; but I held my tongue and let Dick speak. Said he:

'Yonder is the British Museum, where my great-grandfather mostly lives; so I won't say much about it. The building on the left is the Museum Market, and I think we had better turn in there for a minute or two; for Greylocks will be wanting his rest and his oats; and I suppose you will stay with my kinsman the greater part of the day; and to say the truth, there may be some one there whom I particularly want to see, and perhaps have a long talk with.'

He blushed and sighed, not altogether with pleasure, I thought; so of course I said nothing, and he turned the horse under an archway which brought us into a very large paved quadrangle, with a big sycamore tree in each corner and a plashing fountain in the midst. Near the fountain were a few market stalls, with awnings over them of gay striped linen cloth, about which some people, mostly women and children, were moving quietly, looking at the goods exposed there. The ground floor of the building round the quadrangle was occupied by a wide arcade or cloister, whose fanciful but strong architecture I could not enough admire. Here also a few people were sauntering or sitting reading on the benches.

Dick said to me apologetically: 'Here as elsewhere there is little doing to-day; on a Friday you would see it thronged, and gay with people, and in the afternoon there is generally music about the fountain. However, I daresay we shall have a pretty good gathering at our mid-day meal.'

We drove through the quadrangle and by an archway, into a large handsome stable on the other side, where we speedily stalled the old nag and made him happy with horse-meat, and then turned and walked back again through the market, Dick looking rather thoughtful, as it seemed to me.

I noticed that people couldn't help looking at me rather hard; and considering my clothes and theirs, I didn't wonder; but whenever they caught my eye they made me a very friendly sign of greeting.

We walked straight into the forecourt of the Museum, where, except that the railings were gone, and the whispering boughs of the trees were all about, nothing seemed changed; the very pigeons were wheeling about the building and clinging to the ornaments of the pediment as I had seen them of old.

Dick seemed grown a little absent, but he could not forbear giving me an architectural note, and said:

'It is rather an ugly old building, isn't it? Many people have wanted to pull it down and rebuild it: and perhaps if work does really get scarce we may yet do so. But, as my great-grandfather will tell you, it would not be quite a straightforward job; for there are wonderful collections in there of all kinds of antiquities, besides an enormous library with many exceedingly beautiful books in it, and many most useful ones as genuine records, texts of ancient works and the like; and the worry and anxiety, and even risk, there would be in moving all this has saved the buildings themselves. Besides, as we said before, it is not a bad thing to have some record of what our forefathers thought a handsome building. For there is plenty of labour and material in it.'

'I see there is,' said I, 'and I quite agree with you. But now hadn't we better make haste to see your great grand-father?'

In fact, I could not help seeing that he was rather dallying with the time. He said, 'Yes, we will go into the house in a minute. My kinsman is too old to do much work in the Museum, where he was a custodian of the books for many years; but he still lives here a good deal; indeed I think,' said he, smiling, 'that he looks upon himself as a part of the books, or the books a part of him, I don't know which.'

He hesitated a little longer, then flushing up, took my hand, and saying, 'Come along, then!' led me toward the door of one of the old official dwellings.

Chapter IX. Concerning Love

'Your kinsman doesn't much care for beautiful buildings, then,' said I, as we entered the rather dreary classical house; which indeed was as bare as need be, except for some big pots of the June flowers which stood about here and there; though it was very clean and nicely whitewashed.

'O, I don't know,' said Dick, rather absently. 'He is getting old, certainly, for he is over a hundred and five, and no doubt he doesn't care about moving. But of course he could live in a prettier house if he liked: he is not obliged to live in any one place any more than anyone else. This way, Guest.'

And he led the way upstairs, and opening a door we went into a fair-sized room of the old type, as plain as the rest of the house, with a few necessary pieces of furniture, and those very simple and even rude, but solid and with a good deal of carving about them, well designed but rather crudely executed. At the furthest corner of the room, at a desk near the window, sat a little old man in a roomy oak chair, well be-cushioned. He was dressed in a sort of Norfolk jacket of blue serge worn threadbare, with breeches of the same, and grey worsted stockings. He jumped up from his chair, and cried out in a voice of considerable volume for such an old man, 'Welcome, Dick, my lad; Clara is here, and will be more than glad to see you; so keep your heart up.'

'Clara here?' quoth Dick; 'if I had known, I would not have brought—At least I mean I would—'

He was stuttering and confused, clearly because he was anxious to say nothing to make me feel one too many. But the old man, who had not seen me at first, helped him out by coming forward and saying to me in a kind tone:

'Pray pardon me, for I did not notice that Dick, who is big enough to hide anybody, you know, had brought a friend with him. A most hearty welcome to you! All the more, as I almost hope that you are going to amuse an old man by giving him news from over sea for I can see that you are come from over the water and far-off countries.'

He looked at me thoughtfully, almost anxiously, as he said in a changed voice, 'Might I ask you where you come from, as you are so clearly a stranger?'

I said in an absent way: 'I used to live in England, and now I am come back again; and I slept last night at Hammersmith Guest House.'

He bowed gravely, but seemed, I thought, a little disappointed with my answer. As for me, I was now looking at him harder than good manners allowed of, perhaps; for in truth his face, dried-apple-like as it was, seemed strangely familiar to me; as if I had seen it before—in a looking-glass it might be, said I to myself.

'Well,' said the old man, 'wherever you come from, you are come among friends. And I see my kinsman Richard Hammond has an air about him as if he had brought you here for me to do something for you. Is that so, Dick?'

Dick, who was getting still more absent-minded and kept looking uneasily at the door, managed to say, 'Well, yes, kinsman: our guest finds things much altered, and cannot understand it; nor can I; so I thought I would bring him to you since you know more of all that has happened within the last two hundred years than any body else does.—What's that?'

And he turned toward the door again. We heard footsteps outside; the door opened, and in came a very beautiful young woman, who stopped short on seeing Dick, and flushed as red as a rose, but faced him nevertheless. Dick looked at her hard, and half reached out his hand toward her, and his whole face quivered with emotion.

The old man did not leave them long in this shy discomfort, but said, smiling with an old man's mirth: 'Dick, my lad, and you, my dear Clara, I rather think that we two oldsters are in your way; for I think you will have plenty to say to each other. You had better go into Nelson's room up above; I know he has gone out; and he has just been covering the walls all over with mediæval books, so it will be pretty enough even for you two and your renewed pleasure.'

The girl reached out her hand to Dick, and taking his led him out of the room, looking straight before her; but it was easy to see that her blushes came from happiness, not anger; as, indeed, love is far more self-conscious than wrath.

When the door had shut on them the old man turned to me, still smiling, and said:

'Frankly, my dear guest, you will do me a great service if you are come to set my old tongue wagging. My love of talk still abides with me, or rather grows on me; and though it is pleasant enough to see these youngsters moving about and playing together so seriously, as if the whole world depended on their kisses (as indeed it does somewhat), yet I don't think my tales of the past interest them much. The last harvest, the last baby, the last knot of carving in the market-place is history enough for them. It was different, I think, when I was a lad, when we were not so assured of peace and continuous plenty as we are now—Well, well! Without putting you to the question, let me ask you this: Am I to consider you as an enquirer who knows a little of our modern ways of life, or as one who comes from some place where the very foundations of life are different from ours,—do you know anything or nothing about us?'

He looked at me keenly and with growing wonder in his eyes as he spoke; and I answered in a low voice:

'I know only so much of your modern life as I could gather from using my eyes on the way here from Hammersmith and from asking some questions of Richard Hammond, most of which he could hardly understand.'

The old man smiled at this. 'Then,' said he, 'I am to speak to you as—'

'As if I were a being from another planet,' said I.

The old man, whose name, by the bye, like his kinsman's, was Hammond, smiled and nodded, and wheeling his seat round to me, bade me sit in a heavy oak chair, and said, as he saw my eyes fix on its curious carving:

'Yes, I am much tied to the past, *my* past, you understand. These very pieces of furniture belong to a time before my early days; it was my father who got them made; if they had been done within the last fifty years they would have been much cleverer in execution; but I don't think I should have liked them the better. We were almost beginning again in those days: and they were brisk, hot-headed times. But you hear how garrulous I am: ask me questions, ask me questions about anything dear guest; since I *must* talk, make my talk profitable to you.'

I was silent for a minute, and then I said, somewhat nervously: 'Excuse me if I am rude; but I am so much interested in Richard, since he has been so kind to me, a perfect stranger, that I should like to ask a question about him.'

'Well,' said old Hammond, 'if he were not "kind," as you call it, to a perfect stranger he would be thought a strange person, and people would be apt to shun him. But ask on, ask on! Don't be shy of asking.'

Said I: 'That beautiful girl, is he going to be married to her?'

'Well,' said he, 'yes, he is. He has been married to her once already, and now I should say it is pretty clear that he will be married to her again.'

'Indeed,' quoth I, wondering what that meant.

'Here is the whole tale,' said old Hammond; 'a short one enough; and now I hope a happy one: they lived together two years the first time; were both very young; and then she got it into her head that she was in love with somebody else. So she left poor Dick; I say *poor* Dick, because he had not found any one else. But it did not last long, only about a year. Then she came to me, as she was in the habit of bringing her troubles to the old carle, and asked me how Dick was, and whether he was happy, and all the rest of it. So I saw how the land lay, and said that he was very unhappy, and not at all well; which last at any rate was a lie. There, you can guess the rest. Clara came to have a long talk with me to-day, but Dick will serve her turn much better. Indeed, if he hadn't chanced in upon me to-day I should have had to have sent for him tomorrow.'

'Dear me,' said I. 'Have they any children?'

'Yes,' said he, 'two; they are staying with one of my daughters at present, where, indeed, Clara has mostly been. I wouldn't lose sight of her, as I felt sure they would come together again; and Dick, who is the best of good fellows, really took the matter to heart. You see he had no other love to run to, as she had. So I managed it all; as I have done with such-like matters before.'

'Ah,' said I, 'no doubt you wanted to keep them out of the Divorce Court: but I suppose it often has to settle such matters.'

'Then you suppose nonsense,' said he. 'I know that there used to be such lunatic affairs as divorce-courts: but just consider; all the cases that came into them were matters of property quarrels: and I think, dear guest,' said he, smiling, 'that though you do come from another planet, you can see from the mere outside look of our world that quarrels about private property could not go on amongst us in our days.'

Indeed, my drive from Hammersmith to Bloomsbury, and all the quiet happy life I had seen so many hints of, even apart from my shopping, would have been enough to tell me that 'the sacred rights of property,' as we used to think of them, were now no more. So I sat silent while the old man took up the thread of the discourse again, and said:

'Well, then, property quarrels being no longer possible, what remains in these matters that a court of law could deal with? Fancy a court for enforcing a contract of passion or sentiment! If such a thing were needed as a *reductio ad absurdum* of the enforcement of contract, such a folly would do that for us.'

He was silent again a little, and then said: 'You must understand once for all that we have changed these matters; or rather, that our way of looking at them has changed, as we have changed within the last two hundred years. We do not deceive ourselves, indeed, or believe that we can get rid of all the trouble that besets the dealings between the sexes. We know that we must face the unhappiness that comes of man and woman confusing the relations between natural passion, and sentiment, and the friendship which, when things go well, softens the awakening from passing illusions: but we are not so mad as to pile up degradation on that unhappiness by engaging in sordid squabbles about livelihood and position, and the power of tyrannising over the children who have been the result of love or lust.'

Again he paused awhile, and again went on: 'Calf love, mistaken for a heroism that shall be life-long, yet early waning into disappointment; the inexplicable desire that comes on a man of riper years to be the all-in-all to some one woman, whose ordinary human kindness and human beauty he has idealised into superhuman perfection, and made the one object of his desire; or lastly the reasonable longing of a strong and thoughtful man to become the most intimate friend of some beautiful and wise woman, the very type of the beauty and glory of the world which we love so well,—as we exult in all the pleasure and exaltation of spirit which goes with these things, so we set ourselves to bear the sorrow which not unseldom goes with them also; remembering those lines of the ancient poet (I quote roughly from memory one of the many translations of the nineteenth century):

> For this the gods have fashioned man's grief and evil day
> That still for man hereafter might be the tale and the lay.

Well, well, 'tis little likely anyhow that all tales shall be lacking, or all sorrow cured.'

He was silent for some time, and I would not interrupt him. At last he began again: 'But you must know that we of these generations are strong and healthy of body, and live easily; we pass our lives in reasonable strife with nature, exercising not one side of ourselves only, but all sides, taking the keenest pleasure in all the life of the world. So it is a point of honour with us not to be self-centred; not to suppose that the world must cease because one man is sorry; therefore we should think it foolish, or if you will, criminal, to exaggerate these matters of sentiment and sensibility: we are no more inclined to eke out our sentimental sorrows than to cherish our bodily pains; and we recognise that there are other pleasures besides love-making. You must remember, also, that we are long-lived, and that therefore beauty both in man and woman is not so fleeting as it was in the days when we were burdened so heavily by self-inflicted diseases. So we shake off these griefs in a way which perhaps the sentimentalists of other times would think contemptible and unheroic, but which we think necessary and manlike. As on the other hand, therefore, we have ceased to be commercial in our love-matters, so also we have ceased to be *artificially* foolish. The folly which comes by nature, the unwisdom of the immature man, or the older man caught in a trap, we must put up with that, nor are we much ashamed of it; but to be conventionally sensitive or sentimental—my friend, I am old and perhaps disappointed, but at least I think we have cast off *some* of the follies of the older world.'

He paused, as if for some words of mine; but I held my peace: then he went on: 'At least, if we suffer from the tyranny and fickleness of nature or our own want of experience, we neither grimace about it, nor lie. If there must be a sundering betwixt those who meant never to sunder so it must be: but there need be no pretext of unity when the reality of it is gone: nor do we drive those who well know that they are incapable of it to profess an undying sentiment which they cannot really feel: thus it is that as that monstrosity of venal lust is no longer possible, so it is no longer needed. Don't misunderstand me. You did not seem shocked when I told you that there were no law-courts to enforce contracts of sentiment or passion; but so curiously are men made, that perhaps you will be shocked when I tell you that there is no code of public opinion which takes the place of such courts, and which might be as tyrannical and unreasonable as they were. I do not say that people don't judge their neighbours' conduct, sometimes, doubtless, unfairly. But I do say that there is no unvarying conventional set of rules by which people are judged; no bed of Procrustes to stretch or cramp their minds and lives; no hypocritical excommunication which people are *forced* to pronounce, either by unconsidered habit, or by the unexpressed threat of the lesser interdict if they are lax in their hypocrisy. Are you shocked now?'

'N-o—no,' said I, with some hesitation. 'It is all so different.'

'At any rate,' said he, 'one thing I think I can answer for: whatever sentiment there is, it is real—and general; it is not confined to people very specially refined. I am also pretty sure, as I hinted to you just now, that there is not by a great way as much suffering involved in these matters either to men or to women as there used to be. But excuse me for being so prolix on this question! You know you asked to be treated like a being from another planet.'

'Indeed I thank you very much,' said I. 'Now may I ask you about the position of women in your society?'

He laughed very heartily for a man of his years, and said: 'It is not without reason that I have got a reputation as a careful student of history. I believe I really do understand "the Emancipation of Women movement" of the nineteenth century. I doubt if any other man now alive does.'

'Well?' said I, a little bit nettled by his merriment.

'Well,' said he, 'of course you will see that all that is a dead controversy now. The men have no longer any opportunity of tyrannising over the women, or the women over the men; both of which things took place in those old times. The women do what they can do best, and what they like best, and the men are neither jealous of it or injured by it. This is such a commonplace that I am almost ashamed to state it.'

I said, 'O; and legislation? do they take any part in that?'

Hammond smiled and said: 'I think you may wait for an answer to that question till we get on to the subject of legislation. There may be novelties to you in that subject also.'

'Very well,' I said; 'but about this woman question? I saw at the Guest House that the women were waiting on the men: that seems a little like reaction, doesn't it?'

'Does it?' said the old man; 'perhaps you think housekeeping an unimportant occupation, not deserving of respect. I believe that was the opinion of the "advanced" women of the nineteenth century, and their male backers. If it is yours, I recommend to your notice an old Norwegian folk-lore tale called How the Man minded the House, or some such title; the result of which minding was that, after various tribulations, the man and the family cow balanced each other at the end of a rope, the man hanging halfway up the chimney, the cow dangling from the roof, which, after the fashion of the country, was of turf and sloping down low to the ground. Hard on the cow, *I* think. Of course no such mishap could happen to such a superior person as yourself,' he added, chuckling.

I sat somewhat uneasy under this dry gibe. Indeed, his manner of treating this latter part of the question seemed to me a little disrespectful.

'Come, now, my friend,' quoth he, 'don't you know that it is a great pleasure to a clever woman to manage a house skilfully, and to do it so that all the house-mates about her look pleased, and are grateful to her? And then, you know, everybody likes to be ordered about by a pretty woman: why, it is one of the pleasantest forms of flirtation. You are not so old that you cannot remember that. Why, I remember it well.'

And the old fellow chuckled again, and at last fairly burst out laughing.

'Excuse me,' said he, after a while; 'I am not laughing at anything you could be thinking of, but at that silly nineteenth-century fashion, current amongst rich so-called cultivated people, of ignoring all the steps by which their daily dinner was reached, as matters too low for their lofty intelligence. Useless idiots! Come, now, I am a "literary man", as we queer animals used to be called, yet I am a pretty good cook myself.'

'So am I,' said I.

'Well, then,' said he, 'I really think you can understand me better than you would seem to do, judging by your words and your silence.'

Said I: 'Perhaps that is so; but people putting in practice commonly this sense of interest in the ordinary occupations of life rather startles me. I will ask you a question or two presently about that. But I want to return to the position of women amongst you. You have studied the "emancipation of women" business of the nineteenth century: don't you remember that some of the "superior" women wanted to emancipate the more intelligent part of their sex from the bearing of children?'

The old man grew quite serious again. Said he: 'I *do* remember about that strange piece of baseless folly, the result, like all other follies of the period, of the hideous class tyranny which then obtained. What do we think of it now? you would say. My friend, that is a question easy to answer. How could it possibly be but that maternity should be highly honoured amongst us? Surely it is a matter of course that the natural and necessary pains which the mother must go through form a bond of union between man and woman, an extra stimulus to love and affection between them, and that this is universally recognised. For the rest, remember that all the *artificial* burdens of motherhood are now done away with. A mother has no longer any mere sordid anxieties for the future of her children. They may indeed turn out better or worse; they may disappoint her highest hopes; such anxieties as these are a part of the mingled pleasure and pain which goes to make up the life of mankind. But at least she is spared the fear (it was most commonly the certainty) that artificial disabilities would make her children something less than men and women: she knows that they will live and act according to the measure of their own faculties. In times past, it is clear that the "Society" of the day helped its Judaic god, and the "Man of Science" of the time, in visiting the sins of the fathers upon the children. How to reverse this process, how to take the sting out of heredity, has for long been one of the most constant cares of the thoughtful men amongst us. So that, you see, the ordinarily healthy woman (and almost all our women are both healthy and at least comely), respected as a child-bearer and rearer of children, desired as a woman, loved as a companion, unanxious for the future of her children, has far more instinct for maternity than the poor drudge and mother of drudges of past days could ever have had; or than her sister of the upper classes, brought up in affected ignorance of natural facts, reared in an atmosphere of mingled prudery and prurience.'

'You speak warmly,' I said, 'but I can see that you are right.'

'Yes,' he said, 'and I will point out to you a token of all the benefits which we have gained by our freedom. What did you think of the looks of the people whom you have come across to-day?'

Said I: 'I could hardly have believed that there could be so many good-looking people in any civilised country.'

He crowed a little, like the old bird he was. 'What! are we still civilised?' said he. 'Well, as to our looks, the English and Jutish blood, which on the whole is predominant here, used not to produce much beauty. But I think we have improved it. I know a man who has a large collection of portraits printed from photographs of the nineteenth century, and going over them and comparing them with the everyday faces in these times, puts the improvement in our good looks beyond a doubt. Now, there are some people who think it not too fantastic to connect this increase of beauty directly with our freedom and good sense in the matters we have been speaking of: they believe that a child born from the natural and healthy love between a man and a woman, even if that be transient, is likely to turn out better in all ways, and especially in bodily beauty, than the birth of the respectable commercial marriage bed, or of the dull despair of the drudge of that system. They say, Pleasure begets pleasure. What do you think?'

'I am much of that mind,' said I.

Chapter X. Questions and Answers

'Well,' said the old man, shifting in his chair, 'you must get on with your questions, Guest; I have been some time answering this first one.'

Said I: 'I want an extra word or two about your ideas of education; although I gathered from Dick that you let your children run wild and didn't teach them anything; and in short, that you have so refined your education, that now you have none.'

'Then you gathered left-handed,' quoth he. 'But of course I understand your point of view about education, which is that of times past, when "the struggle for life", as men used to phrase it (*i.e.*, the struggle for a slave's rations on one side, and for a bouncing share of the slaveholders' privilege on the other), pinched "education" for most people into a niggardly dole of not very accurate information; something to be swallowed by the beginner in the art of living whether he liked it or not, and was hungry for it or not: and which had been chewed and digested over and over again by people who didn't care about it in order to serve it out to other people who didn't care about it.'

I stopped the old man's rising wrath by a laugh, and said: 'Well, *you* were not taught that way, at any rate, so you may let your anger run off you a little.'

'True, true,' said he smiling. 'I thank you for correcting my ill-temper: I always fancy myself as living in any period of which we may be speaking. But, however, to put it in a cooler way: you expected to see children thrust into schools when they had reached an age conventionally supposed to be the due age, whatever their varying faculties and dispositions might be, and when there, with like disregard to facts to be subjected to a certain conventional course of "learning". My friend, can't you see that such a proceeding means ignoring the fact of *growth*, bodily and mental? No one could come out of such a mill uninjured; and those only would avoid being crushed by it who would have the spirit of rebellion strong in them. Fortunately most children have had that at all times, or I do not know that we should ever have reached our present position. Now you see what it all comes to. In the old times all this was the result of *poverty*. In the nineteenth century, society was so miserably poor, owing to the systematised robbery on which it was founded, that real education was impossible for anybody. The whole theory of their so called education was that it was necessary to shove a little information into a child, even if it were by means of torture, and accompanied by twaddle which it was well known was of no use, or else he would lack information lifelong: the hurry of poverty forbade anything else. All that is past; we are no longer hurried, and the information lies ready to each one's hand when his own inclinations impel him to seek it. In this as in other matters we have become wealthy: we can afford to give ourselves time to grow.'

'Yes,' said I, 'but suppose the child, youth, man, never wants the information, never grows in the direction you might hope him to do: suppose, for instance, he objects to learning arithmetic or mathematics; you can't force him when he *is* grown; can't you force him while he is growing, and oughtn't you to do so?'

'Well,' said he, 'were you forced to learn arithmetic and mathematics?'

'A little,' said I.

'And how old are you now?'

'Say fifty-six,' said I.

'And how much arithmetic and mathematics do you know now?' quoth the old man, smiling rather mockingly.

Said I: 'None whatever, I am sorry to say.'

Hammond laughed quietly, but made no other comment on my admission, and I dropped the subject of education, perceiving him to be hopeless on that side.

I thought a little, and said: 'You were speaking just now of households: that sounded to me a little like the customs of past times; I should have thought you would have lived more in public.'

'Phalangsteries, eh?' said he. 'Well, we live as we like, and we like to live as a rule with certain house-mates that we have got used to. Remember, again, that poverty is extinct, and that the Fourierist phalangsteries and all their kind, as was but natural at the time, implied nothing but a refuge from mere destitution. Such a way of life as that, could only have been conceived of by people surrounded by the worst form of poverty. But you must understand therewith, that though separate households are the rule amongst us, and though they differ in their habits more or less, yet no door is shut to any good-tempered person who is content to live as the other house-mates do: only of course it would be unreasonable for one man to drop into a household and bid the folk of it to alter their habits to please him, since he can go elsewhere and live as he pleases. However, I need not say much about all this, as you are going up the river with Dick, and will find out for yourself by experience how these matters are managed.'

After a pause, I said: 'Your big towns, now; how about them? London, which—which I have read about as the modern Babylon of civilisation, seems to have disappeared.'

'Well, well,' said old Hammond, 'perhaps after all it is more like ancient Babylon now than the "modern Babylon" of the nineteenth century was. But let that pass. After all, there is a good deal of population in places between here and Hammersmith; nor have you seen the most populous part of the town yet.'

'Tell me, then,' said I, 'how is it towards the east?'

Said he: 'Time was when if you mounted a good horse and rode straight away from my door here at a round trot for an hour and a half, you would still be in the thick of London, and the greater part of that would be "slums", as they were called; that is to say, places of torture for innocent men and women;

or worse, stews for rearing and breeding men and women in such degradation that that torture should seem to them mere ordinary and natural life.'

'I know, I know,' I said, rather impatiently, 'That was what was; tell me something of what is. Is there any of that left?'

'Not an inch,' said he; 'but some memory of it abides with us, and I am glad of it. Once a year, on May-day, we hold a solemn feast in those easterly communes of London to commemorate The Clearing of Misery, as it is called. On that day we have music and dancing, and merry games and happy feasting on the site of some of the worst of the old slums, the traditional memory of which we have kept. On that occasion the custom is for the prettiest girls to sing some of the old revolutionary songs, and those which were the groans of the discontent, once so hopeless, on the very spots where those terrible crimes of class-murder were committed day by day for so many years. To a man like me, who have studied the past so diligently, it is a curious and touching sight to see some beautiful girl, daintily clad, and crowned with flowers from the neighbouring meadows, standing amongst the happy people, on some mound where of old time stood the wretched apology for a house, a den in which men and women lived packed amongst the filth like pilchards in a cask; lived in such a way that they could only have endured it, as I said just now, by being degraded out of humanity—to hear the terrible words of threatening and lamentation coming from her sweet and beautiful lips, and she unconscious of their real meaning: to hear her, for instance, singing Hood's Song of the Shirt, and to think that all the time she does not understand what it is all about—a tragedy grown inconceivable to her and her listeners. Think of that, if you can, and of how glorious life is grown!'

'Indeed,' said I, 'it is difficult for me to think of it.'

And I sat watching how his eyes glittered, and how the fresh life seemed to glow in his face, and I wondered how at his age he should think of the happiness of the world, or indeed anything but his coming dinner.

'Tell me in detail,' said I, 'what lies east of Bloomsbury now?'

Said he: 'There are but few houses between this and the outer part of the old city; but in the city we have a thickly-dwelling population. Our forefathers, in the first clearing of the slums, were not in a hurry to pull down the houses in what was called at the end of the nineteenth century the business quarter of the town, and what later got to be known as the Swindling Kens. You see, these houses, though they stood hideously thick on the ground, were roomy and fairly solid in building, and clean, because they were not used for living in, but as mere gambling booths; so the poor people from the cleared slums took them for lodgings and dwelt there, till the folk of those days had time to think of something better for them; so the buildings were pulled down so gradually that people got used to living thicker on the ground there than in most places; therefore it remains the most populous part of London, or perhaps of all these islands. But it is very pleasant there, partly because of the splendour of the architecture, which goes further than what you will see elsewhere. However, this crowding, if it may be called so, does not go further than a street called Aldgate, a name which perhaps you may have heard of. Beyond that the houses are scattered wide about the meadows there, which are very beautiful, especially when you get on to the lovely river Lea (where old Isaak Walton used to fish, you know) about the places called Stratford and Old Ford, names which of course you will not have heard of, though the Romans were busy there once upon a time.'

Not heard of them! thought I to myself. How strange! that I who had seen the very last remnant of the pleasantness of the meadows by the Lea destroyed, should have heard them spoken of with pleasantness come back to them in full measure.

Hammond went on: 'When you get down to the Thames side you come on the Docks, which are works of the nineteenth century, and are still in use, although not so thronged as they once were, since we discourage centralisation all we can, and we have long ago dropped the pretension to be the market of the world. About these Docks are a good few houses, which, however, are not inhabited by many people permanently; I mean, those who use them come and go a good deal, the place being too low and marshy for pleasant dwelling. Past the Docks eastward and landward it is all flat pasture, once marsh, except for a few gardens, and there are very few permanent dwellings there: scarcely anything but a few sheds, and cots for the men who come to look after the great herds of cattle pasturing there. But however, what with the beasts and the men, and the scattered red-tiled roofs and the big hayricks, it does not make a bad holiday to get a quiet pony and ride about there on a sunny afternoon of autumn, and look over the river and the craft passing up and down, and on to Shooters' Hill and the Kentish uplands, and then turn round to the wide green sea of the Essex marshland, with the great domed line of the sky, and the sun shining down in one flood of peaceful light over the long distance. There is a place called Canning's Town, and further out, Silvertown, where the pleasant meadows are at their pleasantest: doubtless they were once slums, and wretched enough.'

The names grated on my ear, but I could not explain why to him. So I said: 'And south of the river, what is it like?'

He said: 'You would find it much the same as the land about Hammersmith. North, again, the land runs up high, and there is an agreeable and well-built town called Hampstead, which fitly ends London on that side. It looks down on the north-western end of the forest you passed through.'

I smiled. 'So much for what was once London,' said I. 'Now tell me about the other towns of the country.'

He said: 'As to the big murky places which were once, as we know, the centres of manufacture, they have, like the brick and mortar desert of London, disappeared; only, since they were the centres of nothing but "manufacture", and served no purpose but that of the gambling market, they have left less signs of their existence than London. Of course, the great change in the use of mechanical force made this an easy matter, and some approach to their break-up as centres would probably have taken place, even if we had not changed our habits so much: but they being such as they were, no sacrifice would have seemed too great a price to pay for getting rid of the "manufacturing districts", as they used to be called. For the rest, whatever coal or mineral we need is brought to grass and sent whither it is needed with as little as possible of dirt, confusion, and the distressing of quiet people's lives. One is tempted to believe from what one has read of the condition of those districts in the nineteenth century, that those who had them under their power worried, befouled, and degraded men out of malice prepense: but it was not so; like the miseducation of which we were talking just now, it came of their dreadful poverty. They were obliged to put up with everything, and even pretend that they liked it; whereas we can now deal with things reasonably, and refuse to be saddled with what we do not want.'

I confess I was not sorry to cut short with a question his glorifications of the age he lived in. Said I: 'How about the smaller towns? I suppose you have swept those away entirely?'

'No, no,' said he, 'it hasn't gone that way. On the contrary, there has been but little clearance, though much rebuilding, in the smaller towns. Their suburbs, indeed, when they had any, have melted away into the general country, and space and elbow-room has been got in their centres: but there are the towns still with their streets and squares and market-places; so that it is by means of these smaller towns that we of to-day can get some kind of idea of what the towns of the older world were like;—I mean to say at their best.'

'Take Oxford, for instance,' said I.

'Yes,' said he, 'I suppose Oxford was beautiful even in the nineteenth century. At present it has the great interest of still preserving a great mass of pre-commercial building, and is a very beautiful place, yet there are many towns which have become scarcely less beautiful.' Said I: 'In passing, may I ask if it is still a place of learning?'

'Still?' said he, smiling. 'Well, it has reverted to some of its best traditions; so you may imagine how far it is from its nineteenth-century position. It is real learning, knowledge cultivated for its own sake—the Art of Knowledge, in short—which is followed there, not the Commercial learning of the past. Though perhaps you do not know that in the nineteenth century Oxford and its less interesting sister Cambridge became definitely commercial. They (and especially Oxford) were the breeding places of a peculiar class of parasites, who called themselves cultivated people; they were indeed cynical enough, as the so-called educated classes of the day generally were; but they affected an exaggeration of cynicism in order that they might be thought knowing and worldly-wise. The rich middle classes (they had no relation with the working-classes) treated them with the kind of contemptuous toleration with which a mediæval baron treated his jester; though it must be said that they were by no means so pleasant as the old jesters were, being, in fact, *the* bores of society. They were laughed at, despised—and paid. Which last was what they aimed at.'

Dear me! thought I, how apt history is to reverse contemporary judgements. Surely only the worst of them were as bad as that. But I must admit that they were mostly prigs, and they *were* commercial. I said aloud, though more to myself than to Hammond, 'Well, how could they be better than the age that made them?'

'True,' he said, 'but their pretensions were higher.'

'Were they?' said I, smiling.

'You drive me from corner to corner,' said he, smiling in turn. 'Let me say at least that they were a poor sequence to the aspirations of Oxford of "the barbarous Middle Ages." '

'Yes, that will do,' said I.

'Also,' said Hammond, 'what I have been saying of them is true in the main. But ask on!'

I said: 'We have heard about London and the manufacturing districts and the ordinary towns: how about the villages?'

Said Hammond: 'You must know that toward the end of the nineteenth century the villages were almost destroyed, unless where they became mere adjuncts to the manufacturing districts, or formed a sort of minor manufacturing district themselves. Houses were allowed to fall into decay and actual ruin; trees were cut down for the sake of the few shillings which the poor sticks would fetch; the building became inexpressibly mean and hideous. Labour was scarce; but wages fell nevertheless. All the small country arts of life which once added to the little pleasures of country people were lost. The country produce which passed through the hands of the husbandmen never got so far as their mouths. Incredible shabbiness and niggardly pinching reigned over the fields and acres which, in spite of the rude and careless husbandry of the times, were so kind and bountiful. Had you any inkling of all this?'

'I have heard that it was so,' said I; 'but what followed?'

'The change,' said Hammond, 'which in these matters took place very early in our epoch, was most strangely rapid. People flocked into the country villages, and, so to say, flung themselves upon the freed land like a wild beast upon his prey; and in a very little time the villages of England were more populous than they had been since the fourteenth century, and were still growing fast. Of course, this invasion of the country was awkward to deal with, and would have created much misery, if the folk had still been under the bondage of class monopoly. But as it was, things soon righted themselves. People found out what they were fit for, and gave up attempting to push themselves into occupations in which they must needs fail. The town invaded the country; but the invaders, like the warlike invaders of early days, yielded to the influence of their surroundings, and became country people; and in their turn, as they became more numerous than the townsmen, influenced them also; so that the difference between town and country grew less and less; and it was indeed this world of the country vivified by the thought and briskness of town-bred folk which has produced that happy and leisurely but eager life of which you have had a first taste. Again I say, many blunders were made, but we have had time to set them right. Much was left for the men of my earlier life to deal with. The crude ideas of the first half of the twentieth century, when men were still oppressed by the fear of poverty, and did not look enough to the present pleasure of ordinary daily life, spoilt a great deal of what the commercial age had left us of external beauty: and I admit that it was but slowly that men recovered from the injuries that they inflicted on themselves even after they became free. But slowly as the recovery came, it *did* come; and the more you see of us, the clearer it will be to you that we are happy. That we live amidst beauty without any fear of becoming effeminate; that we have plenty to do, and on the whole enjoy doing it. What more can we ask of life?'

He paused, as if he were seeking for words with which to express his thought. Then he said:

'This is how we stand. England was once a country of clearings amongst the woods and wastes, with a few towns interspersed, which were fortresses for the feudal army, markets for the folk, gathering places for the craftsmen. It then became a country of huge and foul workshops and fouler gambling-dens, surrounded by an ill-kept, poverty-stricken farm, pillaged by the masters of the workshops. It is now a garden, where nothing is wasted and nothing is spoilt, with the necessary dwellings, sheds, and workshops scattered up and down the country, all trim and neat and pretty. For, indeed, we should be too much ashamed of ourselves if we allowed the making of goods, even on a large scale, to carry with it the appearance, even, of desolation and misery. Why, my friend, those housewives we were talking of just now would teach us better than that.'

Said I: 'This side of your change is certainly for the better. But though I shall soon see some of these villages, tell me in a word or two what they are like, just to prepare me.'

'Perhaps,' said he, 'you have seen a tolerable picture of these villages as they were before the end of the nineteenth century. Such things exist.'

'I have seen several of such pictures,' said I.

'Well,' said Hammond, 'our villages are something like the best of such places, with the church or mote-house of the neighbours for their chief building. Only note that there are no tokens of poverty about them: no tumble-down picturesque; which, to tell you the truth, the artist usually availed himself of to veil his incapacity for drawing architecture. Such things do not please us, even when they indicate no misery. Like the mediævals, we like everything trim and clean, and orderly and bright; as people always do when they have any sense of architectural power; because then they know that they can have what they want, and they won't stand any nonsense from Nature in their dealings with her.'

'Besides the villages, are there any scattered country houses?' said I.

'Yes, plenty,' said Hammond; 'in fact, except in the wastes and forests and amongst the sand-hills (like Hindhead in Surrey), it is not easy to be out of sight of a house; and where the houses are thinly scattered they run large, and are more like the old colleges than ordinary houses as they used to be. That is done for the sake of society, for a good many people can dwell in such houses, as the country dwellers are not necessarily husbandmen; though they almost all help in such work at times. The life that goes on in these big dwellings in the country is very pleasant, especially as some of the most studious men of our time live in them, and altogether there is a great variety of mind and mood to be found in them which brightens and quickens the society there.'

'I am rather surprised,' said I, 'by all this, for it seems to me that after all the country must be tolerably populous.'

'Certainly,' said he; 'the population is pretty much the same as it was at the end of the nineteenth century; we have spread it, that is all. Of course, also, we have helped to populate other countries—where we were wanted and were called for.'

Said I: 'One thing, it seems to me, does not go with your word of "garden" for the country. You have spoken of wastes and forests, and I myself have seen the beginning of your Middlesex and Essex forest. Why do you keep such things in a garden? and isn't it very wasteful to do so?'

'My friend,' he said, 'we like these pieces of wild nature, and can afford them, so we have them; let alone that as to the forests, we need a great deal of timber, and suppose that our sons and sons' sons will do the like. As to the land being a garden, I have heard that they used to have shrubberies and rockeries in gardens once; and though I might not like the artificial ones, I assure you that some of the natural rockeries of our garden are worth seeing. Go north this summer and look at the Cumberland and Westmoreland ones,—where, by the way, you will see some sheep-feeding, so that they are not so wasteful as you think; not so wasteful as forcing-grounds for fruit out of season, *I* think. Go and have a look at the sheep-walks high up in the slopes between Ingleborough and Pen-y-gwent, and tell me if you think we *waste* the land there by not covering it with factories for making things that nobody wants, which was the chief business of the nineteenth century.'

'I will try to go there,' said I.

'It won't take much trying,' said he.

Chapter XI. Concerning Government

'Now,' said I, 'I have come to the point of asking questions which I suppose will be dry for you to answer and difficult for you to explain; but I have foreseen for some time past that I must ask them, will I 'nill I. What kind of a government have you? Has republicanism finally triumphed? or have you come to a mere dictatorship, which some persons in the nineteenth century used to prophesy as the ultimate outcome of democracy? Indeed, this last question does not seem so very unreasonable, since you have turned your Parliament House into a dung-market. Or where do you house your present Parliament?'

The old man answered my smile with a hearty laugh, and said: 'Well, well, dung is not the worst kind of corruption; fertility may come of that, whereas mere dearth came from the other kind, of which those walls once held the great supporters. Now, dear guest, let me tell you that our present parliament would be hard to house in one place, because the whole people is our parliament.'

'I don't understand,' said I.

'No, I suppose not,' said he. 'I must now shock you by telling you that we have no longer anything which you, a native of another planet, would call a government.'

'I am not so much shocked as you might think,' said I, 'as I know something about governments. But tell me, how do you manage, and how have you come to this state of things?'

Said he: 'It is true that we have to make some arrangements about our affairs, concerning which you can ask presently; and it is also true that everybody does not always agree with the details of these arrangements; but, further, it is true that a man no more needs an elaborate system of government, with its army, navy, and police, to force him to give way to the will of the majority of his *equals*, than he wants a similar machinery to make him understand that his head and a stone wall cannot occupy the same space at the same moment. Do you want further explanation?'

'Well, yes, I do,' quoth I.

Old Hammond settled himself in his chair with a look of enjoyment which rather alarmed me, and made me dread a scientific disquisition: so I sighed and abided. He said:

'I suppose you know pretty well what the process of government was in the bad old times?'

'I am supposed to know,' said I.

(Hammond) What was the government of those days? Was it really the Parliament or any part of it?

(1) No.

(H.) Was not the Parliament on the one side a kind of watch-committee sitting to see that the interests of the Upper Classes took no hurt; and on the other side a sort of blind to delude the people into supposing that they had some share in the management of their own affairs?

(I) History seems to show us this.

(H.) To what extent did the people manage their own affairs?

(I) I judge from what I have heard that sometimes they forced the Parliament to make a law to legalise some alteration which had already taken place.

(H.) Anything else?

(I) I think not. As I am informed, if the people made any attempt to deal with the *cause* of their grievances, the law stepped in and said, this is sedition, revolt, or what not, and slew or tortured the ringleaders of such attempts.

(H.) If Parliament was not the government then, nor the people either, what was the government?

(I) Can you tell me?

(H.) I think we shall not be far wrong if we say that government was the Law-Courts, backed up by the executive, which handled the brute force that deluded people allowed them to use for their own purposes; I mean the army, navy, and police.

(I) Reasonable men must needs think you are right.

(H.) Now as to those Law-Courts. Were they places of fair dealing according to the ideas of the day? Had a poor man a good chance of defending his property and person in them?

(I) It is a commonplace that even rich men looked upon a law-suit as a dire misfortune, even if they gained the case; and as for a poor one— why, it was considered a miracle of justice and beneficence if a poor man who had once got into the clutches of the law escaped prison or utter ruin.

(H.) It seems, then, my son, that the government by law-courts and police, which was the real government of the nineteenth century, was not a great success even to the people of that day, living under a class system which proclaimed inequality and poverty as the law of God and the bond which held the world together.

(I) So it seems, indeed.

(H.) And now that all this is changed, and the 'rights of property,' which mean the clenching the fist on a piece of goods and crying out to the neighbours, You shan't have this!—now that all this has disappeared so utterly that it is no longer possible even to jest upon its absurdity, is such a Government possible?

(I) It is impossible.

(H.) Yes, happily. But for what other purpose than the protection of the rich from the poor, the strong from the weak, did this Government exist?

(I) I have heard that it was said that their office was to defend their own citizens against attack from other countries.

(H.) It was said; but was any one expected to believe this? For instance, did the English Government defend the English citizen against the French?

(I) So it was said.

(H.) Then if the French had invaded England and conquered it, they would not have allowed the English workmen to live well?

(I, laughing) As far as I can make out, the English masters of the English workmen saw to that: they took from their workmen as much of their livelihood as they dared, because they wanted it for themselves.

(H.) But if the French had conquered, would they not have taken more still from the English workmen?

(I) I do not think so; for in that case the English workmen would have died of starvation; and then the French conquest would have ruined the French, just as if the English horses and cattle had died of under-feeding. So that after all, the English *workmen* would have been no worse off for the conquest: their French masters could have got no more from them than their English masters did.

(H.) This is true; and we may admit that the pretensions of the government to defend the poor (*i.e.*, the useful) people against other countries come to nothing. But that is but natural; for we have seen already that it was the function of the government to protect the rich against the poor. But did not the government defend its rich men against other nations?

(I) I do not remember to have heard that the rich needed defence; because it is said that even when two nations were at war, the rich men of each nation gambled with each other pretty much as usual, and even sold each other weapons wherewith to kill their own countrymen.

(H.) In short, it comes to this, that whereas the so-called government of protection of property by means of the law-courts meant destruction of wealth, this defence of the citizens of one country against those of another country by means of war or the threat of war meant pretty much the same thing.

(I) I cannot deny it.

(H.) Therefore the government really existed for the destruction of wealth?

(I) So it seems. And yet—

(H.) Yet what?

(I) There were many rich people in those times.

(H.) You see the consequences of that fact?

(I) I think I do. But tell me what they were.

(H.) If the government habitually destroyed wealth, the country must have been poor?

(I) Yes, certainly.

(H.) Yet amidst this poverty the persons for the sake of whom the government existed insisted on being rich whatever might happen?

(I) So it was.

(H.) What *must* happen if in a poor country some people insist on being rich at the expense of others?

(I) Unutterable poverty for the others. All this misery, then, was caused by the destructive government of which we have been speaking?

(H.) Nay, it would be incorrect to say so. The government itself was but the necessary result of the careless, aimless tyranny of the times; it was but the machinery of tyranny. Now tyranny has come to an end, and we no longer need such machinery; we could not possibly use it since we are free. Therefore in your sense of the word we have no government. Do you understand this now?

(I) Yes, I do. But I will ask you some more questions as to how you as free men manage your affairs.

(H.) With all my heart. Ask away.

Chapter XII. Concerning the Arrangement of Life

'Well,' I said, 'about those "arrangements" which you spoke of as taking the place of government, could you give me any account of them?'

'Neighbour,' he said, 'although we have simplified our lives a great deal from what they were, and have got rid of many conventionalities and many sham wants, which used to give our forefathers much trouble, yet our life is too complex for me to tell you in detail by means of words how it is arranged; you must find that out by living amongst us. It is true that I can better tell you what we don't do, than what we do do.'

'Well?' said I.

'This is the way to put it,' said he: 'We have been living for a hundred and fifty years, at least, more or less in our present manner, and a tradition or habit of life has been growing on us; and that habit has become a habit of acting on the whole for the best. It is easy for us to live without robbing each other. It would be possible for us to contend with and rob each other, but it would be harder for us than refraining from strife and robbery. That is in short the foundation of our life and our happiness.'

'Whereas in the old days,' said I, 'it was very hard to live without strife and robbery. That's what you mean, isn't it, by giving me the negative side of your good conditions?'

'Yes,' he said, 'it was so hard, that those who habitually acted fairly to their neighbours were celebrated as saints and heroes, and were looked up to with the greatest reverence.'

'While they were alive?' said I.

'No,' said he, 'after they were dead.'

'But as to these days,' I said; 'you don't mean to tell me that no one ever transgresses this habit of good fellowship?'

'Certainly not,' said Hammond, 'but when the transgressions occur, everybody, transgressors and all, know them for what they are; the errors of friends, not the habitual actions of persons driven into enmity against society.'

'I see,' said I; 'you mean that you have no "criminal" classes.'

'How could we have them,' said he, 'since there is no rich class to breed enemies against the state by means of the injustice of the state?'

Said I: 'I thought that I understood from something that fell from you a little while ago that you had abolished civil law. Is that so, literally?'

'It abolished itself, my friend,' said he. 'As I said before, the civil law-courts were upheld for the defence of private property; for nobody ever pretended that it was possible to make people act fairly to each other by means of brute force. Well, private property being abolished, all the laws and all the legal "crimes" which it had manufactured of course came to an end. Thou shalt not steal, had to be translated into, Thou shalt work in order to live happily. Is there any need to enforce that commandment by violence?'

'Well,' said I, 'that is understood, and I agree with it; but how about the crimes of violence? would not their occurrence (and you admit that they occur) make criminal law necessary?'

Said he: 'In your sense of the word, we have no criminal law either. Let us look at the matter closer, and see whence crimes of violence spring. By far the greater part of these in past days were the result of the laws of private property, which forbade the satisfaction of their natural desires to all but a privileged few, and of the general visible coercion which came of those laws. All *that* cause of violent crime is gone. Again, many violent acts came from the artificial perversion of the sexual passions, which caused over-weening jealousy and the like miseries. Now, when you look carefully into these, you will find that what lay at the bottom of them was mostly the idea (a law-made idea) of the woman being the property of the man, whether he were husband, father, brother, or what not. *That* idea has of course vanished with private property, as well as certain follies about the "ruin" of women for following their natural desires in an illegal way, which of course was a convention caused by the laws of private property.'

'Another cognate cause of crimes of violence was the family tyranny, which was the subject of so many novels and stories of the past and which once more was the result of private property. Of course that is all ended, since families are held together by no bond of coercion, legal or social, but by mutual liking and affection, and everybody is free to come or go as he or she pleases. Furthermore, our standards of honour and public estimation are very different from the old ones; success in besting our neighbours is a road to renown now closed, let us hope for ever. Each man is free to exercise his special faculty to the utmost and every one encourages him in so doing. So that we have got rid of the scowling envy, coupled by the poets with hatred, and surely with good reason; heaps of unhappiness and ill-blood were caused by it, which with irritable and passionate men—*i.e.*, energetic and active men—often led to violence.'

I laughed, and said: 'So that you now withdraw your admission, and say that there is no violence amongst you?'

'No,' said he, 'I withdraw nothing; as I told you, such things will happen. Hot blood will err sometimes. A man may strike another, and the stricken strike back again, and the result be a homicide, to put it at the worst. But what then? Shall we the neighbours make it worse still? Shall we think so poorly of each other as to suppose that the slain man calls on us to revenge him, when we *know* that if he had been maimed, he would, when in cold blood and able to weigh all the circumstances, have forgiven his maimer? Or will the death of the slayer bring the slain man to life again and cure the unhappiness his loss has caused?'

'Yes,' I said, 'but consider, must not the safety of society be safeguarded by some punishment?'

'There, neighbour!' said the old man, with some exultation. 'You have hit the mark. That *punishment* of which men used to talk so wisely and act so foolishly, what was it but the expression of their fear? And they had need to fear, since *they*—*i.e.*, the rulers of society—were dwelling like an armed band in a hostile country. But we who live amongst our friends need neither fear nor punish. Surely if we, in dread of an occasional rare homicide, an occasional rough blow, were solemnly and legally to commit homicide and violence, we could only be a society of ferocious cowards. Don't you think so, neighbour?'

'Yes, I do, when I come to think of it from that side,' said I.

'Yet you must understand,' said the old man, 'that when any violence is committed, we expect the transgressor to make any atonement possible to him, and he himself expects it. But again, think if the destruction or serious injury of a man momentarily overcome by wrath or folly can be any atonement to the commonwealth? Surely it can only be an additional injury to it.'

Said I: 'But suppose the man has a habit of violence,—kills a man a year, for instance?'

'Such a thing is unknown,' said he. 'In a society where there is no punishment to evade, no law to triumph over, remorse will certainly follow transgression.'

'And lesser outbreaks of violence,' said I 'how do you deal with them? for hitherto we have been talking of great tragedies, I suppose?'

Said Hammond: 'If the ill-doer is not sick or mad (in which case he must be restrained till his sickness or madness is cured) it is clear that grief and humiliation must follow the ill-deed; and society in general will make that pretty clear to the ill-doer if he should chance to be dull to it; and again, some kind of atonement will follow,—at the least, an open acknowledgement of the grief and humiliation. Is it so hard to say, I ask your pardon, neighbour?— Well, sometimes it is hard—and let it be.'

'You think that enough?' said I.

'Yes,' said he, 'and moreover it is all that we *can* do. If in addition we torture the man, we turn his grief into anger, and the humiliation he would otherwise feel for *his* wrong-doing is swallowed up by a hope of revenge for *our* wrongdoing to him. He has paid the legal penalty, and can "go and sin again" with comfort. Shall we commit such a folly, then? Remember Jesus had got the legal penalty remitted before he said "Go and sin no more." Let alone that in a society of equals you will not find any one to play the part of torturer or jailer, though many to act as nurse or doctor.'

'So,' said I, 'you consider crime a mere spasmodic disease, which requires no body of criminal law to deal with it?'

'Pretty much so,' said he; 'and since, as I have told you we are a healthy people generally, so we are not likely to be much troubled with *this* disease.'

'Well, you have no civil law, and no criminal law. But have you no laws of the market, so to say—no regulation for the exchange of wares? for you must exchange, even if you have no property.'

Said he: 'We have no obvious individual exchange, as you saw this morning when you went a-shopping; but of course there are regulations of the markets, varying according to the circumstances and guided by general custom. But as these are matters of general assent, which nobody dreams of objecting to, so also we have made no provision for enforcing them: therefore I don't call them laws. In law, whether it be criminal or civil, execution always follows judgement, and someone must suffer. When you see the judge on his bench, you see through him, as clearly as if he were made of glass, the policeman to emprison, and the soldier to slay some actual living person. Such follies would make an agreeable market, wouldn't they?'

'Certainly,' said I, 'that means turning the market into a mere battle-field, in which many people must suffer as much as in the battle-field of bullet and bayonet. And from what I have seen, I should suppose that your marketing, great and little, is carried on in a way that makes it a pleasant occupation.'

'You are right, neighbour,' said he. 'Although there are so many, indeed by far the greater number amongst us, who would be unhappy if they were not engaged in actually making things, and things which turn out beautiful under their hands,—there are many, like the housekeepers I was speaking of, whose delight is in administration and organisation to use long-tailed words; I mean people who like keeping things together, avoiding waste, seeing that nothing sticks fast uselessly. Such people are thoroughly happy in their business, all the more as they are dealing with actual facts, and not merely passing counters round to see what share they shall have in the privileged taxation of useful people which was the business of the commercial folk in past days. Well, what are you going to ask me next?'

Chapter XIII. Concerning Politics

Said I: 'How do you manage with politics?'

Said Hammond, smiling: 'I am glad that it is of *me* that you ask that question; I do believe that anybody else would make you explain yourself, or try to do so, till you were sickened of asking questions. Indeed, I believe I am the only man in England who would know what you mean; and since I know, I will answer your question briefly by saying that we are very well off as to politics,—because we have none. If ever you make a book out of this conversation, put this in a chapter by itself, after the model of old Horrebow's Snakes in Iceland.'

'I will,' said I.

Chapter XIV. How Matters Are Managed

Said I: 'How about your relations with foreign nations?'

'I will not affect not to know what you mean,' said he, 'but I will tell you at once that the whole system of rival and contending nations which played so great a part in the "government" of the world of civilisation has disappeared along with the inequality betwixt man and man in society.'

'Does not that make the world duller?' said I.

'Why?' said the old man.

'The obliteration of national variety,' said I.

'Nonsense,' he said, somewhat snappishly. 'Cross the water and see. You will find plenty of variety: the landscape, the building, the diet, the amusements, all various. The men and women varying in looks as well as in habits of thought; the costume far more various than in the commercial period. How should it add to the variety or dispel the dulness, to coerce certain families or tribes, often heterogeneous and jarring with one another, into certain artificial and mechanical groups, and call them nations, and stimulate their patriotism— i.e., their foolish and envious prejudices?'

'Well—I don't know how,' said I.

'That's right,' said Hammond cheerily; 'you can easily understand that now we are freed from this folly it is obvious to us that by means of this very diversity the different strains of blood in the world can be serviceable and pleasant to each other, without in the least wanting to rob each other: we are all bent on the same enterprise, making the most of our lives. And I must tell you whatever quarrels or misunderstandings arise, they very seldom take place between people of different race; and consequently since there is less unreason in them, they are the more readily appeased.'

'Good,' said I, 'but as to those matters of politics; as to general differences of opinion in one and the same community. Do you assert that there are none?'

'No, not at all,' said he, somewhat snappishly; 'but I do say that differences of opinion about real solid things need not, and with us do not, crystallise people into parties permanently hostile to one another, with different theories as to the build of the universe and the progress of time. Isn't that what politics used to mean?'

'H'm, well,' said I, 'I am not so sure of that.'

Said he: 'I take you, neighbour; they only *pretended* to this serious difference of opinion; for if it had existed they could not have dealt together in the ordinary business of life; couldn't have eaten together, bought and sold together, gambled together, cheated other people together, but must have fought whenever they met: which would not have suited them at all. The game of the masters of politics was to cajole or force the public to pay the expense of a luxurious life and exciting amusement for a few cliques of ambitious persons: and the *pretence* of serious difference of opinion, belied by every action of their lives, was quite good enough for that. What has all that got to do with us?'

Said I: 'Why nothing, I should hope. But I fear—In short, I have been told that political strife was a necessary result of human nature.'

'Human nature!' cried the old boy, impetuously; 'what human nature? The human nature of paupers, of slaves, of slave-holders, or the human nature of wealthy freemen? Which? Come, tell me that!'

'Well,' said I, 'I suppose there would be a difference according to circumstances in people's action about these matters.'

'I should think so, indeed,' said he. 'At all events, experience shows that it is so. Amongst us, our differences concern matters of business, and passing events as to them, and could not divide men permanently. As a rule, the immediate outcome shows which opinion on a given subject is the right one; it is a matter of fact, not of speculation. For instance, it is clearly not easy to knock up a political party on the question as to whether haymaking in such and such a country-side shall begin this week or next, when all men agree that it must at latest begin the week after next, and when any man can go down into the fields himself and see whether the seeds are ripe enough for the cutting.'

Said I: 'And you settle these differences, great and small, by the will of the majority, I suppose?'

'Certainly,' said he; 'how else could we settle them? You see in matters which are merely personal which do not affect the welfare of the community—how a man shall dress, what he shall eat and drink, what he shall write and read, and so forth—there can be no difference of opinion, and everybody does as he pleases. But when the matter is of common interest to the whole community, and the doing or not doing something affects everybody, the majority must have their way; unless the minority were to take up arms and show by force that they were the effective or real majority; which, however, in a society of men who are free and equal is little likely to happen; because in such a community the apparent majority *is* the real majority, and the others, as I have hinted before, know that too well to obstruct from mere pigheadedness; especially as they have had plenty of opportunity of putting forward their side of the question.'

'How is that managed?' said I.

'Well,' said he, 'let us take one of our units of management, a commune, or a ward, or a parish (for we have all three names, indicating little real distinction between them now, though time was there was a good deal). In such a district, as you would call it, some neighbours think that something ought to be done or undone: a new town-hall built; a clearance of inconvenient houses; or say a stone bridge substituted for some ugly old iron one,—there you have undoing and doing in one. Well, at the next ordinary meeting of the neighbours, or Mote, as we call it, according to the ancient tongue of the times before bureaucracy, a neighbour proposes the change and of course, if everybody agrees, there is an end of discussion, except about details. Equally, if no one backs the proposer—"seconds him", it used to be called—the matter drops for the time being; a thing not likely to happen amongst reasonable men however, as the proposer is sure to have talked it over with others before the Mote. But supposing the affair proposed and seconded, if a few of the neighbours disagree to it, if they think that the beastly iron bridge will serve a little longer and they don't want to be bothered with building a new one just then, they don't count heads that time, but put off the formal discussion to the next Mote; and meantime arguments *pro* and *con* are flying about, and some get printed, so that everybody knows what is going on; and when the Mote comes together again there is a regular discussion and at last a vote by show of hands. If the division is a close one, the question is again put off for further discussion; if the division is a wide one, the minority are asked if they will yield to the more general opinion, which they often, nay, most commonly do. If they refuse, the question is debated a third time, when, if the minority has not perceptibly grown, they always give way; though I believe there is some half-forgotten rule by which they might still carry it on further; but I say, what always happens is that they are convinced not perhaps that their view is the wrong one, but they cannot persuade or force the community to adopt it.'

'Very good,' said I; 'but what happens if the divisions are still narrow?'

Said he: 'As a matter of principle and according to the rule of such cases, the question must then lapse, and the majority, if so narrow, has to submit to sitting down under the *status quo*. But I must tell you that in point of fact the minority very seldom enforces this rule, but generally yields in a friendly manner.'

'But do you know,' said I, 'that there is something in all this very like democracy; and I thought that democracy was considered to be in a moribund condition many, many years ago.'

The old boy's eyes twinkled. 'I grant you that our methods have that drawback. But what is to be done? We can't get *anyone* amongst us to complain of his not always having his own way in the teeth of the community, when it is clear that *everybody* cannot have that indulgence. What *is* to be done?'

'Well,' said I, 'I don't know.'

Said he: 'The only alternatives to our method that I can conceive of are these. First, that we should choose out, or breed, a class of superior persons capable of judging on all matters without consulting the neighbours; that, in short, we should get for ourselves what used to be called an aristocracy of intellect; or, secondly, that for the purpose of safe-guarding the freedom of the individual will we should revert to a system of private property again, and have slaves and slave-holders once more. What do you think of those two expedients?'

'Well,' said I, 'there is a third possibility—to wit, that every man should be quite independent of every other, and that thus the tyranny of society should be abolished.'

He looked hard at me for a second or two, and then burst out laughing very heartily; and I confess that I joined him. When he recovered himself he nodded at me, and said: 'Yes, yes, I quite agree with you—and so we all do.'

'Yes,' I said, 'and besides, it does not press hardly on the minority: for, take this matter of the bridge, no man is obliged to work on it if he doesn't agree to its building. At least I suppose not.'

He smiled, and said: 'Shrewdly put; and yet from the point of view of another planet. If the man of the minority does find his feelings hurt, doubtless he may relieve them by refusing to help in building the bridge. But, dear neighbour, that is not a very effective salve for the wound caused by the "tyranny of a majority" in our society; because all work that is done is either beneficial or hurtful to every member of society. The man is benefited by the bridge-building if it turns out a good thing, and hurt by it if it turns out a bad one, whether he puts a hand to it or not; and meanwhile he is benefiting the bridge-builders by his work, whatever that may be. In fact, I see no help for him except the pleasure of saying "I told you so" if the bridge-building turns out to be a mistake and hurts him; if it benefits him he must suffer in silence. A terrible tyranny our Communism, is it not? Folk used often to be warned against this very unhappiness in times past, when for every well-fed, contented person you saw a thousand miserable starvelings. Whereas for us, we grow fat and well-liking on the tyranny; a tyranny, to say the truth, not to be made visible by any microscope I know. Don't be afraid, my friend; we are not going to seek for troubles by calling our peace and plenty and happiness by ill names whose very meaning we have forgotten!'

He sat musing for a little, and then started and said: 'Are there any more questions, dear guest? The morning is waning fast amidst my garrulity.'

Chapter XV. On the Lack of Incentive to Labour in a Communist Society

'Yes,' said I. 'I was expecting Dick and Clara to make their appearance any moment: but is there time to ask just one or two questions before they come?'

'Try it, dear neighbour—try it,' said old Hammond. 'For the more you ask me the better I am pleased; and at any rate if they do come and find me in the middle of an answer, they must sit quiet and pretend to listen till I come to an end. It won't hurt them; they will find it quite amusing enough to sit side by side, conscious of their proximity to each other.'

I smiled, as I was bound to, and said: 'Good; I will go on talking without noticing them when they come in. Now, this is what I want to ask you about—to wit, how you get people to work when there is no reward of labour, and especially how you get them to work strenuously?'

'But no reward of labour?' said Hammond, gravely. 'The reward of labour is *life*. Is that not enough?'

'But no reward for especially good work,' quoth I.

'Plenty of reward,' said he—'the reward of creation. The wages which God gets, as people might have said time agone. If you are going to ask to be paid for the pleasure of creation, which is what excellence in work means, the next thing we shall hear of will be a bill sent in for the begetting of children.'

'Well, but,' said I, 'the man of the nineteenth century would say there is a natural desire towards the procreation of children, and a natural desire not to work.'

'Yes, yes,' said he, 'I know the ancient platitude,—wholly untrue; indeed, to us quite meaningless. Fourier, whom all men laughed at, understood the matter better.'

'Why is it meaningless to you?' said I.

He said: 'Because it implies that all work is suffering, and we are so far from thinking that, that, as you may have noticed, whereas we are not short of wealth, there is a kind of fear growing up amongst us that we shall one day be short of work. It is a pleasure which we are afraid of losing, not a pain.'

'Yes,' said I, 'I have noticed that, and I was going to ask you about that also. But in the meantime, what do you positively mean to assert about the pleasurableness of work amongst you?'

'This, that *all* work is now pleasureable; either because of the hope of gain in honour and wealth with which the work is done, which causes pleasurable excitement, even when the actual work is not pleasant; or else because it has grown into a pleasurable *habit*, as in the case with what you may call mechanical work; and lastly (and most of our work is of this kind) because there is conscious sensuous pleasure in the work itself; it is done, that is, by artists.'

'I see,' said I. 'Can you now tell me how you have come to this happy condition? For, to speak plainly, this change from the conditions of the older world seems to me far greater and more important than all the other changes you have told me about as to crime, politics, property, marriage.'

'You are right there,' said he. 'Indeed, you may say rather that it is this change which makes all the others possible. What is the object of Revolution? Surely to make people happy. Revolution having brought its foredoomed change about, how can you prevent the counter-revolution from setting in except by making people happy? What! shall we expect peace and stability from unhappiness? The gathering of grapes from thorns and figs from thistles is a reasonable expectation compared with that! And happiness without happy daily work is impossible.'

'Most obviously true,' said I: for I thought the old boy was preaching a little. 'But answer my question, as to how you gained this happiness.'

'Briefly,' said he, 'by the absence of artificial coercion, and the freedom for every man to do what he can do best, joined to the knowledge of what productions of labour we really wanted. I must admit that this knowledge we reached slowly and painfully.'

'Go on,' said I, 'give me more detail; explain more fully. For this subject interests me intensely.'

'Yes, I will,' said he; 'but in order to do so I must weary you by talking a little about the past. Contrast is necessary for this explanation. Do you mind?'

'No, no,' said I.

Said he, settling himself in his chair again for a long talk: 'It is clear from all that we hear and read, that in the last age of civilisation men had got into a vicious circle in the matter of production of wares. They had reached a wonderful facility of production, and in order to make the most of that facility they had gradually created (or allowed to grow, rather) a most elaborate system of buying and selling, which has been called the World-Market; and that World-Market, once set a-going, forced them to go on making more and more of these wares, whether they needed them or not. So that while (of course) they could not free themselves from the toil of making real necessities, they created in a never-ending series sham or artificial necessaries, which became, under the iron rule of the aforesaid World-Market, of equal importance to them with the real necessaries which supported life. By all this they burdened themselves with a prodigious mass of work merely for the sake of keeping their wretched system going.'

'Yes—and then?' said I.

'Why, then, once they had forced themselves to stagger along under this horrible burden of unnecessary production, it became impossible for them to look upon labour and its results from any other point of view than one—to wit, the ceaseless endeavour to expend the least possible amount of labour on any article made, and yet at the same time to make as many articles as possible. To this "cheapening of production," as it was called, everything was sacrificed: the happiness of the workman at his work, nay, his most elementary comfort and bare health, his food, his clothes, his dwelling, his leisure, his amusement, his education— his life, in short—did not weigh a grain of sand in the balance against this dire necessity of "cheap production" of things, a great part of which were not worth producing at all. Nay, we are told, and we must believe it, so overwhelming is the evidence, though many of our people scarcely *can* believe it, that even rich and powerful men, the masters of the poor devils aforesaid, submitted to live amidst sights and sounds and smells which it is in the very nature of man to abhor and flee from, in order that their riches might bolster up this supreme folly. The whole community, in fact, was cast into the jaws of this ravening monster, "the cheap production" forced upon it by the World-Market.'

'Dear me!' said I. 'But what happened? Did not their cleverness and facility in production master this chaos of misery at last? Couldn't they catch up with the World-Market, and then set to work to devise means for relieving themselves from this fearful task of extra labour?'

He smiled bitterly. 'Did they even try to?' said he. 'I am not sure. You know that according to the old saw the beetle gets used to living in dung; and these people whether they found the dung sweet or not, certainly lived in it.'

His estimate of the life of the nineteenth century made me catch my breath a little; and I said feebly, 'But the labour-saving machines?'

'Heyday!' quoth he. 'What's that you are saying? the labour-saving machines? Yes, they were meant to "save labour" (or, to speak more plainly, the lives of men) on one piece of work in order that it might be expended—I will say wasted—on another, probably useless, piece of work. Friend, all their devices for cheapening labour simply resulted in increasing the burden of labour. The appetite of the World-Market grew with what it fed on: the countries within the ring of "civilisation" (that is, organised misery) were glutted with the abortions of the market, and force and fraud were used unsparingly to "open up" countries *outside* that pale. This process of "opening up" is a strange one to those who have read the professions of the men of that period and do not understand their practice; and perhaps shows us at its worst the great vice of the nineteenth century, the use of hypocrisy and cant to evade the responsibility of vicarious ferocity. When the civilised World-Market coveted a country not yet in its clutches some transparent pretext was found—the suppression of a slavery different from, and not so cruel as that of commerce; the pushing of a religion no longer believed in by its promoters; the "rescue" of some desperado or homicidal madman whose misdeeds had got him into trouble amongst the natives of the "barbarous" country—any stick, in short, which would beat the dog at all. Then some bold, unprincipled, ignorant adventurer was found (no difficult task in the days of competition), and he was bribed to "create a market" by breaking up whatever traditional society there might be in the doomed country, and by destroying whatever leisure or pleasure he found there. He forced wares on the natives which they did not want, and took their natural products in "exchange", as this form of robbery was called, and thereby he "created new wants", to supply which (that is, to be allowed to live by their new masters) the hapless, helpless people had to sell themselves into the slavery of hopeless toil so that they might have something wherewith to purchase the nullities of "civilisation." Ah', said the old man, pointing to the Museum, 'I have read books and papers in there, telling strange stories indeed of the dealings of civilisation (or organised misery) with "non-civilisation"; from the time when the British Government deliberately sent blankets infected with small-pox as choice gifts to inconvenient tribes of Red-skins, to the time when Africa was infested by a man named Stanley, who—'

'Excuse me,' said I, 'but as you know, time presses; and I want to keep our question on the straightest line possible; and I want at once to ask this about these wares made for the World-Market—how about their quality; these people who were so clever about making goods, I suppose they made them well?'

'Quality!' said the old man crustily, for he was rather peevish at being cut short in his story; 'how could they possibly attend to such trifles as the quality of the wares they sold? The best of them were of a lowish average, the worst were transparent make-shifts for the things asked for, which nobody would have put up with if they could have got anything else. It was the current jest of the time that the wares were made to sell and not to use; a jest which you, as coming from another planet, may understand, but which our folk could not.'

Said I: 'What! did they make nothing well?'

'Why, yes,' said he, 'there was one class of goods which they did make thoroughly well, and that was the class of machines which were used for making things. These were usually quite perfect pieces of workmanship, admirably adapted to the end in view. So that it may be fairly said that the great achievement of the nineteenth century was the making of machines which were wonders of invention, skill, and patience, and which were used for the production of measureless quantities of worthless make-shifts. In truth, the owners of the machines did not consider anything which they made as wares, but simply as means for the enrichment of themselves. Of course, the only admitted test of utility in wares was the finding of buyers for them—wise men or fools, as it might chance.'

'And people put up with this?' said I.

'For a time,' said he.

'And then?'

'And then the overturn,' said the old man, smiling, 'and the nineteenth century saw itself as a man who has lost his clothes whilst bathing, and has to walk naked through the town.'

'You are very bitter about that unlucky nineteenth century,' said I.

'Naturally,' said he, 'since I know so much about it.'

He was silent a little, and then said: 'There are traditions—nay, real histories—in our family about it: my grandfather was one of its victims. If you know something about it, you will understand what he suffered when I tell you that he was in those days a genuine artist, a man of genius, and a revolutionist.'

'I think I do understand,' said I: 'but now, as it seems, you have reversed all this?'

'Pretty much so,' said he. 'The wares which we make are made because they are needed: men make for their neighbours' use as if they were making for themselves, not for a vague market of which they know nothing, and over which they have no control: as there is no buying and selling, it would be mere insanity to make goods on the chance of their being wanted; for there is no longer any one who can be *compelled* to buy them. So that whatever is made is good, and thoroughly fit for its purpose. Nothing *can* be made except for genuine use; therefore no inferior goods are made. Moreover, as aforesaid, we have now found out what we want, so we make no more than we want; and as we are not driven to make a vast quantity of useless things, we have time and resources enough to consider our pleasure in making them. All work which would be irksome to do by hand is done by immensely improved machinery; and in all work which it is a pleasure to do by hand machinery is done without. There is no difficulty in finding work which suits the special turn of mind of everybody; so that no man is sacrificed to the wants of another. From time to time, when we have found out that some piece of work was too disagreeable or troublesome, we have given it up and done altogether without the thing produced by it. Now, surely you can see that under these circumstances all the work that we do is an exercise of the mind and body more or less pleasant to be done: so that instead of avoiding work everybody seeks it: and, since people have got defter in doing the work generation after generation, it has become so easy to do, that it seems as if there were less done, though probably more is produced. I suppose this explains that fear, which I hinted at just now, of a possible scarcity in work, which perhaps you have already noticed, and which is a feeling on the increase, and has been for a score of years.'

'But do you think,' said I, 'that there is any fear of a work-famine amongst you?'

'No, I do not,' said he, 'and I will tell why; it is each man's business to make his own work pleasanter and pleasanter, which of course tends towards raising the standard of excellence, as no man enjoys turning out work which is not a credit to him, and also to greater deliberation in turning it out; and there is such a vast number of things which can be treated as works of art, that this alone gives employment to a host of deft people. Again, if art be inexhaustible, so is science also; and though it is no longer the only innocent occupation which is thought worth an intelligent man spending his time upon, as it once was, yet there are, and I suppose will be, many people who are excited by its conquest of difficulties, and care for it more than for anything else. Again, as more and more of pleasure is imported into work, I think we shall take up kinds of work which produce desirable wares, but which we gave up because we could not carry them on pleasantly. Moreover, I think that it is only in parts of Europe which are more advanced than the rest of the world that you will hear this talk of the fear of a work-famine. Those lands which were once the colonies of Great Britain, for instance, and especially America—that part of it, above all, which was once the United States—are now and will be for a long while a great resource to us. For these lands, and, I say, especially the northern parts of America, suffered so terribly from the full force of the last days of civilisation, and became such horrible places to live in, that they are now very backward in all that makes life pleasant. Indeed, one may say that for nearly a hundred years the people of the northern parts of America have been engaged in gradually making a dwelling-place out of a stinking dust-heap; and there is still a great deal to do, especially as the country is so big.'

'Well,' said I, 'I am exceedingly glad to think that you have such a prospect of happiness before you. But I should like to ask a few more questions, and then I have done for to-day.'

Chapter XVI. Dinner in the Hall of the Bloomsbury Market

As I spoke, I heard footsteps near the door; the latch yielded, and in came our two lovers, looking so handsome that one had no feeling of shame in looking on at their little-concealed love-making; for indeed it seemed as if all the world must be in love with them. As for old Hammond, he looked on them like an artist who has just painted a picture nearly as well as he thought he could when he began it, and was perfectly happy. He said:

'Sit down, sit down, young folk, and don't make a noise. Our guest here has still some questions to ask me.'

'Well, I should suppose so,' said Dick; 'you have only been three hours and a half together; and it isn't to be hoped that the history of two centuries could be told in three hours and a half: let alone that, for all I know, you may have been wandering into the realms of geography and craftsmanship.'

'As to noise, my dear kinsman,' said Clara, 'You will very soon be disturbed by the noise of the dinner-bell, which I should think will be very pleasant music to our guest, who breakfasted early, it seems, and probably had a tiring day yesterday.'

I said: 'Well, since you have spoken the word, I begin to feel that it is so; but I have been feeding myself with wonder this long time past: really, it's quite true,' quoth I, as I saw her smile, O so prettily!

But just then from some tower high up in the air came the sound of silvery chimes playing a sweet clear tune, that sounded to my unaccustomed ears like the song of the first blackbird in the spring, and called a rush of memories to my mind, some of bad times, some of good, but all sweetened now into mere pleasure.

'No more questions now before dinner,' said Clara; and she took my hand as an affectionate child would, and led me out of the room and down stairs into the forecourt of the Museum, leaving the two Hammonds to follow as they pleased.

We went into the market-place which I had been in before, a thinnish stream of elegantly* dressed people going in along with us. We turned into the cloister and came to a richly moulded and carved doorway, where a very pretty dark-haired young girl gave us each a beautiful bunch of summer flowers, and we entered a hall much bigger than that of the Hammersmith Guest House, more elaborate in its architecture and perhaps more beautiful. I found it difficult to keep my eyes off the wall-pictures (for I thought it bad manners to stare at Clara all the time, though she was quite worth it). I saw at a glance that their subjects were taken from queer old-world myths and imaginations which in yesterday's world only about half a dozen people in the country knew anything about; and when the two Hammonds sat down opposite to us, I said to the old man, pointing to the frieze:

'How strange to see such subjects here!'

'Why?' said he. 'I don't see why you should be surprised; everybody knows the tales; and they are graceful and pleasant subjects, not too tragic for a place where people mostly eat and drink and amuse themselves, and yet full of incident.'

I smiled, and said: 'Well, I scarcely expected to find record of the Seven Swans and the King of the Golden Mountain and Faithful Henry, and such curious pleasant imaginations as Jacob Grimm got together from the

---

* 'Elegant,' I mean, as a Persian pattern is elegant; not like a rich 'elegant' lady out for a morning call. I should rather call that *genteel*.

childhood of the world, barely lingering even in his time: I should have thought you would have forgotten such childishness by this time.'

The old man smiled, and said nothing; but Dick turned rather red, and broke out:

'What *do* you mean, guest? I think them very beautiful, I mean not only the pictures, but the stories; and when we were children we used to imagine them going on in every wood-end, by the bight of every stream: every house in the fields was the Fairyland King's House to us. Don't you remember, Clara?'

'Yes,' she said; and it seemed to me as if a slight cloud came over her fair face. I was going to speak to her on the subject, when the pretty waitresses came to us smiling, and chattering sweetly like reed warblers by the river-side, and fell to giving us our dinner. As to this, as at our breakfast, everything was cooked and served with a daintiness which showed that those who had prepared it were interested in it; but there was no excess either of quantity or of gourmandise; everything was simple, though so excellent of its kind; and it was made clear to us that this was no feast, only an ordinary meal. The glass, crockery, and plate were very beautiful to my eyes, used to the study of mediæval art; but a nineteenth century club-haunter would, I daresay, have found them rough and lacking in finish; the crockery being lead-glazed pot-ware, though beautifully ornamented; the only porcelain being here and there a piece of old oriental ware. The glass, again, though elegant and quaint, and very varied in form, was somewhat bubbled and hornier in texture than the commercial articles of the nineteenth century. The furniture and general fittings of the hall were much of a piece with the table-gear, beautiful in form and highly ornamented, but without the commercial "finish" of the joiners and cabinet-makers of our time. Withal, there was a total absence of what the nineteenth century calls "comfort"—that is, stuffy inconvenience; so that, even apart from the delightful excitement of the day I had never eaten my dinner so pleasantly before.

When we had done eating, and were sitting a little while, with a bottle of very good Bordeaux wine before us, Clara came back to the question of the subject-matter of the pictures, as though it had troubled her.

She looked up at them, and said: 'How is it that though we are so interested with our life for the most part, yet when people take to writing poems or painting pictures they seldom deal with our modern life, or if they do, take good care to make their poems or pictures unlike that life? Are we not good enough to paint ourselves? How is it that we find the dreadful times of the past so interesting to us—in pictures and poetry?'

Old Hammond smiled. 'It always was so, and I suppose always will be,' said he, 'however it may be explained. It is true that in the nineteenth century, when there was so little art and so much talk about it, there was a theory that art and imaginative literature ought to deal with contemporary life; but they never did so; for, if there was any pretence of it, the author always took care (as Clara hinted just now) to disguise, or exaggerate, or idealise, and in some way or another make it strange; so that, for all the verisimilitude there was, he might just as well have dealt with the times of the Pharaohs.'

'Well,' said Dick, 'surely it is but natural to like these things strange; just as when we were children, as I said just now, we used to pretend to be so-and-so in such-and-such a place. That's what these pictures and poems do; and why shouldn't they?'

'Thou hast hit it, Dick,' quoth old Hammond; 'it is the child-like part of us that produces works of imagination. When we are children time passes so slow with us that we seem to have time for everything.'

He sighed, and then smiled and said: 'At least let us rejoice that we have got back our childhood again. I drink to the days that are!'

'Second childhood,' said I in a low voice, and then blushed at my double rudeness, and hoped that he hadn't heard. But he had, and turned to me smiling, and said: 'Yes why not? And for my part, I hope it may last long; and that the world's next period of wise and unhappy manhood, if that should happen, will speedily lead us to a third childhood: if indeed this age be not our third. Meantime, my friend, you must know that we are too happy, both individually and collectively, to trouble ourselves about what is to come hereafter.'

'Well, for my part,' said Clara, 'I wish we were interesting enough to be written or painted about.'

Dick answered her with some lover's speech, impossible to be written down, and then we sat quiet a little.

Chapter XVII. How the Change Came

Dick broke the silence at last, saying: 'Guest, forgive us for a little after-dinner dulness. What would you like to do? Shall we have out Greylocks and trot back to Hammersmith? or will you come with us and hear some Welsh folk sing in a hall close by here? or would you like presently to come with me into the City and see some really fine building? or—what shall it be?'

'Well,' said I, 'as I am a stranger, I must let you choose for me.'

In point of fact, I did not by any means want to be 'amused' just then; and also I rather felt as if the old man, with his knowledge of past times, and even a kind of inverted sympathy for them caused by his active hatred of them, was as it were a blanket for me against the cold of this very new world, where I was, so to say, stripped bare of every habitual thought and way of acting; and I did not want to leave him too soon. He came to my rescue at once, and said—

'Wait a bit, Dick; there is someone else to be consulted besides you and the guest here, and that is I. I am not going to lose the pleasure of his company just now, especially since I know he has something else to ask me. So go to your Welshmen, by all means; but first of all bring us another bottle of wine to this nook, and then be off as soon as you like; and come again and fetch our friend to go westward, but not too soon.'

Dick nodded smilingly, and the old man and I were soon alone in the great hall, the afternoon sun was gleaming on the red wine in our tall quaint-shaped glasses. Then said Hammond:

'Does anything especially puzzle you about our way of living, now you have heard a good deal and seen a little of it?'

Said I: 'I think what puzzles me most is how it all came about.'

'It well may,' said he, 'so great as the change is. It would be difficult indeed to tell you the whole story, perhaps impossible: knowledge, discontent, treachery, disappointment, ruin, misery, despair—those who worked for the change because they could see further than other people went through all these phases of suffering; and doubtless all the time the most of men looked on, not knowing what was doing, thinking it all a matter of course, like the rising and setting of the sun—and indeed it was so.'

'Tell me one thing, if you can,' said I. 'Did the change, the "revolution" it used to be called, come peacefully?'

'Peacefully?' said he; 'what peace was there amongst those poor confused wretches of the nineteenth century? It was war from beginning to end: bitter war, till hope and pleasure put an end to it.'

'Do you mean actual fighting with weapons?' said I, 'or the strikes and lock-outs and starvation of which we have heard?'

'Both, both,' he said. 'As a matter of fact, the history of the terrible period of transition from commercial slavery to freedom may thus be summarised. When the hope of realising a communal condition of life for all men arose, quite late in the nineteenth century, the power of the middle classes, the then tyrants of society, was so enormous and crushing, that to almost all men, even those who had, you may say despite themselves, despite their reason and judgement, conceived such hopes, it seemed a dream. So much was this the case that some of those more enlightened men who were then called Socialists, although they well knew, and even stated in public, that the only reasonable condition of Society was that of pure Communism (such as you now see around you), yet shrunk from what seemed to them the barren task of preaching the realisation of a happy dream. Looking back now, we can see that the great motive-power of the change was a longing for freedom and equality, akin if you please to the unreasonable passion of the lover; a sickness of heart that rejected with loathing the aimless solitary life of the well-to-do educated men of that time: phrases, my dear friend, which have lost their meaning to us of the present day; so far removed we are from the dreadful facts which they represent.

'Well, these men, though conscious of this feeling, had no faith in it, as a means of bringing about the change. Nor was that wonderful: for looking around them they saw the huge mass of the oppressed classes too much burdened with the misery of their lives, and too much overwhelmed by the selfishness of misery, to be able to form a conception of any escape from it except by the ordinary way prescribed by the system of slavery under which they lived; which was nothing more than a remote chance of climbing out of the oppressed into the oppressing class.

'Therefore, though they knew that the only reasonable aim for those who would better the world was a condition of equality; in their impatience and despair they managed to convince themselves that if they could by hook or by crook get the machinery of production and the management of property so altered that the "lower classes" (so the horrible word ran) might have their slavery somewhat ameliorated, they would be ready to fit into this machinery, and would use it for bettering their condition still more and still more, until at last the result would be a practical equality (they were very fond of using the word "practical"), because "the rich" would be forced to pay so much for keeping "the poor" in a tolerable condition that the condition of riches would become no longer valuable and would gradually die out. Do you follow me?'

'Partly,' said I. 'Go on.'

Said old Hammond: 'Well, since you follow me, you will see that as a theory this was not altogether unreasonable; but "practically", it turned out a failure.'

'How so?' said I.

'Well, don't you see,' said he, 'because it involved the making of a machinery by those who didn't know what they wanted the machines to do. So far as the masses of the oppressed class furthered this scheme of improvement, they did it to get themselves improved slave-rations—as many of them as could. And if those classes had really been incapable of being touched by that instinct which produced the passion for freedom and equality aforesaid, what would have happened, I think, would have been this: that a certain part of the working-classes would have been so far improved in condition that they would have approached the condition of the middling rich men; but below them would have been a great class of most miserable slaves, whose slavery would have been far more hopeless than the older class-slavery had been.'

'What stood in the way of this?' said I.

'Why, of course,' said he, 'just that instinct for freedom aforesaid. It is true that the slave-class could not conceive the happiness of a free life. Yet they grew to understand (and very speedily too) that they were oppressed by their masters, and they assumed, you see how justly, that they could do without them, though perhaps they scarce knew how; so that it came to this, that though they could not look forward to the happiness or peace of the freeman, they did at least look forward to the war which a vague hope told them would bring that peace about.'

'Could you tell me rather more closely what actually took place?' said I; for I thought *him* rather vague here.

'Yes,' he said, 'I can. That machinery of life for the use of people who didn't know what they wanted of it, and which was known at the time as State Socialism, was partly put in motion, though in a very piecemeal way. But it did not work smoothly; it was, of course, resisted at every turn by the capitalists; and no wonder, for it tended more and more to upset the commercial system I have told you of, without providing anything really effective in its place. The result was growing confusion, great suffering amongst the working classes, and, as a consequence, great discontent. For a long time matters went on like this. The power of the upper classes had lessened, as their command over wealth lessened, and they could not carry things wholly by the high hand as they had been used to in earlier days. So far the State Socialists were justified by the result. On the other hand, the working classes were ill-organised, and growing poorer in reality, in spite of the gains (also real in the long run) which they had forced from the masters. Thus matters hung in the balance; the masters could not reduce their slaves to complete subjection, though they put down some feeble and partial riots easily enough. The workers forced their masters to grant them ameliorations, real or imaginary, of their condition, but could not force freedom from them. At last came a great crash. To explain this you must understand that very great progress had been made amongst the workers, though as before said but little in the direction of improved livelihood.'

I played the innocent and said: 'In what direction could they improve, if not in livelihood?'

Said he: 'In the power to bring about a state of things in which livelihood would be full, and easy to gain. They had at last learned how to combine after a long period of mistakes and disasters. The workmen had now a regular organisation in the struggle against their masters, a struggle which for more than half a century had been accepted as an inevitable part of the conditions of the modern system of labour and production. This combination had now taken the form of a federation of all or almost all the recognised wage-paid employments, and it was by its means that those betterments of the condition of the workmen had been forced from the masters: and though they were not seldom mixed up with the rioting that happened, especially in the earlier days of their organisation, it by no means formed an essential part of their tactics; indeed at the time I am now speaking of they had got to be so strong that most commonly the mere threat of a "strike" was enough to gain any minor point: because they had given up the foolish tactics of the ancient trades unions of calling out of work a part only of the workers of such and such an industry, and supporting them while out of work on the labour of those that remained in. By this time they had a biggish fund of money for the support of strikes, and could stop a certain industry altogether for a time if they so determined.'

Said I: 'Was there not a serious danger of such moneys being misused—of jobbery in fact?'

Old Hammond wriggled uneasily on his seat, and said:

'Though all this happened so long ago, I still feel the pain of mere shame when I have to tell you that it was more than a danger: that such rascality often happened; indeed more than once the whole combination seemed dropping to pieces because of it: but at the time of which I am telling, things looked so threatening, and to the workmen at least the necessity of their dealing with the fast-gathering trouble which the labour-struggle had brought about, was so clear, that the conditions of the times had begot a deep seriousness amongst all reasonable people; a determination which put aside all non-essentials, and which to thinking men was ominous of the swiftly-approaching change: such an element was too dangerous for mere traitors and self-seekers, and one by one they were thrust out and mostly joined the declared reactionaries.'

'How about those ameliorations,' said I; 'what were they? or rather of what nature?'

Said he: 'Some of them, and these of the most practical importance to the men's livelihood, were yielded by the masters by direct compulsion on the part of the men; the new conditions of labour so gained were indeed only customary, enforced by no law: but, once established, the masters durst not attempt to withdraw them in face of the growing power of the combined workers. Some again were steps on the path of "State Socialism"; the most important of which can be speedily summed up. At the end of the nineteenth century the cry arose for compelling the masters to employ their men a less number of hours in the day: this cry gathered volume quickly, and the masters had to yield to it. But it was, of course, clear that unless this meant a higher price for the work per hour, it would be a mere nullity, and that the masters, unless forced, would reduce it to that. Therefore after a long struggle another law was passed fixing a minimum price for labour in the most important industries; which again had to be supplemented by a law fixing the maximum price on the chief wares then considered necessary for a workman's life.'

'You were getting perilously near to the late Roman poor-rates,' said I, smiling, 'and the doling out of bread to the proletariat.'

'So many said at the time,' said the old man drily; 'and it has long been a commonplace that that slough awaits State Socialism in the end, if it gets to the end, which as you know it did not with us. However it went further than this minimum and maximum business, which by the by we can now see was necessary. The government now found it imperative on them to meet the outcry of the master class at the approaching destruction of commerce (as desirable, had they known it, as the extinction of the cholera, which has since happily taken place). And they were forced to meet it by a measure hostile to the masters, the establishment of government factories for the production of necessary wares, and markets for their sale. These measures taken altogether did do something: they were in fact of the nature of regulations made by the commander of a beleaguered city. But of course to the privileged classes it seemed as if the end of the world were come when such laws were enacted.'

'Nor was that altogether without a warrant: the spread of communistic theories and the partial practice of State Socialism had at first disturbed, and at last almost paralysed the marvellous system of commerce under which the old world had lived so feverishly, and had produced for some few a life of gambler's pleasure, and for many, or most, a life of mere misery: over and over again came "bad times" as they were called, and indeed they were bad enough for the wage-slaves. The year 1952 was one of the worst of these times; the workmen suffered dreadfully: the partial, inefficient government factories, which were terribly jobbed, all but broke down, and a vast part of the population had for the time being to be fed on undisguised "charity" as it was called.'

'The Combined Workers watched the situation with mingled hope and anxiety. They had already formulated their general demands; but now by a solemn and universal vote of the whole of their federated societies, they insisted on the first step being taken toward carrying out their demands: this step would have led directly to handing over the management of the whole natural resources of the country, together with the machinery for using them into the power of the Combined Workers, and the reduction of the privileged classes into the position of pensioners obviously dependent on the pleasure of the workers. The "Resolution", as it was called, which was widely published in the newspapers of the day was in fact a declaration of war, and was so accepted by the master class. They began henceforward to prepare for a firm stand against the "brutal and ferocious communism of the day", as they phrased it. And as they were in many ways still very powerful, or seemed so to be, they still hoped by means of brute force to regain some of what they had lost, and perhaps in the end the whole of it. It was said amongst them on all hands that it had been a great mistake of the various governments not to have resisted sooner; and the liberals and radicals (the name as perhaps you may know of the more democratically inclined part of the ruling classes) were much blamed for having led the world to this pass by their mis-timed pedantry and foolish sentimentality: and one Gladstone, or Gledstein (probably, judging by this name, of Scandinavian descent), a notable politician of the nineteenth century, was especially singled out for reprobation in this respect. I need scarcely point out to you the absurdity of all this. But terrible tragedy lay hidden behind this grinning through a horse-collar of the reactionary party. "The insatiable greed of the lower classes must be repressed"—"The people must be taught a lesson"—these were the sacramental phrases current amongst the reactionists, and ominous enough they were.'

The old man stopped to look keenly at my attentive and wondering face; and then said:

'I know, dear guest, that I have been using words and phrases which few people amongst us could understand without long and laborious explanation; and not even then perhaps. But since you have not yet gone to sleep, and since I am speaking to you as to a being from another planet, I may venture to ask you if you have followed me thus far?'

'O yes,' said I, 'I quite understand: pray go on; a great deal of what you have been saying was commonplace with us—when—when—'

'Yes,' said he gravely, 'when you were dwelling in the other planet. Well, now for the crash aforesaid.

'On some comparatively trifling occasion a great meeting was summoned by the workmen leaders to meet in Trafalgar Square (about the right to meet in which place there had for years and years been bickering). The civic bourgeois guard (called the police) attacked the said meeting with bludgeons, according to their custom; many people were hurt in the *mêlée*, of whom five in all died, either trampled to death on the spot, or from the effects of their cudgelling; the meeting was scattered, and some hundreds of prisoners cast into gaol. A similar meeting had been treated in the same way a few days before at a place called Manchester, which has now disappeared. Thus the "lesson" began. The whole country was thrown into a ferment by this; meetings were held which attempted some rough organisation for the holding of another meeting to retort on the authorities. A huge crowd assembled in Trafalgar Square and the neighbourhood (then a place of crowded streets), and was too big for the bludgeon-armed police to cope with; there was a good deal of dry-blow fighting; three or four of the people were killed, and half a score of policemen were crushed to death in the throng, and the rest got away as they could. This was a victory for the people as far as it went. The next day all London (remember what it was in those days) was in a state of turmoil. Many of the rich fled into the country; the executive got together soldiery, but did not dare to use them; and the police could not be massed in any one place, because riots or threats of riots were everywhere. But in Manchester, where the people were not so courageous or not so desperate as in London, several of the popular leaders were arrested. In London a convention of leaders was got together from the Federation of Combined Workmen, and sat under the old revolutionary name of the Committee of Public Safety; but as they had no drilled and armed body of men to direct, they attempted no aggressive measures, but only placarded the walls with somewhat vague appeals to the workmen not to allow themselves to be trampled upon. However, they called a meeting in Trafalgar Square for the day fortnight of the last-mentioned skirmish.

'Meantime the town grew no quieter, and business came pretty much to an end. The newspapers—then, as always hitherto, almost entirely in the hands of the masters—clamoured to the Government for repressive measures; the rich citizens were enrolled as an extra body of police, and armed with bludgeons like them; many of these were strong, well-fed, full-blooded young men, and had plenty of stomach for fighting; but the Government did not dare to use them, and contented itself with getting full powers voted to it by the Parliament for suppressing any revolt, and bringing up more and more soldiers to London. Thus passed the week after the great meeting; almost as large a one was held on the Sunday, which went off peaceably on the whole, as no opposition to it was offered, and again the people cried "victory". But on the Monday the people woke up to find that they were hungry. During the last few days there had been groups of men parading the streets asking (or, if you please, demanding) money to buy food; and what for goodwill, what for fear, the richer people gave them a good deal. The authorities of the parishes also (I haven't time to explain that phrase at present) gave willy-nilly what provisions they could to wandering people; and the Government, by means of its feeble national workshops, also fed a good number of half-starved folk. But in addition to this, several bakers' shops and other provision stores had been emptied without a great deal of disturbance. So far, so good. But on the Monday in question the Committee of Public Safety, on the one hand afraid of general unorganised pillage, and on the other emboldened by the wavering conduct of the authorities, sent a deputation provided with carts and all necessary gear to clear out two or three big provision stores in the centre of the town, leaving papers with the shop managers promising to pay the price of them: and also in the part of the town where they were strongest they took possession of several bakers' shops and set men at work in them for the benefit of the people;—all of which was done with little or no disturbance, the police assisting in keeping order at the sack of the stores, as they would have done at a big fire.

'But at this last stroke, the reactionaries were so alarmed, that they were determined to force the executive into action. The newspapers next day all blazed into the fury of frightened people, and threatened the people, the Government, and everybody they could think of, unless "order were at once restored". A deputation of leading commercial people waited on the Government and told them that if they did not at once arrest the Committee of Public Safety, they themselves would gather a body of men, arm them, and fall on "the incendiaries", as they called them.

'They, together with a number of the newspaper editors, had a long interview with the heads of the Government and two or three military men, the deftest in their art that the country could furnish. The deputation came away from that interview, says a contemporary eye-witness, smiling and satisfied, and said no more about raising an anti-popular army, but that afternoon left London with their families for their country seats or elsewhere.

'The next morning the government proclaimed a state of siege in London,—a thing common enough amongst the absolutist governments on the Continent, but unheard-of in England in those days. They appointed the youngest and cleverest of their generals to command the proclaimed district; a man who had won a certain sort of reputation in the disgraceful wars in which the country had been long engaged from time to time. The newspapers were in ecstasies, and all the most fervent of the reactionaries now came to the front; men who in ordinary times were forced to keep their opinions to themselves or their immediate circle, but who began to look forward to crushing once for all the Socialist, and even the democratic tendencies, which, said they, had been treated with such foolish indulgence for the last sixty years.

'But the clever general took no visible action; and yet only a few of the minor newspapers abused him; thoughtful men gathered from this that a plot was hatching. As for the Committee of Public Safety, whatever they thought of their position, they had now gone too far to draw back; and many of them, it seems, thought that the government would not act. They went on quietly organising their food supply, which was a miserable driblet when all is said; and also as a retort to the state of siege, they armed as many men as they could in the quarter where they were strongest, but did not attempt to drill or organise them, thinking, perhaps, that they could not at the best turn them into trained soldiers till they had some breathing space. The clever general, his soldiers, and the police did not meddle with all this in the least in the world; and things were quieter in London that week-end; though there were riots in many places of the provinces, which were quelled by the authorities without much trouble. The most serious of these were at Glasgow and Bristol.

'Well, the Sunday of the meeting came, and great crowds came to Trafalgar Square in procession, the greater part of the Committee amongst them, surrounded by their band of men armed somehow or other. The streets were quite peaceful and quiet, though there were many spectators to see the procession pass. Trafalgar Square had no body of police in it; the people took quiet possession of it, and the meeting began. The armed men stood round the principal platform, and there were a few others armed amidst the general crowd; but by far the greater part were unarmed.

'Most people thought the meeting would go off peaceably; but the members of the Committee had heard from various quarters that something would be attempted against them; but these rumours were vague, and they had no idea of what threatened. They soon found out.

'For before the streets about the square were filled, a body of soldiers poured into it from the north-west corner and took up their places by the houses that stood on the west side. The people growled at the sight of the redcoats; the armed men of the Committee stood undecided, not knowing what to do; and indeed this new influx so jammed the crowd together that, unorganised as they were, they had little chance of working through it. They had scarcely grasped the fact of their enemies being there, when another column of soldiers, pouring out of the streets which led into the great southern road going down to the Parliament House (still existing, and called the Dung

Market), and also from the embankment by the side of the Thames, marched up, pushing the crowd into a denser and denser mass, and formed along the south side of the Square. Then any of those who could see what was going on, knew at once that they were in a trap, and could only wonder what would be done with them.

'The closely-packed crowd would not or could not budge, except under the influence of the height of terror, which was soon to be supplied to them. A few of the armed men struggled to the front, or climbed up to the base of the monument which then stood there, that they might face the wall of hidden fire before them; and to most men (there were many women amongst them) it seemed as if the end of the world had come, and to-day seemed strangely different from yesterday. No sooner were the soldiers drawn up aforesaid than, says an eye-witness, "a glittering officer on horseback came prancing out from the ranks on the south, and read something from a paper which he held in his hand; which something, very few heard; but I was told afterwards that it was an order for us to disperse, and a warning that he had a legal right to fire on the crowd else, and that he would do so. The crowd took it as a challenge of some sort, and a hoarse threatening roar went up from them; and after that there was comparative silence for a little, till the officer had got back into the ranks. I was near the edge of the crowd, towards the soldiers," says this eye-witness, "and I saw three little machines being wheeled out in front of the ranks, which I knew for mechanical guns. I cried out, 'Throw yourselves down! they are going to fire!' But no one scarcely could throw himself down, so tight as the crowd were packed, I heard a sharp order given, and wondered where I should be the next minute; and then—It was as if the earth had opened, and hell had come up bodily amidst us. It is no use trying to describe the scene that followed. Deep lanes were mowed amidst the thick crowd; the dead and dying covered the ground, and the shrieks and wails and cries of horror filled all the air, till it seemed as if there were nothing else in the world but murder and death. Those of our armed men who were still unhurt cheered wildly and opened a scattering fire on the soldiers. One or two soldiers fell; and I saw the officers going up and down the ranks urging the men to fire again; but they received the orders in sullen silence, and let the butts of their guns fall. Only one sergeant ran to a machine-gun and began to set it going; but a tall young man, an officer too, ran out of the ranks and dragged him back by the collar; and the soldiers stood there motionless while the horror-stricken crowd, nearly wholly unarmed (for most of the armed men had fallen in that first discharge), drifted out of the Square. I was told afterwards that the soldiers on the west side had fired also, and done their part of the slaughter. How I got out of the Square I scarcely know; I went, not feeling the ground under me, what with rage and terror and despair."

'So says our eye-witness. The number of the slain on the side of the people in that shooting during a minute was prodigious; but it was not easy to come at the truth about it; it was probably between one and two thousand. Of the soldiers, six were killed outright, and a dozen wounded.'

I listened, trembling with excitement. The old man's eyes glittered and his face flushed as he spoke, and told the tale of what I had often thought might happen. Yet I wondered that he should have got so elated about a mere massacre, and I said:

'How fearful! And I suppose that this massacre put an end to the whole revolution for that time?'

'No, no,' cried old Hammond; 'it began it!'

He filled his glass and mine, and stood up and cried out, 'Drink this glass to the memory of those who died there, for indeed it would be a long tale to tell how much we owe them.'

I drank, and he sat down again and went on.

'That massacre of Trafalgar Square began the civil war, though, like all such events, it gathered head slowly, and people scarcely knew what a crisis they were acting in.

'Terrible as the massacre was, and hideous and overpowering as the first terror had been, when the people had time to think about it, their feeling was one of anger rather than fear; although the military organisation of the state of siege was now carried out without shrinking by the clever young general. For though the ruling-classes when the news spread next morning felt one gasp of horror and even dread, yet the Government and their immediate backers felt that now the wine was drawn and must be drunk. However, even the most reactionary of the capitalist papers, with two exceptions, stunned by the tremendous news, simply gave an account of what had taken place, without making any comment upon it. The exceptions were one, a so-called "liberal" paper (the Government of the day was of that complexion), which, after a preamble in which it declared its undeviating sympathy with the cause of labour, proceeded to point out that in times of revolutionary disturbance it behoved the government to be just but firm, and that by far the most merciful way of dealing with the poor madmen who were attacking the very foundations of society (which had made them mad and poor) was to shoot them at once, so as to stop others from drifting into a position in which they would run a chance of being shot. In short, it praised the determined action of the Government as the *acme* of human wisdom and mercy, and exulted in the inauguration of an epoch of reasonable democracy free from the tyrannical fads of Socialism.

'The other exception was a paper thought to be one of the most violent opponents of democracy, and so it was; but the editor of it found his manhood, and spoke for himself and not for his paper. In a few simple, indignant words he asked people to consider what a society was worth which had to be defended by the massacre of unarmed citizens, and called on the Government to withdraw their state of siege and put the general and his officers who fired on the people on their trial for murder. He went further, and declared that whatever his opinion might be as to the doctrines of the Socialists, he for one should throw in his lot with the people, until the Government atoned for their atrocity by showing that they were prepared to listen to the demands of men who knew what they wanted, and whom the decrepitude of society forced into pushing their demands in some way or other.

'Of course, this editor was immediately arrested by the military power; but his bold words were already in the hands of the public, and produced a great effect: so great an effect that the Government, after some vacillation, withdrew the state of siege; though at the same time it strengthened the military organisation and made it more stringent. Three of the Committee of Public Safety had been slain in Trafalgar Square: of the rest, the greater part went back to their old place of meeting, and there awaited the event calmly. They were arrested there on the Monday morning, and would have been shot at once by the general, who was a mere military machine, if the Government had not shrunk before the responsibility of killing men without any trial. There was at first a talk of trying them by a special commission of judges, as it was called—*i.e.*, before a set of men bound to find them guilty, and whose business it was to do so. But with the Government the cold fit had succeeded to the hot one; and the prisoners were brought before a jury at the assizes. There a fresh blow awaited the Government; for in spite of the judge's charge, which distinctly instructed the jury to find the prisoners guilty, they were acquitted, and the jury added to their verdict a presentment, in which they condemned the action of the soldiery, in the queer phraseology of the day, as "rash, unfortunate, and unnecessary". The Committee of Public Safety renewed its sittings, and from thenceforth was a popular rallying-point in opposition to the Parliament. The Government now gave way on all sides, and made a show of yielding to the demands of the people, though there was a wide-spread plot for effecting a *coup d'état* set on foot between the leaders of the two so-called opposing parties in the parliamentary faction fight. The well-meaning part of the public was overjoyed, and thought that all danger of a civil war was over. The victory of the people was celebrated by huge meetings held in the parks and elsewhere, in memory of the victims of the great massacre.

'But the measures passed for the relief of the workers, though to the upper classes they seemed ruinously revolutionary, were not thorough enough to give the people food and a decent life and they had to be supplemented by unwritten enactments without legality to back them. Although the Government and Parliament had the law-courts, the army, and "society" at their backs, the Committee of Public Safety began to be a force in the country, and really represented the producing classes. It began to improve immensely in the days which followed on the acquittal of its members. Its old members had little administrative capacity, though with the exception of a few self-seekers and traitors, they were honest, courageous men, and many of them

were endowed with considerable talent of other kinds. But now that the times
called for immediate action, came forward the men capable of setting it on
foot; and a new network of workmen's associations grew up very speedily,
whose avowed single object was the tiding over of the ship of the community
into a simple condition of Communism; and as they practically undertook
also the management of the ordinary labour-war, they soon became the
mouthpiece and intermediary of the whole of the working classes; and the
manufacturing profit-grinders now found themselves powerless before this
combination; unless *their* committee, Parliament, plucked up courage to
begin the civil war again, and to shoot right and left, they were bound to yield
to the demands of the men whom they employed, and pay higher and higher
wages for shorter and shorter day's work. Yet one ally they had, and that was
the rapidly approaching breakdown of the whole system founded on the
World-Market and its supply; which now became so clear to all people,
that the middle classes, shocked for the moment into condemnation of the
Government for the great massacre, turned round nearly in a mass, and called
on the Government to look to matters, and put an end to the tyranny of the
Socialist leaders.

'Thus stimulated, the reactionist plot exploded probably before it was ripe;
but this time the people and their leaders were forewarned, and, before the
reactionaries could get under way, had taken the steps they thought necessary.

'The Liberal Government (clearly by collusion) was beaten by the
Conservatives, though the latter were nominally much in the minority. The
popular representatives in the House understood pretty well what this meant,
and after an attempt to fight the matter out by divisions in the House of
Commons, they made a protest, left the House, and came in a body to the
Committee of Public Safety: and the civil war began again in good earnest.

'Yet its first act was not one of mere fighting. The new Tory Government
determined to act, yet durst not re-enact the state of siege, but it sent a body
of soldiers and police to arrest the Committee of Public Safety in the lump.
They made no resistance, though they might have done so, as they had now
a considerable body of men who were quite prepared for extremities. But
they were determined to try first a weapon which they thought stronger than
street fighting.

'The members of the Committee went off quietly to prison; but they had
left their soul and their organisation behind them. For they depended not on
a carefully arranged centre with all kinds of checks and counter-checks about
it, but on a huge mass of people in thorough sympathy with the movement,
bound together by a great number of links of small centres with very simple
instructions. These instructions were now carried out.

'The next morning, when the leaders of the reaction were chuckling at the
effect which the report in the newspapers of their stroke would have upon the
public—no newspapers appeared; and it was only towards noon that a few

straggling sheets, about the size of the gazettes of the seventeenth century, worked by policemen, soldiers, managers, and press-writers, were dribbled through the streets. They were greedily seized on and read; but by this time the serious part of their news was stale, and people did not need to be told that the GENERAL STRIKE had begun. The railways did not run, the telegraph-wires were unserved; flesh, fish, and green stuff brought to market was allowed to lie there still packed and perishing; the thousands of middle-class families, who were utterly dependent for the next meal on the workers, made frantic efforts through their more energetic members to cater for the needs of the day, and amongst those of them who could throw off the fear of what was to follow, there was, I am told, a certain enjoyment of this unexpected picnic—a forecast of the days to come, in which all labour grew pleasant.

'So passed the first day, and towards evening the Government grew quite distracted. They had but one resource for putting down any popular movement—to wit, mere brute-force; but there was nothing for them against which to use their army and police: no armed bodies appeared in the streets; the offices of the Federated Workmen were now, in appearance, at least, turned into places for the relief of people thrown out of work, and under the circumstances, they durst not arrest the men engaged in such business, all the more, as even that night many quite respectable people applied at these offices for relief, and swallowed down the charity of the revolutionists along with their supper. So the Government massed soldiers and police here and there—and sat still for that night, fully expecting on the morrow some manifesto from "the rebels", as they now began to be called, which would give them an opportunity of acting in some way or another. They were disappointed. The ordinary newspapers gave up the struggle that morning, and only one very violent reactionary paper (called the *Daily Telegraph*) attempted an appearance, and rated "the rebels" in good set terms for their folly and ingratitude in tearing out the bowels of their "common mother", the English Nation, for the benefit of a few greedy paid agitators, and the fools whom they were deluding. On the other hand, the Socialist papers (of which three only, representing somewhat different schools, were published in London) came out full to the throat of well-printed matter. They were greedily bought by the whole public who, of course, like the Government, expected a manifesto in them. But they found no word of reference to the great subject. It seemed as if their editors had ransacked their drawers for articles which would have been in place forty years before, under the technical name of educational articles. Most of these were admirable and straightforward expositions of the doctrines and practice of Socialism, free from haste and spite and hard words, and came upon the public with a kind of May-day freshness, amidst the worry and terror of the moment; and though the knowing well understood that the meaning of this move in the game was mere defiance, and a token of irreconcilable hostility to the then rulers of society, and though, also, they were meant for nothing else by "the rebels", yet they really had their effect as "educational articles". However, "education" of another kind was acting upon the public with irresistible power, and probably cleared their heads a little.

'As to the Government, they were absolutely terrified by this act of "boycotting" (the slang word then current for such acts of abstention). Their counsels became wild and vacillating to the last degree: one hour they were for giving way for the present till they could hatch another plot; the next they all but sent an order for the arrest in the lump of all the workmen's committees; the next they were on the point of ordering their brisk young general to take any excuse that offered for another massacre. But when they called to mind that the soldiery in that "Battle" of Trafalgar Square were so daunted by the slaughter which they had made, that they could not be got to fire a second volley, they shrank back again from the dreadful courage necessary for carrying out another massacre. Meantime the prisoners, brought the second time before the magistrates under a strong escort of soldiers, were the second time remanded.

'The strike went on this day also. The workmen's committees were extended, and gave relief to great numbers of people, for they had organised a considerable amount of production of food by men whom they could depend upon. Quite a number of well-to-do people were now compelled to seek relief of them. But another curious thing happened: a band of young men of the upper classes armed themselves and coolly went marauding in the streets, taking what suited them of such eatables and portables that they came across in the shops which had ventured to open. This operation they carried out in Oxford Street, then a great street of shops of all kinds. The Government, being at that hour in one of their yielding moods, thought this a fine opportunity for showing their impartiality in the maintenance of "order" and sent to arrest these hungry rich youths; who, however, surprised the police by a valiant resistance, so that all but three escaped. The Government did not gain the reputation for impartiality which they expected from this move; for they forgot that there were no evening papers; and the account of the skirmish spread wide indeed but in a distorted form; for it was mostly told simply as an exploit of the starving people from the East-end; and everybody thought it was but natural for the Government to put them down when and where they could.

'That evening the rebel prisoners were visited in their cells by *very* polite and sympathetic persons, who pointed out to them what a suicidal course they were following, and how dangerous these extreme courses were for the popular cause. Says one of the prisoners: "It was great sport comparing notes when we came out anent the attempt of the Government to 'get at' us separately in prison, and how we answered the blandishments of the highly 'intelligent and refined' persons set on to pump us. One laughed; another told extravagant long-bow stories to the envoy; a third held a sulky silence; a fourth damned the polite spy and bade him hold his jaw—and that was all they got out of us."

'So passed the second day of the great strike. It was clear to all thinking people that the third day would bring on the crisis; for the present suspense and ill-concealed terror was unendurable. The ruling classes, and the middle-class non-politicians who had been their real strength and support, were as sheep lacking a shepherd; they literally did not know what to do.

'One thing they found they had to do: try to get the "rebels" to do something. So the next morning, the morning of the third day of the strike, when the members of the Committee of Public Safety appeared again before the magistrate, they found themselves treated with the greatest possible courtesy—in fact, rather as envoys and ambassadors than prisoners. In short, the magistrate had received his orders; and with no more to do than might come of a long stupid speech, which might have been written by Dickens in mockery, he discharged the prisoners, who went back to their meeting-place and at once began a due sitting. It was high time. For this third day the mass was fermenting indeed. There was, of course, a vast number of working people who were not organised in the least in the world; men who had been used to act as their masters drove them, or rather as the system drove, of which their masters were a part. That system was now falling to pieces, and the old pressure of the master having been taken off these poor men, it seemed likely that nothing but the mere animal necessities and passions of men would have any hold on them and that mere general overturn would be the result. Doubtless this would have happened if it had not been that the huge mass had been leavened by Socialist opinion in the first place, and in the second place by actual contact with declared Socialists, many or indeed most of whom were members of those bodies of workmen above said.

'If anything of this kind had happened some years before, when the masters of labour were still looked upon as the natural rulers of the people, and even the poorest and most ignorant man leaned upon them for support, while they submitted to their fleecing, the entire break-up of all society would have followed. But the long series of years during which the workmen had learned to despise their rulers, had done away with their dependence upon them, and they were now beginning to trust (somewhat dangerously, as events proved) in the non-legal leaders whom events had thrust forward; and though most of these were now become mere figure-heads, their names and reputations were useful in this crisis as a stop-gap.

'The effect of the news, therefore, of the release of the Committee gave the Government some breathing time: for it was received with the greatest joy by the workers, and even the well-to-do saw in it a respite from the mere destruction which they had begun to dread, and the fear of which most of them attributed to the weakness of the Government. As far as the passing hour went, perhaps they were right in this.'

'How do you mean?' said I. 'What could the Government have done? I often used to think that they would be helpless in such a crisis.'

Said old Hammond: 'Of course I don't doubt that in the long run matters would have come about as they did. But if the Government could have treated their army as a real army, and used them strategically as a general would have done, looking on the people as a mere open enemy to be shot at and dispersed wherever they turned up, they would probably have gained a victory at the time.'

'But would the soldiers have acted against the people in this way?' said I.

Said he: 'I think from all I have heard that they would have done so if they had met bodies of men armed however badly, and however badly they had been organised. It seems also as if before the Trafalgar Square massacre they might as a whole have been depended upon to fire upon an unarmed crowd, though they were much honeycombed by Socialism. The reason for this was that they dreaded the use by apparently unarmed men of an explosive called dynamite of which many loud boasts were made by the workers on the eve of these events; although it turned out to be of little use as a material for war in the way that was expected. Of course the officers of the soldiery fanned this fear to the utmost, so that the rank and file probably thought on that occasion that they were being led into a desperate battle with men who were really armed, and whose weapon was the more dreadful, because it was concealed. After that massacre, however, it was at all times doubtful if the regular soldiers would fire upon an unarmed or half-armed crowd.'

Said I: 'The regular soldiers? Then there were other combatants against the people?'

'Yes,' said he, 'we shall come to that presently.'

'Certainly,' I said, 'you had better go on straight with your story. I see that time is wearing.'

Said Hammond: 'The Government lost no time in coming to terms with the Committee of Public Safety; for indeed they could think of nothing else than the danger of the moment. They sent a duly accredited envoy to treat with these men, who somehow had obtained dominion over people's minds, while the formal rulers had no hold except over their bodies. There is no need at present to go into the details of the truce (for such it was) between these high contracting parties, the Government of the empire of Great Britain and a handful of working-men (as they were called in scorn in those days), amongst whom, indeed, were some very capable and "square-headed" persons, though, as aforesaid, the abler men were not then the recognised leaders. The upshot of it was that all the definite claims of the people had to be granted. We can now see that most of these claims were of themselves not worth either demanding or resisting; but they were looked on at that time as most important, and they were at least tokens of revolt against the miserable system of life which was then beginning to tumble to pieces. One claim, however, was of the utmost immediate importance, and this the Government tried hard to evade; but as they were not dealing with fools, they had to yield at last. This was the claim of recognition and formal status for the Committee of Public Safety, and all the associations which it fostered under its wing. This it is clear meant two things: first, amnesty for the "rebels", great and small, who, without a distinct act of civil war, could no longer be attacked; and next, a continuance of the organised revolution. Only one point the Government could gain, and that was a name. The dreadful revolutionary title was dropped, and the body, with its branches, acted under the respectable name of the "Board of Conciliation and its local offices". Carrying this name, it became the leader of the people in the civil war which soon followed.'

'O,' said I, somewhat startled, 'so the civil war went on, in spite of all that had happened?'

'So it was,' said he. 'In fact, it was this very legal recognition which made the civil war possible in the ordinary sense of war; it took the struggle out of the element of mere massacres on one side, and endurance plus strikes on the other.'

'And can you tell me in what kind of way the war was carried on?' said I.

'Yes,' he said; 'we have records and to spare of all that; and the essence of them I can give you in a few words. As I told you, the rank and file of the army was not to be trusted by the reactionists; but the officers generally were prepared for anything, for they were mostly the very stupidest men in the country. Whatever the Government might do, a great part of the upper and middle classes were determined to set on foot a counter revolution; for the Communism which now loomed ahead seemed quite unendurable to them. Bands of young men, like the marauders in the great strike of whom I told you just now, armed themselves and drilled and began on any opportunity or pretence to skirmish with the people in the streets. The Government neither helped them nor put them down, but stood by, hoping that something might come of it. These "Friends of Order", as they were called, had some successes at first, and grew bolder; they got many officers of the regular army to help them, and by their means laid hold of munitions of war of all kinds. One part of their tactics consisted in their guarding and even garrisoning the big factories of the period: they held at one time, for instance, the whole of that place called Manchester which I spoke of just now. A sort of irregular war was carried on with varied success all over the country; and at last the Government, which at first pretended to ignore the struggle, or treat it as mere rioting, definitely declared for "the Friends of Order", and joined to their bands whatsoever of the regular army they could get together and made a desperate effort to overwhelm "the rebels", as they were now once more called, and as indeed they called themselves.

'It was too late. All ideas of peace on a basis of compromise had disappeared on either side. The end, it was seen clearly, must be either absolute slavery for all but the privileged, or a system of life founded on equality and Communism. The sloth, the hopelessness, and, if I may say so, the cowardice of the last century, had given place to the eager, restless heroism of a declared revolutionary period. I will not say that the people of that time foresaw the life we are leading now, but there was a general instinct amongst them towards the essential part of that life, and many men saw clearly beyond the desperate struggle of the day into the peace which it was to bring about. The men of that day who were on the side of freedom were not unhappy, I think, though they were harassed by hopes and fears, and sometimes torn by doubts, and the conflict of duties hard to reconcile.'

'But how did the people, the revolutionists, carry on the war? What were the elements of success on their side?'

I put this question, because I wanted to bring the old man back to the definite history, and take him out of the musing mood so natural to an old man.

He answered: 'Well, they did not lack organisers; for the very conflict itself, in days when, as I told you, men of any strength of mind cast away all consideration for the ordinary business of life, developed the necessary talent amongst them. Indeed, from all I have read and heard, I much doubt whether, without this seemingly dreadful civil war, the due talent for administration would have been developed amongst the working men. Anyhow, it was there, and they soon got leaders far more than equal to the best men amongst the reactionaries. For the rest, they had no difficulty about the material of their army; for that revolutionary instinct so acted on the ordinary soldier in the ranks that the greater part, certainly the best part, of the soldiers joined the side of the people. But the main element of their success was this, that wherever the working people were not coerced, they worked, not for the reactionists, but for "the rebels". The reactionists could get no work done for them outside districts where they were all-powerful: and even in those districts they were harassed by continual risings; and in all cases and everywhere got nothing done without obstruction and black looks and sulkiness; so that not only were their armies quite worn out with the difficulties which they had to meet, but the non-combatants who were on their side were so worried and beset with hatred and a thousand little troubles and annoyances that life became almost unendurable to them on those terms. Not a few of them actually died of the worry; many committed suicide. Of course, a vast number of them joined actively in the cause of reaction, and found some solace to their misery in the eagerness of conflict. Lastly, many thousands gave way and submitted to "the rebels"; and as the numbers of these latter increased, it became clear to all men that the cause which was once hopeless, was now triumphant, and that the hopeless cause was that of slavery and privilege.'

Chapter XVIII. The Beginning of the New Life

'Well,' said I, 'so you got clear out of all your trouble. Were people satisfied with the new order of things when it came?'

'People?' he said. 'Well, surely all must have been glad of peace when it came; especially when they found, as they must have found, that after all, they—even the once rich—were not living very badly. As to those who had been poor, all through the war, which lasted about two years, their condition had been bettering, in spite of the struggle; and when peace came at last, in a very short time they made great strides towards a decent life. The great difficulty was that the once-poor had such a feeble conception of the real pleasure of life: so to say, they did not ask enough, did not know how to ask enough, from the new state of things. It was perhaps rather a good than an evil thing that the necessity for restoring the wealth destroyed during the war forced them into working at first almost as hard as they had been used to before the Revolution. For all historians are agreed that there never was a war in which there was so much destruction of wares, and instruments for making them as in this civil war.'

'I am rather surprised at that,' said I.

'Are you? I don't see why,' said Hammond.

'Why,' I said, 'because the party of order would surely look upon the wealth as their own property, no share of which, if they could help it, should go to their slaves, supposing they conquered. And on the other hand, it was just for the possession of that wealth that "the rebels" were fighting, and I should have thought, especially when they saw that they were winning, that they would have been careful to destroy as little as possible of what was so soon to be their own.'

'It was as I have told you, however,' said he. 'The party of order, when they recovered from their first cowardice of surprise—or, if you please, when they fairly saw that, whatever happened, they would be ruined, fought with great bitterness, and cared little what they did, so long as they injured the enemies who had destroyed the sweets of life for them. As to "the rebels," I have told you that the outbreak of actual war made them careless of trying to save the wretched scraps of wealth that they had. It was a common saying amongst them, Let the country be cleared of everything except valiant living men, rather than that we fall into slavery again!'

He sat silently thinking a little while, and then said:

'When the conflict was once really begun, it was seen how little of any value there was in the old world of slavery and inequality. Don't you see what it means? In the times which you are thinking of, and of which you seem to know so much, there was no hope; nothing but the dull jog of the mill-horse under compulsion of collar and whip; but in that fighting-time that followed, all was hope: "the rebels" at least felt themselves strong enough to build up the world again from its dry bones,—and they did it too!' said the old man, his eyes glittering under his beetling brows. He went on: 'And their opponents at least and at last learned something about the reality of life, and its sorrows, which they—their class, I mean—had once known nothing of. In short, the two combatants, the workman and the gentleman, between them—'

'Between them,' I said quickly, 'they destroyed commercialism!'

'Yes, yes, YES,' said he; 'that is it. Nor could it have been destroyed otherwise; except, perhaps, by the whole of society gradually falling into lower depths, till it should at last reach a condition as rude as barbarism. Surely the sharper, shorter remedy was the happiest.'

'Most surely,' said I.

'Yes,' said the old man, 'the world was being brought to its second birth; how could that take place without a tragedy? Moreover, think of it. The spirit of the new days, of our days, was to be delight in the life of the world; intense and overweening love of the very skin and surface of the earth on which man dwells, such as a lover has in the fair flesh of the woman he loves; this, I say, was to be the new spirit of the time. All other moods save this had been exhausted: the unceasing criticism, the boundless curiosity in the ways and thoughts of man, which was the mood of the ancient Greek, to whom these things were not so much a means, as an end, was gone past recovery; nor had there been really any shadow of it in the so-called science of the nineteenth century, which, as you must know, was in the main an appendage to the commercial system; nay, not seldom an appendage to the police of that system. In spite of appearances, it was limited and cowardly, because it did not really believe in itself. It was the outcome, as it was the sole relief, of the unhappiness of the period which made life so bitter even to the rich, and which, as you may see with your bodily eyes, the great change has swept away. More akin to our way of looking at life was the spirit of the Middle Ages, to whom heaven and the life of the next world was such a reality, that it became to them a part of the life upon the earth; which accordingly they loved and adorned, in spite of the ascetic doctrines of their formal creed which bade them contemn it.'

'But that also, with its assured belief in heaven and hell as two countries in which to live, has gone, and now we do, both in word and in deed, believe in the continuous life of the world of men, and as it were, add every day of that common life to the little stock of days which our own mere individual experience wins for us: and consequently we are happy. Do you wonder at it? In times past, indeed, men were told to love their kind, to believe in the religion of humanity, and so forth. But look you, just in the degree that a man had elevation of mind and refinement enough to be able to value this idea, was he repelled by the obvious aspect of the individuals composing the mass which he was to worship; and he could only evade that repulsion by making a conventional abstraction of mankind that had little actual or historical relation to the race; which to his eyes was divided into blind tyrants on the one hand and apathetic degraded slaves on the other. But now, where is the difficulty in accepting the religion of humanity, when the men and women who go to make up humanity are free, happy, and energetic at least, and most commonly beautiful of body also, and surrounded by beautiful things of their own fashioning, and a nature bettered and not worsened by contact with mankind? This is what this age of the world has reserved for us.'

'It seems true,' said I, 'Or ought to be, if what my eyes have seen is a token of the general life you lead. Can you now tell me anything of your progress after the years of the struggle?'

Said he: 'I could easily tell you more than you have time to listen to; but I can at least hint at one of the chief difficulties which had to be met: and that was, that when men began to settle down after the war, and their labour had pretty much filled up the gap in wealth caused by the destruction of that war, a kind of disappointment seemed coming over us, and the prophecies of some of the reactionists of past times seemed as if they would come true, and a dull level of utilitarian comfort be the end for a while of our aspirations and success. The loss of the competitive spur to exertion had not, indeed, done anything to interfere with the necessary production of the community, but how if it should make men dull by giving them too much time for thought or idle musing? But, after all, this dull thunder-cloud only threatened us, and then passed over. Probably, from what I have told you before, you will have a guess at the remedy for such a disaster; remembering always that many of the things which used to be produced—slave-wares for the poor and mere wealth-wasting wares for the rich—ceased to be made. That remedy was, in short, the production of what used to be called art, but which has no name amongst us now, because it has become a necessary part of the labour of every man who produces.'

Said I: 'What! had men any time or opportunity for cultivating the fine arts amidst the desperate struggle for life and freedom that you have told me of?'

Said Hammond: 'You must not suppose that the new form of art was founded chiefly on the memory of the art of the past; although, strange to say, the civil war was much less destructive of art than of other things, and though what of art existed under the old forms, revived in a wonderful way during the latter part of the struggle, especially as regards music and poetry. The art or work-pleasure, as one ought to call it, of which I am now speaking, sprung up almost spontaneously, it seems, from a kind of instinct amongst people, no longer driven desperately to painful and terrible overwork, to do the best they could with the work in hand—to make it excellent of its kind; and when that had gone on for a little, a craving for beauty seemed to awaken in men's minds, and they began rudely and awkwardly to ornament the wares which they made; and when they had once set to work at that, it soon began to grow.

All this was much helped by the abolition of the squalor which our immediate ancestors put up with so coolly; and by the leisurely, but not stupid, country-life which now grew (as I told you before) to be common amongst us. Thus at last and by slow degrees we got pleasure into our work; then we became conscious of that pleasure, and cultivated it, and took care that we had our fill of it; and then all was gained, and we were happy. So may it be for ages and ages!'

The old man fell into a reverie, not altogether without melancholy I thought; but I would not break it. Suddenly he started, and said: 'Well, dear guest, here are come Dick and Clara to fetch you away, and there is an end of my talk; which I daresay you will not be sorry for; the long day is coming to an end, and you will have a pleasant ride back to Hammersmith.'

Chapter XIX. *The Drive Back to Hammersmith*

I said nothing, for I was not inclined for mere politeness to him after such very serious talk; but in fact I should like to have gone on talking with the older man, who could understand something at least of my wonted ways of looking at life, whereas, with the younger people, in spite of all their kindness, I really was a being from another planet. However, I made the best of it, and smiled as amiably as I could on the young couple; and Dick returned the smile by saying, 'Well, Guest, I am glad to have you again, and to find that you and my kinsman have not quite talked yourselves into another world; I was half suspecting as I was listening to the Welshmen yonder that you would presently be vanishing away from us, and began to picture my kinsman sitting in the hall staring at nothing and finding that he had been talking a while past to nobody.'

I felt rather uncomfortable at this speech, for suddenly the picture of the sordid squabble, the dirty and miserable tragedy of the life I had left for a while, came before my eyes; and I had, as it were, a vision of all my longings for rest and peace in the past, and I loathed the idea of going back to it again. But the old man chuckled and said:

'Don't be afraid, Dick. In any case, I have not been talking to thin air; nor, indeed to this new friend of ours only. Who knows but I may not have been talking to many people? For perhaps our guest may someday go back to the people he has come from, and may take a message from us which may bear fruit for them, and consequently for us.'

Dick looked puzzled, and said: 'Well, gaffer, I do not quite understand what you mean. All I can say is, that I hope he will not leave us: for don't you see, he is another kind of man to what we are used to, and somehow he makes us think of all kind of things; and already I feel as if I could understand Dickens the better for having talked with him.'

'Yes,' said Clara, 'and I think in a few months we shall make him look younger; and I should like to see what he was like with the wrinkles smoothed out of his face. Don't you think he will look younger after a little time with us?'

The old man shook his head, and looked earnestly at me, but did not answer her, and for a moment or two we were all silent. Then Clara broke out:

'Kinsman, I don't like this: something or another troubles me, and I feel as if something untoward were going to happen. You have been talking of past miseries to the guest, and have been living in past unhappy times, and it is in the air all round us, and makes us feel as if we were longing for something we cannot have.'

The old man smiled on her kindly, and said: 'Well, my child, if that be so, go and live in the present, and you will soon shake it off.' Then he turned to me, and said: 'Do you remember anything like that, guest, in the country from which you come?'

The lovers had turned aside now, and were talking together softly, and not heeding us; so I said, but in a low voice: 'Yes, when I was a happy child on a sunny holiday, and had everything that I could think of.'

'So it is,' said he. 'You remember just now you twitted me with living in the second childhood of the world. You will find it a happy world to live in; you will be happy there—for a while.'

Again I did not like his scarcely veiled threat, and was beginning to trouble myself with trying to remember how I had got amongst this curious people, when the old man called out in a cheery voice: 'Now, my children, take your guest away, and make much of him; for it is your business to make him sleek of skin and peaceful of mind: he has by no means been as lucky as you have. Farewell, guest!' and he grasped my hand warmly.

'Good-bye,' said I, 'and thank you very much for all that you have told me. I will come and see you as soon as I come back to London. May I?'

'Yes,' he said, 'come by all means—if you can.'

'It won't be for some time yet,' quoth Dick, in his cheery voice; 'for when the hay is in up the river, I shall be for taking him a round through the country between hay and wheat harvest, to see how our friends live in the north country. Then in the wheat harvest we shall do a good stroke of work, I should hope,—in Wiltshire by preference; for he will be getting a little hard with all the open-air living, and I shall be as tough as nails.'

'But you will take me along, won't you, Dick?' said Clara, laying her pretty hand on his shoulder.

'Will I not?' said Dick, somewhat boisterously, 'And we will manage to send you to bed pretty tired every night; and you will look so beautiful with your neck all brown, and your hands too, and you under your gown as white as privet, that you will get some of those strange discontented whims out of your head, my dear. However, our week's haymaking will do all that for you.'

The girl reddened very prettily, and not for shame but for pleasure; and the old man laughed, and said:

'Guest, I see that you will be as comfortable as need be; for you need not fear that those two will be too officious with you: they will be so busy with each other, that they will leave you a good deal to yourself, I am sure, and that is a real kindness to a guest, after all. O, you need not be afraid of being one too many, either: it is just what these birds in a nest like, to have a good convenient friend to turn to, so that they may relieve the ecstasies of love with the solid commonplace of friendship. Besides, Dick, and much more Clara, likes a little talking at times; and you know lovers do not talk unless they get into trouble, they only prattle. Good-bye guest; may you be happy!'

Clara went up to old Hammond, threw her arms about his neck and kissed him heartily, and said: 'You are a dear old man, and may have your jest about me as much as you please; and it won't be long before we see you again; and you may be sure we shall make our guest happy; though, mind you, there is some truth in what you say.'

Then I shook hands again, and we went out of the hall and into the cloisters, and so in the street found Greylocks in the shafts waiting for us. He was well looked after; for a little lad of about seven years old had his hand on the rein and was solemnly looking up into his face; on his back, withal, was a girl of fourteen, holding a three-year-old sister on before her; while another girl, about a year older than the boy, hung on behind. The three were occupied partly with eating cherries, partly with patting and punching Greylocks, who took all their caresses in good part, but pricked up his ears when Dick made his appearance. The girls got off quietly, and going up to Clara, made much of her and snuggled up to her. And then we got into the carriage, Dick shook the reins, and we got under way at once, Greylocks trotting soberly between the lovely trees of the London streets, that were sending floods of fragrance into the cool evening air; for it was now getting toward sunset.

We could hardly go but fair and softly all the way, as there were a great many people abroad in that cool hour. Seeing so many people made me notice their looks the more; and I must say, my taste cultivated in the sombre greyness, or rather brownness, of the nineteenth century, was rather apt to condemn the gaiety and brightness of the raiment; and I even ventured to say as much to Clara. She seemed rather surprised, and even slightly indignant, and said: 'Well, well, what's the matter? They are not about any dirty work; they are only amusing themselves in the fine evening; there is nothing to foul their clothes. Come, doesn't it all look very pretty? It isn't gaudy, you know.'

Indeed that was true; for many of the people were clad in colours that were sober enough, though beautiful, and the harmony of the colours was perfect and most delightful.

I said, 'Yes, that is so; but how can everybody afford such costly garments? Look! there goes a middle-aged man in a sober grey dress; but I can see from here that it is made of very fine woollen stuff, and is covered with silk embroidery.'

Said Clara: 'He could wear shabby clothes if he pleased,—that is, if he didn't think he would hurt people's feelings by doing so.'

'But please tell me,' said I, 'how can they afford it?'

As soon as I had spoken I perceived that I had got back to my old blunder; for I saw Dick's shoulders shaking with laughter; but he wouldn't say a word, but handed me over to the tender mercies of Clara, who said—

'Why, I don't know what you mean. Of course we can afford it, or else we shouldn't do it. It would be easy enough for us to say, we will only spend our labour on making our clothes comfortable: but we don't choose to stop there. Why do you find fault with us? Does it seem to you as if we starved ourselves of food in order to make ourselves fine clothes? or do you think there is anything wrong in liking to see the coverings of our bodies beautiful like our bodies are?—just as a deer's or an otter's skin has been made beautiful from the first? Come, what is wrong with you?'

I bowed before the storm, and mumbled out some excuse or other. I must say, I might have known that people who were so fond of architecture generally, would not be backward in ornamenting themselves; all the more as the shape of their raiment, apart from its colour, was both beautiful and reasonable—veiling the form, without either muffling or caricaturing it.

Clara was soon mollified; and as we drove along toward the wood before mentioned, she said to Dick—

'I tell you what, Dick: now that our kinsman Hammond the Elder has seen our guest in his queer clothes, I think we ought to find him something decent to put on for our journey to-morrow: especially since, if we do not, we shall have to answer all sorts of questions as to his clothes and where they came from. Besides,' she said slily, 'when he is clad in handsome garments he will not be so quick to blame us for our childishness in wasting our time in making ourselves look pleasant to each other.'

'All right, Clara,' said Dick; 'he shall have everything that you—that he wants to have. I will look something out for him before he gets up tomorrow.'

Chapter XX. The Hammersmith Guest House Again

Amidst such talk, driving quietly through the balmy evening, we came to Hammersmith, and were well received by our friends there. Boffin, in a fresh suit of clothes, welcomed me back with stately courtesy; the weaver wanted to button-hole me and get out of me what old Hammond had said, but was very friendly and cheerful when Dick warned him off; Annie shook hands with me, and hoped I had had a pleasant day—so kindly, that I felt a slight pang as our hands parted; for to say the truth, I liked her better than Clara, who seemed to be always a little on the defensive, whereas Annie was as frank as could be, and seemed to get honest pleasure from everything and everybody about her without the least effort.

We had quite a little feast that evening, partly in my honour, and partly, I suspect, though nothing was said about it, in honour of Dick and Clara coming together again. The wine was of the best; the hall was redolent of rich summer flowers; and after supper we not only had music (Annie, to my mind, surpassing all the others for sweetness and clearness of voice, as well as for feeling and meaning), but at last we even got to telling stories, and sat there listening, with no other light but that of the summer moon streaming through the beautiful traceries of the windows, as if we had belonged to time long passed, when books were scarce and the art of reading somewhat rare. Indeed, I may say here, that, though, as you will have noted, my friends had mostly something to say about books, yet they were not great readers, considering the refinement of their manners and the great amount of leisure which they obviously had. In fact, when Dick, especially, mentioned a book, he did so with an air of a man who has accomplished an achievement; as much as to say, 'There, you see, I have actually read that!'

The evening passed all too quickly for me; since that day, for the first time in my life, I was having my fill of pleasure of the eyes without any of that sense of incongruity, that dread of approaching ruin, which had always beset me hitherto when I had been amongst the beautiful works of art of the past, mingled with the lovely nature of the present; both of them, in fact, the result of the long centuries of tradition, which had compelled men to produce the art, and compelled nature to run into the mould of the ages. Here I could enjoy everything without an afterthought of the injustice and miserable toil which made my leisure; the ignorance and dulness of life which went to make my keen appreciation of history; the tyranny and the struggle full of fear and mishap which went to make my romance. The only weight I had upon my heart was a vague fear as it drew toward bed-time concerning the place wherein I should wake on the morrow: but I choked that down, and went to bed happy, and in a very few moments was in a dreamless sleep.

Chapter XXI. Going up the River

When I did wake, to a beautiful sunny morning, I leapt out of bed with my over-night apprehension still clinging to me, which vanished delightfully however in a moment as I looked around my little sleeping chamber and saw the pale but pure-coloured figures painted on the plaster of the wall, with verses written underneath them which I knew somewhat over well. I dressed speedily, in a suit of blue laid ready for me, so handsome that I quite blushed when I had got into it, feeling as I did so that excited pleasure of anticipation of a holiday, which, well-remembered as it was, I had not felt since I was a boy, new come home for the summer holidays.

It seemed quite early in the morning, and I expected to have the hall to myself when I came into it out of the corridor wherein was my sleeping chamber; but I met Annie at once, who let fall her broom and gave me a kiss, quite meaningless I fear, except as betokening friendship, though she reddened as she did it, not from shyness, but from friendly pleasure, and then stood and picked up her broom again, and went on with her sweeping, nodding to me as if to bid me stand out of the way and look on; which, to say the truth, I thought amusing enough, as there were five other girls helping her, and their graceful figures engaged in the leisurely work were worth going a long way to see, and their merry talk and laughing as they swept in quite a scientific manner was worth going a long way to hear. But Annie presently threw me back a word or two as she went on to the other end of the hall: 'Guest,' she said, 'I am glad that you are up early, though we wouldn't disturb you; for our Thames is a lovely river at half-past six on a June morning: and as it would be a pity for you to lose it, I am told just to give you a cup of milk and a bit of bread outside there, and put you into the boat: for Dick and Clara are all ready now. Wait half a minute till I have swept down this row.'

So presently she let her broom drop again, and came and took me by the hand and led me out on to the terrace above the river, to a little table under the boughs, where my bread and milk took the form of as dainty a breakfast as any one could desire, and then sat by me as I ate. And in a minute or two Dick and Clara came to me, the latter looking most fresh and beautiful in a light silk embroidered gown, which to my unused eyes was extravagantly gay and bright; while Dick was also handsomely dressed in white flannel prettily embroidered. Clara raised her gown in her hands as she gave me the morning greeting, and said laughingly: 'Look, Guest! you see we are at least as fine as any of the people you felt inclined to scold last night; you see we are not going to make the bright day and the flowers feel ashamed of themselves. Now scold me!'

Quoth I: 'No, indeed; the pair of you seem as if you were born out of the summer day itself; and I will scold you when I scold it.'

'Well, you know,' said Dick, 'this is a special day—all these days are, I mean. The hay-harvest is in some ways better than corn-harvest because of the beautiful weather; and really, unless you had worked in the hayfield in fine weather, you couldn't tell what pleasant work it is. The women look so pretty at it, too,' he said, shyly; 'so all things considered, I think we are right to adorn it in a simple manner.'

'Do the women work at it in silk dresses?' said I, smiling.

Dick was going to answer me soberly; but Clara put her hand over his mouth, and said, 'No, no, Dick; not too much information for him, or I shall think that you are your old kinsman again. Let him find out for himself: he will not have long to wait.'

'Yes,' quoth Annie, 'don't make your description of the picture too fine, or else he will be disappointed when the curtain is drawn. I don't want him to be disappointed. But now it's time for you to be gone, if you are to have the best of the tide, and also of the sunny morning. Good-bye, guest.'

She kissed me in her frank friendly way, and almost took away from me my desire for the expedition thereby; but I had to get over that, as it was clear that so delightful a woman would hardly be without a due lover of her own age. We went down the steps of the landing-stage, and got into a pretty boat, not too light to hold us and our belongings comfortably, and handsomely ornamented; and just as we got in, down came Boffin and the weaver to see us off. The former had now veiled his splendour in a due suit of working clothes, crowned with a fantail hat, which he took off, however, to wave us farewell with his grave old-Spanish-like courtesy. Then Dick pushed off into the stream, and bent vigorously to his sculls, and Hammersmith, with its noble trees and beautiful water-side houses, began to slip away from us.

As we went, I could not help putting beside his promised picture of the hayfield as it was then the picture of it as I remembered it, and especially the images of the women engaged in the work rose up before me: the row of gaunt figures, lean, flat-breasted, ugly, without a grace of form or face about them; dressed in wretched skimpy print gowns, and hideous flapping sun-bonnets, moving their rakes in a listless mechanical way. How often had that marred the loveliness of the June day to me; how often had I longed to see the hay-fields peopled with men and women worthy of the sweet abundance of midsummer, of its endless wealth of beautiful sights, and delicious sounds and scents. And now, the world had grown old and wiser, and I was to see my hope realised at last!

Chapter XXII. Hampton Court and a Praiser of Past Times

So on we went, Dick rowing in an easy tireless way, and Clara sitting by my side admiring his manly beauty and heartily good-natured face, and thinking, I fancy, of nothing else. As we went higher up the river, there was less difference between the Thames of that day and Thames as I remembered it; for setting aside the hideous vulgarity of the cockney villas of the well-to-do, stockbrokers and other such, which in older time marred the beauty of the bough-hung banks, even this beginning of the country Thames was always beautiful; and as we slipped between the lovely summer greenery, I almost felt my youth come back to me, and as if I were on one of those water excursions which I used to enjoy so much in the days when I was too happy to think that there could be much amiss anywhere.

At last we came to a reach of the river where on the left hand a very pretty little village with some old houses in it came down to the edge of the water, over which was a ferry; and beyond these houses the elm-beset meadows ended in a fringe of tall willows, while on the right hand went the tow-path and a clear space before a row of trees, which rose up behind huge and ancient, the ornaments of a great park: but these drew back still further from the river at the end of the reach to make way for a little town of quaint and pretty houses, some new, some old, dominated by the long walls and sharp gables of a great red-brick pile of building, partly of the latest Gothic, partly of the court-style of Dutch William, but so blended together by the bright sun and beautiful surroundings, including the bright blue river, which it looked down upon, that even amidst the beautiful buildings of that new happy time it had a strange charm about it. A great wave of fragrance, amidst which the lime-tree blossom was clearly to be distinguished, came down to us from its unseen gardens, as Clara sat up in her place, and said:

'O Dick, dear, couldn't we stop at Hampton Court for to-day, and take the guest about the park a little, and show him those sweet old buildings? Somehow, I suppose because you have lived so near it, you have seldom taken me to Hampton Court.'

Dick rested on his oars a little, and said: 'Well, well, Clara, you are lazy today. I didn't feel like stopping short of Shepperton for the night; suppose we just go and have our dinner at the Court, and go on again about five o'clock?'

'Well,' she said, 'so be it; but I should like the guest to have spent an hour or two in the Park.'

'The Park!' said Dick; 'why, the whole Thames-side is a park this time of the year; and for my part, I had rather lie under an elm-tree on the borders of a wheat-field, with the bees humming about me and the corn-crake crying from furrow to furrow, than in any park in England. Besides—'

'Besides,' said she, 'you want to get on to your dearly-loved upper Thames, and show your prowess down the heavy swathes of the mowing grass.'

She looked at him fondly, and I could tell that she was seeing him in her mind's eye showing his splendid form at its best amidst the rhymed strokes of the scythes; and she looked down at her own pretty feet with a half sigh, as though she were contrasting her slight woman's beauty with his man's beauty; as women will when they are really in love, and are not spoiled with conventional sentiment.

As for Dick, he looked at her admiringly a while, and then said at last: 'Well, Clara, I do wish we were there! But, hilloa! we are getting back way.' And he set to work sculling again, and in two minutes we were all standing on the gravelly strand below the bridge, which, as you may imagine, was no longer the old hideous iron abortion, but a handsome piece of very solid oak framing.

We went into the Court and straight into the great hall, so well remembered, where there were tables spread for dinner, and everything arranged much as in Hammersmith Guest Hall. Dinner over, we sauntered through the ancient rooms, where the pictures and tapestry were still preserved, and nothing was much changed, except that the people whom we met there had an indefinable kind of look of being at home and at ease, which communicated itself to me, so that I felt that the beautiful old place was mine in the best sense of the word; and my pleasure of past days seemed to add itself to that of to-day, and filled my whole soul with content.

Dick (who, in spite of Clara's gibe, knew the place very well) told me that the beautiful old Tudor rooms, which I remembered had been the dwellings of the lesser fry of Court flunkies, were now much used by people coming and going; for, beautiful as architecture had now become, and although the whole face of the country had quite recovered its beauty, there was still a sort of tradition of pleasure and beauty which clung to that group of buildings, and people thought going to Hampton Court a necessary summer outing, as they did in the days when London was so grimy and miserable. We went into some of the rooms looking into the old garden, and were well received by the people in them, who got speedily into talk with us, and looked with politely half-concealed wonder at my strange face. Besides these birds of passage, and a few regular dwellers in the place, we saw out in the meadows near the garden, down 'the Long Water,' as it used to be called, many gay tents with men, women, and children round about them. As it seemed, this pleasure-loving people were fond of tent-life, with all its inconveniences, which, indeed, they turned into pleasure also.

We left this old friend by the time appointed, and I made some feeble show of taking the sculls; but Dick repulsed me, not much to my grief, I must say, as I found I had quite enough to do between the enjoyment of the beautiful time and my own lazily blended thoughts.

As to Dick, it was quite right to let him pull, for he was as strong as a horse, and had the greatest delight in bodily exercise, whatever it was. We really had some difficulty in getting him to stop when it was getting rather more than dusk, and the moon was brightening just as we were off Runnymede. We landed there, and were looking about for a place whereon to pitch our tents (for we had brought two with us), when an old man came up to us, bade us good evening, and asked if we were housed for that night; and finding that we were not, bade us home to his house. Nothing loth, we went with him, and Clara took his hand in a coaxing way which I noticed she used with old men; and as we went on our way, made some commonplace remark about the beauty of the day. The old man stopped short, and looked at her and said: 'You really like it then?'

'Yes,' she said, looking very much astonished, 'don't you?'

'Well,' said he, 'perhaps I do. I did, at any rate, when I was younger; but now I think I should like it cooler.'

She said nothing, and went on, the night growing about as dark as it would be; till just at the rise of the hill we came to a hedge with a gate in it, which the old man unlatched and led us into a garden at the end of which we could see a little house, one of whose little windows was already yellow with candle-light. We could see even under the doubtful light of the moon and the last of the western glow that the garden was stuffed full of flowers; and the fragrance it gave out in the gathering coolness was so wonderfully sweet, that it seemed the very heart of the delight of the June dusk; so that we three stopped instinctively and Clara gave forth a little sweet 'O,' like a bird beginning to sing.

'What's the matter?' said the old man, a little testily, and pulling at her hand. 'There's no dog; or have you trodden on a thorn and hurt your foot?'

'No, no, neighbour,' she said; 'but how sweet, how sweet it is!'

'Of course it is,' said he, 'but do you care so much for that?'

She laughed out musically, and we followed suit in our gruffer voices; and then she said: 'of course I do, neighbour; don't you?'

'Well, I don't know,' quoth the old fellow; then he added, as if somewhat ashamed of himself: 'Besides, you know, when the waters are out and all Runnymede is flooded, it's none so pleasant.'

'*I* should like it,' quoth Dick. 'What a jolly sail one would get about here on the floods on a bright frosty January morning!'

'*Would* you like it?' said our host. 'Well, I won't argue with you, neighbour; it isn't worth while. Come in and have some supper.'

We went up a paved path between the roses, and straight into a very pretty room, panelled and carved, and as clean as a new pin; but the chief ornament of which was a young woman, light-haired and grey-eyed, but with her face and hands and bare feet tanned quite brown with the sun. Though she was very lightly clad, that was clearly from choice, not from poverty, though these were the first cottage-dwellers I had come across; for her gown was of silk, and on her wrists were bracelets that seemed to me of great value. She was lying on a sheep-skin near the window, but jumped up as soon as we entered, and when she saw the guests behind the old man, she clapped her hands and cried out with pleasure, and when she got us into the middle of the room, fairly danced round us in delight of our company.

'What!' said the old man, 'you are pleased, are you Ellen?'

The girl danced up to him and threw her arms round him, and said: 'Yes I am, and so ought you to be, grandfather.'

'Well, well, I am,' said he, 'as much as I can be pleased. Guests, please be seated.'

This seemed rather strange to us; stranger, I suspect, to my friends than to me; but Dick took the opportunity of both the host and his grand-daughter being out of the room to say to me softly: 'A grumbler: there are a few of them still. Once upon a time, I am told, they were quite a nuisance.'

The old man came in as he spoke and sat down beside us with a sigh, which, indeed, seemed fetched up as if he wanted us to take notice of it; but just then the girl came in with the victuals, and the carle missed his mark, what between our hunger generally and that I was pretty busy watching the grand-daughter moving about as beautiful as a picture.

Everything to eat and drink, though it was somewhat different to what we had had in London, was better than good, but the old man eyed rather sulkily the chief dish on the table, on which lay a leash of fine perch, and said:

'H'm, perch! I am sorry we can't do better for you, guests. The time was when we might have had a good piece of salmon up from London for you; but the times have grown mean and petty.'

'Yes, but you might have had it now,' said the girl, giggling, 'if you had known that they were coming.'

'It's our fault for not bringing it with us, neighbours,' said Dick, good-humouredly. 'But if the times have grown petty, at any rate the perch haven't; that fellow in the middle there must have weighed a good two pounds when he was showing his dark stripes and red fins to the minnows yonder. And as to the salmon, why, neighbour, my friend here, who comes from the outlands, was quite surprised yesterday morning when I told him we had plenty of salmon at Hammersmith. I am sure I have heard nothing of the times worsening.'

He looked a little uncomfortable. And the old man, turning to me, said very courteously:

'Well, sir, I am happy to see a man from over the water; but I really must appeal to you to say whether on the whole you are not better off in your country; where I suppose, from what our guest says, you are brisker and more alive, because you have not wholly got rid of competition. You see, I have read not a few books of the past days, and certainly *they* are much more alive than those which are written now; and good sound unlimited competition was the condition under which they were written,—if we didn't know that from the record of history, we should know it from the books themselves. There is a spirit of adventure in them, and signs of a capacity to extract good out of evil which our literature quite lacks now; and I cannot help thinking that our moralists and historians exaggerate hugely the unhappiness of the past days, in which such splendid works of imagination and intellect were produced.'

Clara listened to him with restless eyes, as if she were excited and pleased; Dick knitted his brow and looked still more uncomfortable, but said nothing. Indeed, the old man gradually, as he warmed to his subject, dropped his sneering manner, and both spoke and looked very seriously. But the girl broke out before I could deliver myself of the answer I was framing:

'Books, books! always books, grandfather! When will you understand that after all it is the world we live in which interests us; the world of which we are a part and which we can never love too much? Look!' she said, throwing open the casement wider and showing us the white light sparkling between the black shadows of the moonlit garden, through which ran a little shiver of the summer night-wind, 'look! these are our books these days!—and these,' she said, stepping lightly up to the two lovers and laying a hand on each of their shoulders; 'and the guest there, with his over-sea knowledge and experience;— yes, and even you, grandfather' (a smile ran over her face as she spoke), 'with all your grumbling and wishing yourself back again in the good old days,—in which, as far as I can make out, a harmless and lazy old man like you would either have pretty nearly starved, or have had to pay soldiers and people to take the folk's victuals and clothes and houses away from them by force. Yes, these are our books; and if we want more, can we not find work to do in the beautiful buildings that we raise up all over the country (and I know there was nothing like them in past times), wherein a man can put forth whatever is in him, and make his hands set forth his mind and his soul.'

She paused a little, and I for my part could not help staring at her, and thinking that if she were a book, the pictures in it were most lovely. The colour mantled in her delicate sunburnt cheeks; her grey eyes, light amidst the tan of her face, kindly looked on us all as she spoke. She paused, and said again:

'As for your books, they were well enough for times when intelligent people had but little else in which they could take pleasure, and when they must needs supplement the sordid miseries of their own lives with imaginations of the lives of other people. But I say flatly that in spite of all their cleverness and vigour, and capacity for story-telling, there is something loathsome about them. Some of them, indeed, do here and there show some feeling for those whom the history-books call "poor", and of the misery of whose lives we have some inkling; but presently they give it up, and towards the end of the story we must be contented to see the hero and heroine living happily in an island of bliss on other people's troubles; and that after a long series of sham troubles (or mostly sham) of their own making, illustrated by dreary introspective nonsense about their feelings and aspirations, and all the rest of it; while the world must even then have gone on its way, and dug and sewed and baked and built and carpentered round about these useless—animals.'

'There!' said the old man, reverting to his dry sulky manner again. 'There's eloquence! I suppose you like it?'

'Yes,' said I, very emphatically.

'Well,' said he, 'now the storm of eloquence has lulled for a little, suppose you answer my question?—that is, if you like, you know,' quoth he, with a sudden access of courtesy.

'What question?' said I. For I must confess that Ellen's strange and almost wild beauty had put it out of my head.

Said he: 'First of all (excuse my catechising), is there competition in life, after the old kind, in the country whence you come?'

'Yes,' said I, 'it is the rule there.' And I wondered as I spoke what fresh complications I should get into as a result of this answer.

'Question two,' said the carle: 'Are you not on the whole much freer, more energetic—in a word, healthier and happier—for it?'

I smiled. 'You wouldn't talk so if you had any idea of our life. To me you seem here as if you were living in heaven compared with us of the country from which I came.'

'Heaven?' said he: 'you like heaven, do you?'

'Yes,' said I—snappishly, I am afraid; for I was beginning rather to resent his formula.

'Well, I am far from sure that I do,' quoth he. 'I think one may do more with one's life than sitting on a damp cloud and singing hymns.'

I was rather nettled by this inconsequence, and said: 'Well, neighbour, to be short, and without using metaphors, in the land whence I come, where the competition which produced those literary works which you admire so much is still the rule, most people are thoroughly unhappy; here, to me at least, most people seem thoroughly happy.'

'No offence, guest—no offence,' said he; 'but let me ask you; you like that, do you?'

His formula, put with such obstinate persistence, made us all laugh heartily; and even the old man joined in the laughter on the sly. However, he was by no means beaten, and said presently:

'From all I can hear, I should judge that a young woman so beautiful as my dear Ellen yonder would have been a lady, as they called it in the old time, and wouldn't have had to wear a few rags of silk as she does now, or to have browned herself in the sun as she has to do now. What do you say to that, eh?'

Here Clara, who had been pretty much silent hitherto, struck in, and said: 'Well, really, I don't think that you would have mended matters, or that they want mending. Don't you see that she is dressed deliciously for this beautiful weather? And as for the sun-burning of your hay-fields, why, I hope to pick up some of that for myself when we get a little higher up the river. Look if I don't need a little sun on my pasty white skin!'

And she stripped up the sleeve from her arm and laid it beside Ellen's who was now sitting next her. To say the truth, it was rather amusing to me to see Clara putting herself forward as a town-bred fine lady, for she was as well-knit and clean-skinned a girl as might be met with anywhere at the best. Dick stroked the beautiful arm rather shyly, and pulled down the sleeve again, while she blushed at his touch; and the old man said laughingly: 'Well, I suppose you *do* like that; don't you?'

Ellen kissed her new friend, and we all sat silent for a little, till she broke out into a sweet shrill song, and held us all entranced with the wonder of her clear voice; and the old grumbler sat looking at her lovingly. The other young

people sang also in due time; and then Ellen showed us to our beds in small
cottage chambers, fragrant and clean as the ideal of the old pastoral poets;
and the pleasure of the evening quite extinguished my fear of the last night,
that I should wake up in the old miserable world of worn-out pleasures, and
hopes that were half fears.

Chapter XXIII. An Early Morning by Runnymede

Though there were no rough noises to wake me, I could not lie long abed
the next morning, where the world seemed so well awake, and, despite the
old grumbler, so happy; so I got up, and found that, early as it was, someone
had been stirring, since all was trim and in its place in the little parlour, and
the table laid for the morning meal. Nobody was afoot in the house as then,
however, so I went out a-doors, and after a turn or two round the superabundant
garden, I wandered down over the meadow to the river-side, where lay our
boat, looking quite familiar and friendly to me. I walked up stream a little,
watching the light mist curling up from the river till the sun gained power to
draw it all away; saw the bleak speckling the water under the willow boughs,
whence the tiny flies they fed on were falling in myriads; heard the great chub
splashing here and there at some belated moth or other, and felt almost back
again in my boyhood. Then I went back again to the boat, and loitered there
a minute or two, and then walked slowly up the meadow towards the little
house. I noted now that there were four more houses of about the same size
on the slope away from the river. The meadow in which I was going was not
up for hay; but a row of flake-hurdles ran up the slope not far from me on
each side, and in the field so parted off from ours on the left they were making
hay busily by now, in the simple fashion of the days when I was a boy. My feet
turned that way instinctively, as I wanted to see how haymakers looked in
these new and better times, and also I rather expected to see Ellen there.
I came to the hurdles and stood looking over into the hayfield, and was close
to the end of the long line of haymakers who were spreading the low ridges to
dry off the night dew. The majority of these were young women clad much
like Ellen last night, though not mostly in silk, but in light woollen most gaily
embroidered; the men being all clad in white flannel embroidered in bright
colours. The meadow looked like a gigantic tulip-bed because of them. All
hands were working deliberately but well and steadily, though they were as
noisy with merry talk as a grove of autumn starlings. Half a dozen of them,
men and women, came up to me and shook hands, gave me the sele of the
morning, and asked a few questions as to whence and whither, and wishing me
good luck, went back to their work. Ellen, to my disappointment, was not
amongst them, but presently I saw a light figure come out of the hayfield
higher up the slope, and make for our house; and that was Ellen, holding

a basket in her hand. But before she had come to the garden gate, out came Dick and Clara, who, after a minute's pause, came down to meet me, leaving Ellen in the garden; then we three went down to the boat, talking mere morning prattle. We stayed there a little, Dick arranging some of the matters in her, for we had only taken up to the house such things as we thought the dew might damage; and then we went toward the house again; but when we came near the garden, Dick stopped us by laying a hand on my arm and said,

'Just look a moment.'

I looked, and over the low hedge saw Ellen, shading her eyes against the sun as she looked toward the hayfield, a light wind stirring in her tawny hair, her eyes like light jewels amidst her sunburnt face, which looked as if the warmth of the sun were yet in it.

'Look, Guest,' said Dick; 'doesn't it all look like one of those very stories out of Grimm that we were talking about up in Bloomsbury? Here are we two lovers wandering about the world, and we have come to a fairy garden, and there is the very fairy herself amidst of it: I wonder what she will do for us.'

Said Clara demurely, but not stiffly: 'Is she a good fairy, Dick?'

'O, yes,' said he; 'and according to the card, she would do better, if it were not for the gnome or wood-spirit, our grumbling friend of last night.'

We laughed at this; and I said, 'I hope you see that you have left me out of the tale.'

'Well,' said he, 'that's true. You had better consider that you have got the cap of darkness, and are seeing everything, yourself invisible.'

That touched me on my weak side of not feeling sure of my position in this beautiful new country; so in order not to make matters worse, I held my tongue, and we all went into the garden and up to the house together. I noticed by the way that Clara must really rather have felt the contrast between herself as a town madam and this piece of the summer country that we all admired so, for she had rather dressed after Ellen that morning as to thinness and scantiness, and went barefoot also, except for light sandals.

The old man greeted us kindly in the parlour, and said: 'Well, guests, so you have been looking about to search into the nakedness of the land: I suppose your illusions of last night have given way a bit before the morning light? Do you still like it, eh?'

'Very much,' said I, doggedly; 'it is one of the prettiest places on the lower Thames.'

'Oho!' said he; 'so you know the Thames, do you?'

I reddened, for I saw Dick and Clara looking at me, and scarcely knew what to say. However, since I had said in our early intercourse with my Hammersmith friends that I had known Epping Forest, I thought a hasty generalisation might be better in avoiding complications than a downright lie; so I said—

'I have been in this country before; and I have been on the Thames in those days.'

'O,' said the old man, eagerly, 'so you have been in this country before. Now really, don't you *find* it (apart from all theory, you know) much changed for the worse?'

'No, not at all,' said I; 'I find it much changed for the better.'

'Ah,' quoth he, 'I fear that you have been prejudiced by some theory or another. However, of course the time when you were here before must have been so near our own days that the deterioration might not be very great: as then we were, of course, still living under the same customs as we are now. I was thinking of earlier days than that.'

'In short,' said Clara, 'you have *theories* about the change which has taken place.'

'I have facts as well,' said he. 'Look here! from this hill you can see just four little houses, including this one. Well, I know for certain that in old times, even in the summer, when the leaves were thickest, you could see from the same place six quite big and fine houses; and higher up the water, garden joined garden right up to Windsor; and there were big houses in all the gardens. Ah! England was an important place in those days.'

I was getting nettled, and said: 'What you mean is that you de-cockneyised the place, and sent the damned flunkies packing, and that everybody can live comfortably and happily, and not a few damned thieves only, who were centres of vulgarity and corruption wherever they were, and who, as to this lovely river, destroyed its beauty morally, and had almost destroyed it physically, when they were thrown out of it.'

There was silence after this outburst, which for the life of me I could not help, remembering how I had suffered from cockneyism and its cause on those same waters of old time. But at last the old man said, quite coolly:

'My dear guest, I really don't know what you mean by either cockneys, or flunkies, or thieves, or damned; or how only a few people could live happily and comfortably in a wealthy country. All I can see is that you are angry, and I fear with me: so if you like we will change the subject.'

I thought this kind and hospitable in him, considering his obstinacy about his theory; and hastened to say that I did not mean to be angry, only emphatic. He bowed gravely, and I thought the storm was over, when suddenly Ellen broke in:

'Grandfather, our guest is reticent from courtesy; but really what he has in his mind to say to you ought to be said; so as I know pretty well what it is, I will say it for him: for as you know, I have been taught these things by people who—'

'Yes,' said the old man, 'by the sage of Bloomsbury, and others.'

'O,' said Dick, 'so you know my old kinsman Hammond?'

'Yes,' said she, 'and other people too, as my grandfather says, and they have taught me things: and this is the upshot of it. We live in a little house now, not because we have nothing grander to do than working in the fields, but because we please; for if we liked, we could go and live in a big house amongst pleasant companions.'

Grumbled the old man: 'Just so! As if I would live amongst those conceited fellows; all of them looking down upon me!'

She smiled on him kindly, but went on as if he had not spoken. 'In the past times, when those big houses of which grandfather speaks were so plenty, we *must* have lived in a cottage whether we liked it or not; and the said cottage, instead of having in it everything we want, would have been bare and empty. We should not have got enough to eat; our clothes would have been ugly to look at, dirty and frowsy. You, grandfather, have done no hard work for years now, but wander about and read your books and have nothing to worry you; and as for me, I work hard when I like it, because I like it, and think it does me good, and knits up my muscles, and makes me prettier to look at, and healthier and happier. But in those past days you, grandfather, would have had to work hard after you were old; and would have been always afraid of having to be shut up in a kind of prison along with other old men, half-starved and without amusement. And as for me, I am twenty years old. In those days my middle age would be beginning now, and in a few years I should be pinched, thin, and haggard, beset with troubles and miseries, so that no one could have guessed that I was once a beautiful girl.'

'Is this what you have had in your mind, guest?' said she, the tears in her eyes at thought of the past miseries of people like herself.

'Yes,' said I, much moved; 'that and more. Often—in my country I have seen that wretched change you have spoken of, from the fresh handsome country lass to the poor draggle-tailed country woman.'

The old man sat silent for a little, but presently recovered himself and took comfort in his old phrase of 'Well, you like it so, do you?'

'Yes,' said Ellen, 'I love life better than death.'

'O, you do, do you?' said he. 'Well, for my part I like reading a good old book with plenty of fun in it, like Thackeray's "Vanity Fair". Why don't you write books like that now? Ask that question of your Bloomsbury sage.'

Seeing Dick's cheeks reddening a little at this sally, and noting that silence followed, I thought I had better do something. So I said: 'I am only the guest, friends; but I know you want to show me your river at its best, so don't you think we had better be moving presently, as it is certainly going to be a hot day?'

Chapter XXIV. Up The Thames: The Second Day

They were not slow to take my hint; and indeed, as to the mere time of day, it was best for us to be off, as it was past seven o'clock, and the day promised to be very hot. So we got up and went down to our boat—Ellen thoughtful and abstracted; the old man very kind and courteous, as if to make up for his crabbedness of opinion. Clara was cheerful and natural, but a little subdued, I thought; and she at least was not sorry to be gone, and often looked shyly and timidly at Ellen and her strange wild beauty. So we got into the boat, Dick saying as he took his place, 'Well, it *is* a fine day!' and the old man answering, 'What! you like that, do you?' once more; and presently Dick was sending the bows swiftly through the slow weed-checked stream. I turned round as we got into mid-stream, and waving my hand to our hosts, saw Ellen leaning on the old man's shoulder, and caressing his healthy apple-red cheek, and quite a keen pang smote me as thought how I should never see the beautiful girl again. Presently I insisted on taking the sculls, and I rowed a good deal that day; which no doubt accounts for the fact that we got very late to the place which Dick had aimed at. Clara was particularly affectionate to Dick, as I noticed from the rowing thwart; but as for him, he was as frankly kind and merry as ever; and I was glad to see it, as a man of his temperament could not have taken her caresses cheerfully and without embarrassment if he had been at all entangled by the fairy of our last night's abode.

I need say little about the lovely reaches of the river here. I duly noted that absence of cockney villas which the old man had lamented; and I saw with pleasure that my old enemies the 'Gothic' cast-iron bridges had been replaced by handsome oak and stone ones. Also the banks of the forest that we passed through had lost their courtly game-keeperish trimness, and were as wild and beautiful as need be, though the trees were clearly well seen to. I thought it best, in order to get the most direct information, to play the innocent about Eton and Windsor; but Dick volunteered his knowledge to me as we lay in Datchet lock about the first. Quoth he:

'Up yonder are some beautiful old buildings, which were built for a great college or teaching-place by one of the mediæval kings—Edward the Sixth, I think' (I smiled to myself at his rather natural blunder). 'He meant poor people's sons to be taught there what knowledge was going in his days; but it was a matter of course that in the times of which you seem to know so much they spoilt whatever good there was in the founder's intentions. My old kinsman says that they treated them in a very simple way, and instead of teaching poor men's sons to know something, they taught rich men's sons to know nothing. It seems from what he says that it was a place for the "aristocracy" (if you know what that word means; I have been told its meaning) to get rid of their male children for a great part of the year. I daresay old Hammond would give you plenty of information in detail about it.'

'What is it used for now?' said I.

'Well,' said he, 'the buildings were a good deal spoilt by the last few generations of aristocrats, who seem to have had a great hatred against beautiful old buildings, and indeed all records of past history; but it is still a delightful place. Of course, we cannot use it quite as the founder intended, since our ideas about teaching young people are so changed from the ideas of his time; so it is used now as a dwelling for people engaged in learning; and folk from round about come and get taught things that they want to learn; and there is a great library there of the best books. So that I don't think that the old dead king would be much hurt if he were to come to life and see what we are doing there.'

'Well,' said Clara, laughing, 'I think he would miss the boys.'

'Not always, my dear,' said Dick, 'for there are often plenty of boys there, who come to get taught; and also,' said he, smiling, 'to learn boating and swimming. I wish we could stop there: but perhaps we had better do that coming down the water.'

The lock-gates opened as he spoke, and out we went, and on. And as for Windsor, he said nothing till I lay on my oars (for I was sculling then) in Clewer reach, and looking up, said, 'What is all that building up there?'

Said he: 'There, I thought I would wait till you asked, yourself. That is Windsor Castle: that also I thought I would keep for you till we come down the water. It looks fine from here, doesn't it? But a great deal of it has been built or skinned in the time of the Degradation, and we wouldn't pull the buildings down, since they were there; just as with the buildings of the Dung-Market. You know, of course, that it was the palace of our old mediæval kings, and was used later on for the same purpose by the parliamentary commercial sham-kings, as my old kinsman calls them.'

'Yes,' said I, 'I know all that. What is it used for now?'

'A great many people live there,' said he, 'as, with all drawbacks, it is a pleasant place; there is also a well-arranged store of antiquities of various kinds that have seemed worth keeping—a museum, it would have been called in the times you understand so well.'

I drew my sculls through the water at that last word, and pulled as if I were fleeing from those times which I understood so well; and we were soon going up the once sorely be-cockneyed reaches of the river about Maidenhead, which now looked as pleasant and enjoyable as the up-river reaches.

The morning was now getting on, the morning of a jewel of a summer day; one of those days which, if they were commoner in these islands, would make our climate the best of all climates, without dispute. A light wind blew from the west; the little clouds that had arisen at about our breakfast time had seemed to get higher and higher in the heavens; and in spite of the burning sun we no more longed for rain than we feared it. Burning as the sun was, there was a fresh feeling in the air that almost set us a-longing for the rest of the hot afternoon, and the stretch of blossoming wheat seen from the shadow of the boughs. No one unburdened with very heavy anxieties could have felt otherwise than happy that morning: and it must be said that whatever anxieties might lie beneath the surface of things, we didn't seem to come across any of them.

We passed by several fields where haymaking was going on, but Dick, and especially Clara, were so jealous of our up-river festival that they would not allow me to have much to say to them. I could only notice that the people in the fields looked strong and handsome, both men and women, and that so far from there being any appearance of sordidness about their attire, they seemed to be dressed specially for the occasion,—lightly, of course, but gaily and with plenty of adornment.

Both on this day as well as yesterday we had, as you may think, met and passed and been passed by many craft of one kind and another. The most part of these were being rowed like ourselves, or were sailing, in the sort of way that sailing is managed on the upper reaches of the river; but every now and then we came on barges, laden with hay or other country produce, or carrying bricks, lime, timber, and the like, and these were going on their way without any means of propulsion visible to me—just a man at the tiller, with often a friend or two laughing and talking with him. Dick, seeing on one occasion this day, that I was looking rather hard on one of these, said: 'That is one of our force-barges; it is quite as easy to work vehicles by force by water as by land.'

I understood pretty well that these 'force vehicles' had taken the place of our old steam-power carrying; but I took good care not to ask any questions about them, as I knew well enough both that I should never be able to understand how they were worked, and that in attempting to do so I should betray myself, or get into some complication impossible to explain; so I merely said, 'Yes, of course, I understand.'

We went ashore at Bisham, where the remains of the old Abbey and the Elizabethan house that had been added to them yet remained, none the worse for many years of careful and appreciative habitation. The folk of the place, however, were mostly in the fields that day, both men and women; so we met only two old men there, and a younger one who had stayed at home to get on with some literary work, which I imagine we considerably interrupted. Yet I also think that the hard-working man who received us was not very sorry for the interruption. Anyhow, he kept on pressing us to stay over and over again, till at last we did not get away till the cool of the evening.

However, that mattered little to us; the nights were light, for the moon was shining in her third quarter, and it was all one to Dick whether he sculled or sat quiet in the boat: so we went away a great pace. The evening sun shone bright on the remains of the old buildings at Medmenham; close beside which arose an irregular pile of building which Dick told us was a very pleasant house; and there were plenty of houses visible on the wide meadows opposite, under the hill; for, as it seems that the beauty of Hurley had compelled people to build and live there a good deal. The sun very low down showed us Henley little altered in outward aspect from what I remembered it. Actual daylight failed us as we passed through the lovely reaches of Wargrave and Shiplake;

but the moon rose behind us presently. I should like to have seen with my eyes what success the new order of things had had in getting rid of the sprawling mess with which commercialism had littered the banks of the wide stream about Reading and Caversham: certainly everything smelt too deliciously in the early night for there to be any of the old careless sordidness of so-called manufacture; and in answer to my question as to what sort of a place Reading was, Dick answered:

'O, a nice town enough in its way; mostly rebuilt within the last hundred years; and there are a good many houses, as you can see by the lights just down under the hills yonder. In fact, it is one of the most populous places on the Thames round about here. Keep up your spirits, guest! we are close to our journey's end for the night. I ought to ask your pardon for not stopping at one of the houses here or higher up; but a friend, who is living in a very pleasant house in the Maple-Durham meads, particularly wanted me and Clara to come and see him on our way up the Thames; and I thought you wouldn't mind this bit of night travelling.'

He need not have adjured me to keep up my spirits, which were as high as possible; though the strangeness and excitement of the happy and quiet life which I saw everywhere around me was, it is true, a little wearing off, yet a deep content, as different as possible from languid acquiescence, was taking its place, and I was, as it were, really new-born.

We landed presently just where I remembered the river making an elbow to the north towards the ancient house of the Blunts; with the wide meadows spreading on the right-hand side, and on the left the long line of beautiful trees overhanging the water. As we got out of the boat, I said to Dick—

'Is it the old house we are going to?'

'No,' he said, 'though that is standing still in green old age, and is well inhabited. I see, by the way, that you know your Thames well. But my friend Walter Allen, who asked me to stop here, lives in a house, not very big, which has been built here lately, because these meadows are so much liked, especially in summer, that there was getting to be rather too much of tenting on the open field; so the parishes hereabout, who rather objected to that, built three houses between this and Caversham, and quite a large one at Basildon, a little higher up. Look, yonder are the lights of Walter Allen's house!'

So we walked over the grass of the meadows under a flood of moonlight, and soon came to the house, which was low and built around a quadrangle big enough to get plenty of sunshine in it. Walter Allen, Dick's friend, was leaning against the jamb of the doorway waiting for us, and took us into the hall without overplus of words. There were not many people in it, as some of the dwellers there were away at the haymaking in the neighbourhood, and some, as Walter told us, were wandering about the meadow enjoying the beautiful moonlit night. Dick's friend looked to be a man of about forty; tall, black-haired, very kind-looking and thoughtful; but rather to my surprise there was a shade of melancholy on his face, and he seemed a little abstracted and inattentive to our chat, in spite of obvious efforts to listen.

Dick looked on him from time to time, and seemed troubled; and at last he said: 'I say, old fellow, if there is anything the matter which we didn't know of when you wrote to me, don't you think you had better tell us about it at once? or else we shall think we have come here at an unlucky time, and are not quite wanted.'

Walter turned red, and seemed to have some difficulty in restraining his tears, but said at last: 'Of course everybody here is very glad to see you, Dick, and your friends; but it is true that we are not at our best, in spite of the fine weather and the glorious hay-crop. We have had a death here.'

Said Dick: 'Well, you should get over that, neighbour: such things must be.'

'Yes,' Walter said, 'but this was a death by violence, and it seems likely to lead to at least one more; and somehow it makes us feel rather shy of one another; and to say the truth, that is one reason why there are so few of us present to-night.'

'Tell us the story, Walter,' said Dick; 'perhaps telling it will help you to shake off your sadness.'

Said Walter: 'Well, I will; and I will make it short enough, though I daresay it might be spun out into a long one, as used to be done with such subjects in the old novels. There is a very charming girl here whom we all like, and whom some of us do more than like; and she very naturally liked one of us better than anybody else. And another of us (I won't name him) got fairly bitten with love-madness, and used to go about making himself as unpleasant as he could—not of malice prepense, of course; so that the girl, who liked him well enough at first, though she didn't love him, began fairly to dislike him. Of course, those of us who knew him best—myself amongst others—advised him to go away, as he was making matters worse and worse for himself every day. Well, he wouldn't take our advice (that also, I suppose, was a matter of course), so we had to tell him that he *must* go, or the inevitable sending to Coventry would follow; for his individual trouble had so overmastered him that we felt that *we* must go if he did not.'

'He took that better than we expected, when something or other—an interview with the girl, I think, and some hot words with the successful lover following close upon it, threw him quite off his balance; and he got hold of an axe and fell upon his rival when there was no one by; and in the struggle that followed the man attacked, hit him an unlucky blow and killed him. And now the slayer in his turn is so upset that he is like to kill himself; and if he does, the girl will do as much, I fear. And all this we could no more help than the earthquake of the year before last.'

'It is very unhappy,' said Dick; 'but since the man is dead, and cannot be brought to life again, and since the slayer had no malice in him, I cannot for the life of me see why he shouldn't get over it before long. Besides, it was the right man that was killed and not the wrong. Why should a man brood over a mere accident for ever? And the girl?'

'As to her,' said Walter, 'the whole thing seems to have inspired her with terror rather than grief. What you say about the man is true, or it should be; but then, you see, the excitement and jealousy that was the prelude to this tragedy had made an evil and feverish element round about him, from which he does not seem to be able to escape. However, we have advised him to go away—in fact, to cross the seas; but he is in such a state that I do not think he *can* go unless someone *takes* him, and I think it will fall to my lot to do so; which is scarcely a cheerful outlook for me.'

'O, you will find a certain kind of interest in it,' said Dick. 'And of course he *must* soon look upon the affair from a reasonable point of view sooner or later.'

'Well, at any rate,' quoth Walter, 'now that I have eased my mind by making you uncomfortable, let us have an end of the subject for the present. Are you going to take your guest to Oxford?'

'Why, of course we must pass through it,' said Dick, smiling, 'as we are going into the upper waters: but I thought that we wouldn't stop there, or we shall be belated as to the haymaking up our way. So Oxford and my learned lecture on it, all got at second-hand from my old kinsman, must wait till we come down the water a fortnight hence.'

I listened to this story with much surprise, and could not help wondering at first that the man who had slain the other had not been put in custody till it could be proved that he killed his rival in self-defence only. However, the more I thought of it, the plainer it grew to me that no amount of examination of witnesses, who had witnessed nothing but the ill-blood between the two rivals, would have done anything to clear up the case. I could not help thinking, also, that the remorse of this homicide gave point to what old Hammond had said to me about the way in which this strange people dealt with what I had been used to hear called crimes. Truly, the remorse was exaggerated; but it was quite clear that the slayer took the whole consequences of the act upon himself, and did not expect society to whitewash him by punishing him. I had no fear any longer that 'the sacredness of human life' was likely to suffer amongst my friends from the absence of gallows and prison.

Chapter XXV. The Third Day on the Thames

As we went down to the boat next morning, Walter could not quite keep off the subject of last night, though he was more hopeful than he had been then, and seemed to think that if the unlucky homicide could not be got to go oversea, he might at any rate go and live somewhere in the neighbourhood pretty much by himself; at any rate, that was what he himself had proposed. To Dick, and I must say to me also, this seemed a strange remedy; and Dick said as much. Quoth he:

'Friend Walter, don't set the man brooding on the tragedy by letting him live alone. That will only strengthen his idea that he had committed a crime, and you will have him killing himself in good earnest.'

Said Clara: 'I don't know. If I may say what I think of it, it is that he had better have his fill of gloom now, and, so to say, wake up presently to see how little need there has been for it; and then he will live happily afterwards. As for his killing himself, you need not be afraid of that; for, from all you tell me, he is really very much in love with the woman; and to speak plainly, until his love is satisfied, he will not only stick to life as tightly as he can, but will also make the most of every event of his life—will, so to say, hug himself up in it; and I think that this is the real explanation of his taking the whole matter with such an excess of tragedy.'

Walter looked thoughtful, and said: 'Well, you may be right; and perhaps we should have treated it all more lightly: but you see, guest' (turning to me), 'such things happen so seldom, that when they do happen, we cannot help being much taken up with it. For the rest, we are all inclined to excuse our poor friend for making us so unhappy, on the ground that he does it out of an exaggerated respect for human life and its happiness. Well, I will say no more about it; only this: will you give me a cast up stream, as I want to look after a lonely habitation for the poor fellow, since he will have it so, and I hear that there is one which would suit us very well on the downs beyond Streatley; so if you will put me ashore there I will walk up the hill and look to it.'

'Is the house in question empty?' said I.

'No,' said Walter, 'but the man who lives there will go out of it, of course, when he hears that we want it. You see, we think that the fresh air of the downs and the very emptiness of the landscape will do our friend good.'

'Yes,' said Clara, smiling, 'and he will not be so far from his beloved that they cannot easily meet if they have a mind to—as they certainly will.'

This talk had brought us down to the boat, and we were presently afloat on the beautiful broad stream, Dick driving the prow swiftly through the windless water of the early summer morning, for it was not yet six o'clock. We were at the lock in a very little time; and as we lay rising and rising on the in-coming water, I could not help wondering that my old friend the pound-lock, and that of the very simplest and most rural kind, should hold its place there; so I said:

'I have been wondering, as we passed lock after lock, that you people, so prosperous as you are, and especially since you are so anxious for pleasant work to do, have not invented something which would get rid of this clumsy business of going up-stairs by means of these rude contrivances.'

Dick laughed. 'My dear friend,' said he, 'as long as water has the clumsy habit of running down hill, I fear we must humour it by going up-stairs when we have our faces turned from the sea. And really I don't see why you should fall foul of Maple-Durham lock, which I think a very pretty place.'

There was no doubt about the latter assertion, I thought, as I looked up at the overhanging boughs of the great trees, with the sun coming glittering through the leaves, and listened to the song of the summer blackbirds as it mingled with the sound of the backwater near us. So not being able to say why I wanted the locks away—which, indeed, I didn't do at all—I held my peace. But Walter said—

'You see, guest, this is not an age of inventions. The last epoch did all that for us, and we are now content to use such of its inventions as we find handy, and leaving those alone which we don't want. I believe, as a matter of fact, that some time ago (I can't give you a date) some elaborate machinery was used for the locks, though people did not go so far as try to make the water run uphill. However, it was troublesome, I suppose, and the simple hatches, and the gates, with a big counterpoising beam, were found to answer every purpose, and were easily mended when wanted with material always to hand: so here they are, as you see.'

'Besides,' said Dick, 'this kind of lock is pretty, as you can see; and I can't help thinking that your machine-lock, winding up like a watch, would have been ugly and would have spoiled the look of the river: and that is surely reason enough for keeping such locks as these. Good-bye, old fellow!' said he to the lock, as he pushed us out through the now open gates by a vigorous stroke of the boat-hook. 'May you live long, and have your green old age renewed for ever!'

On we went; and the water had the familiar aspect to me of the days before Pangbourne had been thoroughly cocknified, as I have seen it. It (Pangbourne) was distinctly a village still—*i.e.* a definite group of houses, and as pretty as might be. The beech-woods still covered the hill that rose above Basildon; but the flat fields beneath them were much more populous than I remembered them, as there were five large houses in sight, very carefully designed so as not to hurt the character of the country. Down on the green lip of the river, just where the water turns toward the Goring and Streatley reaches, were half a dozen girls playing about on the grass. They hailed us as we were about passing them, as they noted that we were travellers, and we stopped a minute to talk with them. They had been bathing, and were light clad and barefooted, and were bound for the meadows on the Berkshire side, where the haymaking had begun, and were passing the time merrily enough till the Berkshire folk came in their punt to fetch them. At first nothing would content them but we must go with them into the hayfield, and breakfast with them; but Dick put forward his theory of beginning the hay-harvest higher up the water, and not spoiling my pleasure therein by giving me a taste of it elsewhere, and they gave way, though unwillingly. In revenge they asked me a great many questions about the country I came from and the manners of life there, which I found rather puzzling to answer; and doubtless what answers I did give were puzzling enough to them. I noticed both with these pretty girls and with everybody else we met, that in default of serious news, such as we had heard at Maple-Durham, they were eager to discuss all the little details of life; the weather, the hay-crop, the last new house, the plenty or lack of such and such birds, and so on; and they talked of these things not in a fatuous and conventional way, but as taking, I say, real interest in them. Moreover, I found that the women knew as much about all these things as the men: could name a flower, and knew its qualities; could tell you the habitat of such and such birds and fish, and the like.

It is almost strange what a difference this intelligence made in my estimate of the country life of that day; for it used to be said in past times, and on the whole truly, that outside their daily work country people knew little of the country, and at least could tell you nothing about it; while here were these people as eager about all the goings on in the fields and woods and downs as if they had been Cockneys newly escaped from the tyranny of bricks and mortar.

I may mention as a detail worth noticing that not only did there seem to be a great many more birds about of the non-predatory kinds, but their enemies the birds of prey were also commoner. A kite hung over our heads as we passed Medmenham yesterday; magpies were quite common in the hedgerows; I saw several sparrow-hawks, and I think a merlin; and now just as we were passing the pretty bridge which had taken the place of Basildon railway-bridge, a couple of ravens croaked above our boat, as they sailed off to the higher ground of the downs. I concluded from all this that the days of the gamekeeper were over, and did not even need to ask Dick a question about it.

Chapter XXVI. The Obstinate Refusers

Before we parted from these girls we saw two sturdy young men and a woman putting off from the Berkshire shore, and then Dick bethought him of a little banter of the girls, and asked them how it was that there was nobody of the male kind to go with them across the water, and where their boats were gone to. Said one, the youngest of the party: 'O, they have got the big punt to lead stone from up the water.'

'Who do you mean by "they," dear child?' said Dick.

Said an older girl, laughing: 'You had better go and see them. Look there,' and she pointed north-west, 'don't you see the building going on there?'

'Yes,' said Dick, 'and I am rather surprised at this time of the year; why are they not haymaking with you?'

The girls all laughed at this, and before their laugh was over, the Berkshire boat had run on to the grass and the girls stepped in lightly, still sniggering, while the newcomers gave us the sele of the day. But before they were under way again, the tall girl said: 'Excuse us for laughing, dear neighbours, but we have had some friendly bickering with the builders up yonder, and as we have no time to tell you the story, you had better go and ask them: they will be glad to see you—if you don't hinder their work.'

They all laughed again at that, and waved us a pretty farewell as the punters set them over toward the other shore, and left us standing on the bank beside our boat.

'Let us go and see them,' said Clara; 'that is, if you are not in a hurry to get to Streatley, Walter?'

'O no,' said Walter, 'I shall be glad of the excuse to have a little more of your company.'

So we left the boat moored there, and went on up the slow slope of the hill; but I said to Dick on the way, being somewhat mystified: 'What was all that laughing about? What was the joke?'

'I can guess pretty well,' said Dick; 'some of them up there have got a piece of work which interests them, and they won't go to the haymaking, which doesn't matter at all, because there are plenty of people to do such easy-hard work as that; only, since haymaking is a regular festival, the neighbours find it amusing to jeer good-humouredly at them.'

'I see,' said I, 'much as if in Dickens's time some young people were so wrapped up in their work that they wouldn't keep Christmas.'

'Just so,' said Dick, 'only these people need not be young either.'

'But what did you mean by easy-hard work?' said I.

Quoth Dick: 'Did I say that? I mean work that tries the muscles and hardens them and sends you pleasantly weary to bed, but which isn't trying in other ways: doesn't harass you in short. Such work is always pleasant if you don't overdo it. Only, mind you, good mowing requires some little skill. I'm a pretty good mower.'

This talk brought us up to the house that was a-building, not a large one, which stood at the end of a beautiful orchard surrounded by an old stone wall.

'O yes, I see,' said Dick; 'I remember, a beautiful place for a house: but a starveling of a nineteenth century house stood there: I am glad they are rebuilding: it's all stone too, though it need not have been in this part of the country: my word, though, they are making a neat job of it: but I wouldn't have made it all ashlar.'

Walter and Clara were already talking to a tall man clad in his mason's blouse, who looked about forty, but was, I daresay, older, who had his mallet and chisel in hand; there were at work in the shed and on the scaffold about half a dozen men and two women, blouse-clad like the carles, while a very pretty woman who was not in the work but was dressed in an elegant suit of blue linen came sauntering up to us with her knitting in her hand. She welcomed us and said, smiling: 'So you are come up from the water to see the Obstinate Refusers: where are you going haymaking, neighbours?'

'O, right up above Oxford,' said Dick; 'it is rather a late country. But what share have you got with the Refusers, pretty neighbour?'

Said she, with a laugh: 'O, I am the lucky one who doesn't want to work; though sometimes I get it, for I serve as model to Mistress Philippa there when she wants one: she is our head carver; come and see her.'

She led us up to the door of the unfinished house, where a rather little woman was working with mallet and chisel on the wall nearby. She seemed very intent on what she was doing, and did not turn round when we came up; but a taller woman, quite a girl she seemed, who was at work nearby, had already knocked off, and was standing looking from Clara to Dick with delighted eyes. None of the others paid much heed to us.

The blue-clad girl laid her hand on the carver's shoulder and said: 'Now, Philippa, if you gobble up your work like that, you will soon have none to do; and what will become of you then?'

The carver turned round hurriedly and showed us the face of a woman of forty (or so she seemed), and said rather pettishly, but in a sweet voice:

'Don't talk nonsense, Kate, and don't interrupt me if you can help it.' She stopped short when she saw us, then went on with the kind smile of welcome which never failed us. 'Thank you for coming to see us, neighbours; but I am sure that you won't think me unkind if I go on with my work, especially when I tell you that I was ill and unable to do anything all through April and May; and this open-air and the sun and the work together, and my feeling well again too, make a mere delight of every hour to me; and excuse me, I must go on.'

She fell to work accordingly on a carving in low relief of flowers and figures, but talked on amidst her mallet strokes: 'You see, we all think this the prettiest place for a house up and down these reaches; and the site has been so long encumbered with an unworthy one, that we masons were determined to pay off fate and destiny for once, and build the prettiest house we could compass here—and so—and so—'

Here she lapsed into mere carving, but the tall foreman came up and said: 'Yes, neighbours, that is it: so it is going to be all ashlar because we want to carve a kind of a wreath of flowers and figures all round it; and we have been much hindered by one thing or other—Philippa's illness amongst others,— and though we could have managed our wreath without her—'

'Could you, though?' grumbled the last-named from the face of the wall.

'Well, at any rate, she is our best carver, and it would not have been kind to begin the carving without her. So you see,' said he, looking at Dick and me, 'we really couldn't go haymaking, could we, neighbours? But you see, we are getting on so fast now with this splendid weather, that I think we may well spare a week or ten days at wheat-harvest and won't we go at *that* work then! Come down then to the acres that lie north and by west at our backs and you shall see good harvesters, neighbours.'

'Hurrah, for a good brag!' called a voice from the scaffold above us; 'our foreman thinks that an easier job than putting one stone on another!'

There was a general laugh at this sally, in which the tall foreman joined; and with that we saw a lad bringing out a little table into the shadow of the stone-shed, which he set down there, and then going back, came out again with the inevitable big wickered flask and tall glasses, whereon the foreman led us up to due seats on blocks of stone, and said:

'Well, neighbours, drink to my brag coming true, or I shall think you don't believe me! Up there!' said he, hailing the scaffold, 'are you coming down for a glass?' Three of the workmen came running down the ladder as men with good 'building legs' will do; but the others didn't answer, except the joker (if he must so be called), who called out without turning round: 'Excuse me, neighbours, for not getting down. I must get on: my work is not superintending, like the gaffer's yonder; but, you fellows, send us up a glass to drink the haymakers' health.' Of course, Philippa would not turn away from her beloved work; but the other woman carver came; she turned out to be Philippa's daughter, but was a tall strong girl, black-haired and gipsey-like of face and curiously solemn of manner. The rest gathered round us and clinked glasses, and the men on the scaffold turned about and drank to our healths; but the busy little woman by the door would have none of it all, but only shrugged her shoulders when her daughter came up to her and touched her.

So we shook hands and turned our backs on the Obstinate Refusers, went down the slope to our boat, and before we had gone many steps heard the full tune of tinkling trowels mingle with the humming of the bees and the singing of the larks above the little plain of Basildon.

Chapter XXVII. The Upper Waters

We set Walter ashore on the Berkshire side, amidst all the beauties of Streatley, and so went our ways into what once would have been the deeper country under the foothills of the White Horse; and though the contrast between half-cocknified and wholly unsophisticated country existed no longer, a feeling of exultation rose within me (as it used to do) at sight of the familiar and still unchanged hills of the Berkshire range.

We stopped at Wallingford for our mid-day meal; of course, all signs of squalor and poverty had disappeared from the streets of the ancient town, and many ugly houses had been taken down and many pretty new ones built, but I thought it curious, that the town still looked like the old place I remembered so well; for indeed it looked like that ought to have looked.

At dinner we fell in with an old, but very bright and intelligent man, who seemed in a country way to be another edition of old Hammond. He had an extraordinary detailed knowledge of the ancient history of the countryside from the time of Alfred to the days of the Parliamentary Wars, many events of which, as you may know, were enacted round about Wallingford. But, what was more interesting to us, he had detailed record of the period of the change to the present state of things, and told us a great deal about it, and especially of that exodus of the people from the town to the country, and the gradual recovery by the town-bred people on one side, and the country-bred people on the other, of those arts of life which they had each lost; which loss, as he told us, had at one time gone so far that not only was it impossible to find a carpenter or a smith in a village or a small country town, but that people in such places had even forgotten how to bake bread, and that at Wallingford, for instance, the bread came down with the newspapers by an early train from London, worked in some way, the explanation of which I could not understand. He told us also that the townspeople who came into the country used to pick up the agricultural arts by carefully watching the way in which the machines worked, gathering an idea of handicraft from machinery; because at that time almost everything in and about the fields was done by elaborate machines used quite unintelligently by the labourers. On the other hand, the old men amongst the labourers managed to teach the younger ones gradually a little artisanship, such as the use of the saw and the plane, the work of the smithy, and so forth; for once more, by that time it was as much as—or rather, more than—a man could do to fix an ash pole to a rake by handiwork; so that it would take a machine worth a thousand pounds, a group of workmen, and a half a day's travelling, to do five shillings' worth of work. He showed us, among other things, an account of a certain village council who were working hard at all this business; and the record of their intense earnestness in getting to the bottom of some matter which in time past would have been thought quite trivial, as, for example, the due proportions of alkali and oil for soap-making for the village wash, or the exact heat of the water into which a leg of mutton should be plunged for boiling—all this joined to the utter absence of anything like party feeling, which even in a village assembly would certainly have made its appearance in an earlier epoch, was very amusing, and at the same time instructive.

This old man, whose name was Henry Morsom, took us, after our meal and a rest, into a biggish hall which contained a large collection of articles of manufacture and art from the last days of the machine period to that day; and he went over them with us, and explained them with great care. They also were very interesting, showing the transition from the make-shift work of the machines (which was at about its worst a little after the Civil War before told of) into the first years of the new handicraft period. Of course, there was much overlapping of the periods: and at first the new handwork came in very slowly.

'You must remember,' said the old antiquary, 'that the handicraft was not the result of what used to be called material necessity: on the contrary, by that time the machines had been so much improved that almost all necessary work might have been done by them: and indeed many people at that time, and before it, used to think that machinery would entirely supersede handicraft; which certainly, on the face of it, seemed more than likely. But there was another opinion, far less logical, prevalent amongst the rich people before the days of freedom, which did not die out at once after that epoch had begun. This opinion, which from all I can learn seemed as natural then, as it seems absurd now, was, that while the ordinary daily work of the world would be done entirely by automatic machinery, the energies of the more intelligent part of mankind would be set free to follow the higher forms of the arts, as well as science and the study of history. It was strange, was it not, that they should thus ignore that aspiration after complete equality which we now recognise as the bond of all happy human society?'

I did not answer, but thought the more. Dick looked thoughtful, and said:

'Strange, neighbour? Well, I don't know. I have often heard my old kinsman say the one aim of all people before our time was to avoid work, or at least they thought it was; so of course the work which their daily life *forced* them to do, seemed more like work than that which they *seemed* to choose for themselves.'

'True enough,' said Morsom. 'Anyhow, they soon began to find out their mistake, and that only slaves and slave-holders could live solely by setting machines going.'

Clara broke in here, flushing a little as she spoke: 'Was not their mistake once more bred of the life of slavery that they had been living?—a life which was always looking upon everything, except mankind, animate and inanimate—"nature," as people used to call it—as one thing, and mankind as another. It was natural to people thinking in this way, that they should try to make "nature" their slave, since they thought "nature" was something outside them.'

'Surely,' said Morsom; 'and they were puzzled as to what to do, till they found the feeling against a mechanical life, which had begun before the Great Change amongst people who had leisure to think of such things, was spreading insensibly; till at last under the guise of pleasure that was not supposed to be work, work that was pleasure began to push out the mechanical toil, which they had once hoped at the best to reduce to narrow limits indeed, but never to get rid of; and which, moreover, they found they could not limit as they had hoped to do.'

'When did this new revolution gather head?' said I.

'In the half-century that followed the Great Change,' said Morsom, 'it began to be noteworthy; machine after machine was quietly dropped under the excuse that the machines could not produce works of art, and that works of art were more and more called for. Look here,' he said, 'here are some of the works of that time—rough and unskilful in handiwork, but solid and showing some sense of pleasure in the making.'

'They are very curious,' said I, taking up a piece of pottery from amongst the specimens which the antiquary was showing us; 'not a bit like the work of either savages or barbarians, and yet with what would once have been called a hatred of civilisation impressed upon them.'

'Yes,' said Morsom, 'you must not look for delicacy there: in that period you could only have got that from a man who was practically a slave. But now, you see,' said he, leading me on a little, 'we have learned the trick of handicraft, and have added the utmost refinement of workmanship to the freedom of fancy and imagination.'

I looked, and wondered indeed at the deftness and abundance of beauty of the work of men who had at last learned to accept life itself as a pleasure, and the satisfaction of the common needs of mankind and the preparation for them, as work fit for the best of the race. I mused silently; but at last I said:

'What is to come after this?'

The old man laughed. 'I don't know,' said he; 'we will meet it when it comes.'

'Meanwhile,' quoth Dick, 'we have got to meet the rest of our day's journey; so out into the street and down to the strand! Will you come a turn with us, neighbour? Our friend is greedy of your stories.'

'I will go as far as Oxford with you,' said he; 'I want a book or two out of the Bodleian Library. I suppose you will sleep in the old city?'

'No,' said Dick, 'we are going higher up; the hay is waiting us there, you know.'

Morsom nodded, and we all went into the street together, and got into the boat a little above the town bridge. But just as Dick was getting the sculls into the rowlocks, the bows of another boat came thrusting through the low arch. Even at first sight it was a gay little craft indeed—bright green, and painted over with elegantly drawn flowers. As it cleared the arch, a figure as bright and gay-clad as the boat rose up in it; a slim girl dressed in light blue silk that fluttered in the draughty wind of the bridge. I thought I knew the figure, and sure enough, as she turned her head to us, and showed her beautiful face, I saw with joy that it was none other than the fairy godmother from the abundant garden on Runnymede—Ellen, to wit.

We all stopped to receive her. Dick rose in the boat and cried out a genial good morrow; I tried to be as genial as Dick, but failed; Clara waved a delicate hand to her; and Morsom nodded and looked on with interest. As to Ellen, the beautiful brown of her face was deepened by a flush, as she brought the gunwale of her boat alongside ours, and said:

'You see, neighbours, I had some doubt if you would all three come back past Runnymede, or if you did, whether you would stop there; and besides, I am not sure whether we—my father and I—shall not be away in a week or two, for he wants to see a brother of his in the north country, and I should not like him to go without me. So I thought I might never see you again, and that seemed uncomfortable to me, and—and so I came after you.'

'Well,' said Dick, 'I am sure we are all very glad of that; although you may be sure that as for Clara and me, we should have made a point of coming to see you, and of coming the second time, if we had found you away the first. But, dear neighbour, there you are alone in the boat, and you have been sculling pretty hard, I should think, and might find a little quiet sitting pleasant; so we had better part our company into two.'

'Yes,' said Ellen, 'I thought you would do that, so I have brought a rudder for my boat: will you help me to ship it, please?'

And she went aft in her boat and pushed along our side till she had brought the stern close to Dick's hand. He knelt down in our boat and she in hers, and the usual fumbling took place over hanging the rudder on its hooks; for, as you may imagine, no change had taken place in the arrangement of such an unimportant matter as the rudder of a pleasure-boat. As the two beautiful young faces bent over the rudder, they seemed to me to be very close together, and though it only lasted a moment, a sort of pang shot through me as I looked on. Clara sat in her place and did not look round, but presently she said, with just the least stiffness in her tone:

'How shall we divide? Won't you go into Ellen's boat, Dick, since, without offence to our guest, you are the better sculler?'

Dick stood up and laid his hand on her shoulder, and said: 'No, no; let Guest try what he can do—he ought to be getting into training now. Besides, we are in no hurry: we are not going far above Oxford; and even if we are benighted, we shall have the moon, which will give us nothing worse of a night than a greyer day.'

'Besides,' said I, 'I may manage to do a little more with my sculling than merely keeping the boat from drifting down stream.'

They all laughed at this, as if it had been a very good joke; and I thought that Ellen's laugh, even amongst the others, was one of the pleasantest sounds I had ever heard.

To be short, I got into the new-come boat, not a little elated, and taking the sculls, set to work to show off a little. For—must I say it?—I felt as if even that happy world were made happier for my being so near this strange girl; although I must say that of all persons I had seen in that world renewed, she was the most unfamiliar to me, the most unlike what I could have thought of. Clara, for instance, beautiful and bright as she was, was not unlike a *very* pleasant and unaffected young lady; and the other girls also seemed nothing more than specimens of very much improved types which I had known in other times. But this girl was not only beautiful with a beauty quite different from that of 'a young lady,' but was in all ways so strangely interesting; so that I kept wondering what she would say or do next to surprise and please me. Not, indeed, that there was anything startling in what she actually said or did;

but it was all done in a new way, and always with that indefinable interest and pleasure of life, which I had noticed more or less in everybody, but which in her was more marked and more charming than in any one else that I had seen.

We were soon under way and going at a fair pace through the beautiful reaches of the river, between Bensington and Dorchester. It was now about the middle of the afternoon, warm rather than hot, and quite windless; the clouds high up and light, pearly white, and gleaming, softened the sun's burning, but did not hide the pale blue in most places, though they seemed to give it height and consistency; the sky, in short, looked really like a vault, as poets have sometimes called it, and not like mere limitless air, but a vault so vast and full of light that it did not in any way oppress the spirits. It was the sort of afternoon that Tennyson must have been thinking about, when he said of the Lotos-Eaters' land that it was a land where it was always afternoon.

Ellen leaned back in the stern and seemed to enjoy herself thoroughly. I could see that she was really looking at things and let nothing escape her, and as I watched her, an uncomfortable feeling that she had been a little touched by love of the deft, ready, and handsome Dick, and that she had been constrained to follow us because of it, faded out of my mind; since if it had been so, she surely could not have been so excitedly pleased, even with the beautiful scenes we were passing through. For some time she did not say much, but at last, as we had passed under Shillingford Bridge (new built, but somewhat on its old lines), she bade me hold the boat while she had a good look at the landscape through the graceful arch. Then she turned about to me and said:

'I do not know whether to be sorry or glad that this is the first time that I have been in these reaches. It is true that it is a great pleasure to see all this for the first time; but if I had had a year or two of memory of it, how sweetly it would all have mingled with my life, waking or dreaming! I am so glad Dick has been pulling slowly, so as to linger out the time here. How do you feel about your first visit to these waters?'

I do not suppose she meant a trap for me, but anyhow I fell into it, and said: 'My first visit! It is not my first visit by many a time. I know these reaches well; indeed, I may say that I know every yard of the Thames from Hammersmith to Cricklade.'

I saw the complications that might follow, as her eyes fixed mine with a curious look in them, that I had seen before at Runnymede, when I had said something which made it difficult for others to understand my present position amongst these people. I reddened, and said, in order to cover my mistake: 'I wonder you have never been up so high as this, since you live on the Thames, and moreover row so well that it would be no great labour to you. Let alone,' quoth I, insinuatingly, 'that anybody would be glad to row you.'

She laughed, clearly not at my compliment (as I am sure she need not have done, since it was a very commonplace fact), but at something which was stirring in her mind; and she still looked at me kindly, but with the above-said keen look in her eyes, and then she said:

'Well, perhaps it is strange, though I have a good deal to do at home, what with looking after my father, and dealing with two or three young men who have taken a special liking to me, and all of whom I cannot please at once. But you, dear neighbour; it seems to me stranger that you should know the upper river, than that I should not know it; for, as I understand, you have only been in England a few days. But perhaps you mean that you have read about it in books, and seen pictures of it?—though that does not come to much, either.'

'Truly,' said I. 'Besides, I have not read any books about the Thames: it was one of the minor stupidities of our time that no one thought fit to write a decent book about what may fairly be called our only English river.'

The words were no sooner out of my mouth than I saw that I had made another mistake; and I felt really annoyed with myself, as I did not want to go into a long explanation just then, or begin another series of Odyssean lies. Somehow, Ellen seemed to see this, and she took no advantage of my slip; her piercing look changed into one of mere frank kindness, and she said:

'Well, anyhow I am glad that I am travelling these waters with you, since you know our river so well, and I know little of it past Pangbourne, for you can tell me all I want to know about it.' She paused a minute, and then said: 'Yet you must understand that the part I do know, I know as thoroughly as you do. I should be sorry for you to think that I am careless of a thing so beautiful and interesting as the Thames.'

She said this quite earnestly, and with an air of affectionate appeal to me which pleased me very much; but I could see that she was only keeping her doubts about me for another time.

Presently we came to Day's Lock, where Dick and his two sitters had waited for us. He would have me go ashore, as if to show me something which I had never seen before; and nothing loth I followed him, Ellen by my side, to the well-remembered Dykes, and the long church beyond them, which was still used for various purposes by the good folk of Dorchester: where, by the way, the village guest-house still had the sign of the Fleur-de-luce which it used to bear in the days when hospitality had to be bought and sold. This time, however, I made no sign of all this being familiar to me: though as we sat for a while on the mound of the Dykes looking up at Sinodun and its clear-cut trench, and its sister *mamelon* of Whittenham, I felt somewhat uncomfortable under Ellen's serious attentive look, which almost drew from me the cry, 'How little anything is changed here!'

We stopped again at Abingdon, which, like Wallingford, was in a way both old and new to me, since it had been lifted out of its nineteenth-century degradation, and otherwise was as little altered as might be.

Sunset was in the sky as we skirted Oxford by Oseney; we stopped a minute or two hard by the ancient castle to put Henry Morsom ashore. It was a matter of course that so far as they could be seen from the river, I missed none of the towers and spires of that once don-beridden city; but the meadows all round which, when I had last passed through them, were getting daily more and more squalid, more and more impressed with the seal of the 'stir and intellectual life of the nineteenth century,' were no longer intellectual, but had once again become as beautiful as they should be, and the little hill of Hinksey, with two or three very pretty stone houses new-grown on it (I use the word advisedly; for they seemed to belong to it) looked down happily on the full streams and waving grass, grey now, but for the sunset, with its fast-ripening seeds.

The railway having disappeared, and therewith the various level bridges over the streams of Thames, we were soon through Medley Lock and in the wide water that washes Port Meadow, with its numerous population of geese nowise diminished; and I thought with interest how its name and use had survived from the older imperfect communal period, through the time of the confused struggle and tyranny of the rights of property, into the present rest and happiness of complete Communism.

I was taken ashore again at Godstow, to see the remains of the old nunnery, pretty nearly in the same condition as I had remembered them; and from the high bridge over the cut close by, I could see, even in the twilight, how beautiful the little village with its grey stone houses had become; for we had now come into the stone-country, in which every house must be either built, walls and roof, of grey stone or be a blot on the landscape.

We still rowed on after this, Ellen taking the sculls in my boat; we passed a weir a little higher up, and about three miles beyond it came by moonlight again to a little town, where we slept at a house thinly inhabited, as its folk were mostly tented in the hayfields.

Chapter XXVIII. The Little River

We started before six o'clock the next morning, as we were still twenty-five miles from our resting place, and Dick wanted to be there before dusk. The journey was pleasant, though to those who do not know the upper Thames, there is little to say about it. Ellen and I were once more together in her boat, though Dick, for fairness' sake, was for having me in his, and letting the two women scull the green toy. Ellen, however, would not allow this, but claimed me as the interesting person of the company. 'After having come so far,' said she, 'I will not be put off with a companion who will always be thinking of somebody else than me: the guest is the only person who can amuse me properly. I mean that really,' said she, turning to me, 'and have not said it merely as a pretty saying.'

Clara blushed and looked very happy at all this; for I think up to this time she had been rather frightened of Ellen. As for me I felt young again, and strange hopes of my youth were mingling with the pleasure of the present; almost destroying it, and quickening it into something like pain.

As we passed through the short and winding reaches of the now quickly lessening stream, Ellen said: 'How pleasant this little river is to me, who am used to a great wide wash of water; it almost seems as if we shall have to stop at every reach-end. I expect before I get home this evening I shall have realised what a little country England is, since we can so soon get to the end of its biggest river.'

'It is not big,' said I, 'but it is pretty.'

'Yes,' she said, 'and don't you find it difficult to imagine the times when this little pretty country was treated by its folk as if it had been an ugly characterless waste, with no delicate beauty to be guarded, with no heed taken of the ever fresh pleasure of the recurring seasons, and changeful weather, and diverse quality of the soil, and so forth? How could people be so cruel to themselves?'

'And to each other,' said I. Then a sudden resolution took hold of me, and I said: 'Dear neighbour, I may as well tell you at once that I find it easier to imagine all that ugly past than you do, because I myself have been part of it. I see both that you have divined something of this in me; and also I think you will believe me when I tell you of it, so that I am going to hide nothing from you at all.'

She was silent a little, and then she said: 'My friend, you have guessed right about me; and to tell you the truth I have followed you up from Runnymede in order that I might ask you many questions, and because I saw that you were not one of us; and that interested and pleased me, and I wanted to make you as happy as you could be. To say the truth, there was a risk in it,' said she, blushing—'I mean as to Dick and Clara; for I must tell you, since we are going to be such close friends, that even amongst us, where there are so many beautiful women, I have often troubled men's minds disastrously. That is one reason why I was living alone with my father in the cottage at Runnymede. But it did not answer on that score; for of course people came there, as the place is not a desert, and they seemed to find me all the more interesting for living alone like that, and fell to making stories of me to themselves—like I know you did, my friend. Well, let that pass. This evening, or to-morrow morning, I shall make a proposal to you to do something which would please me very much, and I think would not hurt you.'

I broke in eagerly, saying that I would do anything in the world for her; for indeed, in spite of my years and the too obvious signs of them (though that feeling of renewed youth was not a mere passing sensation, I think)—in spite of my years, I say, I felt altogether too happy in the company of this delightful girl, and was prepared to take her confidences for more than they meant perhaps.

She laughed now, but looked very kindly on me. 'Well,' she said, 'meantime for the present we will let it be; for I must look at this new country that we are passing through. See how the river has changed character again: it is broad now, and the reaches are long and very slow-running. And look, there is a ferry!'

I told her the name of it, as I slowed off to put the ferry-chain over our heads; and on we went passing by a bank clad with oak trees on our left hand, till the stream narrowed again and deepened, and we rowed on between walls of tall reeds, whose population of reed sparrows and warblers were delightfully restless, twittering and chuckling as the wash of the boats stirred the reeds from the water upward in the still, hot morning.

She smiled with pleasure, and her lazy enjoyment of the new scene seemed to bring out her beauty doubly as she leaned back amidst the cushions, though she was far from languid; her idleness being the idleness of a person, strong and well-knit both in body and mind, deliberately resting.

'Look!' she said, springing up suddenly from her place without any obvious effort, and balancing herself with exquisite grace and ease; 'look at the beautiful old bridge ahead!'

'I need scarcely look at that,' said I, not turning my head away from her beauty. 'I know what it is; though' (with a smile) 'we used not to call it the Old Bridge time agone.'

She looked down upon me kindly, and said, 'How well we get on now you are no longer on your guard against me!'

And she stood looking thoughtfully at me still, till she had to sit down as we passed under the middle one of the row of little pointed arches of the oldest bridge across the Thames.

'O the beautiful fields!' she said; 'I had no idea of the charm of a very small river like this. The smallness of the scale of everything, the short reaches, and the speedy change of the banks, give one a feeling of going somewhere, of coming to something strange, a feeling of adventure which I have not felt in bigger waters.'

I looked up at her delightedly; for her voice, saying the very thing that I was thinking, was like a caress to me. She caught my eye and her cheeks reddened under their tan, and she said simply:

'I must tell you, my friend, that when my father leaves the Thames this summer he will take me away to a place near the Roman wall in Cumberland; so that this voyage of mine is farewell to the south; of course with my goodwill in a way; and yet I am sorry for it. I hadn't the heart to tell Dick yesterday that we were as good as gone from the Thames-side; but somehow to you I must needs tell it.'

She stopped and seemed very thoughtful for a while, and then said smiling:

'I must say that I don't like moving about from one home to another; one gets so pleasantly used to all the detail of the life about one; it fits so

harmoniously and happily into one's own life, that beginning again, even in a
small way, is a kind of pain. But I daresay in the country which you come
from, you would think this petty and unadventurous and would think the
worse of me for it.'

She smiled at me caressingly as she spoke, and I made haste to answer:
'O, no, indeed; again you echo my very thoughts. But I hardly expected to
hear you speak so. I gathered from all I have heard that there was a great deal
of changing of abode amongst you in this country.'

'Well,' she said, 'of course people are free to move about; but except for
pleasure-parties, especially in harvest and hay-time, like this of ours, I don't
think they do so much. I admit that I also have other moods than that of stay-
at-home, as I hinted just now, and I should like to go with you all through the
west country—thinking of nothing,' concluded she smiling.

'I should have plenty to think of,' said I.

Chapter XXIX. A Resting-Place on the Upper Thames

Presently at a place where the river flowed round a headland of the meadows,
we stopped a while for rest and victuals, and settled ourselves on a beautiful
bank which almost reached the dignity of a hill-side: the wide meadows
spread before us, and already the scythe was busy amidst the hay. One change
I noticed amidst the quiet beauty of the fields—to wit, that they were planted
with trees here and there, often fruit-trees, and that there was none of the
niggardly begrudging of space to a handsome tree which I remembered too
well; and though the willows were often polled (or shrowded, as they call it in
that country-side), this was done with some regard to beauty: I mean that
there was no polling of rows on rows so as to destroy the pleasantness of half
a mile of country, but a thoughtful sequence in the cutting, that prevented a
sudden bareness anywhere. To be short, the fields were everywhere treated as
a garden made for the pleasure as well as the livelihood of all, as old Hammond
told me was the case.

On this bank or bent of the hill, then, we had our mid-day meal; somewhat
early for dinner, if that mattered, but we had been stirring early: the slender
stream of the Thames winding below us between the garden of a country
I have been telling of; a furlong from us was a beautiful little islet begrown
with graceful trees; on the slopes westward of us was a wood of varied growth
overhanging the narrow meadow on the south side of the river; while to the
north was a wide stretch of mead rising very gradually from the river's edge.
A delicate spire of an ancient building rose up from out of the trees in the
middle distance, with a few grey houses clustered about it; while nearer
to us, in fact not half a furlong from the water, was a quite modern stone

house—a wide quadrangle of one story, the buildings that made it being quite low. There was no garden between it and the river, nothing but a row of pear-trees still quite young and slender; and though there did not seem to be much ornament about it, it had a sort of natural elegance, like that of the trees themselves.

As we sat looking down on all this in the sweet June day, rather happy than merry, Ellen, who sat next me, her hand clasped about one knee, leaned sideways to me, and said in a low voice which Dick and Clara might have noted if they had not been busy in happy wordless love-making: 'Friend, in your country were the houses of your field-labourers anything like that?'

I said: 'Well, at any rate the houses of our rich men were not; they were mere blots upon the face of the land.'

'I find that hard to understand,' she said. 'I can see why the workmen, who were so oppressed, should not have been able to live in beautiful houses; for it takes time and leisure, and minds not over-burdened with care, to make beautiful dwellings; and I quite understand that these poor people were not allowed to live in such a way as to have these (to us) necessary good things. But why the rich men, who had the time and the leisure and the materials for building, as it would be in this case, should not have housed themselves well, I do not understand as yet. I know what you are meaning to say to me,' she said, looking me full in the eyes and blushing, 'to wit that their houses and all belonging to them were generally ugly and base, unless they chanced to be ancient like yonder remnant of our forefathers' work' (pointing to the spire); 'that they were—let me see; what is the word?'

'Vulgar,' said I. 'We used to say,' said I, 'that the ugliness and vulgarity of the rich men's dwellings was a necessary reflection from the sordidness and bareness of life which they forced upon the poor people.'

She knit her brows as in thought; then turned a brightened face on me, as if she had caught the idea, and said: 'Yes, friend, I see what you mean. We have sometimes—those of us who look into these things—talked this very matter over; because, to say the truth, we have plenty of record of the so-called arts of the time before Equality of Life; and there are not wanting people who say that the state of that society was not the cause of all that ugliness; that they were ugly in their life because they liked to be, and could have had beautiful things about them if they had chosen; just as a man or a body of men now may, if they please, make things more or less beautiful—Stop! I know what you are going to say.'

'Do you?' said I, smiling, yet with a beating heart.

'Yes,' she said; 'you are answering me, teaching me, in some way or another, although you have not spoken the words aloud. You are going to say that in times of inequality it was an essential condition of the life of these rich men that they should not themselves make what they wanted for the adornment of their lives, but should force those to make them whom they forced to live pinched and sordid lives; and that as a necessary consequence the sordidness and pinching, the ugly barrenness of those ruined lives, were worked up into the adornment of the lives of the rich, and art died out amongst men? Was that what you would say, my friend?'

'Yes, yes,' I said, looking at her eagerly; for she had risen and was standing on the edge of the bent, the light wind stirring her dainty raiment, one hand laid on her bosom, the other arm stretched downward and clenched in her earnestness.

'It is true,' she said, 'it is true! We have proved it true!'

I think amidst my—something more than interest in her, and admiration for her, I was beginning to wonder how it would all end. I had a glimmering of fear of what might follow; of anxiety as to the remedy which this new age might offer for the missing of something one might set one's heart on. But now Dick rose to his feet and cried out in his hearty manner: 'Neighbour Ellen, are you quarrelling with the guest, or are you worrying him to tell you things which he cannot properly explain to our ignorance?'

'Neither, dear neighbour,' she said. 'I was so far from quarrelling with him that I think I have been making him good friends both with himself and me. Is it so, dear guest?' she said, looking down at me with a delightful smile of confidence in being understood.

'Indeed it is,' said I.

'Well, moreover,' she said, 'I must say for him that he has explained himself to me very well indeed, so that I quite understand him.'

'All right,' quoth Dick. 'When I first set eyes on you at Runnymede I knew that there was something wonderful in your keenness of wits. I don't say that as a mere pretty speech to please you,' said he quickly, 'but because it is true; and it made me want to see more of you. But, come, we ought to be going; for we are not half way, and we ought to be in well before sunset.'

And therewith he took Clara's hand, and led her down the bent. But Ellen stood thoughtfully looking down for a little, and as I took her hand to follow Dick, she turned round to me and said:

'You might tell me a great deal and make many things clear to me, if you would.'

'Yes,' said I, 'I am pretty well fit for that,—and for nothing else—an old man like me.'

She did not notice the bitterness which, whether I liked it or not, was in my voice as I spoke, but went on: 'It is not so much for myself; I should be quite content to dream about past times, and if I could not idealise them, yet at least idealise some of the people who lived in them. But I think sometimes people are too careless of the history of the past—too apt to leave it in the hands of old learned men like Hammond. Who knows? happy as we are, times may alter; we may be bitten with some impulse towards change, and many things may seem too wonderful for us to resist, too exciting not to catch at, if we do not know that they are but phases of what has been before; and withal ruinous, deceitful, and sordid.'

As we went slowly down toward the boats she said again: 'Not for myself alone, dear friend; I shall have children; perhaps before the end a good many;—I hope so. And though of course I cannot force any special kind of knowledge upon them, yet, my friend, I cannot help thinking that just as they might be like me in body, so I might impress upon them some part of my ways of thinking; that is, indeed, some of the essential part of myself; that part which was not mere moods, created by matters and events round about me. What do you think?'

Of one thing I was sure, that her beauty and kindness and eagerness combined, forced me to think as she did, when she was not earnestly laying herself open to receive my thoughts. I said, what at the time was true, that I thought it most important; and presently stood entranced by the wonder of her grace as she stepped into the light boat and held out her hand to me. And so on we went up the Thames still—or whither?

Chapter XXX. The Journey's End

On we went. In spite of my new-born excitement about Ellen, and my gathering fear of where it would land me, I could not help taking abundant interest in the condition of the river and its banks; all the more as she never seemed weary of the changing picture, but looked at every yard of flowery bank and gurgling eddy with the same kind of affectionate interest which I myself once had so fully, as I used to think, and perhaps had not altogether lost even in this strangely changed society with all its wonders. Ellen seemed delighted with my pleasure at this, that, or the other piece of carefulness in dealing with the river: the nursing of pretty corners; the ingenuity in dealing with difficulties of water-engineering so that the most obviously useful works looked beautiful and natural also. All this, I say, pleased me hugely, and she was pleased at my pleasure—but rather puzzled too.

'You seem astonished,' she said, just after we had passed a mill* which spanned all the stream save the water-way for traffic, but which was as beautiful in its way as a Gothic cathedral—'you seem astonished at this being so pleasant to look at.'

'Yes,' I said, 'in a way I am; though I don't see why it should not be.'

---

* I should have said that all along the Thames there were abundance of mills used for various purposes; none of which were in any degree unsightly, and many strikingly beautiful; and the gardens about them marvels of loveliness.

'Ah!' she said, looking at me admiringly, yet with a lurking smile in her face, 'you know all about the history of the past. Were they not always careful about this little stream which now adds so much pleasantness to the countryside? It would always be easy to manage this little river. Ah! I forgot, though,' she said, as her eye caught mine, 'in the days we are thinking of pleasure was wholly neglected in such matters. But how did they manage the river in the days that you—' Lived in she was going to say; but correcting herself, said— 'in the days of which you have record?'

'They *mis*managed it,' quoth I. 'Up to the first half of the nineteenth century, when it was still more or less of a highway for the country people, some care was taken of the river and its banks; and though I don't suppose any one troubled himself about its aspect, yet it was trim and beautiful. But when the railways—of which no doubt you have heard—came into power, they would not allow the people of the country to use either the natural or artificial waterways, of which the latter there were a great many. I suppose when we get higher up we shall see one of these; a very important one, which one of these railways entirely closed to the public, so that they might force people to send their goods by their private road, and so tax them as heavily as they could.'

Ellen laughed heartily. 'Well,' she said, 'that is not stated clearly enough in our history-books, and it is worth knowing. But certainly the people of those days must have been a curiously lazy set. We are not either fidgety or quarrelsome now, but if any one tried such a piece of folly on us, we should use the said waterways, whoever gainsaid us: surely that would be simple enough. However, I remember other cases of this stupidity: when I was on the Rhine two years ago, I remember they showed us ruins of old castles, which, according to what we heard, must have been made for pretty much the same purpose as the railways were. But I am interrupting your history of the river: pray go on.'

'It is both short and stupid enough,' said I. 'The river having lost its practical or commercial value—that is, being of no use to make money of—'

She nodded. 'I understand what that queer phrase means,' said she. 'Go on!'

'Well, it was utterly neglected, till at last it became a nuisance—'

'Yes,' quoth Ellen, 'I understand: like the railways and the robber knights. Yes?'

'So then they turned the makeshift business on to it, and handed it over to a body up in London, who from time to time, in order to show that they had something to do, did some damage here and there,—cut down trees, destroying the banks thereby; dredged the river (where it was not needed always), and threw the dredgings on the fields so as to spoil them; and so forth. But for the most part they practised "masterly inactivity", as it was then called—that is, they drew their salaries, and let things alone.'

'Drew their salaries,' she said. 'I know that means that they were allowed to take an extra lot of other people's goods for doing nothing. And if that had been all, it really might have been worth while to let them do so, if you couldn't find any other way of keeping them quiet; but it seems to me that being so paid, they could not help doing something, and that something was bound to be mischief,—because,' said she, kindling with sudden anger, 'the whole business was founded on lies and false pretensions. I don't mean only these river-guardians, but all these master-people I have read of.'

'Yes,' said I, 'how happy you are to have got out of the parsimony of oppression!'

'Why do you sigh?' she said, kindly and somewhat anxiously. 'You seem to think that it will not last?'

'It will last for you,' quoth I.

'But why not for you?' said she. 'Surely it is for all the world; and if your country is somewhat backward, it will come into line before long. Or,' she said quickly, 'are you thinking that you must soon go back again? I will make my proposal which I told you of at once, and so perhaps put an end to your anxiety. I was going to propose that you should live with us where we are going. I feel quite old friends with you, and should be sorry to lose you.' Then she smiled on me, and said: 'Do you know, I begin to suspect you of wanting to nurse a sham sorrow, like the ridiculous characters in some of those queer old novels that I have come across now and then.'

I really had almost begun to suspect it myself, but I refused to admit so much; so I sighed no more, but fell to giving my delightful companion what little pieces of history I knew about the river and its borderlands; and the time passed pleasantly enough; and between the two of us (she was a better sculler than I was, and seemed quite tireless) we kept up fairly well with Dick, hot as the afternoon was, and swallowed up the way at a great rate. At last we passed under another ancient bridge; and through meadows bordered at first with huge elm-trees mingled with sweet chestnut of younger but very elegant growth; and the meadows widened out so much that it seemed as if the trees must now be on the bents only, or about the houses except for the growth of willows on the immediate banks; so that the wide stretch of grass was little broken here. Dick got very much excited now, and often stood up in the boat to cry out to us that this was such and such a field, and so forth; and we caught fire at his enthusiasm for the hayfield and its harvest, and pulled our best.

At last we were passing through a reach of the river where on the side of the towing-path was a highish bank with a thick whispering bed of reeds before it, and on the other side a higher bank, clothed with willows that dipped into the stream and crowned by ancient elm-trees, we saw bright figures coming along close to the bank, as if they were looking for something; as, indeed, they were, and we—that is, Dick and his company—were what they were looking for.

Dick lay on his oars, and we followed his example. He gave a joyous shout to the people on the bank, which was echoed back from it in many voices, deep and sweetly shrill; for there were above a dozen persons, both men, women, and children. A tall handsome woman, with black wavy hair and deep-set grey eyes, came forward on the bank and waved her hand gracefully to us, and said:

'Dick, my friend, we have almost had to wait for you! What excuse have you to make for your slavish punctuality? Why didn't you take us by surprise, and come yesterday?'

'O,' said Dick, with an almost imperceptible jerk of his head toward our boat, 'we didn't want to come too quick up the water; there is so much to see for those who have not been up here before.'

'True, true,' said the stately lady, for stately is the word that must be used for her; 'and we want them to get to know the wet way from the east thoroughly well, since they must often use it now. But come ashore at once, Dick, and you, dear neighbours; there is a break in the reeds and a good landing-place just round the corner. We can carry up your things, or send some of the lads after them.'

'No, no,' said Dick; 'it is easier going by water, though it is but a step. Besides, I want to bring my friend here to the proper place. We will go on to the Ford; and you can talk to us from the bank as we paddle along.'

He pulled his sculls through the water, and on we went, turning a sharp angle and going north a little. Presently we saw before us a bank of elm-trees, which told us of a house amidst them, though I looked in vain for the grey walls that I expected to see there. As we went, the folk on the bank talked indeed, mingling their kind voices with the cuckoo's song, the sweet strong whistle of the blackbirds, and the ceaseless note of the corn-crake as he crept through the long grass of the mowing-field; whence came the waves of fragrance from the flowering clover amidst of the ripe grass.

In a few minutes we had passed through a deep eddying pool into the sharp stream that ran from the ford, and beached our craft on a tiny strand of limestone-gravel, and stepped ashore into the arms of our up-river friend, our journey done.

I disentangled myself from the merry throng, and mounting on the cart-road that ran along the river some feet above the water, I looked round about me. The river came down through a wide meadow on my left, which was grey now with the ripened seeding grasses; the gleaming water was lost presently by a turn of the bank, but over the meadow I could see the mingled gables of a building where I knew the lock must be, and which now seemed to combine a mill with it. A low wooded ridge bounded the river-plain to the south and south-east, whence we had come, and a few low houses lay about its feet and up its slope. I turned a little to my right, and through the hawthorn sprays and long shoots of the wild roses could see the flat country spreading out far away under the sun of the calm evening, till something that might be called hills with a look of sheep-pastures about them bounded it with a soft blue line. Before me, the elm-boughs still hid most of what houses there might be in this river-side dwelling of men; but to the right of the cart-road a few grey buildings of the simplest kind showed here and there.

There I stood in a dreamy mood, and rubbed my eyes as if I were not wholly awake, and half expected to see the gay-clad company of beautiful men and women change to two or three spindle-legged back-bowed men and haggard, hollow-eyed, ill-favoured women, who once wore down the soil of this land with their heavy hopeless feet, from day to day, and season to season, and year to year. But no change came as yet, and my heart swelled with joy as I thought of all the beautiful grey villages, from the river to the plain and the plain to the uplands, which I could picture to myself so well, all peopled now with this happy and lovely folk, who had cast away riches and attained to wealth.

Chapter XXXI. An Old House amongst New Folk

As I stood there Ellen detached herself from our happy friends who still stood on the little strand and came up to me. She took me by the hand, and said softly, 'Take me on to the house at once; we need not wait for the others: I had rather not.'

I had a mind to say that I did not know the way thither, and that the river-side dwellers should lead; but almost without my will my feet moved on along the road they knew. The raised way led us into a little field bounded by a backwater of the river on one side; on the right hand we could see a cluster of small houses and barns, new and old, and before us a grey stone barn and a wall partly overgrown with ivy, over which a few grey gables showed. The village road ended in the shallow of the aforesaid backwater. We crossed the road, and again almost without my will my hand raised the latch of a door in the wall, and we stood presently on a stone path which led up to the old house to which fate in the shape of Dick had so strangely brought me in this new world of men. My companion gave a sigh of pleased surprise and enjoyment; nor did I wonder, for the garden between the wall and the house was redolent of the June flowers, and the roses were rolling over one another with that delicious superabundance of small well-tended gardens which at first sight takes away all thought from the beholder save that of beauty. The blackbirds were singing their loudest, the doves were cooing on the roof-ridge, the rooks in the high elm-trees beyond were garrulous among the young leaves, and the swifts wheeled whining about the gables. And the house itself was a fit guardian for all the beauty of this heart of summer.

Once again Ellen echoed my thoughts as she said: 'Yes, friend, this is what I came out for to see; this many-gabled old house built by the simple country-folk of the long-past times, regardless of all the turmoil that was going on in cities and courts, is lovely still amidst all the beauty which these latter days have created; and I do not wonder at our friends tending it carefully and making much of it. It seems to me as if it had waited for these happy days, and held in it the gathered crumbs of happiness of the confused and turbulent past.'

She led me up close to the house, and laid her shapely sun-browned hand and arm on the lichened wall as if to embrace it, and cried out, 'O me! O me! How I love the earth, and the seasons, and weather, and all things that deal with it, and all that grows out of it,—as this has done!'

I could not answer her, or say a word. Her exultation and pleasure were so keen and exquisite, and her beauty, so delicate, yet so interfused with energy, expressed it so fully, that any added word would have been commonplace and futile. I dreaded lest the others should come in suddenly and break the spell she had cast about me; but we stood there a while by the corner of the big gable of the house, and no one came. I heard the merry voices some way off presently, and knew that they were going along the river to the great meadow on the other side of the house and garden.

We drew back a little, and looked up at the house: the door and the windows were open to the fragrant sun-cured air; from the upper window-sills hung festoons of flowers in honour of the festival, as if the others shared in the love for the old house.

'Come in,' said Ellen. 'I hope nothing will spoil it inside; but I don't think it will. Come! we must go back presently to the others. They have gone on to the tents; for surely they must have tents pitched for the haymakers—the house would not hold a tithe of the folk, I am sure.'

She led me to the door, murmuring little above her breath as she did so, 'The earth and the growth of it and the life of it! If I could but say or show how I love it!'

We went in, and found no soul in any room as we wandered from room to room,—from the rose-covered porch to the strange and quaint garrets amongst the great timbers of the roof, where of old time the tillers and herdsmen of the manor slept, but which a-nights seemed now, by the small size of the beds, and the litter of useless and disregarded matters—bunches of drying flowers, feathers of birds, shells of starlings' eggs, caddis worms in mugs, and the like—seemed to be inhabited for the time by children.

Everywhere there was but little furniture, and that only the most necessary, and of the simplest forms. The extravagant love of ornament which I had noted in this people elsewhere seemed here to have given place to the feeling that the house itself and its associations was the ornament of the country life amidst which it had been left stranded from old times, and that to re-ornament it would but take away its use as a piece of natural beauty.

We sat down at last in a room over the wall which Ellen had caressed, and which was still hung with old tapestry, originally of no artistic value, but now faded into pleasant grey tones which harmonised thoroughly well with the quiet of the place, and which would have been ill supplanted by brighter and more striking decoration.

I asked a few random questions of Ellen as we sat there, but scarcely listened to her answers, and presently became silent, and then scarce conscious of anything, but that I was there in that old room, the doves crooning from the roofs of the barn and dovecot beyond the window opposite to me.

My thought returned to me after what I think was but a minute or two, but which, as in a vivid dream, seemed as if it had lasted a long time, when I saw Ellen sitting, looking all the fuller of life and pleasure and desire from the contrast with the grey faded tapestry with its futile design, which was now only bearable because it had grown so faint and feeble.

She looked at me kindly, but as if she read me through and through. She said: 'You have begun again your never-ending contrast between the past and this present. Is that not so?'

'True,' said I. 'I was thinking of what you, with your capacity and intelligence, joined to your love of pleasure, and your impatience of unreasonable restraint— of what you would have been in that past. And even now, when all is won and has been for a long time, my heart is sickened with thinking of all the waste of life that has gone on for so many years.'

'So many centuries,' she said, 'so many ages!'

'True,' I said; 'too true,' and sat silent again.

She rose up and said: 'Come, I must not let you go off into a dream again so soon. If we must lose you, I want you to see all that you can see first before you go back again.'

'Lose me?' I said—'go back again? Am I not to go up to the North with you? What do you mean?'

She smiled somewhat sadly, and said: 'Not yet; we will not talk of that yet. Only, what were you thinking of just now?'

I said falteringly: 'I was saying to myself, The past, the present? Should she not have said the contrast of the present with the future: of blind despair with hope?'

'I knew it,' she said. Then she caught my hand and said excitedly, 'Come while there is yet time! Come!' And she led me out of the room; and as we were going downstairs and out of the house into the garden by a little side door which opened out of a curious lobby, she said in a calm voice, as if she wished me to forget her sudden nervousness: 'Come! we ought to join the others before they come here looking for us. And let me tell you, my friend, that I can see you are too apt to fall into mere dreamy musing: no doubt because you are not yet used to our life of repose amidst of energy; of work which is pleasure and pleasure which is work.'

She paused a little, and as we came out into the lovely garden again, she said: 'My friend, you were saying that you wondered what I should have been if I had lived in those past days of turmoil and oppression. Well, I think I have studied the history of them to know pretty well. I should have been one of the poor, for my father when he was working was a mere tiller of the soil. Well, I could not have borne that; therefore my beauty and cleverness and brightness' (she spoke with no blush or simper of false shame) 'would have been sold to rich men, and my life would have been wasted indeed; for I know enough of that to know that I should have had no choice, no power of will over my life; and that I should never have bought pleasure from the rich men, or even opportunity of action, whereby I might have won some true excitement. I should have wrecked and wasted in one way or another, either by penury or by luxury. Is it not so?'

'Indeed it is,' said I.

She was going to say something else, when a little gate in the fence, which led into a small elm-shaded field, was opened, and Dick came with hasty cheerfulness up the garden path, and was presently standing between us, a hand laid on the shoulder of each. He said: 'Well, neighbours, I thought you two would like to see the old house quietly without a crowd in it. Isn't it a jewel of a house after its kind? Well, come along, for it is getting towards dinner-time. Perhaps you, guest, would like a swim before we sit down to what I fancy will be a pretty long feast?'

'Yes,' I said, 'I should like that.'

'Well, good-bye for the present, neighbour Ellen,' said Dick. 'Here comes Clara to take care of you, as I fancy she is more at home amongst our friends here.'

Clara came out of the fields as he spoke; and with one look at Ellen I turned and went with Dick, doubting, if I must say the truth, whether I should see her again.

Chapter XXXII. The Feast's Beginning—The End

Dick brought me at once into the little field which, as I had seen from the garden, was covered with gaily-coloured tents arranged in orderly lanes, about which were sitting and lying in the grass some fifty or sixty men, women, and children, all of them in the height of good temper and enjoyment—with their holiday mood on, so to say.

'You are thinking that we don't make a great show as to numbers,' said Dick; 'but you must remember that we shall have more to-morrow; because in this haymaking work there is room for a great many people who are not over-skilled in country matters: and there are many who lead sedentary lives, whom it would be unkind to deprive of their pleasure in the hayfield— scientific men and close students generally: so that the skilled workmen, outside those who are wanted as mowers, and foremen of the haymaking, stand aside, and take a little downright rest, which you know is good for them, whether they like it or not: or else they go to other countrysides, as I am doing here. You see, the scientific men and historians, and students generally, will not be wanted till we are fairly in the midst of the tedding, which of course will not be till the day after to-morrow.' With that he brought me out of the little field on to a kind of causeway above the riverside meadow, and thence turning to the left on to a path through the mowing grass, which was thick and very tall, led on till we came to the river above the weir and its mill. There we had a delightful swim in the broad piece of water above the lock, where the river looked much bigger than its natural size from its being dammed up by the weir.

'Now we are in a fit mood for dinner,' said Dick, when we had dressed and were going through the grass again; 'and certainly of all the cheerful meals in the year, this one of haysel is the cheerfullest; not even excepting the corn-harvest feast; for then the year is beginning to fail, and one cannot help having a feeling behind all the gaiety, of the coming of the dark days, and the shorn fields and empty gardens; and the spring is almost too far off to look forward to. It is, then, in the autumn, when one almost believes in death.'

'How strangely you talk,' said I, 'of such a constantly recurring and consequently commonplace matter as the sequence of the seasons.' And indeed these people were like children about such things, and had what seemed to me a quite exaggerated interest in the weather, a fine day, a dark night, or a brilliant one, and the like.

'Strangely?' said he. 'Is it strange to sympathise with the year and its gains and losses?'

'At any rate,' said I, 'if you look upon the course of the year as a beautiful and interesting drama, which is what I think you do, you should be as much pleased and interested with the winter and its trouble and pain as with this wonderful summer luxury.'

'And am I not?' said Dick, rather warmly; 'only I can't look upon it as if I were sitting in a theatre seeing the play going on before me, myself taking no part of it. It is difficult,' said he, smiling good-humouredly, 'for a non-literary man like me to explain myself properly, like that dear girl Ellen would; but I mean that I am part of it all, and feel the pain was well as the pleasure in my own person. It is not done for me by somebody else, merely that I may eat and drink and sleep; but I myself do my share of it.'

In his way also, as Ellen in hers, I could see that Dick had that passionate love of the earth which was common to but few people at least, in the days I knew; in which the prevailing feeling amongst intellectual persons was a kind of sour distaste for the changing drama of the year, for the life of earth and its dealings with men. Indeed, in those days it was thought poetic and imaginative to look upon life as a thing to be borne, rather than enjoyed.

So I mused till Dick's laugh brought me back into the Oxfordshire hayfields. 'One thing seems strange to me,' said he—'that I must needs trouble myself about the winter and its scantiness, in the midst of the summer abundance. If it hadn't happened to me before, I should have thought it was your doing, guest; that you had thrown a kind of evil charm over me. Now, you know,' said he, suddenly, 'that's only a joke, so you mustn't take it to heart.'

'All right,' said I; 'I don't.' Yet I did feel somewhat uneasy at his words, after all.

We crossed the causeway this time, and did not turn back to the house, but went along a path beside a field of wheat now almost ready to blossom. I said: 'We do not dine in the house or garden, then? for I can see that the houses are mostly very small.'

'Yes,' said Dick, 'you are right, they are small in this country-side: there are so many good old houses left, that people dwell a good deal in such small detached houses. As to our dinner, we are going to have our feast in the church. I wish, for your sake, it were as big and handsome as that of the old Roman town to the west, or the forest town to the north;* but, however, it will hold us all; and though it is a little thing, it is beautiful in its way.'

This was somewhat new to me, this dinner in a church, and I thought of the church-ales of the Middle Ages; but I said nothing, and presently we came out into the road which ran through the village. Dick looked up and down it, and seeing only two straggling groups before us, said: 'It seems as if we must be somewhat late; they are all gone on; and they will be sure to make a point of waiting for you, as the guest of guests, since you come from so far.'

He hastened as he spoke, and I kept up with him, and presently we came to a little avenue of lime-trees which led us straight to the church porch, from whose open door came the sound of cheerful voices and laughter, and varied merriment.

'Yes,' said Dick, 'it's the coolest place for one thing, this hot evening. Come along; they will be glad to see you.'

Indeed, in spite of my bath, I felt the weather more sultry and oppressive than on any day of our journey yet.

We went into the church, which was a simple little building with one little aisle divided from the nave by three rounded arches, a chancel, and a rather roomy transept for so small a building, the windows mostly of the graceful Oxfordshire fourteenth-century type. There was no modern architectural decoration in it; it looked, indeed, as if none had been attempted since the Puritans whitewashed the mediæval saints and histories on the wall. It was, however, gaily dressed up for this latter-day festival, with festoons of flowers from arch to arch, and great pitchers of flowers standing about on the floor;

---

* Cirencester and Burford he must have meant.

while under the west window hung two cross scythes, their blades polished white, and gleaming from out of the flowers that wreathed them. But its best ornament was the crowd of handsome, happy-looking men and women that were set down to table, and who, with their bright faces and rich hair over their gay holiday raiment, looked, as the Persian poet puts it, like a bed of tulips in the sun. Though the church was a small one, there was plenty of room; for a small church makes a biggish house; and on this evening there was no need to set cross tables along the transepts; though doubtless these would be wanted next day, when the learned men of whom Dick has been speaking should be come to take their more humble part in the haymaking.

I stood on the threshold with the expectant smile on my face of a man who is going to take part in a festivity which he is really prepared to enjoy. Dick, standing by me was looking round the company with an air of proprietorship in them, I thought. Opposite me sat Clara and Ellen, with Dick's place open between them: they were smiling, but their beautiful faces were each turned towards the neighbours on either side, who were talking to them, and they did not seem to see me. I turned to Dick, expecting him to lead me forward, and he turned his face to me; but strange to say, though it was as smiling and cheerful as ever, it made no response to my glance—nay, he seemed to take no heed at all of my presence, and I noticed that none of the company looked at me. A pang shot through me, as of some disaster long expected and suddenly realised. Dick moved on a little without a word to me. I was not three yards from the two women who, though they had been my companions for such a short time, had really, as I thought, become my friends. Clara's face was turned full upon me now, but she also did not seem to see me, though I know I was trying to catch her eye with an appealing look. I turned to Ellen, and she *did* seem to recognise me for an instant; but her bright face turned sad directly, and she shook her head with a mournful look, and the next moment all consciousness of my presence had faded from her face.

I felt lonely and sick at heart past the power of words to describe. I hung about a minute longer, and then turned and went out of the porch again and through the lime-avenue into the road, while blackbirds sang their strongest from the bushes about me in the hot June evening.

Once more without any conscious effort of will I set my face toward the old house by the ford, but as I turned round the corner which led to the remains of the village cross, I came upon a figure strangely contrasting with the joyous, beautiful people I had left behind in the church. It was a man who looked old, but whom I knew from habit, now half-forgotten, was really not much more than fifty. His face was rugged, and grimed rather than dirty; his eyes dull and bleared; his body bent, his calves thin and spindly, his feet dragging and limping. His clothing was a mixture of dirt and rags long over-familiar to me. As I passed him he touched his hat with some real goodwill and courtesy, and much servility.

Inexpressibly shocked, I hurried past him and hastened along the road that led to the river and the lower end of the village; but suddenly I saw as it were a black cloud rolling along to meet me, like a nightmare of my childish days; and for a while I was conscious of nothing else than being in the dark, and whether I was walking, or sitting, or lying down, I could not tell.

****

I lay in my bed in my house at dingy Hammersmith thinking about it all; and trying to consider if I was overwhelmed with despair at finding I had been dreaming a dream; and strange to say, I found that I was not so despairing.

Or indeed *was* it a dream? If so, why was I so conscious all along that I was really seeing all that new life from the outside, still wrapped up in the prejudices, the anxieties, the distrust of this time of doubt and struggle?

All along, though those friends were so real to me, I had been feeling as if I had no business amongst them: as though the time would come when they would reject me, and say, as Ellen's last mournful look seemed to say, 'No, it will not do; you cannot be of us; you belong so entirely to the unhappiness of the past that our happiness even would weary you. Go back again, now you have seen us, and your outward eyes have learned that in spite of all the infallible maxims of your day there is yet a time of rest in store for the world, when mastery has changed into fellowship—but not before. Go back again, then, and while you live you will see all round you people engaged in making others live lives which are not their own, while they themselves care nothing for their own real lives—men who hate life though they fear death. Go back and be the happier for having seen us, for having added a little hope to your struggle. Go on living while you may, striving, with whatsoever pain and labour needs must be, to build up little by little the new day of fellowship, and rest, and happiness.'

Yes, surely! and if others can see it as I have seen it, then it may be called a vision rather than a dream.

HOW I BECAME A SOCIALIST

I am asked by the Editor to give some sort of a history of the above conversion, and I feel that it may be of some use to do so, if any readers will look upon me as a type of a certain group of people, but not so easy to do clearly, briefly and truly. Let me, however, try. But first, I will say what I mean by being a Socialist, since I am told that the word no longer expresses definitely and with certainty what it did ten years ago. Well, what I mean by Socialism is a condition of society in which there should be neither rich nor poor, neither master nor master's man, neither idle nor overworked, neither brain-sick brain-workers nor heart-sick hand workers, in a word in which all men would be living in equality of condition, and would manage their affairs unwastefully, and with the full consciousness that harm to one would mean harm to all—the realisation at last of the meaning of the word COMMONWEALTH.

Now this view of Socialism, which I hold to-day, and hope to die holding, is what I began with; I had no transitional period, unless you may call such a brief period of political radicalism during which I saw my ideal clear enough, but had no hope of any realisation of it. That came to an end some months before I joined the (then) Democratic Federation, and the meaning of my joining that body was that I had conceived a hope of the realisation of my ideal. If you ask me how much of a hope, or what I thought we Socialists then living and working would accomplish towards it, or when there would be effected any change in the face of society, I must say, I do not know. I can only say that I did not measure my hope, nor the joy that it brought me at the time. For the rest when I took that step I was blankly ignorant of economics; I had never so much as opened Adam Smith or heard of Ricardo, or of Karl Marx. Oddly enough I *had* read some of Mill, to wit, those posthumous papers of his (published was it in the *Westminster Review*, or the *Fortnightly*?) in which he attacks Socialism in its Fourierist guise. In those papers he put the arguments, as far as they go, clearly and honestly, and the result so far as I was concerned was to convince me that Socialism was a necessary change, and that it was possible to bring it about in our own days. Those papers put the finishing touch to my conversion to Socialism. Well, having joined a Socialist body (for the Federation soon became definitely Socialist), I put some conscience into trying to learn the economical side of Socialism, and even tackled Marx, though I must confess that, whereas I thoroughly enjoyed the historical side of 'Capital', I suffered agonies of confusion of the brain over reading the pure economics of that great work. Anyhow, I read what I could, and will hope that some information stuck to me from my reading; but more, I must think, from continuous conversation with such friends as Bax and Hyndman and Scheu, and the brisk course of propaganda meetings which were going on at the time, and in which I took my share. Such finish to what of education in practical Socialism as I am capable of I received afterwards from some of my Anarchist friends, from whom I learned, quite against their intention, that Anarchism was impossible, much as I learned from Mill against *his* intention that Socialism was necessary.

But in thus telling how I fell into *practical* Socialism I have begun, as I perceive, in the middle, for in my position [as] a well-to-do man not suffering from the disabilities which oppress a working man at every step, I feel that I might never have been drawn into the practical side of the question if an ideal had not forced me to seek towards it. For politics as politics, ie, not regarded as a necessary if cumbersome and disgustful means to an end, would never have attracted me, nor when I had become conscious of the wrongs of society as it now is, and the oppression of poor people, could I have ever believed in the possibility of a *partial* setting right of those wrongs. In other words, I could never have been such a fool as to believe in the happy and 'respectable' poor.

If therefore my ideal forced me to look for practical Socialism, what was it that forced me to conceive of an ideal? Now here comes in what I said of my being (in this paper) a type of a certain group of mind.

Before the uprising of *modern* Socialism, almost all intelligent people either were, or professed themselves to be, quite contented with the civilisation of this century. Again, almost all of these really were thus contented, and saw nothing to do but to perfect the said civilisation by getting rid of a few ridiculous survivals of the barbarous ages. To be short, this was the *Whig* frame of mind, natural to the modern prosperous middle-class men, who in fact, as far as mechanical progress is concerned, have nothing to ask for, if only Socialism would leave them alone to enjoy their plentiful stye.

But besides these contented ones there were others who were not really contented, but had a vague sentiment of repulsion to the triumph of civilisation, but were coerced into silence by the measureless power of Whiggery. Lastly there were a few who were in open rebellion against the said Whiggery—a few, say two, Carlyle and Ruskin. The latter, before my days of practical Socialism, was my master towards the ideal aforesaid, and, looking backward, I cannot help saying, by the way, how deadly dull the world would have been twenty years ago but for Ruskin! It was through him that I learned to give form to my discontent, which I must say was not by any means vague. Apart from the desire to produce beautiful things, the leading passion of my life has been and is hatred of modern civilisation. What shall I say of it now, when the words are put into my mouth, my hope of its destruction—and what shall I say of its supplanting by Socialism.

What shall I say concerning its mastery of, and its waste of mechanical power, its commonwealth so poor, its enemies of the commonwealth so rich, its stupendous organisation—for the misery of life. Its contempt for simple pleasures which everyone could enjoy but for its folly. Its eyeless vulgarity which has destroyed art, the one certain solace of labour? All this I felt then as now, but I did not know why it was so. The hope of the past times was gone, the struggles of mankind for many ages had produced nothing but this sordid, aimless, ugly confusion; the immediate future seemed to me likely to intensify all the present evils by sweeping away the last survivals of the days before the dull squalor of civilisation had settled down on the world. This was a bad look out indeed, and, if I may mention myself as a personality and not as a mere type, especially so to a man of my disposition, careless of metaphysics and religion as well as of scientific analysis, but with a deep love of the earth and the life on it, and a passion for the history of the past of mankind. Think of it. Was it all to end in a counting-house on the top of a cinder heap, with Podsnap's drawing room in the office, and a Whig committee dealing out champagne to the rich and margarine to the poor in such convenient proportions as would make men contented together, though the pleasure of the eyes was taken from the world, and the place of Homer was to be taken by Huxley. Yet believe me, in my heart when I really forced myself to look towards the future, that is what I saw in it, and as far as I could tell scarce any one seemed to think it worth while to struggle against such a consummation of civilisation. So there I was in for a fine pessimistic end of life, if it had not somehow dawned on me, that amidst all this filth of civilisation the seeds of a great change, what we others call Social Revolution, were beginning to germinate. The whole face of things was changed to me by that discovery, and all I had to do then in order to become a Socialist, was to hook myself on to the practical movement, which as beforesaid, I have tried to do as well as I could.

To sum up then, the study of history and the love and practice of art forced me into a hatred of the civilisation, which if things were to stop as they are would turn history into inconsequent nonsense, and make art a collection of the curiosities of the past, which would have no serious relation to the life of the present.

But the consciousness of revolution stirring amidst our hateful modern society prevented me, luckier than many others of artistic perception, from crystallising into a mere railer against 'progress' on one hand, and on the other from wanting time and energy in any of the numerous schemes by which the quasi-artistic of the middle-classes hope to make art grow when it has no longer any root, and thus I became a practical Socialist.

A last word or two. Perhaps some of our friends will say, what have we to do with these matters of history and art? We want by means of Social-Democracy to win a decent livelihood, we want in some sort to live and that at once. Surely anyone who professes to think that the question of art and cultivation must go before that of the knife and fork (and there are some who do propose that) does not understand what art means, or how that its roots must have a soil of a thriving and unanxious life. Yet it must be remembered that civilisation has reduced the workman to such a skinny and pitiful existence, that he scarcely knows how to frame a desire for any life much better than that which he now endures perforce. It is the province of art to set the true ideal of a full and reasonable life before him, a life to which the perception and creation of beauty, the enjoyment of real pleasure that is, shall be felt to be as necessary to man as his daily bread, and that no man, and no set of men can be deprived of this except by mere oppression, which should be resisted to the utmost.

ON EPPING FOREST

Letter to the Editor of the *Daily Chronicle*, 22 April 1895

Sir,

I venture to ask you to allow me a few words on the subject of the present treatment of Epping Forest. I was born and bred in its neighbourhood (Walthamstow and Woodford), and when I was a boy and young man, knew it yard by yard from Wanstead to the Theydons, and from Hale End to the Fairlop Oak. In those days it had no worse foes than the gravel stealer and the rolling fence maker, and was always interesting and often very beautiful. From what I can hear it is years since the greater part of it has been destroyed, and I fear, Sir, that in spite of your late optimistic note on the subject, what is left of it now runs the danger of further ruin.

The special character of it was derived from the fact that by far the greater part was a wood of hornbeams, a tree not common save in Essex and Herts. It was certainly the biggest hornbeam wood in these islands, and I suppose in the world. The said hornbeams were all pollards, being shrouded every four or six years, and were interspersed in many places with holly thickets; and the result was a very curious and characteristic wood, such as can be seen nowhere else. And I submit that no treatment of it can be tolerable which does not maintain this hornbeam wood intact.

But the hornbeam, though an interesting tree to an artist and reasonable person, is no favourite with the landscape gardener, and I very much fear that the intention of the authorities is to clear the forest of its native trees, and to plant vile weeds like deodars and outlandish conifers instead.

We are told that a committee of 'experts' has been formed to sit in judgement on Epping Forest; but, Sir, I decline to be gagged by the word 'expert' and I call on the public generally to take the same position. An 'expert' may be a very dangerous person because he is likely to narrow his views to the particular business (usually a commercial one) which he represents. In this case, for instance, we do not want to be under the thumb of either a wood bailiff, whose business is to grow timber for the market, or of a botanist whose business is to collect specimens for a botanical garden; or of a landscape-gardener whose business is to vulgarise a garden or landscape to the utmost extent that his patron's purse will allow of. What we want is reasonable men of real artistic taste to take into consideration what the essential needs of the case are, and to advise accordingly.

Now it seems to me that the authorities who have Epping Forest in hand may have two intentions as to it. First, they may intend to landscape garden it, or turn it into golf grounds (and I very much fear that even the latter nuisance may be in their minds); or second, they may really think it necessary (as you suggest) to thin the hornbeams, so as to give them a better chance of growing. The first alternative we Londoners should protest against to the utmost, for if it be carried out then Epping Forest is turned into a mere piece of vulgarity, is destroyed in fact.

As to the second, to put our minds at rest, we ought to be assured that the cleared spaces would be planted again, and that almost wholly with hornbeam. And, further, the greatest possible care should be taken that not a single tree should be felled, unless it were necessary for the growth of its fellows. Because, mind you, with comparatively small trees, the really beautiful effect of them can only be got by their standing as close together as the exigencies of growth will allow. We want a thicket, not a park, from Epping Forest.

In short, a great and practically irreparable mistake will be made, if under the shelter of the opinion of experts, from mere carelessness and thoughtlessness, we let the matter slip out of the hands of the thoughtful part of the public: the essential character of one of the greatest ornaments of London will disappear, and no one will have even a sample left to show what the great north-eastern forest was like.

I am sir,
Yours obediently,
William Morris

From *The Sundering Flood*

Chapter I. Of a River Called the Sundering Flood, and of the Folk that Dwelt thereby

It is told that there was once a mighty river which ran south into the sea, and at the mouth thereof was a great and rich city, which had been builded and had waxed and thriven because of the great and most excellent haven which the river aforesaid made where it fell into the sea. And now it was like looking at a huge wood of barked and smoothened fir-trees when one saw the masts of the ships that lay in the said haven.

But up this river ran the flood of tide a long way, so that the biggest of dromonds and round-ships might fare up it, and oft they lay amid pleasant up-country places, with their yards all but touching the windows of the husbandman's stead, and their bowsprits thrusting forth amongst the middens, and the routing swine, and querulous hens; and the uneasy lads and lasses sitting at high-mass of the Sunday in the grey village church would see the tall masts dimly amidst the painted saints of the aisle windows, and their minds would wander from the mass-hackled priest and the words and the gestures of him, and see visions of far countries and outlandish folk, and some would be heart-smitten with that desire of wandering and looking on new things which so oft the sea-beat board and the wind-strained pine bear with them to the dwellings of the stay-at-homes: and to some it seemed as if, when they went from out the church, they should fall in with St. Thomas of India stepping over the gangway, and come to visit their uplandish Christmas and the Yule-feast of the field-abiders of mid-winter frost. And moreover, when the tide failed, and there was no longer a flood to bear the sea-going keels up-stream (and that was hard on an hundred of miles from the sea), yet was this great river a noble and wide-spreading water, and the downlong stream thereof not so heavy nor so fierce but that the barges and lesser keels might well spread their sails when the south-west blew, and fare on without beating; or if the wind were fouler for them, they that were loth to reach from shore to shore, might be tracked up by the draught of horses and bullocks, and bear the wares of the merchants to many a cheaping.

Other rivers moreover not a few fell into this main flood, and of them were some no lesser than the Thames is at Abingdon, where I, who gathered this tale, dwell in the House of the Black Canons; blessed be St. William, and St. Richard, and the Holy Austin our candle in the dark! Yea and some were even bigger, so that the land was well furnished both of fisheries and water-ways.

Now the name of this river was the Sundering Flood, and the city at the mouth thereof was called the City of the Sundering Flood. And it is no wonder, considering all that I have told concerning the wares and chaffer that it bore up-country, though the folk of the City and its lands, and the city-folk in special, knew no cause for this name. Nay, oft they jested and gibed and gabbed, for they loved their river much and were proud of it; wherefore they said it was no sunderer but a uniter; that it joined land to land and shore to shore; that it had peopled the wilderness and made the waste places blossom, and that no highway for wheels and beasts in all the land was so full of blessings and joys as was their own wet Highway of the Flood. Nevertheless, as meseemeth that no name is given to any town or mountain or river causeless, but that men are moved to name all steads for a remembrance of deeds that have been done and tidings that have befallen, or some due cause, even so might it well be with the Sundering Flood, and whereas also I wot something of that cause I shall now presently show you the same.

For ye must know that all this welfare of the said mighty river was during that while that it flowed through the plain country a-nigh the city, or the fertile pastures and acres of hill and dale and down, further to the north. But one who should follow it up further and further would reach at last the place where it came forth from the mountains. There, though it be far smaller than lower down, yet is it still a mighty great water, and it is then well two hundred miles from the main sea. Now from the mountains it cometh in three great forces, and many smaller ones, and perilous and awful is it to behold; for betwixt those forces it filleth all the mountain ghyll, and there is no foothold for man, nay for goat, save at a hundred foot or more above the water, and that evil and perilous; and as is the running of a winter mill-stream to the beetles and shrew-mice that haunt the greensward beside it, so is the running of that flood to the sons of Adam and the beasts that serve them: and none has been so bold as to strive to cast a bridge across it.

But when ye have journeyed with much toil and no little peril over the mountain-necks, for by the gorge of the river, as aforesaid, no man may go, and have come out of the mountains once more, then again ye have the flood before you, cleaving a great waste of rocks mingled with sand, where groweth neither tree nor bush nor grass; and now the flood floweth wide and shallow but swift, so that no words may tell of its swiftness, and on either side the water are great wastes of tumbled stones that the spates have borne down from the higher ground. And ye shall know that from this place upward to its very wells in the higher mountains, the flood decreaseth not much in body or might, though it be wider or narrower as it is shallower or deeper, for nought but mere trickles of water fall into it in the space of this sandy waste, and what feeding it hath is from the bents and hills on either side as you wend toward the mountains to the north, where, as aforesaid, are its chiefest wells.

Now when ye have journeyed over this waste for some sixty miles the land begins to better, and there is grass again, yet no trees, and it rises into bents, which go back on each side, east and west, from the flood, and the said bents are grass also up to the tops, where they are crested with sheer rocks black of colour. As for the flood itself, it is now gathered into straiter compass, and is deep, and exceeding strong; high banks it hath on either side thereof of twenty foot and upward of black rock going down sheer to the water; and thus it is for a long way, save that the banks be higher and higher as the great valley of the river rises toward the northern mountains.

But as it rises the land betters yet, and is well grassed, and in divers nooks and crannies groweth small wood of birch and whiles of quicken tree; but ever the best of the grass waxeth nigh unto the lips of the Sundering Flood, where it rises a little from the Dale to the water; and what little acre-land there is, and it is but little, is up on knolls that lie nearer to the bent, and be turned somewhat southward; or on the east side of the flood (which runneth here nigh due north to south), on the bent-side itself, where, as it windeth and turneth, certain slopes lie turned to south-west. And in these places be a few garths, fenced against the deer, wherein grow rye, and some little barley whereof to make malt for beer and ale, whereas the folk of this high-up windy valley may have no comfort of wine. And it is to be said that ever is the land better and the getting more on the east side of the Sundering Flood than on the west.

As to the folk of this land, they are but few even now, and belike were fewer yet in the time of my tale. There was no great man amongst them, neither King, nor Earl, nor Alderman, and it had been hard living for a strong-thief in the Dale. Yet folk there were both on the east side and the west of the flood. On neither side were they utterly cut off from the world outside the Dale; for though it were toilsome it was not perilous to climb the bents and so wend over the necks east and west, where some forty miles from the west bank and fifty from the east you might come down into a valley fairly well peopled, wherein were two or three cheaping-towns: and to these towns the dalesmen had some resort, that they might sell such of their wool as they needed not to weave for themselves, and other small chaffer, so that they might buy wrought wares such as cutlery and pots, and above all boards and timber, whereof they had nought at home.

But this you must wot and understand, that howsoever the Sundering Flood might be misnamed down below, up in the Dale and down away to the southern mountains it was such that better named it might not be, and that nought might cross its waters undrowned save the fowl flying. Nay and if one went up-stream to where it welled forth from the great mountains, he were no nearer to passing from one side to the other, for there would be nought before him but a wall of sheer rock, and above that rent and tumbled crags, the safe strong-houses of erne and osprey and gerfalcon. Wherefore all the dealings which the folk on the east Dale and the west might have with each other was but shouting and crying across the swirling and gurgling eddies of the black water, which themselves the while seemed to be talking together in some dread and unknown tongue.

True it is that on certain feast days, and above all on Midsummer night, the folk would pluck up a heart, and gather together as gaily clad as might be where the flood was the narrowest, save at one place, whereof more hereafter, and there on each side would trundle the fire-wheel, and do other Midsummer games, and make music of string-play and horns, and sing songs of old time and drink to each other, and depart at last to their own homes blessing each other. But never might any man on the east touch the hand of any on the west, save it were that by some strange wandering from the cheaping-towns aforesaid they might meet at last, far and far off from the Dale of the Sundering Flood.

Chapter II. Of Wethermel and the Child Osberne

Draw we nigher now to the heart of our tale, and tell how on the east side of the Sundering Flood was erewhile a stead hight Wethermel: a stead more lonely than most even in that Dale, the last house but one, and that was but a cot, toward the mountains at the head of the Dale. It was not ill set down, for its houses stood beneath a low spreading knoll, the broader side whereof was turned to the south-west, and where by consequence was good increase of corn year by year. The said knoll of Wethermel was amidst of the plain of the Dale a mile from the water-side, and all round about it the pasture was good for kine and horses and sheep all to the water's lip on the west and half way up the bent on the east; while towards the crown of the bent was a wood of bushes good for firewood and charcoal, and even beyond the crown of the bent was good sheep-land a long way.

Nevertheless, though its land was fruitful as for that country, yet had Wethermel no great name for luck, and folk who had the choice would liever dwell otherwise, so that it was hard for the goodman to get men to work there for hire. Many folk deemed that this ill-luck came because the knoll had been of old time a dwelling of the Dwarfs or the Land-wights, and that they grudged it that the children of Adam had supplanted them, and that corn grew on the very roof of their ancient house. But however that might be, there was little thriving there for the most part: and at least it was noted by some, that if there were any good hap it ever missed one generation, and went not from father to son, but from grandsire to grandson: and even so it was now at the beginning of this tale.

For he who had been master of Wethermel had died a young man, and his wife followed him in a month or two, and there was left in the house but the father and mother of these twain, hale and stout folk, he of fifty winters, she of forty-five; an old woman of seventy, a kinswoman of the house who had fostered the late goodman; and a little lad who had to name Osberne, now twelve winters old, a child strong and bold, tall, bright and beauteous. These four were all the folk of Wethermel, save now and then a hired man who was hard-pressed for livelihood would be got to abide there some six months or so.

It must be told further that there was no house within ten miles either up or down the water on that side, save the little cot abovesaid nigher to the mountains, and that was four miles up-stream; it hight Burcot, and was somewhat kenspeckle. Withal as to those Cloven Motes, as they were called, which were between the folk on either side, they were holden at a stead seven miles below Wethermel. So that in all wise was it a lonely and scantly-manned abode: and because of this every man on the stead must work somewhat hard and long day by day, and even Osberne the little lad must do his share; and up to this time we tell of, his work was chiefly about the houses, or else it was on the knoll, or round about it, scaring fowl from the corn; weeding the acre-ground, or tending the old horses that fed near the garth; or goose-herding at whiles. Forsooth, the two elders, who loved and treasured the little carle exceedingly, were loth to trust him far out of sight because of his bold heart and wilful spirit; and there were perils in the Dale, and in special at that rough and wild end of thereof, though they came not from weaponed reivers for the more part, though now and again some desperate outcast from the thicker peopled lands had strayed into it; and there was talk from time to time of outlaws who lay out over the mountain-necks, and might not always do to lack a sheep or a neat or a horse. Other perils more of every-day there were for a young child, as the deep and hurrying stream of the Sundering Flood, and the wolves which haunted the bent and the foothills of the mountains; and ever moreover there was the peril from creatures seldom seen, Dwarfs and Land-wights to wit, who, as all tales told, might be well pleased to have away into their realm so fair a child of the sons of Adam as was this Osberne.

Forsooth for the most part the lad kept within bounds, for love's sake rather than fear, though he wotted well that beating abode bound-breaking; but ye may well wot that this quietness might not always be. And one while amongst others he was missing for long, and when his grandsire sought him he found him at last half way between grass and water above the fierce swirling stream of the river; for he had clomb down the sheer rock of the bank, which all along the water is fashioned into staves, as it were organ-pipes, but here and there broken by I wot not what mighty power. There then was my lad in an ingle-nook of the rock, and not able either to go down or come up, till the goodman let a rope down to him and hauled him on to the grass.

Belike he was a little cowed by the peril, and the beating he got for putting his folk in such fear; but though he was somewhat moved by his grandame's tears and lamentations over him, and no less by the old carline's bewailing for his days that he would so surely shorten, yet this was not by a many the last time he strayed from the stead away into peril. On a time he was missing again night-long, but in the morning came into the house blithe and merry, but exceeding hungry, and when the goodman asked him where he had been and bade him whipping-cheer, he said that he cared little if beaten he were, so merry a time he had had; for he had gone a long way up the Dale, and about twilight (this was in mid-May) had fallen in with a merry lad somewhat bigger than himself, who had shown him many merry plays, and at last had brought him to his house, 'which is not builded of stone and turf, like to ours', saith he, 'but is in a hole in the rock; and there we wore away the night, and there was no one there but we two, and again he showed me more strange plays, which were wondrous; but some did frighten me.'

Then his grandsire asked him what like those plays were. Said Osberne: 'He took a stone and stroked it, and mumbled, and it turned into a mouse, and played with us nought afraid a while; but presently it grew much bigger, till it was bigger than a hare; and great game meseemed that was, till on a sudden it stood on its hind-legs, and lo it was become a little child, and O, but so much littler than I; and then it ran away from us into the dark, squealing the while like a mouse behind the panel, only louder. Well, thereafter, my playmate took a big knife, and said: "Now, drudgling, I shall show thee a good game indeed." And so he did, for he set the edge of the said knife against his neck, and off came his head; but there came no blood, nor did he tumble down, but took up his head and stuck it on again, and then he stood crowing like our big red cock. Then he said: "Poultry, Cockerel, now will I do the like by thee." And he came to me with the knife; but I was afraid, and gat hold of his hand and had the knife from him; and then I wrestled with him and gave him a fall; but I must needs let him get up again presently, whereas he grew stronger under my hand; then he thrust me from him and laughed exceeding much, and said: "Here is a champion come into my house forsooth! Well, I will leave thine head on thy shoulders, for belike I might not be able to stick it on again, which were a pity of thee, for a champion shalt thou verily be in the days to come." After this all his play with me was to sit down and bid me hearken; and then he took out a little pipe, and put it to his mouth, and made music out of it, which was both sweet and merry. And then he left that, and fell to telling me tales about the woods where big trees grow, and how his kindred had used to dwell therein, and fashioned most fair things in smith's work of gold and silver and iron; and all this liked me well, and he said: "I tell thee that one day thou shalt have a sword of my father's father's fashioning, and that will be an old one, for they both were long-lived." And as he spake I deemed that he was not like a child any more, but a little, little old man, white-haired and wrinkle-faced, but without a beard, and his hair shone like glass. And then, then I went to sleep, and when I woke up again it was morning, and I looked around and there was no one with me. So I arose and came home to you, and I am safe and sound if thou beat me not, kinsman.'

Now ye may judge if his fore-elders were not scared by the lad's tale, for they knew that he had fallen in with one of the Dwarf-kin, and his grandame caught him up and hugged him and kissed him well favouredly; and the carline, whose name was Bridget, followed on the like road; and then she said:

'See you, kinsmen, if it be not my doing that the blessed bairn has come back to us. Tell us, sweetheart, what thou hast round thy neck under thy shirt.' Osberne laughed. Said he: 'Thou didst hang on me a morsel of parchment with signs drawn thereon, and it is done in a silk bag. Fear not, foster-mother, but that I will wear it yet, since thou makest such to-do over it.'

'Ah! the kind lad thou art, my dear,' said the carline. 'I will tell you, kinsmen, that I had that said parchment from our priest, and it is strong neckguard against all evil things, for on it is scored the Holy Rood, and thereon are the names of the three Holy Kings, and other writing withal which I may not read, for it is in clerks' Latin.' And again the two women made much of the little lad, while the goodman stood by grumbling and grunting; but this time did Osberne escape his beating, though he was promised a drubbing which should give him much to think on if he went that way again; and the women prayed and besought him to be obedient to the goodman herein.

But one thing he had not told his kinsfolk, to wit, that the Dwarf had given him for a gift that same knife wherewith he had played the game of heads-off, and a fair sheath thereto, and he had done him to wit that most like luck would go with it. Wherefore little Osberne had the said knife hidden under his raiment, along with the parchment whereon was scored the Holy Rood and the good words of wisdom written.

[...]

Chapter VII. Of a Newcomer, and his Gift to Osberne

Now when spring came again, needs must Osberne drive the sheep up to the bents, though he had liefer haunted the riverside, for sore he desired to cross the flood and find out tidings there. And though he were a child, yet he would by his own choice have fared to seek out the pretty maiden whose hand he had held on the edge of the river that even, but livelihood drave him to look to the sheep now that the spring grass was growing.

So on a certain day when March was wearing towards April he drave his sheep up over the crown of the bent; and there he went with them a way where, the land still rising, the ground was hard and rocky but clean, and the grass sweet for as scanty as it was, growing in little hollows and shelters round about the rocks. Wherefore the sheep were nimble in their feeding, and led him on long, till they and he were come into a grassy little dale with a stream running through it. There they were neither to hold nor to bind, but strayed all up and down the dale and over the crest of the bent thereof, and would not come to his call; and his dog was young and not very wise, and could do little to help him. So he began to think he had best gather what of the sheep he could, and drive them home and fold them, and then come back and hunt for the rest, perhaps with the help of his grandsire; but as the ones he could get at were all close anigh, and he was hot and weary with running hither and thither and holloaing to sheep and dog, he would go down to the stream and drink and rest awhile first. And even so he did, and lay down by the water and drank a long draught; but while he was about it he thought he heard footsteps coming down the hill-side over the greensward.

Howsoever, he had his drink out, and then rose to his knees and looked up, and therewith sprang hastily to his feet, for a tall man was coming on toward him not ten yards from the stream, on the further side of it. He was not, so to say, afeard by the sight, yet somewhat startled, for the man was not his grandsire, nor forsooth did he seem to be one of the Dale-dwellers. For he was so clad that he had a grey hauberk on him of fine ringmail, and a scarlet coat thereunder embroidered goodly; a big gold ring was on his left arm, a bright basnet on his head; he was girt with a sword, and bare a bow in his hand, and a quiver hung at his back. He was a goodly man, young by seeming, bright-faced and grey-eyed; his hair was yellow and as fine as silk, and it hung down over his shoulders.

Now Osberne put as good a face on the meeting as he might, and gave the newcomer the sele of the day, and he hailed him again in a clear loud voice, and they stood looking on each other across the stream a while. Then the newcomer laughed pleasantly and said: 'Hast thou any name that I may call thee by?'

'I am Osberne of Wethermel,' said the youngling. 'Aha,' said the man, 'art thou he that slew the leash of great grey wolves last autumn, who had put two armed men to flight the day before?' Said Osberne, reddening: 'Well, what was I to do? There fell a leash of hill-dogs on our sheep, and I made them forbear. Was it a scathe to thee, lord?' The newcomer laughed again: 'Nay, my lad,' said he, 'I love them no more than ye do; they were no dogs of mine. But what doest thou here?'

'Thou seest,' said the youngling, 'that I am shepherding our sheep; and a many have run from me, and I cannot bring them back to me. So I was going home with those that be left.'

'Well,' says the man, 'we can soon mend that. Rest thou here and abide my coming back again, and I will fetch them for thee.'

'With a good will,' says Osberne, 'and I shall can thee many thanks therefor.'

So the man strode on and through the stream, and went his ways up the further bent, and Osberne sat down on a stone and abode him in no little wonder. The man was gone somewhat more than an hour, and then Osberne sees the sheep topping the crest of the bent and pouring down into the dale, and the newcomer came next driving them down; and when they came to the stream they stood there and moved no more than if they were penned.

Then the newcomer came through them up to Osberne, and said in a kind voice, though it was loud: 'What, art thou here yet? I deemed that thou wouldst have run home.'

'Why should I have run?' said the lad. 'For fear of me,' said the other. Said Osberne: 'I was somewhat afeard when I first saw thee, and thou with the grey byrny and the gleaming helm; but then I saw that thou wert no ill man, and I feared thee no longer. Withal I was fain to see thee again; for thou art goodly and fair to behold, and I am fain to remember thee.'

Said the man: 'Even so have others said ere now.' 'Were they women?' said Osberne. 'Thou art brisk and keen, youngling,' said the man. 'Yes, they were women: but it was long ago.' 'Yet thou lookest no old man,' said Osberne. 'I have seen old men: they be nought like to thee.'

'Heed thou not that,' said the helmed man; 'but tell me, how old a man art thou?' Said Osberne: 'When this April is three days old I shall be thirteen years old.'

Said the man of the waste: 'Well, thou art stalwart for thy years, and that liketh me well, and meseems that we shall be friends hereafter: and when thou art a grown man I shall seem no older to thee; nay, we shall be as brothers. Belike I shall see thee again before long; meanwhile, I give thee this rede: when thou mayest, seek thou to the side of the Sundering Flood, for meseemeth that there lieth thy weird. Now there is this last word to be said, that I came hither today to see thee, and in token thereof I have brought thee a gift. Canst thou shoot in the bow aught?' Said Osberne: 'There is one at home, and my grandsire hath bent it for me at whiles, and taught me how to shoot somewhat; but I am little deft therein.'

Then the man betook him the bow which he had in his hand and said: 'Here is one that shall make thee deft; for whoso hath this as a gift from me shall hit what he shooteth at if he use my shafts withal, and here be three which I will give thee; and if thou take heed, thou shalt not find them easy to lose, since ever they shall go home. But if ever thou lose two of them, then take the third and go into some waste place where there is neither meadow nor acre, and turn to the north-east and shoot upward toward the heavens, and say this rhyme:

> A shaft to the north,
> Come, ye three, come ye forth;
> A shaft to the east,
> Come three at the least;
> A shaft to the sky,
> Come swift, come anigh!
> Come one one and one,
> And the tale is all done.

5

And then shalt thou find the arrows lying at thy feet. Now take the bow and arrows, and drive we thy sheep betwixt us to the top of the bent that looks down on Wethermel.'

Then Osberne took the bow and shafts, and he all quivering with joy and delight; and then the two of them together went back across the waste with the sheep before them, and as they went side by side the man said many things, and this at last: 'Now that I know thy name, it is like that thou wouldst know mine and who I am; but my very name I may not tell thee, for thy tongue has no word for it, but now and when we meet again thou mayst call me Steelhead: and thou shalt know that when next we meet I shall be arrayed all otherwise than now. In that array I deem thou wilt know me, but look to it that thou show no sign thereof before other men; and as to the bow, thou wilt not be eager belike to say of whom thou hadst it. Lo now! we have opened up Wethermel; fare thou well, bold bairn, and forget not my redes.'

And therewith he turned about and gat him gone into the waste again, striding hugely; and the lad was sorry to lack him, for he deemed him the goodliest and best man that he had ever met.

Chapter VIII. The Goodman Gets a New Hired Man

Now when he came home to Wethermel he found tidings there, for the goodman had gotten a new hired man, and he showed him to Osberne, who greeted him well: he was a tall man, mild of aspect and speech, flaxen-haired and blue-eyed, and seemed a stark carle. He had come to the stead that morning while the goodman was away, and had craved guesting of the women, who made him welcome and set him down to meat. He told them that his name was Stephen, that he had been born in the country-side, but had gone thence in his early youth to East Cheaping, which was the market town whither that folk had resort; and that he had grown up there and there wedded a wife; but that when she died in childing with her first bairn, and the bairn had not lived, he loathed the place, and came back again into the Dale.

So when the goodman came home this Stephen offered himself to him, and said that he deemed he could do as good a stroke of work as another, and that he was not for any great wage, but he must not be stinted of his meat, whereas he was a heavy feeder. The goodman liked the looks of him, and they struck the bargain betwixt them straightway, and Stephen had hansel of a second dinner, and ate well thereat; and henceforth is he called Stephen the Eater.

Now when the goodman saw Osberne bring in his new weapon, he asked him whence he had it, and the lad told him that he had been far in the waste, and had found it there. The goodman eyed him, but said nought. Forsooth, he misdoubted him that the bow was somewhat unked, and that the lad had had some new dealings with the Dwarf-kin or other strange wights. But then he bethought him of Osberne's luck, and withal it came to his mind that now he had gotten this victual-waster, it would not be ill if his lad should shoot them some venison or fowl now and again; and by the look of the bow he deemed it like to be a lucky one. But Stephen reached out for the bow, and handled it and turned it about, and spake: 'This is a handy weapon, and they who made it were not without craft, and it pleases me to see it; for now, when it brings home prey in the evening, the goodman will deem my maw the less burdensome to him. By my rede, goodman, ye will do well to make thy youngling the hunter to us all, for such bows as this may be shot in only by them that be fated thereto.' And he nodded and smiled on Osberne, and the lad deemed that the new man would be friendly to him. So then was supper brought in, and Stephen the Eater played as good a part as if he had eaten nought since sunrise.

But the next day, when Stephen was bound for driving the sheep to the bent, he said to Osberne: 'Come thou with me, young master, to show me the way; and bring thy bow and arrows withal, and see if thou canst shoot us something toothsome, for both of feathers and fur there is foison on the hill-side.' So they went together, and betwixt whiles of the shepherding Osberne shot a whole string of heathfowl and whimbrel; and ever he hit that which he shot at, so that the arrows were indeed easy to find, since they never failed to be in the quarry.

The goodman was well pleased with his catch, and Stephen licked his lips over the look of the larder. And the next day the lad let Stephen go alone to the hill, and he himself took a horse and went up the water a ten mile toward the mountain, and there he slew a hart of ten tines with one arrow, and brought the quarry home across the horse, to the joy of all the household, and the goodman was not rueing his bargain with Stephen the Eater. So it went on that every two or three days Osberne fared afield after catch, and but seldom came home empty-handed, and the other days he did as he would and went where he listed. And now he began to follow the rede of Steelhead, and went oftenest by the side of the Sundering Flood, but as yet he had gone up the water and not down.

Chapter IX. The Bight of the Cloven Knoll

And now it was mid-April, and the goodman dight him to ride to a mote of the neighbours at a stead hight Bull-meads, where the Dalesmen were wont to gather in the spring, that they might ride thence all together to the town of East Cheaping and sell the autumn clip of wool and do other chaffer. So the carle goes his ways alone, and will be one night at Bull-meads and two at East Cheaping, and then another at Bull-meads, and be back on the fifth day. And when he was gone, comes Stephen to Osberne, and says: 'Young master, I am going presently to the hill with the sheep, and thou needest neither to go with me nor fare a-hunting today, since the house is full of meat; so thou art free, and were I in thy shoes I would go straight from this door down to the water-side, and see if thou mayst not happen on something fair or seldom seen. [And it were not amiss to do on thy coat of scarlet.] But hearken to my rede, if thou comest on aught such, thou hast no need to tell of it to any one, not even to me.

Osberne thanks him, and takes his bow and arrows and goes his way and comes to the riverside and turns his face south, and goes slowly along the very edge of the water; and the water itself drew his eyes down to gaze on the dark green deeps and fierce downlong swirl of the stream, with its sharp clean lines as if they were carven in steel, and the curling and upheaval and sudden changing of the talking eddies: so that he scarce might see the familiar greensward of the further shore.

At last, when he had gone thus more than two miles from where he first hit the water, a long straight reach lay before him, and as he looked down it, it seemed as if the river came presently to an end; but in sooth there was a sharp turn to the east by which the water ran, but narrowing much; and this narrowing was made by the thrusting forth of the western bank into a sharp ness, which, from where Osberne now stood, showed a wide flank facing, as it seemed, the whole hurrying stream of the flood; but the stream turned ere it smote the cliff, and striving for the narrow outgate made a prodigious eddy or whirlpool ere it might clear itself of the under-water foot of the ness and make eastward so as to rush on toward the sea. But in the face of the wall, in the bight where the whirlpool turned from it, was a cave the height of a tall man, and some four feet athwart; and below it a ledge, thrust out from the sheer rock and hanging over the terrible water, and it was but a yard wide or so. It was but ten feet above the water, and from it to the grass above must have been a matter of forty feet. But the ness as it thrust forth into the river rose also, so that its crest was a score of feet higher where it went down into the water than its base amidst the green grass. Then came the strait passage of the water, some thirty feet across, and then the bank of the eastern side, which, though it thrust not out, but rather was as it were driven back by the stream, yet it rose toward the water, though not so much as the ness over against it. It was as if some-one had cast down a knoll across the Sundering Flood, and the stream had washed away the sloped side thereof, and then had sheared its way through by the east side where the ground was the softest. Forsooth so it seemed to the Dalesmen, for on either side they called it the Bight of the Cloven Knoll.

Osberne stood amazed right over against the cave in the cliff-side, and stared at the boiling waters beneath him, that seemed mighty enough to have made a hole in the ship of the world and sunk it in the deep. And he wondered at the cave, whether it were there by chance hap, or that some hands had wrought it for an habitation.

And as he stood gazing there, on a sudden there came out of the cave a shape as of man, and stood upon the ledge above the water, and the lad saw at once that it was a little maiden of about his own age, with ruddy golden hair streaming down from her head, and she was clad in a short coat of dark blue stuff and no more raiment, as far as he could see. Now as aforesaid, Osberne was in his holiday raiment of red scarlet by the bidding of Stephen. Now the maiden looks up and sees the lad standing on the eastern shore, and starts back astonished. Then she came forward again and looked under the sharp of her hand, for the sun shone from the south and was cast back dazzling from the water. There was but some thirty feet of water between them, but all gurgling and rushing and talking, so the child raised a shrill and clear voice as she clapped her hands together and cried: 'O thou beauteous creature, what art thou?' Osberne laughed, and said in a loud voice: 'I am a man, but young of years, so that they call me a boy, and a bairn, and a lad. But what art thou?'

'Nay, nay,' she said, 'I must be nigher to thee; it is over-wide here amidst the waters' speech. Fare up to the top on thy side, and so will I.' And therewith she turned about and fell to climbing up the side of the cliff by the broken black staves and the shaly slips. And though Osberne were a boy, yea and a tough one in some ways, he trembled and his heart beat quick to see the little creature wending that perilous upright road, and he might not take his eyes off her till she had landed safely on the greensward; then he turned and went swiftly up the eastern knoll, and reached the edge of the sheer rock just as the maiden came running up the ness on her side.

He spake not, for he was eyeing her closely, and she might not speak for a while for lack of breath. At last she said: 'Now are we as near to each other as we may be today; yea for many days, or it may be for all our lives long: so now let us talk.' She set her two feet together and held her hands in front of her, and so stood as if she looked for him to begin. But the words came not speedily to his mouth, and at last she said: 'I wonder why thou wilt not speak again; for thy laugh was as the voice of a dear bird; and thy voice is beauteous, so loud and clear.'

He laughed, and said: 'Well then, I will speak. Tell me what thou art. Art thou of the Faery? for thou art too well shapen to be of the Dwarf-kin.' She clapped her hands together and laughed; then she said: 'I laughed not as mocking thy question, but for joy to hear thy voice again. Nay, nay, I am no faery, but of the children of men. But thou, art thou not of the sons of the Land-wights?'

'No more than thou art,' said he. 'I am a goodman's son, but my father is dead, and my mother also, and I live at home at Wethermel up the water, with my grandsire and grandame.'

Said she: 'Are they kind to thee?' The lad drew himself up: 'I am kind to them,' said he. 'How goodly thou art!' she said; 'that was why I dreamed thou must be of the Land-wights, because I have seen divers men, some old, some young like to thee, but none half so goodly.' He smiled, and said: 'Well,

I thought thou wert of the Faery because thou art goodly and little. I have seen a pretty maid not long since, but she was older than thou, I deem, and far taller. But tell me, how old art thou?' She said: 'When May is half worn I shall be of thirteen winters.'

'Lo now,' said he, 'we be nigh of an age; I was thirteen in early April. But thou hast not told me where thou dwellest, and how.' She said: 'I dwell at Hartshaw Knolls hard by. I am the daughter of a goodman, as thou art, and my father and mother are dead, so that my father I never saw, and now I dwell with my two aunts, and they be both older than was my mother.'

'Are they kind to thee?' said the lad, laughing that he must cast back her question. 'Whiles,' said she, laughing also, 'and whiles not: maybe that is because I am not always kind to them, as thou art to thy folk.' He answered nought, and she was silent a while; then he said: 'What is in thy mind, maiden?' 'This,' she said, 'that I am thinking how fair a chance it was that I should have seen thee, for thou hast made me so glad.' Said he: 'We can see each other again belike and make it less of a chance.' 'O yea,' she said, and was silent a while. Said he: 'I wot not why it was that thou wert in the cave: and tell me, is it not exceeding perilous, the climbing up and down? why wilt thou do that? Also I must tell thee, that this was another cause why I thought thou wert of faery, that thou camest out of the cave.'

Said she: 'I will tell thee all about the cave; but first as to the peril of going thither and coming thence: wouldst thou be very sorry if I were lost on the way?' 'Yea,' said he, 'exceeding sorry.' 'Well,' said she, 'then fear it not, for it is so much a wont of mine that to me there is no peril therein: yet am I glad that thou wert afraid for me.' 'I was sore afraid,' said Osberne. 'Now as to the cave,' said the maiden. 'I found it out two years ago, when I was very little, and the women had been less than kind to me. And thither may I go whenas I would that they should seek me not; because folk say that it is a dwelling of the Dwarfs, and they fear to enter it. Besides, when I think of my kinswomen coming down the rock to find me therein, and they be tall, and one stiff, as if she were cut out of timber, and the other exceeding fat, that makes me merry!'

And therewith she sat down on the very edge of the cliff with her little legs hanging over the water, and laughed, rocking to and fro in her laughter, and Osberne laughed also. But he said: 'But art thou not afraid of the Dwarfs?' She said: 'Dear bairn, or boy, I had been there many times before I heard tell of the Dwarfs, and I gat no harm, and after I had heard the tale I went still, and still gat no harm; nay I will tell thee somewhat: I gat gifts, or such they seemed unto me. First I had to herd the sheep and take them to the best grass, and whiles they strayed and were wearisome to me, and I came home with divers missing, and then would I be wyted or even whipped for what was no fault of mine. And one such time, I betook me to the cave and sat therein and wept, and complained to myself of my harm, and when I went out of the cave I saw on the ledge close to my foot a thing lying, and I took it up, and saw that it was a pipe with seven holes therein, and when I blew into it it made sweet and merry little music. So I thought it great prize, and went away home with it with all my sorrows well healed. But the next day I drave my sheep to grass, as my business was, and, as oft happened, they strayed, and I followed them and gat nothing done; so I was weary, and afraid of what would betide at home in the stead. So I sat down on a stone, and when I had wept a little I thought I would comfort myself with the music of the pipe. But lo, a wonder! For no sooner had a note or two sounded than all the sheep came running up to me, bleating and mowing, and would rub against my sides as I sat piping, and home I brought every head in all glee. And even so has it befallen ever since; and that was hard on a year agone. Fair boy, what dost thou think I am doing now?' Osberne laughed. 'Disporting thee in speech with a friend,' said he. 'Nay,' said she, 'but I am shepherding sheep.'

And she drew forth the pipe from her bosom and fell to playing it, and a ravishing sweet melody came thence, and so merry that the lad himself began to shift his feet as one moving to measure, and straightway he heard a sound of bleating, and sheep came running toward the maiden from all about. Then she arose and ran to them, lest they should shove each other into the water; and she danced before them, lifting up her scanty blue skirts and twinkling her bare feet and legs, while her hair danced about her, and the sheep, they too capered and danced about as if she had bidden them. And the boy looked on and laughed without stint, and he deemed it the best of games to behold. But when she was weary she came back to the head of the ness and sat down again as before, and let the sheep go where they would.

NOTE BY WILLIAM MORRIS ON HIS AIMS IN FOUNDING THE KELMSCOTT PRESS

I began printing books with the hope of producing some which would have a definite claim to beauty, while at the same time they should be easy to read and should not dazzle the eye, or trouble the intellect of the reader by eccentricity of form in the letters.

I have always been a great admirer of the calligraphy of the Middle Ages and of the earlier printing which took its place. As to the fifteenth century books I had noticed that they were always beautiful by force of the mere typography, even without the added ornament, with which many of them are so lavishly supplied. And it was the essence of my undertaking to produce books which it would be a pleasure to look upon as pieces of printing and arrangement of type.

Looking at my adventure from this point of view then, I found I had to consider chiefly the following things: the paper, the form of the type, the relative spacing of the letters, the words, and the lines; and lastly the position of the printed matter on the page.

It was a matter of course that I should consider it necessary that the paper should be hand-made, both for the sake of durability and appearance. It would be a very false economy to stint in the quality of the paper for the sake of the price: so I had only to think about the kind of hand-made paper. On this head I came to two conclusions: 1st, that the paper must be wholly of linen (most hand-made papers are of cotton today), and must be quite 'hard', ie thoroughly well sized,— and 2nd that, though it must be 'laid' and not 'wove' (ie made on a mould made of obvious wires), the lines caused by the wires of the mould must not be too strong, so as to give a ribbed appearance. I found that on these points I was at one with the practice of the papermakers of the fifteenth century; so I took as my model a Bolognese paper of about 1473. My friend Mr Batchelor of Little Chart, Kent, carried out my views very satisfactorily, and produced from the first the excellent paper which I still use.

Next as to type: by instinct rather than by conscious thinking it over, I began by getting myself a fount of Roman type. And here what I wanted was letter pure in form; severe, without needless excrescences; solid, without the thickening and thinning of the line, which is the essential fault of the ordinary modern type, and which makes it difficult to read; and not compressed laterally, as all later type has grown to be, owing to commercial exigencies.

There was only one source from which to take examples of this perfected Roman type, to wit, the works of the great Venetian printers of the fifteenth century, of whom Nicholas Jenson produced the completest and most Roman characters from 1470 to 1476.

This type I studied with much care, getting it photographed to a big scale, and drawing it over many times before I began designing my own letter: so that though I think I mastered the essence of it, I did not copy it servilely. In fact, my Roman type, especially in the lower case, tends rather more to the Gothic than does Jenson's.

After a while I felt that I must have a Gothic as well as a Roman fount; and herein the task I set myself was to redeem the Gothic character from the charge of unreadableness which is commonly brought against it. And I felt that this charge could not be reasonably brought against the types of the first two decades of printing; that Shoeffer at Mainz, Mentelin at Strasburg, and Gunther Zainer at Augsburg avoided the spiky ends and undue compression which lay some of the later type open to the above charge. Only the earlier printers (naturally following therein the practice of their predecessors the Scribes) were very liberal of contractions, and used an excess of 'tied' letters, which, by the way, are very useful to the compositor. So I entirely eschewed contractions, except for the '&' and had very few 'tied' letters, in fact none but the absolutely necessary ones. Keeping my end steadily in view, I designed a black-letter type which I think I may claim to be as readable as a Roman one, and to say the truth, I prefer it to the Roman.

This type is of the size we call 'Great primer' over here (the Roman type is of 'English' size); but later on I was driven by the necessities of the 'Chaucer' (a double-columned book) to get a small Gothic type of 'pica' size.

The punches for all these types were cut for me with great intelligence and skill, and render my designs most satisfactorily.

Now as to the spacing: 1st, the 'face' of the letter should be as nearly coterminous with the 'body' as possible, so as to avoid undue whites between the letters; 2nd, the lateral spaces between the words should be (a) no more than is necessary to distinguish clearly the division into words, and (b) should be as nearly equal as possible. Modern printers, even the best, pay very little heed to these two essentials of seemly composition, and the inferior ones run riot in licentious spacing, thereby producing, *inter alia*, those ugly rivers of lines running about the page which are such a blemish to decent printing; 3rd, the whites between the lines should not be excessive: the modern practice of 'leading' should be used as little as possible, and never without some definite reason, such as marking some special piece of printing. The only leading I have allowed myself is a hair lead between the lines of my Gothic pica type; and not even this in the smaller paged books.

Lastly, but by no means least, comes the position of the printed matter on the page. This should always leave the inner margin the narrowest, the top

KELMSCOTT PRESS, UPPER
MALL, HAMMERSMITH.

February 16th, 1897.

Note. This is the Golden type.
This is the Troy type.
This is the Chaucer type.

Secretary:
S. C. Cockerell, Kelmscott Press, Upper Mall,
Hammersmith, London, W., to whom all
letters should be addressed.

FIGURE 12. Cover of an advertising circular list of books produced by the
Kelmscott Press, showing the three fonts Morris designed for the Press. Alamy.

somewhat wider, the outside (fore edge) wider still, and the bottom widest of
all. This rule is never departed from in mediæval books, written or printed;
modern printers systematically transgress against it, thus apparently
contradicting the fact that the unit of a book is not *one* page but a *pair* of
pages. A friend, the librarian of one of our most important private libraries,
tells me that after careful testing he has come to the conclusion that the
mediæval rule was to make a difference of 20 per cent from margin to margin.

Now these matters of spacing and position are of the greatest importance
in the production of beautiful books; if they are properly considered they will

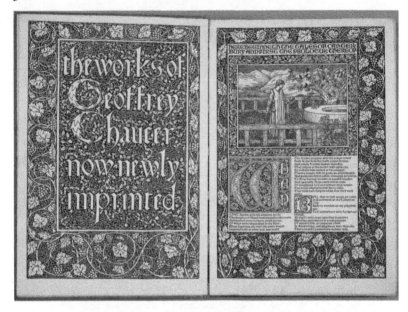

FIGURE 13. Opening spread from the Kelmscott Chaucer, 1896, set in the Chaucer typeface. William Morris Society.

make a book printed in quite ordinary type at least decent and pleasant to the eye. The disregard of them will spoil the effect of the best designed type.

It was only natural that I, a decorator by profession, should attempt to ornament my books suitably: about this matter, I will only say that I have always tried to keep in mind the necessity for making my decoration a part of the page of type. I may add that in designing the magnificent and inimitable woodcuts which have adorned several of my books, and will above all adorn the Chaucer which is now drawing near completion, my friend Sir Edward Burne-Jones has never lost sight of this important point, so that his work will not only give us a series of most beautiful and imaginative pictures, but will form the most harmonious decoration possible to the printed book.

NOTES

LETTERS TO CORMELL (CROM) PRICE, 1855

LETTER TO CORMELL PRICE, 3 APRIL 1855

Text from Mackail, I, 53–6. Price was a lifelong friend of Morris's whom he first met at Oxford, and who later became headteacher of the United Services College, a boarding school which Rudyard Kipling attended as a boy. Shortly after writing this letter, Morris abandoned his plans to go into the Church of England and decided to become an architect instead.

p. 3 *Ted*: Edward Burne-Jones, whom Morris met in his early days at Oxford and with whom he remained friends for the rest of this life.

exceedingly seedy: a further letter to Price about the poem goes on: 'It is very foolish, but I have a tenderness for that thing, I was so happy writing it, which I did on Good Friday...For those bad rhymes, I don't like them, though perhaps I don't feel them hurt me so much as they seem to do you.' Mackail, I, 57.

l. 6 *Gethsemane*: the garden where Jesus and some of his disciples gathered before he was betrayed to his death by Judas.

l. 45 *Woful*: archaic spelling of woeful.

p. 5 *don't spare me*: although Morris burned all of the early poems not included in his first collection, *The Defence of Guenvere, and Other Poems* (London, 1858), some copies, including this one, were kept by friends and relations. A few other early poems were published by May Morris in *CW*, XXI, xxx–xxxi, and in *AWS*, I, 517–32.

a-brassing: brass rubbing, rubbing with an ink pad onto paper over the effigies cut into brass in churches to make copies of them.

LETTER TO CORMELL PRICE, 10 AUGUST 1855

Text from Mackail, I, 73–8. Morris, Burne-Jones, and another Oxford friend, William Fulford, set off on a tour of northern France on 19 July 1855. Price had been due to join them but had to pull out at the last minute.

p. 6 *flamboyant*: a particularly ornate form of late Gothic architecture developed particularly in France and Spain between 1375 and 1500.

Deo gratias: (Latin) thank God. Morris's objection to the restoration of old buildings was a lifelong passion and resulted in 1877 in the formation of the Society for the Protection of Ancient Buildings, or SPAB, known by Morris and his circle as Anti-Scrape. The 1877 'Manifesto of the SPAB' describes restoration as 'a strange and most fatal idea, which by its very name implies that it is possible to strip from a building this, that and the other part of its history—of its life that is,...and leave it still historical, living, and even as it once was' (*AWS*, I, 111).

p. 7 *Chartres...Invalides*: John Ruskin, whose work Morris had discovered and read aloud to his friends at Oxford, describes Chartres as a key example of 'Northern

Gothic' and Rouen, 'with the associated Norman cities, Caen, Bayeux, and Coutances', as representing 'the entire range of Northern architecture from the Romanesque to Flamboyant'. Ruskin, Preface to the First Edition (1849), *The Seven Lamps of Architecture*, in *Works*, VIII, 12; 6.

p. 7 *Versailles*: Baroque royal palace just outside Paris.

the Dome of the Invalides: Baroque chapel built in the 1670s on the same complex as a hospital for injured soldiers (*les invalides*).

p. 8 *Newcomes…book*: William Thackeray, *The Newcomes*, published in 1855 by the German publisher Tauchnitz, who produced English texts for distribution beyond Britain. Later, reading Thackeray's *Esmond* in 1869, Morris writes to Philip Webb: 'Thackeray's *style* I think so precious bad' (*CL*, I, 85).

FROM *THE OXFORD AND CAMBRIDGE MAGAZINE*

THE HOLLOW LAND: A TALE

First published in the September and October numbers of the *Oxford and Cambridge Magazine*, 1856, 565–77 and 632–41. The magazine was conceived, written and edited by Morris and his undergraduate friends. Twelve monthly numbers, priced at a shilling each, were published by Bell and Daldy before the magazine folded. Morris variously uses 'House of the Lilies' and 'house of the Lilies' in this first edition of the story. I have standardized throughout to House of the Lilies.

l. 4 *Recken…know*: Thomas Carlyle keeps the German word here, using the plural of *Recke*, seasoned hero or warrior.

Mote: might/may.

p. 10 *Nibelungen Lied…Miscellanies*: Carlyle, 'The Nibelungen Lied', in Carlyle, XXXVII: *Critical and Miscellaneous Essays*, 2, 216–73. It is a medieval Germanic epic of dynasty, love, betrayal, and revenge. In 1869 Morris began a translation of it. May Morris notes that after two hundred and sixteen stanzas he 'wisely turned to more sympathetic tasks' (*CW*, VII, xxxiii). In 1870 he and Icelandic scholar Eiríkr Magnússon translated the Icelandic version of the tale, the *Völsunga Saga*: 'older I suppose and, to my mind, without measure nobler and grander', wrote Morris (*CL*, I, 98).

lime: the common lime or linden, *tilia x europaea*, native to Europe.

p. 12 *albs*: long white robes worn by clergy.

l. 9 *Mariae Virginis*: (Latin, as used by the medieval church in Europe) the Virgin Mary.

l. 12 *planets seven*: in medieval thinking the seven planets were Saturn, Jupiter, Mars, Venus, Mercury, and the sun and moon.

p. 17 *I trow*: I believe.

from base to cope: from the lowest part of the castle to the highest. Cope here means the coping or capping of the walls, their very top.

p. 18 *helves*: handles.

the 'Kyrie': *Kyrie eleison* (Latin), meaning Lord have mercy. One of the regular prayers of both Roman Catholic and Protestant churches.

p. 19 *Exsurgat Deus*: (Latin) May God arise. Another common prayer in church liturgies, from Psalm 68:1; the line goes on *dissipentur inimici* 'may his enemies be scattered'.

the judgment of God: the medieval concept of trial by combat. Morris comes back repeatedly to this idea and uses it as the title of a poem in *The Defence* (1858).

p. 22 *mail-coif*: a close-fitting cap of chain mail usually worn under the helmet and sometimes covering the back and sides of the head.

p. 23 *undern*: archaism for the third hour of the day, 9 a.m.

p. 24 *'my heart...melting wax'*: from Psalm 22.14.

p. 25 *Fytte*: canto, chapter, or section.

p. 29 *leal*: loyal.

p. 34 *we painted...altered*: Mackail, I, 104, comments: 'that this is what actually happens from the yellowing of the crystalline lens of the eye in advanced life was only discovered by specialists many years later. How did Morris know, or divine it?'

p. 35 *Propter amnen Babylonis*: 'By the rivers of Babylon', from Psalm 137. This is an unusual form of the well-known Latin Psalm, and curious given Morris's familiarity with church psalmody. May Morris changes it to the more common '*Super flumina Babylonis*' (*CW*, I, 288).

THE STORY OF THE UNKNOWN CHURCH

First published in the *Oxford and Cambridge Magazine* in January 1856, pp. 28–33. The details of landscape and architecture draw closely on Morris's tour of the churches of northern France in the summer of 1855. See his August 1855 letter to Crom Price, 5–8. Like 'The Hollow Land', this tale was not published again in Morris's lifetime.

p. 38 May Morris breaks up Morris's paragraphs into more conventional lengths in *CW*, I, 254–90. It may be the exigencies of space in the magazine that resulted in this headlong format, but it seems aptly to suggest something of Morris's experimental interest in form and space. This number of the magazine, unlike subsequent ones, was edited by Morris himself.

pp. 38–9 *The Abbey where we built...windings*: Morris's letter of August 1855 (5–8 above) describes just such a scene of corn and flowers in the countryside around Dreux.

p. 40 *quatrefoils*: four-leaved shapes common in Gothic architecture.

p. 42 *holy wars*: the Crusades, a long-running series of military campaigns across the eleventh, twelfth, and thirteenth centuries, instigated by European nations in the cause of claiming the Holy Land for Christianity, wresting it from Muslim control.

FROM *THE DEFENCE OF GUENEVERE,*
AND OTHER POEMS

Morris's first collection of poems, published by Bell and Daldy in 1858. Text for all of the following poems is taken from this edition. Minor textual changes are indicated in the notes for each, including changes suggested in an errata slip included with the first edition. Obvious typos have been silently corrected.

THE DEFENCE OF GUENEVERE

First published in *The Defence*, 1–17. In 1855 Morris bought and delighted in a copy of Southey's 1817 edition of Malory's *Morte Darthur* (1485), which includes the tale of King Arthur's queen, Guenevere, her relationship with his knight, Sir Launcelot, and its consequences (*MA*, II, 20, 1–8). Morris's telling picks up Malory's coy assertion that 'the quene and Launcelot were to gyders. And whether they were a bedde or at other maner of disportes, me lyst not hereof make no mencyon, for love that time was not as is now a days (*MA*, II, 20, 3).

l. 1 *But...speak*: Guenevere is on trial for her relationship with Launcelot. The introduction to *CW*, I, xx–xxi includes an unpublished fragment which May Morris suggests was originally intended to begin the poem.

l. 8 *Gauwaine*: one of the knights of the Round Table, himself guilty of betraying a fellow-knight by wooing his lover for himself, in Malory's tale (*MA*, I, 4, 23). Morris focuses not on the accusations of Guenevere by her enemies, but on her refusal of Gauwaine's authority as judge.

l. 64 *King Ban of Benwick*: or Benoïc, father to Launcelot, brother to King Bors, both allies to Arthur.

l. 153 *your mother*: the adulterous Queen Morgause, who was murdered by one of her sons. In Malory (*MA*, II, 10, 14), it is Gaheris who murders her, but Morris, like the French Arthurian poet, Chretien de Troyes, makes a different son, Agravaine, the murderer.

l. 169 *la Fausse Garde*: the Castle of Falseness, from old French, adapting the name of Launcelot's castle, La Joyeuse Gard, or Joyous Gard as it is in *MA*, II, 10, 52.

l. 173 *Mellyagraunce*: knight who abducts Guenevere and some of her women. They are rescued by Launcelot, who makes peace with Mellyagraunce and spends the night with Guenevere. Blood from the hand he had injured breaking the bars of her room during the rescue ends up on her bedcovers. Mellyagraunce, seeing the blood, impugns her honour. Launcelot goes into combat with him in her defence and kills Mellyagraunce at her urging (*MA*, II, 19, 1–9).

l. 201 *I weet*: I know. 1858 has a full stop here.

l. 205 *the lists*: in medieval tournaments, the field or area in which the jousting takes place.

l. 211 *caitiff*: a vile wretch. The term carries a sense of scorn on the part of the speaker.

l. 220 *shent*: disgraced.

l. 225 *to grey*: 1858 has 'the grey'. An errata slip in the first edition notes this correction, but it is not made in subsequent editions.

GOLDEN WINGS

First published in *The Defence*, 202–14, although a short story of the same name was published in the *Oxford and Cambridge Magazine* in December 1856.

l. 2 *poplar*: quick-growing trees native to Europe and much of the northern hemisphere.

l. 23 *aspens*: *Populus tremula*, a species of poplar with particularly rustling leaves.

l. 32 *meat*: food.

l. 47 *Jehane du Castel beau*: Joan of the beautiful castle.

l. 51 *fille de fay*: here fay is a form of the French *foi or foy*, that is, faith or faithfulness, as her name also suggests.

l. 58 *Ladies' Gard*: the Ladies' Castle.

l. 74 *Undern*: see note to p. 23.

ll. 87–8 *Arthur...Avallon*: In *MA*, II, 21, 5, Arthur, wounded in battle, is carried off on a mysterious barge, saying 'I wyl into the vale of avylyon to hele me of my grevous wounde'. Tennyson's *Morte d'Arthur* in *Poems* II, 3–19, with which Morris was deeply familiar, borrows closely from Malory's telling. Morris spells Avallon variously with single or double l.

l. 99 *coverlit*: bedspread, from French.

l. 174 *pennon*: a long triangular or forked-tail flag, usually attached to knight's spear to identify him.

THE HAYSTACK IN THE FLOODS

First published in *The Defence*, 215–22. Set just outside the English-held territory of Gascony in south-western France during the Hundred Years War, a series of battles between the English and French fought between 1337 and 1453 over disputed rights to the French crown and French lands. The poem draws on Froissart's medieval French *Chronicles* (1369) for background and is set after the English victory at Poitiers in 1356. Morris read Froissart in translation as a young man and continued to do so all his life: May Morris records him frequently reading aloud from 'Lord Berners' Froissart' (*CW*, XXII, xxi). At his death he was working on an edition of the *Chronicles*.

l. 9 *kirtle*: the long skirt of her dress. It is hitched up to allow her to ride better.

ll. 34–5 *Judas*: the disciple who betrayed Jesus.

three / Red running lions: the arms of the English royalty from the time of Richard I onwards.

l. 42 *coif*: head covering, most likely here the part of the helmet that covers the skull.

l. 45 *Poictiers*: a city in Poictou (Poitou). The Battle of Poitiers, fought on 19 September 1356, ended in a significant victory for the English.

l. 47 *The Gascon frontier*: the border between French and English-held land. Gascony was held by England, so they are almost in safe territory.

l. 52 *the Chatelet*: the castle in Paris where cases of treason were tried.

ll. 57–8 *All this...at last*: Jehane suggests she would be tried for treason if she is returned to France, but would be damned by heaven for betraying Robert if she were to become Godmar's mistress as he wishes.

l. 61 *St George for Marny!*: he is asserting the right of England, represented by St. George, to French land. The cry identifies him as Robert Marny, or de Marny, a soldier from Essex who fought in the Battle of Poitiers on 19 September 1356.

l. 109 *gag me Robert*: in 1858, this reads, *gag me, Robert*; the change is noted in an errata slip but not made in later editions.

l. 153 *first fitte*: the first stanza, or section. See note to p. 26.

SIR PETER HARPDON'S END

First published in *The Defence*, pp. 69–109. Like 'The Haystack in the Floods' the poem is set in the Hundred Years War and draws on Froissart in its references to major French and English military leaders and events, though the story itself is Morris's. May Morris publishes an omitted scene in *CW*, I, xxvi–xxxi. St Denis is spelled St Dennis each time in *The Defence*, but changed in KP 1892, as it is here.

p. 67 *Poictou*: province of southwest France, in which the Battle of Poitiers took place in 1356. See note on l. 45, 'The Haystack in the Floods'.

Gascon...service: Sir Peter is on the English side in the war.

l. 30 *villaynes*: peasants.

l. 32 *Clisson or Sanxere*: Olivier de Clisson fought first on the English, then on the French side; Louis de Sancerre, a Marshal of France.

ll. 39–41 *Chandos...Charterhouse*: Sir John Chandos, an English knight killed at a skirmish at Lussac Bridge in 1370. *Pembroke*: the Earl of Pembroke, John Hastings, commander of the English fleet in the battle of La Rochelle; *Phelton*: William Felton, an English knight who fought at the Battle of Poitiers and was appointed to a court position as seneschal of Poitou; *Manny*: Walter Manny, an English knight who fought at Poitiers, founder of the Charterhouse monastery, friend and patron of Froissart.

l. 59 *Guesclin*: Sir Bertrand du Guesclin, much-admired French soldier and military leader; from 1370 until his death in 1380 he was constable of France.

l. 64 *petrariae*: devices to hurl stones, often against the walls of a besieged city.

l. 67 *glaives*: a generic term which covers a wide range of spears, swords (including a two-edged sword) or lances.

l. 114 *I am...blame*: a reference to Malory's tale of Balin le Savage, a knight who slays the holy King Pellam with a 'dolorous stroke' (*MA*, I, 2, 15) and in doing so lays waste to Pellam's castle and all the surrounding lands. He also later kills his brother Balan, unable to escape that fate revealed to him in a prophecy by Merlin (*MA*, I, 2, 18).

l. 119 *marish*: archaism for marsh.

l. 138 *gard*: in *The Defence*, this is *yard*. KP 1892 changes it to *gard*, as the 1858 errata note suggests.

l. 156 *Paul...blade*: most likely the apostle Paul, often depicted with a sword in his hand, as a reminder of his martyrdom by beheading.

l. 160 *archgays*: iron-tipped spears or lances, also known as lancegays.

l. 181 *two Edwards*: Edward III, king of England and his son, Edward the Black Prince, who fought in the victorious English army at Crécy and Poitiers.

l. 192 *siege of Troy*: from Homer's *Iliad*. May Morris notes that in 1857 or 1858 Morris began a long poem 'in blank verse with lyrics interspersed' (*CW*, II, xiv); it was entitled *Scenes from the Fall of Troy* and was not published until 1915, in *CW*, XXIV; he also translated in 1887 some 200 lines of the *Iliad*, as part of a projected but unfinished volume, following his 1887 translation of *The Odyssey*.

l. 208 *Hector*: great Trojan warrior, King Priam's son.

l. 307 *Job*: in the biblical book of this name, Job is tested by God to see if he remains righteous when he loses all his possessions, his family, and everything he holds dear.

l. 330 *harm*: *The Defence* has *harms*. The correction is noted in the 1858 errata slip.

l. 338 *for*: *The Defence* has *than*; KP 1892 and *CW* amend to *for*.

l. 381 *Laurence*: Friar Laurence in *Romeo and Juliet*.

l. 389 *the constable*: commander of the royal armies, responsible for overseeing the implementation of the law.

l. 394 *Rather…see*: by contrast with Jesus who spits on the eyes of a blind man to make him see, in Mark 8:23.

l. 421 *Considering…salt*: even at this early stage of his career Morris is alert to the economics of daily life.

l. 537 *Avalon*: land of dreams and perfection. See note on l. 88, 'Golden Wings'.

l. 582 *St. George Guienne*: Guienne was a province of France, so this pairing of St George with Guienne claims it decisively for England.

l. 583 *Jericho's of old*: in the Biblical book of Joshua, Joshua is instructed to walk seven times around the walls of Jericho, blowing a trumpet, and on the seventh time round, the walls will fall flat. Joshua 6:1–27.

ll. 595–6 *Using his left hand…now-a-days*: use of the left hand, or both hands, is a recurring sign of creativity and power for Morris.

l. 667 *apse*: an arched or domed recess in a building.

l. 668 *go:* in 1858, 'yo'. Corrected in the 1875 edition by Ellis and White.

ll. 711–12 *as wight… Wade*: wight means courageous, valiant in battle; see Malory, 'were thou as wyzte [wight] as ever was Wade or Launcelot' (*MA*, I, 7, 9).

l. 722 *whan*: an archaic form of when.

l. 741 *muckle of worth*: of great worth, using a variant of the Old English *mickle*.

l. 745 *fitte*: see note to p. 26.

CONCERNING GEFFRAY TESTE NOIRE

First published in *The Defence*, 135–47. Draws on Froissart, taking real but disparate events and figures—the siege of Ventadour; a castle in Auvergne, France, belonging to Geffray Teste Noire (i.e. Tête Noire, or Black Head); the people's uprising of 1358 known as the Jacquerie; and the figure of John of Chateauneuf (or Castel Neuf [New Castle])—and connecting them to shape the poem.

l. 1 *Canon of Chimay*: Froissart was Canon of Chimay in the Low Countries and is believed to have been buried there.

l. 3 *John of Castel Neuf*: a figure who appears in passing in Froissart I. 609.

l. 5 *Gascon*: belonging to the English-owned lands of Gascony.

l. 7 *Pilled*: pillaged.

were lief: owed allegiance to.

l. 13 *bastides:* temporary towers erected as part of a siege.

l. 26 *camaille:* a chain mail covering for the neck and upper back, attached to the helmet.

l. 47 *Carcassone:* a city in southern France.

ll. 52–3 *the horse…sound:* see Job 39:25, where the powerful horse, 'saith among the trumpets, Ha, ha; and he smelleth the battle afar off, the thunder of the captains, and the shouting'.

l. 78 *rowels:* small spiked wheels on the back of a spur.

l. 99 *The Jacquerie:* a peasant uprising in France in 1358. Froissart, I, 240–41 emphasizes the many acts of burning—of people and buildings—that took place.

l. 107 Morris visited the church at Beauvais on his walking tour of northern France in the summer of 1854.

THE EVE OF CRECY

First published in *The Defence*, 166–8. Froissart I, 164–8 gives a detailed account of the battle of Crécy of 1346, between the English, commanded by Edward III, and the French under Philip VI.

l. 4 *Ah, qu'elle est belle La Margeurite:* ah, how beautiful Margaret is.

l. 14 *arriere-ban:* the summons to battle from the king to his vassals.

l. 15 *basnet:* (also spelled basinet or bascinet) a light, rounded steel headpiece rising to a point, with a visor to cover the face.

l. 26 *varlets:* servants or grooms to a knight.

l. 41 *perdie:* from French, *par Dieu*, by God.

l. 46 *banneret:* a high-ranking knight.

l. 51 *St. Ives:* a town in Cornwall, south-west England.

NEAR AVALON

First published in *The Defence*, 239–40. In *MA*, II, 21, 5, Arthur is borne away to Avalon for the healing of his wounds on a ship steered by three ladies in mourning, wearing black hoods.

l. 11 *heaumes:* large helmets coming down to rest on the shoulders, with only small slits to see through.

IN PRISON

First published as part of a short story, 'Frank's Sealed Letter' in *O and C*, April 1856, 230. My source text is *The Defence*, 247–8.

l. 1 *Wearily, drearily:* an echo of the 'dreary / aweary' rhyme in Tennyson's 'Mariana' of 1830 (*Poems*, I, 205–7).

FROM *THE EARTHLY PARADISE*

Published by F. S. Ellis in four parts between 1868 and 1870, this long narrative poem, with its Chaucerian structure, consists of a Prologue by the 'singer' of the poem, followed by a series of tales told to each other, month by month, by northern European wanderers and the southern European elders of an island on which the wanderers are shipwrecked in their flight from the plague. Unlike *The Defence*, *The Earthly Paradise* was received rapturously by the literary press and the public. The *Temple Bar* was typical in hailing Morris as 'the singer of, perhaps, the most unvarying sweetness and sustained tenderness of soul that ever caressed the chords of the lyre.' 'The Poetry of the Period', *Temple Bar*, 27 (November 1869), 45. The text here is taken from the first edition of 1868–70, in which parts I and II are in one bound volume; Lemire, 26–8, explains the complicated publishing history of early editions of the text.

APOLOGY

Published in Part I, 1868.

FROM THE PROLOGUE—THE WANDERERS

Published in Part I, 1868.

l. 8 *Levantine staves*: rods protruding from the prow of the boat.

l. 103 *twibil*: can mean a number of different weapons, but here probably a double-edged battle axe.

l. 109 *Væringers*: Norse bodyguards of the Emperor Constantine.

ll. 112–13 *Swithiod the Greater*: Norse king in the *Ynglinga Saga*, in *Heimskringla* by Snorri Sturluson (1178–1241). Morris read it first in translation and between 1893 and 1905 the Saga Library published a four-volume edition translated by Morris and Icelandic scholar Eiríkr Magnússon.

l. 113 *Odin*: chief of the Norse gods.

l. 122 *Asagard*: usually Asgard, home of the Norse gods.

l. 125 *Lazarus' finger*: reference to the biblical story of the poor man, Lazarus, to whom a rich man denies sustenance; after both their deaths, Lazarus is in heaven and the rich man, in hell, calls out, asking Abraham to 'send Lazarus, that he may dip the tip of his finger in water, and cool my tongue; for I am tormented in this flame'. Abraham denies him, saying that 'now he is comforted, and thou art tormented' (Luke 16:24–5).

l. 130 *dromond*: a large ship.

l. 153 *Swabian*: from southwest Germany.

l. 159 *Kaiser Redbeard*: Frederick I, Duke of Swabia, King of Germany and Italy, and Holy Roman Emperor from 1155–90. Legends grew up after his death in Turkey that he lived on in a mountain range in Thuringia, Germany.

l. 188 *fisher-cobles*: flat-bottomed fishing boats.

MARCH

Published in Part I, 1868.

l. 54 *St. Luke's short summer*: a period of calm dry weather around St. Luke's Day, 18 October.

NOVEMBER

Published in Part III, brought out in November 1869 but dated 1870.

FEBRUARY

Published in Part IV, 1870.

FROM THE WATCHING OF THE FALCON

Published in Part II, bound in one volume with Part I in 1868.

l. 67 *seneschal*: chief household official in a royal establishment.

l. 74 *Dorsar*: (archaic) ornamental cloth or hanging.

l. 78 *dight for*: prepared for.

l. 130 *losel*: scoundrel, specifically with the suggestion that this is a layabout or wastrel.

LETTER TO CHARLES ELIOT NORTON

From Norman Kelvin, *Collected Letters of William Morris*, 4 vols (Princeton: Princeton University Press, 1984–96), I, 151–133. © 1984. Reprinted by permission of Princeton University Press via Copyright Clearance Center.

p. 121 See figure 11 for an illustration based on Kelmscott Manor.

FROM *SIGURD THE VOLSUNG*

First published by Ellis and White in late 1876 (but dated 1877), the edition from which this text is taken. It draws on the *Völsunga Saga*, translated by Morris and Magnússon in 1870. In December 1869 Morris wrote to Charles Eliot Norton: 'the Völsunga has rather swallowed me up...—I had it in my head to write an epic of it, but though I still hanker after it, I see clearly it would be foolish, for no verse could render the best parts of it, and it would only be a flatter and tamer version of a thing already existing' (*CL*, I, 99). When he eventually did write his own epic, after two visits to Iceland, it was, May Morris notes, 'the darling of his heart', the work 'that he held most highly and wishes to be remembered by' (*CW*, XII, xi; xxiii).

l. 26 *Branstock*: Burne-Jones made a woodcut of the Branstock as one of two illustrations for the Kelmscott Press edition of *Sigurd* published in 1898, after Morris's death.

l. 69 *norland main*: northern sea.

l. 76 *the field of the fishes*: the sea. Morris uses the Old Icelandic form of the kenning, a descriptive periphrastic phrase or compound noun.

l. 78 *the bath of the swan*: the sea.

l. 83 *written*: inscribed or engraved. Morris notes in a letter of 1868 'the practice of the early Scandinavians of scoring their weapons with runes' (*CL*, I, 71).

l. 91 *dight*: Morris uses this verb, which has variations of meaning centred around dressing or preparing, frequently and in different ways across the poem. Here, it means to cook or prepare food.

ll. 124–5 *One-eyed…gleaming grey*: Morris and Magnússon's note in the *Völsunga Saga* reads 'The man is Odin, who is always so represented, because he gave his eye as a pledge for a draught from the fountain of Mimir, the source of all wisdom' (*CW*, VII, 481).

l. 126 *sundog*: the appearance of a halo around the sun in a cloudy sky.

l. 127 *bill*: bill-hook, a heavy knife with a curved end.

l. 128 *flame of the sea*: gold.

l. 130 *the wold*: the world, or the earth.

l. 144 *battle-acre*: the field of battle.

l. 159 *Volsung Children*: here and elsewhere in *Sigurd*, children means young men.

l. 204 *peace-strings*: these occur in a number of Norse sagas; they are thongs tied around a sword so that it cannot be drawn in haste.

l. 251 *the woven…sea*: cloth dyed with purple that came from sea-snails off the coast of Tyre, Lebanon; it was a difficult and expensive process, so that purple fabric signified wealth and status. Morris was in the midst of his own dyeing experiments for his work with the Firm as he wrote *Sigurd*.

l. 259 *purple-selling men*: men selling purple-dyed fabric.

l. 261 *bast of the linden*: the bark of the lime or linden tree, used since prehistoric times in Nordic countries to make rope for ships, baskets, and mats.

ll. 284–5 *roof over…dragons*: cover the sea with our ships, which have dragons at the prow.

l. 291 *Ran*: goddess of the sea in Norse mythology.

l. 304 *wotted*: knew.

l. 339 *Norns*: Morris and Magnússon's footnote in the *Völsunga Saga* reads: 'Nornir are the fates of the northern mythology. They are three—*Urdr*, the past; *Verdandi*, the present; and *Skuld*, the future. They sit beside the fountain of Urd (*Urdarbrienur*), which is below one of the roots of *Yggdrasil*, the world-tree, which tree their office it is to nourish by sprinkling it with the water of the fountain' (*CW*, VII, 481).

l. 350 *dight*: ready.

l. 400 *swan-bath*: sea.

l. 404 *halers of the hawsers*: pullers on the ships ropes and cables.

l. 407 *Ægir's Acre*: the sea; Ægir is husband of Ran, goddess of the sea.

l. 451 *holt*: a wooded hill.

l. 452 *bent:* a grassy slope.

l. 455 *wedge-array*: a v-shaped battle formation much used by the ancient Goths.

l. 476 *Odin's door*: a shield.

l. 577 *hopples*: fetters.

l. 724 *Baldur*: Son of Odin, described by Snorri Sturluson in his thirteenth-century collection of Norse myths, the *Prose Edda* (London, 2005), 33, as 'so beautiful and bright that light shines from him'.

l. 821 *worms*: snakes.

l. 839 *neat*: cattle.

l. 848 *the sons of... the sons of Kings*: the Volsungs are descendants of the gods.

ll. 869–70 *Æsir... Dwarf-kind*: the Æsir and Vanir are the gods in Norse mythology. Sturluson (22) notes that 'the dwarves had come to life in the soil under the earth, like maggots... but by a decision of the gods they acquired human understanding and assumed the likeness of men'.

l. 934 *water-ouzels*: *Cinclus cinclus*, small water birds; known in Britain as white-throated dippers and in the United States as American dippers.

l. 990 *eel-grig*: a young eel.

l. 1047 *chaffering*: trading.

l. 1158 *sackless*: i.e. sacklessly, without good cause.

l. 1169 *whittles*: knives.

war-flame: sword.

l. 1172 *garth of murder*: the space of murder, here standing in for the people fighting.

l. 1224 *gride*: scrape with a jarring sound.

l. 1226 *earth-bone*: stone.

l. 1360 *many... rent*: ravens were common symbols on Norse banners of war; the warflame is Sinfiotli's sword, with which he cuts through enemy ranks, the wall of ravens.

l. 1380 *hight*: named (from Old English; Germanic in origin).

l. 1386 *griping*: grasping (from Old English; Germanic in origin).

l. 1405 *carle and queen*: man and woman.

l. 1427 *the pale... wands*: the enclosure fenced with woven hazel wood, which is supple and easy to manipulate.

l. 1433 *holm*: here, hill (from Old Saxon); as the *OED* notes, holm can also (and more commonly) mean the opposite, low-lying ground.

l. 1434 *hall of mould*: burial hall.

l. 1459 *weregild*: an amount of gold, determined by rank, paid to release someone from guilt or responsibility for wrongdoing in ancient Norse, Germanic, and British law. From the old English.

l. 1520 *Baldur dead*: in Norse myth, mistletoe is the only thing that can kill Baldur, who is impervious to spears and arrows. Mischievous god Loki gives the unsuspecting blind Hodi a mistletoe branch to throw at Baldur and it kills him (Sturluson, 66–7). Matthew Arnold's 1855 poem, *Balder Dead*, had brought the figure of Balder/Baldur to a Victorian readership.

l. 1697 *river of strife*: an image Morris returns to frequently in his own thinking. See letter to Robert Thomson, 24 July 1884, 291–3 in this volume, in which he notes the necessity of crossing a 'river of violence'.

l. 1702 *twi-bill*: a double-bladed axe.

l. 1744 *Norns*: see note on l. 339.

ll. 1838–39 *the many-pictured-floor...hangings of delight:* see 'Some Hints on Pattern-Designing', 275–6 in this volume, for Morris's strictures on the decoration of houses with hangings and stories.

l. 1931 *cunning*: skilful.

l. 1933 *o'er-well warded...fight*: guarded by more than weapons; the suggestion is there is some supernatural protection here.

l. 1946 *changed...homes*: when the world is created the giants are defeated by the gods and relegated to the edges of the world (Sturluson, 17).

l. 1964 *trowed*: believed.

l. 1979 *weary and happy breast*: see also l. 2055, where Sigurd 'cherished her breast'. Ancient Nordic culture stressed the importance of the first breastfeeding, as well as naming by the father, as a sign of a child's acceptance and place in the family and community. Nonetheless Morris departs from his saga sources in insistently drawing attention to it.

l. 2041 *astonied*: bewildered, or dazed with astonishment.

l. 2070 *sea-beat bent*: stiff grasses or reeds on the shoreline beaten down by waves.

l. 2090 *mirk-wood*: see also *The House of the Wolfings*, 402–404 in this volume.

l. 2193 *ernes*: sea eagles.

l. 2231 *mews:* gulls, especially sea gulls common in northern Europe.

l. 2285 *When the bonds...his chain*: the beginnings of the end of the world. Fenrir, a powerful wolf who is the offspring of mischief-making trickster god Loki, is bound with a magical chain until Ragnarök, the Twilight of the Gods, the events that begin the end of the world. Loki is also bound by his fellow gods until Ragnarök.

ll. 2399–400 *Hænir...began*: in the Eddas, Hænir (usually spelled Hœnir in the Eddas) is a minor god who helps Odin to create humans.

l. 2450 *the tooth of the whale*: narwhal tusk, considered very precious and much used and traded in the Middle Ages.

l. 2457 *folk of the firth*: fish.

l. 2487 *wold*: land.

highway wet: river or sea.

l. 2734 *Frey*: the god responsible for rain and sunshine, crops and wealth; twin of Freyia.

l. 2738 *Thor*: the strongest of all gods, equipped with a hammer, Mjölnir, a powerful belt and iron gloves.

l. 2740 *shuttle-race*: a ledge to pass the shuttle along through the two levels of warp threads (the shed) on a handloom.

l. 2742 *Freyia*: twin of Frey; goddess to whom belong half the people slain in battle (the other half belong to Odin); she is also associated with love (Sturluson, 35). Frigg, wife of Odin, is sometimes conflated with Freyia and because she 'knows the fates of men' (Sturluson, 30) is sometimes said to weave fates or events.

l. 2747 *Bragi*: god of poetry and music.

scald: ancient Nordic poet.

l. 2863 *bewray*: betray

l. 3038 *peace-strings*: see note on l. 204.

l. 3046 *mead-lark*: meadow lark, another name for the meadow pipit (*Anthus pratensis*), found across Western Europe, rather than what is more commonly known today as the meadow lark (belonging to the genera *Sturnella* or *Leistes*), not found in Europe.

l. 3051 *ness*: a headland or promontory.

l. 3066 *the tooth of the sea-beast*: narwhal tusk. See note on l. 2427.

l. 3150 *Baldur riseth in peace*: in Norse myth, after Ragnarök, the end of the world, Baldur will rise from the dead.

l. 3246 *though... hall*: as though the wind were howling round the curves of the mountains.

l. 3349 *loose and bind*: see Matthew 16:19.

l. 3358 *meres*: lakes or pools.

l. 3507 *Surt*: a footnote in Morris and Magnússon's *Völsunga Saga* reads 'a fire-giant, who will destroy the world at the Ragnarok, or destruction of all things' (*CW*, VII, 482).

l. 3508 *child*: young man.

l. 3763 *river of fire*: an image Morris re-uses metaphorically in later work, including 'The Prospects of Architecture in Civilization', *CW*, XXII,131.

ll. 3814–15 *Shield-burg... Odin*: a fortress (burg) walled with shields, the tiles of Odin.

l. 3858 *deem*: judge.

l. 4069 *bight*: bend.

FROM THE LESSER ARTS

Delivered as a lecture to the Trades Guild of Learning at the Cooperative Institute, London, on 4 December 1877, entitled 'The Decorative Arts: Their Relation to Modern Life and Progress'. It was published in *The Architect* on 8 December 1877, with its original title, then brought out as a pamphlet by Ellis and White in February 1878. After that Morris renamed it 'The Lesser Arts' and published it in *Hopes* in 1882. This text uses the *Hopes* edition; there are minor changes from the earlier editions, notably switching the new title into the early part of the essay.

p. 242 *you will read... the subject*: see Ruskin, *The Nature of Gothic* in *Works*, X: *The Stones of Venice*, ii, 180–269. Morris returns repeatedly in his work to Ruskin's emphasis on pleasure in labour and on imperfection as a sign of vitality and creativity.

p. 243 *St. Sophia*: built as a church for the Emperor Justinian, it had by Morris's time been converted into a mosque.

p. 245 *vainglory... half*: Morris repeatedly laments contemporary additions and alterations to Westminster Abbey, including the addition of monuments inside it. See 'Mr Shaw Lefevre's Monumental Chapel', 000–00.

p. 246 *axle-tree*: originally the pole at each end of which a carriage wheel sits, hence metaphorically, the centre around which things revolve.

p. 248 *Sirs... men?*: Ruskin notes 'you must either make a tool of the creature, or a man of him. You cannot make both. Men were not intended to work with the accuracy of tools, to be precise and perfect in all their actions' (*The Nature of Gothic*, 192).

p. 252 *I believe that...sordid cares*: Morris invokes here the values of the French Revolution of 1789–93: Liberté, Egalité, Fraternité.

THE BEAUTY OF LIFE

Delivered as a lecture on 19 February 1880 in Birmingham Town Hall, under the title 'Labour and Pleasure *versus* Labour and Sorrow'. It was first published in May of that year as a pamphlet of that name by the Birmingham Society of Arts and School of Design, who had invited Morris, its President from 1878–9, to give the lecture. Morris later edited it slightly, retitled it 'The Beauty of Life' and published it in 1882 in *Hopes*, from which this text is taken.

p. 253 *—propter vitam vivendi perdere causas*: for the sake of your life lose the reasons for living. In Juvenal this quotation is preceded by 'nec', so that it becomes an instruction: do not for the sake...In the first pamphlet edition of the lecture, the epigraph is taken not from Juvenal but from Daniel Defoe, *Farther Adventures*, and reads: 'And the men of labour spent their strength in daily strugglings for breath to maintain the vital strength they laboured with: so living with a daily circulation of sorrow, living but to work, and working but to live, as if daily bread were the only end of a wearisome life, and a wearisome life the only occasion of daily bread' (*Labour and Pleasure* [n.p.]). In *Hopes*, this epigraph is transferred to 'The Art of the People', Morris's lecture to the same group a year earlier, 19 February 1879.

p. 256 *a joy...user*: in 'Art under Plutocracy' (1883), Morris similarly argues: 'Art is man's expression of his joy in labour. If those are not Professor Ruskin's words they embody at least his teaching on this subject' (*CW*, XXIII, 176). See also 268, 274.

p. 257 *New Birth*: the Renaissance.

p. 258 *dimming...Renaissance*: in a lecture of 24 October 1891 Morris describes the period after the artist Raphael, who died in 1520, as 'that the period when art became academical, *i.e.*, inorganic; the so-called renaissance' (*AWS*, I, 302).

the music...Coleridge: Morris includes Blake and Coleridge in his short list of 'modern poets' in a longer list of favourite books for the *Pall Mall Gazette* in 1886 (*CL*, II, 517); in three separate letters of the 1880s he quotes from Blake's 'The Poison Tree' in the context of expressing political differences (*CL*, II, 308, 357, 381); Coleridge, he notes in a letter of 1894, 'was a muddle-brained metaphysician who by some strange freak of fortune turned out a few real poems amongst the dreary flood of inanity which was his wont' (*CL*, IV, 119).

the Heart of Midlothian: Walter Scott's 1818 novel of working-class Scottish life and the pursuit of justice for the poor in the 1730s.

pp. 258–9 *that little knot...now*: the Pre-Raphaelite Brotherhood, a group of artists including Dante Gabriel Rossetti, William Holman Hunt, and John Everett Millais, formed in 1848 to challenge contemporary forms and ideals of art through looking back to the period before Raphael for their ideals. Morris and Edward Burne-Jones's work became associated with the movement.

p. 259 *since the tide... art:* Ruskin publicly defended the Pre-Raphaelites, praising their attention to nature and truth, when their art was first exhibited to shocked public reactions.

p. 262 *Salamis and Thermopylæ*: at the Battle of Salamis in 480 BC a small army of Greek city states overthrew the much larger and more powerful Persian army, following a defeat at Thermoplyae where the Greeks nonetheless held back the Persian army at a narrow pass for a week before being betrayed and overtaken.

little knot... Roman Empire: Morris refers here to the coming of Christianity in the ancient world; the Galilean peasants are the disciples of Jesus, whose small, obscure religious movement became within a few hundred years the dominant force in the Roman empire under Constantine.

residuum: originally meaning waste material left over from industrial processes. The term was widely used in public discourse in the Victorian period to refer to an underclass of the poor who did not work.

its elder sister: Rome.

p. 263 *last year I told you*: in his lecture 'The Art of the People' delivered on 19 February 1879, to the Birmingham Society of Arts and School of Design. Published in *Hopes* in 1882.

p. 264 *I had the honour... Venice*: on 13 November 1879, Morris spoke at the Birmingham and Midlands Institute in Birmingham about the proposed restoration of the west front of St. Mark's, Venice. He also wrote to Ruskin, Browning, Disraeli, and Gladstone, urging them to take action against the restoration, which, as he noted in a letter to the *Daily News* of 31 October, was to take the form of pulling down the west front (*CL*, II, 530, 534, 538, 528). The SPAB and a newly formed St. Mark's Committee continued to campaign vigorously against the restoration.

p. 266 *Bradford*: a city in the north of England, a thriving centre of the textile industry, particularly trading in wool, from the middle of the nineteenth century. Morris lectured there on 17 February 1884.

Saltaire: a model village built just outside Bradford by textile manufacturer Titus Salt for the workers in his factory.

Or Manchester... talked of: The Manchester Association for the Prevention of Smoke was established in 1842 and, like similar committees in other towns, including Birmingham, tried over the following forty years to ensure the local enforcement of a series of national acts aimed at abating smoke pollution from factories, but with little success.

p. 267 *Hampton Court*: Tudor palace built in 1514 with large formal grounds and mazes.

pp. 272–3 *even when it was a Christian church*: see note on p. 602.

p. 273 *Stamboul*: Istanbul, the name informally used for Constantinople, the capital of the Ottoman Empire, although not adopted as the city's official name until 1930.

p. 274 *to have breasted... Leyden*: the Siege of Leiden, or Leyden, of 1573–4 saw the citizens of this Dutch town hold out against a sustained Spanish attack.

Oliver: probably the wise and brave warrior Olivier, companion of the Frankish hero Roland in the twelfth-century epic poem *Chanson de Roland*. The poem dramatizes the battle of Charlemagne's army to hold back Basque forces at a narrow pass during the Battle of Roncevaux in 778, fighting to the death against a greater force.

FROM SOME HINTS ON PATTERN-DESIGNING

Delivered as a lecture at the Working Men's College, London, on 10 December 1881. The College, established in 1854 under the principalship of the Christian Socialist F. D. Maurice and with Ruskin as a regular lecturer, aimed to provide a broad liberal education for working men. The lecture was published in *The Architect*, 17 and 24 December 1881, 391–4 and 408–10. I have used *The Architect* edition as my source text. Where there are significant differences between the lecture manuscript (BL MS 45331), and the published form of the text, I have noted them. I have silently corrected minor errors of spelling or punctuation, comparing the manuscript, *The Architect* and May Morris's text (*CW*, XXII, 175–205).

p. 278 *breaks the clouds on them*: *CW*, XXII, 178, adds [through] in square brackets here after *breaks*. But the sentence is not present in Morris's MS, where there is a more international and less soft image here. See following footnote.

Is it not…Picardy: in MS 45331, 130, Morris has: 'Look! Is it not better to be reminded of the close vine-trellis by the waterside of Nile, or the tulips standing thick in the fields of the Persian spring, or the wild-woods and their streams and the hunting dogs panting beside them; or the swallows sweeping between the garden boughs and the house-eaves where their nestlings are.'

hint: *The Architect*, 392, misprints as 'limit'. MS 45331, 130, and *CW*, XXII, 178 have 'hint'.

something…callousness: MS 45331, 130, reads: 'either to think of things which would move us too much or to be callous in thinking of them'. Given the importance of ideas of rest and unrest for Morris, it is worth noting that being too much moved becomes unrest here. See also p. 276 on callousness.

p. 279 *ryot*: a peasant farmer, especially in South Asia (the word has Urdu and Persian origins).

p. 281 *thrums of worsted*: odds and ends of worsted, a smooth yarn spun from wool in which the fibres have been combed to run in the same direction; cloth made from this yarn is also called worsted.

p. 281 *Mr. Parnell…fireworks*: MS 45331, 134 is more politically specific about immediate events: 'of Sir Garnet Wolsey [Wolseley] in burnt sugar or done in fireworks Mr Parnell in Kilmainham Jail'. Irish Republican and MP Charles Stewart Parnell had been imprisoned in October 1881 on charges of interfering with the maintenance of law and order; in 1881 the Anglo-Irish Sir Garnet Wolseley was Quartermaster-General to the British Forces.

p. 282 *Yes…his keep*: this responds to Luke 10:7.

construction of a wall: *CW*, XXII, 184, notes that in the lecture, 'the following notes on the construction of designs were illustrated by a series of diagrams and by drawings of historic patterns on a greatly enlarged scale.'

diapers: repeating patterns or designs on a flat surface.

p. 284 *this Italian one*: Morris was lecturing with illustrations, so this would have been accompanied by a drawing.

p. 286 *bull*: a bull is a self-contradictory term; Morris uses it because the Gothic is originally associated with the Goths, from Western Europe, rather than with the East.

a perfection...attainable: an argument closely related to one made by Ruskin in *The Nature of Gothic* (1853).

barbarians...Europe: the Goths and other Germanic tribes whose risings against the Romans signalled the beginning of the end of the Roman Empire. In 'The Development of Modern Society', Morris and his co-author Ernest Belfort Bax urge readers to 'throw off ' the fear of death that runs alongside tolerance of capitalist oppression; in doing so, they note, 'shall we be our own Goths, and at whatever cost break up again the new tyrannous Empire of Capitalism' (*Commonweal*, 16 August 1890, 261).

p. 288 *Well,...did not*: a wry reference to Morris's own business, Morris and Co., which made furnishings for wealthy middle-class homes, among other things.

The first part of Morris's lecture in *The Architect* ends on 394. It begins again on 408. I have omitted 408–9 of *The Architect* edition, covering other arts such as paper staining for wallpapers, printing on cloth, carpet designing and decorative embroidery. This text picks up again on 410 of *The Architect*, beginning with 'I must ask'.

p. 289 *flunkies*: originally upper servants in uniform; metaphorically, people submitting spinelessly to those above them.

I believe...duty of: added in a posthumous pamphlet edition of *Some Hints* (Longmans Green & Co, 1899), 43, and retained in *CW*, XXII, 204.

p. 290 *barbarous waste*: MS 45331, 155 adds here: 'And first we have to show that we love art and know what it means by casting barbarous luxury from us those of us that are rich by taking for our standard of the comfort of life something which all people might attain to if society were resettled on a basis of justice and good will.'

LETTER TO ROBERT THOMSON

From Norman Kelvin, *Collected Letters of William Morris*, 4 vols (Princeton: Princeton University Press, 1984–1996), II, 305–307. © 1987. Reprinted by permission of Princeton University Press via Copyright Clearance Center. Elbert Hubbard notes that Thomson was 'a strayed American of southern birth and Scotch antecedents who had become stranded in London', where he joined the Democratic Federation. He adds that 'Mr Thomson being much interested in Ruskin's program, especially the feature of "national workshops" [...] broached this subject in a letter to Morris' (Hubbard, 62, 63).

p. 291 *nor could it...could*: as Kelvin notes, the mention of Ruskin's account of his childhood refers to *Fors Clavigera* (1878) and his idea of national workshops appears in *Unto this Last* (1860–62) (*CL*, II, 307).

pp. 291–2 *it is...time*: Morris refers here to H. M. Hyndman's 'stepping stones' to 'a happier period', of which the eight-hour day was one. The stepping stones were set out in 1883 in *Socialism Made Plain: Being the Social and Political Manifesto of the Democratic Federation* (London: W. Reeves, 1883), 5–6.

p. 292 *Monday's*: a 'Great Reform Demonstration' held in Hyde Park on 21 July 1884, called by the London Trades Council when Parliament rejected the Third Reform Bill to extend the franchise. Thompson, 328–9 gives an account of the day but gives the date as Monday 23rd. *CL*, II, 304 accurately corrects it to Monday 21 July. Morris attended and distributed socialist literature with other SDF members; they clashed with supporters of the Liberal John Bright.

p. 293 *<controul>*: Kelvin uses these brackets to indicate a word crossed out in Morris's handwritten form.

USEFUL WORK *VERSUS* USELESS TOIL

Delivered as a lecture at the Hampstead Liberal Club on 16 January 1884. Printed as a pamphlet in 1885, as the second of a numbered sequence of 7 pamphlets by various authors, entitled *The Socialist Platform*. As Lemire (105) notes, it was a popular lecture and was reprinted in a number of different pamphlets in London, Chicago, Sydney, Moscow, and New York. This text is taken from *Signs*, 1888.

p. 299 *labour-power*: a term Marx uses in *Capital*, i, 177 to mean 'capacity for labour', or 'the aggregate of those mental and physical capabilities existing in a human being', which can be exchanged as a commodity for money.

p. 300 *Such... Co-operation (so-called)*: there was much debate in socialist circles at this time about the Cooperative movement which developed in Britain across the mid-1800s. Morris consistently saw it as ineffective in the cause of labour justice. The 'Manifesto of the Socialist League' in *Commonweal*, February 1885, 1, notes: 'Co-operation so called—that is, competitive co-operation for profit—would merely increase the number of small joint-stock capitalists, under the mask of creating an aristocracy of labour, while it would intensify the severity of labour by its temptations to overwork.'

p. 306 *commission de lunatico*: (Latin, *commission de lunatico inquirendo*) a commission to inquire into someone's sanity of mind, to determine whether another person ought to take over their affairs.

p. 307 *glorious drama... winter*: see *News*, 559, on the changing drama of the year.

p. 308 *plush breeches... wear them*: Victorian upper servants such as footmen would conventionally wear outfits of low-quality velvet known as plush.

oleo-margarine: a fatty substance obtained by extracting the liquid portion from purified beef fat under pressure and allowing it to solidify, which formed the basis of the original butter substitute, margarine (made from it by adding milk, etc., and churning). *OED*.

HOW WE LIVE AND HOW WE MIGHT LIVE

This lecture was delivered on 11 January 1885, and first published in five consecutive parts in *Commonweal*, between 4 June and 2 July 1887; Morris's footnote on 4 June

(177) records that 'this paper has been delivered as a lecture on several occasions; and I have been often asked to reprint it: hence its appearance in *Commonweal*'. My text is taken from the slightly edited version published as one of seven essays in *Signs* in 1888, in which Morris again notes, 'if any excuse be needed for their publication . . . the one I have to offer is, that I have often been asked by persons among my audiences to publish them' (*Signs*, v).

p. 311 *Legree*: Simon Legree, a particularly cruel and vicious plantation owner in Harriet Beecher Stowe's influential abolitionist text *Uncle Tom's Cabin* (1852).

p. 313 *Jingoes*: nationalistic warmongers. The term dates back to a music-hall song about those who energetically supported a war against Russian incursions into Turkey in 1878, shortly after Morris first became involved in politics on the opposing side.

p. 315 *a steam-engine . . . shoddy*: Manchester was a major centre of the textile industry, particularly the cotton industry, in the Victorian period. China-clay or kaolin was used in the manufacture of textiles, to make the cloth thicker through a process of *fulling*, kneading water and clay into the cloth to tighten the fibres and absorb impurities (Fuller's earth, similar to china-clay, was also used in this process). Shoddy is cloth made from yarns pulled from old woollen goods and re-woven, then fulled.

Asiatic worker . . . ruined him: Morris is always alert to the international implications of working conditions. See *News*, 481–2.

p. 317 *combination*: as Morris uses it here, an early term for trades-unionism. From 1799 onwards, a series of Combination Acts were passed in Britain (1799, 1800, 1825) to prevent workers striking or taking other action to bargain for better conditions. In 1871 trade unions were made legal for the first time, although picketing was outlawed.

pp. 320–21 *a distinguished physicist has said*: *Commonweal*, 18 June 1887, 195 has, 'I have heard a distinguished surgeon say . . .'

p. 322 *Socialist Community*: in *Commonweal*, 25 June 1887, 202, 'Socialist State'.

Procrustean bed: in Greek mythology, the rogue Procrustes made people fit a one-size iron bed by either stretching them or cutting off their legs. Morris uses this image again in *News*, 458.

UNATTRACTIVE LABOUR

Published in May 1885 as the first of a two-part serial supplement to *Commonweal* in its first year, followed by 'Attractive Labour'. It sets out Morris's analysis of contemporary conditions of work and their solutions in easily accessible terms.

p. 330 *Factory Acts*: a series of statutes passed from 1833 onwards, aimed at limiting factory working hours, first for children, then for women and young people over 13 and, very much later, for all workers. Although conditions of work varied across industries, by 1885 women and young people between 14 and 18 routinely worked over 56 hours a week, while men usually worked sixty-hour weeks across ten-hour days.

ATTRACTIVE LABOUR

The June 1885 sequel to 'Unattractive Labour', a supplement to *Commonweal*. The title echoes French utopian thinker Charles Fourier's theory of attractive labour (1808), which emphasizes variety as a source of pleasure in labour. See Fourier, 163–70.

p. 334 *barbarous countries*: barbarism is a positive concept for Morris, suggesting an opposite to the artificiality and oppression of civilization. See his letter of 13 May 1885 to Georgiana Burne-Jones, 337 in this volume.

p. 335 *phalangstery*: Fourier proposed that society should be organized not by families, but into cooperative communities (phalanxes, housed in phalansteries) of 1,500 or so workers with a wide variety of skills, status, character, and knowledge, including peasant farmers and capitalists. Fourier, 137–54.

p. 336 *whose descendants... energy*: as indeed is the case in *News*, 444–5

our friend, and not our enemy: see 'How We Live and How We Might Live', 319, on the conquest of Nature.

FROM TWO LETTERS TO GEORGIANA BURNE-JONES

Text from Mackail, II, 143–4. Morris corresponded regularly with Georgiana Burne-Jones, wife of Edward Burne-Jones and a friend of Morris's in her own right, with intimate ease and on a variety of topics right up until his death.

p. 337 *Millthorpe*: smallholding home of socialist poet, writer, and advocate of social equality and sexual liberation, Edward Carpenter, between Sheffield and Chesterfield.

Carlisle to Settle: railway line opened in 1876.

Kirkby Stephen: village on the route of the railway. In a letter to his daughter Jenny, Morris comments: 'I think it is the loveliest part of all England' (*CL*, II, 427).

After London: Richard Jefferies's 1885 novel, set in the wake of an ecological disaster that has destroyed London and returned the country to a wilderness inhabited by disparate groups surviving off the land.

more faith than a grain of mustard seed: Morris is drawing on Matthew 17:20: 'if ye have faith as a grain of mustard seed, ye shall say unto this mountain, "Remove hence to yonder place," and it shall remove. And nothing shall be impossible unto you.' Kelvin suggests he means '[no] more faith', in *CL*, II, 436.

as ...days of Noë: the days of apparent normality in a world gone wrong before the flood that, in the biblical story, wiped out most of the world, apart from those saved by Noah. This wording comes from Luke 17:26–7.

THE VULGARIZATION OF OXFORD

Text from *Daily News*, 20 November 1885, 2. Morris had campaigned against the widening of Magdalen Bridge in 1881. Summer 1885 saw the beginning of construction

of the Pitt Rivers Museum on the east side of the University Museum and an extension
to New College.

p. 339 *Holywell-street*: Jane Burden, Morris's wife-to-be, lived a house in St. Helen's
Passage, just off Holywell Street, as a child. In 1885 New College, which had extended
to its west into Holywell Street in 1875–7, built a further extension on its east side,
demolishing houses at 87 and 88 Holywell Street.

Dr Hornby and Eton: James John Hornby was headmaster of Eton College from
1868 and in 1884 became its Provost. Henderson notes that Hornby had 'decided to
pull down the school library and the old houses on the western side of Weston's Yard,
among which was the fine sixteenth-century Headmaster's house' (*Letters*, 243). See
also Kelvin's further notes in *CL*, II, 494.

THE DAY IS COMING

First published by Reeves in September 1883 as a penny pamphlet, *Chants for
Socialists*, No. 1. Included in the first collected edition of *Chants for Socialists*, 1885, a
pamphlet of six songs written by Morris and published in London by the Socialist
League Office for use at meetings and demonstrations. *Chants* went through several
editions over the following ten years. The text here is from *Chants* (1885), 3–5.

ALL FOR THE CAUSE

First published in *Justice*, 19 April 1884, 4, and then in the collected *Chants* (1885),
8–9. In 'The Beauty of Life', 273 above, Morris argued that the 'cause for which to
strive... is the Democracy of Art, the ennobling of daily and common work'. Here 'the
Cause' is socialism, but Morris's vision of it is continuous with his earlier definition.

l. 2 *some... die*: see 'The Beauty of Life', 274: 'few men can be so lucky as to die for
a cause, without having first of all lived for it.'

THE MARCH OF THE WORKERS

First published in *Commonweal*, February 1885, 5, and then in *Chants* (1885), 11–12.
May Morris notes that 'the measure of The March of the Workers is very heavy for the
air—"John Brown's body lies mouldering in the Grave," but someone unluckily
furnished my father not with the original words as a guide, but with another set of verses,
the long racing metre of which he followed. When he found out how much simpler the
original John Brown song was, he was rather vexed about it' (*CW*, XXIV, xxxii–xxxiii).

A DREAM OF JOHN BALL

First published as a serial in *Commonweal*, between 13 November 1886 and 22 January
1887. Morris made minor revisions and brought it out in book form with Reeves and

Turner in 1888. This is my source text here. All the chapter titles and divisions were added in 1888; other changes, apart from minor rearrangements of paragraphing or punctuation, are identified in the notes. The tale tells the story of the 1381 Peasants' Rising or Peasants' Revolt against the oppression of the landowners, represented by the introduction of a third new poll tax in five years in 1380. The uprising, though unsuccessful, was seen by nineteenth-century historians as marking the beginning of the end of feudalism.

p. 349 *Some... Victoria*: a house from the time of Queen Elizabeth (1558–1603) with earlier remnants and later additions, which Morris saw as destructive. Queen Anne reigned from 1702–14, Silly Billy—a popular nickname for William IV—from 1830 to 1837, when Victoria ascended to the throne.

churchwardened: repaired, whitewashed, plastered, or restored in a way that does damage to the original features of the building. In the Church of England, the church warden is responsible for the care of the fabric of the building, among other duties.

cob: a mixture of clay with straw and gravel, used in ancient times (and revived in the twentieth century) for building in certain parts of England, including Wiltshire in the south-west, an area Morris knew well from his youth at Marlborough College, from where he records frequent escapes into the countryside.

William Cobbett: (1763–1835) pamphleteer, journalist, farmer, anti-Corn Law Leaguer, medievalist, and supporter of the 1832 Reform Act; from 1832 he was Radical MP for Oldham. He was actively pro-Catholic and casually anti-Semitic in his writings. In *Rural Rides* (1830) he documented the beauties and mores of the English countryside, alongside what he saw as its destruction. Riding into Wiltshire and looking over Milton and Pewsey, Cobbett notes, 'I never before saw anything to please me like this valley of the Avon.' *Rural Rides*, II, 56.

the foothills... horse: an area on the borders of Berkshire and Oxfordshire, west of London, named after the Uffington white horse, a prehistoric figure carved into the hillside. Morris knew the area well from boyhood onwards and visited often.

All this: *Commonweal* picks up the tale here, beginning 'All these I have seen'.

Manchester... Sunday: Morris had strong links with Manchester: he delivered at least twenty-nine separate lectures or speeches in the city across the course of the 1880s and 1890s. Morris & Co opened two shops there in 1883. Mitcham Fair Green is in Surrey, near Morris's dyeing works at Merton Abbey, over 200 miles from Manchester. *Commonweal* records regular Socialist League propaganda meetings there in 1886 and 1887.

p. 350 *early apples*: *Commonweal*, 13 November 1886, 257, has simply *apples*, thus setting the story later. As Nicholas Salmon points out, the events of the Peasants' Revolt took place in the second and third weeks of June, 1381. 'The Revision of *A Dream of John Ball*', *Journal of William Morris Studies*, 10.2 (1993), 16.

quick: a shortening of quickbeam, from the Old English *cuicbeam* or *cwicbeam*: rowan or mountain ash.

bill-hook: see note on *Sigurd*, l. 127. Traditionally an agricultural tool for cutting shrubs and trees. Spikes were sometimes added to it for use in warfare.

leet: a court held annually by the lord of the manor.

p. 351 *only…dire necessity*: the dreamer's clothing indicates he is a scribe rather than a soldier.

midsummer: in *Commonweal*, 13 November 1886, 257 this is rendered *late summer*. See note on early apples, p. 350.

St. Clement: patron saint of metalworkers and blacksmiths.

p. 352 *John the Miller…all*: these phrases were included in a letter from John Ball; they seem to have been circulated as a secret sign of belonging to the uprising as well as to spread its message. Victorian Liberal historian John R. Green notes that 'in the rude jingle of these lines began for England the literature of political controversy' (Green, i, 266).

p. 353 *Essex*: 'a party of insurgents in Essex gave the signal for open revolt by crossing the Thames under Jack Straw and calling Kent to revolt' (Green, i, 265).

p. 354 *poll-groat bailiffs*: men who collect the poll (per-head) tax of a groat, a coin worth four pence.

soccage: socage tenants lived on a lord's land and paid regular rents of money or services. Morris contrasts them with villeins who were peasants wholly subject to the lord and without any tenancy rights to land or property.

bever-time: mealtime.

Lollards: labouring-class followers of John Wycliffe, a Roman Catholic priest critical of the hierarchical and sacramental practices of the Catholic Church. He translated the Bible, usually read in Latin, into English and advocated separating the church from secular hierarchies of power. Green, i, 264, notes that John Ball 'had for twenty years been preaching a Lollardry of coarser and more popular type than that of Wyclif'.

If a man…eat?: See 2 Thessalonians 3.10: 'if any would not work, neither should he eat'.

John Litster: leader of the people's rising in Norfolk in 1381. He was a dyer by trade.

woad: a traditional blue, plant-based dye; Morris notes in 1875 that 'indigo seems scarcely to have been known in Europe (as a dye) till the end of the 16th century, and before that time nothing but woad was used for blue as far as I can make out' (*CL*, I, 279).

madder: a plant-based dye much used in medieval times, one of the many natural sources of dye Morris used at his own works at Merton Abbey. He discusses its uses in 'Dyeing as an Art', *The Decorator and Furnisher*, 19.6 (1892), 217.

p. 355 *A vision…to him*: Morris was a student at Exeter College, Oxford, 1853–6. In 1887 he noted that 'the memory of its grey streets as they then were has been an abiding influence and pleasure in my life'. *The Aims of Art* (London: Office of the Commonweal, 1887), 13.

night-long rain: the section that follows, including the song, was added for the 1888 book version. In *Commonweal*, 20 November 1886, 267, this sentence is followed by 'but there the song dropped'.

l. 5 *the lily lea*: the lea is arable land or open grassland; here the lily seems to suggest not the flower but its association with purity, so that it means untouched, uncultivated land.

l. 22 *grey-goose wing:* arrow.

p. 356 *boiled... hardened: Commonweal*, 20 November 1886, 267, has *circles of boiled and hardened leather*.

ll. 31–2 *When Adam... gentleman*: see Edward Burne-Jones's woodcut frontispiece to *A Dream of John Ball* (figure 10).

p. 359 *And who... rich man*: from Luke 10:29.

p. 360 *gossip*: a close friend.

the proud... fellow: this story would have evoked for many of Morris's first readers the well-known biblical tale of Lazarus and the rich man (Dives). See note on p. 597.

accolade: the act of conferring a knighthood by a combination of word and symbolic gesture.

p. 361 *holpen*: helped.

hedge-priest: a little-educated priest, with low standing in the church hierarchy, no parish of his own, and social status equivalent to the peasantry rather than the clergy. Froissart (I, 652) calls him 'a crazy priest'. The usage is contemptuous, but Morris's Ball reclaims the term.

p. 362 *hopples*: fetters.

p. 363 *losels*: wastrels or scoundrels.

Senlac: the hill on which Harold Godwinson is said to have deployed his troops in the Battle of Hastings, 1066; here it signifies the triumph of William the Conqueror, the overthrow of Saxon Britain and the idea of 'the Norman Yoke' (a phrase with a long history, but used influentially by Walter Scott in *Ivanhoe* in 1820), that is, the development of feudalism and oppression instead of native freedom.

p. 364 *churl*: man.

p. 366 *long-bow and cloth-yard shaft*: the long bow was a particularly English weapon, as opposed to the French crossbow; a cloth-yard shaft is the arrow that fits the long bow, so called because it as long as the yard used for measuring cloth.

did me to wit: let me know.

Sir John Newton... Rochester Castle: in Froissart I, 655 the peasants 'advanced to the castle', seized 'a knight called sir John de Newtoun' and forced him to go with them to London.

p. 367 *billmen*: men carrying bill-hooks to use in the battle.

stour: conflict.

arbalestiers: soldiers armed with crossbows.

Jack Straw: Froissart I, 658 refers to the 'leaders' of the common people in the uprising as 'John Ball, Jack Straw and Wat Tyler'.

p. 368 *fagot*: a bundle of sticks bound together to use for fuel.

Plashed: that is, the rowan (known as quick) branches had been bent over and interwoven to form a strong fence-like hedge.

p. 369 *two... arrows: Commonweal*, 11 December 1886, 290, has *a dozen*.

p. 370 *Crecy field*: Crécy was the site of a battle between France and England in August 1346, during the Hundred Years War. See 'The Eve of Crecy' 94–5).

p. 371 *bushment*: (ambushment) the arrangement of soldiers ready for an ambush.

one... Essex: because little is known about him, it has been suggested the name was a pseudonym, hence it might be used by many.

p. 371 *glaives*: see note on p. 594.

p. 372 *King's Son of Heaven*: Christ.

Apollo's bow: Homer, *The Iliad*, II, ll. 33–50, describes the power and force of Apollo's arrows fired in anger.

p. 375 *French wars*: the Hundred Years War between England and France, beginning in 1337.

p. 376 *cots*: cottages.

p. 377 *let the dead ... dead*: see Luke 9:60. More than any of Morris's other works, *John Ball* is steeped in biblical allusion, fitting for the medieval setting and voice of John Ball.

I were fain of: I would like.

p. 378 *chantrey priests*: priests employed to chant masses, usually for their patron, but also for the dead, in a designated chapel or area of the monastery, the chantry. (Morris's spelling is idiosyncratic here.)

chamber or loft above: Commonweal, 18 December 1886, 298, has *rooms above*.

p. 379 *with ... woven into it*: As indeed Morris suggests is the best kind of decoration. See notes on p. 272 and p. 276.

p. 380 *mazer*: a wooden drinking bowl.

plough-shares ... spears: a reversal of the biblical image of a peaceful future in Isaiah 2:4.

delator: informer.

p. 384 *He changed his life*: Malory uses this phrase for Arthur's death in *MA*, II, 21, 7.
cantle: a portion cut off the greater whole.

p. 386 *the years ... sickness*: the Black Death or bubonic plague of 1348–9. It halved the population of Britain in a few short years, and as a result 'the whole organisation of labour was thrown out of gear' (Green, i, 263).

taken the tonsure: become a monk.

p. 387 *chaffering*: bartering or haggling.

p. 388 *the power of labour*: this draws on Marx's concept of labour-power, explained to *Commonweal* readers by Edward Aveling in 'Lessons in Socialism', *Commonweal*, January 1886, 5.

the residue ... himself: this tallies with Marx's concept of surplus value, explained by Aveling in 'Lessons in Socialism', 5.

p. 389 *whip ... Egypt*: see Exodus 1–5.

p. 393 *sley*: part of a weaving loom used to push back and tighten the woven threads. As Wilmer notes, Morris had taught himself how to use a handloom, largely superseded in his own time by industrial-revolution-era machinery (Wilmer, 408).

The Hunt's Up!: traditional folk tune.

p. 394 *husbandmen*: caretakers or managers of the fields and crops.

p. 395 *the parish*: the smallest administrative district in England. It is an ecclesiastical term, meaning the area for which one church is responsible.

the hundred: an administrative unit larger than a parish, but smaller than a shire or county, having its own court.

p. 395 *forestalling and regrating*: see Morris's note on p. 390.

p. 399 *Thames Conservancy*: the body responsible for maintaining the river Thames. In 1895 Morris wrote to the secretary of the Thames Conservancy Board about a proposed building, suggesting how it could be made to blend in with the landscape and already existing architecture (*CL*, IV, 294).

bight of the river: curved stretch of the river.

the 'Great Wen': Cobbett uses this term for London in *Rural Rides*, i, 52.

'work' … 'play': Morris, unlike most working-class labourers of his day, has pleasure in his work; he suggests here that Ruskin, as a serious artist and proponent of pleasure in work, would see Morris's art as both work and play, equally valid.

FROM *THE HOUSE OF THE WOLFINGS*

Text from the first edition, published by Reeves and Turner in December 1888, dated 1889. Morris wrote in a letter of 1888 that 'it is a story of the life of the Gothic tribes on their way through middle Europe, and their first meeting with the Romans in war. It is meant to illustrate the melting of the individual into the society of the tribes: I mean apart from the artistic side of things that is its moral—if it has one. It is written partly in prose and partly in verse: but the verse is always spoken by the actors in the tale, though they do not always talk verse; much as it is in the Sagas, though it cannot be said to be formed on their model' (*CL*, II, 836).

p. 402 *Thames at Sheene*: Sheene, site of a medieval Carthusian priory and royal residence, was renamed Richmond in the fifteenth century, under the rule of Henry VII. The Thames is particularly wide at Teddington, just before Richmond, at around 100 metres across. Its narrowest point is at Lechlade, near Morris's house, Kelmscott Manor.

wains: large open farm carts

kine: cattle.

p. 404 *wainburg*: the arrangement of wains to form a kind of burg, or fortress, around the people.

chapiter: the top part of a pillar, which supports the roof.

luffer: usually a domed chimney-like structure with slits across it, characteristic of medieval buildings.

p. 405 *Things*: meetings of the people for communal government. The *OED* notes that *thing* is a word 'of multiple origins', Scandinavian and Icelandic.

Doom was given: judgement was pronounced.

p. 406 *neat-herd*: cowherd.

milch-kine: dairy cows.

p. 407 *humble-bee*: (archaism) bumble-bee.

sea-whale of the North: narwhal, found in waters off Greenland and Russia.

p. 409 *splintered War-shaft … aspen*: arrow.

p. 410 *stithies*: forges.

MR SHAW LEFEVRE'S MONUMENTAL CHAPEL

First published, under this heading, in the *Daily News* of 30 January 1889, 3. Morris is responding to a plan by Liberal MP for Bradford Central, George Shaw Lefevre, to put before parliament a bill for building an additional chapel onto Westminster Abbey as there was no space in the Abbey itself for further monuments. Hansard reports that on 3 May 1889 Shaw Lefevre withdrew the bill after the government instituted an independent inquiry into the question of space in the Abbey.

p. 411 *fanes*: (Latin) temple or place of worship.

p. 412 *Cockney*: Morris uses cockney here as Cobbett used it *Rural Rides*, i, 332, and elsewhere to mean something characterized by artificiality and vulgarity. Morris's epigraph to 'The Prospects of Architecture in Civilization' (*CW*, XXII, 119) is a quotation from Carlyle also using the term in this way: 'the horrible doctrine that this universe is a Cockney Nightmare'.

LOOKING BACKWARD

First published in *Commonweal*, 22 June 1889, 194–5, reviewing the American Edward Bellamy's hugely popular 1888 utopian novel of State Socialism, *Looking Backward*. In a letter of 13 May 1889, Morris comments that he 'had to [read it], having promised to lecture on it. Thank you, I wouldn't care to live in such a cockney paradise as he imagines' (*CL*, III, 59). He did give his lecture on the text that month, as *Commonweal* records on 18 May 1889, 159.

p. 414 *Mr Bradlaugh…Maxse*: Charles Bradlaugh, founder of the National Secular Society, published *Some Objections to Socialism* in 1884. Across four weeks in May and June 1888 Bradlaugh and socialist author and editor Ernest Belfort Bax engaged in 'a written debate' in *Commonweal*, entitled 'Will Socialism Benefit the English People?' Bradlaugh concluded not; Gladstone, Liberal politician and prime minister at the time of Morris's first active engagement with politics over the Eastern Question in 1876, and again PM in 1880–5 and then 1886: Morris, who at first admired him, refers to him in letters of 1885 as 'that old villain' and 'that canting old scoundrel' (*CL*, II, 488, 500); Admiral Maxse was an advocate of cooperation and land reform, and an unsuccessful Liberal candidate for Parliament in 1868 and 1874. He is described in *Commonweal* as 'a very hard-shell Coercionist' (12 January 1889, 12) and a 'very hard-shell Radical' (4 May 1889, 140).

'How shall we live then?': Morris gave a lecture with this title on 1 and 3 March 1889 (Lemire, *Unpublished Lectures*, 278), as well as on subsequent occasions. It was first published by Paul Meier as *An Unpublished Lecture by William Morris* in the *International Review of Social History*, 16 (1971), 217–40.

John Ruskin…bourgeois: Morris elsewhere suggests that Ruskin 'has done serious and solid work towards the new birth of Society, without which genuine art, the expression of man's pleasure in his handiwork, must inevitably cease altogether'. *The Nature of Gothic* (Kelmscott Press, 1893), v.

NEWS FROM NOWHERE

First published as a weekly serial in *Commonweal*, from 11 January 1890 until 4 October 1890. On 7 October 1890 Morris wrote to Scottish Socialist League member John Bruce Glasier: 'I shall now presently begin to touch up N from N for its book form, & will publish it for 1s/o. It has amused me very much writing it: but you may depend upon it, it won't sell' (*CL*, III, 218). It was brought out by Reeves and Turner in 1891, edited by Morris. This is the source text I have used here. Significant changes from the *Commonweal* edition are noted below.

p. 420 *Up at the League*: the Socialist League, which Morris founded with a provisional council of twenty-three others, including Eleanor Marx, Edward Aveling, and Ernest Belfort Bax, in December 1884, publishing a first edition of the League newspaper, *Commonweal*, in February 1885.

damning all the rest for fools: Morris's own impatience and sudden but wholly unmalicious furies are attested to by friends, family, and his own letters. George Bernard Shaw noted his habit, 'when annoyed by some foolish speaker', of pulling single hairs violently from his moustache and growling "damned fool!"' (*AWS*, II, xiii).

a carriage...railway: the first part of the London underground was opened in 1863, made up of steam-powered engines pulling gas-lit carriages; in 1886 further excavations began and November 1890, just as *Commonweal* published the last parts of *News*, saw the opening of the first deep-tunnel part of the railway, powered by electricity.

his own...Thames: Morris's own London house, Kelmscott House, stood on the banks of the Thames near Hammersmith Bridge, which had been built in 1887.

p. 421 *Eyot*: small island in a river.

p. 422 *sculls*: lightweight oars.

p. 423 *Barn Elms*: a manor house and estate along the Thames at Barnes, originally belonging to the dean and chapter of St. Paul's Cathedral; by 1890 the grounds were planted not only with elms but with London plane trees (*Platanus x acerifolia*), pollution-resistant hybrids widely planted in London across the 1800s.

damascened: ornamented metal, usually steel, with carved watery patterns filled in with gold or silver.

we don't want...season: by 1890 there had not been salmon in the Thames for almost fifty years, due to pollution. Morris is always attentive to matters relating to fish and fishing. In one of his earliest letters to his sister Emma from school he discusses buying a fishing rod (*CL*, I, 6).

Thorneycroft's: shipbuilding firm based in Chiswick.

p. 423 *Ponte Vecchio*: a bridge across the Arno River in Florence, built in 1345, after a flood destroyed the bridge that was previously there. Morris and Burne-Jones visited Florence in 1873.

p. 424 *2003*: in *Commonweal*, 18 January 1890, 18, the date is 1971.

p. 426 *Colney Hatch*: a lunatic asylum in Barnet, London, built in 1851.

p. 426 *filagree*: now commonly spelled filigree. 'Jewel work of a delicate kind made with threads and beads, usually of gold and silver' (*Encycl. Brit.*). *OED*.

p. 427 *very particularly familiar with them*: again, clearly Morris's own house on the Thames at Hammersmith.

Crosby Hall: built in 1466 by Sir John Crosby, a textile merchant, in Bishopsgate. It later belonged to Thomas More, author of *Utopia* (1516).

p. 428 *never a dressy person*: as indeed Morris himself was not; both he and others frequently make note of his inattention to details of dress.

Guest-hall...memory: the coach house of Kelmscott House was turned into a hall and regularly used for meetings of the Socialist League.

p. 429 *pollards*: trees that have been cut back to retain a particular shape or size.

Queen Elizabeth's Lodge...landscape garden it: Queen's Elizabeth's lodge was first built by Henry VIII in 1543. Morris describes, in a lecture of 1882, 'my first acquaintance with a room hung with faded greenery at Queen Elizabeth's Lodge by Chingford Hatch in Epping Forest' (*CW*, XXII, 254).

High Beech: High Beech is the only village in Epping Forest.

Epping Forest...boy: like Guest, Morris, born in Walthamstow, spent many childhood hours in Epping Forest.

p. 430 *political economy*: this negative view of political economy echoes Ruskin's in *The Roots of Honour*, in *Works*, XVII, 25–42.

p. 431 *as Scott says*: Walter Scott, the novelist, with whose works Morris was deeply familiar, having read them since early childhood.

Ne quid nimis: (Latin) nothing in excess.

p. 432 *wherry*: a light rowing boat mainly used on rivers.

Boffin: named after a kind-hearted character in Dickens's *Our Mutual Friend* (1865), uneducated but fond of literature and nicknamed 'the golden dustman' after he comes into an unexpected inheritance from his master, who trades in dust (used in the 1800s for making bricks, among other things).

p. 434 *the Baptistry at Florence*: an octagonal basilica built on the foundations of a Roman baptistry; it is the oldest religious building in Florence, consecrated in 1059, officially named the Baptistry of Florence in 1128.

Mote-House: a meeting hall for decisions of the people. From Old Norse/ Scandinavian and Old English.

p. 436 *why 'gardens' I don't know*: Kensington Gardens was in Morris's time a formal pleasure garden forming part of the grounds around Kensington Palace, adjoining Hyde Park.

p. 438 *slaves*: the working class, 'wage-slaves' as they were called in *Commonweal* and more generally by socialists of Morris's day.

Westminster Abbey: Morris laments the restoration of and addition of monuments to Westminster Abbey in a series of letters across the 1880s and 1890s. See pp. 411–12 in this volume.

p. 440 *queer antiquarian...nuisances*: a nod to the Society for the Protection of Ancient Buildings (SPAB).

p. 441 *blue duds...purser*: Guest's clothes are similar to the blue serge outfit that Morris frequently wore.

p. 442 *Latakia*: tobacco named after the port city in Syria where it was originally prepared.

p. 443 *Japanese work*: lacquer work, imported to and imitated by Europeans from the 1680s.

p. 447 *ward-mote*: meeting of a small group of people to make decisions about their area; the ward is the local area.

pp. 447–50 *I held...pondered*: the rest of this chapter is added in 1891. *Commonweal*, 22 February 1890, 59, finishes here, and the story picks up again on 1 March 1890, 66, at Chapter VIII: 'An Old Friend'.

p. 450 *Spell ho*: let's take a short break (spell).

pondered silently: the foregoing scene reworks Ford Madox Brown's 1852–65 painting 'Work', which has many of these elements, but in which workers and children are clearly poverty-stricken. There is also perhaps a reference to Ruskin's short-lived 1874 project of rebuilding a stretch of the North Hinksey Road with some Oxford students.

p. 451 *the old Jewish proverb-book*: the Old Testament book of Psalms. Psalm 90.10: 'the days of our years are threescore years and ten'.

Richard III: although the Bishop of Ely features in *Richard III*, his house is not mentioned, and it seems likely that Morris means *Richard II*, in which John of Gaunt's 'sceptr'd isle' speech in Act 2. Sc. 1 is delivered at Ely House.

p. 453 *jacket...stockings*: Hammond's outfit, like Guest's, closely mirrors Morris's own habitual outfit.

p. 456 *reductio ad absurdum*: (Latin) reduction to absurdity, i.e. demonstration of faults in an argument through taking it to a ridiculous extreme.

p. 457 *For this...the lay*: slightly misquoted from Morris's own edition of *The Odyssey of Homer, done into English Verse*, viii, ll. 579–80, in *CW*, XII, 117.

p. 458 *bed of Procrustes*: See note on p. 322.

p. 459 *some such title*: 'The Man who was to Mind the House' was a Norse folk tale translated in *Popular Tales from the Norse* (Edinburgh, 1858) by George Webbe Dasent, whose work Morris enjoyed.

it is a great pleasure...her: on women's work, Morris writes in a letter of 24 April 1886: 'Of course we must claim absolute equality of condition between women & men, as between other groups, but it would be poor economy setting women to do men's work (as unluckily they often do now) or vice versa' (*CL*, II, 545).

p. 461 *left-handed*: wrongly, in error.

p. 462 *Phalangsteries*: see note on p. 335 on phalansteries. It is the centrally organized structure of phalansteries to which Old Hammond, like Morris, objects.

the modern Babylon of civilisation: a common designation for London in the late 1800s, suggesting by association the excesses and immorality of the biblical Babylon of the book of Revelation.

p. 463 *Hood's Song of the Shirt*: Thomas Hood's popular poem 'The Song of the Shirt' (1843) tells the tale of an impoverished seamstress.

p. 464 *the lovely river Lea*: the River Lea runs through Walthamstow where Morris grew up.

p. 464 *Isaak Walton*: Izaak Walton's classic *The Compleat Angler* (1653) extols the joys of fishing and gives careful accounts of various kinds of fish, their habitats, and the best means of catching them.

Canning's Town and Silvertown...to him: both slum areas along the East London docks in Morris's time, with overcrowded housing and evil-smelling factories for the manufacture of oil, varnish, and printer's ink, as well as the spinning of guts into strings for racquets.

p. 465 *less interesting... Cambridge*: as a student at Oxford, Morris noted in 1855: 'As to Cambridge, it is rather a hole of a place, and can't compare for a moment with Oxford'; it was an opinion he seems never to have revised (*CL*, I, 13).

cultivated people: academics, or dons. Morris writes disparagingly of dons in general. See his letter to the *Daily News*, 20 November 1885, 339 in this volume. In another letter he writes of 'the sordid blackguards of "Dons" who pretend to educate people' at Oxford (*CL*, III, 154).

p. 467 *picturesque*: in the aesthetic theory of the picturesque developed by art critics such as Uvedale Price (1794), ruined or tumbledown buildings were seen as enhancing the appeal of a landscape.

p. 469 *Ingleborough and Pen-y-gwent*: mountains in north Yorkshire where sheep farmers pasture their herds.

p. 476 *Horrebow's Snakes in Iceland*: Chapter 72 of Niels Horrebow's *The Natural History of Iceland*, trans. by Johann Anderson (1758), 91, reads, in its entirety: 'No snakes of any kind are to be met with throughout the whole island'.

How Matters Are Managed: the first section of this chapter, up to ' "Good", said I' (477) is added in 1891.

p. 477 *'but as... none?'*: this instalment in *Commonweal*, 26 April 1890, 130 begins 'How Matters Are Managed', here, but with a slightly altered sentence: ' "But", quoth I, "is there no difference of opinion amongst you? Is that your assertion?" ' Like the other additions of 1891, this assertion of the interdependent individuality of nations gestures towards more complexity and diversity than is in the *Commonweal* version.

p. 480 *The reward of labour is life*: cf. Ruskin's dictum in *Unto this Last* that 'there is no wealth but life' (*Works*, XVII, 105).

Fourier... better: Fourier particularly stressed the importance of people following their passions and desires, which should be pleasurable in work, as well as in sexual relationships.

p. 481 *The gathering... that*: see Matthew 7:16: 'Do men gather grapes of thorns, or figs of thistles?'

p. 483 *desperado*: in 1887, Henry Morton Stanley, the journalist and explorer who famously tracked down missing missionary explorer David Livingstone in 1871, was sent out to rescue Emin Pasha, a Polish Ottoman doctor who was governor of Equatoria in Egyptian Sudan, from attack by local militias. Pasha had been put in place by an earlier 'desperado', Charles Gordon, governor-general of the Sudan, whose colonial exploits had been discussed and critiqued in *Commonweal* in 1885. Stanley made trade agreements as he went on his rescue mission and was lauded as a heroic Christian adventurer on his return in May 1890.

p. 483 *Stanley*: Stanley features frequently in *Commonweal* in 1890, described by Sergius Stepniak as 'this God-appointed (which is to say self-appointed) apostle of rum, rifles, and religion (1 February 1890, 33), and by Morris as a 'rifle-and-bible newspaper correspondent' (3 May 1890, 140).

p. 484 *done by immensely improved machinery . . . produced by it*: similarly, 'Useful Work *versus* Useless Toil', 309, suggests leaving undone any work too repulsive to be done voluntarily.

p. 486 *Jacob Grimm*: Morris includes Grimm's folk tales in a list of his favourite books provided to the *Pall Mall Gazette* in 1886 for their series on the favourite books of famous figures (*CL*, II, 515).

p. 487 *bight*: stretch of river between land; bend (from Old English).

p. 489 *strikes…starvation*: such as are reported weekly in *Commonweal* throughout 1890.

p. 491 *great crash*: the *Commonweal* version of the tale stops here, and picks up again at 'On some comparatively trifling occasion' (494 in this edition), which in *Commonweal* reads, 'On some trifling occasion' (24 May 1890, 161).

p. 492 *jobbery*: misuse of public office or money for personal advantage.

At the end of the nineteenth century… reduce it to that: the campaign for an eight-hour working day was gathering force by 1890. While Morris supported the idea early on—see his letter of 24 Jul. 1884 to Robert Thomson in this volume—by 1890 he was arguing that it did not further the cause of socialism and would be 'nothing more than an amelioration in the lot of—slaves' (*Commonweal*, 17 May 1890, 154).

p. 493 *Gladstone… respect*: Morris had a particular aversion to Gladstone. See note on p. 414.

grinning through a horse-collar: posing and behaving ridiculously. The term derives from a traditional entertainment at country fairs where young men would compete at putting their face into a horse collar and making foolish expressions.

p. 494 *On some… cast into gaol*: Morris borrows here from the events of Bloody Sunday, 13 November 1887, in which he participated. Socialist, radical, and Irish republican groups, demanding release for Irish republican William O'Brien, freedom to assemble, and better conditions for the unemployed, marched in separate columns to converge on Trafalgar Square. They were met by mounted police who violently dispersed them and injured hundreds. One man later died of his injuries. A week later, law-writer Alfred Linnell died in similar circumstances at another demonstration. There is also an echo of the Peterloo massacre of peaceful protestors in 1819 in this account of clashes between people's uprising and violent state suppression.

Manchester… disappeared: on Morris' knowledge of Manchester, centre of Britain's northern textile industry and urban poverty, see note on p. 349.

Committee of Public Safety: as Leopold (196) notes, this was a term first used in 1793, during the years of the French Revolution, but became associated with the abuses of the Terror; it was used again under the Paris Commune of 1871, a socialist and anarchist local people's government set up in opposition to the state and murderously suppressed by the central government at Versailles, an event commemorated annually by the Socialist League in London.

p. 496 *disgraceful wars…time to time*: the wars of empire, such as those in India, South Africa, Egypt, and Sudan which Morris and his Socialist League colleagues attack repeatedly in *Commonweal*. Sir Charles Warren, who oversaw policing of the Bloody Sunday events, had previously been in the military.

last sixty years: in *Commonweal* the time frame is 'the last twenty years' (24 May 1890, 162).

Glasgow and Bristol: two cities with particularly active socialist groups in Morris's own time. Morris had visited the Socialist Leaguers in Glasgow himself at least once a year between 1884 and 1889; Bristol, where Morris delivered a lecture on 'Art and Labour' in 1885, had an active Socialist Society and saw a wave of labour strikes in 1889–90.

red-coats: soldiers.

p. 501 *the gazettes of the seventeenth century*: gazettes were the forerunners of today's broadsheets. *The Oxford Gazette* (later the *London Gazette*), the first British gazette, came out in 1665.

GENERAL STRIKE: a reference that would have resonated with Morris's first readers. In 1889 and 1890 the idea of a general strike as a means of initiating social change came increasingly to the fore in *Commonweal*, including in the 7 June 1890 issue in which this instalment of the tale appears.

rated: berated.

published in London: In Morris's day socialist newspapers were beginning to proliferate but the key London papers in 1890, alongside Morris's *Commonweal*, were *Justice* and *To-Day*, for both of which Morris wrote at various times. *To-Day* folded in 1889. As Leopold (197) notes, the anarchist-communist journal *Freedom*, established in 1886, was also a significant London paper by 1890.

p. 502 *anent*: with reference to.

p. 504 *dynamite*: patented in 1867. *Commonweal* reported satirically on a number of dynamite scares associated with anarchists in particular across the later 1880s and 1890s, including in an article of June 1890 about a 'sham dynamite sensation' in the United States (*Commonweal*, 28 June 1890, 203).

"square-headed": sensible, level-headed.

p. 505 *"Friends of Order"*: oppression under the guise of 'order' is a recurring theme in *Commonweal*.

p. 512 *white as privet*: the privet plant has white flowers. Gerard's *Herball* quotes Virgil on the *alba ligustra*, the white privet.

p. 514 *somewhat over well*: Morris's own walls seem to be evoked here. He and his friends painted the walls of the Red House, his home from 1860–5, with stories and figures, mythical and biblical.

p. 516 *cockney villas*: showy, ugly houses.

Hampton Court: see note on p. 267.

p. 517 *Dutch William*: William of Orange, King of England, 1689–1702.

I had rather…England: Morris's article, 'Under an Elm-Tree; Or, Thoughts on the Countryside', *Commonweal*, 6 July 1889, 212–13, foreshadows Dick's comments.

p. 518 *flunkies*: obsequious hangers-on.

p. 520 *leash of fine perch*: a number of this freshwater fish, held together by grass or string through the mouth.

p. 520 *minnows*: tiny fish on which the perch feed.

p. 523 *bleak*: small fish, which live on insect larvae as well as aquatic invertebrates.
chub: omnivorous, medium-sized, freshwater fish.

flake-hurdles: fences made by wattling, i.e. interweaving branches of willow or hazel through upright sticks of wood.

p. 525 *de-cockneyised...packing*: got rid of those committed to luxury, artificiality, and ugliness.

p. 526 *'Vanity Fair'*: William Thackeray's satirical 1848 novel exposes the hypocrisies of well-to-do society.

p. 527 *thwart*: a boat-seat used by the rower.

Up yonder...blunder: Eton College was in fact built in 1440 under the aegis of Henry VI. In Morris's time, it was a school for the sons of the wealthy. It remains one of the most expensive of the British fee-paying public schools.

p. 528 *Maidenhead*: as Leopold (200) notes, this town on the Thames had a reputation in the 1890s as a place for pleasure outings, snobbery, and showiness. Morris's objection, however, seems to relate specifically to the river itself, and so perhaps is at least as much to Isambard Kingdom Brunel's generally admired red brick railway bridge across the river, built in 1838. On a trip following this same route down the Thames by boat with his friends in 1880, he had also noted that Cliefden Woods, just after Maidenhead, seemed to him 'rather artificial' (*CL*, I, 582).

p. 530 *Reading and Caversham*: Reading was heavily industrialized in the Victorian period, with a major brewery, a biscuit factory, and its own Reading Sauce factory. Caversham was home to a Norman manor-house modified over centuries and, after a fire, rebuilt in 1850 in a mixture of styles inspired by Italian baroque.

the ancient house of the Blunts: Mapledurham House, an Elizabethan manor house.

p. 531 *sending to Coventry*: ostracizing, particularly by refusing to speak to someone or acknowledge them when they speak.

p. 533 *pound-lock*: a river lock with a gate and sluice for controlling water levels.

p. 535 *Cockneys*: here Morris uses Cockneys in its conventional sense of East End Londoners.

their enemies...the days of the gamekeeper were over: there are no longer gamekeepers keeping the population of birds of prey in check and managing wildlife on behalf of the aristocracy and landed gentry. There is a nod here to matters of land ownership hotly debated across the political spectrum from the 1870s onwards, fuelled by the publication of John Bateman's census, *The Great Landowners of Great Britain and Ireland* (London, 1876).

The Obstinate Refusers: this chapter was added in 1891.

p. 536 *gave us the sele of the day*: greeted us, or wished us good day (from Old English, sǽl, which can mean either season, time of day, or happiness.)

ashlar: a stone hewn into a square to use for building.

p. 538 *Wallingford*: on their 1880 boat trip Morris and his friends stayed in 'stuffy, grubby little Wallingford' (*CL*, I, 583).

p. 539 *from the time...Parliamentary Wars*: from the time of Alfred the Great, 871–99, to the English Civil War 1641–51, fought between the armies of Parliament and the armies of King Charles I.

p. 541 *a hatred of civilisation impressed upon them*: Morris notes elsewhere that 'the leading passion of my life has been and is hatred of modern civilisation' ('How I Became a Socialist', 564).

Bodleian Library: the main library of the University of Oxford.

p. 543 *always afternoon*: 'In the afternoon they came unto a land | In which it seemèd always afternoon'. Tennyson, 'The Lotos-eaters' (1832), in *Poems*, I, 468.

I know... Cricklade: Cricklade is a village on the Thames in Wiltshire, between Cirencester and Swindon.

p. 544 *Odyssean lies*: In 'The Influence of the North', Morris draws attention to Odysseus delighting Athene with 'an intricate series of lies' (*AWS*, I, 452).

Day's Lock: near Dorchester-on-Thames.

mamelon: a rounded hillock (borrowed from French, unusually for Morris who tends to prefer Northern and Germanic words).

p. 548 *polled (or... country-side)*: to poll is to cut the top off a tree but also more generally to prune to a particular shape.

p. 555 *And the house... summer*: The house is based on Morris's own Oxfordshire home, Kelmscott Manor. See figure 11.

p. 559 *tedding*: spreading out the freshly mown grass to dry in the sun.

haysel: the haymaking season (from the combination of hay with Old English *sǽl*, or season, the same word on which Morris draws for 'the sele of the day'. See note to p. 536.)

p. 560 *This was somewhat new to me... Middle Ages*: this sentence was added in 1891. As Wilmer (417) notes, church-ales were medieval festivals, named after the drink.

p. 561 *Persian poet... sun*: as Leopold notes, probably the *Shahnameh* by the medieval Persian poet Abdul Qasim Mansur Ferdowsī (*c*.920–1020). In Julius Mohl's French translation, which Morris discusses reading in an 1883 letter to his daughter May (*CL*, II, 153), when spring comes, it is as though 'l'air sema des tulipes sur la surface du sol' [the air sowed tulips on the ground] (Ferdowsī, V, 609). Ferdowsī describes the beauty of beds of tulips and other flowers on several occasions and also compares beautiful women, beautiful men, and the bloodied battlefield (Ferdowsī, I, 257; IV, 9; II, 11, 31 to tulips. Morris translated part of the text, he owned at least one illustrated edition in Persian from the seventeenth century, and in 1886 included the *Shahnameh* in his list of favourite books for the *Pall Mall Gazette*, under 'the kind of book which Mazzini called "Bibles"' (*CL*, II, 515).

all consciousness... face: on 7 October 1890, Morris wrote to Glasier: 'I have been down at Kelmscott (where Ellen vanished you know)'. This last instalment of *News* appeared in *Commonweal* just days earlier, on 4 October 1890.

HOW I BECAME A SOCIALIST

First published in *Justice*, 16 June 1894, 6, from which this text is taken. In the same year Morris contributed to a series known as the 'Why I Ams', published by the Scottish anarchist-Communist James Tochatti, entitled 'Why I Am a Communist' (Liberty Press, 1894).

p. 563 *COMMONWEALTH*: Morris returns repeatedly to this idea of the common good. In his introduction to Thomas More's 1516 *Utopia* he writes of More's evocation of: 'the longing for a society of equality of condition; a society in which the individual man can scarcely conceive of his existence apart from the Commonwealth of which he forms a portion. This, which is the essence of his book, is the essence also of the struggle in which we are engaged' (Introduction to Thomas More, *Utopia*, Kelmscott Press, 1893, viii).

I had no...realisation of it: in a letter in 1883, Morris writes: 'I used to think that one might further real socialistic progress by doing what one could on the lines of ordinary middle-class Radicalism.' Now, he says, he realizes: 'it is made for and by the middle classes and will always be under the control of rich capitalists' (*CL*, II, 199).

Adam Smith, Ricardo, Karl Marx: Adam Smith, political economist, author of *The Wealth of Nations* (1776), and proponent of the idea of the 'invisible hand' of the self-regulating market; David Ricardo, political economist, author of *On The Principles of Political Economy and Taxation* (1817), who developed the idea of the wage fund and proposed the labour theory of value, arguing that the worth of a commodity depends at least in part on how much labour went into producing it; Karl Marx, communist and author of *Capital* (1867) which critiques capitalism and earlier models of the labour theory of value.

Fourierist: relating to beliefs based on the ideas of Charles Fourier. See notes to 335, 462, 480.

p. 564 *Bax and Hyndman and Scheu*: fellow socialists in London. Morris collaborated with Bax in writing 'The Development of Modern Society' in *Commonweal* in 1890, collaborated with Hyndman on the *Manifesto of the Social Democratic Federation* in 1883–4, before he left the SDF, and worked closely with the Austrian refugee and Socialist League member Andreas Scheu, who also contributed to *Commonweal*.

the Whig frame of mind: the Whig party had merged, with Radicals, free-traders, and reformists, into the Liberal party in 1859, but Morris uses the term to denote a Liberal view of history as progress, support of free trade, and protection of the economic interests of the middle class.

p. 565 *Podsnap*: in Dickens's *Our Mutual Friend* (1865), Podsnap is a bourgeois city financier, self-satisfied, unimaginative, prudish, and conventional. Morris uses Podsnap repeatedly to stand for all that is morally and physically ugly, pinching and concerned with money over values of community and beauty; see, for instance, 'The Revival of Architecture', *Fortnightly Review*, May 1888, 671.

the place of Homer...Huxley: the art of the people, represented by Homer, to be replaced by science, represented by Morris's contemporary, the biologist and Darwinist Thomas Henry Huxley.

ON EPPING FOREST

Text taken from the *Daily Chronicle*, 23 April 1895, 3. Morris follows this up with two further letters, one on 27 April, responding to an article challenging his views, and one on 9 May reporting on a recent visit to Epping Forest in further defence of his view, noting that 'that though no doubt acting with the best intentions, the management of the forest is going on a wrong tack: it is making war on the natural aspect of the forest.' *Daily Chronicle*, 9 May 1895, 3.

p. 567 *pollards*: see note on p. 429.
shrouded: cut back.
deodars: large cedar trees with drooping branches. Native to the Himalayas.

FROM *THE SUNDERING FLOOD*

Morris's last work, almost completely finished but not yet edited on his death. Morris dictated the last lines of the book from his sickbed in September 1896 (Lemire, 221; *CW*, XXI, xiv). This text is taken from the Kelmscott Press edition, printed in November 1897, issued for sale in 1898. The colophon to this edition notes that 'it was overseen by May Morris'. Where it differs significantly from Morris's manuscript, Add MS 45326, held in the British Library, or from the later *Collected Works* edition, I have noted this.

p. 570 *dromonds*: large medieval ships.
bowsprits: long spars extending out from the central body of the ship.
middens: rubbish tips or heaps of refuse.
mass-hackled: wearing a chasuble, a sleeveless priestly robe put on over other robes.
St. Thomas of India: one of Jesus's disciples, believed by some to have travelled to India; nineteenth-century archaeological discoveries led to renewed interest in this idea.
Black Canons: an order of Augustinian clerics in the Roman Catholic church, so-called because of the black cloak they wear at certain times of year.
chaffer: goods for trade or sale.
p. 571 *peopled...blossom*: see Isaiah 35:1: 'The wilderness and the solitary place shall be glad for them; and the desert shall rejoice, and blossom as the rose.'
spates: floods, or rushing waters.
bents: hillsides.
p. 572 *quicken tree*: archaic usage for the rowan or mountain-ash. See note to p. 350.
erne: sea eagle.
cheaping-towns: trading towns.
pp. 572–81 *Dalesmen*: Morris uses a mixture of lower-case and upper-case initial letters for dalesmen across the tale in his manuscript. The early editions retain this idiosyncrasy as I have done here.
p. 573 *trundle the fire-wheel*: set in motion a firework that spins round.
hight: named.
cot: cottage.
liever: rather.
Land-wights: spirits of a particular place in Norse mythology.

p. 574 *kenspeckle*: conspicuous.

Cloven Motes: self-governing administrative and organizational meetings of the people (motes) divided by the river.

carle: man or boy.

reivers: marauding thieves.

neat: cattle.

ingle-nook: a corner, usually beside a chimney but here made by a cleft in the rock.

carline: woman.

p. 575 *grandame* (also *grandam*): grandmother.

(this was in mid-May): KP has commas instead of brackets in keeping with the press style. Add MS 45326, 9, and *CW*, XXI, 8 have brackets.

squealing: KP, 17 has *squeaking*, but *CW*, XXI, 8, uses 'squealing': in Add MS 45326, 10, the handwriting is unclear, but looks closer to squealing than squeaking.

p. 576 *bairn*: child.

Holy Rood: the cross of Christ.

[. . .]: In the intervening chapters, Osberne shows his bravery in taking care of the flocks, kills some wolves that threaten them, and has an encounter with a woman at the Cloven Mote.

he had liefer: he had rather.

p. 577 *so to say*: KP has 'he was not to say afeared' (48) as does *CW*, XXI, 24, but Add MS 45326 has 'he was not so to say' (28), a phrase Morris uses frequently in his work, so I have kept it here and punctuated it in Morris's usual style.

hauberk: a protective coat of chain mail.

basnet: see note to p. 94, l. 15.

the sele of the day: see note to p. 536.

scathe: hurt or harm.

can thee many thanks: thank you profusely.

p. 578 *rede*: advice.

weird: fate.

drive we thy sheep: KP, 53 and *CW*, XXI, 27 have 'drive me thy sheep', but Add MS 45326, 31 has 'drive we thy sheep'. This seems to fit best the sense of the passage.

p. 579 *and there wedded a wife*: KP, 55 has *and then. CW*, XXI, 28 has *and there*, reading the slightly illegible second word in Add MS 45326, 32 as it is clearly intended, given the rhythm of the sentence.

had hansel of: had as a gift.

unked: unnatural or with supernatural and disturbing influence or origin.

wights: people.

p. 580 *foison*: plentiful supply.

heathfowl: ground birds, most commonly grouse.

whimbrel: a coastal wading bird with a long curved beak, similar to a curlew; sometimes the names are used interchangeably.

Bight of the Cloven Knoll: here, bight means a stretch of river running through the middle of a knoll or hillock.

p. 580 *chaffer*: trade.

p. 581 *And it were...scarlet*: This is an addition to Morris's manuscript, included at this point in KP, 59, and at the end of this paragraph in *CW*, XXI, 30. It makes sense of a later comment in this chapter about Osberne's scarlet coat.

ness: a promontory or headland.

thirty feet across: KP, 61, has 'fifty feet across' here, clearly in error. Add MS 45326, 35, and *CW*, XXI, 32, have '30 feet', fitting the description of the 'strait' passage.

p. 582 *red scarlet*: See note to p. 581 for earlier mention of this coat.

thirty feet: KP, 63 has *fifty feet*; Add MS 45326, 36, has *thirty yards*; *CW*, XXI, 31, has *thirty feet*, in keeping with Morris's description of the eastern shore above.

p. 583 *Whiles*: sometimes.

harm...somewhat: KP, 68, has 'harm. May I tell thee somewhat?' Add MS45326, 39 has it as it is here.

wyted: blamed.

p. 584 *drave*: Add MS 45326, 39, and *CW*, XXI, 35, have 'drave', using Morris's preferred archaic past here, while KP, 69, uses 'drove'.

mowing: uttering animal sounds.

NOTE BY WILLIAM MORRIS ON HIS AIMS IN FOUNDING THE KELMSCOTT PRESS

The text here is taken from the first printed version, in the Boston journal, *Modern Art*, 4 (April 1896), 36–9, in which it was entitled simply 'The Kelmscott Press'. Sydney Cockerell, Morris's executor, notes in the posthumous 1898 edition of the text, that 'the foregoing article was written at the request of a London bookseller for an American client who was about to read a paper on the Kelmscott Press.' Lemire (223–4) notes that the American client was Carl Edelheim who gave this note 'as the body of a paper read to the Philobiblon Club of Philadelphia on 29 Jan. 1896'. The *Modern Art* text is prefaced with a note by Edelheim who comments that on communicating with Morris via his friend Bernard Quaritch, the bookseller and collector, he received not only printed materials about the Kelmscott Press, 'but also a lengthy paper by Mr. Morris himself', and, he notes, 'I cannot possibly do better than give you the contents of this paper in toto' (*Modern Art*, 36). The whereabouts of Cockerell's transcript of Morris's autograph manuscript is now unknown, having been sold by Christie's, but the journal text is almost identical with the KP text. Slight differences, with the exception of punctuation and layout, are noted below. For illustrations of typefaces see figure 12.

p. 585 *for the sake of the price*: KP, 2, has 'as to price' here.

p. 586 *from 1470 to 1476*: *Modern Art*, 37, inserts here: '[This is the old Jenson. Ed]'.

my Roman type...Jenson's: *Modern Art*, 37, inserts here: '[Mr. Morris christened his the 'Golden' type. Ed.]'. It was first called by Morris, as Peterson notes, 'the regenerate type or Jenson-Morris'. William S. Peterson, *The Kelmscott Press: A History of William Morris's Typographical Adventure* (Oxford, 1991), 84.

p. 586 *I prefer it to the Roman*: *Modern Art*, 38, has inserted: '[This he called the Troy type]'.

of the size ... here: KP, 4, not addressing a specifically American audience so directly, has: 'This type is of the size called Great Primer (the Roman...)'.

'Great Primer'... 'pica' size: the Troy type size is Great Primer, which we now call 18 point, the Golden Type (Roman) is 14 point, and the Chaucer, a smaller Troy, is 12 point. See figure 12.

with great intelligence and skill: KP, 4, has 'by Mr E. P. Prince'.

The only ... books: KP, 5, is more technical here: 'The only leading I have allowed myself is a "thin" lead ... in the Chaucer and the double-columned books I have used a "hair" lead ... and not even this in the 16mo books.'

p. 588 *printed book*: KP concludes with: Kelmscott House, Upper Mall, Hammersmith, Nov. 11, 1895.

INDEX OF TITLES AND FIRST LINES

Titles of works are shown in italics.